T0202761

Lecture Notes in Computer Science 14356

Founding Editors

Gerhard Goos
Juris Hartmanis

The series Lecture Notes in Computer Science (LNCS), including its subseries Lecture Notes in Artificial Intelligence (LNAI) and Lecture Notes in Bioinformatics (LNBI), has established itself as a medium for the publication of new developments in computer science and information technology research, teaching, and education.

LNCS enjoys close cooperation with the computer science R & D community, the series counts many renowned academics among its volume editors and paper authors, and collaborates with prestigious societies. Its mission is to serve this international community by providing an invaluable service, mainly focused on the publication of conference and workshop proceedings and postproceedings. LNCS commenced publication in 1973.

Huchuan Lu · Wanli Ouyang · Hui Huang ·
Jiwen Lu · Risheng Liu · Jing Dong · Min Xu
Editors

Image
and Graphics

12th International Conference, ICIG 2023
Nanjing, China, September 22–24, 2023
Proceedings, Part II

Editors
Huchuan Lu 🆔
Dalian University of Technology
Dalian, China

Hui Huang 🆔
Shenzhen University
Shenzhen, China

Risheng Liu 🆔
Dalian University of Technology
Dalian, China

Min Xu 🆔
University of Technology Sydney
Sydney, NSW, Australia

Wanli Ouyang 🆔
University of Sydney
Sydney, NSW, Australia

Jiwen Lu 🆔
Tsinghua University
Beijing, China

Jing Dong 🆔
Institute of Automation, CAS
Beijing, China

ISSN 0302-9743   ISSN 1611-3349 (electronic)
Lecture Notes in Computer Science
ISBN 978-3-031-46307-5   ISBN 978-3-031-46308-2 (eBook)
https://doi.org/10.1007/978-3-031-46308-2

This Springer imprint is published by the registered company Springer Nature Switzerland AG
The registered company address is: Gewerbestrasse 11, 6330 Cham, Switzerland

Paper in this product is recyclable.

Preface

These are the proceedings of the 12th International Conference on Image and Graphics (ICIG 2023), which was held in Nanjing, China, on September 22–24, 2023. The Conference was hosted by China Society of Image and Graphics (CSIG), organized by Nanjing University of Posts & Telecommunications, co-organized by Nanjing University of Science & Technology and Nanjing University of Information Science and Technology, supported by Springer.

ICIG is a biennial conference that focuses on innovative technologies of image, video, and graphics processing and fostering innovation, entrepreneurship, and networking. ICIG 2023 featured world-class plenary speakers, exhibits, and high-quality peer-reviewed oral and poster presentations.

CSIG has hosted the series of ICIG conference since 2000. Details about the past conferences are as follows:

Conference	Place	Date	Submitted	Proceedings
First (ICIG 2000)	Tianjin, China	August 16–18	220	156
Second (ICIG 2002)	Hefei, China	August 15–18	280	166
Third (ICIG 2004)	Hong Kong, China	December 17–19	460	140
4th (ICIG 2007)	Chengdu, China	August 22–24	525	184
5th (ICIG 2009)	Xi'an, China	September 20–23	362	179
6th (ICIG 2011)	Hefei, China	August 12–15	329	183
7th (ICIG 2013)	Qingdao, China	July 26–28	346	181
8th (ICIG 2015)	Tianjin, China	August 13–16	345	170
9th (ICIG 2017)	Shanghai, China	September 13–15	370	172
10th (ICIG 2019)	Beijing, China	August 23–25	384	183
11th (ICIG 2021)	Haikou, China	December 26–28	421	198

For ICIG 2023, 409 submissions were received and 166 papers were accepted. To ease the search for a required paper in these proceedings, the accepted papers have been arranged into different sections according to their topic.

We sincerely thank all the contributors, who came from around the world to present their advanced work at this event. We would also like to thank all the reviewers, who carefully reviewed all submissions and made their valuable comments for improving the accepted papers. The proceedings could not have been produced without the invaluable efforts of the members of the Organizing Committee, and a number of active members of CSIG.

September 2023

Huchuan Lu
Wanli Ouyang
Hui Huang
Jiwen Lu
Risheng Liu
Jing Dong
Min Xu

Organization

Organizing Committee

General Chairs

Yaonan Wang	Hunan University, China
Qingshan Liu	Nanjing University of Posts & Telecommunications, China
Ramesh Jain	University of California, Irvine, USA
Alberto Del Bimbo	University of Florence, Italy

Technical Program Chairs

Huchuan Lu	Dalian University of Technology, China
Wanli Ouyang	University of Sydney, Australia
Hui Huang	Shenzhen University, China
Jiwen Lu	Tsinghua University, China

Organizing Committee Chairs

Yuxin Peng	Peking University, China
Xucheng Yin	University of Science and Technology Beijing, China
Bo Du	Wuhan University, China
Bingkun Bao	Nanjing University of Posts & Telecommunications, China

Publicity Chairs

Abdulmotaleb El Saddik	University of Ottawa, Canada
Phoebe Chen	La Trobe University, Australia
Kun Zhou	Zhejiang University, China
Xiaojun Wu	Jiangnan University, China

Award Chairs

Changsheng Xu   Institute of Automation, CAS, China
Shiguang Shan   Institute of Computing Technology, CAS, China
Mohan Kankanhalli   National University of Singapore, Singapore

Publication Chairs

Risheng Liu   Dalian University of Technology, China
Jing Dong   Institute of Automation, CAS, China
Min Xu   University of Technology Sydney, Australia

Workshop Chairs

Yugang Jiang   Fudan University, China
Kai Xu   National University of Defense Technology,
                                 China
Zhu Li   University of Missouri, USA
Oliver Deussen   Universität Konstanz, Germany

Exhibits Chairs

Qi Tian   Huawei Cloud, China
Wu Liu   JD.COM, China
Weishi Zheng   Sun Yat-sen University, China
Kun Xu   Tsinghua University, China

Tutorial Chairs

Weiwei Xu   Zhejiang University, China
Nannan Wang   Xidian University, China
Shengsheng Qian   Institute of Automation, CAS, China
Klaus Schöffmann   Klagenfurt University, Austria

Sponsorship Chairs

Xiang Bai   Huazhong University of Science and Technology,
                                 China
Mingming Cheng   Nankai University, China

Finance Chairs

Lifang Wu	Beijing University of Technology, China
Yubao Sun	Nanjing University of Information Science & Technology, China
Miao Hong	CSIG, China

Social Media Chairs

Zhenwei Shi	Beihang University, China
Wei Jia	Hefei University of Technology, China
Feifei Zhang	Tianjin University of Technology, China

Local Chairs

Jian Cheng	Institute of Automation, CAS, China
Xiaotong Yuan	Nanjing University of Information Science & Technology, China
Yifan Jiao	Nanjing University of Posts & Telecommunications, China

Website Chairs

Rui Huang	Chinese University of Hong Kong, Shenzhen, China
Jie Wang	Nanjing University of Posts & Telecommunications, China

Area Chairs

Yuchao Dai	Xi Peng	Yong Xia
Yulan Guo	Boxin Shi	Shiqing Xin
Xiaoguang Han	Dong Wang	Feng Xu
Tong He	Lijun Wang	Jia Xu
Gao Huang	Limin Wang	Kun Xu
Meina Kan	Nannan Wang	Yongchao Xu
Yu-Kun Lai	Xinchao Wang	Junchi Yan
Li Liu	Xinggang Wang	Shiqi Yu
Huimin Lu	Yunhai Wang	Jian Zhang
Jinshan Pan	Baoyuan Wu	Pingping Zhang
Houwen Peng	Jiazhi Xia	Shanshan Zhang

Additional Reviewers

Bingkun Bao	Zhiheng Fu	Hao Ju
Yulong Bian	Wei Gai	Yongzhen Ke
Chunjuan Bo	Ziliang Gan	Lingshun Kong
Zi-Hao Bo	Changxin Gao	Jian-Huang Lai
JIntong Cai	Qing Gao	Yu-Kun Lai
Zhanchuan Cai	Shang Gao	Xingyu Lan
Mingwei Cao	Zhifan Gao	Yang Lang
Jianhui Chang	Tong Ge	Wentao Lei
Yakun Chang	Shenjian Gong	Yang Lei
Bin Chen	Guanghua Gu	Baohua Li
Guang Chen	Yuliang Gu	Bocen Li
Hongrui Chen	Shihui Guo	Boyang Li
Jianchuan Chen	Yahong Han	Chao Li
Junsong Chen	Yizeng Han	Chenghong Li
Siming Chen	Yufei Han	Dachong Li
Xiang Chen	Junwen He	Feng Li
Xin Chen	Mengqi He	Gang Li
Ziyang Chen	Xiaowei He	Guanbin Li
Jinghao Cheng	Yulia Hicks	Guorong Li
Lechao Cheng	Yuchen Hong	Guozheng Li
Ming-Ming Cheng	Ruibing Hou	Hao Li
Jiaming Chu	Shouming Hou	Hongjun Li
Hainan Cui	Donghui Hu	Kunhong Li
Yutao Cui	Fuyuan Hu	Li Li
Enyan Dai	Lanqing Hu	Manyi Li
Tao Dai	Qiming Hu	Ming Li
Jisheng Dang	Ruimin Hu	Mingjia Li
Sagnik Das	Yang Hu	Qifeng Li
Xinhao Deng	Yupeng Hu	Shifeng Li
Haiwen Diao	Bao Hua	Shutao Li
Jian Ding	Guanjie Huang	Siheng Li
Wenhui Dong	Le Hui	Xiaoyan Li
Xiaoyu Dong	Chengtao Ji	Yanchun Li
Shuguang Dou	Naye Ji	Yang Li
Zheng-Jun Du	Xiaosong Jia	Yi Li
Peiqi Duan	Xu Jia	Ying Li
Qingnan Fan	Chaohui Jiang	Yue Li
Yongxian Fan	Haoyi Jiang	Yunhao Li
Zhenfeng Fan	Peng Jiang	Zihan Li
Gongfan Fang	Runqing Jiang	Dongze Lian
Kun Fang	Zhiying Jiang	Jinxiu Liang
Sheng Fang	Leyang Jin	Junhao Liang
Xianyong Fang	Yongcheng Jing	Tian Liang

Zhengyu Liang

Zhifang Liang

Bencheng Liao

Zehui Liao

Chuan Lin

Feng Lin

Qifeng Lin

Weilin Lin

Wenbin Lin

Xiaotian Lin

Yiqun Lin

Jingwang Ling

Qiu Lingteng

Aohan Liu

Chang Liu

Cheng-Lin Liu

Haolin Liu

Jingxin Liu

Jinyuan Liu

Kenkun Liu

Lei Liu

Long Liu

Meng Liu

Min Liu

Qingshan Liu

Risheng Liu

Shengli Liu

Shiguang Liu

Shuaiqi Liu

Songhua Liu

Wei Liu

Wenrui Liu

Wenyu Liu

Xuehu Liu

Yiguang Liu

Yijing Liu

Yipeng Liu

Yong Liu

Yu Liu

Yunan Liu

Zhenguang Liu

Zilin Lu

Weiqi Luo

Yong Luo

Zhaofan Luo

Zhongjin Luo

Yunqiu Lv

Junfeng Lyu

Youwei Lyu

Chunyan Ma

Fengji Ma

Huimin Ma

Tianlei Ma

Xinke Ma

Qirong Mao

Yuxin Mao

Wei Miao

Yongwei Miao

Weidong Min

Jiawen Ming

Weihua Ou

Jinshan Pan

Yun Pei

Zongju Peng

Hongxing Qin

Liangdong Qiu

Xinkuan Qiu

Yuda Qiu

Zhong Qu

Weisong Ren

Nong Sang

Guangcun Shan

Linlin Shen

Zhiqiang Shen

Jiamu Sheng

Jun Shi

Zhenghao Shi

Zhenwei Shi

Chengfang Song

Jiechong Song

Jifei Song

Yong Song

Zhengyao Song

Qingtang Su

Jiande Sun

Long Sun

Xuran Sun

Zhixing Sun

Gary Tam

Hongchen Tan

Jing Tan

Jiajun Tang

Jin Tang

Shiyu Tang

Minggui Teng

Yao Teng

Yanling Tian

Zhigang Tu

Matthew Vowels

Bo Wang

Dong Wang

Dongsheng Wang

Haiting Wang

Hao Wang

Jingyi Wang

Jinjia Wang

Jinting Wang

Jinwei Wang

Junyu Wang

Lijun Wang

Longguang Wang

Meng Wang

Miao Wang

Peizhen Wang

Pengjie Wang

Rui Wang

Ruiqi Wang

Ruotong Wang

Shengjin Wang

Shijie Wang

Tao Wang

Xiaoxing Wang

Xin Wang

Xingce Wang

Yili Wang

Yingquan Wang

Yongfang Wang

Yue Wang

Yun Wang

Zi Wang

Hongjiang Wei

Shaokui Wei

Xiu-Shen Wei

Ziyu Wei

Shuchen Weng

Zhi Weng

Qian Wenhua

Jianlong Wu

Lianjun Wu

Tao Wu

Yadong Wu

Yanmin Wu

Ye Wu

Yu Wu

Yushuang Wu

Di Xiao

Yuxuan Xiao

Jin Xie

Jingfen Xie

Jiu-Cheng Xie

Yutong Xie

Jiankai Xing

Bo Xu

Hongming Xu

Jie Xu

Xiaowei Xu

Yi Xu

Mingliang Xue

Xiangyang Xue

Difei Yan

Xin Yan

Yichao Yan

Zizheng Yan

Bin Yang

Cheng Yang

Jialin Yang

Kang Yang

Min Yang

Shuo Yang

Shuzhou Yang

Xingyi Yang

Xue Yang

Yang Yang

Yiqian Yang

Zhongbao Yang

Chao Yao

Chengtang Yao

Jingfeng Yao

Chongjie Ye

Dingqiang Ye

Jingwen Ye

Yiwen Ye

Xinyu Yi

Xinyi Ying

Di You

Bohan Yu

Chenyang Yu

Jiwen Yu

Runpeng Yu

Songsong Yu

Danni Yuan

Yang Yue

Lin Yushun

Qingjie Zeng

Qiong Zeng

Yaopei Zeng

Yinwei Zhan

Dawei Zhang

Guozhen Zhang

Jianpeng Zhang

Jiawan Zhang

Jing Zhang

Mingda Zhang

Pengyu Zhang

Pingping Zhang

Xiao-Yong Zhang

Xinpeng Zhang

Xuanyu Zhang

Yanan Zhang

Yang Zhang

Ye Zhang

Yuanhang Zhang

Zaibin Zhang

ZhiHao Zhang

Jie Zhao

Sicheng Zhao

Yuchao Zheng

Shuaifeng Zhi

Fan Zhong

Chu Zhou

Feng Zhou

JiaYuan Zhou

Jingyi Zhou

Tao Zhou

Yang Zhou

Zhanping Zhou

Minfeng Zhu

Mingli Zhu

Mingrui Zhu

Xu Zhu

Zihao Zhu

Shinan Zou

Contents – Part II

Computer Vision and Pattern Recognition

Temporal Global Re-detection Based on Interaction-Fusion Attention in Long-Term Visual Tracking

Jingyuan Ma[1,2]($\boxtimes$), Zhiqiang Hou[1,2], Ruoxue Han[1,2], and Sugang Ma[1,2]

[1] School of Computer Science and Technology, Xi'an University of Posts and Telecommunications, Xi'an 710121, China
mjy2022030163.com
[2] Key Laboratory of Network Data Analysis and Intelligent Processing of Shaanxi Province, Xi'an 710121, China

Abstract. In long-term visual tracking, target occlusion and out-of-view are common problems that lead to target drift, adding re-detection to short-term tracking algorithms is a general solution. To better handle the problem of target disappearing and reappearing in long-term visual tracking, this paper proposes a temporal global re-detection method based on interaction-fusion attention. Firstly, ResNet50 is used as the feature extraction network to obtain the depth features of the template and the search region. Then, a new interaction-fusion attention is added to extract the connection of different dimensionality of features. Finally, Temporal ROI Align is introduced to select candidate boxes, increasing the use of historical information by re-detection method, and improving the accuracy of target localization. STMTrack algorithm is selected as the short-term tracking algorithm, which works with the proposed re-detection method to construct a long-term tracking algorithm, and experiments are conducted on the UAV123, LaSOT, UAV20L, and VOT2018-LT datasets, and the effectiveness of this re-detection method can be seen from the experimental results.

Keywords: Long-Term visual tracking · Global re-detection · Attention mechanism

1 Introduction

In recent years, more and more experts and scholars have begun to research long-term visual tracking [1], and the consequent long-term visual tracking datasets [2–5] have become increasingly challenging. In the long-term visual tracking process, there are a large number of difficult situations such as target occlusion and out-of-view, when the target reappears, it is difficult to retrieve the target by the tracking algorithm because the location is uncertain and the

Supported by the National Natural Science Foundation of China under grant no. 62072370 and the Natural Science Foundation of Shaanxi Province under grant no. 2023-JC-YB-598.

change of scale. To solve these problems, experts began to study the re-detection method.

Most of the early long-term tracking algorithms based on correlation filtering [6,7] used feature points and classifiers for re-detection. However, these methods only use manual features, the precision is greatly affected. In the recent long-term visual tracking algorithms based on deep learning, there are many new re-detection methods to be proposed. Zhu et al. proposed the DaSiamRPN [8], it retrieves the target by expanding the search area. The MBMD [9] proposed by Zhang et al. combines local and global sliding window search to achieve re-detection. Yan et al. proposed the SPLT [10] to re-detect the search area by updating the Skimming-Perusal framework. Huang et al. proposed Global-Track [11] using global tracking methods, each frame is independent of the historical frame. However, the method that expanding the search area [8] has the situation that the target is still out of view during re-detection. The global sliding window search [9] can find the target globally but cannot achieve real-time tracking speed. Updating the search area [10] has uncertainty about whether the target is within the selected search area. GlobalTrack [11] lacks feature enhancement processing when locating targets, and its global search without relying on history frames can limit the accuracy of target localization.

To address the above issues, inspired by the GlobalTrack algorithm, this paper proposes a global re-detection method, which can effectively improve the accuracy of the re-detection method. Firstly, the local features extracted through convolutional neural networks do not contain the relationship between the target and the global image features. To this end, Interaction-Fusion Attention Module (IFAM) is introduced to obtain spatial and channel information, enhancing the ability to model target features. In addition, to utilize historical information, Temporal ROI Align (TRA) [12] is introduced to extract candidate frames. Through IFAM and TRA, the proposed re-detection method can more accurately locate the target.

2   Method

2.1   Long-Term Visual Tracking Algorithm Framework

The framework of the long-term tracking algorithm in this paper is shown in Fig. 1, which is divided into a visual tracking module and a post-processing module.

In the visual tracking module, STMTrack [13] is selected as the short-term tracking algorithm to obtain the initial tracking result in this paper. In the post-processing module, F_{max} is used to determine whether the initial tracking result drifts, where F_{max} is the maximum response value generated during the tracking process. To reduce the error of F_{max}, it is set that the target is considered lost when F_{max} is less than the threshold l_o for 5 consecutive frames. When the target is determined to be missing, it is re-searched in the whole image using global re-detection. The global re-detection used in the post-processing module is the method proposed in this paper. The final tracking result output by the

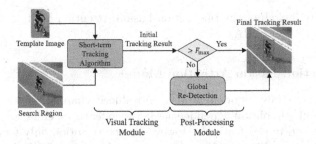

Fig. 1. Long-term visual tracking algorithm framework.

re-detection is no longer subject to result determination. If the output result is still incorrect, the target is searched again in the subsequent frames using global re-detection. In the following, we will introduce our global re-detection method.

2.2 Global Re-detection Method

The global re-detection method in this paper is based on the GlobalTrack algorithm [11], and improves the accuracy of target positioning by adding Interaction-Fusion Attention Module (IFAM) and Temporal ROI Align (TRA). The specific framework is shown in Fig. 2.

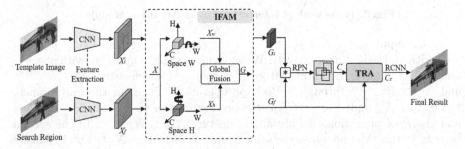

Fig. 2. Framework of the global re-detection method.

Firstly, the template image and the search region image are input into a convolutional neural network (CNN) to extract image features, and the template image feature X_t and the search region image feature X_f are obtained. Secondly, the extracted features X_t and X_f are input into the Interaction-Fusion Attention Module (IFAM), and richer feature information is obtained through interactive processing and global fusion of different spaces. G_t and G_f are the results of interactive fusion of attention for template image feature X_t and search area image feature X_f. Next, the feature G_t and G_f are subjected to cross correlation operations and processed by a Region Proposal Network (RPN) to obtain feature C; Then, feature C is passed through Temporal ROI Align (TRA) to obtain the temporal characteristics and laws of historical frames, and a feature C_T containing temporal information is obtained; Finally, the feature C_T is processed by RCNN and the final tracking result is output. In the following, we will specifically introduce the Interaction-Fusion Attention Module (IFAM) and Temporal ROI Align (TRA).

2.3   Interaction-Fusion Attention Module

In recent years, many algorithms have introduced channel, spatial, or fusion attention modules to obtain dependencies between features, enhancing their ability to extract and model features. However, most attention only focuses on the interaction between different features, such as channel space fusion attention, while ignoring the relationship between the various dimensions of the feature. Therefore, this paper proposes a interaction-fusion attention to better extract feature information. The specific process is shown in Fig. 3.

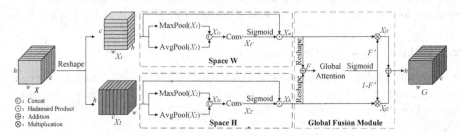

Fig. 3. Framework of Interaction-Fusion Attention Module.

In the input tensor $X \in R^{c \times w \times h}$, c is the channel space, and spaces w and h are width and height, respectively. When channel space c interacts with space w and space h, firstly, the input feature X is reshaped into features $X_1 \in R^{h \times w \times c}$ and $X_2 \in R^{w \times c \times h}$ through a Reshape operation; Then, in the first branch, the feature X_1 undergoes a $Concat$ operation on the results of the $MaxPool$ and $AvgPool$ operations, to obtain the feature $X_{1c} \in R^{2 \times w \times c}$. In the second branch, feature X_2 undergoes the same operation as feature X_1 to obtain feature $X_{2c} \in R^{2 \times c \times h}$. After two pooling operations, the obtained features aggregate the maximum and average features of the original features, with rich feature information. The process of acquiring feature X_{1c} is shown in Eq. (1):

$$X_{1c} = Concat(MaxPool(X_1), AvgPool(X_1)) \tag{1}$$

Next, the feature X_{1c} undergoes a convolution operation ($Conv$), performs normalization layer processing on the feature, and passes through the activation function $Sigmoid$ to obtain the feature $X_{1'} \in R^{1 \times w \times c}$. Similarly, the feature X_{2c} undergoes the above process to obtain the feature $X_{2'} \in R^{1 \times c \times h}$. Finally, the feature $X_{1'}$ is multiplied by the original feature X_1 element by element to obtain the feature $X_w \in R^{h \times w \times c}$ after interacting with the spatial w; Multiply feature $X_{2'}$ and original feature X_2 element by element to obtain feature $X_h \in R^{w \times c \times h}$ after interacting with spatial h. The obtained features X_w and X_h include the interactive dependency between the spatial dimensions w, h and the channel space c. This better enhances the modeling capability of the features.

The interaction process between space c and space w is shown in Eq. (2), and the interaction process between space c and h is the same as Eq. (2).

$$X_w = Sigmoid(Conv(X_{1c})) \qquad (2)$$

In the global fusion module, the feature fusion process is as follows:

Firstly, we reshape the interaction features X_w and X_h obtained from the above spatial interaction process to convert the feature dimension to $c \times w \times h$, and then add the two features together to get the feature $F \in R^{c \times w \times h}$. The calculation of eigenvalue F can be represented by Eq. (3):

$$F = Reshape(X_w) + Reshape(X_h) \qquad (3)$$

Then, the feature F is passed through the global attention and activation function $Sigmoid$ to obtain the vector $F' \in R^{c \times 1 \times 1}$. F' is the weight vector after weighting the channels with different importance levels for feature F, and the interval of vector F' is $[0, 1]$. The above calculation is shown in Eq. (4):

$$F' = Sigmoid(GLA(F)) \qquad (4)$$

where, GLA is Global Attention, and the process is shown in Fig. 4. The feature F is subjected to a GlobalAvgPooling operation to obtain a vector $F_g \in R^{c \times 1 \times 1}$ with global information. Then, a vector $F_p \in R^{\frac{c}{4} \times 1 \times 1}$ with smaller data volume is obtained through pointwise convolution and BatchNorm2d normalization (BN) operations. After the pointwise convolution operation, the channel dimension c is reduced to a quarter of the original size. Use point by point convolution and BatchNorm2d normalization to focus on channel scale and data issues to reduce data volume and maintain network stability. Next, the vector F_p is processed through the activation function ReLU to eliminate the gradient disappearance problem during training. Finally, the final output $F' \in R^{c \times 1 \times 1}$ of Global Attention is obtained by restoring dimension c through pointwise convolution. The above process is shown in Eq. (5):

$$GLA(F) = Conv(ReLU(BN(Conv(GlobalAvgPooling(F))))) \qquad (5)$$

where, $Conv$ is a pointwise convolution operation.

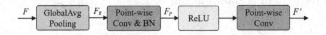

Fig. 4. Framework of Global Attention Module.

Next, the vector F' obtained through the Global Attention and activation function Sigmoid is multiplied by the feature X_w to obtain the feature $X_{f1} \in R^{c \times w \times h}$. In order to select weights more flexibly, let the network determine their respective weights, change the vector F' to $1 - F'$, and then multiply it with the feature X_h to obtain the feature $X_{f2} \in R^{c \times w \times h}$. Finally, the features X_{f1} and X_{f2} are added to obtain the final enhanced feature $G \in R^{c \times w \times h}$. Feature G

contains the interdependencies between different spaces within the global scope, which can better highlight the target features. The above process is shown in Eq. (6):

$$G = X_w \times F' + X_h \times (1 - F') \tag{6}$$

To better prove the effectiveness of the Global Fusion Module (GFM), this paper compares it with the common fusion method (Addition). The results on OTB100 [14] are shown in Table 1. Parentheses indicate the fusion methods used in attention. Specifically, the first behavior uses the results of the original GlobalTrack algorithm [11], the second behavior uses the results of ordinary fusion methods (Addition), and the last behavior uses the results of the Global Fusion Module (GFM).

Table 1. Effect of different fusion methods on tracking performance on OTB100.

Method	Precision	Success
GlobalTrack	0.761	0.610
GlobalTrack+IFAM (Addition)	0.769	0.615
GlobalTrack+IFAM (GFM)	0.774	0.621

The processing of feature through the Interaction-Fusion Attention Module (IFAM) enables the output features to aggregate interactive information from different spatial dimensions, while maintaining global feature dependencies. This improves feature modeling capabilities, more prominent target features, and more accurate target positioning.

2.4   Temporal ROI Align

The GlobalTrack algorithm only uses the template and the feature information of the current image to locate the target. Considering the extraction and utilization of historical information during the tracking process, we introduce Temporal ROI Align [12]. It uses the similarity of features to extract the ROI region features of the current frame from the feature map of other frames, and extracts temporal information of the ROI region during the tracking process. The process of Temporal ROI Align is shown in Fig. 5.

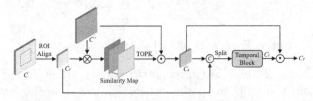

Fig. 5. Framework of Temporal ROI Align.

Firstly, perform the ROI Align operation on the input feature C to extract the region of interest feature C_r.

Then, input the feature map C' with target information in the previous frame and multiply it by C_r to calculate a similar feature map group of ROI features. Through the TOPK operation, select the first K most similar features from the similar feature map group, and multiply with C' element by element to obtain the feature C_s. By extracting the similarity between different frames, the C_s aggregate the features at each spatial location that are most similar to the feature of interest C_r in the current frame, including rich historical information.

Next, in order to fuse the current frame information and historical information, performing a Concat operation on the features C_s and C_r, the obtained result is input into the temporal attention, obtaining temporal features in different frames, and obtaining the feature C_t with temporal information. In temporal block, multiple temporal attention module is used to process and extract temporal features, and Softmax is used to suppress erroneous features in historical frames to better enhance the accuracy of timing information.

Finally, the feature C_t and C_s are fused to obtain final output feature C_T.

Through the processing of features using Temporal ROI Align, it is possible to fully obtain information about historical frames and extract the similarity change rules of features in historical frames. At the same time, it can also suppress error information, making ROI features more accurate, and improving the accuracy of subsequent target positioning.

3 Experiment and Analysis

3.1 Experimental Configuration

The global re-detection method in this paper is implemented using the Python 3.7, PyTorch 1.6.0 programming environment, and CUDA10.1 deep learning architecture. The experimental platform operating system is Ubuntu 16.04, the CPU is Intel Corei5-8400 2.80 GHz, and the GPU is GeForce RTX 2080Ti.

This paper conducted ablation experiments on OTB100 [14]. To verify the effectiveness of the global re-detection method in this paper, the STMTrack [13] is selected as the short-term tracking algorithm in the long-term tracking framework, and our global re-detection method is added to the post processing module. A performance comparison with the original GlobalTrack was conducted on UAV20L [2], and long-term tracking performance experimental evaluations were conducted on UAV123 [2], LaSOT [3], UAV20L [2], and VOT2018-LT [4].

3.2 Ablation Experiment

We chose to perform ablation experiments on OTB100 [14] to demonstrate the effectiveness of the modules used in the global re detection method in this paper and their impact on speed. The experimental results are shown in Table 2. It can be seen that the modules used in the global re-detection method in this paper can effectively improve the performance of the method, and after combining the two modules, better results can be achieved.

Table 2. Results of ablation experiment.

GlobalTrack	IFAM	TRA	Precision	Success	FPS
✓			0.761	0.610	7
✓	✓		0.774	0.621	6.1
✓		✓	0.770	0.616	5.5
✓	✓	✓	0.786	0.627	4.9

3.3   Performance Comparison

To prove the effectiveness of the global re-detection method in this paper and its impact on the long-term tracking speed, the STMTrack [13] is selected as the short-term tracking algorithm based on which the performance of the global re-detection method in this paper is compared with the original GlobalTrack algorithm [11] on four datasets. The experimental results are shown in Table 3. It can be seen that the global re-detection method in this paper is effective. Compared to adding the original GlobalTrack, the average tracking speed of our global re-detection method has not significantly changed, enabling the tracking algorithm to achieve real-time results.

Table 3. Performance comparison as a re-detection method.

Tracker	UAV123		LaSOT			UAV20L		VOT2018-LT			FPS
	Pr.	Succ.	Pr.	N-Pr.	Succ.	Pr.	Succ.	Pr.	Recall	F-score	
STMTrack	0.825	0.647	0.633	0.693	0.606	0.747	0.592	0.630	0.523	0.572	37
STMTrack+GlobalTrack	0.835	0.648	0.644	0.701	0.619	0.833	0.641	0.656	0.600	0.628	36
STMTrack+Ours	0.843	0.650	0.658	0.712	0.631	0.856	0.668	0.674	0.619	0.646	35.4

3.4   Qualitative Analysis

To qualitatively analyze the performance of our global re-detection method, four groups of videos were selected from VOT2018-LT [4] for comparison. Figure 6 shows the partial visual tracking results of adding the global re-detection method and the other 5 comparison algorithms to the STMTrack algorithm [13]. We conduct qualitative analysis of various interference situations in long-term visual tracking, such as out-of-view, partial occlusion, full occlusion, shape scale variation, and background clutters. The four video sequences shown in the figure are *bicycle*, *freestyle*, *rightrope*, and *uav*1 from top to bottom. Due to the small size of the target in *uav*1, we zoomed in on it, using black dotted lines to indicate the enlarged area. As can be seen from Fig. 6, compared to the original STMTrack algorithm, adding the global re-detection method in this paper can effectively deal with multiple interference factors in long-term tracking, enabling the tracking algorithm to track targets more accurately.

GroundTruth   STMTrack+Ours   STMTrack   MBMD   SPLT   GlobalTrack   FuCoLoT

Fig. 6. Tracking effect of selected video sequences in VOT2018-LT.

3.5 Quantitative Analysis

UAV123. This paper compares the original results of the STMTrack [13] with the results after adding our global re-detection method (Ours) on UAV123 [2], and compares the other nine representative tracking algorithms, DaSiamRPN [8], GlobalTrack [11], SiamRPN++ [15], SiamBAN [16], SiamGAT [17], SiamR-CNN [18], AutoMatch [19], CLNet [20], and HiFT [21]. As can be seen from Fig. 7, after adding our re-detection method, the target can be re-searched in time when target drift occurs during the tracking process, effectively improving the performance of the original tracking algorithm in relatively difficult

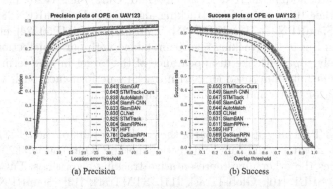

(a) Precision   (b) Success

Fig. 7. UAV123 tracking result evaluation curve.

short-term tracking, and improving the accuracy by 1.8%. SiamR-CNN combines object detection algorithm, which is a long-term tracking algorithm with better performance. Adding our global re-detection method to STMTrack can make the algorithm performance higher than SiamR-CNN, further proving the effectiveness of the global re-detection method in this paper.

LaSOT. This paper compares the original results of the STMTrack on LaSOT [3] with the results after adding our re-detection method (Ours), and compares 12 other representative tracking algorithms, SPLT [10], GlobalTrack [11], SiamRPN++ [15], SiamBAN [16], SiamGAT [17], CLNet [20], SiamRN [22], Ocean [23], DiMP50 [24], LTMU [25], SiamCAR [26], ROAM++ [27]. Figure 8 shows a comparison diagram of the above tracking algorithms on LaSOT. It can be seen that for a large dataset with many interference factors, the addition of our re-detection method can make the tracking algorithm more robust during tracking, improving precision, normalization precision, and success rate by 2.5%, 1.9%, and 2.5%, respectively.

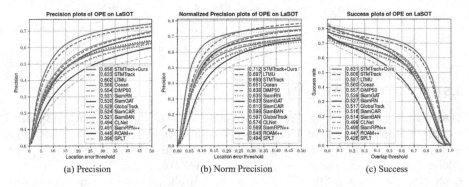

(a) Precision   (b) Norm Precision   (c) Success

Fig. 8. LaSOT tracking result evaluation curve.

UAV20L. This paper compares the original results of the STMTrack [13] with the results after adding our re-detection method (Ours) on UAV20L [2], and compares the other 10 representative tracking algorithms, DaSiamRPN [8], GlobalTrack [11], SiamRPN++ [15], HiFT [21], SiamRN [22], DiMP50 [24], etc. As can be seen from Fig. 9, the tracking algorithm added with our re-detection method can effectively cope with the disappearance of the target in long-term tracking, and has significantly improved long-term tracking performance, with a precision improvement of 10.9% and a success rate improvement of 7.6%.

VOT2018-LT. This paper compares the original results of the STMTrack [13] with the results after adding our re-detection method (Ours) on VOT2018-LT [4], and compares the other nine representative tracking algorithms, FuCoLoT [7], MBMD [9], SPLT [10], GlobalTrack [11], STMTrack [13], SiamRPN++ [15], DiMP50 [24], etc. Figure 10 shows the tracking result evaluation curve of

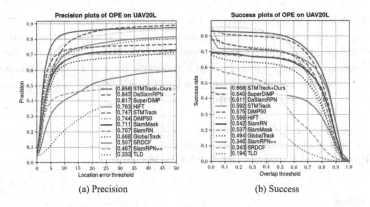

(a) Precision   (b) Success

Fig. 9. UAV20L tracking result evaluation curve.

each visual tracking algorithm on VOT2018-LT. Overall, adding a re-detection method can effectively address issues in long-term tracking and significantly improves the performance of the tracking algorithm on VOT2018-LT. Adding our re-detection method to the STMTrack algorithm can increase the Precision vs. Recall rate by 5.8%.

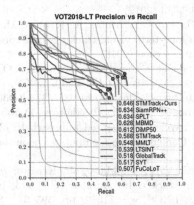

Fig. 10. VOT2018-LT tracking result evaluation curve.

4 Conclusion

To solve the problem of insufficient feature representation and insufficient use of context information in re-detection methods, this paper proposes a temporal global re-detection method based on interaction-fusion attention. A new interaction-fusion attention is introduced to obtain interactive dependency information between different spaces in the feature, enhancing the feature information. The Temporal ROI Align is added to select candidate boxes, increasing the utilization of historical information. The proposed methods improve the accuracy of the re-detection method by enhancing feature information and adding historical information and have achieved good results. In future research, we will continue to conduct more in-depth research on the re-detection method, further improve the accuracy of this method, and explore a more convenient plug-and-play re-detection method.

Acknowledgements. This work is supported by the National Natural Science Foundation of China under grant no. 62072370 and the Natural Science Foundation of Shaanxi Province under grant no. 2023-JC-YB-598.

References

1. Liu, C., Chen, X.F., Bo, C.J., Wang, D.: Long-term visual tracking: review and experimental comparison. Mach. Intell. Res. **19**, 1–19 (2022)
2. Mueller, M., Smith, N., Ghanem, B.: A benchmark and simulator for UAV tracking. In: Leibe, B., Matas, J., Sebe, N., Welling, M. (eds.) ECCV 2016. LNCS, vol. 9905, pp. 445–461. Springer, Cham (2016). https://doi.org/10.1007/978-3-319-46448-0_27
3. Fan, H., et al.: LaSOT: a high-quality benchmark for large-scale single object tracking. In: Proceedings of the IEEE Conference on Computer Vision and Pattern Recognition, pp. 5374–5383 (2019)
4. Lukežič, A., Zajc, L.Č., Vojíř, T., Matas, J., Kristan, M.: Now you see me: evaluating performance in long-term visual tracking. In: Proceedings of the European Conference on Computer Vision (2018)
5. Kristan, M., et al.: The eighth visual object tracking VOT2020 challenge results. In: Bartoli, A., Fusiello, A. (eds.) ECCV 2020. LNCS, vol. 12539, pp. 547–601. Springer, Cham (2020). https://doi.org/10.1007/978-3-030-68238-5_39
6. Hong, Z., Chen, Z., Wang, C., Mei, X., Prokhorov, D., Tao, D.: Multi-store tracker (muster): a cognitive psychology inspired approach to object tracking. In: Proceedings of the IEEE Conference on Computer Vision and Pattern Recognition, pp. 749–758 (2015)
7. Lukežič, A., Zajc, L.Č, Vojíř, T., Matas, J., Kristan, M.: FuCoLoT – a fully-correlational long-term tracker. In: Jawahar, C.V., Li, H., Mori, G., Schindler, K. (eds.) ACCV 2018. LNCS, vol. 11362, pp. 595–611. Springer, Cham (2019). https://doi.org/10.1007/978-3-030-20890-5_38
8. Zhu, Z., Wang, Q., Li, B., Wu, W., Yan, J., Hu, W.: Distractor-aware Siamese networks for visual object tracking. In: Proceedings of the European Conference on Computer Vision, pp. 101–117 (2018)
9. Zhang, Y., Wang, D., Wang, L., Qi, J., Lu, H.: Learning regression and verification networks for long-term visual tracking. arXiv preprint arXiv:1809.04320 (2018)
10. Yan, B., Zhao, H., Wang, D., Lu, H., Yang, X.: 'Skimming-Perusal' tracking: a framework for real-time and robust long-term tracking. In: Proceedings of the IEEE/CVF International Conference on Computer Vision, pp. 2385–2393 (2019)
11. Huang, L., Zhao, X., Huang, K.: GlobalTrack: a simple and strong baseline for long-term tracking. In: Proceedings of the AAAI Conference on Artificial Intelligence, vol. 34, no. 07, pp. 11037–11044 (2020)

12. Gong, T., Chen, K., Wang, X., et al.: Temporal ROI align for video object recognition. In: Proceedings of the AAAI Conference on Artificial Intelligence, vol. 35, no. 2, pp. 1442–1450 (2021)
13. Fu, Z., Liu, Q., Fu, Z., Wang, Y.: STMTrack: template-free visual tracking with space-time memory networks. In: Proceedings of the IEEE Conference on Computer Vision and Pattern Recognition, pp. 13774–13783 (2021)
14. Wu, Y., Lim, J., Yang, M.H.: Online object tracking: a benchmark. In: Proceedings of the IEEE Conference on Computer Vision and Pattern Recognition, pp. 2411–2418 (2013)
15. Li, B., Wu, W., Wang, Q., Zhang, F., Xing, J., Yan, J.: SiamRPN++: evolution of Siamese visual tracking with very deep networks. In: Proceedings of the IEEE Conference on Computer Vision and Pattern Recognition, pp. 4282–4291 (2019)
16. Chen, Z., Zhong, B., Li, G., Zhang, S., Ji, R.: Siamese box adaptive network for visual tracking. In: Proceedings of the IEEE Conference on Computer Vision and Pattern Recognition, pp. 6668–6677 (2020)
17. Guo, D., Shao, Y., Cui, Y., Wang, Z., Zhang, L., Shen, C.: Graph attention tracking. In: Proceedings of the IEEE Conference on Computer Vision and Pattern Recognition, pp. 9543–9552 (2021)
18. Voigtlaender, P., Luiten, J., Torr, P.H.S., Leibe, B.: Siam R-CNN: visual tracking by re-detection. In: Proceedings of the IEEE Conference on Computer Vision and Pattern Recognition, pp. 6578–6588 (2020)
19. Zhang, Z., Liu, Y., Wang, X., Li, B., Hu, W.: Learn to match: automatic matching network design for visual tracking. In: Proceedings of the IEEE/CVF International Conference on Computer Vision, pp. 13339–13348 (2021)
20. Dong, X., Shen, J., Shao, L., Porikli, F.: CLNet: a compact latent network for fast adjusting Siamese trackers. In: Vedaldi, A., Bischof, H., Brox, T., Frahm, J.-M. (eds.) ECCV 2020. LNCS, vol. 12365, pp. 378–395. Springer, Cham (2020). https://doi.org/10.1007/978-3-030-58565-5_23
21. Cao, Z., Fu, C., Ye, J., Li, B., Li, Y.: HiFT: hierarchical feature transformer for aerial tracking. In: Proceedings of the IEEE/CVF International Conference on Computer Vision, pp. 15457–15466 (2021)
22. Cheng, S., Zhong, B., Li, G., Liu, X., Tang, Z., Li, X., Wang, J.: Learning to filter: Siamese relation network for robust tracking. In: Proceedings of the IEEE Conference on Computer Vision and Pattern Recognition, pp. 4421–4431 (2021)
23. Zhang, Z., Peng, H., Fu, J., Li, B., Hu, W.: Ocean: object-aware anchor-free tracking. In: Vedaldi, A., Bischof, H., Brox, T., Frahm, J.-M. (eds.) ECCV 2020. LNCS, vol. 12366, pp. 771–787. Springer, Cham (2020). https://doi.org/10.1007/978-3-030-58589-1_46
24. Bhat, G., Danelljan, M., Gool, L.V., Timofte, R.: Learning discriminative model prediction for tracking. In: Proceedings of the IEEE/CVF International Conference on Computer Vision, pp. 6181–6190 (2019)
25. Dai, K., Zhang, Y., Wang, D., Li, J., Lu, H., Yang, X.: High-performance long-term tracking with meta-updater. In: Proceedings of the IEEE Conference on Computer Vision and Pattern Recognition, pp. 6298–6307 (2020)
26. Guo, D., Wang, J., Cui, Y., Wang, Z., Chen, S.: SiamCAR: Siamese fully convolutional classification and regression for visual tracking. In: Proceedings of the IEEE Conference on Computer Vision and Pattern Recognition, pp. 6269–6277 (2020)
27. Yang, T., Xu, P., Hu, R., Chai, H., Chan, A.B.: ROAM: recurrently optimizing tracking model. In: Proceedings of the IEEE Conference on Computer Vision and Pattern Recognition, pp. 6718–6727 (2020)

VLNet: A Multi-task Network for Joint Vehicle and Lane Detection

Aiqi Feng, Haodong Liu, Tianyang Xu, Donglin Zhang, and Xiao-Jun Wu[✉]

Jiangsu Provincial Engineering Laboratory of Pattern Recognition and
Computational Intelligence, Jiangnan University, Wuxi 214122, Jiangsu, China
wu_xiaojun@jiangnan.edu.cn

Abstract. Visual perception is a crucial component of autonomous
driving. Fully understanding the road environment is conducive to the
safe driving of vehicles. However, most existing methods are usually
unable to simultaneously accomplish multiple visual perception tasks,
limiting the promotion and utilization. To this end, we propose VLNet:
a novel and effective multi-task road environment perception network,
which can perform vehicle and lane detection simultaneously. Specifically, VLNet consists of a shared feature extraction network and two
detection branches for specific tasks. The vehicle detection branch uses
a multi-scale method to detect vehicles, and the lane detection branch
outputs instance-level segmentation map of lanes. Considering the correlation between vehicles and lanes, we leverage the semantic clues of
the lane branch to assist vehicle detection. Compared with single-task
networks, the proposed method reduces memory and computing costs
effectively. Finally, experiments on the challenging Boxy vehicle detection dataset and the LLAMAS lane detection dataset demonstrate the
efficacy of the developed model.

Keywords: Visual perception · Vehicle detection · Lane detection ·
Multi-task network · Semantic clue

1 Introduction

Advanced Driving Assistance System (ADAS) needs properly comprehend the
road environment, such as pedestrians, vehicles and lanes around the current
vehicle. With the development of deep learning, numerous algorithms with good
performance have emerged to perform these visual perception tasks. However,
most existing methods usually only focus on a single task. For example, for
the task of traffic object detection, researchers have achieved good detection
performance by using object detection methods such as Faster R-CNN [17], SSD
[11] and YOLO [16]. These object detection algorithms are usually also used in
subsequent tracking [12,22–24]. Lane detection is an important part of automatic
driving. For lane detection, recent typical methods such as SCNN [14], LaneNet

This work is supported in part by the National Natural Science Foundation of China
(Grant No.62020106012, 62106089).

H. Lu et al. (Eds.): ICIG 2023, LNCS 14356, pp. 16–28, 2023.
https://doi.org/10.1007/978-3-031-46308-2_2

[13], and LaneAF [1] consider lane detection as a pixel-level segmentation task, and achieve accurate segmentation of lanes.

Although the above approaches have shown good performance on a single task, in real applications, deploying multiple environment perception models to embedded devices will take up a large amount of memory and computation, slowing down the inference time. Therefore, building an effective multi-task network is crucial for road environment perception. Generally speaking, compared with the single-task network, the multi-task network consists of multiple task heads that can share the feature extraction network and perform multiple prediction tasks at the same time, thereby reducing memory and computing costs. Furthermore, different tasks in road scenes are frequently associated, such as vehicles are typically placed between two lane lines. Therefore, the detection performance may be enhanced by investigating the correlation between multiple tasks.

To this end, we propose a joint vehicle and lane detection network, VLNet for short. VLNet is a simple and efficient multi-task network, which can reduce the cost of memory and calculation. Specifically, we use ResNet-34 to extract features at different scales first, and the Feature Pyramid Network (FPN) [10] is leveraged to fuse features of different scales. Moreover, the vehicle detection branch adopts the multi-scale strategy to detect vehicles, and the lane detection branch outputs the instance-level segmentation map of lanes. To explore the correlation between vehicles and lanes, we use the semantic clues of the lane branch to assist vehicle detection, which can improve detection performance. In summary, the contributions of this paper can be summarized as follows:

1) We propose a simple and effective multi-task network VLNet, which can complete vehicle and lane detection at the same time. It can effectively reduce memory and computing costs.
2) We use the semantic clues from the lane detection branch to guide the vehicle detection, improving the detection accuracy of the vehicle detection branch.
3) Different from the existing multi-task network for road environment perception, the proposed method can achieve instance-level segmentation and can identify varying numbers of lanes.
4) The developed VLNet achieves good performance on both the vehicle detection task and the lane detection task.

The remainder of this paper is organized as follows. Section 2 reviews related works. In Sect. 3, we introduce the developed VLNet in detail. Section 4 analyzes the experimental results. Finally, the summary of this paper is given in Sect. 5.

2   Related Work

With the rapid development of deep learning, some CNN (Convolutional Neural Networks) based methods for visual perception have been proposed and attracted considerable attention. In this section, we briefly review the related works of vehicle detection, lane detection and multi-task detection methods based on CNN.

2.1 Vehicle Detection

Vehicle detection is a fundamental task in ADAS. Object detection algorithms based on CNN can be divided into two-stage object detection algorithms based on proposals and one-stage object detection algorithms based on regression. The two-stage object detection algorithms are mainly based on a series of R-CNN [6] algorithms, such as Faster R-CNN [17], Mask R-CNN [7], and Cascade R-CNN [4], etc. These methods firstly use Region Proposal Network (RPN) to select Region of Interests (RoI) that may contain objects, and then classify and locate the candidate RoI. Due to using RPN to screen candidate regions, the detection accuracy is high, but speed is low. The one-stage detectors regard object detection as a regression task, and directly regress bounding boxes on the image and predict the corresponding category. These methods have a simple structure and fast detection speed, which can meet the real-time detection requirements, and is more suitable for applications with limited memory and computation in embedded devices. Representative algorithms include SSD-series [5,11], and YOLO-series [9,16,20] algorithms, etc. As a continuously iterative YOLO-series algorithm, it achieves fast and accurate detection by introducing anchor mechanism, refined network structure, FPN, multi-scale detection and other techniques.

2.2 Lane Detection

Lane detection is crucial for lane keeping, lane departure, trajectory planning and decision-making in ADAS. Recent methods based on deep learning usually treat lane detection as a pixel-level segmentation task [1,8,13,14,25,27]. SCNN [14] proposes a message passing mechanism to collect global contextual information to improve the accuracy of lane detection. However, it also introduces a large amount of calculation. In order to reduce computation of backbone network, Hou et al. [8] proposed a self-attention distillation module to aggregate contextual information, achieving high detection accuracy and real-time performance on a lightweight backbone network. LaneNet [13] combines the binary segmentation branch and the embedding branch to realize lane instance-level segmentation, but the post-clustering process is time-consuming and difficult to meet the real-time detection requirements. LLNet [27] uses the instance segmentation map instead of the binary segmentation map in LaneNet to filter falsely detected pixels and further improve the detection accuracy. LaneAF [1] clusters lane pixels to corresponding lane instances by predicting binary segmentation maps and affinity fields, and is able to detect a variable number of lanes.

2.3 Multi-task Detection

Aiming at the problem that multiple single-task networks will occupy a large amount of memory and calculation, many researchers try to build a multi-task network to complete multiple visual perception tasks. Compared with the single-task network, the multi-task network can effectively reduce the amount of memory and calculation because multiple task branches share the feature extraction network. More importantly, the detection performance can be further improved by using the correlation information between multiple tasks. In order to complete multiple road environment perception tasks, MultiNet [19] designs a multi-task network with a shared encoder and three independent decoders. It simultaneously completes three traffic scene perception tasks of scene classification, object detection and drivable area segmentation. DLT-Net [15] inherits the encoder-decoder structure in MultiNet, explores the correlation between each task, and constructs contextual tensors between each decoder to realize mutual complementation of information. YOLOP [21] adds a drivable area segmentation head and a lane segmentation head on the basis of the lightweight YOLOv5 detector to achieve joint detection of multiple tasks and has high real-time performance. However, its decoders are independent of each other, and each task cannot benefit from other tasks to improve performance.

Although the above multi-task networks can achieve good performance on multiple visual perception tasks, these methods are all trained on homologous datasets, namely, one sample contains multiple labels. However, the acquisition cost and labeling cost of strictly homologous datasets are huge. Therefore, multi-task learning under non-homologous datasets has also become a difficulty. Moreover, for lane detection, the above visual perception multi-task networks only segment lane in semantic level. In order to promote research in the field of autonomous driving visual perception, Bosch released multiple large-scale single-task datasets, such as the Boxy [2] vehicle detection dataset containing 200k high-resolution images and the LLAMAS [3] lane detection dataset containing 100k images. Lanes in the LLAMAS are marked at the instance level. We use non-homologous datasets to train an end-to-end multi-task network, which can simultaneously detect vehicles and lanes. More importantly, it can achieve instance-level segmentation of lanes.

3   Method

In this section, we elaborately introduce the proposed method. The overall architecture of VLNet is shown in Fig. 1, which consists of a shared feature extraction network, the vehicle detection branch and the lane detection branch. Moreover, the semantic clues of the lane branch are utilized to guide vehicle detection.

3.1   Vehicle Detection Branch

Similar to the YOLO algorithm, we adopt a multi-scale object detection strategy based on the anchor mechanism. The image is divided into $S \times S$ grids, and each grid presets 3 anchor boxes. First, RestNet-34 is used to extract semantic feature maps (C_2, C_3 and C_4) at different levels. Then these feature maps are fed into FPN for further feature fusion, which combines deep semantic information and shallow position information to enhance the feature representation. The fused multi-scale feature maps (P_2, P_3 and P_4) are input into the vehicle detection head.

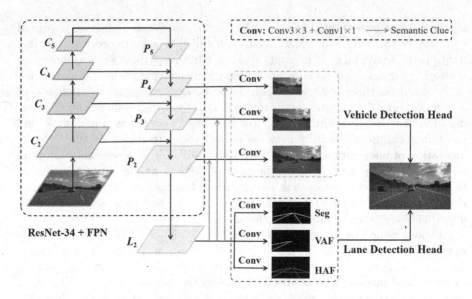

Fig. 1. The framework of our VLNet.

For the part of vehicle detection head, the output feature maps are mapped to $S \times S$ grids, and each grid is responsible for predicting the regression parameters, confidence and category probability of three detection boxes. For each feature map, we use one 3×3 convolution to further extract features, and then use one 1×1 convolution to modulate the channel to the dimension of the prediction vector. Correspond to the four regression parameters of the object (center point offset parameter and scaling parameters), object confidence and category probability. Finally, redundant bounding boxes are eliminated through Non-Maximum Suppression.

3.2 Lane Detection Branch

Drawing on the prediction branch in LaneAF, the lane detection branch in this paper also predicts a binary segmentation mask and the horizontal affinity field (HAF) and vertical affinity field (VAF) of each pixel. The affinity field refers to a vector field that can map any location on the image to a two-dimensional unit vector. A unit vector in the VAF encodes the direction in which the next set of lane pixels above it is located. While the unit vector in HAF points to the center of the current lane, therefore lanes of arbitrary width can be clustered. The lane detection head adopts a single scale, and the 1/4 scale feature map of the original image as input. The specific prediction network is very simple. A binary segmentation mask, HAF and VAF are obtained by one 3×3 and one 1×1 convolution. Finally, the foreground pixels are clustered into lane instances through a simple row-by-row decoding process from bottom to top.

3.3   Semantic Clues

It can be observed from the driving scene that the vehicles frequently are in the middle of two lane lines. Considering the correlation between vehicles and lanes, the semantic clues of lanes can be exploited to assist in vehicle detection. As shown in Fig. 1, the green arrow represents the semantic clue features of the lanes. The semantic clue features are added to each detection branch of vehicle detection. For feature maps of different sizes, the downsampling operation is used to adjust them to the same scale. Since the feature map dimensions of the lane detection branch and the vehicle detection branch are both 256 dimensions, a simple addition operation is used to enhance the features of the vehicle detection branch. We verify the effectiveness of semantic clues of lanes in the ablation experiment part.

3.4   Loss Function

The loss function of VLNet consists of vehicle detection loss and lane detection loss.

Vehicle Detection Loss. The vehicle detection loss function is a weighted sum of confidence loss, classification loss, and localization loss as in Eq. 1.

$$L_{vehicle} = \lambda_{obj} L_{obj} + \lambda_{cls} L_{cls} + \lambda_{box} L_{box}, \tag{1}$$

where L_{obj} and L_{cls} are confidence loss and classification loss respectively, both of which use cross-entropy loss. Localization loss adopts CIoU loss. CIoU further considers the center point distance and aspect ratio consistency between bounding boxes and ground truth, which can effectively improve localization accuracy and speed up convergence. λ_{obj}, λ_{cls} and λ_{box} are trade-off factors.

Lane Detection Loss. The loss function of lane detection includes L_{BCE}, L_{IoU} and L_{AF}, defined as Eq. 2.

$$L_{lane} = L_{BCE} + L_{IoU} + L_{AF}. \tag{2}$$

The lane detection head outputs a binary segmentation map, vertical and horizontal affinity fields. For the binary segmentation map, in order to alleviate the unbalanced foreground and background pixels, the weighted binary cross-entropy loss and IoU loss are jointly used to constrain the classification error between the binary segmentation map and ground truth. For the vertical and horizontal affinity field branches, apply L_1 loss only to foreground pixels. The calculation of the affinity field loss is shown in Eq. 3.

$$L_{AF} = \frac{1}{N_{fg}} \sum_i \left[\left| t_i^{haf} - o_i^{haf} \right| + \left| t_i^{vaf} - o_i^{vaf} \right| \right]. \tag{3}$$

In conclusion, the final loss of VLNet is as follows:

$$L_{total} = L_{vehicle} + L_{lane}. \tag{4}$$

4   Experiments and Analysis

We use the large-scale vehicle detection dataset Boxy [2] and the lane detection dataset LLAMAS [3] released by Bosch to jointly train the multi-task network. The training samples are extracted separately through the data loader for joint training. Table 1 shows the attributes of Boxy and LLAMAS dataset.

Table 1. Attributes of the datasets used in this work.

Dataset	Frames	Train	Validation	Test	Resolution	Scenarios
Boxy [2]	200000	135398	28746	35856	1232 × 1028	highway
LLAMAS [3]	100042	58269	20844	20929	1280 × 717	highway

4.1   Implementation Details

ResNet-34 is adopted as backbone network, and we use the pre-trained weights on ImageNet as initialization. During training, the input image resolution is 640 × 352. We use Adam optimizer with learning rate of 0.0001, weight decay of 0.001. Batch size is set as 8, and total training epochs are 40. Furthermore, we also make use of data augmentation strategy, including random crops, scales, rotations and horizontal flips. The entire network is implemented based on Pytorch and trained on a single GTX 2080Ti GPU.

4.2   Boxy

Dataset Description. Boxy [2] is a large and challenging vehicle detection dataset, which contains 200k high-resolution images. These images are collected in highway scenarios, covering various driving environments such as sunny, cloudy, rainy, dusk and night. The average vehicle label size only occupies about 0.3% of the image. Due to the limitation of experimental conditions, only one image is selected for one sequence of images in Boxy. Finally, a total of 18041 training images are selected. Experimental validation is performed on the standard validation set of Boxy.

Evaluation Metric. The average precision of the standard COCO format is used to evaluate the vehicle detection accuracy, including mAP with IoU at [0.5: 0.95] and AP_{50} with IoU at 0.5.

Quantitative Results. Table 2 compares the detection performance of the vehicle detection on Boxy. The mainstream object detection algorithms Faster R-CNN and Cascade R-CNN are selected for comparison. Table 2 shows that VLNet proposed in this paper are 45.5%and 74.5% on mAP and AP50, respectively. Compared with Faster R-CNN and Cascade R-CNN, the mAP is increased by 10.3% and 6.9%, respectively.

Table 2. Comparison of vehicle detection results of different methods on Boxy.

Method	Backbone	mAP	AP50
Faster R-CNN [17]	ResNet-34	35.2	45.5
Cascade R-CNN [4]	ResNet-34	38.6	51.1
VLNet	ResNet-34	**45.5**	**74.5**

Qualitative Results. The visual results of vehicle detection of VLNet on Boxy dataset are shown in Fig. 2, and good detection results have been achieved in different lighting driving environments. Since the proposed method in this paper can jointly detect vehicles and lanes, Fig. 3 shows the visualization of lane detection on Boxy. Although without training the lane detection branch on Boxy, VLNet can still detect lane instances in different road scenarios.

4.3 LLAMAS

Dataset Description. LLAMAS [3] is a large lane detection dataset with approximately 100k images. All images are collected from highway scenarios, covering different lighting conditions. Since the labels of test set are not public, we conducts experimental verification on validation set.

Evaluation Metric. Using F_1 score as the evaluation indicator of LLAMAS dataset. The predicted lane is regarded as a true example when IoU between the predicted lane and ground truth is greater than 0.5. $F_1 = \frac{2 \times Precision \times Recall}{Precision + Recall}$, where $Precision = \frac{TP}{TP+FP}$, $Recall = \frac{TP}{TP+FN}$, TP is the number of correctly predicted lane points, FP is the number of wrong predictions, and FN represents the number of missing points.

Quantitative Results. Table 3 reports the detection results of our method and other advanced lane detection methods on the LLAMAS validation set. It can be observed that comparing LaneATT and LaneAF lane detection algorithms, VLNet can achieve the best performance in Precision, Recall and F1 score, demonstrating the efficacy of the proposed model.

Fig. 2. Visual results of vehicle detection on Boxy dataset.

Table 3. Comparison of lane detection results of different methods on LLAMAS.

Method	Backbone	Precision	Recall	F1
LaneATT [18]	ResNet-34	-	-	94.96
LaneAF [1]	ResNet-34	96.35	96.63	96.49
VLNet	ResNet-34	**96.57**	**96.76**	**96.66**

Qualitative Results. Figure 4 shows the lane detection results of VLNet on LLAMAS validation set. For challenging scenarios such as unclear lanes, shadows, occlusions, and curves, the proposed method can still accurately predict each lane instance. We also provide the visual results of vehicle detection on LLAMAS, as shown in Fig. 5.

4.4 BDD100K

BDD100K [26] is a public dataset for autonomous driving research. It contains multiple task labels such as traffic objects, lanes and drivable areas, etc. We presents the visualization results of the model trained on Boxy and LLAMAS datasets on BDD100K, as shown in Fig. 6. The visualization results show that the proposed method has a certain generalization ability.

4.5 Ablation Study

The Effectiveness of Multi-task Network. We also perform some experiments to verify the effectiveness of the multi-task network proposed. The experimental results are given in Table 4, which reports the performance of the multi-task network and the single-task network. It can be seen that the performance

Fig. 3. Visual results of lane detection on Boxy dataset.

of the multi-task network proposed in this work is close to that of the corresponding single task on vehicle detection and lane detection. More importantly, multi-task networks can save a large amount of memory and computation compared to executing each task individually.

The Effectiveness of Semantic Clues. In order to verify the effectiveness of the semantic clues proposed scheme. We carry out some experiments. The results are given in Table 4. Specifically, the last row of Table 4 indicates that the multi-task network adds semantic clues. We can see that the semantic clues scheme can enhance the detection performance. To be specific, the mAP and AP50 of vehicle detection are increased by 0.4% and 0.7%, respectively, indicating that the lane semantic clues strategy can effectively improve the performance of vehicle detection.

Table 4. Ablation experiments.

Vehicle branch	Lane branch	Semantic clue	mAP	AP50	Precision	Recall	F1
√			44.8	74.0	-	-	-
	√		-	-	**96.67**	96.63	96.65
√	√		45.1	73.8	96.52	96.70	96.61
√	√	√	**45.5**	**74.5**	96.57	**96.76**	**96.66**

Fig. 4. Visual results of lane detection on LLAMAS dataset.

Fig. 5. Visual results of vehicle detection on LLAMAS dataset.

Fig. 6. Visual results of joint vehicle and lane detection on BDD100K dataset.

5   Conclusion

In this paper, we propose a simple and effective multi-task network (VLNet) for end-to-end vehicle and lane detection. VLNet consists of a shared feature extraction network and two detection branches. Compared with the single-task network, the proposed VLNet can effectively reduce a large amount of memory and calculating costs, improving the inference speed of the network. Furthermore, we leverage the semantic clues of the lane branch to assist detect vehicles. Experimental results show that VLNet has achieved good performance on both the Boxy vehicle detection dataset and the LLAMAS lane detection dataset. Most importantly, compared with existing multi-task networks for visual perception tasks, our method is capable of instance-level lane segmentation and can identify varying numbers of lanes.

Acknowledgement. This work was supported by the National Natural Science Foundation of China (62020106012, 62202204, U1836218), the Fundamental Research Funds for the Central Universities (JUSRP123032) and the 111 Project of Ministry of Education of China (B12018).

References

1. Abualsaud, H., Liu, S., Lu, D.B., Situ, K., Rangesh, A., Trivedi, M.M.: LaneAF: robust multi-lane detection with affinity fields. IEEE Robot. Autom. Lett. **6**(4), 7477–7484 (2021)
2. Behrendt, K.: Boxy vehicle detection in large images. In: Proceedings of the IEEE/CVF International Conference on Computer Vision Workshops (2019)
3. Behrendt, K., Soussan, R.: Unsupervised labeled lane markers using maps. In: Proceedings of the IEEE/CVF International Conference on Computer Vision Workshops (2019)
4. Cai, Z., Vasconcelos, N.: Cascade R-CNN: high quality object detection and instance segmentation. IEEE Trans. Pattern Anal. Mach. Intell. **43**(5), 1483–1498 (2019)
5. Fu, C.Y., Liu, W., Ranga, A., Tyagi, A., Berg, A.C.: DSSD: deconvolutional single shot detector. arXiv preprint arXiv:1701.06659 (2017)
6. Girshick, R., Donahue, J., Darrell, T., Malik, J.: Rich feature hierarchies for accurate object detection and semantic segmentation. In: Proceedings of the IEEE Conference on Computer Vision and Pattern Recognition, pp. 580–587 (2014)
7. He, K., Gkioxari, G., Dollár, P., Girshick, R.: Mask R-CNN. IEEE Trans. Pattern Anal. Mach. Intell. **42**(2), 386–397 (2018)
8. Hou, Y., Ma, Z., Liu, C., Loy, C.C.: Learning lightweight lane detection CNNs by self attention distillation. In: Proceedings of the IEEE/CVF International Conference on Computer Vision, pp. 1013–1021 (2019)
9. Li, C., et al.: YOLOv6 v3. 0: a full-scale reloading. arXiv preprint arXiv:2301.05586 (2023)
10. Lin, T.Y., Dollár, P., Girshick, R., He, K., Hariharan, B., Belongie, S.: Feature pyramid networks for object detection. In: Proceedings of the IEEE Conference on Computer Vision and Pattern Recognition, pp. 2117–2125 (2017)

11. Liu, W., et al.: SSD: single shot multibox detector. In: Leibe, B., Matas, J., Sebe, N., Welling, M. (eds.) ECCV 2016. LNCS, vol. 9905, pp. 21–37. Springer, Cham (2016). https://doi.org/10.1007/978-3-319-46448-0_2

12. Meinhardt, T., Kirillov, A., Leal-Taixe, L., Feichtenhofer, C.: TrackFormer: multi-object tracking with transformers. In: The IEEE Conference on Computer Vision and Pattern Recognition (CVPR) (2022)

13. Neven, D., De Brabandere, B., Georgoulis, S., Proesmans, M., Van Gool, L.: Towards end-to-end lane detection: an instance segmentation approach. In: 2018 IEEE Intelligent Vehicles Symposium (IV), pp. 286–291. IEEE (2018)

14. Pan, X., Shi, J., Luo, P., Wang, X., Tang, X.: Spatial as deep: spatial CNN for traffic scene understanding. In: Proceedings of the AAAI Conference on Artificial Intelligence, vol. 32 (2018)

15. Qian, Y., Dolan, J.M., Yang, M.: DLT-Net: joint detection of drivable areas, lane lines, and traffic objects. IEEE Trans. Intell. Transp. Syst. **21**(11), 4670–4679 (2019)

16. Redmon, J., Divvala, S., Girshick, R., Farhadi, A.: You only look once: unified, real-time object detection. In: Proceedings of the IEEE Conference on Computer Vision and Pattern Recognition, pp. 779–788 (2016)

17. Ren, S., He, K., Girshick, R., Sun, J.: Faster R-CNN: towards real-time object detection with region proposal networks. IEEE Trans. Pattern Anal. Mach. Intell. **39**(6), 1137–1149 (2017)

18. Tabelini, L., Berriel, R., Paixao, T.M., Badue, C., Souza, A.F.D., Oliveira-Santos, T.: Keep your eyes on the lane: real-time attention-guided lane detection. In: Computer Vision and Pattern Recognition (2021)

19. Teichmann, M., Weber, M., Zoellner, M., Cipolla, R., Urtasun, R.: MultiNet: real-time joint semantic reasoning for autonomous driving. In: 2018 IEEE intelligent vehicles symposium (IV), pp. 1013–1020. IEEE (2018)

20. Wang, C.Y., Bochkovskiy, A., Liao, H.Y.M.: YOLOv7: trainable bag-of-freebies sets new state-of-the-art for real-time object detectors. arXiv preprint arXiv:2207.02696 (2022)

21. Wu, D., et al.: YOLOP: you only look once for panoptic driving perception. Mach. Intell. Res. **19**, 550–562 (2022). https://doi.org/10.1007/s11633-022-1339-y

22. Xu, T., Feng, Z.H., Wu, X.J., Kittler, J.: An accelerated correlation filter tracker. Pattern Recogn. **102**, 107172 (2020)

23. Xu, T., Feng, Z., Wu, X.J., Kittler, J.: Adaptive channel selection for robust visual object tracking with discriminative correlation filters. Int. J. Comput. Vision **129**, 1359–1375 (2021)

24. Xu, T., Feng, Z., Wu, X.J., Kittler, J.: Toward robust visual object tracking with independent target-agnostic detection and effective Siamese cross-task interaction. IEEE Trans. Image Process. **32**, 1541–1554 (2023)

25. Yang, J., Zhang, L., Lu, H.: Lane detection with versatile AtrousFormer and local semantic guidance. Pattern Recogn. **133**, 109053 (2023)

26. Yu, F., et al.: BDD100K: a diverse driving video database with scalable annotation tooling. arXiv preprint arXiv:1805.04687 2(5), 6 (2018)

27. Zhang, L., Kong, B., Wang, C.: LLNet: a lightweight lane line detection network. In: Peng, Y., Hu, S.-M., Gabbouj, M., Zhou, K., Elad, M., Xu, K. (eds.) ICIG 2021. LNCS, vol. 12888, pp. 355–369. Springer, Cham (2021). https://doi.org/10.1007/978-3-030-87355-4_30

Adaptive Cost Aggregation in Iterative Depth Estimation for Efficient Multi-view Stereo

Xiang Wang, Xiao Bai$^{(\boxtimes)}$, and Chen Wang

School of Computer Science and Engineering, State Key Laboratory of Software Development Environment, Jiangxi Research Institute, Beihang University, Beijing, China
baixiao@buaa.edu.cn

Abstract. The deep multi-view stereo (MVS) approaches generally construct 3D cost volumes to regularize and regress the depth map. These methods are limited with high-resolution outputs since the memory and time costs grow cubically as the volume resolution increases. In this paper, we presented an multi-stage iterative depth map estimation method for MVS. In our network, the cost volume is iteratively processed by lightweight 2D convolution based GRU modules, and the multi-stage coarse-to-fine structure is adopted to speed up the depth estimation process. To further improve the 3D reconstruction quality, we make improvements from two different perspectives of adaptive cost aggregation: a view-adaptive weighting module is proposed to account for the occlusion problem in cost volume fusion, and a spatial-adaptive deformable geometric feature encoding module is introduced to the cost volume feature encoding before feeding into GRUs for stronger modeling capability. Experiments on the DTU dataset demonstrated the effectiveness of the proposed network in accuracy with remarkable efficiency performance.

Keywords: Multi-view stereo · Iterative network · Coarse-to-fine · 3D reconstruction

1 Introduction

Multi-view Stereo (MVS) aims to reconstruct the high-quality 3D models of the observed scene given a series of overlapping calibrated images. Multi-view stereo is a fundamental task in 3D computer vision, which plays an important role in augmented/virtual reality, autonomous driving, robotics and 3D modeling. Predicting depth maps from given views and fusing them into a point cloud is the most common pipeline of MVS.

Recent remarkable progresses have been made with the successes of deep neural networks in 3D perception and reconstruction [20,36,37,39]. MVSNet [31] has paved the way for most multi-view stereo networks that predict the depth map of the reference view from multiple images, which decomposed the whole process into four main steps: (1) extracting feature maps from multi-view images,

© The Author(s), under exclusive license to Springer Nature Switzerland AG 2023
H. Lu et al. (Eds.): ICIG 2023, LNCS 14356, pp. 29–41, 2023.
https://doi.org/10.1007/978-3-031-46308-2_3

(2) constructing a cost volume in the frustum of the reference view by aggregating multi-view features, (3) regularizing the cost volume to produce the probability volume, and (4) regressing the depth map from the probability volume. Note that cost volume regularization, the key step for good accuracy, consists of a 3D CNN, is known to be costly in terms of computation time and memory. Recently, several attempts have been made to solve this problem, from multi-stage coarse-to-fine methods [4,10,30] to recurrent methods [25,29,32]. Nevertheless, it is still difficult to reach a great trade-off between 3D reconstruction quality and computational cost.

Notable progresses come from the idea of iteratively updating the depth map of the reference view. Wang et al. [22] introduced the classical PatchMatch [2] method to the end-to-end trainable network, enabling updating depth maps with high efficiency. Recently, RAFT [18] proposed to estimate optical flow by iteratively updating a motion field through a series of GRU modules, which emulated the steps of a first-order optimization algorithm. Several works [15, 21,23] were inspired from this work and utilized the GRU to iteratively update the depth map. By only retrieving local cost information and using only 2D convolution in the GRU updater, the time and memory efficiency are greatly boosted. Specifically, Wang et al. [23] also adopted the coarse-to-fine framework, further boosting the reconstruction quality.

In this work, we follow the GRU-based depth map updater works and make some key modifications that improves the reconstruction quality with negligible computation burden increase. First, occlusion from different views raises a severe problem for precise matching, thus affects the quality of cost volume construction. Taking visibility information into account could be beneficial to reduce the negative influence of mismatched pixels in the cost volume. We propose a view-adaptive weighting module during multiple cost volume fusion, which exploits the similarity between reference and source features to explicitly model the visibility. Second, the cost volume is embedded into geometric features before fed into the GRU update module. To better describe boundary and texture-less regions when embedding matching information, we leverage the deformable convolutions [6,40] that adaptively sample the aggregating locations for better cost aggregation. These two modules shows notable performance boost over the multi-stage iterative depth update method [23], while only introduce minimal learnable parameters and modest additional computational cost in memory and time.

In summary, the main contributions of this paper are: (1) The view adaptive weighting module for cost volume fusion is introduced into the GRU based iterative depth update architecture, which explicitly accounts for the visibility information. (2) A deformable convolution is applied to the cost encoding procedure before feeding into the GRU depth updater, better preserving the geometric information along boundaries. (3) With little additional computation, the proposed method achieve better reconstruction performance over recent iterative MVS networks.

2   Related Work

2.1   Traditional Methods

Traditional MVS methods can be divided into four main categories according to the output scene representations: voxel based [17,19], surface based [7,14], patch based [8] and depth map based methods [9,16,27]. Among those methods, the depth map based methods are more concise, flexible and scalable. Following the classical PatchMatch Stereo method [2], many MVS algorithms estimate high quality depth maps by view selection, local propagation and aggregation strategies. Galliani et al. [9] presented Gipuma, which utilized a checkerboard-based propagation scheme that enabled parallel message-passing during propagation. Schönberger et al. [16] presented COLMAP, which jointly estimated pixel-wise view selection, depth map and surface normal to enhance the robustness of the algorithm. Recently, Xu et al. proposed ACMM [27], which extended the MVS framework to multi-scale, accompanied with adaptive checkerboard propagation and multi-hypothesis joint view selection. Although these methods can obtain robust 3D reconstruction results, their reconstruction quality are not satisfactory.

2.2   Learning-Based Methods

With the recent development of deep learning, multi-view stereo methods have benefited from the powerful representation learning ability of deep networks, empowered by training data. Yao et al. [31] proposed a depth-map based multi-view stereo network, which consisted of four steps: a feature extraction network, a cost volume construction module, a cost aggregation network and a depth estimation module. Such a network architecture has formed the basic paradigm for the depth map-based MVS networks. However, the cost regularization with a 3D CNN causes the main bottleneck in efficiency as the memory and run-time grow cubically with increasing resolution. To reduce the memory consumption when dealing with high-resolution images, recurrent methods [25,29,32] split the cost volume into 2D slices along the depth dimension and sequentially process the cost information, while sacrificing run-time. The coarse to fine strategy, processing a cost volume pyramid with decreasing depth range instead of the whole cost volume, has been adopted in several latest works [4,10,30] to reduce the memory consumption and improve the accuracy and speed. Despite their impressive performance, coarse-to-fine methods have difficulty in recovering from errors introduced at coarse resolutions [35]. RAFT [18] has witnessed the great progress in optical flow. Its key idea, updating current depth map using the information of iteratively retrieved local cost volumes and the historical cost information encoded in hidden states of GRUs, has inspired several efficient MVS networks [15,21,23]. In particular, [21] formulated the RAFT-like structure in a coarse-to-fine manner, reaching a good trade-off between effectiveness and efficiency. We further introduce several modules to this structure that improve the reconstruction results without sacrificing efficiency. Please refer to [24] for a detailed review.

3 Method

In this section, we presented our proposed multi-view stereo framework. The network architecture is illustrated in Fig. 1(a). The network consists of a feature extraction network, a context network, a depth initialization network based on a 3D CNN, and a cascade depth estimation framework with multiple iterative GRU optimizer units.

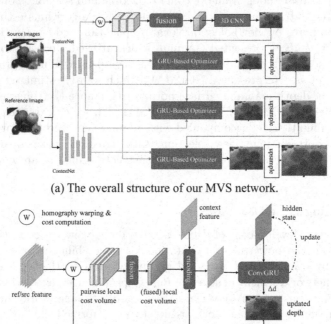

(a) The overall structure of our MVS network.

(b) The detailed structure of GRU-Based Optimizer.

Fig. 1. The framework of the proposed multi-stage iterative MVS networks and the detail of the GRU-based depth optimizer.

3.1 Multi-scale Feature Extraction Network and Cost Volume Computation

The input images of size $H \times W$ include a reference image and $\mathbf{I}_0$ and $N-1$ source images $\{\mathbf{I}_i\}_{i=1,\dots N-1}$. All the images are passed through a Feature Pyramid Network to extract multi-scale matching features. Specifically, a feature map $\mathbf{F}_i^k$ of size $\frac{H}{2^{3-k}} \times \frac{W}{2^{3-k}}$ is extracted from the stage k, $k = 0, 1, 2$. Another Feature Pyramid Network is leveraged to extract multi-scale context features from only $\mathbf{I}_0$, which provides the context features, $\mathbf{CT}_i^k$ and initial hidden states $\mathbf{h}_i^k$ for the iterative GRU units at corresponding stages. The context FPN shares the same structure as the feature FPN, while not sharing parameters.

Similar to other depth map based deep multi-view stereo methods [10,22,31, 32], We adopt the plane sweep stereo principle [5] that establish several front-to-parallel planes in the reference view. Given the camera intrinsic parameters

$\{\mathbf{K}_i\}_{i=0,...N-1}$ and relative transformations $\{\mathbf{R}_0, i | \mathbf{t}_0, i\}_{i=1,...N-1}$ between the reference view and the source view i, for a pixel $\mathbf{p}$ with the depth hypothesis d in the reference view, the projected pixel in the source view can be found at:

$$\mathbf{p}_{i,d} = \mathbf{K}_i \cdot (\mathbf{R}_{0,i} \cdot (\mathbf{K}_0^{-1} \cdot \mathbf{p} \cdot d) + \mathbf{t}_{0,i}) \tag{1}$$

By interpolating features at pixel $\mathbf{p}_{i,d}$, we can get warped features $\hat{\mathbf{F}}_i(\mathbf{p}_{i,d})$ and compare with the reference feature. The cost $\mathbf{c}_{i,d}$ denote the similarity of the reference feature and the warped feature, forming the pairwise volumes. The pairwise volumes are then fused into a single volume, presenting matching cost of depth hypotheses for the reference view.

3.2 Multi-stage Iterative Depth Estimation

We adopt the multi-scale iterative structure to predict the depth map for the reference view iteratively. Our network generates multi-resolution depth map in a coarse-to-fine manner, and in each stage, it produces residual depth to refine the depth maps. By using lightweight GRU units to regularize the cost rather than using the 3D CNN, our network gains much time and memory efficiency.

Depth Initialization Network. The iterative GRU optimizer refine the depth progressively, requiring a large number of steps if the initial depth is given improperly or failing to predict a reliable depth in textureless or occluded regions. Thus, we use a 3D CNN based depth estimation network as [31] at the coarsest stage for depth initialization. It produce a probability volume $\mathbf{P}_d$ over a depth hypothesis set, which is small but covering the whole depth range. The initial depth estimation is computed as the weighted sum of all considered depth hypotheses. Considering that we only use the 3D regularization network at the coarsest stage, the computation cost is relatively small.

Cascade GRU-Based Depth Optimizer. Our GRU-based depth optimizer produces a sequence of depth maps for the reference view from the initial depth. In each optimizer step, it produces a residual depth map that update the current depth: $d_{t+1}^k = d_t^k + \Delta d_t^k$. After the last optimizer step T^k in stage k, the depth map d_T^k is upsampled to the resolution of the next stage d_0^{k+1}.

The detailed structure of a GRU-based Depth Optimizer is illustrated in Fig. 1(b). In each stage k, the optimizer unit receives a local cost volume $\mathbf{C}_0^k$, a context feature $\mathbf{CT}^k$ and the initial hidden state $\mathbf{h}_0^k$, the latter two of which are from the context network. At each step t, the local cost volume $\mathbf{C}_t^k$ (see Sec. 3.3) is retrieved according to the current depth d_t^k estimate and is constructed on the fly, saving much memory usage. $\mathbf{C}_t^k$, $\mathbf{CT}^k$ and d_t^k are passed through a feature encoding module (see Sec. 3.4) to produce a geometric-aware feature, which is then fed into the ConvGRU module. A single ConvGRU module with small 2d convolutions updates the hidden state $\mathbf{h}_{t+1}^k$, from which the residual depth Δd_t^k is produced that updates the current depth estimate. We update the depth map

T times in each stage, and then d_T^k is upsampled via convex upsampling as in [18]. After the last iteration at stage 2 and upsampling, the final depth map of resolution $H \times W$ can be obtained. The parameters of ConvGRU modules are shared within the same stage but differ across stages.

Loss Function. The network produces a sequence of depth predictions, including a depth map d_0^0 from the initialization network, multi-scale depth map series from the GRU optimizers $\{d_i^k\}_{i=1,...,T}$ and the upsampled depth maps from the last step of each stage $\{d_0^{k+1}\}$, $k = 0, 1, 2$. L_1 losses are used on all output depth maps and the ground truth depth maps of corresponding scales. Specifically, all depth maps outputs $\{d_i^k, d_0^{k+1}\}_{i=1,...,T}$ and their losses L_m are organized as a sequence according to the output order. The loss function is the weighted sum of all depth losses:

$$L = L_0 + \sum_{m=1}^{M-1} \lambda^{M-1-m} L_m \tag{2}$$

where L_0 is the loss from the depth initialization network, M is the size of the depth map sequence and m is the depth map index. We adopt the exponentially increasing weights for the depth map loss sequence following [18], where $\lambda = 0.9$.

3.3   View-Adaptive Weighting for Cost Volume Fusion

A key factor affecting the accuracy of MVS is the occlusion caused by large changes of camera viewpoints. Occlusion causes feature inconsistency between matched pixels and thus unreliable costs for correct matches. Explicitly accounting for visibility information is necessary for reliable cost volume construction. Several works [3,22,25,34,38] compute the visibility from pairwise volumes or via additional networks and use it as weights on cost volume fusion. We find that the pairwise cost volumes have already captured depth-wise 3D associations between different views, and use them directly as fusing weights is reasonable. Given pairwise volumes $\{C_i \in \mathbb{R}^{C \times D \times H \times W}\}_{i=1,...,N-1}$ computed using groupwise correlation [28], the fusing weights are calculated as:

$$\mathbf{w}_i = \text{softmax}(\frac{\sum_c C_i}{t_e \sqrt{C}}) \tag{3}$$

where t_e is the temperature parameter and softmax is performed along the depth dimension. The fused cost volume is then computed as the weighted sum as:

$$C = \frac{\sum_{i=1}^{N-1} \mathbf{w}_i C_i}{\sum_{i=1}^{N-1} \mathbf{w}_i} \tag{4}$$

Such view-adaptive weighting mechanism doesn't introduce additional network parameters. Note that the cost volume exactly provides C cost slices, each of which inherently provides a combination of view weights. Average operation could be applied to these cost slices When treating them equally. For more flexible view aggregating, we can treat these slices differently and highlight more significant ones. Specifically, the slice-specific weights w_c are computed from source feature maps $\mathbf{F}_i$ using an Squeeze-and-Excitation (SE) block [11]. Then the numerator of Eq. 3 becomes $\sum_c w_c \mathbf{C}_i$. The detailed architecture is shown in Fig. 2(a), and we validate that both kinds of cost slice combination options (average & slice-adaptive) improve the reconstruction with little additional cost.

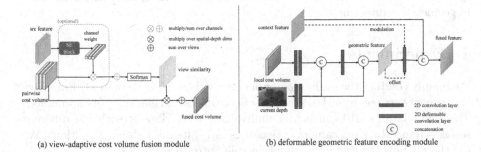

(a) view-adaptive cost volume fusion module   (b) deformable geometric feature encoding module

Fig. 2. The details of the proposed view-adaptive weighting module for cost volume fusion and the deformable geometric feature encoding module.

3.4   Deformable Geometric Feature Encoding

Different from MVSNet [31], only local cost volumes of size $C \times D \times H \times W$ are sampled in narrow depth ranges and reshaped into a feature map of size $C \times D \times HW$. A module with strong modeling capability is required to process such 2D geometric features. Instead of propagating geometric information naively from a static set of neighbors as in conventional 2D convolutions, we leverage the deformable convolution [6,40] to aggregate geometric features from adaptively sampled neighboring locations. As illustrated in Fig. 2(b), the geometric features $\mathbf{g}_t^k$, collected from the cost features and depth features, are processed by one-stride deformable convolutions with exclusive parameters. The definition of the deformable convolution is as:

$$\mathbf{g'}_t^k(p) = \sum_n w_n^k \cdot \mathbf{g}_t^k(\mathbf{p} + \mathbf{p}_n + \Delta \mathbf{p}_n(\mathbf{g}_t^k)) \cdot \Delta m_n(\mathbf{CT}^k) \tag{5}$$

where $\mathbf{g}_t^k(\mathbf{p})$ denotes the geometric feature at pixel $\mathbf{p}$ in the step t of stage k; w_n and $\mathbf{p}_n$ denote the kernel parameter and fixed offset defined in a common 2D convolution; $\Delta \mathbf{p}_n$ and Δm_n are the offset and modulation weight yielded adaptively by learnable sub-networks. Specifically, we use the geometric feature $\mathbf{g}_t^k$ itself at each step to compute the offset, while use the context feature at the corresponding stage $\mathbf{CT}^k$ to compute the modulation weight shared for all steps within the stage. The context features provide information about the semantic structure and is useful for reweighting geometric features. Also, sharing modulation weights within the stage saves computation. This deformable geometric feature encoding module could effectively avoid aggregating across surface boundaries and preserve good matching information.

There are also works that utilizing deformable convolutions for better cost computation. [13,25] use DCN to generate better features for subsequent cost computation, while our method applied adaptive sampling on the geometric encoding after constructing cost volume. [26] also uses DCN on cost volumes, but our method leverages the context features, rather than the cost volume itself, to generate modulation weights, letting the semantic information involved in geometric refinement.

4 Experiments

We mainly conduct the evaluation of our method on DTU [1] dataset. Extensive experiments are conducted to show the effectiveness and efficiency of our method. The DTU dataset [1] is an indoor multi-view stereo dataset with 124 different scenes scanned by fixed camera trajectories in 7 different lighting conditions. We use the training, testing and validation split introduced in [12].

4.1 Implementations

Train. We set the resolution of input images to 640×512 and the number of input images to 5 when training on the DTU training set. The depth hypotheses are sampled in the inverse depth range. The global cost volume covering the whole range is constructed at stage 0 with the depth hypothesis number of 48. Local cost volumes are dynamically constructed with the depth hypothesis number of 4 for all the stage. The depth hypotheses intervals at stages 0, 1, 2 are set to $4I_m, 2I_m, I_m$, where $I_m = (1/d_{min} - 1/d_{max})/Z$ is the minimum interval of inverse depth ($Z = 384$). The iteration number of GRU depth optimizers are all set to 3 at stage 0, 1, 2. The network is trained on NVIDIA GeForce RTX 3080 GPUs.

Test. We evaluate our method on the DTU evaluation set with 5 input views of resolution 1184×1600. Similar to other learning-based MVS methods, photometric and geometric consistencies are leveraged to filter the output depth maps before fusing them into a single point cloud. We follow the implementation of [23] that uses the absolute depth error between reprojected source depth and reference depth as the geometric consistency criterion and uses the upsampled confidence from depth initialization network as the photometric consistency criterion. We follow the evaluation metrics provided by the DTU dataset [1].

4.2 Performance Evaluation

Quantitative comparison on the DTU dataset is shown in Table 1. Our method has promising performance on the accuracy and completeness, and outperforms

Table 1. Quantitative results of different methods on DTU dataset [1]. The distance metrics, including accuracy (Acc.), completeness (Comp.) and the overall score (Overall), measure the reconstruction quality. Running time (Time) and memory consumption (Mem.) show the efficiency. The best result in each column is highlighted in bold, and the second best is underlined. (lower is better)

Method	Acc. (mm)	Comp. (mm)	Overall (mm)	Time (s)	Mem. (GB)
COLMAP [16]	0.400	0.664	0.532	–	–
MVSNet [31]	0.396	0.527	0.462	–	–
R-MVSNet [32]	0.385	0.459	0.422	–	–
D^{2}HC-RMVSNet [29]	0.395	0.378	0.386	–	–
Point-MVSNet [3]	0.342	0.411	0.376	–	–
Vis-MVSNet [38]	0.369	0.361	0.365	0.61	5.6
Fast-MVSNet [35]	0.336	0.403	0.370	0.52	7.0
AA-RMVSNet [25]	0.376	0.339	0.357	–	–
CVP-MVSNet [30]	**0.296**	0.406	0.351	1.51	8.8
CasMVSNet [10]	0.325	0.385	0.355	0.55	9.1
UCSNet [4]	0.338	0.349	0.344	0.54	6.6
PatchmatchNet [22]	0.427	**0.277**	0.352	0.25	3.6
IterMVS [21]	0.373	0.354	0.363	**0.17**	**3.1**
Effi-MVS [23]	0.321	0.313	<u>0.317</u>	<u>0.19</u>	**3.1**
Ours	<u>0.316</u>	<u>0.296</u>	**0.306**	0.20	<u>3.3</u>

other methods on the overall metric, demonstrating the effectiveness of our method. Comparing with [23], which also follows the coarse-to-fine iterative depth estimation framework, our method has greatly improved the completeness and the overall scores. We show a reconstruction example of DTU dataset in Fig. 3 for qualitative illustration. Our method could better reconstructed textureless regions and thin structures.

We also compare several learning-based multi-view stereo methods in terms of running time and memory consumption. Our method consumes slightly more runtime and memory usages over the most efficient method [21,23], while achieving the best reconstruction results.

We further validate the effectiveness of our proposed adaptive cost aggregation modules in the ablation study. All experiments have the same hyperparameters. As shown in Table 2, both the view-adaptive weighting module and the deformable geometric feature encoding module improved the overall performance. The average and slice-adaptive versions of view weight generation perform similarly, and the latter one has a slightly better result.

To evaluate the generalization performance of our proposed method, we follow the setting in [23] and reconstruct the point clouds of Tanks & Temples dataset using the model trained on DTU without any fine-tuning. The mean F-scores of intermediate and advanced sequences are 54.98 and 34.60 respectively, which is comparable to the result of Effi-MVS (56.88 and 34.39). With finetuning on BlendedMVS dataset [33] following the common protocol, the results can be improved to 60.51 and 38.29. Further improvements on this dataset are left for future works.

Table 2. Ablation studies of the proposed adaptive cost aggregation modules.

View Weight Generation	Deformable Encoding	Acc. (mm)	Comp. (mm)	Overall (mm)
No	No	0.321	0.313	0.317
average	No	0.320	0.299	0.310
slice-adaptive	No	0.317	0.300	0.309
average	Yes	0.318	0.296	0.308
slice-adaptive	Yes	0.316	0.296	0.306

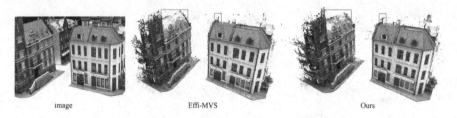

image   Effi-MVS   Ours

Fig. 3. Qualitative results of scan 29 of DTU dataset [1]. As highlighted, our method generates more completed point cloud in the textureless roof and thin structures.

5 Conclusion

In this paper, we presented an multi-stage iterative depth map estimation method for MVS. Two different modules for adaptive cost aggregation, the view-adaptive weighting module and the deformable geometric feature encoding module, are introduced to the iterative network that improve the reconstruction quality with negligible additional computational cost. Experiments on the DTU dataset demonstrated the significant improvement of the proposed network in accuracy with remarkable efficiency performance.

Acknowledgement. This work is supported by the National Natural Science Foundation of China (No. 62276016).

References

1. Aanæs, H., Jensen, R.R., Vogiatzis, G., Tola, E., Dahl, A.B.: Large-scale data for multiple-view stereopsis. Int. J. Comput. Vision **120**, 153–168 (2016)
2. Barnes, C., Shechtman, E., Finkelstein, A., Goldman, D.B.: PatchMatch: a randomized correspondence algorithm for structural image editing. ACM Trans. Graph. **28**(3), 24 (2009)
3. Chen, R., Han, S., Xu, J., Su, H.: Visibility-aware point-based multi-view stereo network. IEEE Trans. Pattern Anal. Mach. Intell. **43**(10), 3695–3708 (2020)
4. Cheng, S., et al.: Deep stereo using adaptive thin volume representation with uncertainty awareness. In: Proceedings of the IEEE/CVF Conference on Computer Vision and Pattern Recognition, pp. 2524–2534 (2020)

5. Collins, R.T.: A space-sweep approach to true multi-image matching. In: Proceedings of the IEEE/CVF Conference on Computer Vision and Pattern Recognition, pp. 358–363. IEEE (1996)
6. Dai, J., et al.: Deformable convolutional networks. In: Proceedings of the IEEE/CVF International Conference on Computer Vision, pp. 764–773 (2017)
7. Furukawa, Y., Ponce, J.: Carved visual hulls for image-based modeling. In: Leonardis, A., Bischof, H., Pinz, A. (eds.) ECCV 2006. LNCS, vol. 3951, pp. 564–577. Springer, Heidelberg (2006). https://doi.org/10.1007/11744023_44
8. Furukawa, Y., Ponce, J.: Accurate, dense, and robust multiview stereopsis. IEEE Trans. Pattern Anal. Mach. Intell. **32**(8), 1362–1376 (2009)
9. Galliani, S., Lasinger, K., Schindler, K.: Massively parallel multiview stereopsis by surface normal diffusion. In: Proceedings of the IEEE International Conference on Computer Vision, pp. 873–881 (2015)
10. Gu, X., Fan, Z., Zhu, S., Dai, Z., Tan, F., Tan, P.: Cascade cost volume for high-resolution multi-view stereo and stereo matching. In: Proceedings of the IEEE/CVF Conference on Computer Vision and Pattern Recognition, pp. 2495–2504 (2020)
11. Hu, J., Shen, L., Sun, G.: Squeeze-and-excitation networks. In: Proceedings of the IEEE/CVF Conference on Computer Vision and Pattern Recognition, pp. 7132–7141 (2018)
12. Ji, M., Gall, J., Zheng, H., Liu, Y., Fang, L.: SurfaceNet: an end-to-end 3d neural network for multiview stereopsis. In: Proceedings of the IEEE/CVF International Conference on Computer Vision, pp. 2307–2315 (2017)
13. Li, J., et al.: Practical stereo matching via cascaded recurrent network with adaptive correlation. In: Proceedings of the IEEE/CVF Conference on Computer Vision and Pattern Recognition, pp. 16263–16272 (2022)
14. Li, Z., Wang, K., Zuo, W., Meng, D., Zhang, L.: Detail-preserving and content-aware variational multi-view stereo reconstruction. IEEE Trans. Image Process. **25**(2), 864–877 (2015)
15. Ma, Z., Teed, Z., Deng, J.: Multiview stereo with cascaded epipolar RAFT. In: Avidan, S., Brostow, G., Cissé, M., Farinella, G.M., Hassner, T. (eds.) ECCV 2022. LNCS, vol. 13691, pp. 734–750. Springer, Cham (2022). https://doi.org/10.1007/978-3-031-19821-2_42
16. Schonberger, J.L., Frahm, J.M.: Structure-from-motion revisited. In: Proceedings of the IEEE Conference on Computer Vision and Pattern Recognition, pp. 4104–4113 (2016)
17. Sinha, S.N., Mordohai, P., Pollefeys, M.: Multi-view stereo via graph cuts on the dual of an adaptive tetrahedral mesh. In: Proceedings of the IEEE/CVF International Conference on Computer Vision, pp. 1–8. IEEE (2007)
18. Teed, Z., Deng, J.: RAFT: recurrent all-pairs field transforms for optical flow. In: Vedaldi, A., Bischof, H., Brox, T., Frahm, J.-M. (eds.) ECCV 2020. LNCS, vol. 12347, pp. 402–419. Springer, Cham (2020). https://doi.org/10.1007/978-3-030-58536-5_24
19. Ulusoy, A.O., Black, M.J., Geiger, A.: Semantic multi-view stereo: jointly estimating objects and voxels. In: Proceedings of the IEEE/CVF Conference on Computer Vision and Pattern Recognition, pp. 4531–4540. IEEE (2017)
20. Wang, C., et al.: Uncertainty estimation for stereo matching based on evidential deep learning. Pattern Recogn. **124**, 108498 (2022)
21. Wang, F., Galliani, S., Vogel, C., Pollefeys, M.: IterMVS: iterative probability estimation for efficient multi-view stereo. In: Proceedings of the IEEE/CVF Conference on Computer Vision and Pattern Recognition, pp. 8606–8615 (2022)

22. Wang, F., Galliani, S., Vogel, C., Speciale, P., Pollefeys, M.: PatchMatchNet: learned multi-view patchmatch stereo. In: Proceedings of the IEEE/CVF Conference on Computer Vision and Pattern Recognition, pp. 14194–14203 (2021)

23. Wang, S., Li, B., Dai, Y.: Efficient multi-view stereo by iterative dynamic cost volume. In: Proceedings of the IEEE/CVF Conference on Computer Vision and Pattern Recognition, pp. 8655–8664 (2022)

24. Wang, X., et al.: Multi-view stereo in the deep learning era: a comprehensive review. Displays **70**, 102102 (2021)

25. Wei, Z., Zhu, Q., Min, C., Chen, Y., Wang, G.: AA-RMVSNet: adaptive aggregation recurrent multi-view stereo network. In: Proceedings of the IEEE/CVF International Conference on Computer Vision, pp. 6187–6196 (2021)

26. Xu, H., Zhang, J.: AANet: adaptive aggregation network for efficient stereo matching. In: Proceedings of the IEEE/CVF Conference on Computer Vision and Pattern Recognition, pp. 1959–1968 (2020)

27. Xu, Q., Tao, W.: Multi-scale geometric consistency guided multi-view stereo. In: Proceedings of the IEEE/CVF Conference on Computer Vision and Pattern Recognition, pp. 5483–5492 (2019)

28. Xu, Q., Tao, W.: Learning inverse depth regression for multi-view stereo with correlation cost volume. In: Proceedings of the AAAI Conference on Artificial Intelligence, vol. 34, pp. 12508–12515 (2020)

29. Yan, J., et al.: Dense hybrid recurrent multi-view stereo net with dynamic consistency checking. In: Vedaldi, A., Bischof, H., Brox, T., Frahm, J.-M. (eds.) ECCV 2020. LNCS, vol. 12349, pp. 674–689. Springer, Cham (2020). https://doi.org/10.1007/978-3-030-58548-8_39

30. Yang, J., Mao, W., Alvarez, J.M., Liu, M.: Cost volume pyramid based depth inference for multi-view stereo. In: Proceedings of the IEEE/CVF Conference on Computer Vision and Pattern Recognition, pp. 4877–4886 (2020)

31. Yao, Y., Luo, Z., Li, S., Fang, T., Quan, L.: MVSNet: depth inference for unstructured multi-view stereo. In: Proceedings of the European Conference on Computer Vision (ECCV), pp. 767–783 (2018)

32. Yao, Y., Luo, Z., Li, S., Shen, T., Fang, T., Quan, L.: Recurrent MVSNet for high-resolution multi-view stereo depth inference. In: Proceedings of the IEEE/CVF Conference on Computer Vision and Pattern Recognition, pp. 5525–5534 (2019)

33. Yao, Y., et al.: BlendedMVS: a large-scale dataset for generalized multi-view stereo networks. In: Proceedings of the IEEE/CVF Conference on Computer Vision and Pattern Recognition, pp. 1790–1799 (2020)

34. Yi, H., et al.: Pyramid multi-view stereo net with self-adaptive view aggregation. In: Vedaldi, A., Bischof, H., Brox, T., Frahm, J.-M. (eds.) ECCV 2020. LNCS, vol. 12354, pp. 766–782. Springer, Cham (2020). https://doi.org/10.1007/978-3-030-58545-7_44

35. Yu, Z., Gao, S.: Fast-MVSNet: sparse-to-dense multi-view stereo with learned propagation and gauss-newton refinement. In: Proceedings of the IEEE/CVF Conference on Computer Vision and Pattern Recognition, pp. 1949–1958 (2020)

36. Zhang, H., et al.: Deep learning-based 3D point cloud classification: a systematic survey and outlook. Displays 102456 (2023)

37. Zhang, J., et al.: Revisiting domain generalized stereo matching networks from a feature consistency perspective. In: Proceedings of the IEEE/CVF Conference on Computer Vision and Pattern Recognition, pp. 13001–13011 (2022)

38. Zhang, J., Yao, Y., Li, S., Luo, Z., Fang, T.: Visibility-aware multi-view stereo network. In: The British Machine Vision Conference (2020)

39. Zhang, P., et al.: Learning multi-view visual correspondences with self-supervision. Displays **72**, 102160 (2022)
40. Zhu, X., Hu, H., Lin, S., Dai, J.: Deformable convnets V2: more deformable, better results. In: Proceedings of the IEEE/CVF Conference on Computer Vision and Pattern Recognition, pp. 9308–9316 (2019)

A Novel Semantic Segmentation Method for High-Resolution Remote Sensing Images Based on Visual Attention Network

Wentao Wang and Xili Wang[✉]

Shaanxi Normal University, Xi'an 710119, Shaanxi, China
wangxili@snnu.edu.cn

Abstract. With a small receptive field, convolutional neural network (CNN) cannot effectively capture long-range dependencies in remote sensing (RS) images, which are particularly important for segmentation. The Transformer-based segmentation methods can obtain global dependencies while bring a large computational burden. To efficiently capture the long-range dependencies, we design a novel RS image segmentation model SegVAN with encoder-decoder structure by introducing Visual Attention Network (VAN). Firstly, the encoder makes use of the large kernel attention in VAN to obtain a wider range of contextual information. Secondly, a simple and efficient decoder is designed to restore the original resolution of the image to obtain the segmentation map. Specifically in the decoding process, in order to obtain high-level semantic information while preserving detailed information, we propose a feature alignment fusion module (FAFM) to align and fuse high-level features and low-level features, and the coordinate attention module (CAM) is used to enhance the fused features. Finally, during training, we propose a hybrid loss function to alleviate the accuracy degradation caused by class imbalance in RS images. The proposed SegVAN is verified on two public RS datasets of Vaihingen and Potsdam, and the mIoU reaches 84.03% and 87.29%, respectively. SegVAN significantly reduces computational complexity while achieving high accuracy compared to the state-of-the-art Transformer-based methods.

Keywords: Remote sensing image · Semantic segmentation · Visual attention network · Feature alignment

1 Introduction

With the rapid development of satellite remote sensing technology, the number of RS images is increasing [1], among which urban RS images have high resolution, which play a great role in urban construction planning, environmental protection, and have great research value. Image semantic segmentation refers to pixel-level recognition of the input image to determine the semantic category of each pixel. With the development of deep learning technology, the mainstream semantic segmentation methods have changed from traditional machine learning methods

H. Lu et al. (Eds.): ICIG 2023, LNCS 14356, pp. 42–53, 2023.
https://doi.org/10.1007/978-3-031-46308-2_4

to deep neural network methods. CNN-based methods [2,3] make full use of the advantage that the convolution operation can accurately capture local details, and have achieved great success in image semantic segmentation.

There are three difficulties in semantic segmentation of RS images: 1) The spectrum of different objects may be extremely similar, and some objects are occluded by trees and shadows. Small receptive fields can only capture local fine-grained information, which is easy to cause misclassification. 2) In the process of feature extraction, the low-level features obtained from the shallow layers of the network contain more detailed information, and the high-level features obtained from the deep layers of the network contain rich semantic information. In order to obtain high-level features, it is usually necessary to perform multiple down-sampling on the input image, which will cause the loss of small objects and detailed information. 3) For RS images, there is often a phenomenon of class imbalance. Taking Vaihingen dataset as an example, the samples of impervious surface account for 27.94%, and the samples of car account for 1.79%. As a result, the model is prone to optimize the categories with more samples during training, while the accuracy of the classes with fewer samples is difficult to improve.

For the first difficulty, the same class of objects may be repeated in different locations in a RS image. Capturing long-range dependencies in an image will help to determine the category of pixels, thus effectively alleviating the misclassification. At present, there are two main ways to obtain the long-range dependencies of feature maps: one is increasing the receptive field of CNN, such as the multi-scale dilated convolution [4], and large convolution kernel [5], but they bring more computation. The other way is introducing attention mechanism, such as DANet [6], CCNet [7] and MANet [8]. While these methods of introducing attention aggregate long-range dependencies from local information captured by CNN, instead of encoding long-range dependencies directly.

It has to be mentioned that Transformer [9] has powerful global information modeling capability thanks to self-attention, some studies [10,11] have applied Transformer to image segmentation tasks and achieved remarkable results. However, Transformer-based segmentation models generally require large amount of computation and memory, which are difficult to generalize.

Visual Attention Network (VAN) [12] decomposes the large kernel convolution, and proposes large kernel attention (LKA) from the decomposed large kernel convolution, which is not only able to capture long-range dependencies, but also has significantly lower computational complexity than large kernel convolution. However, the effectiveness of VAN in RS images has not been fully studied.

For the second difficulty, in order to obtain high-level features while preserving detailed information, it is effective to fuse high-level features and low-level features. Many methods, such as Swin-Unet [13] and ST-UNet [14], adopt the skip-connection similar to the U-Net, during the upsampling process, gradually concatenate the feature maps of the same size generated by the encoder. This just stacks high-level and low-level features together, without making a connection between semantic information and detailed information for each pixel in the feature map. In addition, each skip-connection can only fuse feature maps of one scale, and low-level features can only participate in fusion after high-level features.

For the third difficulty, classes with a small number of samples are usually more difficult to classify than those with a large number of samples. The common method is to improve the loss function, design a reasonable loss function to optimize the training objective. WCE loss [15] gives bigger weights to difficult categories than simple categories in loss, while Focal loss [16] uses a dynamic scaling factor to make the model pay less attention to easy categories and focus on difficult categories. These two methods can alleviate the problem of class imbalance, but the additional introduced parameters need to be adjusted manually, which increases the difficulty of training.

To address the above problems, we propose a segmentation model based on the VAN named SegVAN, which uses VAN as the encoder to capture long-range dependencies. In the decoder, the feature alignment fusion module (FAFM) is designed to align and fuse features of different scales, rationally use features of different scales and retain detailed information, then the coordinate attention module (CAM) is used to enhance the fused features. Finally, a hybrid loss function is designed to alleviate the class imbalance problem of RS images.

The main contributions of this paper are:

1) We introduce VAN into the field of RS image semantic segmentation. The large kernel attention in the VAN is used to capture the long-range dependencies of the feature map, which can reduce the misclassification, verifying the effectiveness of VAN in RS images.
2) We propose a simple and effective decoding structure. The feature alignment fusion module in the decoder can make full use of the features of different scales and better preserve the detail information to improve the accuracy.
3) We conduct experiments on two well-known urban RS datasets of Vaihingen and Potsdam, and the mIoU reaches 84.03% and 87.29%, respectively. SegVAN achieves high accuracy while greatly reducing computation compared with the latest Transformer-based methods.

2   Methods

Our proposed SegVAN includes the encoder VAN, as well as a lightweight decoder consisting of FAFM and CAM.

2.1   SegVAN

Figure 1 depicts the encoder-decoder structure of the SegVAN. To extract features from an input $X \in R^{H \times W \times 3}$, VAN is employed. The encoding process incorporates four times downsampling, leading to a reduction in the resolution of the feature map and an increase in the number of channels. As a result, four feature maps, namely F_1, F_2, F_3, and F_4, are obtained. The resolution of F_n is

$(H/(2^{n+1}) \times (W/(2^{n+1}))$, where $n = 1, 2, 3, 4$. The number of channels of the feature map in each stage depends on the version of the VAN we used. During decoding, the FAFM in the decoder aligns the feature maps of the four stages to the same size in resolution and channel, and adds them element-by-element for fusion. Then the CAM is used to enhance the fused features in space and channel. Finally, the segmentation map with the same resolution as the original image is obtained by upsample operation.

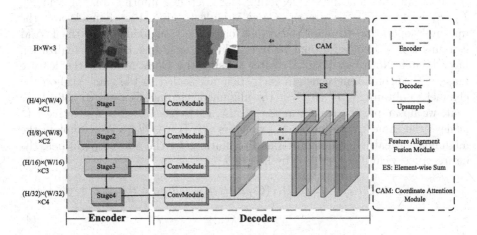

Fig. 1. SegVAN network structure.

2.2 Encoder

The encoder of SegVAN is VAN. In order to take advantage of large kernel convolution to capture long-range dependencies and save computing resources, VAN uses a depth-wise convolution, a deep-wise dilation convolution and a 1×1 convolution to decompose large kernel convolution, and thus large kernel attention is proposed. The decomposed large kernel convolution is used to calculate the attention map for the input, the process is shown in Eqs. 1 and 2.

$$Attention = Conv_{1 \times 1}(DW - D - Conv(DW - Conv(F))), \qquad (1)$$

$$Output = Attention \otimes F, \qquad (2)$$

where $DW - Conv$ stands for depth-wise convolution, $DW - D - Conv$ stands for depth-wise dilation convolution, $Conv_{1 \times 1}$ stands for 1×1 convolution, $\otimes$ means element-wise product. The input F goes through three decomposition of the large kernel convolution to get the attention value, and then the attention value and the input are multiplied element-wise to obtain the output.

VAN takes large kernel attention as the core and adopts an architecture like hierarchical Transformer. According to different scales, VAN provides seven versions of VAN_B0 to VAN_B6, we adopt VAN_B3 pre-trained on ImageNet as the backbone of SegVAN, with a parameters of 44.8M. In Fig. 1, the feature map channels output by the four stages of VAN_B3 are 64,128,320,512, respectively.

2.3   Feature Alignment Fusion Module

The FAFM is the yellow part in Fig. 2. For the four-stage feature maps F_1, F_2, F_3, F_4 obtained by the encoder, F_2, F_3, F_4 compared to F_1 having more semantic information and F_1 retaining more detailed information, we add F_2, F_3, F_4 back to F_1. We use the Conv Module to align the channels and the upsample operation to align the resolutions. The Conv Module in the FAFM contains a 3×3 convolutional layer (stride is 1, padding is 1), normalization layer (Batch Norm) and ReLU. After passing the Conv Module, the feature maps with inconsistent scales in each stage are scaled to the same size on the channel to obtain F_1', F_2', F_3', F_4', the alignment channel C is set to 256. After that, we upsample the feature maps F_2', F_3', F_4' by $2\times$, $4\times$, $8\times$ respectively to achieve the same resolution as F_1', which is $(H/4) \times (W/4)$. We complete the alignment of features on channels and resolutions by the above operations, the entire process can be described by Eqs. 3–5.

$$F_n' = f(F_n) = Relu(BN(Conv(F_n))), \; where \; n = 1, 2, 3, 4. \tag{3}$$

$$S_1 = F_1', \tag{4}$$

$$S_n = U_{2^{n-1}}(F_n'), \tag{5}$$

where $n = 2, 3, 4$, U represents upsample and $U_{2^{n-1}}$ represents upsample by a factor of 2^{n-1}.

After aligning the four-stage features output by VAN, the four feature maps S_1, S_2, S_3, S_4 with the same resolution and the same number of channels are fused element-by-element to obtain the fused feature AS ($AS \in R^{\frac{H}{4} \times \frac{W}{4} \times C}$), as shown in Eq. 6.

$$AS = S_1 \oplus S_2 \oplus S_3 \oplus S_4, \tag{6}$$

where $\oplus$ stands for element-wise addition.

2.4   Coordinate Attention Module

The structure of CAM is shown in Fig. 2, which carries out the pooling operation in the horizontal and the vertical directions respectively to embed the position information into the channel. The pooling operation is as follows: for the input $X \in R^{H \times W \times C}$, coordinate attention [17] adopts two $1D$ convolutions to encode each feature channel along the horizontal and vertical directions, the output $z_c^h(h)$ of the c-th channel with height h is shown in Eq. 7, the output $z_c^w(w)$ of the c-th channel with width w is shown in Eq. 8:

$$z_c^h(h) = \frac{1}{W} \sum_{0 \le i \le W} x_c(h, i), \tag{7}$$

$$z_c^w(w) = \frac{1}{H} \sum_{0 \le i \le H} x_c(j, w), \tag{8}$$

where W and H represents the height and width of the input, respectively.

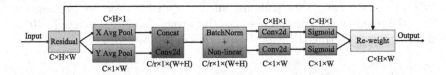

Fig. 2. Coordinate Attention Module. (Color figure online)

Two feature maps can be obtained by pooling the input features in two different directions. One contains the horizontal information and the other contains the vertical information. After that, these two feature maps are respectively encoded into two attention maps, which are then multiplied to the input feature map to enhance the representation of the feature map.

For CAM, the fused feature map $AS \in R^{\frac{H}{4} \times \frac{W}{4} \times C}$ is taken as input and an enhanced feature map AS' with the same size of AS is output. The segmentation map can be obtained by upsampling the AS'.

2.5 Loss Functions

We combine Dice loss [18] and cross-entropy loss to form a hybrid loss function, which can make the model pay more attention to those categories with fewer samples, and improve the performance of the model on class-imbalanced datasets. The cross-entropy loss function, Dice loss function and hybrid loss function are shown in Eqs. 9, 10 and 11 respectively.

$$L_{CE} = -\frac{1}{N} \sum_{i=1}^{N} \sum_{c=1}^{C} y_c^{(i)} \log \hat{y}_c^{(i)} + (1 - y_c^{(i)}) \log(1 - \hat{y}_c^{(i)}), \tag{9}$$

$$L_{Dice} = 1 - \frac{2}{N} \sum_{i=1}^{N} \sum_{c=1}^{C} \frac{\hat{y}_c^{(i)} y_c^{(i)}}{\hat{y}_c^{(i)} + y_c^{(i)}}, \tag{10}$$

$$L = L_{CE} + L_{Dice}, \tag{11}$$

where N represents the number of samples and C represents the number of classes, y represents the true label and $\hat{y}$ represents the prediction.

3 Experiments

3.1 Dataset

We test the effectiveness of the proposed SegVAN on Vaihingen and Potsdam datasets. The Vaihingen dataset consists of 33 true orthophoto (TOP) images with average size of 2494 × 2064 pixels, each with three multispectral bands (red, green, near infrared) and a digital surface Model (DSM). The Potsdam dataset consists of 38 true orthophoto (TOP) images with size 6000 × 6000 pixels, each with four multispectral bands (red, green, blue, near infrared) as well as DSM and normalized DSM. As in previous work [11], for Vaihingen, we use 17 images for testing and 16 images for training, and for Potsdam, we use 14 images for testing, the remaining 23 images (besides the wrong annotated image 7_10) are used for training. During the experiment, we do not use DSM.

3.2   Evaluation Metrics

We measure model precision by using overall accuracy (OA), mean Union intersection (mIoU), and F1 score (F1), and model complexity by parameters of model and floating point operation count (Flops).

$$OA = \frac{\sum_{k=1}^{N} TP_k}{\sum_{k=1}^{N} TP_k + FP_k + TN_k + FN_k}, \tag{12}$$

$$mIoU = \frac{1}{N} \sum_{k=1}^{N} \frac{TP_k}{TP_k + FP_k + FN_k}, \tag{13}$$

$$precision = \frac{1}{N} \sum_{k=1}^{N} \frac{TP_k}{TP_k + FP_k}, \tag{14}$$

$$recall = \frac{1}{N} \sum_{k=1}^{N} \frac{TP_k}{TP_k + FN_k}, \tag{15}$$

$$F1 = 2 \times \frac{precision \times recall}{precision + recall}, \tag{16}$$

where TP stands for true positive, FP for false positive, TN for true negative, and FN for false negative, N stands for the number of classes.

3.3   Experimental Setup

All models in the experiment are implemented with PyTorch. The optimizer is AdamW and the initial learning rate is 6e−4, the cosine strategy is used to adjust the learning rate. For two datasets, the large images are cropped to 512 × 512 pixels. During training, augmentation techniques such as random scale (0.5, 0.75, 1.0, 1.25, 1.5), random vertical flip, random horizontal flip, and random rotation are used with a training epoch of 60 and a batch size of 4. In the testing phase, Test-time Augmentation (TTA) techniques such as multi-scale and random flip augmentation are used.

3.4   Experimental Results and Analysis

The comparison methods include CNN-based methods U-Net [3], DeepLabV3+ [4], MANet [8], and Transformer-based methods DC-Swin [19], FT-UNetFormer [11]. The backbone of SegVAN with a parameter of 44.8M, to ensure a fair comparison, CNN-based methods use ResNet101 [20] (45M parameters) as the backbone, transformer-based methods use Swin-Small [21] (50M parameters) as the backbone. For all the compared methods, the hybrid loss mentioned before is used for training and test-time augmentation is used at test time.

Table 1 lists the segmentation results of different methods on the Vaihigen dataset. SegVAN achieves 91.20 in Mean F1, 91.49% in OA and 84.03% in mIoU, it outperforms CNN-based methods which using small-scale convolution in the encoding process, indicating the effectiveness of capturing long-range dependencies. Comparing SegVAN with DC-Swin, which extracts multi-scale relationships in feature fusion, and FT-UNetFormer, which uses skip-connection to fuse features, SegVAN achieves comparable performance to them on four classes, while achieving 1.5% improvement on the car category with small size, indicating the effectiveness of the feature fusion method adopted in the SegVAN.

Table 1. Segmentation results on the Vaihingen dataset.

Method	Para. ↓	FLOPs ↓	Imp. Surf.	Building	Low veg.	Tree	Car	Mean F1	OA (%)	mIoU (%)
U-Net	47.9M	58.6G	92.91	95.39	84.97	90.44	80.11	90.36	91.08	82.62
DeepLabv3+	58.8M	241.7G	93.08	96.03	85.21	90.35	89.26	90.79	91.30	83.33
MANet	54.9M	73.7G	93.00	95.60	84.93	90.32	88.60	90.49	91.13	82.84
DC-Swin	66.9M	72.2G	**93.63**	96.22	**85.57**	**90.42**	89.45	91.06	**91.66**	83.80
FT-UNetFormer	57.5M	88.6G	93.47	**96.24**	85.48	90.39	89.41	91.00	91.58	83.69
SegVAN	**47.3M**	**51.5G**	93.36	96.21	85.20	90.32	**90.92**	**91.20**	91.49	**84.03**

Table 2. Segmentation results on the Potsdam dataset.

Method	Para. ↓	FLOPs ↓	Imp. Surf.	Building	Low veg.	Tree	Car	Mean F1	OA (%)	mIoU (%)
U-Net	47.9M	58.6G	91.76	95.59	87.05	88.85	96.35	91.92	90.10	85.26
DeepLabv3+	58.8M	241.7G	92.61	96.22	87.80	89.22	95.92	92.35	90.86	85.98
MANet	54.9M	73.7G	93.02	96.37	87.98	89.16	95.98	92.50	91.06	86.17
DC-Swin	66.9M	72.2G	**93.58**	96.88	88.00	89.55	96.39	92.88	91.49	86.92
FT-UNetFormer	57.5M	88.6G	93.42	96.76	88.31	89.44	96.25	92.84	91.43	86.82
SegVAN	**47.3M**	**51.5G**	93.42	**97.15**	**88.78**	**89.75**	**96.42**	**93.10**	**91.68**	**87.29**

Table 2 shows the results on the Potsdam dataset. Our proposed SegVAN achieves 93.10 in Mean F1, 91.68% in OA and 87.29% in mIoU with the minimum 47.3M parameters and 51.5G floating-point operations. It outperforms two advanced transformer-based SegVANs in accuracy, and note that there is a 30%

to 40% reduction in floating point counts, which demonstrates the superiority of SegVAN. In short, our proposed SegVAN is the best in overall performance. Figure 3 shows some segmentation maps of the cropped test images, and Fig. 4 shows the prediction results for large image of ID 2 in Vaihingen dataset and ID 3_14 in Potsdam dataset.

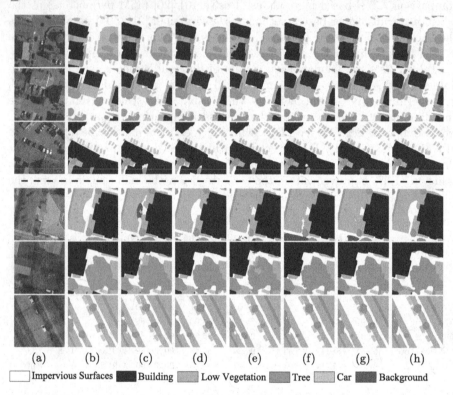

| (a) | (b) | (c) | (d) | (e) | (f) | (g) | (h) |

☐ Impervious Surfaces ■ Building ☐ Low Vegetation ■ Tree ☐ Car ■ Background

Fig. 3. Segmentation maps obtained by different methods on the Vaihigen (top) and Potsdam (bottom) test set, (a) Input Image, (b) Ground Truth, (c) U-Net, (d) DeepLabV3+, (e) MANet, (f) DC-Swin, (g) FT-UNetFormer, (h) SegVAN.

3.5 Ablation Study

The effectiveness of VAN, FAFM, CAM and hybrid loss function is verified by ablation experiments, we select ResNet101 with the direct upsample operation as the baseline. The results are shown in Table 3. Comparing ResNet101+Upsample with VAN+Upsample, the mIoU of the latter is 3% higher. The F1 score of each category is improved, indicating the effectiveness of capturing long-range dependencies. Comparing VAN+Upsample with VAN+FAFM, the difference between them is whether there is a FAFM or not. The latter improve in F1 in every category, with the car category showing a 7.6% increase in F1 score. The overall mIoU is increased by 3.1%, which fully demonstrates the effectiveness of FAFM. Comparing VAN+FAFM with VAN+FAFM+CAM, the latter has different degrees of improvement in Mean F1, OA and mIoU. This shows the effectiveness of CAM, which enhances the fused features to further improve the accuracy.

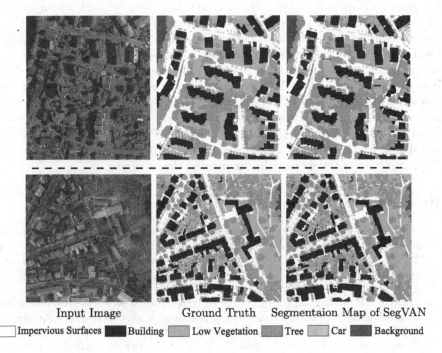

Input Image   Ground Truth   Segmentaion Map of SegVAN

☐ Impervious Surfaces ■ Building ☐ Low Vegetation ■ Tree ☐ Car ■ Background

Fig. 4. Visualization results of ID 2 (top) in Vaihingen test set and ID 2_13 (bottom) in Potsdam test set.

Table 3. Ablation experiments on the Vaihingen dataset.

Method	Imp. Surf.	Building	Low veg.	Tree	Car	Mean F1	OA (%)	mIoU (%)
ResNet101+Upsample	91.15	95.02	83.73	89.41	75.89	87.04	89.86	77.65
VAN+Upsample	92.50	95.76	84.69	89.60	83.05	89.12	90.76	80.70
VAN+FAFM	93.16	96.09	85.20	**90.37**	90.60	91.09	91.42	83.83
VAN+FAFM+CAM	**93.36**	**96.21**	**85.20**	90.32	**90.92**	**91.20**	**91.49**	**84.03**
CE Loss	93.26	96.15	85.17	90.32	89.78	90.94	91.43	83.59
Dice Loss	90.86	94.82	84.10	89.77	89.59	89.28	90.02	81.71
CE Loss+Dice Loss	**93.36**	**96.21**	**85.20**	**90.32**	**90.92**	**91.20**	**91.49**	**84.03**

We adopt different loss functions to train SegVAN to test the performance of different loss functions. It can be seen from Table 3 that the hybrid loss function has achieved the highest results in F1 in each category, compared with CE loss and Dice loss, the F1 of car is increased by 1.1% and 1.3% respectively. The car has the least samples among the five classes, indicating that the hybrid loss function is indeed helpful to improve the class with fewer samples.

4   Conclusion

For urban RS images, we introduce Visual Attention Network as an encoder to capture long-range dependencies, and design a simple and effective decoding structure to make full use of features at different scales. The feature alignment fusion module and coordinate attention module can effectively improve the accuracy of RS images segmentation. Experiments on Vaihingen and Potsdam datasets have proved the effectiveness of the proposed method. The model can reach high accuracy while achieving simple structure and saving computing resources, which is a very competitive method in semantic segmentation of urban RS data. We hope that in the field of RS images, there will be more research to deeply explore the potential of Visual Attention Network and reduce the complexity of the model while improving the accuracy.

References

1. Zhu, M., Wan, S., Jin, P., Xu, J.: A similarity constraint divergent activation method for weakly supervised object detection in remote sensing images. In: Peng, Y., Hu, S.M., Gabbouj, M., Zhou, K., Elad, M., Xu, K. (eds.) Image and Graphics, pp. 418–430. Springer, Cham (2021). https://doi.org/10.1007/978-3-030-87355-4_35

2. Long, J., Shelhamer, E., Darrell, T.: Fully convolutional networks for semantic segmentation. In: 2015 IEEE Conference on Computer Vision and Pattern Recognition (CVPR), pp. 3431–3440 (2015). https://doi.org/10.1109/CVPR.2015.7298965

3. Ronneberger, O., Fischer, P., Brox, T.: U-Net: convolutional networks for biomedical image segmentation. In: Navab, N., Hornegger, J., Wells, W.M., Frangi, A.F. (eds.) Medical Image Computing and Computer-Assisted Intervention - MICCAI 2015, pp. 234–241. Springer, Cham (2015). https://doi.org/10.1007/978-3-319-24574-4_28

4. Firdaus-Nawi, M., Noraini, O., Sabri, M., Siti-Zahrah, A., Zamri-Saad, M., Latifah, H.: DeepLabV3+ _encoder-decoder with atrous separable convolution for semantic image segmentation. Pertanika J. Trop. Agric. Sci. **34**(1), 137–143 (2011)

5. Ding, X., Zhang, X., Han, J., Ding, G.: Scaling up your kernels to 31×31: revisiting large kernel design in CNNs. In: 2022 IEEE/CVF Conference on Computer Vision and Pattern Recognition (CVPR), pp. 11953–11965 (2022). https://doi.org/10.1109/CVPR52688.2022.01166

6. Fu, J., et al.: Dual attention network for scene segmentation. In: 2019 IEEE/CVF Conference on Computer Vision and Pattern Recognition (CVPR), pp. 3141–3149 (2019). https://doi.org/10.1109/CVPR.2019.00326

7. Huang, Z., Wang, X., Huang, L., Huang, C., Wei, Y., Liu, W.: CCNet: criss-cross attention for semantic segmentation. In: 2019 IEEE/CVF International Conference on Computer Vision (ICCV), pp. 603–612 (2019). https://doi.org/10.1109/ICCV.2019.00069

8. Li, R., et al.: Multiattention network for semantic segmentation of fine-resolution remote sensing images. IEEE Trans. Geosci. Remote Sens. **60**, 1–13 (2022). https://doi.org/10.1109/TGRS.2021.3093977

9. Vaswani, A., et al.: Attention is all you need. In: Proceedings of the 31st International Conference on Neural Information Processing Systems, NIPS 2017, pp. 6000–6010. Curran Associates Inc., Red Hook, NY, USA (2017)

10. Zheng, S., et al.: Rethinking semantic segmentation from a sequence-to-sequence perspective with transformers. In: 2021 IEEE/CVF Conference on Computer Vision and Pattern Recognition (CVPR), pp. 6877–6886 (2021). https://doi.org/10.1109/CVPR46437.2021.00681

11. Wang, L., et al.: UNetFormer: a UNet-like transformer for efficient semantic segmentation of remote sensing urban scene imagery. ISPRS J. Photogramm. Remote. Sens. **190**, 196–214 (2022). https://doi.org/10.1016/j.isprsjprs.2022.06.008

12. Guo, M.H., Lu, C.Z., Liu, Z.N., Cheng, M.M., Hu, S.M.: Visual attention network. arXiv preprint arXiv:2202.09741 (2022)

13. Cao, H., et al.: Swin-Unet: Unet-like pure transformer for medical image segmentation. In: Karlinsky, L., Michaeli, T., Nishino, K. (eds.) Computer Vision – ECCV 2022 Workshops. ECCV 2022. LNCS, vol. 13803. Springer, Cham (2021). https://doi.org/10.1007/978-3-031-25066-8_9

14. He, X., Zhou, Y., Zhao, J., Zhang, D., Yao, R., Xue, Y.: Swin transformer embedding UNet for remote sensing image semantic segmentation. IEEE Trans. Geosci. Remote Sens. **60**, 1–15 (2022). https://doi.org/10.1109/TGRS.2022.3144165

15. Sudre, C.H., Li, W., Vercauteren, T., Ourselin, S., Jorge Cardoso, M.: Generalised dice overlap as a deep learning loss function for highly unbalanced segmentations. In: Cardoso, M.J., et al. (eds.) DLMIA/ML-CDS -2017. LNCS, vol. 10553, pp. 240–248. Springer, Cham (2017). https://doi.org/10.1007/978-3-319-67558-9_28

16. Lin, T.Y., Goyal, P., Girshick, R.B., He, K., Dollár, P.: Focal loss for dense object detection. In: 2017 IEEE International Conference on Computer Vision (ICCV), pp. 2999–3007 (2017)

17. Hou, Q., Zhou, D., Feng, J.: Coordinate attention for efficient mobile network design. In: 2021 IEEE/CVF Conference on Computer Vision and Pattern Recognition (CVPR), pp. 13708–13717 (2021). https://doi.org/10.1109/CVPR46437.2021.01350

18. Li, X., Sun, X., Meng, Y., Liang, J., Wu, F., Li, J.: Dice loss for data-imbalanced NLP tasks. In: Annual Meeting of the Association for Computational Linguistics (2019)

19. Wang, L., Li, R., Duan, C., Zhang, C., Meng, X., Fang, S.: A novel transformer based semantic segmentation scheme for fine-resolution remote sensing images. IEEE Geosci. Remote Sens. Lett. **19**, 1–5 (2022)

20. He, K., Zhang, X., Ren, S., Sun, J.: Deep residual learning for image recognition. In: 2016 IEEE Conference on Computer Vision and Pattern Recognition (CVPR), pp. 770–778 (2015)

21. Liu, Z., et al.: Swin transformer: hierarchical vision transformer using shifted windows. In: 2021 IEEE/CVF International Conference on Computer Vision (ICCV), pp. 9992–10002 (2021). https://doi.org/10.1109/ICCV48922.2021.00986

Efficient Few-Shot Image Generation via Lightweight Octave Generative Adversarial Networks

Sihao Liu, Yuanbo Li, and Cong Hu[✉]

School of Artificial Intelligence and Computer Science, Jiangnan University, Wuxi, China
conghu@jiangnan.edu.cn

Abstract. Generating high-quality images from few-shot image is always a challenging task. FastGAN achieves great success in few-shot image generation task by using a lightweight network structure with incorporating a self-supervised discriminator and skip-layer channel-wise excitation module. However, FastGAN still has defect that the generated image is severe distortion. To tackle this problem, this work proposes a novel few-shot generation method called Octave Generative Adversarial Network (OctGAN) which using octave convolution in the unconditional generation task. Specifically, octave convolution is utilized to directly decouple high and low frequency features at the feature level, thereby high frequency features are used to enhance the generator's image generation quality and low frequency features are used to increase the discriminator's receptive field. Through qualitative and quantitative experimental analysis on multiple datasets covering a wide variety of image domains demonstrate that this work proves OctGAN not only has better image generation ability but also has less parameters and computational complexity.

Keywords: Generative adversarial network · Few-shot image generation · Feature decoupling

1 Introduction

Generative Adversarial Networks (GANs) show remarkable success in image generation tasks such as image editing, image conversion, and style transfer [13,17]. However, their performance heavily relies on large amounts of training data. If they are used for few-shot image generation tasks, their effectiveness will be greatly reduced, even leading to training failure. The primary reason for this is that the discriminator can easily overfit to the small training datasets, making it difficult to provide useful gradient flow to optimize the generator. To overcome this difficulty, researchers propose using pre-trained models to guide few-shot image generation, either through fine-tuning [25] or by adding extra fully-connected layers [20]. One early breakthrough in this area is made by Mine-GAN [24], which employs an additional fully connected layer to extract prior knowledge from a pre-trained model for guiding few-shot image generation. Li

H. Lu et al. (Eds.): ICIG 2023, LNCS 14356, pp. 54–65, 2023.
https://doi.org/10.1007/978-3-031-46308-2_5

et al. [14] find that adding an elastic regularization term to different convolution layers can significantly improve the overfitting problem of GANs. Ojha [19] which was inspired by DistanceGAN [22] maintains a paired distance between images before and after adaptation to prevent overfitting. While these methods are effective in addressing the overfitting problem of few-shot generation, they rely on finding a compatible pre-training dataset. The generation performance is likely to be poor without this [19, 28].

Recent research work [18] highlights the advantages of feature decoupling in high and low frequency domains in generating high-quality images. However, the approach proposed, which uses wavelet-based feature decoupling, is a limiting factor for few-shot image generation task. It requires applying decoupling on lots of real images and incurs high computational cost. In this paper, we propose to implement a novel generative adversarial network by utilizing octave convolution [2] to directly decouple features in the feature domain, and explore the potential of octave convolution in unconditional generation tasks. Our main contribution is summarized as follows:

- We design a novel GAN model (OctGAN) which uses octave convolution to achieve a more lightweight GAN for few-shot image generation tasks. In terms of the number of model parameters and computational complexity, our model has better advantages.
- To the best of my knowledge, it's first time octave applied on unconditional generation tasks. To examine its impact, we developed a generator and self-supervised discriminator with feature decoupling based on octave convolution properties. Our experiments demonstrate that incorporating both high and low-frequency features in these models leads to significant performance gains.
- We conduct extensive experiments on multiple high-fidelity datasets and achieved significant improvements in FID scores, especially in datasets of size 1024^2.

2   Related Work

Few-Shot Image Generation: In recent years, few-shot image generation has become an increasingly popular area of research. The main challenge is that the discriminator is prone to overfitting and quickly memorizes all the real data when there is limited real data available. This hinders the effective transmission of gradients to the generator, making it difficult to train the generator effectively [4]. To address this issue, most approaches are using pre-trained models and fine-tuning method [19, 24]. Additionally, feature fusion has also been utilized in recent years to address this problem, but such methods require similar semantics between the training sets, otherwise the generated images may suffer from significant artifacts [6, 7]. This work focuses on retraining GANs against a background of limited image data, which poses a greater risk of discriminator overfitting and generator mode collapse. To overcome these difficulties, FastGAN [15] employs a lightweight StyleGAN model [13] model, along with a self-supervised discriminator and a skip-layer channel-wise excitation module, to achieve significant success in few-shot image generation tasks. This work will continue to explore the ability of GANs in few-shot image generation tasks.

Multi-scale Representation Learning: In order to achieve great efficient models in mobile and embedded devices, MobileNets [8] improve the vanilla convolution by introducing a deeply separable convolution that can construct lightweight deep neural networks. Octave convolution [2] divides features into high frequency features and low frequency features, which not only reduces the computational complexity of convolution but also implements the decoupling of high and low frequency features. MUXConv [16] further reduces the computational complexity of convolution by channel multiplexing and spatial multiplexing.

Stabilize The GAN Training: Due to the limited number of training samples, there is a high risk of overfitting in the discriminator (D) during training, which may result in a highly unstable generator (G) and a significant risk of mode collapse. While previous approaches solve this issue are employing regularization [4,23] and data augmentation [10,11,26,28] to mitigate overfitting, their efficacy diminishes as the size of the training set is reduced. In this work, a new feature decoupling method is explored to stabilize D training.

Feature Decoupling: In recent years, feature decoupling has garnered attention in image editing and GAN inversion tasks [1,9]. The attribute group editing method [3] employs average feature representation to depict all common attributes in these images. Further, it utilizes sparse dictionary to learn and store all class-independent attributes of images, thereby facilitating the modification of image attributes in different degrees from varying directions. In addition, the method [5] uses wavelet transform to extract high-frequency features and guides the generator to produce high-quality images with more details by inputting them into a discriminator. In contrast, One-Shot GAN [21] employs feature decoupling via average pooling layer and 1×1 convolution. This work is inspired by the use of feature decoupling to enhance generation tasks and adopt a similar approach. However, instead of using the previous methods, this work applies octave convolution for decoupling directly at the feature level.

3   Methodology

3.1   Motivation

Based on previous research, researchers propose two ideas to improve the unconditional generation task. The first idea is to enhance the detailed feature generation capability of the generator, and the second idea is to strengthen the representation learning ability of the discriminator to prevent overfitting. To enhance the generator's ability to generate fine details, recent developments based on feature decoupling are integrated. However, this work is working on few-shot image generation task and recent feature decoupling methods rely on a good deal of real images, so this work decides to perform feature decoupling directly at the feature level to consider both real and fake images during training. To achieve this, octave convolution is used. Given that the low-frequency feature stream of octave convolution can effectively expand the convolution field of reception, it is applied to the discriminator to improve its encoding performance and supervise the generator based on high and low-frequency features.

3.2 Stabilize the Octave Convolution

Octave convolution is initially designed to enable efficient and robust gradient flow in recognition tasks, facilitating rapid convergence towards high recognition accuracy. However, in the context of unconditional adversarial generation tasks, excessive gradient flow may result in training failure, with either the generator or discriminator dominating the training. To ensure smooth gradient flow and prevent overfitting, the gradient flow generated by octave convolution is constrained. Specifically, spectral-normalization [27] is introduced to the octave convolution, satisfying the 1-Lipschitz condition to limit the gradient flow and stabilize the training process:

$$\frac{||f(x) - f(x')||_2}{||x - x'||_2} \leq K(K = 1) \tag{1}$$

Which f and x are the function and input, k is a constant and satisfies the 1-Lipschitz condition when k is set to 1.

3.3 OctGAN

Octave convolution (OctConv) has not been studied in unconditional generation tasks. Specifically, OctConv can directly replace the original convolution, but during the convolution process, it separates features into high-frequency and low-frequency components. High-frequency features represent areas of the image where pixel changes are large, such as the fine details of the image, while low-frequency features represent areas where pixel changes are small, such as the contours and backgrounds of the image. In theory, the ability of OctConv to disentangle features can be effectively used in the generator and discriminator to enhance the generation capability of GANs.

Formally, let $X \in \mathbb{R}^{c \times h \times w}$ represents the input feature tensor. OctConv performs an explicit channel-wise decomposition on X as $X = X_L, X_H$ at first. For the low-frequency features X_L, it reduces the size of the image dimensions, i.e., height and width, by half, and performs convolution separately on the high-frequency and low-frequency features. According to this feature, we can use it to reduce the number of parameters and computational complexity of GANs network, so as to achieve the effect of accelerating training. There is also communication between the high-frequency and low-frequency features. The forward calculation is defined as follows:

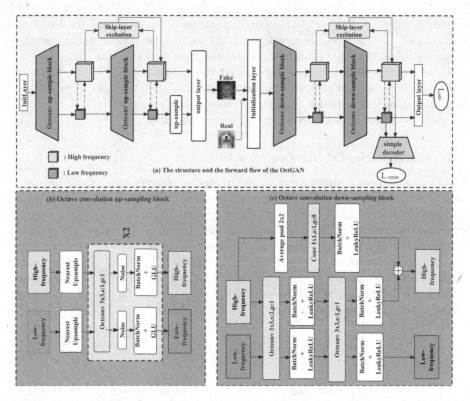

Fig. 1. The structure of OctGAN and two convolution blocks improved by octave convolution. The dashed lines represent information exchange between high and low frequency features.

$$Y_H = f(X_H; W^{H \to H}) + upsample(f(X_L; W^{L \to H}), 2)$$
$$Y_L = f(X_L; W^{L \to L}) + f(pool(X_H, 2); W^{H \to L}) \tag{2}$$

where $f(X; W)$ denotes a convolution with parameters W, $pool(X, k)$ is an average pooling operation with kernel size $k \times k$ and stride k. $Upsample(X, k)$ is an up-sampling operation by a factor of k via nearest interpolation.

Figure 1 illustrates the structure of OctGAN and two convolution blocks improved by octave convolution. For the generator part of OctGAN, in addition to directly replacing the vanilla convolution in all up-sampling blocks with octave convolution, the skip-layer excitation module is also added to the high-frequency features at the three layers of the feature map with the sizes of 64^2, 128^2 and 256^2 respectively, so as to provide a faster and more robust gradient flow for high-frequency features. Ensure that the generator has better image detail generation ability. The improved skip-layer excitation module is defined as:

$$Y = F(f(X_{low}; W^{H \to H}), W_i) * f(X_{high}; W^{H \to H}) \tag{3}$$

where X and Y are input and output feature-maps. The low resolution feature-maps and high resolution feature-maps are decomposed into high frequency features through octave convolution operation f. Then function F converts the high frequency features of X_{low} to the same number of high frequency feature channels of x_{high} through the learnable parameter W_i.

In the output layer, the setting of alpha-out equals 0 is not used in the octave convolution, otherwise it means that the low frequency features are abandoned in the last OctConv layer. Although such a setting can effectively improve the accuracy of the recognition task, the low frequency features should be retained in the generation tasks to provide richer channel information for the generator.

For the discriminator part of OctGAN, in addition to replacing the vanilla convolution and adding skip-layers excitation module to the high frequency features, this work also investigates how to add self-supervised learning to the discriminator based OctConv and how to use the high and low frequency features more reasonably at the output layer. The purpose of self-supervised learning is to enable the discriminator to learn more comprehensive representation extraction ability by reconstructing the feature-maps of low spatial dimension encoded by the discriminator. Compared with the vanilla convolution, the low-frequency features in the octave convolution can effectively amplify the receiving field twice in the process of convolution, which can help the discriminator to capture more context information from a further location and improve its representation extraction ability. So instead of just putting in the high-frequency features, the high frequency should need to be combined with low frequency features and put back into the reconstruction task. The reconstruction loss function of the self-supervised stage is defined as follows:

$$\mathcal{L}_{recons} = \mathbb{E}_{f_H, f_L \sim D_{encode}(X), x \sim I_{real}} [|||\mathcal{G}(concat(f_H, f_L)) - \mathcal{T}(x)|||] \qquad (4)$$

where f is the intermediate feature-maps from D, the function G contains the reconstruction processing on f and the decoder, and the function T represents the processing of sample x from real images I_{real}.

Only high frequency features at the output layer can significantly improve the recognition ability. However, in the unconditional generation task, the discriminator will always have an advantage over the generator, resulting in the overfitting of the discriminator which can no longer provide an effective gradient flow for the generator. Therefore, the setting of alpha-out equals 0 is also not used in the output layer, and high and low frequency features are combined into the output layer. This method can make the model obtain better representation extraction ability while maintaining the stability of training.

In summary, the following is the complete loss function:

$$\mathcal{L}_D = -\mathbb{E}_{x \sim I_{real}}[min(0, -1| + D(x))] - \mathbb{E}_{\hat{x} \sim G(z)}[min(0, -1 - D(\hat{x}))] + \mathcal{L}_{recons} \qquad (5)$$
$$\mathcal{L}_G = -\mathbb{E}_{z \sim \mathcal{N}[D(G(z))]} \qquad (6)$$

where D's loss function is the hinge version of the adversarial loss add the reconstruction loss.

3.4 Efficiency Analysis

From the perspective of computational efficiency, low-frequency features in octave convolution contain a lot of redundant information. Reducing the spatial dimension of low-frequency features is means reducing the spatial redundancy, thus reducing the number of parameters and the amount of computation in each convolution. As a result, OctGAN is much more compact than FastGAN, uses less computational costs and memory consumption during training, and the overall training process is much faster. Table 1 shows the theoretical calculation cost and memory consumption of OctGAN and FastGAN.

Table 1. Comparison of the number of model parameters and computational complexity between FastGAN and OctGAN.

	Params (M)	FLOPs (M)
FastGAN'G	29.13	79271.04
Our'G	**27.56**	**36341.93**
FastGAN'D	8.39	13229.01
Ours'D	**5.97**	**11092.24**

Table 2. FID comparison at 256^2 resolution on few-shot datasets.

	Animal Face-Dog	Animal Face-Cat	Obama	Panda	Grumpy-cat
Image number	389	160	100	100	100
StyleGAN2	58.85	42.44	46.87	12.06	27.08
StyleGAN2 finetune	61.03	46.07	35.75	14.5	29.34
FastGAN	**50.66**	**35.11**	41.05	**10.03**	**26.65**
Ours	55.31	36.54	**40.87**	10.10	32.10

4 Experiments

4.1 Experimental Setup

Dataset. The experimental setup is as same as FastGAN's setup and rans the experiment on multiple datasets with a wide range of content categories, including Animal-Face Dog and Cat, 100-shot-Obama, 100-shot-panda, and Grumpy-cat [28], at 256×256 resolution. The 1024×1024 resolution datasets includes Flickr Face-HQ (FFHQ) [12], Oxford-flowers, art paintings, photographs on natural landscape, Pokemon, anime face, skull and shell. These datasets vary in style and content, which is a good way to verify that OctGAN is still generalizing.

Table 3. FID comparison at 1024^2 resolution on few-shot datasets.

	Skull	Shell	Anime-Face	Pokemon	Art-painting	Flowers	FFHQ
Image number	100	60	120	800	1000	1000	1000
StyleGAN2	127.98	241.37	152.73	190.23	74.56	45.23	25.66
StyleGAN2 finetune	107.68	220.45	61.23	60.12	N/A	N/A	36.72
FastGAN	130.05	155.47	**59.38**	57.19	45.08	25.66	**24.45**
Ours	**106.72**	**152.72**	64.41	**48.8**	**44.75**	**25.55**	29.25

Metrics. For image generation quality, Frechet Inception Distance which is mainly used to evaluate image quality is used to measure the image distance between the real data and the generated data. We let each class of generating model generates 5,000 images and calculate the FID between the generated image and the entire training dataset. All datasets are trained five times using random seeds and reported the highest scores. In addition, the theoretical computing costs and memory consumption of OctGAN and FastGAN are calculated and compared.

Baselines. We conduct comparative experiments with FastGAN [15], StyleGAN2 [11] and StyleGAN2 finetune on different datasets of different categories and sizes to demonstrate the effectiveness of our model.

4.2 Few-Shot Generation

The advantage of OctGAN becomes more clear from the qualitative comparisons in Fig. 2. The model parameters are saved every 10k iterations and reported the best FID from those model parameters. It is shown in Table 2 and Table 3 that OctGAN has better or similar generation capacity in most datasets. It is worth noting that OctGAN has more advantages in the number of model parameters, computational cost and memory consumption.Table 1 shows the detailed comparison between OctGAN and FastGAN in various aspects.

4.3 Ablation Study

For the discriminator and generator, the original model's G and D are replaced separately for the ablation experiment. It will reflect the improved performance of the two modules over the FastGAN. In the self-supervised learning stage, different methods are used to investigate the use of high and low frequency features here. Specifically, high frequency or low frequency features can be input in the self-supervised learning stage alone, or combine high and low frequency features in self-supervised learning stage. The same idea is tested at the output layer to see how discriminator can use the decoupled features for optimal performance.

Table 4 shows the generator contribute the most in terms of generated quality. It shows that the decoupling of octave convolution in terms of feature frequencies enables the generator to know how to generate pictures with better

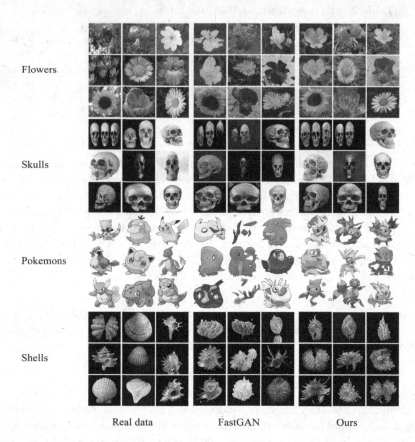

Flowers

Skulls

Pokemons

Shells

Real data   FastGAN   Ours

Fig. 2. Qualitative comparison between our model and FastGAN on 1024^2 resolution datasets. The left-most panel shows the training images, and the right two panels show the uncurated samples from FastGAN and OctGAN. Both models are trained from scratch for 10 h with a batch-size of 8. The samples are generated from the checkpoint with the lowest FID.

Table 4. FID comparison at 1024^2 resolution on few-shot datasets. Dorigin and Gorigin represent the original D and G of FastGAN, and OctD and OctG represent the D and G of OctGAN.

	Skull	Shell	Pokemon
Baseline	130.05	155.47	57.19
Dorigin+OctG	114.72	153.94	50.92
OctD+Gorigin	127.2	158.23	55.52
Ours	**106.72**	**152.72**	**48.8**

image quality. Specifically, OctGAN uses octave convolution to dismantle the generation task of the generator. The high-frequency part is only responsible for generating image details, while the low-frequency part is only responsible for generating image background. The details of the image are hard to generate, so the model assigns more parameters, and the background of the image is easy to generate, so it assigns fewer parameters. Therefore, the feature decoupling splits a generation task into two relatively simple generation tasks, each of them can focus more on its own generation part and reduce the possibility of generating redundant data and incorrect data. Table 5 shows that combining the high and low-frequency features at the self-supervised reconstruction stage and the output layer leads to the greatest performance improvement, which also validates our explanation of the method. As the suspect, investing only in high-frequency features results in an overly powerful discriminator that overfits the data. Investing only in low-frequency features results in a weak discriminator that cannot provide effective gradient flow for the generator. However, when combining high and low-frequency features and investing them in the output layer, will obtain a discriminator with appropriate discriminative power that effectively guides the generator's training. Finally, three channel-wise excitation modules are deployed on the high-frequency feature route to achieve the best image generation effect with the least computational cost.

Table 5. The FID comparison was performed at 1024^2 resolution using different frequency features input to the output layer and self-supervised reconstruction stage.

	Skull	Shell	Pokemon
Baseline	130.05	155.47	57.19
High frequency	153.2	187.64	87.82
Low frequency	218.47	238.78	124.94
High+low frequency	**106.72**	**152.72**	**48.8**

5 Conclusion

In this paper, we propose a novel few-shot generation model, named Octave Generative Adversarial Network (OctGAN). By using octave convolution in the unconditional generation task, the quality of image generation is improved. In theory, the feature decoupling ability of octave convolution can improve the generation ability of the generator and the representation learning ability of the discriminator, and further accelerate the training speed. Experiments are conducted on thirteen datasets, showing that our OctGAN has a better ability to generate realistic images. In the future, we will explore these interesting issues and hope that this work can benefit various downstream tasks of GANs and provide a new research direction for subsequent research.

Acknowledgements. This work was supported in part by the National Natural Science Foundation of China (Grant No. 62006097, U1836218), in part by the Natural Science Foundation of Jiangsu Province (Grant No. BK20200593) and in part by the China Postdoctoral Science Foundation (Grant No. 2021M701456)

References

1. Chen, B., Gan, Y., Bao, B.K.: Multi-pose facial expression recognition based on unpaired images. In: Peng, Y., Hu, SM., Gabbouj, M., Zhou, K., Elad, M., Xu, K. (eds.) Image and Graphics: 11th International Conference, ICIG 2021, Haikou, China, 6–8 August 2021, Proceedings, Part II 11, vol. 12889, pp. 374–385. Springer, Cham (2021). https://doi.org/10.1007/978-3-030-87358-5_30
2. Chen, Y., et al.: Drop an octave: reducing spatial redundancy in convolutional neural networks with octave convolution. In: Proceedings of the IEEE/CVF International Conference on Computer Vision, pp. 3435–3444 (2019)
3. Ding, G., et al.: Attribute group editing for reliable few-shot image generation. In: Proceedings of the IEEE/CVF Conference on Computer Vision and Pattern Recognition, pp. 11194–11203 (2022)
4. Engelmann, J., Lessmann, S.: Conditional Wasserstein GAN-based oversampling of tabular data for imbalanced learning. Expert Syst. Appl. **174**, 114582 (2021)
5. Gao, Y., et al.: High-fidelity and arbitrary face editing. In: Proceedings of the IEEE/CVF Conference on Computer Vision and Pattern Recognition, pp. 16115–16124 (2021)
6. Gu, Z., Li, W., Huo, J., Wang, L., Gao, Y.: LoFGAN: fusing local representations for few-shot image generation. In: Proceedings of the IEEE/CVF International Conference on Computer Vision, pp. 8463–8471 (2021)
7. Hong, Y., Niu, L., Zhang, J., Zhao, W., Fu, C., Zhang, L.: F2GAN: fusing-and-filling GAN for few-shot image generation. In: Proceedings of the 28th ACM International Conference on Multimedia, pp. 2535–2543 (2020)
8. Howard, A.G., et al.: MobileNets: efficient convolutional neural networks for mobile vision applications. arXiv preprint arXiv:1704.04861 (2017)
9. Huang, C., Song, Y., Zhang, Y.: Feature separation GAN for cross view Gait recognition. In: Peng, Y., Hu, S.-M., Gabbouj, M., Zhou, K., Elad, M., Xu, K. (eds.) ICIG 2021. LNCS, vol. 12888, pp. 65–76. Springer, Cham (2021). https://doi.org/10.1007/978-3-030-87355-4_6
10. Jiang, L., Dai, B., Wu, W., Loy, C.C.: Deceive D: adaptive pseudo augmentation for GAN training with limited data. Adv. Neural. Inf. Process. Syst. **34**, 21655–21667 (2021)
11. Karras, T., Aittala, M., Hellsten, J., Laine, S., Lehtinen, J., Aila, T.: Training generative adversarial networks with limited data. Adv. Neural. Inf. Process. Syst. **33**, 12104–12114 (2020)
12. Karras, T., Laine, S., Aila, T.: A style-based generator architecture for generative adversarial networks. In: Proceedings of the IEEE/CVF Conference on Computer Vision and Pattern Recognition, pp. 4401–4410 (2019)
13. Karras, T., Laine, S., Aittala, M., Hellsten, J., Lehtinen, J., Aila, T.: Analyzing and improving the image quality of StyleGAN. In: Proceedings of the IEEE/CVF Conference on Computer Vision and Pattern Recognition, pp. 8110–8119 (2020)
14. Li, Y., Zhang, R., Lu, J., Shechtman, E.: Few-shot image generation with elastic weight consolidation. arXiv preprint arXiv:2012.02780 (2020)

15. Liu, B., Zhu, Y., Song, K., Elgammal, A.: Towards faster and stabilized GAN training for high-fidelity few-shot image synthesis. In: International Conference on Learning Representations (2021)
16. Lu, Z., Deb, K., Boddeti, V.N.: MUXConv: information multiplexing in convolutional neural networks. In: Proceedings of the IEEE/CVF Conference on Computer Vision and Pattern Recognition, pp. 12044–12053 (2020)
17. Ma, F., Xia, G., Liu, Q.: Spatial consistency constrained GAN for human motion transfer. IEEE Trans. Circuits Syst. Video Technol. **32**(2), 730–742 (2021)
18. Moon, S.J., Kim, C., Park, G.M.: WaGI: wavelet-based GAN inversion for preserving high-frequency image details. arXiv preprint arXiv:2210.09655 (2022)
19. Ojha, U., et al.: Few-shot image generation via cross-domain correspondence. In: Proceedings of the IEEE/CVF Conference on Computer Vision and Pattern Recognition, pp. 10743–10752 (2021)
20. Shao, H.C., Liu, K.Y., Su, W.T., Lin, C.W., Lu, J.: DotFAN: a domain-transferred face augmentation net. IEEE Trans. Image Process. **30**, 8759–8772 (2021)
21. Sushko, V., Gall, J., Khoreva, A.: One-Shot GAN: learning to generate samples from single images and videos. In: Proceedings of the IEEE/CVF Conference on Computer Vision and Pattern Recognition, pp. 2596–2600 (2021)
22. Tran, N.-T., Bui, T.-A., Cheung, N.-M.: Dist-GAN: an improved GAN using distance constraints. In: Ferrari, V., Hebert, M., Sminchisescu, C., Weiss, Y. (eds.) Computer Vision – ECCV 2018. LNCS, vol. 11218, pp. 387–401. Springer, Cham (2018). https://doi.org/10.1007/978-3-030-01264-9_23
23. Tseng, H.Y., Jiang, L., Liu, C., Yang, M.H., Yang, W.: Regularizing generative adversarial networks under limited data. In: Proceedings of the IEEE/CVF Conference on Computer Vision and Pattern Recognition, pp. 7921–7931 (2021)
24. Wang, Y., Gonzalez-Garcia, A., Berga, D., Herranz, L., Khan, F.S., van de Weijer, J.: MineGAN: effective knowledge transfer from GANs to target domains with few images. In: Proceedings of the IEEE/CVF Conference on Computer Vision and Pattern Recognition, pp. 9332–9341 (2020)
25. Xiao, J., Li, L., Wang, C., Zha, Z.J., Huang, Q.: Few shot generative model adaption via relaxed spatial structural alignment. In: Proceedings of the IEEE/CVF Conference on Computer Vision and Pattern Recognition, pp. 11204–11213 (2022)
26. Yin, X., Gu, X., Chang, H., Ma, B., Chen, X.: Attribute-aware pedestrian image editing. In: Zhao, Y., Barnes, N., Chen, B., Westermann, R., Kong, X., Lin, C. (eds.) Image and Graphics: 10th International Conference, ICIG 2019, Beijing, China, 23–25 August 2019, Proceedings, Part I, vol. 11901, pp. 44–56. Springer, Cham (2019). https://doi.org/10.1007/978-3-030-34120-6_4
27. Yoshida, Y., Miyato, T.: Spectral norm regularization for improving the generalizability of deep learning. arXiv preprint arXiv:1705.10941 (2017)
28. Zhao, S., Liu, Z., Lin, J., Zhu, J.Y., Han, S.: Differentiable augmentation for data-efficient GAN training. Adv. Neural. Inf. Process. Syst. **33**, 7559–7570 (2020)

Incorporating Global Correlation and Local Aggregation for Efficient Visual Localization

Dong Xie, Jianfeng Lu$^{(\boxtimes)}$, Zhenbo Song, and Xuanzhu Chen

Nanjing University of Science and Technology, Nanjing 210094, China
lujf@njust.edu.cn

Abstract. Scene coordinate regression has made significant improvements in visual localization by voting with segmentation strategy, which first segments landmark patches and then votes landmark points within each patch. However, such method ignores global correlations between patches and lacks local aggregation of voting directions. In this paper, we present a new visual localization framework based on an efficient vision transformer and voting aggregation loss. Specifically, we introduce a global correlation feature extractor to capture the correlated features of global information and employ differentiable angular loss to enhance the aggregation of local voting directions, thus improving the accuracy and robustness of visual localization. Extensive experiments are conducted on the 7-scenes and Cambridge Landmarks datasets. Results show that our method is superior to the scene coordinate regression method on both datasets, demonstrating the effectiveness of this framework.

Keywords: Visual localization · Global Correlation · Local Aggregation

1 Introduction

Visual localization [23,34], a critical technique in augmented reality (AR), virtual reality (VR), autonomous driving, has garnered extensive attention from the computer vision community. The primary goal in visual localization is to estimate the precise 6-DoF camera pose with respect to a known environment. Currently, the common approach for visual localization involves scene coordinate regression methods [3,4,14,28,30], which directly regress 3D scene coordinates from an image by learning a neural network, and the 6-DoF camera pose can be computed through RANSAC-PnP [9]. Instead of directly regressing 3D scene coordinates, feature-based approach [24,25] builds correspondences between 2D feature points in the image and 3D points in the pre-built scene by matching local visual descriptors [2,6,16,21]. In addition, the pixel-level vector voting-based approach [10,11,19,33] accomplishes visual localization by identifying and locating a series of predefined keypoints, in which all 3D keypoints need to be specified manually and all pixels on the image are involved in voting for the predefined 2D keypoints to build correspondences.

© The Author(s), under exclusive license to Springer Nature Switzerland AG 2023
H. Lu et al. (Eds.): ICIG 2023, LNCS 14356, pp. 66–78, 2023.
https://doi.org/10.1007/978-3-031-46308-2_6

(a) Query Image   (b) Feature Map of VS-Net   (c) Feature Map of ours

Fig. 1. Comparison of features captured between our method and VS-Net.

Existing scene coordinate regression method only relies on limited receptive field of the input image to extract feature, resulting in only local regions being considered in prediction process. Similarly, the feature-based method only provides accurate localization at the position of prior feature points, causing errors in regions lacking distinct features. Instead of using points, VS-Net [11] first uniformly divided the 3D scene and images into patches to increase the localization robustness. However, this method still sacrifices the continuity of contextual information and loses the correlation between patches.

To address this issue, we propose a novel visual localization framework that leverages both global correlation and local aggregation based on semantic patch segmentation and pixel voting techniques. To capture global information, we introduce a global correlation feature extractor based on attention mechanism [7,17,31] that generates multi-scale feature maps of the input image for subsequent semantic segmentation and pixel voting process. By considering the correlation of global semantic information, features could preserve continuity within the whole image, such as object position and size. Figure 1 demonstrates feature maps from the proposed method and the VS-Net [11]. It is noticed that our method extracts features with more global correlations, *i.e.* continuous contours of the whole building, potentially benefiting subsequent segmentation and voting. Then to enhance the aggregation of pixel voting in each patch, we adopt a differentiable angular loss that regularizes all voting pixels to tend in the direction towards keypoints. Hence, our method localizes keypoints with the most votes from pixel vectors, even inferring keypoints outside the image, while maintaining angle aggregation within patches. By combining the two techniques, we achieve competitive accuracy and robustness in visual localization. Furthermore, as the large number of parameters typically required by visual localization models, we introduce a lightweight architecture model that significantly reduces the number of network parameters and computational complexity while maintaining good performance. We evaluate our approach on the 7-scenes [28] and Cambridge Landmarks [12] datasets and compare it with existing visual localization methods. The results show that our method outperforms the scene coordinate regression on both datasets, demonstrating the effectiveness of this framework.

In summary, the contributions of this paper are as follows:

- We introduce an efficient global correlation feature extractor with multi-scale fusion to capture the correlated features for semantic patch segmentation.

- We present a differentiable angular loss to enhance the aggregation of voting directions for each patch, which decreases the keypoint regression error.
- We propose a lightweight visual localization pipeline that significantly reduces the number of network parameters and computational complexity while maintaining good performance and improving computing efficiency.

2 Related Work

Visual Localization. Visual localization aims to predict the 6-DoF camera pose for a query image. The prevailing methods are typically through establishing 2D-3D correspondences between 2D image positions and 3D scene coordinates and the final pose is generated by the RANSAC-PNP method. Traditional visual localization frameworks often involve the Structure from Motion techniques (SfM) [27,32,37,40] to estimate the camera's position and orientation in 3D environment. The SfM-based approach requires capturing a series of images in the scene, extracting and matching these feature points [2,6,16,21] between different images to achieve 3D reconstruction and visual localization. With the development of deep neural networks, many feature-based methods [23–26] have been proposed that adopt local descriptors to establish such correspondences between 2D image feature points and 3D scene points. Another alternative approach is scene coordinate regression [3,4,14], which takes 2D image features to directly predict 3D scene points for achieving better performance on small datasets. Recently, Liu et al. [41] proposes a novel visual localization method based on direct matching between the implicit 3D descriptors and the 2D image with transformer. And Zhou et al. [42] presents GoMatch that only relies on visual bearing vector descriptors matching between a query image and a 3D point cloud.

Semantic Segmentation. Semantic segmentation [5,15,20,35,38], which aims to assign a semantic label to each pixel for achieving fine recognition of objects in an image, has been widely applied in computer vision. In visual localization, semantic segmentation can be utilized to enhance the perception and understanding of the environment [8,13,29,39] and even replace the role of descriptors [29]. For example, in VS-Net [11], the 3D scene and images are uniformly divided into many patches, and semantic segmentation is applied to predict the patch category ID to which each pixel belongs. Only pixels of the same category ID can participate in voting for keypoints. However, the uniform division of image patches can lead to a loss of continuity in contextual information. Inspired by the global attention mechanism in transformer [31], we introduce a global correlation feature extractor to enhance the model's understanding between patches.

Voting-Based Pose Estimation. In visual localization, the predicted poses may be inaccurate due to the existence of occlusion and severe changes. To counteract these variations, voting strategy [10,11,19,33] is introduced to locate the keypoints by selecting the pixels with the most number of votes, thereby improving the accuracy of pose estimation. Yu et al. [36] propose a differentiable proxy voting loss that considers the distances between pixel voting vectors and keypoints to optimize the results. Meanwhile, we argue that there is lack of aggregation inside the patch, and inspired by this, we introduce a differentiable angular voting loss to improve the aggregation within patches. We believe that the critical factor for the final keypoints lies in the direction, as it is used to calculate the intersection point with the highest number of votes.

3   Method

3.1   Framework of Segmentation and Voting

This work builds upon the VS-Net [11] framework to establish the 2D-3D correspondences, in which the 3D scene surfaces are uniformly divided into multiple patches, with each patch center is manually defined as 3D keypoint q_i. Correspondingly, the 2D images are also divided into many patches by the 3D scene's projection and each pixel in the image is assigned its associated patch id. The 2D keypoint coordinate c is computed as follows:

$$c_i = F(q_i, K, R, t), \tag{1}$$

where q_i is the i's 3D keypoint, K represents camera intrinsic, R represents camera pose rotation parameter and t represents camera pose translation parameter. For the i's patch, each pixel p_j has a ground truth direction vector d_j pointing to the 2D keypoint c_i, which can be represented as

$$d_j = \frac{p_j - c_i}{\|p_j - c_i\|_2}. \tag{2}$$

Thus, for a given image, the neural network predicts a patch-id and a voting vector for each pixel. The patch-id denotes the semantic patch in segmentation map, and the voting vector points to the corresponding 2D keypoint in the patch. To determine the 2D keypoints, vectors with the same patch-id i participate in voting and the intersection with the highest number of votes will be selected as the 2D keypoint of i's patch.

3.2   Global Correlation Feature Extraction

To improve the correlation between different patches in the image, we incorporate the global correlation feature extractor based on mobileVitv2 [17] to capture the correlated features. With multi-scale factors in account, our method outputs five feature maps in different scales, providing richer information for subsequent segmentation and voting decoder.

As depicted in Fig. 2, we first take a 2D image as input and apply the attention module to obtain five feature maps, which can be formulated as

$$F_{\times 2}, F_{\times 4}, F_{\times 8}, F_{\times 16}, F_{\times 32} = Att(I), \tag{3}$$

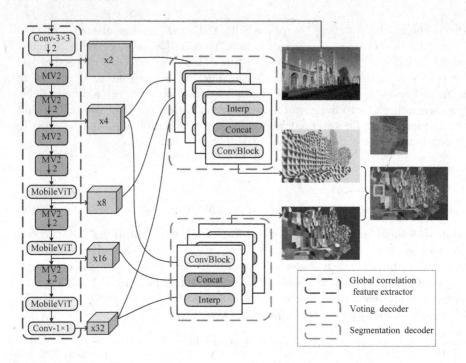

Fig. 2. Pipeline of our method: The global correlation feature extractor generates multi-scale feature maps for segmentation and voting. MV2 denotes MobileNetv2 [22] and MobileVit [17] represents a MobileVit attention module.

where $\mathbf{F}_{\times i}$ denotes the feature map for down-sampling i times. Figure 1 shows that our method is more sensitive to the contour features of objects within the image and can capture them more clearly than VS-Net [11]. Subsequently, $\mathbf{F}_{\times i}(i = \{4, 16, 32\})$ are then fed into segmentation decoder to obtain the segmentation map, which consists of four main modules, each containing three sub-modules: interpolation, concatenation, and convolution. Similarly, $\mathbf{F}_{\times i}(i = \{2, 4, 8, 32\})$ are taken in the voting decoder to obtain the vector map, which consists of three same main modules as segmentation decoder. This two decoders can be expressed as

$$\mathbf{F}_S = \mathbf{S}(\mathbf{F}_{\times 4}, \mathbf{F}_{\times 16}, \mathbf{F}_{\times 32}), \tag{4}$$

$$\mathbf{F}_V = \mathbf{V}(\mathbf{F}_{\times 2}, \mathbf{F}_{\times 4}, \mathbf{F}_{\times 8}, \mathbf{F}_{\times 32}), \tag{5}$$

where $\mathbf{F}_S$ denotes segmentation map, and $\mathbf{F}_V$ denotes vector map. Finally, we merge the segmentation map $\mathbf{F}_S$ and vector map $\mathbf{F}_V$ to compute intersections with the most votes as the 2D keypoints,

$$\{\mathbf{I}_i\} = \Omega(\mathbf{F}_S, \mathbf{F}_V), \tag{6}$$

where $\mathbf{I}_i$ denote all final 2D keypoints.

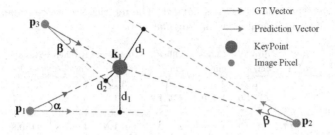

Fig. 3. Directional errors may be larger if pixel is closer to keypoints.

3.3 Local Aggregate Voting

To address the issue of aggregation within patches, we employ differentiable angular loss to increase patch aggregation during the voting process. Given the segmentation map $\mathbf{F}_S$ and vector map $\mathbf{F}_V$, for a patch $\mathbf{Q}$ in segmentation map and the predicted vector $\mathbf{v}$ of each pixel $\mathbf{p}$ in the patch, the differentiable angular loss is as follows:

$$\mathbf{L}_{va} = \sum_{Q \in F_C} \sum_{p \in Q} (1 - \frac{v_Q(p) \cdot d_Q(p)}{\|v_Q(p)\|_2 \cdot \|d_Q(p)\|_2 + \epsilon}), \tag{7}$$

where $d_Q(p)$ represents ground truth vector for pixel $\mathbf{p}$ in patch $\mathbf{Q}$, $v_Q(p)$ represents pixel prediction vector and The value of ϵ is 1e-3. As shown in Fig. 3, for pixel $\mathbf{p}_1$ and $\mathbf{p}_2$, when their distance error between the keypoint and direction vector is same $\mathbf{d}_1$, the directional error α of $\mathbf{p}_1$ is larger as $\mathbf{p}_1$ is closer to the keypoint $\mathbf{k}_1$, especially in low-resolution images. We have appended the angular loss to the segmentation and voting loss, which further accelerates the convergence in training process and improve the localization accuracy. The total loss is calculated as:

$$\mathbf{L} = \mathbf{L}_{seg} + \mathbf{L}_{vote} + \lambda \mathbf{L}_{va}, \tag{8}$$

where $\mathbf{L}_{seg}$ denotes segmentation loss, $\mathbf{L}_{vote}$ denotes voting l_1 loss and λ denotes hyperparameter.

4 Experiment

In this section, we provide a detailed description of our experimental setup, including the datasets used, the specific configuration of the experiments. We evaluate our approach on the 7-scenes [28] and Cambridge Landmarks [12] datasets and compare it with state-of-the-art methods. Furthermore, we conduct an ablation study to further analyze the contributions of angle loss to the model performance.

Table 1. Results on indoor 7-scenes dataset. The metrics we use to evaluate performance are median positional error and angular error.

Method	Chess	Fire	Heads	Office	Pumpkin	Kitchen	Stairs	Avg
	cm, °	cm, °	cm, °	cm, °	cm, °	cm, °	cm, °	cm, °
AS [25]	4, 1.96	3, 1.53	2, 1.45	9, 3.61	8, 3.10	7, 3.37	3, 2.22	5.1, 2.5
HF-Net [23]	2.6, 0.9	2.7, 1.0	1.4, 0.9	4.3, 1.2	5.8, 1.6	5.3, 1.6	7.2, 1.9	4.2, 1.3
GoMatch [42]	4, 1.6	12, 3.7	5, 3.4	7, 1.8	28, 5.6	14, 3.0	58,13.1	18.3, 4.6
HSC-Net [14]	2.1, 0.7	2.2, 0.9	1.2, 0.9	2.7, 0.8	4.0, **1.0**	4.0, 1.8	3.1, 0.8	2.7, 1.0
Reg [14]	2.1, 1.0	2.4, 0.9	1.2, 0.8	3.1, 0.9	4.3, 1.1	4.5, 1.4	3.8, 0.9	3.1, 1.0
DSAC++ [4]	**1.5, 0.5**	2.0, 0.9	1.3, 0.8	2.6, 0.7	4.3, 1.1	3.8, **1.1**	9.1, 2.5	3.5, 1.1
VS-Net [11]	**1.5, 0.5**	**1.9, 0.8**	1.2, **0.7**	**2.1, 0.6**	3.7, **1.0**	**3.6, 1.1**	**2.8, 0.8**	**2.4, 0.8**
Ours	*1.6, 0.6*	*2.0, **0.8***	***1.1**, 0.8*	*2.2, 0.7*	***3.6, 1.0***	***3.6, 1.1***	*3.3, 0.9*	*2.5, 0.9*

Table 2. Results on outdoor Cambridge Landmark dataset. The metrics we use to evaluate performance are median positional error and angular error. This flag (–) represents a failure in GreatCourt.

Method	GreatCourt	KingsCollege	OldHospital	ShopFacade	St.MarysChurch	Avg
	m, °	m, °	m, °	m, °	m, °	m, °
AS [25]	-	0.42, 0.55	0.44, 1.01	0.12, 0.4	0.19, 0.54	-
HF-Net [23]	0.76, 0.3	0.34, 0.4	0.43, 0.6	0.09, 0.4	0.16, 0.5	0.356, 0.31
GoMatch [42]	-	0.25, 0.6	2.83, 8.1	0.48, 4.8	3.35, 9.9	-
HSC-Net [14]	0.28, 0.2	0.18, 0.3	0.19, **0.3**	**0.06, 0.3**	0.09, 0.3	0.160, 0.28
Reg [14]	1.25, 0.6	0.21, 0.3	0.21, **0.3**	**0.06, 0.3**	0.16, 0.5	0.378, 0.40
DSAC++ [4]	0.40, 0.2	0.20, 0.3	0.20, **0.3**	**0.06, 0.3**	0.13, 0.4	0.194, 0.30
VS-Net [11]	**0.22, 0.1**	0.16, **0.2**	**0.16, 0.3**	**0.06, 0.3**	**0.08, 0.3**	**0.136, 0.24**
Ours	*0.24, **0.1***	***0.15**, 0.3*	***0.16, 0.3***	*0.07, **0.3***	*0.13, 0.4*	*0.150, 0.28*

4.1 Experimental Setup

Datasets. We evaluated our method on 7-scenes dataset [28] and Cambridge Landmarks datasets [12]. 7-scenes dataset is a collection of tracked RGB-D camera frames, which contains seven indoor scene data. And the 3D dense model along with the camera poses are implemented by KinectFusion [18]. Cambridge Landmarks dataset is a large-scale outdoor visual relocalisation dataset taken around Cambridge University containing raw video, extracted image frames labelled with their 6-DOF camera pose and a visual reconstruction of the scene.

Implementation Details. We conducted our experiments on a computing system equipped with an Intel(R) Xeon(R) Platinum 8260 CPU and a Tesla V100-SXM2-32 GB GPU. Our model architecture is built upon a U-net encoder-decoder structure, where the encoder contains MobileNetV2 [22], MobileViT [17] block, and convolutional layer modules, while the decoder consists of repeated interpolation, concatenation and convolutional layer modules. During training, we used an Adam optimizer with a learning rate of 1e−4, and set the hyper-parameter for the introduced angle loss to 1e−3. We evaluated our model's performance by two metrics: the translation error (cm/m) and the angle error (degree) with respect to the ground truth pose matrix.

Table 3. Comparison of model complexity between our model and VS-Net on 7-scenes dataset.

Method	FLOPs	Params	Time
VS-Net [11]	144G	62M	0.381 s
Ours	106G	8M	0.014 s

4.2 Localization Results

Feature-based and scene coordinate regression methods are commonly used for visual localization. Feature-based methods such as Active Search [25] use SIFT [16] feature points and a priority-based algorithm for 2D-3D matching. HF-Net [23], on the other hand, utilizes NetVLAD [1] and SuperPoint [6] to compute global and local descriptors for matching. Scene coordinate regression methods, including Reg [14] and DSAC++ [4], are used to regress scene coordinates directly, with the latter incorporating a Reg-based selection algorithm with differentiable bit pose assumptions. HSC-Net [14] uses a coarse-to-fine hierarchical scene prediction to enhance localization performance. And GoMatch [42] is an alternative to visual-based matching that solely relies on geometric information for matching image keypoints to maps, represented as sets of bearing vectors. Additionally, VS-Net [11] utilizes a segmentation and voting framework to establish correspondences for visual localization.

We present experimental outcomes in Tables 1 and 2. Our method has exhibited notable performance on both indoor and outdoor scenarios and outperforms feature-based and scene regression methods in average position error and angle error across all tested scenarios. However, our method is slightly inferior than VS-Net [11] in the Stairs and St.MarysChurch scenarios, which could be attributed to their more challenging nature and the potential limitation of generalization resulting from the smaller number of parameters in our approach compared to VS-Net [11]. Overall, our method has demonstrated notable performance in most scenarios, but further optimization is required to achieve better results in challenging environments.

Comparing the model complexity of our method with VS-Net [11], as shown in Table 3, our method exhibits a significant advantage in floating-point operations (FLOPs), model parameters and model inference time. Specifically, our method requires 25% fewer floating-point operations than the VS-Net model, while the model parameter size of our method is only 8M, which accounts for just 13% of the VS-Net model parameter size. Notably, our method model inference time for per image takes only 3.6% of VS-Net. Taken together, our method is much more lightweight and efficient.

Table 4. Ablation study of Angle Loss. The metrics we use to evaluate performance are median positional error and angular error.

Angle loss	w/o	w
Chess	1.58 cm, 0.53°	1.56 cm, 0.56°
Fire	2.30 cm, 0.91°	1.98 cm, 0.80°
Heads	1.15 cm, 0.79°	1.14 cm, 0.75°
Office	2.52 cm, 0.71°	2.24 cm, 0.67°
Pumpkin	3.63 cm, 1.03°	3.57 cm, 1.03°
Kitchen	3.83 cm, 1.09°	3.58 cm, 1.13°
Stairs	3.49 cm, 0.97°	3.34 cm, 0.88°
Avg	2.64 cm, 0.86°	2.49 cm, 0.83°
GreatCourt	27.4 cm, 0.11°	23.7 cm, 0.10°
KingsCollege	15.1 cm, 0.27°	14.9 cm, 0.27°
OldHospital	18.5 cm, 0.39°	15.8 cm, 0.34°
ShopFacade	8.3 cm, 0.37°	6.5 cm, 0.32°
St.MarysChurch	13.1 cm, 0.43°	12.6 cm, 0.42°
Avg	16.5 cm, 0.31°	14.7 cm, 0.29°

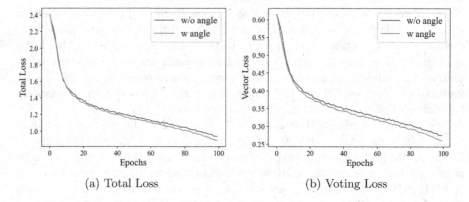

(a) Total Loss   (b) Voting Loss

Fig. 4. Impact of Angle Loss on Model Convergence.

4.3   Ablation Study

In this section, we conducted an analysis to investigate the effect of incorporating angle loss in our method. To this end, we evaluated the position error and angle error on 7-scenes and Cambridge datasets with and without angle loss. The results, as shown in Table 4, indicate a considerable reduction in both position and angle errors after incorporating angle loss, particularly in position error. These findings suggest that the inclusion of angle loss improves the local aggregation within patches, resulting in a more accurate localization.

Furthermore, Fig. 4 illustrates the variations in total loss and vector voting loss with and without angle loss. The results demonstrate that the incorporation of angle loss leads to a slight improvement in both total loss and vector voting loss, thereby enhancing the convergence performance of the model.

5   Conclusion

In this work, we present an efficient visual localization framework that integrates the global correlation feature extractor and the local aggregate loss through voting with segmentation strategy. By introducing the global correlation feature extractor to capture the correlation of global information and employing the differentiable angular loss to enhance the aggregation of local information, we achieve competitive accuracy and robustness in localization compared to existing methods. Additionally, a lightweight pipeline is introduced to reduce the number of model parameters and computational complexity. Experimental results on the 7-scenes and Cambridge Landmarks datasets demonstrate the effectiveness of our method. Future work will focus on further improving the performance by exploring the potential of an end-to-end lightweight framework for visual localization.

Acknowledgement. This work was supported in part by the National Natural Science Foundation of China (No. 62302220), in part by the China Postdoctoral Foundation (No. 2023M731691), and in part by the Jiangsu Funding Program for Excellent Postdoctoral Talent (No. 2022ZB268).

References

1. Arandjelovic, R., Gronat, P., Torii, A., Pajdla, T., Sivic, J.: NetVLAD: CNN architecture for weakly supervised place recognition. In: Proceedings of the IEEE Conference on Computer Vision and Pattern Recognition, pp. 5297–5307 (2016)
2. Bay, H., Tuytelaars, T., Van Gool, L.: SURF: speeded up robust features. In: Leonardis, A., Bischof, H., Pinz, A. (eds.) ECCV 2006. LNCS, vol. 3951, pp. 404–417. Springer, Heidelberg (2006). https://doi.org/10.1007/11744023_32
3. Brachmann, E., et al.: DSAC-differentiable RANSAC for camera localization. In: Proceedings of the IEEE Conference on Computer Vision and Pattern Recognition, pp. 6684–6692 (2017)
4. Brachmann, E., Rother, C.: Learning less is more-6D camera localization via 3D surface regression. In: Proceedings of the IEEE Conference on Computer Vision and Pattern Recognition, pp. 4654–4662 (2018)
5. Chen, L.C., Papandreou, G., Kokkinos, I., Murphy, K., Yuille, A.L.: DeepLab: semantic image segmentation with deep convolutional nets, atrous convolution, and fully connected CRFs. IEEE Trans. Pattern Anal. Mach. Intell. **40**(4), 834–848 (2017)

6. DeTone, D., Malisiewicz, T., Rabinovich, A.: SuperPoint: self-supervised interest point detection and description. In: Proceedings of the IEEE Conference on Computer Vision and Pattern Recognition Workshops, pp. 224–236 (2018)

7. Dosovitskiy, A., et al.: An image is worth 16 × 16 words: transformers for image recognition at scale. arXiv preprint arXiv:2010.11929 (2020)

8. Fan, H., Zhou, Y., Li, A., Gao, S., Li, J., Guo, Y.: Visual localization using semantic segmentation and depth prediction. arXiv preprint arXiv:2005.11922 (2020)

9. Fischler, M.A., Bolles, R.C.: Random sample consensus: a paradigm for model fitting with applications to image analysis and automated cartography. Commun. ACM **24**(6), 381–395 (1981)

10. Hu, Y., Hugonot, J., Fua, P., Salzmann, M.: Segmentation-driven 6D object pose estimation. In: Proceedings of the IEEE/CVF Conference on Computer Vision and Pattern Recognition, pp. 3385–3394 (2019)

11. Huang, Z., et al.: VS-Net: voting with segmentation for visual localization. In: Proceedings of the IEEE/CVF Conference on Computer Vision and Pattern Recognition, pp. 6101–6111 (2021)

12. Kendall, A., Grimes, M., Cipolla, R.: PoseNet: a convolutional network for real-time 6-DOF camera relocalization. In: Proceedings of the IEEE International Conference on Computer Vision, pp. 2938–2946 (2015)

13. Larsson, M., Stenborg, E., Toft, C., Hammarstrand, L., Sattler, T., Kahl, F.: Fine-grained segmentation networks: self-supervised segmentation for improved long-term visual localization. In: Proceedings of the IEEE/CVF International Conference on Computer Vision, pp. 31–41 (2019)

14. Li, X., Wang, S., Zhao, Y., Verbeek, J., Kannala, J.: Hierarchical scene coordinate classification and regression for visual localization. In: Proceedings of the IEEE/CVF Conference on Computer Vision and Pattern Recognition, pp. 11983–11992 (2020)

15. Long, J., Shelhamer, E., Darrell, T.: Fully convolutional networks for semantic segmentation. In: Proceedings of the IEEE Conference on Computer Vision and Pattern Recognition, pp. 3431–3440 (2015)

16. Lowe, D.G.: Distinctive image features from scale-invariant keypoints. Int. J. Comput. Vision **60**, 91–110 (2004)

17. Mehta, S., Rastegari, M.: Separable self-attention for mobile vision transformers. arXiv preprint arXiv:2206.02680 (2022)

18. Newcombe, R.A., et al.: KinectFusion: real-time dense surface mapping and tracking. In: 2011 10th IEEE International Symposium on Mixed and Augmented Reality, pp. 127–136. IEEE (2011)

19. Peng, S., Liu, Y., Huang, Q., Zhou, X., Bao, H.: PVNet: pixel-wise voting network for 6DoF pose estimation. In: Proceedings of the IEEE/CVF Conference on Computer Vision and Pattern Recognition, pp. 4561–4570 (2019)

20. Ronneberger, O., Fischer, P., Brox, T.: U-Net: convolutional networks for biomedical image segmentation. In: Navab, N., Hornegger, J., Wells, W., Frangi, A. (eds.) Medical Image Computing and Computer-Assisted Intervention-MICCAI 2015: 18th International Conference, Munich, Germany, 5–9 October 2015, Proceedings, Part III 18, vol. 9351, pp. 234–241. Springer, Cham (2015). https://doi.org/10.1007/978-3-319-24574-4_28

21. Rublee, E., Rabaud, V., Konolige, K., Bradski, G.: ORB: an efficient alternative to SIFT or SURF. In: 2011 International Conference on Computer Vision, pp. 2564–2571. IEEE (2011)

22. Sandler, M., Howard, A., Zhu, M., Zhmoginov, A., Chen, L.C.: MobileNetV 2: inverted residuals and linear bottlenecks. In: Proceedings of the IEEE Conference on Computer Vision and Pattern Recognition, pp. 4510–4520 (2018)

23. Sarlin, P.E., Cadena, C., Siegwart, R., Dymczyk, M.: From coarse to fine: robust hierarchical localization at large scale. In: Proceedings of the IEEE/CVF Conference on Computer Vision and Pattern Recognition, pp. 12716–12725 (2019)

24. Sattler, T., Leibe, B., Kobbelt, L.: Fast image-based localization using direct 2D-to-3D matching. In: 2011 International Conference on Computer Vision, pp. 667–674. IEEE (2011)

25. Sattler, T., Leibe, B., Kobbelt, L.: Improving image-based localization by active correspondence search. In: Fitzgibbon, A., Lazebnik, S., Perona, P., Sato, Y., Schmid, C. (eds.) Computer Vision-ECCV 2012: 12th European Conference on Computer Vision, Florence, Italy, 7–13 October 2012, Proceedings, Part I 12, vol. 7572, pp. 752–765. Springer, Cham (2012). https://doi.org/10.1007/978-3-642-33718-5_54

26. Sattler, T., Leibe, B., Kobbelt, L.: Efficient & effective prioritized matching for large-scale image-based localization. IEEE Trans. Pattern Anal. Mach. Intell. **39**(9), 1744–1756 (2016)

27. Schonberger, J.L., Frahm, J.M.: Structure-from-motion revisited. In: Proceedings of the IEEE Conference on Computer Vision and Pattern Recognition, pp. 4104–4113 (2016)

28. Shotton, J., Glocker, B., Zach, C., Izadi, S., Criminisi, A., Fitzgibbon, A.: Scene coordinate regression forests for camera relocalization in RGB-D images. In: Proceedings of the IEEE Conference on Computer Vision and Pattern Recognition, pp. 2930–2937 (2013)

29. Stenborg, E., Toft, C., Hammarstrand, L.: Long-term visual localization using semantically segmented images. In: 2018 IEEE International Conference on Robotics and Automation (ICRA), pp. 6484–6490. IEEE (2018)

30. Valentin, J., Nießner, M., Shotton, J., Fitzgibbon, A., Izadi, S., Torr, P.H.: Exploiting uncertainty in regression forests for accurate camera relocalization. In: Proceedings of the IEEE Conference on Computer Vision and Pattern Recognition, pp. 4400–4408 (2015)

31. Vaswani, A., et al.: Attention is all you need. In: Advances in Neural Information Processing Systems, vol. 30 (2017)

32. Wu, C.: VisualSFM: a visual structure from motion system (2011). http://www.cs.washington.edu/homes/ccwu/vsfm

33. Xiang, Y., Schmidt, T., Narayanan, V., Fox, D.: PoseCNN: a convolutional neural network for 6D object pose estimation in cluttered scenes. arXiv preprint arXiv:1711.00199 (2017)

34. Xu, Y., et al.: SelfVoxeLO: self-supervised lidar odometry with voxel-based deep neural networks. In: Conference on Robot Learning, pp. 115–125. PMLR (2021)

35. Yu, F., Koltun, V.: Multi-scale context aggregation by dilated convolutions. arXiv preprint arXiv:1511.07122 (2015)

36. Yu, X., Zhuang, Z., Koniusz, P., Li, H.: 6DoF object pose estimation via differentiable proxy voting loss. arXiv preprint arXiv:2002.03923 (2020)

37. Zhang, G., Dong, Z., Jia, J., Wong, T.-T., Bao, H.: Efficient non-consecutive feature tracking for structure-from-motion. In: Daniilidis, K., Maragos, P., Paragios, N. (eds.) ECCV 2010. LNCS, vol. 6315, pp. 422–435. Springer, Heidelberg (2010). https://doi.org/10.1007/978-3-642-15555-0_31

38. Zhong, Z., et al.: Squeeze-and-attention networks for semantic segmentation. In: Proceedings of the IEEE/CVF Conference on Computer Vision and Pattern Recognition, pp. 13065–13074 (2020)

39. Zhou, G., Bescos, B., Dymczyk, M., Pfeiffer, M., Neira, J., Siegwart, R.: Dynamic objects segmentation for visual localization in urban environments. arXiv preprint arXiv:1807.02996 (2018)

40. Zhu, S., et al.: Parallel structure from motion from local increment to global averaging. arXiv preprint arXiv:1702.08601 (2017)

41. Liu, J., Nie, Q., Liu, Y., Wang, C.: NeRF-Loc: visual localization with conditional neural radiance field. CoRR abs/2304.07979 (2023)

42. Zhou, Q., Agostinho, S., Osep, A., Leal-Taix e, L.: Is geometry enough for matching in visual localization? In: Avidan, S., Brostow, G., Cissé, M., Farinella, G.M., Hassner, T. (eds.) Computer Vision - ECCV 2022–17th European Conference, Tel Aviv, Israel, 23–27 October 2022, Proceedings, Part X. LNCS, vol. 13670, pp. 407–425. Springer, Cham (2022). https://doi.org/10.1007/978-3-031-20080-9_24

Deep Interactive Image Semantic and Instance Segmentation

Xuzijing Wu[1], Pengfei Yang[2], Wenteng Shao[1], Tao Wang[1(✉)], and Quansen Sun[1]

[1] School of Computer Science and Engineering, Nanjing University of Science and Technology, Nanjing 210094, China
wangtaoatnjust@163.com

[2] School of Automation, Nanjing University of Science and Technology, Nanjing 210094, China

Abstract. Existing deep interactive segmentation methods only focus on the extraction of specific instance objects. When the target of interest to users is a category, existing methods have to perform more interactions. We take advantages of the relevance between semantic and instance segmentations, and give two definitions based on the interactive mode, i.e. interactive semantic segmentation and interactive instance segmentation, to distinguish the actual requirements of instance objects and semantic categories that users are interested in. Then, a dual-branch-based full convolutional network model is proposed to integrate the above two tasks (similar to a multi-task learning), in which the relevance between the interactive semantic and instance segmentations can be jointly explored along with a simultaneous output of potential interested semantic categories and instance objects. Vast experimental results on GrabCut, Berkeley, SBD and DAVIS datasets verified the effectiveness of the proposed method.

Keywords: Interactive segmentation · Iterative training · Dual-path network · Multitask learning

1 Introduction

As a basic research in computer vision and image processing, interactive image segmentation can extract objects of interest to users based on a small amount of user interaction, which has been widely used in dataset annotation [1], automatic driving [2] and medical image analysis [3].

A large number of interactive image segmentation algorithms have been proposed in the literature [10, 11, 13, 14]. Early interactive segmentation methods are mainly represented by the energy optimization models. The classical algorithms include graph cut [10], random walk [11], shortest path [12], etc. These methods establish the segmentation task as the solution of the objective function in mathematics. However, due to the lack of semantics of the underlying visual features, it is difficult for the above traditional interactive methods to obtain accurate segmentation under limited user interaction. Thanks to the development of deep learning technology, many deep interactive segmentation algorithms have been proposed in recent years [13, 14]. Relying on the strong feature

H. Lu et al. (Eds.): ICIG 2023, LNCS 14356, pp. 79–90, 2023.
https://doi.org/10.1007/978-3-031-46308-2_7

representation ability, such methods can complete segmentation only with a few user click interactions. The algorithm performance has been significantly improved compared with the traditional methods. This paper focuses on the interactive image segmentation task based on deep learning.

As shown in Fig. 1(a), the existing deep interactive method can segment the object of interest to users under limited clicks. However, in practical applications, when the user interacts in a specific object region, the target of interest may also be the entire category to which the object belongs (as shown in Fig. 1(b)). Therefore, the existing deep interactive methods only focus on the segmentation of specific instance objects, while ignoring the segmentation requirements of potential semantic categories. When the user is interested in the whole category, the existing methods have to interact more times to extract all objects belonging to this category, in order to meet the user's segmentation requirements. This paper will explore the above practical problems.

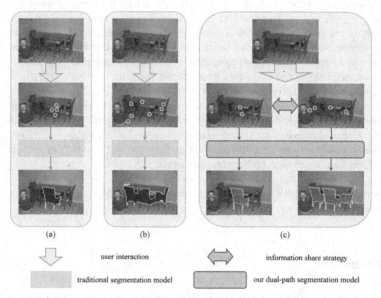

Fig. 1. Interactive segmentation process.

To solve the problems of instance object and semantic category segmentations that users are interested in, this paper first gives two new definitions: interactive image instance segmentation and interactive image semantic segmentation. We define interactive instance segmentation as segmenting specific instance objects of interest to users, and interactive semantic segmentation as segmenting specific semantic categories of interest to users. Unlike the existing image semantic segmentation and instance segmentation methods, their label space is determined by fixed predefined datasets, while in interactive semantic and instance segmentation tasks, the label space is defined by flexible (unfixed) user interaction. From the image panoptic segmentation model [16], the potential association between semantic segmentation and instance segmentation tasks is discovered. Similarly, a potential connection also exists between the interactive semantic and instance segmentation tasks. Therefore, on the basis of distinguishing these two tasks, this paper designs a two-branch symmetric network structure based on convolutional neural network to combine interactive semantic and interactive instance segmentation tasks, and explores the correlation between these two tasks through the shared backbone network (similar to multi-task learning). The segmentation results of instance objects and semantic categories that meet the user's potential requirement can be output simultaneously by these two branches (as shown in Fig. 1(c)). For the interactive training mode, we also explore the relevance of these two tasks in click embedding. For example, clicked labels in interactive semantic segmentation can also assist interactive instance segmentation, and vice versa. The main contributions of this paper are summarized as follows:

1. We gave new concepts of interactive image semantic segmentation and interactive image instance segmentation to distinguish the practical requirements of instance objects and semantic categories that are of interest to users in the interactive segmentation task;
2. We built a two-branch full convolution network model to combine and unify the two tasks of interactive semantic and interactive instance segmentation based on the shared backbone network, which explors the correlation between these two tasks in terms of click embedding and feature learning, and realizes the simultaneous output of potentially interested instance objects and semantic categories. Furthermore, it also verifies the effectiveness of the joint learning compared with the independent learning of these two tasks.

2   Related work

Many deep learning-based interactive image segmentation approaches have been proposed in the literature. Zhang et al. [17] constructed an efficient click-sampling method. Input includes 2 corner points and an optional point of the bounding box object. In order to retain semantic information and local boundary details at the same time, Yao et al. [19] integrated multi-level super-pixel information into the feature map. Mahadevan et al. [21] proposed a new click generation strategy in the iterative training process. Deep GrabCut [22] solves the problem of interactive bounding boxes through an end-to-end training encoder-decoder architecture. Wang et al. [23] expressed the interactive information with geodesic distance to improve the discrimination between adjacent pixels and the label similarity of similar regions. In the fusion of interactive information, early fusion [24] connects the interactive channel with the image RGB three channels as the input of neural network. In addition, Forte et al. [25] combined the soft iou loss and the suggested click location loss to force the network segmentation results to be correct at the click location. Lin et al. [20] proposed the First Click Attention Network (FCA-Net) based on the difference between the initial interaction point and other interaction points, which improved the accuracy of interactive segmentation. Sofiiuk et al. [13] proposed an interactive segmentation method without back propagation and used the mask of the previous step as an additional channel for input. Liu et al. [15] proposed a general interactive segmentation framework, which enables the existing segmentation network to predict the next click (pseudo click) and improve the segmentation mask as the imitation of human click. Li et al. [4] decomposed the slow prediction of the whole image into two kinds of fast reasoning: rough segmentation of the target and local refinement, narrowing the gap between academic methods and industrial needs.

However, almost all the above methods only focus on the instance objects that users are interested in. When users are interested in the semantic categories, they are difficult to get satisfactory segmentation results.

3   Method

As mentioned above, though many deep interactive segmentation methods have been proposed, few of them pay attention to the segmentation of semantic categories. Therefore, in Sect. 3.1 we first design an interactive semantic segmentation model. Based on the similar network structure, we give an interactive instance segmentation design in Sect. 3.2. In Sect. 3.3, we propose a dual-branch network to combine the above two tasks together.

3.1   Interactive Image Semantic Segmentation Model

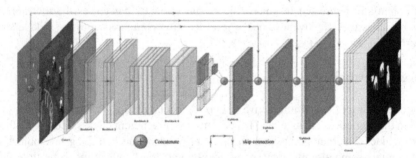

Fig. 2. Our interactive semantic segmentation model.

Network Structure: As shown in Fig. 2, referring to the existing semantic segmentation network [18], the interactive semantic segmentation model built in this paper is composed of four parts: variant residual network [5], Atrous Spatial Pyramid Pooling (ASPP) module [6] with expansion rates of 12, 24 and 36, upsampling module and final classification module. The original image is connected with the positive and negative click maps through the channel, and then it is transferred to the network. After the encoder and decoder, a pixel-level classification head is utilized to obtain the final segmentation.

Encoder: The encoder we adopted is an improved ResNet network [5], which is composed of a common convolution module and a residual module with 2, 3, 5, 2 bottleneck modules. The common convolution module is connected by a 7 * 7 convolution with stride 2, a batch normalization layer, relu activation, and a maxpool layer with stride 2.

Residual module I does not use dilated convolution, and reduces the resolution to 1/4 of the original size. Residual module II uses dilated convolution with an expansion rate of 2 without reducing the resolution. Residual module III does not use dilated convolution, and reduces the resolution to 1/8 of the original size. Residual module IV uses dilated convolution with an expansion rate of 4 without reducing the resolution. Down-sampling operation is executed in the shortcut of the second bottleneck module of each layer, so that the transmission length is consistent with the required length.

Decoder: The outputs of upblock 1、2、3 are upsampled as deep features, and the outputs of original image and the interaction point、Conv1、Resblock2 are used as shallow features. Three sets of deep and shallow features are fused. The last feature is input into a classification header consisting of two sets of 3 * 3 convolutions and one set of 1 * 1 convolutions to obtain the final segmentation result.

3.2 Interactive Image Instance Segmentation Model

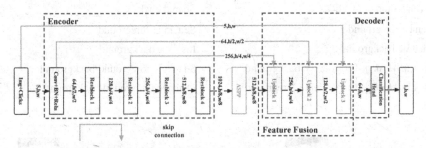

Fig. 3. Our interactive instance segmentation model.

As shown in Fig. 3, we construct the interactive instance segmentation model based on the similar structure with the interactive semantic model. When performing interactive instance segmentation, fine-size receptive fields are used in the ASPP module. The expansion rate of ASPP module in the interactive instance segmentation model is set to 6, 12, and 36 respectively. At the same time, to ensure the accuracy of selection and correction clicks under interactive instance segmentation, we set the disk radius used for instance segmentation to 0.8 times that of semantic segmentation.

3.3 Joint Interactive Semantic and Instance Segmentation Model

Network Structure: Similar to the components in the above single network model, the joint network shares parameters in the residual module. Two network branches are composed of the same ASPP module, upper sampler and classification head. In this paper, user interaction clicks are transformed into four channels: semantic foreground (positive), semantic background (negative), instance foreground (positive), and instance background (negative), and then concatenated with the RGB channels (total 7 channels) input into the network.

Information Sharing: The learning effect of the clicked label on two segmentation tasks intersects. For example, labels of positive clicks in instance segmentation is also the true set of its corresponding semantic category. Therefore, the interaction information for the instance segmentation can be shared for the semantic segmentation, and vice versa. All involved interaction types in our model include semantic foreground clicks, semantic background clicks, instance foreground clicks and instance background clicks. We define $Mask_{ins}$ and $Mask_{cls}$ to represent a single instance and a standard segmentation mask corresponding to a single semantic class. In view of the characteristics between instance individuals and their corresponding semantic masks, the information sharing strategies are summarized in Table 1. Due to the information sharing strategy, the click maps in the four interaction channels is no longer the points obtained by [13], but the enhanced points calculated from the sharing strategy. Based on the strategy, our semantic instance joint training process is shown in Fig. 4.

Table 1. Information sharing strategy.

Original interaction clicks	Shared clicks
Instance foreground	Semantic foreground
Semantic background	Instance background
In/not in $Mask_{cls}$ for instance background	Semantic foreground/background
In/not in $Mask_{ins}$ for semantic foreground	Instance foreground/background

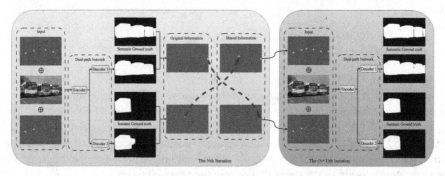

Fig. 4. Semantic-instance joint training process.

In each iteration, the model calculates the most wrong region of both the semantic and instance segmentation simultaneously and takes points. The output segmentations are updated with the added clicks. The iterative collection process stops when the segmentation quality reaches a specific accuracy.

During training, since the semantic and instance ground truth are provided, we can easily determine whether the negative clicks for instance segmentation should be shared with the semantic segmentation, and whether the positive clicks for semantic segmentation should be shared with the instance segmentation. During test, since there is no ground truth, we only share the positive instance clicks with the semantic foreground, and share the negative semantic clicks with the instance background.

3.4 Loss Function

We use the normalized focus loss (NFL) [8] to optimize semantic segmentation and instance segmentation results. Compared to the commonly used binary cross entropy loss (BCE) in image segmentation, this solves the problem of gradient disappearance and has faster convergence speed and higher accuracy.

Let $\widehat{M}$ be the output of semantic segmentation or instance segmentation, $P(\widehat{M})$ be the total weight, and $p_{i,j}$ be the probability that the prediction at point (i, j) is positive. The loss function of a single branch network is as follows:

$$P(\widehat{M}) = \sum_{i,j} (1 - p_{i,j})^{\gamma} \tag{1}$$

$$L_{ins} = L_{sem} = NFL(i, j, \widehat{M}) = -\frac{1}{P(\widehat{M})}(1 - p_{i,j})^{\gamma} log p_{i,j} \tag{2}$$

Let L_{sem} be the loss of semantic segmentation in a dual branch network, and L_{ins} be the loss of instance segmentation. To sum up, the loss function used for training our two-branch network is defined as:

$$L_{dualpath} = \alpha L_{sem} + L_{ins} \tag{3}$$

where α is a balance factor to balance the proportion of semantic loss and instance loss. We set α to 1.2 in our experiment.

4 Experiment

4.1 Experimental Settings

We conducted tests between our single branch network and our dual branch network. To compare with single branch networks (Single-Ins and Single-Sem), we respectively tested instance segmentation (Dualpath-Ins in Sect. 3.3) and semantic segmentation (Dualpath-Sem in Sect. 3.3) of our joint model. To evaluate the performance of the joint model, we also tested the joint model with multitasking learning strategy (Multi-Task in Sect. 3.3) and the joint model without it.

Segmentation models proposed in this paper are based on the DeepLab V3 + [18] backbone. SBD dataset [9] is selected as the training set, which includes 11355 images with both the semantic and instance annotations, 8498 of them are utilized for training, and the remaining 2857 are utilized for test. The strategy in [7] is used to generate the initial click. Random scaling, translation, rotation, expansion and clipping are applied to augment the samples during training. Referring to [13], the iterative training strategy is utilized to train the above network. The radius of the disk at the first correction point is set to the maximum, followed by a decrease (radius = 1:8, 2:6, 3:4 if iteration < 4 else 2). We used Adam with β_1=0.999 and β_2=0.99, and trained the networks for 120 epochs with learning rate 10^{-3}. All experiments were conducted by the PyTorch framework based on two NVIDIA RTX 2080TIs.

The commonly used mean intersection over union (mIoU) is selected to quantitatively evaluate the segmentation quality. Based on the characteristic of interactive segmentation, the mean number of clicks (mNoC) required to reach specific accuracy is also utilized to evaluate the interaction performance, where the maximum number of interactions for each target is fixed as 20.

4.2   Effectiveness Evaluation

As shown in Fig. 5, we test the algorithm performance of the single-path networks (in Sect. 3.1 and 3.2) and the dual-path network (in Sect. 3.3) based on the GrabCut, Berkeley, DAVIS and SBD datasets. From the varying curves of the number of clicks vs. mIoU in Fig. 5, we can find that higher mIoU values are obtained by the dual-branch model with the first few clicks for both the interactive instance (upper) and semantic (down) segmentation compared with the single-branch models. The two curves tend to overlap when the number of clicks increases. From the comparison, the bidirectional learning of these two tasks can promote mutual performance improvement for both interactive instance and semantic segmentation.

As shown in Table 2, the mIoU index is listed to evaluate the performance of the single-branch networks (Sect. 3.1 and 3.2), single-task of dual-branch network (Sect. 3.3), and multi-task of dual-branch network (Sect. 3.3) based on the GrabCut, Berkeley, SBD and DAVIS datasets. Comparing Dualpath-Ins and Dualpath-Sem with Single-Ins and Single-Sem, it can be seen that lower mNoC values are obtained benefited from the joint learning for both interactive instance and semantic segmentation. Comparing Multi-Task with the sum of Dualpath-Ins and Dualpath-Sem, significantly fewer clicks are required to reach 90% (85%) mIoU accuracy on all the datasets when performing both interactive instance and semantic tasks simultaneously, which shows a stronger understanding for objects with joint multi-task learning.

Table 2. Comparison of mNoC for single-path instance model (Single-Ins) in Sect. 3.1, single-path semantic model (Single-Sem) in Sect. 3.2, dual-path instance output (Dualpath-Ins) in Sect. 3.3, dual-path semantic output (Dualpath-Sem) in Sect. 3.3, and the joint segmentation model in Sect. 3.3 on four datasets.

Method	Berkeley mNoC@90%	GrabCut mNoC@90%	DAVIS mNoC@90%	SBD mNoC@85%
Single-Ins	6.61	5.92	9.71	5.19
Single-Sem	6.73	5.51	9.26	7.65
Dualpath-Ins	6.23	5.42	7.35	4.65
Dualpath-Sem	5.67	5.38	7.56	6.74
Multi-Task	9.46	7.46	8.48	8.52

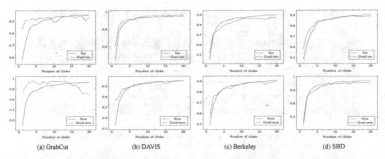

Fig. 5. The number of clicks vs. mean IoU curves of single-path and dual-path networks for interactive instance (upper) and semantic (down) segmentation on GrabCut, Berkeley, SBD and DAVIS datasets.

4.3 Comparison with the State-of-the-Arts

4.3.1 Qualitative Benchmark Results

As shown in Table 3, we qualitatively compare the accuracy and speed of our semantic segmentation model with GraphCut [26], feature backpropagating refinement scheme (f-BRS) [14] and latent diversity based segmentation (LD) [27] on datasets with semantic objects (DAVIS and SBD). Figure 6. Lists the qualitative benchmark results of five images. In the first three images, both f-BRS and our method can complete interactive semantic segmentation with less than 5 clicks. However, compared with our semantic segmentation model, f-BRS performs worse on the boundary of the object (such as the legs of the horse in the 1st and 3rd images) under the same number of clicks. It can be seen that object details can be easily lost when using interactive instance segmetation model in semantic segmentation task. For the fourth and fifth image, f-BRS cannot obtain qualified segmentation results through five interactions, while our model only requires four interactions. For GraphCut and LD method, they cannot complete the segmentation of most images within 5 clicks. Since the ASPP module adopted in our model uses appropriate hole convolution with different expansion rates, targets with different scales can be accurately captured by the proposed method.

Table 3. Comparison of mNoC for GraphCut, f-BRS, LD method and our semantic segmentation model on DAVIS and SBD datasets. Best performanse in bold.

Method	DAVIS mNoC@90%	SBD mNoC@85%
GC	19.46	17.67
LD	14.54	11.26
f-BRS	10.87	7.68
ours	**9.26**	**7.65**

Fig. 6. Performance comparison between GraphCut, f-BRS, LD method and our semantic segmentation model.

4.3.2 Qualitative Benchmark Results

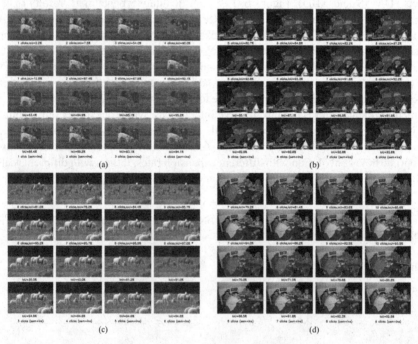

Fig. 7. Performance comparison between single-path and joint dual-path segmentation models. The first and second rows of each small experiment are interactive semantic segmentation and instance segmentation processes, the third and fourth rows are joint segmentation processes.

In Fig. 7, we compare the segmentation performance between the single-branch semantic/instance segmentation and the two-branch joint segmentation model. By comparison, it can be seen that compared with the joint model, speeds of the interactive segmentation convergence for the single-branch methods are significantly slower. For the four test images, at least 6, 9, 10 and 13 clicks are required for the single-branch methods to reach 0.85 IoU accuracy, and only 3, 5, 6 and 9 clicks are needed for the joint model to complete the segmentation processes. The information sharing during the mutual learning helps to improve the interaction efficiency for both interactive instance and semantic segmentation tasks.

5 Conclusion

This paper makes up for the weakness of traditional interactive image segmentation methods in distinguishing between image semantic information and instance individual information, and puts forward a model specially suitable for interactive semantic segmentation and interactive instance segmentation. Based on the optimization of existing methods with better results, a parallel interactive semantic instance segmentation network structure is designed. Through experimental comparison, the correctness of the method of sharing interactive information between semantic segmentation and instance segmentation using multi-task learning strategy is verified, which meets the different needs of users in interactive image segmentation.

Acknowledgement. This work was supported by the Scientific Research Training Program of Nanjing University of Science and Technology under Grant 202210288030 and the National Natural Science Foundation of China under Grant 62172221.

References

1. Acuna, D., Ling, H., Kar, A., Fidler, S.: Efficient interactive annotation of segmentation datasets with Polygon-RNN++. arXiv preprint arXiv:1803.09693 (2018)
2. Hao, Y.: EISeg: an efficient interactive segmentation tool based on PaddlePaddle. arXiv preprint arXiv:2210.08788 (2022)
3. Xu, D., Dogra, P., Ourselin, S., Feng, A., Cardoso, M.J., Diaz-Pinto, A.: MONAI label: a framework for AI-assisted interactive labeling of 3D medical images. arXiv preprint arXiv: 2203.12362 (2022)
4. Chen, X., Zhao, Z.Y., Zhang, Y.L., Duan, M.: FocalClick: towards practical interactive image segmentation arXiv preprint arXiv:2204.02574 (2022)
5. He, K., Zhang, X., Ren, S., Sun, J.: Deep residual learning for image recognition. arXiv preprint arXiv:1512.03385 (2015)
6. Chen, L.C., Papandreou, G., Kokkinos, I., Murphy, K., Yuille, A.L.: Deeplab: semantic image segmentation with deep convolutional nets, atrous convolution, and fully connected CRFs. arXiv preprint arXiv:1606.00915 (2016)
7. Xu, N., Price, B., Cohen, S., Yang, J., Huang, T.: Deep interactive object selection. arXiv preprint arXiv:1603.04042, 2016

8. Sofifiiuk, K., Barinova, O., Konushin, A., Barinova, O.: AdaptIS: adaptive instance selection network. In: 2019 IEEE/CVF International Conference on Computer Vision (ICCV), IEEE, pp. 7355–7363 (2019). https://doi.org/10.1109/iccv.2019.00745

9. Hariharan, B., Arbeláez, P., Bourdev, L., Maji, S., Malik, J.: Semantic contours from inverse detectors. In: 2011 International Conference on Computer Vision, IEEE, pp. 991–998 (2011)

10. Barath, D., Matas, J.: Graph-cut RANSAC. arXiv preprint arXiv:1706.00984 (2017)

11. Grady, L.: Random walks for image segmentation. IEEE Trans. Pattern Anal. Mach. Intell. **28**(11), 1768–1783 (2006)

12. Bai, X.: A geodesic framework for fast interactive image and video segmentation and matting. In: IEEE 11th International Conference on Computer Vision, pp. 1–8 (2007)

13. Sofiiuk, K., Petrov, I.A., Konushin, A.: Reviving iterative training with mask guidance for interactive segmentation. arXiv preprint arXiv:2102.06583 (2021)

14. Sofiiuk, K., Petrov, I., Barinova, O., Konushin, A.: f-brs: rethinking backpropagating refinement for interactive segmentation. In: Proceedings of the IEEE/CVF Conference on Computer Vision and Pattern Recognition, pp. 12234–12244 (2020)

15. Liu, Q., Zheng, M., Planche, B., Karanam, S.: PseudoClick: interactive image segmentation with click imitation. arXiv preprint arXiv:2207.05282 (2022)

16. He, K., Kirillov, A., Girshick, R.: Panoptic feature pyramid networks. arXiv preprint arXiv: 1901.02446 (2019)

17. Zhang, S., Liew, J.H., Wei, Y., Wei, S., Zhao, Y.: Interactive object segmentation with inside-outside guidance. In: Proceedings of the IEEE/CVF Conference on Computer Vision and Pattern Recognition, pp. 12234–12244 (2020)

18. Chen, L.C., Papandreou, G., Schroff, F., Adam, H.: Rethinking atrous convolution for semantic image segmentation. arXiv preprint arXiv:1703.05587 (2017)

19. Majumder, S., Yao, A.: Conten-aware multi-level guidance for interactive instance segmentation. In: Proceedings of the IEEE/CVF Conference on Computer Vision and Pattern Recognition, pp. 11602–11611 (2019)

20. Lin, Z., Zhang, Z., Chen, L.-Z., Cheng, M.-M., Lu, S.-P.: Interactive image segmentation with first click attention. In: Proceedings of the IEEE Conference on Computer Vision and Pattern Recognition, pp.13339–13348 (2020)

21. Mahadevan, S., Voigtlaender, P., Leibe, B.: Iteratively trained interactive segmentation. arXiv preprint arXiv:1805.04398 (2018)

22. Xu, N., Price, B., Cohen, S., Yang, J., Huang, T.: Deep grabcut for object selection. arXiv preprint arXiv:1707.00243 (2017)

23. Wang, G., et al.: DeepGeoS: a deep interactive geodesic framework for medical image segmentation. IEEE Trans. Pattern Anal. Mach. Intell. **41**(7) 1559–1572 (2018)

24. Benenson, R., Popov, S., Ferrari, V.: Large-scale interactive object segmentation with human annotators. In: Proceedings of the IEEE Conference on Computer Vision and Pattern Recognition, pp.11700–11709 (2019)

25. Forte, M., Price, B., Cohen, S., Xu, N., Pitié, F.:Getting to 99% accuracy in interactive segmentation. arXiv preprint arXiv:2003.07932 (2020)

26. Boykov, Y.Y., Jolly, M.-P.: Interactive graph cuts for optimal boundary & region segmentation of objects in ND images. In: IEEE 8th International Conference on Computer Vision, pp.105–112 (2001)

27. Li, Z., Chen, Q., Koltun, V.: Interactive image segmentation with latent diversity. In: Proceedings of the IEEE Conference on Computer Vision and Pattern Recognition, pp.577–585 (2018)

Learning High-Performance Spiking Neural Networks with Multi-Compartment Spiking Neurons

Xinjie Li[1], Jianxiong Tang[1], and Jianhuang Lai[1,2]($\boxtimes$)

[1] School of Computer Science and Engineering, Sun Yat-sen University, Guangzhou, China
tangjx6@mail2.sysu.edu.cn, stsljh@mail.sysu.edu.cn
[2] Key Laboratory of Machine Intelligence and Advanced Computing, Ministry of Education, Guangzhou, China

Abstract. In recent years, spiking neural networks (SNNs) have gained significant attention due to bio-inspired working mechanism. The VGG-like and ResNet-like architectures are widely used for SNNs modeling. However, the spiking features of such architectures are generated by the layer-wise Integrate-and-Fire (IF) dynamics. The firing of deep neurons is independent of the neurons in the shallow layers. In this paper, we propose Multi-Compartment Spiking Neural Network (MC-SNN) that integrates the MPs of the shallow neurons to fire the deep neurons. Specifically, the MC-SNN is modeled by a Multi-Compartment Leaky Integrate-and-Fire (MC-LIF) neuron and an Adaptive Gating Unit (AGU). The MC-LIF neuron models the IF dynamics using the MPs from both deep and shallow layers, and the AGU adaptively scales the MPs of the MC-LIF neuron. These increase the information interaction between spiking neurons and improve the performance of SNNs. Besides, we design the Binarized Synaptic Encoder (BSE) to reduce the computation cost for the input of SNNs. Experimental results show that the MC-SNN performs well on the neuromorphic datasets, reaching 79.52% and 81.24% on CIFAR10-DVS and N-Caltech101, respectively.

Keywords: Deep learning · Spiking neural networks · Multi-Compartment

1 Introduction

In recent years, deep neural networks (DNNs) have been widely adopted in computer vision tasks, such as image classification [1], object segmentation [2], re-identification [3]. However, the superior performance of DNNs often relies on a large number of parameters and computations, which result in energy-inefficient model inference. Although many light weight DNNs [4] have been proposed for computer vision tasks on low-power hardware, most of them lack the ability to handle tasks with temporal context. To address these issues, spiking neural networks (SNNs) [5] have been proposed. The SNNs introduce a bio-reasonable recurrence module to process the temporal information and have

H. Lu et al. (Eds.): ICIG 2023, LNCS 14356, pp. 91–102, 2023.
https://doi.org/10.1007/978-3-031-46308-2_8

the computational efficiency to process the binary spikes. Therefore, SNNs play an important role in the real-time applications on edge devices, especially on neuromorphic chips [6].

The spiking neuron is the basic component of SNNs, and the Leaky Integrate-and-Fire (LIF) neuron [7] is the most commonly used one. It integrates the MPs over T timesteps, and fires a binary spike when the MPs exceed the firing threshold. As a result, the computation of SNNs is more efficient than that of ANNs. The spike-based back-propagation algorithms [8] are popular for direct training of SNNs. It estimates a surrogate gradient of the spiking outputs with respect to the MPs, allowing the training error to propagate on the spatial and temporal topology structure of the SNNs.

Benefiting from the success of spike-based BP, two kinds of architecture are widely applied for SNNs modeling: (a) Spiking VGG and (b) Spiking ResNet. Spiking VGG is a VGG-like model with spiking neurons, and has been demonstrated to be effective in image classification tasks [9]. However, similar to the vanilla VGG, vanishing gradient problem still occurs. To address this issue, Spiking ResNet [10] has been proposed. By adding the skip connections in SNNs, the SNNs go deeper and achieve satisfactory performance. Nonetheless, the spiking features of such architecture are generated by the layer-wise Integrate-and-Fire (IF) dynamics. The firing of deep neurons is independent of the MPs of the neurons in the shallow layers. Furthermore, the current SNNs structures mainly borrow from DNNs, which may result in sub-optimal performance for deep SNNs.

In this paper, we connect the MPs of the shallow spiking neurons with the firing of the deep spiking neurons and propose the Multi-Compartment Spiking Neural Network (MC-SNN). Specifically, the MC-SNN is modeled by a Multi-Compartment Leaky Integrate-and-Fire (MC-LIF) neuron and an Adaptive Gating Unit (AGU). MC-LIF neuron facilitates the MPs of shallow neurons during deep neurons charging, which promoting cooperation and communication between neurons. On this basis, the AGU adaptively scales the MPs of the MC-LIF neuron, which increases the dynamic diversity of the neurons. Finally, we design Binary Synaptic Encoder (BSE) to reduce the computational cost of the input layer of the SNNs. Our contributions are as follows:

- We propose the Multi-Compartment Leaky Integrate-and-Fire (MC-LIF) neuron and Adaptive Gating Unit (AGU) to model the SNNs.
- We design Binary Synaptic Encoder (BSE) to reduce the computational cost of the input layer of the SNNs.
- Extensive experiments on CIFAR10-DVS and N-Caltech101 demonstrate the effectiveness of our proposed methods.

2   Related Work

2.1   Spiking Neural Networks

The spiking neuron is the basic component of the SNNs, and the Leaky Integrate-and-Fire (LIF) is the most widely used. Given a fully connected SNN, the dynamics of the i-th neuron of the n-layer are

$$u_i^{t+1,n} = \tau u_i^{t,n} \left(1 - o_i^{t,n}\right) + \sum_{j=1}^{n-1} w_{ij}^n o_j^{t+1,n-1}, \tag{1}$$

$$o_i^{t+1,n} = \begin{cases} 1, u_i^{t+1,n} - V_{th} > 0, \\ 0, otherwise. \end{cases} \tag{2}$$

$u_i^{t+1,n}$ is the MPs of i-th neuron. w_{ij} is the synaptic weight between i-th neuron and j-th neuron. $o_i^{t+1,n} \in \{0,1\}$ is the spike from the i-th neuron in n-th layer at timestamp $(t + 1)$. The LIF neuron accumulates the MPs in time direction and generates a spike when $u_i^{t+1,n}$ crosses V_{th}. After that, the accumulated MP is reset to 0. In addition, the binary nature of the spikes makes the SNNs suitable for low-power hardware, especially for neuromorphic chips.

Many variants of LIF neurons have been proposed for better SNNs modeling. Yao et al. [11] proposed a GLIF model to enlarge the representation space of neurons by fusing different biological features. Wu et al. [12] relaxed the spiking neuron's outputs to analog values and proposed a Leaky Integrate Analog and Fire neuron to model a LIAF-Net for efficient spatio-temporal processing. Fang et al. [13] designed a Parametric LIF (PLIF) neuron to speed up the learning of SNNs by introducing a learnable decay factor. Although these neurons improve the performance of SNNs, their spiking outputs are generated by the layer-wise IF dynamics. The MPs of the spiking neurons in the shallow layer do not influence the firing of the deep neurons, thus reducing the information interactions of the deep SNNs.

2.2 Input Coding for SNNs

Handcraft encoder and Learnable encoder are widely applied to SNNs. Handcraft encoders are manually designed using different encoding strategies, such as poisson encoding [14], phase encoding [15], and DCT encoding [16]. Although the encoding mechanism of handcrafted encoders is simple and interpretable, most of them require many timesteps for SNNs training and inference. Learnable encoder [17] achieves good performance in SNNs. It reduces the coding time and accelerates the training of SNNs. However, such encoders require additional MAC operations to encode the input data, which degenerates the energy efficiency of the SNNs.

3 Methodology

In this section, we introduce the Multi-Compartment Spiking Neural Network (MC-SNN). We first introduce the Multi-Compartment LIF (MC-LIF) neuron, which integrates the MPs of the shallow neurons to fire the deep neurons. Then, in Sect. 3.2 we design Adaptive Gating Unit (AGU) to adaptively scale the MPs of the MC-LIF neuron. Finally, we design the Binary Synaptic Encoder (BSE) to reduce the computation cost for the input of SNNs.

3.1   Multi-Compartment LIF Neuron

Inspired by the multi-compartment neuron [18–20], we integrate the MPs of the shallow neurons to fire the deep neurons and propose Multi-Compartment LIF neuron (MC-LIF). The dynamics of MC-LIF neuron are as follows:

$$u_i^{t+1,n} = \tau u_i^{t,n}\left(1 - o_i^{t,n}\right) + \sum_{j=1}^{n-1} w_{ij}^n o_j^{t+1,n-1} + u_j^{t+1,n-1}, \qquad (3)$$

where $u_j^{t+1,n-1}$ is the MPs of j-th neuron in $(n-1)$ layer. Compared with Eq. (1), the $u_j^{t+1,n-1}$ of the MC-LIF stores the MPs of all previous layers, enabling the shallow neurons to fire the deep neurons. Therefore, by accumulating the MPs in temporal and spatial dimensions, MC-LIF neuron increases the information interaction, which promotes cooperation and communication between neurons. More clearly, we summarize the difference between LIF and MC-LIF in Fig. 1.

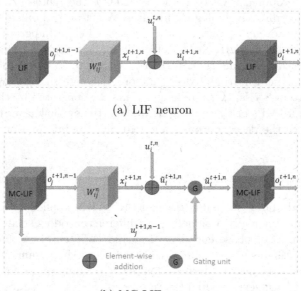

(a) LIF neuron

(b) MC-LIF neuron

Fig. 1. Differences between LIF and MC-LIF neuron.

3.2   Adaptive Gating Unit

To improve the diversity of the spiking neurons, we propose the Adaptive Gating Unit (AGU) to adaptively scale the values of the MPs, which is described as:

$$\widetilde{u}_i^{t+1,n} = \alpha \widetilde{u}_i^{t+1,n} + (1 - \alpha) u_j^{t+1,n-1}, \qquad (4)$$

$$\alpha = \frac{1}{1 + exp(-g)}, \qquad (5)$$

where $\widetilde{u}_i^{t+1,n}$ denotes the MPs of i-th MC-LIF neuron in deep layer. α is the gating factor of gated unit. $g \in \mathbb{R}_c$ is a learnable vector for the MPs of c channels. Based on Eq. (4) and Eq. (5), MC-LIF neuron selectively integrates the MPs from both the shallow layer and the deep layer. Meanwhile, we adopt different gating factors in different channels, thereby increasing the heterogeneity of neurons and the expressiveness of SNNs.

The neuronal dynamics of MC-LIF neuron are summarized as follows:

$$u_i^{t+1,n} = \alpha \left(\tau u_i^{t,n} \left(1 - o_i^{t,n} \right) + \sum_{j=1}^{n-1} w_{ij}^n o_j^{t+1,n-1} \right) + (1 - \alpha) u_j^{t+1,n-1}, \quad (6)$$

$$o_i^{t+1,n} = \begin{cases} 1, u_i^{t+1,n} - V_{th} > 0, \\ 0, otherwise. \end{cases} \quad (7)$$

3.3 Binary Synaptic Encoder

To perform SNNs with few timesteps, previous methods use the first layer of SNNs as the spike encoder. This introduces more multiply-accumulate (MAC) operations and energy cost for the SNNs. To solve this problem, we propose the Binary Synaptic Encoder (BSE) to efficiently encode the image into the spikes. The principles of the BSE are shown in Fig. 2.

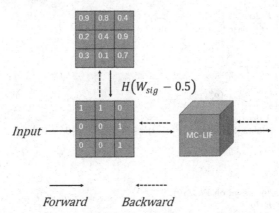

Fig. 2. The principles of the Binary synaptic encoder.

In the forward-propagation, We convert the first convolution layer to binary form W_{BSE}. The formulation for W_{BSE} is given as follows:

$$W_{BSE} = \mathbb{H} \left(W_{sig} - 0.5 \right), \quad (8)$$

$$W_{sig} = \frac{1}{1 + exp(-W_{conv})}, \quad (9)$$

where W_{conv} denotes the weights of first convolution layer. Equation (9) scales W_{conv} into $(0, 1)$. $\mathbb{H}$ is the Heaviside function. If W_{sig} is greater than 0.5, W_{BSE} is set as 1. Otherwise, It's set as 0.

Since the weights of the BSE are binary, the BP training can not be applied for parameter updating. To address this problem, we relax Eq. (8) as follows:

$$W_{BSE} = \mathbb{H}\left(W_{sig} - 0.5\right) + W_{sig} - c, \tag{10}$$

where $c = W_{sig}$ is a constant. Compared with Eq. (8), the gradient of the loss function with respect to W_{BSE} is available through W_{sig}. Therefore, the binary property of W_{BSE} is guaranteed and the BP training ensures its updating.

To train the MC-SNN, we adopt the following loss function, which contains two components: Cross-Entropy Loss ($\mathcal{L}_{ce}$) and Mean-Squared Loss ($\mathcal{L}_{mse}$).

$$\mathcal{L} = \sum_{i=1}^{N} \left(\gamma \sum_{t=1}^{T} \mathcal{L}_{ce}(o_i^{t,L}, y_i) + \beta \mathcal{L}_{mse}(o_i^{L}, y_i) \right), \tag{11}$$

where $o_i^{t,L}$ is the output in last layer at timestamp t. o_i^{L} is the sum of outputs over T timesteps. y_i is the label of image. γ and β are the scaling factors which are set as hyperparameters.

We present the workflow of the MC-SNN in Algorithm 1.

Algorithm 1: MC-SNN Training Pipeline.

Training sample: $(\mathbf{x}_i, \mathbf{y}_i)$, Timesteps: T, Layer number: L, Loss function: $\mathcal{L}$, $\gamma > 0$, $\beta > 0$

STAGE1:

for $t \leftarrow 1$ to T do

    for $l \leftarrow 1$ to L do

        | Calculate $o_i^{t,l}$ based on Eq. (6) and Eq. (7).

    end

    $o_i^{L} = o_i^{L} + o_i^{t,L}$

    $\mathcal{L}_{ce}^{t} = \mathcal{L}_{ce}(o_i^{t,L}, y_i)$

end

$\mathcal{L} = \gamma \sum_{t=1}^{T} \mathcal{L}_{ce}^{t} + \beta \times \mathcal{L}_{mse}(o_i^{L}, y_i)$

for $t \leftarrow T$ to 1 do

    for $l \leftarrow L$ to 1 do

        | Update weights and biases: $W^l \leftarrow W^l - \alpha \frac{\partial \mathcal{L}}{\partial W^l}$, $b^l \leftarrow b^l - \alpha \frac{\partial \mathcal{L}}{\partial b^l}$.

    end

end

STAGE2:

for $t \leftarrow 1$ to T do

    Calculate W_{BSE} based on Eq. (10).

    for $l \leftarrow 1$ to L do

        | Calculate $o_i^{t,l}$ based on Eq. (6) and Eq. (7).

    end

    $o_i^{L} = o_i^{L} + o_i^{t,L}$

    $\mathcal{L}_{ce}^{t} = CE(o_i^{t,L}, y_i)$

end

$\mathcal{L} = \gamma \sum_{t=1}^{T} \mathcal{L}_{ce}^{t} + \beta \times \mathcal{L}_{mse}(o_i^{L}, y_i)$ for $t \leftarrow T$ to 1 do

    for $l \leftarrow L$ to 1 do

        | Update weights and biases: $W^l \leftarrow W^l - \alpha \frac{\partial \mathcal{L}}{\partial W^l}$, $b^l \leftarrow b^l - \alpha \frac{\partial \mathcal{L}}{\partial b^l}$.

    end

end

---

4 Experiments

In this section, we evaluate the performance and efficiency of MC-SNN on two neuromorphic datasets: CIFAR10-DVS and N-Caltech 101. The experimental settings and results are presented in the following subsections.

4.1 Experimental Settings

Network Structure. We adopt a fully convolutional network with 17 layers to model the MC-SNN, whose structure is $[k3c64 - BN] \times 2 - [k3c128 - BN] \times 2 - [k3c256 - BN] \times 3 - MP - [k3c512 - BN] \times 3 - MP - [k3c512 - BN] \times 3 - GAP - FC$. $kNcM$ denotes the convolutional layer with kernel size N and output channels M. The BN, MP, GAP, and FC are the batch normalization, max pooling, global average pooling, and fully connected layers, respectively. The MC-LIF neurons are stacked after all BN layers.

Training Settings. All experiments were conducted on Quadro RTX 8000 (48G). The model is trained for 100 epochs. We use Adam optimizer with original learning rate 0.001, weight decay 5×10^{-4}. For MC-LIF neurons, we set membrane time constant: $\tau = 0.25$, threshold: $V_{th} = 1$, timesteps: $T = 20$, scaling factors: $\gamma = 0.95$, $\beta = 0.05$.

Neuromorphic Datasets. CIFAR10-DVS [21] is an event-based dataset that was created by converting 10,000 frame-based images from CIFAR-10 into 10,000 event streams. The dataset contains 10 different classes, each with 1000 samples, and the camera has a spatial resolution of 128×128. To split CIFAR10-DVS into training and testing set, we randomly select 90% images for training and the remaining 10% for testing.

Caltech101 [22] is a dataset containing 100 different object classes and a background class. For N-Caltech101, the number of samples in each class ranges from 31 (inline skate) to 800 (airplanes). We divide N-Caltech101 into training set and testing set in the same way as CIFAR10-DVS. Accuracy results for all datasets are averaged over 5 runs.

4.2 Comparison with Existing Works

We first compare the performance of our model with other methods in Table 1, demonstrating the effectiveness of the MC-SNN on neuromorphic datasets. For CIFAR10-DVS and N-Caltech101, the MC-SNN achieves average accuracy with 79.52% and 81.24%, respectively, which outperforms other methods. Compared with DSR [24], MC-SNN achieves 2.25% accuracy improvement on CIFAR10-DVS. Meanwhile, MC-SNN achieves 81.24% accuracy, without using any data augmentation.

Table 1. Comparison between MC-SNN and other models.

Model	Architecture	TimeSteps	Accuracy
CIFAR10-DVS			
Tandem Learning [23]	7-layer CNN	20	65.59%
STBP-tdBN [25]	ResNet-19	10	67.80%
PLIF [13]	7-layer CNN	20	74.80%
DSR [24]	VGG-11	20	77.27% ± 0.24%
TED [26]	VGGSNN	10	77.33% ±0.21%
SpikeFormer [27]	Spikformer-4-256	10	78.90%
LTMD [28]	5-layer fully-connected SNN	7	73.30%
IM-Loss [29]	ResNet-19	10	72.60%±0.08%
Ours	**MC-SNN**	**20**	**79.52% ±0.61%**
N-Caltech101			
LSQ [30]	7-layer CNN	-	80.48%
TCJA-SNN [31]	VGGSNN	14	78.50%
SNN-ROE [32]	VGG11-like	-	78.00%
EventMix [33]	Resnet18	10	79.47%
NDA [34]	ResNet-34	10	81.20%
Ours	**MC-SNN**	**20**	**81.24% ±1.28%**

4.3 Energy Analysis

The Energy Efficiency of MC-SNN vs ANN We estimate the compute energy of SNN by computing the energy benefit of SNN over ANN. We replace the MC-LIF neuron in SNN with the ReLU activation in ANN. The input of ANN is a tensor with $(T \times C) \times H \times W$ dimensions.

In ANN, the number of operations in the l-th convolution layer is defined as

$$\#OP_A^l = k_w \times k_h \times c_{in} \times h_{out} \times w_{out} \times c_{out}, \tag{12}$$

where k_w (k_h) is the kernel width (height) of l-th convolution layer, h_{out} (w_{out}) is the output feature's height (width), c_{in} (c_{out}) is the channel of input(output). In SNN, the number of operations in the similar layer as ANN is defined as

$$OP_S^l = SpikeRate_l \times OP_A^l, \tag{13}$$

$$SpikeRate_l = \frac{Totalspike_l}{T \times Neurons_l}. \tag{14}$$

In Eq. (14), $\#SpikeRate_l$ is the spike rate in l-th layer. $\#Totalspike_l$ is the total number of spikes in l-th layer over T timesteps. $Neurons_l$ is the total number of neurons in l-th layer. We compare the energy cost of the hidden layers between MC-SNN and ANN. In 45nm CMOS technology, the energy cost for the MAC operations of the ANN (4.6pJ) is 5.1× more than that of the SNN (0.9pJ). Let E_A and E_S represent the energy of ANN and SNN, respectively. We compute $\frac{E_A}{E_S}$ of hidden layers by

$$\frac{E_A}{E_S} = \frac{4.6 \times \sum_{l=2}^{L-1} OP_A^l}{0.9 \times \sum_{l=2}^{L-1} OP_S^l}. \tag{15}$$

The accuracy and energy consumption of ANN and SNN are presented in Table 2. The energy consumption of the hidden layers of ANN is 118.78× of our method, confirming that our approach can achieve better performance with lower energy consumption.

Table 2. The compute energy of MC-SNN and ANN.

Model	OP	Energy	Accuracy
ANN	1.00	118.78	69.10%
Ours	**0.043**	**1.00**	**80.30%**

Figure 3 shows the layer-wise spike rate of MC-SNN. The MC-SNN achieves a lower spike rate between 0.02 and 0.4, indicating that our model achieves sparse spike activities and low energy cost.

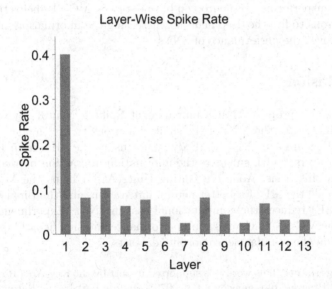

Fig. 3. Layer-wise spike rate for MC-SNN during inference over entire testing set.

The Efficiency of BSE. By comparing the result of stage2 with stage1 in Table 3, we get the efficiency of BSE. Compared to first stage's input, the BSE has achieved a 0.4% increase in accuracy while reducing energy consumption by 0.39 times.

Table 3. The comparisons of accuracy and energy between BSE and learnable encoder.

Method	Accuracy	Energy
Stage1	79.90%	1.00
Stage2	**80.30%**	**0.39**

Table 4. The comparisons of accuracy between MC-LIF and LIF.

Method	CIFAR10-DVS	N-Caltech101
LIF	79.16%	79.12%
MC-LIF	**79.52%**	**81.24%**

4.4 Ablation Study

To demonstrate the effectiveness of MC-LIF neuron, we compare MC-SNN with LIF-based SNN on CIFAR10-DVS and N-Caltech101. As shown in Table 4, MC-LIF neuron outperforms LIF neuron on both datasets. MC-LIF helps the MPs of shallow neurons to fire the deep neurons, increasing the information interaction, thus it improves the performance of SNNs.

5 Conclusion

In this work, we propose Multi-Compartment Spiking Neural Network (MC-SNN) that integrates the MPs of the shallow neurons to fire the deep neurons. The MC-LIF neuron models the IF dynamics using the MPs from both deep and shallow layers, which enhances the information interaction between spiking neurons. On this basis, Adaptive Gating Unit (AGU) helps the MC-SNN to adaptively scale the MPs for better neuron integration, and the Binary synaptic Encoder (BSE) reduces the computational cost in SNNs. Experimental results show that the MC-SNN achieves good performance and significantly reduces the energy cost on the popular neuromorphic datasets.

Acknowledgement. This work was supported in part by the Key-Area Research and Development Program of Guangzhou (202007030004); in part by the National Natural Science Foundation of China(62076258).

References

1. Yang, L., et al.: SimAM: a simple, parameter-free attention module for convolutional neural networks. In: International Conference on Machine Learning, PMLR, pp. 11863–11874 (2021)
2. Chen, Z., Zhou, H., Lai, J., et al.: Contour-aware loss: boundary-aware learning for salient object segmentation. IEEE Trans. Image Process. **30**, 431–443 (2020)

3. Zhang, Q., et al.: Uncertainty modeling with second-order transformer for group re-identification. In: Proceedings of the AAAI Conference on Artificial Intelligence, vol. 36, no. 3, pp. 3318–3325 (2022)

4. Sandler, M., Howard, A., Zhu, M., et al.: MobileNetV2: inverted residuals and linear bottlenecks. In: Proceedings of the IEEE Conference on Computer Vision and Pattern Recognition, pp. 4510–4520 (2018)

5. Maass, W.: Networks of spiking neurons: the third generation of neural network models. Neural Netw. **10**(9), 1659–1671 (1997)

6. He, W., et al.: Comparing SNNs and RNNs on neuromorphic vision datasets: Similarities and differences. Neural Netw. **132**, 108–120 (2020)

7. Gerstner, W., Kistler, W.M.: Spiking Neuron Models: Single Neurons, p. 2. Plasticity, Populations (2002)

8. Zenke, F., Vogels, T.P.: The remarkable robustness of surrogate gradient learning for instilling complex function in spiking neural networks. Neural Comput. **33**(4), 899–925 (2021)

9. Rueckauer, B., Lungu, I.A., Hu, Y.H., et al.: Conversion of continuous-valued deep networks to efficient event-driven networks for image classification. Front. Neurosci. **11**, 682 (2017). https://doi.org/10.3389/fnins.2017.00682

10. Hu, Y., Tang, H., Pan, G.: Spiking deep residual networks. IEEE Transactions on Neural Networks and Learning Systems (2021)

11. Yao, X., et al.: GLIF: a unified gated leaky integrate-and-fire neuron for spiking neural networks. arXiv preprint arXiv:2210.13768 (2022)

12. Wu, Z., Zhang, H., Lin, Y., et al.: LIAF-Net: leaky integrate and analog fire network for lightweight and efficient spatiotemporal information processing. IEEE Trans. Neural Netw. Learn. Syst. **33**(11), 6249–6262 (2021)

13. Fang, W., Yu, Z., Chen, Y., et al.: Incorporating learnable membrane time constant to enhance learning of spiking neural networks. In: Proceedings of the IEEE/CVF International Conference on Computer Vision, pp. 2661–2671 (2021)

14. Han, B., Srinivasan, G., Roy, K.: RMP-SNN: residual membrane potential neuron for enabling deeper high-accuracy and low-latency spiking neural network. In: Proceedings of the IEEE/CVF Conference on Computer Vision and Pattern Recognition, pp. 13558–13567 (2020)

15. Arriandiaga, A., Portillo, E., Espinosa-Ramos, J.I., et al.: Pulsewidth modulation-based algorithm for spike phase encoding and decoding of time-dependent analog data. IEEE Trans. Neural Netw. Learn. Syst. **31**(10), 3920–3931 (2019)

16. Garg, I., Chowdhury, S.S., Roy, K.: DCT-SNN: using DCT to distribute spatial information over time for low-latency spiking neural networks. In: Proceedings of the IEEE/CVF International Conference on Computer Vision, pp. 4671–4680 (2021)

17. Rathi, N., Roy, K.: DIET-SNN: a low-latency spiking neural network with direct input encoding and leakage and threshold optimization. IEEE Trans. Neural Netw. Learn. Syst. (2021)

18. Guerguiev, J., Lillicrap, T.P., Richards, B.A.: Towards deep learning with segregated dendrites eLife 6, e22901 (2017). https://doi.org/10.7554/eLife.22901

19. Sun, Y., Zeng, Y., Zhao, F., et al.: Multi-compartment neuron and population encoding improved spiking neural network for deep distributional reinforcement learning. arXiv preprint arXiv:2301.07275 (2023)

20. Gao, T., Deng, B., Wang, J., et al.: Highly efficient neuromorphic learning system of spiking neural network with multi-compartment leaky integrate-and-fire neurons. Front. Neurosci. **16**, 929644 (2022)

21. Li, H., et al.: CIFAR10-DVS: an event-stream dataset for object classification. Front. Neurosci. **11**, 309–309 (2017)

22. Orchard, G., et al.: Converting static image datasets to spiking neuromorphic datasets using saccades. Front. Neurosci. **9**, 437–437 (2015)

23. Wu, J., Chua, Y., Zhang, M., Li, G., Li, H., Tan, K.C.: A tandem learning rule for effective training and rapid inference of deep spiking neural networks. TNNLS (2021). 2, 3, 7

24. Meng, Q., Xiao, M., Yan, S., et al.: Training high-performance low-latency spiking neural networks by differentiation on spike representation. In: Proceedings of the IEEE/CVF Conference on Computer Vision and Pattern Recognition, pp. 12444–12453 (2022)

25. Zheng, H., Wu, Y., Deng, L., Hu, Y., Li, G.: Going deeper with directly-trained larger spiking neural networks. In: AAAI (2021). 1, 2, 4, 7

26. Deng, S., et al.: Temporal efficient training of spiking neural network via gradient re-weighting. arXiv preprint arXiv:2202.11946 (2022)

27. Zhou, Z., et al.: Spikformer: when Spiking Neural Network Meets Transformer. arXiv preprint arXiv:2209.15425 (2022)

28. Wang, S., Cheng, T.H., Lim, M.H.: LTMD: learning improvement of spiking neural networks with learnable thresholding neurons and moderate dropout. Adv. Neural. Inf. Process. Syst. **35**, 28350–28362 (2022)

29. Guo, Y., Chen, Y., Zhang, L., et al.: IM-Loss: information maximization loss for spiking neural networks. Adv. Neural. Inf. Process. Syst. **35**, 156–166 (2022)

30. Shymyrbay, A., Fouda, M.E., Eltawil, A.: Training-aware low precision quantization in spiking neural networks. In: 2022 56th Asilomar Conference on Signals, Systems, and Computers, pp. 1147–1151. IEEE (2022)

31. Zhu, R.J., Zhao, Q., Zhang, T., et al.: TCJA-SNN: temporal-channel joint attention for spiking neural networks. arXiv preprint arXiv:2206.10177 (2022)

32. Wu, D., et al.: Optimising event-driven spiking neural network with regularisation and cutoff. arXiv preprint arXiv:2301.09522 (2023)

33. Shen, G., Zhao, D., Zeng, Y.: EventMix: an efficient augmentation strategy for event-based data. arXiv preprint arXiv:2205.12054 (2022)

34. Li, Y., et al. Neuromorphic data augmentation for training spiking neural networks. In: Computer Vision–ECCV 2022: 17th European Conference, Tel Aviv, Israel, October 23–27, 2022, Proceedings, Part VII, pp. 631-649. Springer Nature Switzerland, Cham (2022). https://doi.org/10.1007/978-3-031-20071-7_37

Attribute Space Analysis for Image Editing

Yiping Chen, Shuqi Yang, Baodi Liu, and Weifeng Liu[✉]

China University of Petroleum (East China), Qingdao 266580, China
liuwf@upc.edu.cn

Abstract. Image editing is a widely studied topic in computer vision, which enables the modification of specific attributes in images without altering other crucial information. One popular unsupervised technique currently used is feature decomposition in the latent space of Generative Adversarial Networks (GANs), which provides editing directions that can control attribute changes to achieve desired image editing results. However, this method often does not allow for the direct acquisition of the desired editing direction by setting the target attribute in advance. In this work, we propose a method to finding editing directions in the attribute space by analyzing image differences. This enables users to obtain target directions by actively defining the attribute they want to change. Specifically, this method discovers semantic directions suitable for target attribute editing by applying Principal Component Analysis (PCA) on the difference of image latent codes embedded in the latent space. Through experiments, our method can effectively find the target editing direction according to user needs and achieve satisfactory editing effects at the same time.

Keywords: GANs · Image Editing · Attribute Space

1 Introduction

Image editing involves altering specific attributes of an image without affecting other aspects, and has been greatly facilitated by advancements in deep generative models [1–3]. Among the various deep generative models, Generative Adversarial Networks (GANs) [4–6] are the most extensively used in research. GANs have been successful in generating high-quality and realistic images. GANs-based approaches to image editing have achieved remarkable progress, enabling the manipulation of facial attributes while preserving identity information.

Image editing methods based on GANs can be classified into two categories based on their control mechanisms: methods based on conditional GANs and methods based on the latent space of GANs. Conditional GAN-based methods involve training conditional GANs based on user-defined conditions, which are then used to edit images by inputting both the image and the corresponding control conditions. In contrast, methods based on the latent space of GANs aim to identify editing directions with semantic meanings by analyzing the latent

H. Lu et al. (Eds.): ICIG 2023, LNCS 14356, pp. 103–114, 2023.
https://doi.org/10.1007/978-3-031-46308-2_9

Beard on CelebA-HQ Faces   Lipstick on FFHQ Faces

Blue sky on and LSUN Church   Redness on Stanford Car

Fig. 1. The attribute editing direction is obtained by analyzing the attribute space in different domains such as face, church and car. For each set of images, the middle image is the original image, and the left and right are the output images after shifting the latent encode towards the edited direction.

space of GANs. By moving the latent code corresponding to the image along these directions, controllable editing of the image can be achieved.

Image editing based on conditional GANs controls image generation by modeling the conditional distribution of images given certain prior information. For example, some works [7] use semantic segmentation annotations as conditions to guide images for editing, and others [8] allow conditional GANs to control images for editing given text information. [7] proposed MaskGAN, which first learns the style mapping between the image mask and the target image, then models the edits on the source mask, and uses conditional GANs to generate the results. [8] proposed PDF-GAN to improve text-image consistency by fusing semantic information of different granularities and capturing accurate semantics, enabling high-quality editing of text-controlled images. However, while these methods enable desired image editing, they cannot achieve continuous changes during the editing process. Additionally, obtaining prior conditions like semantic segmentation maps is often challenging, with high training costs. Furthermore, text-based approaches have limited control over image details.

The latent space-based method for image editing enables smooth attribute changes in images by exploring the latent space to uncover meaningful directions. This approach can be supervised [9,10] or unsupervised [11,12]. InterFace-GAN [9] is a well-known supervised image editing method, which trains a Support Vector Machine (SVM) [13] on each label, and uses the normal vector of the resulting hyperplane as the latent space editing direction. [10] uses an externally trained estimator function to find directions for cognitive image attributes for a pretrained BigGAN model. Feedback from the evaluator guides the optimization process, and the resulting optimal orientation allows manipulation of the desired cognitive attributes. However, additional training of a classifier or estimator model is typically required, making the process cumbersome and expensive. [11] proposes an unsupervised closed factorization algorithm for latent semantic discovery by directly factorizing pre-trained generator weights. GANSpace [12] is a very classic unsupervised method. This method maps randomly sampled vectors to the GANs space and applies Principal Component Analysis (PCA) [14] to obtain editing directions with different semantics, each direction corresponds to an editing operation. Although the unsupervised method is simple to operate and not constrained by prior conditions, it will simultaneously obtain dozens of semantically meaningful editing directions. This can make it inconvenient for users who need to find a specific editing direction for a target attribute if the index value of the editing direction is not provided beforehand.

In this work, we propose a method for identifying editing directions in attribute space by analyzing image differences. Specifically, we embed paired images that represent changes in the target attribute into the GANs space and then calculate the difference between them to obtain the target attribute representation. Subsequently, we decompose the attribute space to identify editing directions capable of modifying the target attribute. Our method allows the user to actively define the attribute to be edited without requiring any additional training of the classifier, and directly obtaining the editing direction corresponding to the attribute alteration. As shown in Fig. 1, our experiments conducted on multiple datasets exhibit excellent editing results. The contributions of this paper are summarized as follows:

- We propose a method for finding editing directions in attribute space by analyzing image differences. We embed paired images reflecting target attribute changes in the latent space of pre-trained GANs to obtain the difference, and the editing direction can be obtained by decomposing differences.
- Our method allows users to actively define the attributes to be edited, and then use our method to quickly obtain the editing direction of the target attribute without additional training of the classifier.
- Our method is user-friendly. It does not need to change the network structure, and only requires the pre-trained model and simple calculations to achieve excellent editing results on face, church and car datasets.

2   Background

2.1   Generative Adversarial Networks

Over the years, Generative Adversarial Networks (GANs) have made tremendous progress in synthesizing high-quality images. The generator in GANs $G(\cdot)$ learns a mapping from a d-dimensional latent space $\mathcal{Z} \subseteq \mathbb{R}^d$ to a high-dimensional image space $\mathcal{Z} \subseteq \mathbb{R}^{H \times W \times C}$, as $\mathbf{I} = G(z)$. Here, $z \in \mathcal{Z}$, $\mathbf{I} \in \mathcal{I}$ denote the input latent code and output image respectively. StyleGAN [4,5] is one of the most advanced GANs currently used for image synthesis. The Generator of StyleGAN can map latent codes sampled from a standard normal distribution to realistic images. A mapping network consisting of an 8-layer multi-layer perceptron maps the latent code z to an intermediate latent code $w \in \mathcal{W}$. These codes are replicated and fed into each synthesis block of the synthesis network, which outputs deep feature maps for synthesizing images. Thus, the output of each layer of the synthetic network can be expressed as

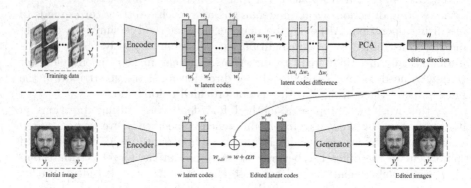

Fig. 2. The pipeline of editing using our method. Given the paired data of target attribute changes, the difference corresponding to w latent encodes is calculated to represent the attribute space. Use PCA to decompose the attribute space to obtain the editing direction. Map the image to be edited to the w space, and move along the obtained editing direction to realize the editing of the target attribute.

$$\mathbf{y}_i = G_i(\mathbf{y}_{i-1}, w) \tag{1}$$

where $w = M(z)$, i is the number of layers, the input $\mathbf{y_0}$ of the first layer is a constant, and M is an 8-layer multilayer perceptron. We can realize image editing by inputting different w_i into corresponding layers.

2.2 Edit in GAN Latent Space

The latent space of GANs contains a wealth of semantic information. The method based on latent space proposes to represent a semantic concept by a certain direction $n \in \mathbb{R}^d$ in the latent space, and these directions can be further applied to image editing with the property of vector operations. Specifically, after inverting the image into the latent space, the GANs latent space is carefully analyzed to find the editable direction that can be interpreted and disentangled, and the editing is realized by the following operation

$$\mathbf{edit}(G(z)) = G(z') = G(z + \alpha n) \tag{2}$$

where $\mathbf{edit}(\cdot)$ represents the editing operation. We can change the target semantics by moving the latent code z linearly along a semantically meaningful direction n. α indicates the editing strength, which is often used in some existing methods [9,11,12]. This requires GAN inversion to obtain a code that can accurately reconstruct the original image. In this way, in subsequent operations, there will be no large deviation between the generated image and the target image due to error accumulation. Several works [15,16] are attempting to address this problem.

Fig. 3. The results of attribute editing on the face dataset exhibit changes in smile and light attributes respectively. The first row corresponds to editing on the FFHQ face image, while the second row corresponds to editing on the CelebA-HQ face image. The input source image is presented in the leftmost column.

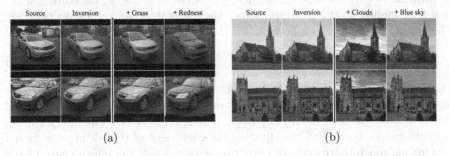

Fig. 4. (a) The result of attribute editing on the car dataset, adding grass, and changing the appearance color to red. (b) The result of attribute editing on the church dataset, adding clouds and blue sky color. The leftmost column is the input source image. (Color figure online)

3   Method

Given an image generated by GANs, it can be mapped to a point in the GANs latent space. Moving this point in a certain direction causes changes to the semantic information of the image. However, the semantic information in high-dimensional image space is highly entangled, making it difficult to achieve precise image editing. To achieve controllable image editing, it is necessary to decompose the latent space and find a suitable editing direction. Our method employs the concept of image difference to represent the attribute space and decomposes it to obtain the target attribute editing direction.

Figure 2 shows the process of discovering latent semantic directions and performing controlled edits by setting the target attribute. Our method is very simple to operate. Initially, we need paired training data, where each pair of images represents a variation of the same target attribute. Next, the image is mapped to the latent space of GANs through an encoder or other inversion methods to obtain the corresponding latent code $(z_{1:i}, z'_{1:i})$. Since the StyleGAN mapping network can map the latent codes into w space, the features in w space have better separability. Modifying the w vector to edit the attributes is less likely to affect other attributes than directly modifying the latent code z. Therefore in this method, we utilize the mapping network to further project the latent encoding into the w space, resulting in pairwise w vectors. Then each pair of vectors is internally subtracted to obtain $\Delta w_{1:i}$ to represent the attribute space, which contains the change information of the attribute. Inspired by GANSpace [12], we apply Principal Component Analysis (PCA) to these differences $\Delta w_{1:i}$, decomposing the attribute space to obtain mutually orthogonal principal axes. They are sorted according to the contribution to the attribute change, and we can obtain the target attribute editing direction n from the principal components corresponding to the dimensions with the largest variance in the data. Typically, the first principal component is the desired editing direction.

Once the editing direction is obtained, the image editing operation can be performed. To edit a new image defined by a latent encoding w, the editing direction n is applied to the w vector before feeding it into the generative network. The editing formula is as follows

$$w_{edit} = w + \alpha n \tag{3}$$

where α is a hyperparameter used to control the editing strength. We apply the modified latent encoding w_{edit} to all 18 layers of the StyleGAN synthetic network simultaneously, instead of only inputting it to specific layers. The image editing strength can be controlled by adjusting the coefficient of the editing direction.

Our approach delves into the attribute space. From the image space to the attribute space, it is equivalent to performing a dimension reduction operation on the attributes, filtering out those attributes that we do not want to edit. Consequently, we only need to decompose the attribute space, and we can easily obtain the principal direction of the target attribute.

4   Experiments

4.1   Datasets, Models and Configurations

We conduct experiments to validate our method on multiple datasets, including faces, churches, and cars. Attribute editing for faces and cars is a conventional practice in image editing, while church attribute editing serves as a typical test for outdoor scene images. We utilized four datasets of FFHQ [4], CelebA-HQ [17], LSUN Church [18] and Stanford Car [19] for experiments.

We selected the state-of-the-art GAN inversion models [15, 16] for projecting images into the latent space. These models employ the pre-trained StyleGAN2 [5] and can directly invert the image to the w space of StyleGAN2. Specifically, [15] is trained on the FFHQ and LSUN Church datasets, and [16] is on the Stanford Cars dataset.

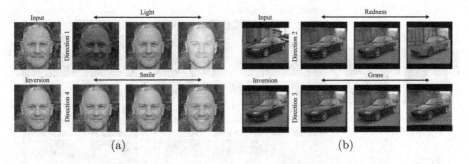

Fig. 5. Results of experiments on the training set where each pair of images represents a variation of two attributes. (a) Realize the decomposition of smile and light combination attributes on face images, and can find the editing direction to change smile or light respectively. (b) Realize the decomposition of redness and grass combined attributes on the car image, and can find the editing direction to add redness or grass respectively.

We cannot use the data in these three datasets directly because they are not paired. To carry out our experiments, we generate pairs of face, church, and car images representing variations in multiple attributes as our datasets. For each training task, we used a dataset size of 2000 image pairs, which may seem small in the field of deep learning, but has nevertheless yielded good results. The batch size during training was set to 1, while other parameter settings remained the same as [15, 16].

4.2   Experiment Results

We designed two types of experiments, which differ in the settings of the training data. In order to evaluate the effectiveness of our method, we created a dataset in which each image pair contains only one variation of a target attribute, such as a smile. In another experiment, we set each pair of images to include changes in two target attributes, such as simle and light, to test whether our method also has the ability to decouple attributes. We created a dataset in which each image pair contains variations of two target attributes, such as a smile and light. This was done to test whether our method can effectively decouple attributes.

In the single attribute editing experiment, we conducted smile and light attribute editing on the face dataset. As shown in Fig. 3, our work enables efficient editing while preserving non-editing attributes. Furthermore, we can control the degree of change of attributes by controlling the edit strength. Additionally, Fig. 4 shows our edits to the car and church images. For the car image, we want to drive the car onto grass or paint the car red. For the church image, we want the sky to be more cloudy or blue. The editing directions of these results are all found in the first three PCA components, as expected. While misalignment of paired training data may affect the order in which the edit directions are obtained, it does not deviate much from the expected direction. This demonstrates that our method can accurately identify the editing direction for the

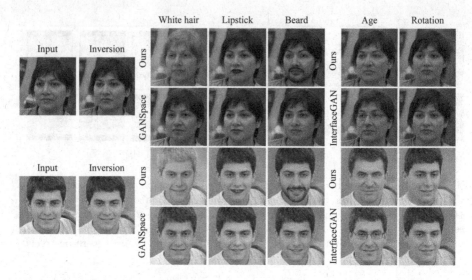

Fig. 6. Qualitative comparison of our method with the editing effects of GANSpace and InterFaceGAN methods. Our method shows satisfactory results. The editing of white hair by GANSpace is not obvious, and the editing of lipstick and beard is entangled with gender. InterFaceGAN also generates glasses when editing age.

target attribute change using pre-defined attributes, and can be applied to edit real images.

To further assess the decoupling ability, we allow each pair of images in the training data to vary in two attributes. For example, in the case of a face image with changes in both smile and light, our method was able to successfully determine the editing direction that changes one of the attributes respectively, as shown in Fig. 5. A similar effect can also be obtained from car images. These results demonstrate that our method has the capacity to handle changes in multiple attributes, enabling attribute disentanglement.

It is important to note that our editing results can also be affected by the inversion process. While the inversion model we utilize is highly effective in reconstructing face images, it may slightly alter the original information when reconstructing car and church images, such as the car model and background. As a result, attributes that are not intended to change during the editing process may be inadvertently modified. However, it is important to recognize that this issue is not caused by our editing method, but rather by the limitations of the inversion process itself.

4.3   Comparison with Other Methods

Qualitative Results. To show our editing effects, we compare our method with current mainstream methods GANSpace [12] and InterFaceGAN [9]. Due to the well-defined face attributes, we conduct experiments on face editing. The results, as shown in Fig. 6 demonstrate that our approach is on par with the other two methods in terms of image authenticity, thus indicating that our method can achieve superior image editing. More importantly, our method can directly obtain the corresponding editing direction by predefining these attributes, and realize controllable editing. In contrast, when exploring the latent space of GANs, the editing results tend to be influenced by the data distribution, as exemplified by women wearing lipstick and men sporting beards. But our method allows men to wear lipstick and women to grow beards. In addition, InterFaceGAN is accompanied by the generation of glasses when editing age, and does not achieve good feature decoupling. However, our method does not appear glasses when editing the age. In summary, our method has achieved highly effective in real image editing.

Table 1. Quantitative analysis on GANSpace and our method where we compare Smile, Lipstick, Beard and eyebrow attributes using FFHQ dataset on StyleGAN2.

Attribute	GANSpace	Ours	Attribute	GANSpace	Ours
+Smile	0.96	0.99	+Lipstick	0.38	0.58
Source	0.69	0.69	Source	0.24	0.24
−Smile	0.18	0.02	−Lipstick	0.23	0.12
+Beard	0.18	0.74	+Eyebrow	0.25	0.29
Source	0.08	0.08	Source	0.04	0.04
−Beard	0.02	0.01	−Eyebrow	0.01	0.01

Quantitative Results. To understand whether our method changes images to desired attributes, we perform quantitative analysis using attribute predictors to compare with baseline. We randomly selected 500 source images from FFHQ and used GANSpace and our method to edit four attributes (smile, lipstick, beard, and eyebrow). Subsequently, we scored the source images and edited results using the pre-trained predictor for the CelebA attribute dataset [20]. The higher the score, the more the image possessed the specific attributes. Table 1 displays the scores for several attributes in positive (+) and negative (−) directions. To see how the scores change, we first score 500 source images. The average predictor score for the smile attribute is 0.69, lipstick is 0.24, beard is 0.08, and eyebrow is 0.04. Moving the latent codes towards the negative direction of the beard and eyebrow attributes, we find that our method and the GANSpace method both drop scores in a similar range. But when moving towards the negative direction of the smile and lipstick attributes, the score degradation of our method is more obvious compared to GANSpace. Both approaches achieve similar attribute changes when moving the latent codes towards the positive direction of the smile and eyebrow attributes. However, our method outperformed GANSpace in editing towards the positive direction of the beard and lipstick attributes.

Direction 1	Direction 2	Direction 3	Direction 4	Direction 5

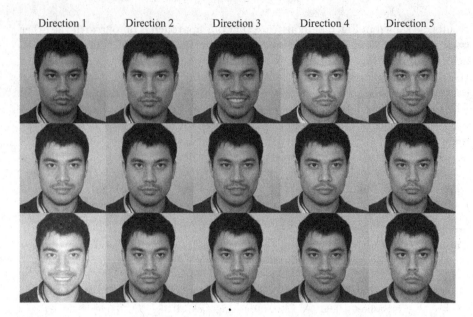

Fig. 7. The experiment was performed after combining the training data with smile change and light change, and the first five PCA components were selected as the editing direction. The first direction produces a common change of the two attributes, and the third direction achieves a smile change. There are almost no changes in other directions, and we have not found the editing direction of the light attribute.

4.4   Further Discussion

We propose a third dataset setting in addition to the two introduced in Sect. 4.2. This type of dataset includes two sets of paired images that reflect different attribute changes. However, the paired images within each set reflect the same attribute changes. We also chose the two attributes of smile and light to conduct experiments, and the experimental results are shown in Fig. 7. The first direction produces a common change in both attributes, while the third direction achieves a change in smile. There are almost no changes in other directions, and we have not found the editing direction of the light attribute. We speculate that this is because in this type of experiment, when PCA decomposes the attribute space, the principal components that contribute more to the degree of attribute change are ranked in front. And one of the attributes was ranked behind because the contribution was not large enough, making it difficult for us to find. PCA does not have the characteristics of classification, so it cannot decompose the required attributes well. It can be considered to use LDA instead of PCA, first separate different attributes, and then find the corresponding editing direction, we leave it to future work.

5 Conclusion

In this work, we propose a method for identifying editing directions in attribute space by analyzing image differences. We embed pairs of images reflecting target attribute changes in the latent space of pre-trained GANs and then subtract them. This allows users to find suitable editing directions by actively defining target attributes. We demonstrate the efficacy of our method on different datasets and compare it with state-of-the-art methods.

Acknowledgements. This work was supported by the Qingdao Natural Science Foundation (No. 23-2-1-161-zyyd-jch), the Shandong Natural Science Foundation (No. ZR2023MF008, No. ZR2023QF046), the Major Scientific and Technological Projects of CNPC (No. ZD2019-183-008) and the National Natural Science Foundation of China (No. 61671480).

References

1. Goodfellow, I., et al.: Generative adversarial networks. Commun. ACM **63**(11), 139–144 (2020)
2. Kingma, D.P., Welling, M.: Auto-encoding variational bayes. arXiv preprint arXiv:1312.6114 (2013)
3. Ho, J., Jain, A., Abbeel, P.: Denoising diffusion probabilistic models. Adv. Neural. Inf. Process. Syst. **33**, 6840–6851 (2020)
4. Karras, T., Laine, S., Aila, T.: A style-based generator architecture for generative adversarial networks. In: Proceedings of the IEEE/CVF Conference on Computer Vision and Pattern Recognition, pp. 4401–4410 (2019)
5. Karras, T., Laine, S., Aittala, M., Hellsten, J., Lehtinen, J., Aila, T.: Analyzing and improving the image quality of styleGAN. In: Proceedings of the IEEE/CVF Conference on Computer Vision and Pattern Recognition, pp. 8110–8119 (2020)
6. Brock, A., Donahue, J., Simonyan, K.: Large scale GAN training for high fidelity natural image synthesis. arXiv preprint arXiv:1809.11096 (2018)
7. Lee, C.H., Liu, Z., Wu, L., Luo, P.: MaskGAN: towards diverse and interactive facial image manipulation. In: Proceedings of the IEEE/CVF Conference on Computer Vision and Pattern Recognition, pp. 5549–5558 (2020)
8. Tan, Z., Ye, Z., Yang, X., Wang, Q., Yan, Y., Huang, K.: Towards better text-image consistency in text-to-image generation. arXiv preprint arXiv:2210.15235 (2022)
9. Shen, Y., Gu, J., Tang, X., Zhou, B.: Interpreting the latent space of GANs for semantic face editing. In: Proceedings of the IEEE/CVF Conference on Computer Vision and Pattern Recognition, pp. 9243–9252 (2020)
10. Goetschalckx, L., Andonian, A., Oliva, A., Isola, P.: GANalyze: toward visual definitions of cognitive image properties. In: Proceedings of the IEEE/CVF International Conference on Computer Vision, pp. 5744–5753 (2019)
11. Shen, Y., Zhou, B.: Closed-form factorization of latent semantics in GANs. In: Proceedings of the IEEE/CVF Conference on Computer Vision and Pattern Recognition, pp. 1532–1540 (2021)
12. Härkönen, E., Hertzmann, A., Lehtinen, J., Paris, S.: GANspace: discovering interpretable GAN controls. Adv. Neural. Inf. Process. Syst. **33**, 9841–9850 (2020)
13. Noble, W.S.: What is a support vector machine? Nat. Biotechnol. **24**(12), 1565–1567 (2006)

14. Wold, S., Esbensen, K., Geladi, P.: Principal component analysis. Chemom. Intell. Lab. Syst. **2**(1–3), 37–52 (1987)
15. Dinh, T.M., Tran, A.T., Nguyen, R., Hua, B.S.: Hyperinverter: improving style-GAN inversion via hypernetwork. In: Proceedings of the IEEE/CVF Conference on Computer Vision and Pattern Recognition, pp. 11389–11398 (2022)
16. Alaluf, Y., Tov, O., Mokady, R., Gal, R., Bermano, A.: HyperStyle: StyleGAN inversion with hypernetworks for real image editing. In: Proceedings of the IEEE/CVF Conference on Computer Vision and Pattern Recognition, pp. 18511–18521 (2022)
17. Karras, T., Aila, T., Laine, S., Lehtinen, J.: Progressive growing of GANs for improved quality, stability, and variation. arXiv preprint arXiv:1710.10196 (2017)
18. Yu, F., Seff, A., Zhang, Y., Song, S., Funkhouser, T., Xiao, J.: LSUN: construction of a large-scale image dataset using deep learning with humans in the loop. arXiv preprint arXiv:1506.03365 (2015)
19. Krause, J., Stark, M., Deng, J., Fei-Fei, L.: 3d object representations for fine-grained categorization. In: Proceedings of the IEEE International Conference on Computer Vision Workshops, pp. 554–561 (2013)
20. Liu, Z., Luo, P., Wang, X., Tang, X.: Deep learning face attributes in the wild. In: Proceedings of the IEEE International Conference on Computer Vision, pp. 3730–3738 (2015)

SAGAN: Self-attention Generative Adversarial Network for RGB-D Saliency Prediction

Yongfang Wang[✉], Shuyu Xiao, and Peng Ye

School of Communication and Information Engineering, Shanghai University, Shanghai 200444, China
yfw@shu.edu.cn

Abstract. A key problem in RGB-D saliency prediction is how to effectively exploit the multi-model cues. In the paper, we propose a self-attention generative adversarial network (SAGAN) for RGB-D saliency prediction, which can extract heterogeneous features from RGB and depth by driving long-range dependency modeling and adversarial training. Specifically, we explore selective fusion based on channel attention (SFA) and prior initialization approach to efficiently learn the salient cues of RGB-D images. SFA is designed to adaptively select and fuse features in different level between RGB and depth, and prior initialization is introduced to reduce the demand for annotated RGB-D datasets and accelerate the convergence of model training by reusing RGB prior weights. Extensive experiments on two publicly available datasets demonstrate the superiority of our approach over other state-of-the-art methods.

Keywords: RGB-D saliency prediction · Selective fusion · Prior initialization · Self-attention generative adversarial network

1 Introduction

Visual attention is an important mechanism of human visual system for selectively processing the most important part in large amount of visual information. Thus, visual attention models (VAMs) which can locate salient areas or objects accurately have a wide range of applications such as visual tracking [1], image semantic segmentation [2] and action recognition [3, 4]. VAMs can be explicitly divided into two branches: saliency prediction [5–11] and salient object detection [12–14] models. The former is used to predict discrete pixel-level saliency intensity map, while the latter is utilized to detect and segment the most salient object in a scene. Generally, existing VAMs are designed via two strategies: bottom-up and top-down. Bottom-up is stimulus-driven and depends on the input images, top-down is task-driven and needs to consider task experience and prior knowledge.

Recently, some convolutional neural networks (CNNs) have been designed to predict visual saliency for RGB images. Typically, SALICON [6] fine-tuned the ImageNet-pretrained CNN via saliency evaluation function and integrated features at different image scales. DeepNet [7] introduced a shallow CNN which is trained from scratch and

© The Author(s), under exclusive license to Springer Nature Switzerland AG 2023
H. Lu et al. (Eds.): ICIG 2023, LNCS 14356, pp. 115–123, 2023.
https://doi.org/10.1007/978-3-031-46308-2_10

a deeper one initialized with the pretrained VGG net. SalGAN [8] proposed an encoder-decoder generative adversarial network (GAN) and introduced the binary cross entropy loss for saliency prediction. DeepGaze2 [9] designed a CNN based contrast model to evaluate the contributions of low-level and high-level features in fixation prediction. SAM [10] adopted a LSTM recursive attention module to enhance saliency features in turn. GazeGAN [11] designed a local and global GANs based saliency model and utilized "skip connection" and "center surround connection" to learn multilevel features.

Although CNN-based saliency prediction on 2D images has achieved great progress, most models cannot directly be applied in 3D images. Depth sensors can provide paired RGB and depth images, which can be used to overcome this. However, CNN-based RGB-D saliency prediction need to address two key issues: 1) how to effectively exploit information of both intra- and cross- modality in RGB-D; 2) how to train a model with limited labeled RGB-D datasets. Zhou et al. [15] proposed a content-aware fusion module to combine global and local-contrast features for RGB-D saliency prediction. Lv et al. [16] combined channel attention mechanism with a three-stream network to predict visual attention on RGB-D images. They used the parameters of ImageNet-pretrained VGG16 or ResNet18 to initialize the proposed model.

Compared to previous methods, our main contributions are summarized as follows: 1) we propose a novel self-attention generative adversarial network to extract heterogeneous features from RGB and depth. 2) we design a selective fusion module for multi-level cross-modal features selection and fusion between RGB and depth information. 3) prior initialization is introduced to alleviate the demand for annotated RGB-D data and speed up the convergence of CNN model. 4) The proposed model achieves excellent performance on two benchmark datasets for RGB-D saliency prediction.

2   Roposed Method

In this paper, a self-attention generative adversarial network (SAGAN) including a selective fusion module (SFA) and a prior initialization is proposed to predict saliency for RGB-D images, as depicted in Fig. 1. SAGAN consists of non-locally enhanced generator and discriminator, the generator is based on encoder-decoder structure, the discriminator acts like a classifier, through their adversarial training we can extract stronger features from RGB and depth. SFAs are placed in the encoder of generator to obtain heterogeneous features and also be used in the decoder through skip connection. Prior initialization intends to use RGB-based prior weights to initialization the proposed RGB-D based model before training. More details are introduced in the following subsection.

2.1   A Subsection Sample Self-attention Generative Adversarial Network

The Generator. The backbone of our generator is the non-locally enhanced encoder-decoder network named NLEDN presented by *Li et al.* [17], which has shown its rationality and superiority in single image de-raining. We extend it for RGB-D saliency prediction. Compared to the generator of GazeGAN [11] and SalGAN [8], our encoder-decoder network consists of a range of non-locally enhanced dense blocks (NEDBs), which not only fully utilizes hierarchical features from proceeding layers [18] but also well models the long-distance dependencies [19]. First, in order to use more detailed information on high-resolution images with acceptable computing cost, As shown in Fig. 1, we design a pair of novel layers: Space to Depth (S2D) and Depth to Space (D2S), and add them on the input and output of our generator.

$$I_0^m = S2D(I^m) \tag{1}$$

$$\widehat{S}_i = D2S\left(Sigm(\widehat{F}_i^m)\right) \tag{2}$$

where I^m is an input image, $m \in \{rgb, d\}$ denotes the RGB and depth, respectively, $\widehat{F}_i^m$ is the i-th output feature of the decoder, $Sigm$ is sigmoid activation function. D2S layer is similar to pixel shuffle [20], and acts mutually as the reverse operation with S2D layer.

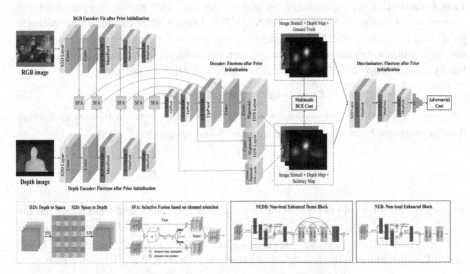

Fig. 1. Architecture of the proposed method.

Further, in order to process RGB and depth image pairs, we replace all pooling indices guided max-pooling layers with bilinear up-sampling layers and build two encoders as RGB and depth encoders in our generator.

$$F_1^m = Conv(I_0^m) \tag{3}$$

$$F_2^m = Conv(F_1^m) \tag{4}$$

$$F_l^m = MaxPool\left(NEDB_{k \times k}(F_{l-1}^m)\right) \tag{5}$$

where I_0^m is output image from S2D layer, F_l^m is the l-th output feature of the encoder, $Conv$ is a 3×3 kernel convolution, $MaxPool$ is a 3×3 max pooling layer and $NEDB_{k \times k}$ denotes $k \times k$ non-locally enhanced dense block.

In addition, skip connections between the encoder and decoder aim to combine RGB and depth features with task-specific features. Firstly, the RGB and depth features from both encoders are adaptively fused by SFA in multiple level, then new multi-scale RGB-D features will be combined in the decoder through skip connection.

The Discriminator. Inspired by [21] and [22], we design an attentive discriminator to make the adversarial training reach more state-of-the-art performance. Our discriminator consists of a S2D layer, three multi-scale NEDBs and three FC layers. NEDBs contain $k \times k$ region-wise nonlocal operations and two 3×3 kernel convolutions with ReLU activations. The number of kernels for three NEDBs are $32, 64, 64$. Three FC layers have neurons of $100, 2, 1$, which is activated by tanh, tanh, sigmoid, respectively. SAGAN is a conditional GAN because the input of our discriminator includes both RGB-D image pair and the saliency map (human gaze).

Loss Function. Existing studies have shown that the combination of adversarial and content losses is effective to train a GAN [11, 21]. During adversarial training, saliency prediction not only approximates human gaze in terms of visual content but also fools the discriminator, we define the total loss function with the combination of multiscale binary cross entropy loss $\mathcal{L}_{MBCE}$ and adversarial loss $D(S, T)$ as follows

$$\mathcal{L}_{GAN} = \alpha \cdot \mathcal{L}_{MBCE} - logD(S, T) \tag{6}$$

where α is set to 0.1 to balance two losses. $D(S, T)$ denotes the probability of fooling the discriminator between generation saliency S and ground truth T [8].

$$\mathcal{L}_{MBCE}\left(\hat{S}, T\right) = \sum_{i=1}^{M} \lambda_i \cdot \mathcal{L}_{BCE}(\hat{S}_i, T_i) \tag{7}$$

where $\hat{S}_i$ is the output of i th layer of the decoder, and T_i is the ground truth which has the same scale with $\hat{S}_i$. $\mathcal{L}_{BCE}(\hat{S}_i, T_i)$ is binary cross entropy loss [8].We utilize the outputs of 1st, 3rd and 4th layers, whose sizes are 1, $\frac{1}{2}$ and $\frac{1}{4}$ of the original size. Because larger scale often has more contextual information, we set λ as $0.6, 0.8, 1.0$, respectively.

2.2   Selective Fusion Based on Channel Attention

Different from most previous works combining cross-modal deep features by undifferentiated concatenation in one stage, we introduce the SFA to extract new RGB-D features in multiple level of the encoder, which can select and fuse complementary features from multi-modality adaptively. For performing the importance of each modality, we first extract the integrated channel-wise global information based on RGB features F^{rgb} and depth features F^d.

$$S = \mathcal{F}_{gp}(F) = \mathcal{F}_{gp}\left(F^{rgb} + F^d\right) \tag{8}$$

where F is integrated features via the element-wise summation of F^{rgb} and F^d. $\mathcal{F}_{gp}$ represents the channel-wise global average pooling and $S \in \mathbb{R}^{c \times 1}$. Then, a fully connected layer is used to create the compact features $Z \in \mathbb{R}^{d \times 1}$ for efficient and adaptive selection.

$$Z = \mathcal{F}_{fc}(S) = \mathcal{R}(\mathcal{B}(WS)) \tag{9}$$

where $\mathcal{R}$ denotes the ReLU function, $\mathcal{B}$ represents the Batch Normalization, $W \in \mathbb{R}^{d \times c}$. $d = max(c/2, 32)$ is a typical set-ting as in [23]. Further, a soft attention across channels guided by the compact features Z is used to adaptively select information of different modality [23].

$$a = \frac{e^{AZ}}{e^{AZ} + e^{BZ}}, b = \frac{e^{BZ}}{e^{AZ} + e^{BZ}} \quad (10).$$

where $a, b \in \mathbb{R}^{c \times 1 \times 1}$ represent the soft attention vector of $F^{rgb}, F^d \in \mathbb{R}^{c \times h \times w}$, and $A, B \in \mathbb{R}^{c \times d}$, respectively. The final RGB-D features are obtained through the attention weighting fusion between RGB and depth.

$$F^{rgb-d} = a \cdot F^{rgb} + b \cdot F^d \quad (11)$$

where $F^{rgb-d} \in \mathbb{R}^{c \times h \times w}$. Note that the proposed SFA can be easily extended from two-branch case to more branches.

2.3 Prior Initialization

Given an input image I, the CNN-based saliency model uses a set of weights θ to produce a saliency map $\hat{S}$, and the saliency value v of location (i, j) in $\hat{S}$ can be formulated as.

$$\hat{S}(i, j) = p(v|R(I, i, j); \theta) \quad (12)$$

where $R(I, i, j)$ denotes the receptive field of pixel (i, j) in I. When the network completes the training process, θ is fixed and used to predict visual saliency of any images.

In order to solve the demand for labeled RGB-D data and speed up the convergence of CNN model, we exploit the RGB dataset SALICON [24] to pretrain a RGB model. The SALICON dataset is the largest saliency prediction benchmark, which contains 10000 training images, 5000 test images and 5000 validation images. The RGB model is the simple version of the proposed SAGAN: the generator remove the depth-specific encoder and SFAs, the discriminator only uses the RGB image and saliency map as the input.

After pretraining the RGB model, we can get the RGB prior weights ω, which can be used to initialization the RGB-D model to guide the post-training weights θ. Thus, the saliency map $\hat{S}^\omega$ with prior guidance can be produced as.

$$\hat{S}^\omega(i, j) = p(v|R(I, i, j); \theta; \omega) \quad (13)$$

Note that we use the weights of RGB encoder to initialize two encoders, RGB encoder choose fix weights and depth encoder is fine-tuned by RGB encoder, as is shown in Fig. 1.

3 Experiment

3.1 Experimental Setup

Datasets. We conduct the experiments to evaluate the effectiveness of proposed model on two publicly available datasets: the NCTU-3DFixation dataset [25] which consists 475 paired RGB and depth images from RGB-D movies and videos, and the NUS-3DSaliency dataset [26] which consists 600 RGB-D images from indoor and outdoor scenes.

Evaluation Metrics. Six metrics including similarity (SIM), Kullback-Leibler divergence (KL), Pearson's Correlation Coefficient (CC), Area under ROC curve -Judd and -Borji (AUC-J and AUC-B), Normalized Scanpath Saliency (NSS), are used to evaluate our model comprehensively. Note that, higher AUC-B, AUC-J, CC, NSS, SIM value and lower KL value indicate better saliency prediction performance.

Implementation Details. We randomly split the NCTU and NUS datasets into two parts: 80% images for training and the rest for testing [15, 16]. Due to the S2D and D2S layers, a batch size of is 6 and RGB-D images is 480 × 640. The AdaGrad optimizers with 0.0001 weight decay are used to train the generator and discriminator alternately, with an initialization learning rate of 0.003 and 0.045, the learning rate of the generator is reduced from 0.003 to 0.001 within 160 epochs. We applied label-preserving augmentation transformations [11] on the RGB-D images to enlarge the dataset for a better prediction performance. The proposed model is implemented on Pytorch 1.0.0 using a PC equipped with a RTX 2080Ti GPU (12G memory).

3.2 Comparison with State-of-the-Art Models

We compare the proposed SAGAN model with 6 deep learning based saliency models, including 4 RGB models (SalGAN [8], DeepGaze2 [9], SAM [10], GazeGAN [11]) and 2 RGB-D models (Zhou [15], Lv [16]).

We present the quantitative results in Table 1, where the top model is highlighted in boldface. Our method performs more competitively with others both different datasets and metrics, and the better performance is achieved especially in terms of CC, NSS and SIM.

Table 1. Performance comparison with other models

Models	NUTU (RGB-D movies and videos)						NUS (RGB-D indoor and outdoor scenes)					
	AUC-B	AUC-J	CC	KL	NSS	SIM	AUC-B	AUC-J	CC	KL	NSS	SIM
SalGAN	0.8868	0.9406	0.7247	0.5843	2.0564	**0.6406**	0.8520	0.9050	0.5685	1.8060	2.2158	0.4703
DeepGaze2	0.8097	0.9236	0.6823	0.7482	1.8967	0.6106	0.7640	0.8917	0.5413	1.7002	2.1155	0.4349
SAM	0.7791	**0.9565**	0.7411	1.4573	2.0804	0.6380	0.7392	0.9039	0.5760	2.9175	2.2597	0.4784
GazeGAN	0.8828	0.9390	0.7312	1.1336	2.0589	0.6387	0.8543	**0.9057**	**0.5881**	2.6514	2.2848	**0.4856**
Zhou	**0.9150**	–	0.8526	**0.2610**	2.3473	–	**0.8752**	–	0.5596	1.3407	2.2881	–
Lv	0.9143	–	**0.8614**	**0.2681**	**2.3795**	–	0.8339	–	0.5579	**1.0903**	**2.3373**	–
SAGAN	**0.9197**	**0.9773**	**0.8705**	0.2821	**2.5294**	**0.7542**	**0.8621**	**0.9211**	**0.6272**	1.1554	**2.4635**	**0.4937**

We provide the visual comparison results in Fig. 2. As shown in the third rows, when there are multiple salient regions, our method successfully captures the varying salient degrees, while many algorithms exist missed or false detection. For a complex scene (fourth row) or a scene with similar foreground and back-ground (fifth row), our method also performs well, while other algorithms are susceptible to some interferences. For common outdoor and indoor scenes (last two rows), our method can obtain more accurate saliency maps which are closer to the ground-truth, compared to other algorithms.

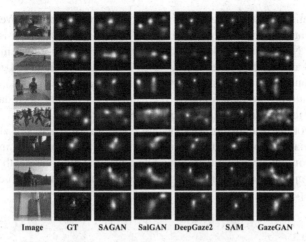

Fig. 2. Visual comparisons with state-of-the-art models

3.3 Ablation Analysis

Table 2. Ablation analysis on the NCTU dataset

Models	AUC-B	CC	KL	NSS	SIM
GD	0.8868	0.7247	0.5843	2.0564	0.6406
AGD	0.8900	0.7553	0.5637	2.1327	0.6630
Prior+	0.9184	0.8527	0.2864	2.4696	0.7339
SFA+	**0.9197**	**0.8705**	**0.2821**	**2.5294**	**0.7542**

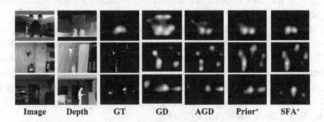

Fig. 3. Visual illustration of ablation analysis.

In this section, we evaluate the contribution of each component of the proposed network. To this end, we construct different variations, including: (1) the baseline model is the SalGAN proposed in [8], namely GD here. (2) we inject the self-attention mechanism into the generator and discriminator, namely AGD. (3) on the basis of AGAD, we first build RGB and depth encoders in the generator, then initialize the RGB-D based generator and discriminator with RGB based prior weights by using prior Initialization approach, namely Prior +. (4) the final model integrates multi-level SFA modules, which contains all the components, namely SFA+.

The quantitative results on the NCTU dataset are shown in Table 2. We can see that all the components can boost the performance by a large margin. Similar results can be obtained on the NUS dataset. The performance gains derive from that, more accurate and robust RGB and depth features are extracted with attention enhanced generator and discriminator, multi-level cross-modal RGB-D features are further explored by SFAs. Besides, prior initialization can improve the results with limited deep data, which is concluded from the considerable improvement of SFA$^+$.

The visual comparison results are shown in Fig. 3. In particular, self-attention generative adversarial network has the ability to focus on the more prominent regions, prior initialization and selective fusion module tend to exploit the depth cue and the cross-modal complementary information to effectively enhance the saliency prediction performance respectively.

4 Conclusion

In this paper, we propose RGB-D saliency prediction based on self-attention generative adversarial network. The proposed method combines long-range dependency modeling and adversarial training, which can effectively learn heterogeneous features from RGB and depth. Besides multi-level cross-modal complementary features can be easily obtained by the SFA. Moreover, Prior initialization makes it easy to extend RGB saliency prediction to RGB-D ones when limited amount of RGB-D datasets. Experimental results have shown the superiority of proposed method on benchmark datasets.

References

1. Liu, Y., Wang, Q., Hu, H., He, Y.: A novel real-time moving target tracking and path planning system for a quadrotor UAV in unknown unstructured outdoor scenes. IEEE Trans. Syst. Man Cybern.: Syst. **49**(11), 2362–2372 (2018)
2. Wei, Y., et al.: STC: a simple to complex framework for weakly-supervised semantic segmentation. IEEE Trans. Pattern Anal. Mach. Intell. **39**(11), 2314–2320 (2016)
3. Wang, X., Gao, L., Song, J., Shen, H.: Beyond frame-level CNN: saliency-aware 3-D CNN with LSTM for video action recognition. IEEE Signal Process. Lett. **24**(4), 510–514 (2016)
4. Kamel, A., Sheng, B., Yang, P., Li, P., Shen, R., Feng, D.D.: Deep convolutional neural networks for human action recognition using depth maps and postures. IEEE Trans. Syst. Man Cybern.: Syst. **49**(9), 1806–1819 (2018)
5. Huang, K., Zhu, C., Li, G.: Saliency detection by adaptive channel fusion. IEEE Signal Process. Lett. **25**(7), 1059–1063 (2018)
6. Huang, X., Shen, C., Boix, X., Zhao, Q.: Salicon: reducing the semantic gap in saliency prediction by adapting deep neural networks. In: IEEE International Conference on Computer Vision, pp. 262–270 (2015)
7. Pan, J., Sayrol, E., Giro-i-Nieto, X., McGuinness, K., O'Connor, N.E.: Shallow and deep convolutional networks for saliency prediction. In: IEEE Conference on Computer Vision and Pattern Recognition, pp. 598–606 (2016)
8. Pan, J., et al.: SalGAN: visual saliency prediction with generative adversarial networks. arXiv preprint arXiv:1701.01081 (2017)

9. Kummerer, M., Wallis, T.S., Gatys, L.A., Bethge, M.: Understanding low-and high-level contributions to fixation prediction. In: IEEE International Conference on Computer Vision, pp. 4789–4798 (2017)

10. Cornia, M., Baraldi, L., Serra, G., Cucchiara, R.: Predicting human eye fixations via an LSTM-based saliency attentive model. IEEE Trans. Image Process. **27**(10), 5142–5154 (2018)

11. Che, Z., Borji, A., Zhai, G., Min, X., Guo, G., Le Callet, P.: How is gaze influenced by image transformations? Dataset and model. IEEE Trans. Image Process. **29**, 2287–2300 (2020)

12. Guan, W., Wang, T., Qi, J., Zhang, L., Lu, H.: Edge-aware convolution neural network based salient object detection. IEEE Signal Process. Lett. **26**(1), 114–118 (2018)

13. Huang, R., Xing, Y., Wang, Z.: RGB-D salient object detection by a CNN with multiple layers fusion. IEEE Signal Process. Lett. **26**(4), 552–556 (2019)

14. Zhu, C., Cai, X., Huang, K., Li, T.H., Li, G.: Pdnet: prior-model guided depth-enhanced network for salient object detection. In: IEEE International Conference on Multimedia and Expo, pp. 199–204 (2019)

15. Zhou, W., Lv, Y., Lei, J., Yu, L.: Global and local-contrast guides content-aware fusion for RGB-D saliency prediction. IEEE Trans. Syst. Man Cybern.: Syst. 1–9 (2019)

16. Lv, Y., Zhou, W., Lei, J., Ye, L., Luo, T.: Attention-based fusion network for human eye-fixation prediction in 3D images. Opt. Express **27**(23), 34056–34066 (2019)

17. Li, G., He, X., Zhang, W., Chang, H., Dong, L., Lin, L.: Non-locally enhanced encoder-decoder network for single image de-raining. In: ACM International Conference on Multimedia, pp. 1056–1064 (2018)

18. Huang, G., Liu, Z., Van Der Maaten, L., Weinberger, K.Q.: Densely connected convolutional networks. In: IEEE Conference on Computer Vision and Pattern Recognition, pp. 4700–4708 (2017)

19. Wang, X., Girshick, R., Gupta, A., He, K.: Non-local neural networks. In: IEEE Conference on Computer Vision and Pattern Recognition, pp. 7794–7803 (2018)

20. Shi, W.: Real-time single image and video super-resolution using an efficient sub-pixel convolutional neural network. In: IEEE Conference on Computer Vision and Pattern Recognition, pp. 1874–1883 (2016)

21. Qian, R., Tan, R.T., Yang, W., Su, J., Liu, J.: Attentive generative adversarial network for raindrop removal from a single image. In: IEEE Conference on Computer Vision and Pattern Recognition, pp. 2482–2491 (2018)

22. Zhang, H., Goodfellow, I., Metaxas, D., Odena, A.: Self-attention generative adversarial networks. arXiv preprint arXiv:1805.08318 (2018)

23. Li, X., Wang, W., Hu, X., Yang, J.: Selective kernel networks. In: IEEE Conference on Computer Vision and Pattern Recognition, pp. 510–519 (2019)

24. Jiang, M., Huang, S., Duan, J., Zhao, Q.: Salicon: saliency in context. In: IEEE Conference on Computer Vision and Pattern Recognition, pp. 1072–1080 (2015)

25. Ma, C.-Y., Hang, H.-M.: Learning-based saliency model with depth information. J. Vis. **15**(6), 19 (2015)

26. Lang, C., Nguyen, T. V., Katti, H., Yadati, K., Kankanhalli, M., Yan, S.: Depth matters: influence of depth cues on visual saliency. In: IEEE European Conference on Computer Vision, pp. 101–115 (2012). https://doi.org/10.1007/978-3-642-33709-3_8

Behavioural State Detection Algorithm for Infants and Toddlers Incorporating Multi-scale Contextual Features

Qisheng Wang[1], Zede Zhu[1,2,3(✉)], Wei Guo[1], and Hao Huang[1]

[1] Lu'an Branch, Anhui Institute of Innovation for Industrial Technology, Lu'an 237000, China
zhuzede@126.com
[2] Hefei Institutes of Physical Science, Chinese Academy of Sciences, Hefei 230000, China
[3] CAS Henan Industrial Technology Innovation and Incubation Center, Henan 450000, China

Abstract. In order to achieve intelligent monitoring of infants and toddlers' behaviour, reduce the risk of accidental injury and ease the caregiver's burden, this paper proposes a behavioural state detection algorithm that incorporates multi-scale contextual features to achieve real-time monitoring of whether infants and toddlers are climbing, crawling, sitting, lying, standing (walking) and lost in a total of six states. To ensure the algorithm's ability to detect targets of interest at multiple scales and to obtain faster detection efficiency, a deep feature fusion network is constructed based on a feature pyramid network structure, In addition, in order to improve the ability of the deep feature fusion network to obtain more global semantic information of the feature map, a contextual feature extraction structure is constructed to mine the contextual valid features of the feature map by residual structure and dilated convolution. The experimental results show that the method achieves a detection speed of 72.18 FPS and a detection accuracy of 95.24%, which enables faster detection of infants and toddlers' behavioural states and slightly better accuracy relative to the baseline algorithm.

Keywords: Convolutional neural networks · Feature pyramid networks · Object detection · Dilated convolution

1 Introduction

A robust fertility rate is of great strategic importance to the future of the country, yet since 2017, China's fertility rate has continued to decline [1]. In addition, in May 2019, the General Office of the State Council issued the Guiding Opinions on Promoting the Development of Infants and Toddlers Care Services for Infants and Toddlers Under the Age of 3, which states that technologies such as the Internet, big data, the Internet of Things and artificial intelligence should be fully utilised to develop and apply information management systems for infants and toddlers care services in conjunction with the actual infants and toddlers

H. Lu et al. (Eds.): ICIG 2023, LNCS 14356, pp. 124–135, 2023.
https://doi.org/10.1007/978-3-031-46308-2_11

care services [2]. Therefore, to take care of the healthy growth of infants and toddlers, it is important to study intelligent infants and toddlers' behavioural state monitoring methods to reduce the risk of accidental injury to infants and toddlers.

A lot of work has been carried out by researchers to effectively acquire human action features in video sequences for behavioural state recognition [3–7]. For example, Simonyan et al. [3] designed a two-stream network structure based on Convolutional Neural Network (CNN) to acquire visible image features and optical flow features respectively; Tran et al. [4] proposed a 3-dimensional convolutional neural network that can extract both spatial and temporal features of a complete human action; Similarly, Donahue et al. [5] used a combination of CNN and Recurrent Neural Network (RNN) to extract spatial and temporal sequence features of a complete action, respectively; Yan et al. [6] used a sequence of human skeletal points as input and used Graph Convolutional Networks (GCN) to extract action features; Duan et al. [7] used a 2-dimensional human skeletal heat map stack as input to extract action and temporal features using 3D convolutional neural networks and achieved excellent performance on short video classification tasks. However, existing video-based action recognition algorithms are mainly used for adult behaviour classification in short videos, where infants and toddlers' action features differ from adult action features, and video data are difficult to obtain and model training and inference are costly.

Based on the above problems and considering the feasibility of using object detection algorithms for human behavioural state detection and recognition [8–12], this paper optimises the baseline object detection algorithm YOLOX-tiny [13] and proposes a behavioural state detection and recognition algorithm for infants and toddlers that incorporates multi-scale contextual features, with a view to ensuring accuracy while obtaining more real-time detection performance. First, in order to improve the efficiency of the baseline algorithm execution and to ensure the detection capability of the final algorithm in this paper for multi-scale targets of interest, a Deep Feature Fusion Network (DFFN) was constructed by redesigning the Path Aggregation Feature Pyramid Network (PAFPN) of the YOLOX-tiny algorithm based on the Feature Pyramid Network (FPN) [14] structure. Finally, to improve the ability of DFFN to obtain more global semantic information, a feature extraction structure that can effectively mine feature graph contextual information was constructed by residual structure and dilated convolution.

2   Principle of Algorithm

2.1   Algorithm Structure

In order to achieve low cost and be able to quickly and accurately detect and identify the behavioral state of infants and toddlers, this paper proposes an infants and toddlers behavioral state detection algorithm incorporating contextual features, which mainly involves a lightweight target detection algorithm, and the overall framework of the algorithm is shown in Fig. 1. Specifically, firstly, the

RGB image is fed into the Darknet53 [15] backbone feature extraction network to obtain the deep feature Dark0, the sub-depth feature Dark1, and the shallow feature Dark2 of the RGB image; Secondly, the obtained three-layer features are fed into a deep feature fusion network that utilizes the Contextual Feature Extraction Structure (CFES) to generate multi-scale feature maps; then, the decoupling head [13] is used to extract the object classification and localization features in the three layers of different scale feature maps respectively; finally, the features output from the three decoupling heads are fused to achieve the precise localization and classification of the object of interest.

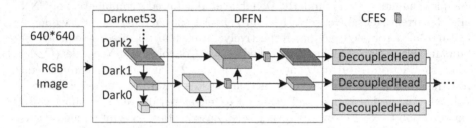

Fig. 1. Overall framework of the algorithm.

2.2 DFFN

The occurrence of dangerous actions of infants and toddlers is sudden, and it is important to accurately grasp the behavioral state of infants and toddlers in real time to reduce the risk of accidental injury of infants and toddlers. Therefore, in this paper, under the premise of guaranteeing the detection accuracy of the algorithm, and with the starting point of improving the actual detection speed of the algorithm, the deep feature fusion network DFFN is constructed to replace the PAFPN structure of the baseline algorithm, and the structure of the DFFN and PAFPN is shown in Fig. 2.

For the PAFPN module, both top-down and bottom-up bidirectional feature fusion networks are used. Experimental studies have found that PAFPN using convolutional kernel size 3 for downsampling brings high computational effort, so only top-down multi-scale feature fusion strategy is used in this paper. The deep feature maps with stronger semantic information are used to enhance the information of the shallow feature maps with stronger texture information, to improve the expressive ability of the shallow output feature maps, and the multi-scale feature maps and decoupling head are utilized to achieve the precise localization and recognition of multi-scale objects of interest.

The DFFN structure consists of convolution, Batch Normalization (BN), SiLU activation function, residual idea [16] and nearest neighbor interpolation upsampling algorithm. Specifically, the CBS structure constructed using a convolution kernel of size 1, BN and SiLU activation function is used to change

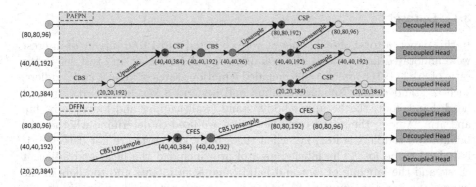

Fig. 2. PAFPN and DFFN structure.

the number of feature map channels; CFES is constructed using CBS, dilation convolution (convolution kernel of size 3 and dilation rate 2), BN, SiLU activation function, and residual structure to enhance the semantic representation of the output feature maps and to change the number of channels; and nearest-neighbor interpolation up-sampling algorithm is used to change the feature map length and width of the feature map, thus realizing the cascading of the up-sampled feature map with sub-deep features in the channel direction. Unlike the CFES structure in this paper, the CSP uses a normal 2D convolution with a convolution kernel size of 3. The CBS and CFES structures are shown below (Fig. 3).

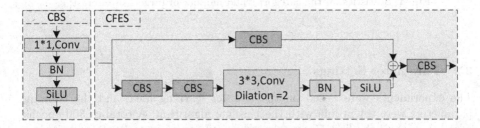

Fig. 3. CBS and CFES network structure diagram.

3   Experiments

The experiments are based on Windows 10 OS with GeForce GTX1660(6 GB) GPU, Intel Core i7-10700 @ 2.9 GHz processor, and Pytorch1.7.0 deep learning framework.

3.1   Dataset

In this paper, a total of 5692 images were collected and 19166 targets of interest were annotated and divided into training set, validation set and test set in the ratio of 8:1:1. 19166 annotations included 5 motion states of infants and toddlers, such as stand (walk), sit, crawl, climb and lie, and 8 key body parts, such as head, hand, foot, the lie upper body, stand (walk) upper and lower body, hip and arm. Among them, the body key parts are used to determine whether the infants and toddlers is lost, i.e. when the 8 body key parts are not detected, it is judged to be lost. The labeled area of arm included the head and adjacent chest, and the labeling of foot and hand came from infants and toddlers in the lying state, and the number of labeling in each category is shown in Fig. 4.

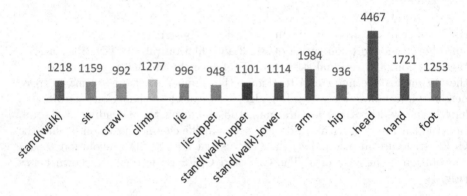

Fig. 4. Statistics on the categories and number of targets of interest.

3.2   Parameter Settings

The experiments were based on the transfer learning idea, and the training parameters were set in line with the baseline algorithm. A total of 300 epochs were set up, and the first 50 eporchs were used for freeze training, and the last 250 eporchs were used for unfreeze training, with a batch size of 16 and 8. The training was performed using a stochastic gradient descent (SGD) optimiser with an initial learning rate of 0.01 and a cosine function to reduce the learning rate, with an SGD momentum was 0.937.

3.3   Objective Evaluation Results

To represent the overall performance difference between the algorithm in this paper and the baseline algorithm, the average detection accuracy (mAP), number of parameters (Params), Giga Floating-point Operations Per Second (GFLOPs) and Frames Per Second (FPS) transmitted by the model are comparison. The result of FPS is calculated by dividing 100 by the time it takes to iteratively inspect the same image 100 times. The relevant results are recorded as shown in Table 1.

Table 1. Model Performance Metrics Comparison.

Model	mAP	Params	GFLOPs	FPS
Baseline	95.17%	5,036,358	15.250G	60.42
Ours	95.24%	3,788,172	13.645G	72.18

As can be seen from Table 1, the algorithm in this paper significantly improves the operation speed of the algorithm compared with the baseline algorithm while ensuring the overall accuracy of the model, and the algorithm in this paper improves the detection speed by 11.76 FPS, which achieves a more real-time detection of the behavioral state of infants and toddlers, thus reducing the risk of accidental injury due to non-real-time signal transmission. In addition, it can be visualized from the table results that DFFN effectively reduces the number of parameters by 24.78% compared to PAFPN.

Generalisation ability is one of the evaluation metrics to measure the effectiveness of a model, so the experiments recorded the variation in accuracy of the baseline algorithm and the algorithm in this paper on the validation set, with results recorded every 10 eporchs. The results were recorded as shown in Fig. 5 below.

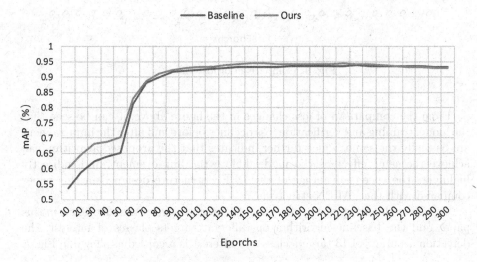

Fig. 5. Validation set detection accuracy comparison.

As can be seen from Fig. 5, both the present algorithm and the baseline algorithm demonstrate good generalization ability based on the dataset constructed in this paper, and the model detection performance increases steadily with the number of training iterations and stabilizes after 100 training iterations. The algorithm achieves higher accuracy than the baseline algorithm at the beginning of training and during the stabilisation period, which also demonstrates the effectiveness of the improved algorithm in this paper.

The change in loss values during model training can reflect the speed of convergence, training efficiency and effectiveness of the model, so this paper records the training and validation losses of the baseline algorithm and this paper's algorithm during model training as shown in Fig. 6 below.

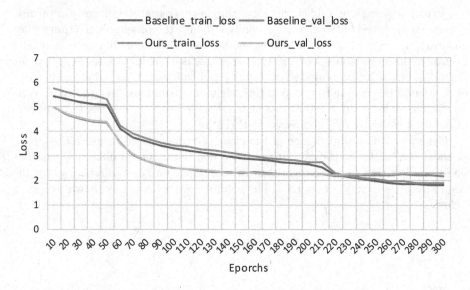

Fig. 6. Comparison of loss values.

From the comparison of loss changes in the figure above, it can be seen that the model training and verification loss declines before and after the improvement are basically the same, which further indicates that the proposed algorithm can achieve the same effect as the model before the improvement, and indirectly highlights the speed advantage of the DFFN structure designed in this paper compared with the PAFPN structure.

To reflect the difference in detection accuracy between the algorithm in this paper and the baseline algorithm on different targets classes of interest, the detection accuracy of 13 targets classes of interest is recorded as shown in Fig. 7.

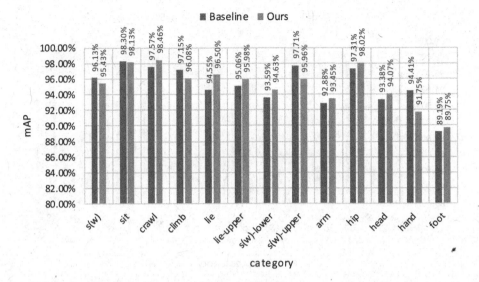

Fig. 7. Comparison of 13 kinds of detection accuracy.

From the comparison results of the detection accuracy of different targets of interest in Fig. 7, it can be seen that the algorithm in this paper improves the detection accuracy of 8 types of targets of interest relative to the baseline algorithm, including 2 larger scale behavioral state targets of infants and toddlers crawling and lying, 4 medium and large scale targets of upper body in lying state, lower body in standing (walking) state, hip and arm, and 2 relatively smaller scale targets of head and foot key parts. This makes it possible to identify the behavioral states of infants and toddlers more accurately.

In order to effectively mine the contextual features of the feature map and expand the receptive field, ablation comparison experiments are conducted for the selection of the dilated convolution parameters, which are set to 1, 2, 3, 4 and 5. When the dilated parameter is 1, it is two-dimensional ordinary convolution, and the experimental results are recorded as shown in Fig. 8, and d in the figure indicates the dilated convolution parameter.

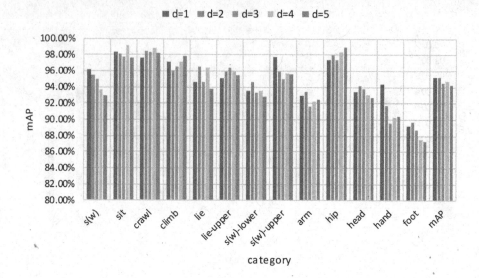

Fig. 8. The results of the ablation comparison test.

From the experimental results in Fig. 8, it can be seen that the selection of the dilated convolution parameters has a certain influence on the detection and recognition of targets of interest at different scales. On the infants and toddlers' state and key body part datasets constructed in this paper, for small-scale targets of interest, the accuracy of small-scale targets decreases with the increase of the dilated convolution parameters, such as the three small-scale targets of head, hand and foot, and on the contrary, for medium and large scale targets, the detection accuracy of most of the targets categories shows an increase or a small floating situation. Therefore, the selection of appropriate dilated convolution parameters for different scales of the targets task of interest has a positive effect on the model performance.

3.4 Subjective Evaluation Results

In order to visually compare the differences between this paper's algorithm and the baseline algorithm for infants and toddlers' behavior state detection, as well as to verify the feasibility of using the object detection method for infants and toddlers' multiple behavior state detection and identification, the experiments randomly selected infants and toddlers' behavior state pictures for detection, and the experimental detection results are shown in Fig. 9.

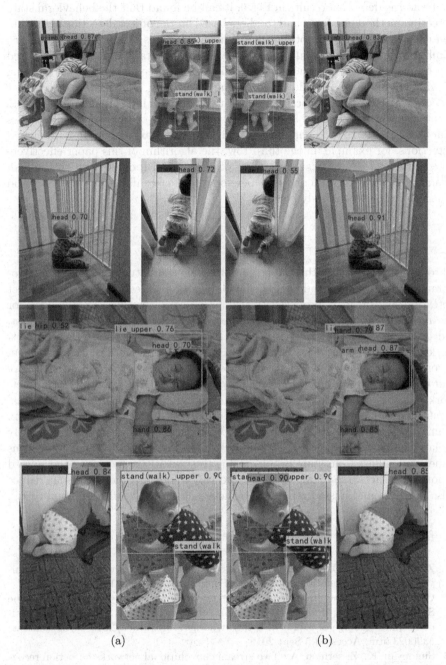

(a)   (b)

Fig. 9. Comparison of subjective test results. (a) shows the detection results of the baseline algorithm and (b) shows the detection results based on the algorithm of this paper.

From the detection results in Fig. 9, it can be found that the behavioral state detection method of infants and toddlers based on the object detection algorithm can effectively identify a total of five behavioral states of infants and toddlers: climb, crawl, lie, stand (walk), and sit, and can accurately detect the exposed key body parts, which provides a prerequisite guarantee for accurate monitoring of whether infants and toddlers lost. The interesting point is that the object detection algorithm can effectively detect the targets of interest and other targets of interest within its range. Further observation of the comparison results shows that the algorithm of this paper can effectively reduce false detections and missed detections, for example, in the third row, the algorithm of this paper effectively detects the exposed critical body parts of infants and toddler lying on the bed; in addition, the algorithm of this paper shows higher confidence in the detection of most of the critical body parts.

4   Conclusions

Through the research in this paper, a multi-scale contextual feature fusion algorithm for infants and toddlers' behavioural state detection based on object detection algorithm is proposed, which provides a new method and idea for the research and application of infants and toddlers action recognition. First, a deep feature fusion network is constructed based on the feature pyramid network structure to achieve faster detection speed with guaranteed accuracy; then, a contextual feature extraction structure is constructed by residual structure and dilation convolution to improve the ability of the deep feature fusion network to obtain more global semantic information of the feature map. The final experimental results show that the detection speed of this paper's algorithm is improved by 11.76 FPS compared to the baseline algorithm, and a slightly higher accuracy is achieved in this paper's task. However, the algorithm in this paper still suffers from state problems due to sudden false positives and missed reports in practice, and we will continue to explore methods that can reduce false positives and missed reports to achieve better results with minimal cost.

References

1. Zhai, Z.W., Jin, G.Z., Zhang, Y.Y.: Reassessment of Chinas fertility level: an analysis of the 7th population census data. Popul. Res. **46**(4), 3–13 (2022)
2. General Office of the State Council of China: Guidance of the General Office of the State Council on promoting the development of care services for infants and toddlers under the age of 3 (2019). http://www.gov.cn/xinwen/2019-05/09/content_5390023.htm. Accessed 5 Sept 2019
3. Simonyan, K., Zisserman, A.: Two-stream convolutional networks for action recognition in videos. Adv. Neural. Inf. Process. Syst. **30**(5), 568–576 (2014)
4. Tran, D., Bourdev, L., Fergus, L., et al.: Learning spatiotemporal features with 3D convolutional networks. In: 2015 IEEE International Conference on Computer Vision (ICCV), pp. 4489–4497. https://doi.org/10.1109/ICCV.2015.510

5. Donahue, J., Anne Hendricks, L., Guadarrama, S., et al.: Long-term recurrent convolutional networks for visual recognition and description. IEEE Trans. Pattern Anal. Mach. Intell. **39**(4), 2625–2624 (2017)
6. Yan, S., Xiong, Y., Lin, D.: Spatial temporal graph convolutional networks for skeleton-based action recognition. In: Proceedings of the AAAI Conference on Artificial Intelligence, vol. 32, no. 1, pp. 7444–7452 (2018)
7. Duan, H., Zhao, Y., Chen, K., et al.: Revisiting skeleton-based action recognition. In: 2022 IEEE/CVF Conference on Computer Vision and Pattern Recognition (CVPR), pp. 2959–2968. https://doi.org/10.1109/CVPR52688.2022.00298
8. Wang, Z.P., Wang, T.: Faster RCNN-based detection method for violations of crossing fences. Comput. Syst. Appl. **31**(4), 346–351 (2022)
9. Wan, L.B.: Research on Smoking Behavior Detection System Based on Deep Learning. Master, University of Electronic Science and Technology of China (2022)
10. Zhou, H.C., Yang, J., Xu, Z.G.: Design of human fall detection system based on YOLOv5 algorithm. J. Jinling Inst. Technol. **38**(2), 22–29 (2022)
11. Li, Z., Xiong, J., Chen, H.: Based on improved yolov3 for college students' classroom behavior recognition. In: 2022 International Conference on Artificial Intelligence and Computer Information Technology (AICIT), pp. 1–4. https://doi.org/10.1109/AICIT55386.2022.9930274
12. Choi, B., An, W., Kang, H.: Human action recognition method using YOLO and OpenPose. In: 2022 13th International Conference on Information and Communication Technology Convergence (ICTC), pp. 1786–1788. https://doi.org/10.1109/ICTC55196.2022.9952808
13. Ge, Z., Liu, S., Wang, F., et al.: YOLOX: exceeding YOLO series in 2021. arXiv e-prints, arXiv: 2107.08430 (2021)
14. Lin, T.-Y., Dollár, P., Girshick, R., et al.: Feature pyramid networks for object detection. In: 2017 IEEE Conference on Computer Vision and Pattern Recognition (CVPR), pp. 936–944. https://doi.org/10.1109/CVPR.2017.106
15. Redmon, J., Farhadi, A.: YOLOv3: an incremental improvement. arXiv preprint arXiv: 1804.02767 (2018)
16. He, K.M., Zhang, X., Ren, S.Q.: Deep residual learning for image recognition. In: 2016 IEEE Conference on Computer Vision and Pattern Recognition (CVPR), pp. 770–778. https://doi.org/10.1109/CVPR.2016.90

Motion-Scenario Decoupling for Rat-Aware Video Position Prediction: Strategy and Benchmark

Xiaofeng Liu[1], Jiaxin Gao[1], Yaohua Liu[1], Nenggan Zheng[2], and Risheng Liu[1(✉)]

[1] Dalian University of Technology, Liaoning, China
rsliu@dlut.edu.cn
[2] Zhejiang University, Zhejiang, China

Abstract. Recently significant progress has been made in human action recognition and behavior prediction using deep learning techniques, leading to improved vision-based semantic understanding. However, there is still a lack of high-quality motion datasets for small bio-robotics, which presents more challenging scenarios for long-term movement prediction and behavior control based on third-person observation. In this study, we introduce RatPose, a bio-robot motion prediction dataset constructed by considering the influence factors of individuals and environments based on predefined annotation rules. To enhance the robustness of motion prediction against these factors, we propose a Dual-stream Motion-Scenario Decoupling (*DMSD*) framework that effectively separates scenario-oriented and motion-oriented features and designs a scenario contrast loss and motion clustering loss for overall training. With such distinctive architecture, the dual-branch feature flow information is interacted and compensated in a decomposition-then-fusion manner. Moreover, we demonstrate significant performance improvements of the proposed *DMSD* framework on different difficulty-level tasks. We also implement long-term discretized trajectory prediction tasks to verify the generalization ability of the proposed dataset.

Keywords: Rat Dataset · Feature Decoupling · Video Prediction

1 Introduction

In recent years, significant advancements in neuroscience and biomedical engineering have facilitated the development of Brain-Computer Interface (BCI) [1–3], which offer potential benefits for rehabilitating neuromotor disorder [4] and controlling small animals [5] such as rats, beetles and doves. These animals endowed with autonomous intelligence and dexterous and agile bodies are allowed to perform special military missions or emergency rescues after natural disasters where human intervention is difficult. However, the intention of animals and the uncertainty associated with changes in the environment and individual organisms pose significant challenges for effective manipulation by humans. Therefore, it is of great significance to acquire high-quality movement data and perform a comprehensive analysis of robotic movement behavior based on varying environmental and individual factors to regulate biological behavior.

The inference and prediction of human motion [6,7] based on visual observation has been an extensively researched topic. Representative works include the HUMAN3.6M dataset [8], which predicts human pose, and the LMBRD dataset [9], which recognizes different behaviors of housed mice. Additionally, the 'something something' dataset [10] is proposed for human-object interaction, which predicts actions performed by humans with respect to different objects. These datasets use videos to capture the meta-action and interaction between the target creatures and their surrounding environment, leading to improved predictions and better understanding of their behavior. However, these datasets generally focus on the current specific actions of organisms, without considering the movement outcomes in the future, which limits the exploration of the organisms' moving motivation.

Deep learning based action recognition methods [11,12] and large-scale video datasets have made significant progress in recent years, and different architectures or modules are proposed to improve the temporal modeling capabilities of deep learning models. TRN [13] introduces a temporal relation network module to learn and reason about temporal dependencies between video frames at multiple time scales. Similarly, TIN [14] improves the temporal feature extraction based on TSM and proposes a temporal interlacing operator to fuse the temporal and spatial information. While these methods have shown some success in action recognition, their limitations in solely focusing on the temporal and spatial features between adjacent frames, without taking into account environmental and biological factors present in the video, thus hinder their performance in predicting the future movement of rats with high levels of uncertainty.

1.1 Our Contribution

To boost the investigation on motion behavior analysis of bio-robots and further research of behavioral control prototype incorporating animal moving intention, we first build a dataset RatPose which focuses on the bio-robot's movement prediction based on collected third-person video sequences. The movement data is collected in consideration of influence factors including varying individuals and different environments (e.g., Open Field and Maze), covering up to 5 scenarios, 6 individuals and 1023 data pairs. We also conduct detailed analysis of the individuals' differences and how it influences the performance of bio-robot's motion prediction. Based on the above analysis, we propose a Dual-stream Motion-Scenario Decoupling (*DMSD*) framework to effectively decompose the scenario-oriented and motion-oriented features. Then we propose a motion clustering loss to measure the distance between features and the nearest simulated cluster center and combine the scenario contrast loss to construct the overall loss function. Finally, we demonstrate the significant performance improvement of the proposed *DMSD* framework on single scenario and multiple scenarios motion prediction tasks. Furthermore, we implement our method to tackle more challenging discretized trajectory prediction based on long-term video sequences to show its generalization performance over different individuals and environments. In summary, our contributions can be summarized as follows:

- Based on predefined annotation rules, we construct the first bio-robot's motion prediction dataset, namely RatPose, with full consideration of varying individuals and environments, and conduct comprehensive analysis of the influence of individuals and prediction intervals for proper task settings, which contributes to further research on the behavioral control prototype incorporating all kinds of uncertainties.
- We propose a Dual-stream Motion-Scenario Decoupling (*DMSD*) framework to decompose the scenario-oriented and motion-oriented features, and design a novel motion clustering loss together with the scenario contrast loss to facilitate the robustness over varying environments and states of individuals.
- Extensive experiments under difference difficulty levels and ablation studies have demonstrate the effectiveness over existing methods (34.3% and 29.6% relative improvement of Top 1 accuracy under single and multiple scenario, respectively). We also verify the generalization performance of this framework on more challenging discretized trajectory prediction tasks.

2   Problem Set-Up

We focus on the long-term movements of rats to monitor their moving intentions, rather than their specific detailed actions, from an overhead perspective. To approximately estimate the intention, we aim to predict the motion patterns of rats and model it into a classification problem, which has potential applications in various fields, including bio-robot controlling.

2.1   Basic Settings

In this study, we address a unique problem that differs from the conventional action recognition tasks. While action recognition typically focuses on identifying what a human is doing or how they are interacting with objects, our goal is to predict the future moving position of rats. Unlike humans, animals do not always act logically or rationally, making this problem more challenging. Moreover, we use a different labeling strategy that is based on the outcome of the motion rather than the motion itself.

In our problem, we aim to classify motion results into five categories, namely top, down, left, right, and middle, as illustrated in Fig. 1. To determine the label of an object, we examine the distance it has moved relative to its body length. If the object moves a short distance, less than a predefined proportion of its body length, we label it as middle, indicating that it has stayed on the ground. Otherwise, we determine the label based on the direction of the body center's movement in pixel level. Specifically, we use θ to denote the counterclockwise angle between the width axis of the image and the motion vector after a short

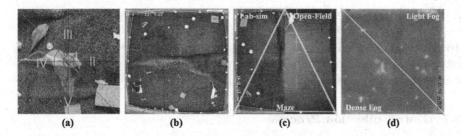

Fig. 1. Problem definition (a) and multi-view task scenario configuration (b)–(d). Subfigure (a) illustrates the classification labels used under different tasks, while subfigures (b)–(d) illustrate three task settings based on the associated difficulty levels: single scenario, multiple scenarios, and more challenging scenarios.

time t, ρ to denote the pixel length of the motion vector, and r to denote the predefined length in pixel level. Then we can define a set of the predicted motions: $\mathcal{M} = \{up : \rho > r, \frac{3}{4}\pi < \theta + 2k\pi < \frac{5}{4}\pi; left : \rho > r, \frac{5}{4}\pi < \theta + 2k\pi < \frac{7}{4}\pi; down : \rho > r, \frac{7}{4}\pi < \theta + 2k\pi < \frac{9}{4}\pi; right : \rho > r, \frac{9}{4}\pi < \theta + 2k\pi < \frac{11}{4}\pi; middle : \rho < r\}$, where $k \in Z$. Here we set $t = 3s$ and r is $1/10$ of the pixel length of the image.

Our problem can be characterized as a classification task with a unique focus and approach. In addition, our approach enables us to extract valuable insights from redundant video data in biological experiments, which may not be suitable for traditional action recognition tasks.

2.2   Advanced Settings

Predicting the motion patterns of animals is a challenging task due to the unpredictable nature of their movements. A range of factors, including environmental, biological, and psychological aspects, contribute to the significant variance in animal motion outcomes. Therefore, it is crucial to consider these factors when developing a solution. In this study, we aim to address this issue by taking into account the visual differences between various scenarios and visual perception difficulties. To achieve this goal, we propose three different problem settings: a single scenario, multiple scenarios, and challenging scenarios ranging from easy to hard, as Fig. 1 reveals. The first problem setting involves collecting data from a few rats in a single scenario, while the second problem setting involves collecting data from a few rats in various scenarios. Finally, the third problem setting involves collecting data in a single scenario where the visual images are affected by simulated smoke using a mask placed on the camera. Except the visual challenge, there only exists 1 video per class for training or finetune in the challenging setting. By incorporating these settings, we hope to develop a comprehensive understanding of animal motion patterns and contribute to the advancement of related research fields.

3   The RatPose Dataset

To better understanding rat's behaviors from visual perspective from a wide range of diverse environments and generalize to new settings, we propose Rat-Pose, a dataset for sharing different rats' moving experience in various scenarios.

3.1   Data Collection Process

Visual data was collected using an overhead camera to capture a vertical view of the environment, as illustrated in Fig. 2. To enhance the diversity of the data, videos were recorded of rats in various environments, including a simple maze with eight arms (Maze), a laboratory simulation of the real environment (Lab-sim), and an open field environment in a gym (Open Field). In order to expand the range of scenarios and increase the variability of the data, we considered the open-field environment as the baseline and introduced variations such as adding grass as the ground or placing toys as barriers.

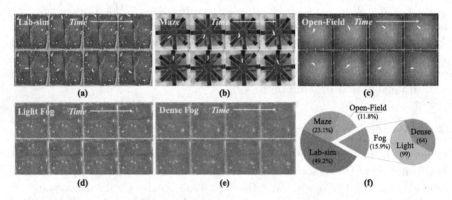

Fig. 2. A glimpse of the RatPose video dataset. Scenario trajectories (a)–(e): Lab-sim, Maze, Open-Field, Light Fog and Dense Fog. (f): Data distribution.

3.2   Dataset Features

RatPose is full of challenging, and the challenging mainly comes from the natural insurance affected by many factors. We primarily consider the influences caused by individual differences, and differences in individual states. In order to demonstrate individual differences involved in modeling rat locomotor behavior, we utilize video data collected from six distinct rats. As shown in 3, the dataset is randomly partitioned into training and testing sets based on the individual rat, and a baseline model is trained using the training set and evaluated on multiple testing sets. Analysis of the resulting correlation matrix indicates that the model performs well in predicting the behavior of the corresponding rat, but struggles

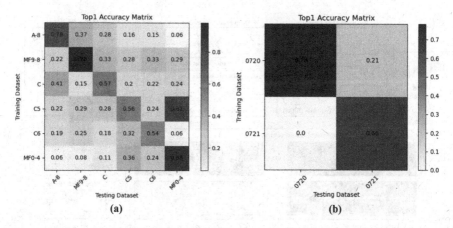

Fig. 3. Performance using different data sets to train and test baseline model, each of which contains hundreds samples. (a): Testing performance using different rats, named A-8, MF9-8, C, C5, C6 and MF0-4, to build data sets. (b): Testing performance using one rat, A-8, but in different time.

to generalize to new rats. And in the right subfigure, although the video data is collected with only a one-day time interval, there are notable variations in the state of the rat under observation. The observed heterogeneity in the rat's condition results in a substantial discrepancy between the predicted and actual outcomes of its behavioral actions. These features suggest when facing the situation lack of sufficient data, model is fragile when meeting data full of diversity, especially in the situation that test data is not identically distributed.

4 The Proposed Method

This section describes the workflow of the Dual-stream Motion-Scenario Decoupling (*DMSD*) framework and the training loss. The overall architecture is shown in Fig. 4, mainly including three parts: the pre-decoupling operator, deep feature extractor, and the future motion predictor.

4.1 Dual-Stream Motion-Scenario Decoupling (DMSD)

As illustrated, pre-decoupling operator contains Motion Removal Module (MRM) denoted by ϕ and Scenario Removal Module (SRM) as ψ to get the scenario relative input $\mathbf{u}$ and the motion relative input $\mathbf{v}$. We then input the parallel pre-decoupling terms $\mathbf{u}$ and $\mathbf{v}$ into the dual feature extractor to obtain the deep scenario features $\mathbf{s}$ and the deep motion features $\mathbf{m}$ for prediction, with the guidance of scenario contrast loss and motion clustering loss. The pre-decoupling operator and deep feature extractor compose a dual branch, jointly parameterized by θ and serves as the backbone to extract features. The future

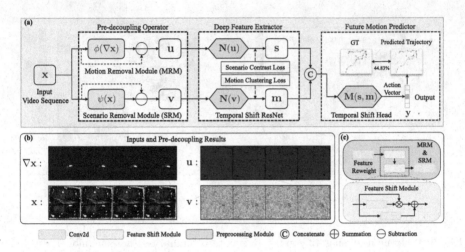

Fig. 4. Overview of the proposed Dual-stream Motion-Scenario Decoupling (*DMSD*) framework. (a): Network architecture, including pre-decoupling operation, deep feature extractor and future motion predictor. (b): Visual images of the input and pre-decoupling results. (c): General network architecture of MRM and SRM.

motion predictor uses temporal shift head[1] denoted as **M** to fuse and output the action vector to predict the motion probability **y**. The process can be formulated as

$$\mathbf{y} = M\big((N(\mathbf{x} - \phi(\nabla\mathbf{x})), N(\mathbf{x} - \psi(\mathbf{x})))\big), \tag{1}$$

where $\mathbf{x} = \{I_t | t = 0, 1, 2, 3...\}$ presents the input video sequence and $\nabla\mathbf{x} = \{I_t - I_0 | t = 0, 1, 2, 3...\}$ presents the differences among $\mathbf{x}$, indicating movement of the target.

Pre-decoupling Operator. To decompose the mixture components in a natural manner, we initially use MRM and SRM to decouple the input image sequences into different terms **v** and **u**. The MRM module is compromised by a convolution layer designed to expand the dimension, two feature shift module dedicated to recombining features and feature reweighting, and a convolution layer intended to reduce the dimension. We apply MRM module ϕ on $\nabla\mathbf{x}$ and a residual-like subtraction operation to obtain the scenario relative term **u**. We get this term by removing the motion component from the input sequences, enabling us to extract scenario features effectively. The SRM module shares the same network architecture with MRM while it has different parameters and input. We apply SRM module ψ directly on **x** to get a general representation of the input scenario. Similarly, we use the subtraction operator as well as SRM to remove scenario information and obtain the motion relative term **v** by removing the background component from the original input. As shown in Fig. 4, for input sequence **x**, **u** present the scenario information and show the viable domain for

---

[1] See work [15] for the detailed implementation of temporal shift head.

rat's movement as the unreachable part is filled in black. Meanwhile, $\mathbf{v}$ represents the movement of the rat in pixel space, with its spatial information. By doing so, we pre-decouple the input sequence into different terms concentrated on different factors.

Deep Feature Extractor. In addition to the pre-decoupling function, we use deep feature extractor for deep feature extraction and better factors decoupling. The deep feature extractor the deep feature extractor contains two temporal shift resnet[2] denoted as $\mathbf{N}$ to extract and fuse the temporal and spatial features of $\mathbf{u}$ and $\mathbf{v}$. Besides, we propose the scenario contrast loss and motion clustering loss[3] to better detect the correlations among data and decouple the coupling relationship between $\mathbf{s}$ and $\mathbf{m}$.

Future Motion Predictor. After applying the dual branch, we utilize the Future Motion Predictor to fuse $\mathbf{s}$ and $\mathbf{m}$ features and generate the predicted output $\mathbf{y}$. Future Motion Predictor facilitates the integration and decoding of temporal and spatial features, alongside motion and scenario features, to yield robust and effective prediction outcomes. Notably, our approach demonstrate remarkable resilience to changes in environmental perspectives, with a prediction accuracy of up to 48.8% even under such conditions.

4.2 Loss Function

We propose several losses to explore the similarity of action behaviors in different scenarios and the differences in scenario factors under different states. Among them, we optimize both dual-branch network's parameters θ and the clustering centers $\mathbf{r}$ using the feature decoupling loss L_f, which is expressed as follows:

$$L_f = \lambda_s \cdot L_{sc} + \lambda_m \cdot L_{mc}, \tag{2}$$

where L_{sc} and L_{mc} are the proposed scenario contrast loss and motion clustering loss. λ_s and λ_m are the corresponding weights. In our training, we empirically set $\lambda_s = 0.1$ and $\lambda_m = 1$. In addition, we introduce the classification loss L_{cls} optimize the whole networks parameters θ and ω. The process of optimization is carried out alternately in every iteration step.

Scenario Contrast Loss: In order to increase the sensitivity of the scene feature representation to slight changes in the environment, we utilize the technique of contrastive learning. We consider videos captured in the same scenario at the same time as positive samples, denoted as $\mathbf{s}^+$, while all others are considered as negative samples, denoted as $\mathbf{s}^-$. Drawing inspiration from contrastive learning for visual representations [17], we formulate scenario contrast loss as:

$$L_{sc} = -\log \frac{exp(sim(\boldsymbol{s}, \boldsymbol{s}^+))}{\sum_{\boldsymbol{s}' \in \boldsymbol{s}^-} exp(sim(\boldsymbol{s}, \boldsymbol{s}'))}. \tag{3}$$

---

[2] See work [15,16] for the detailed implementation of temporal shift resnet.

[3] We provide more details about the proposed scenario contrast loss and motion clustering loss in Sect. 4.2.

Motion Clustering Loss: We employ a series of trainable representation clustering centers $\mathbf{r}_c$ with label c. To measure the distance between each feature and the nearest cluster center, we calculate the minimum $L2$ distance between the feature and the center as the nearest auxiliary distance:

$$D(\mathbf{m}|c) = \min_{\mathbf{r}} ||\mathbf{m} - \mathbf{r}||_2 \quad s.t. \quad \mathbf{r} \in \mathbf{r}_c. \tag{4}$$

Next, we use the softmax function on the opposite number of the nearest auxiliary distance between each class feature center as the probability and apply cross-entropy to obtain the final motion clustering loss. This approach allows us to learn distributions of feature representations and obtain better decision boundaries:

$$L_{mc} = CE(\frac{e^{-D(\mathbf{m}|\mathbf{z})}}{\sum_k e^{-D(\mathbf{m}|\mathbf{z})}}, \mathbf{z}). \tag{5}$$

Here, $\mathbf{z}$ denotes the ground truth label, and CE denotes the cross-entropy loss.

5 Experiments

In this study, all models are trained and tested on a server equipped with an Intel(R) Xeon(R) Gold 5218 CPU @ 2.30GHz and an NVIDIA A40 GPU. The training process is conducted using the mmaction framework [18] with default training hyper-parameters. We adopt a sampling strategy where every 8th frame of the video is selected and resized to 224×224. For each video, we sample the last 8 frames according to this rule. For longer video online prediction, we predict the position distribution every 3 s for the subsequent 3 s.

5.1 Quantitative Evaluation

Table 1. Quantitative comparison of rat location prediction accuracy for state-of-the-art methods in Single and Multiple Scenarios.

Metric		Setting									
		Single					Multiple				
		TRN	TSM	TIN	TSF	Ours	TRN	TSM	TIN	TSF	Ours
Acc	Mean↑	37.39	37.39	39.92	33.68	44.66	40.45	40.00	36.58	38.40	46.68
	Std↓	49.63	49.63	30.49	35.18	5.01	37.39	42.23	28.21	27.66	10.71
Top1Acc↑		30.10	30.10	33.98	29.13	45.63	34.98	34.98	32.51	34.48	45.32

In order to evaluate the effectiveness of our proposed method, we conducted experiments on both single and multiple scenarios tasks, as Table 1 reveals. To demonstrate the superiority of our approach, we performed a quantitative comparison with four state-of-the-art methods, namely TRN [13], TSM [15], TIN [14], and TSF [19]. The experimental results clearly indicate that our method achieves significantly better performance than the other methods in terms of both mean class accuracy and top-1-accuracy, providing strong evidence for the effectiveness of our proposed approach.

We conduct ablation experiments on our auxiliary loss, as Table 2 reveals. The S_1 approach represents the network trained solely with the classification loss, while S_2 and S_3 show the results obtained by integrating the Scenario Contrast and the Motion Clustering Loss, respectively. Acc_s and Acc_m represent the top-1 accuracy in single scenario and multiple scenarios respectively. To train the approaches other than S_1 an iterative joint training strategy was applied.

Table 2. Ablation analysis of different loss functions in our proposed *DMSD* training: Impact of Scenario Contrast Loss and Motion Clustering Loss.

	L_{cls}	L_{sc}	L_{mc}	$Acc_s\uparrow$	$Acc_m\uparrow$
S_1	✔	✘	✘	30.10	42.36
S_2	✔	✔	✘	38.83	41.38
S_3	✔	✘	✔	39.81	44.83
Ours	✔	✔	✔	46.68	45.32

To demonstrate the efficacy of our training strategy, we conducted a comprehensive comparative analysis against several state-of-the-art few shot learning techniques, including RHG [20], BDA [21], and IAPTT [22]. In this context, we regarded the feature extraction layer as an upper-level challenge while considering the subsequent classification layer as a lower-level problem. Employing a bilevel optimization approach facilitated the seamless acquisition of a robust universal feature extraction module. As evident from the results presented in Table 3, traditional methods for few-shot learning struggle to acquire a viable representation and, in some cases, even perform worse than direct training. In stark contrast, our proposed approach not only surpasses the performance of other methods but also significantly enhances the final outcome. The superiority of our technique in capturing essential features and its ability to adapt to limited training data highlight its potential as a groundbreaking solution in the field of few-shot learning.

Table 3. Quantitative comparison of rat location prediction accuracy for state-of-the-art methods with Different Training Strategies.

	Setting								
Metric	TIN				DMSD				
	RHG	BDA	IAPTT	-	RHG	BDA	IAPTT	-	Ours
MeanAcc↑	27.53	28.08	34.55	39.92	23.47	27.98	28.03	42.36	46.68
Top1Acc↑	26.11	28.57	29.06	33.98	25.12	26.60	27.59	30.10	45.32

We observe that utilizing the motion clustering loss and scenario contrast loss resulted in significant improvements in one or more of the evaluation metrics presented in the table. Furthermore, the combined use of these two losses during training leads to a substantial increase in the performance of the final model, particularly in a single scenario setting, where the top-1 accuracy is improved by approximately 52% compared to the basic dual-branch model. This indicates that the motion clustering loss and scenario contrast loss are effective in improving the overall performance of the model.

5.2 Qualitative Evaluation

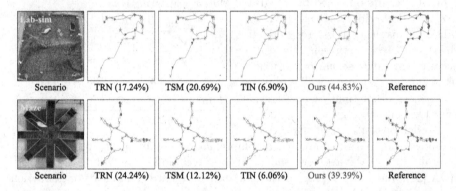

Fig. 5. Qualitative comparison for tracking and predicting the movement trajectory of rats in different camera scenario views. Gray lines depict the trajectory of rat movement, circles indicate stationary positions, while triangles in up, down, left, and right directions represent the rat's movement. The red crosses signify prediction errors, and the yellow star pattern denotes the rat's starting position. The numerical value represents the top-1 accuracy on this trajectory. (Color figure online)

To illustrate the generalizability and robustness of our method, we conduct qualitative evaluation employ several highly challenging video segments for practical experimentation. Notably, the data in these segments differs not only in the individual rats used for data collection but also in the camera angles employed for filming, as compared to those present in the RatPose training set.

As depicted in Fig. 5, the first row of the figure shows a difference between the shooting angle of the video footage and the angle of the training data. Despite this slight visual discrepancy, the prediction accuracy of TRN and other methods considerably decline. In contrast, our method is found to be robust to changes in shooting angles, as its prediction accuracy remained unaffected.

Additionally, the rats in the second row of the figure display more vigorous movements than those in the dataset, performing complex activities within a short period in the maze environment. This leads to a decrease in prediction accuracy for all methods, reflecting the notable individual differences among rats and the difficulty of real-time prediction of their movement intentions. Nonetheless, our method was able to maintain a relatively reasonable level of prediction accuracy even under these challenging circumstances, further attesting to the superiority of our approach.

6   Conclusion

In conclusion, recent advancements in bio-robotics with Brain-Computer Interface (BCI) techniques have made it possible to directly control animals such as rats, beetles, and doves by humans. However, the highly unpredictable and difficult to control behaviors of these animals make it crucial to develop accurate and effective methods for predicting their movements. This paper proposes a novel dataset called RatPose for predicting the heading direction of rats' movement, which shifts the attention towards forecasting the future movement outcomes of organisms. The paper also proposes a visual prediction model that effectively decouples motion from the environment for this dataset, achieving superior performance when compared to state-of-the-art action recognition methods.

Acknowledgements. This work is partially supported by the National Key R&D Program of China (2020YFB1313503), the National Natural Science Foundation of China (U22B2052), the Fundamental Research Funds for the Central Universities and the Major Key Project of PCL (PCL2021A12).

References

1. Wolpaw, J.R., et al.: Brain-computer interface technology: a review of the first international meeting. IEEE Trans. Rehabilitation Eng. **8**(2), 164–173 (2000)
2. Nicolas-Alonso, L.F., Gomez-Gil, J.: Brain computer interfaces, a review. Sensors **12**(2), 1211–1279 (2012)
3. Roy, A.M.: Adaptive transfer learning-based multiscale feature fused deep convolutional neural network for eeg mi multiclassification in brain-computer interface. Eng. Appl. Artif. Intell. **116**, 105347 (2022)
4. Zhang, R., Li, Y., Yan, Y., Zhang, H., Shaoyu, W., Tianyou, Yu., Zhenghui, G.: Control of a wheelchair in an indoor environment based on a brain-computer interface and automated navigation. IEEE Trans. Neural Syst. Rehabil. Eng. **24**(1), 128–139 (2015)
5. Gupta, A., et al.: A hierarchical meta-model for multi-class mental task based brain-computer interfaces. Neurocomputing, **389**, 207–217 (2020)
6. Moeslund, T.B., Hilton, A., Krüger, V., Sigal, L.: Visual analysis of humans. Springer (2011)
7. Klette, R.: Dimitris N Metaxas, and Bodo Rosenhahn. Understanding, Modelling, Capture, and Animation. Springer, Human Motion (2008)
8. Ionescu, C., Papava, D., Olaru, V., Sminchisescu, C.: Human3. 6m: large scale datasets and predictive methods for 3d human sensing in natural environments. IEEE Trans. Pattern Anal. Mach. Intell. **36**(7), 1325–1339 (2013)
9. Jhuang, D., et al.: Automated home-cage behavioural phenotyping of mice. Nature Commun. **1**(1), 1–10 (2010)

10. Goyal, R., et al.: The "something something" video database for learning and evaluating visual common sense. In: Proceedings of the IEEE International Conference on Computer Vision, pp. 5842–5850 (2017)

11. Zolfaghari, M., Singh, K., Brox, T.: Eco: efficient convolutional network for online video understanding. In: Proceedings of the European Conference on Computer Vision (ECCV), pp. 695–712 (2018)

12. Zhou, B., Andonian, A., Oliva, A., Torralba, A.: Temporal relational reasoning in videos. In: Proceedings of the European conference on computer vision (ECCV), pp. 803–818 (2018)

13. Zhou, B., Andonian, A., Oliva, A., Torralba, A.: Temporal relational reasoning in videos. European Conference on Computer Vision (2018)

14. Shao, H., Qian, S., Liu, Y.: Temporal interlacing network. AAAI (2020)

15. Lin, J., Gan, C., Han, S.: Tsm: temporal shift module for efficient video understanding. In: Proceedings of the IEEE International Conference on Computer Vision (2019)

16. He, K., Zhang, X., Ren, S., Sun, J.: Deep residual learning for image recognition. In: Proceedings of the IEEE Conference on Computer Vision and Pattern Recognition, pp. 770–778 (2016)

17. Chen, T., Kornblith, S., Norouzi, M., Hinton, G.: A simple framework for contrastive learning of visual representations. In: International Conference on Machine Learning, pp. 1597–1607. PMLR (2020)

18. MMAction2 Contributors. Openmmlab's next generation video understanding toolbox and benchmark (2020). https://github.com/open-mmlab/mmaction2

19. Bertasius, G., Wang, H., Torresani, L.: Is space-time attention all you need for video understanding? In: ICML, vol. 2, p. 4 (2021)

20. Franceschi, L., Donini, M., Frasconi, P., Pontil, M.: Forward and reverse gradient-based hyperparameter optimization. In: Precup, D., Teh, Y.W. (eds.) Proceedings of the 34th International Conference on Machine Learning. Proceedings of Machine Learning Research, vol. 70, pp. 1165–1173. PMLR, 06–11 Aug 2017

21. Liu, R., Pan, M., Yuan, X., Zeng, S., Zhang, J.: A general descent aggregation framework for gradient-based bi-level optimization. IEEE Trans. Pattern Anal. Mach. Intell. **45**(1), 38–57 (2023)

22. Liu, R., Liu, Y., Zeng, S., Zhang, J.: Methodology, analysis and extensions, augmenting iterative trajectory for bilevel optimization (2023)

Dual Fusion Network for Hyperspectral Semantic Segmentation

Xuan Ding, Shuo Gu, and Jian Yang[(✉)]

PCA Laboratory, Key Laboratory of Intelligent Perception and Systems for High-Dimensional Information of Ministry of Education, Jiangsu Key Laboratory of Image and Video Understanding for Social Security, School of Computer Science and Engineering, Nanjing University of Science and Technology, Nanjing, China
csjyang@njust.edu.cn

Abstract. With the development of imaging technology, it becomes increasingly easy to obtain hyperspectral images (HSI) containing rich spectral information. The application of hyperspectral images in autonomous driving is expected to become a reality. Hyperspectral images have higher dimensions and more information than RGB images, which brings the challenge of training with limited samples. It is not easy to train satisfactory semantic segmentation models directly from hyperspectral images. In this paper, we propose a hyperspectral dual-fusion (hyperDF) network that can fully utilize the pre-training knowledge of the RGB modality to improve the performance of hyperspectral semantic segmentation. Specifically, we generate pseudo-color images from hyperspectral images to simulate RGB signals in order to make better use of the pre-trained RGB semantic segmentation models. The pseudo-color and hyperspectral images are processed in a dual encoder structure and then fused through a channel-wise attention fusion module. Finally, a multi-scale decoder injected with low-level features is used to predict the semantic segmentation results. Experimental results on the Hyperspectral City V2.0 dataset show that our method achieves state-of-the-art results, with a mIoU of 51.68%.

Keywords: Hyperspectral Image · Semantic Segmentation · Pseudo-color

1 Introduction

Semantic segmentation is a fundamental task in computer vision. The most commonly used input data is RGB image, which works well in simple environments. However, it only contains three bands of information in the visible spectrum. Therefore metamerism [4] makes it challenging to distinguish between similar colors. RGB image is also highly susceptible to different light conditions, such as night, rain, or fog. In recent years, with the advancement of technology, hyperspectral images can be obtained in real-time through snapshot sensors [23], mak-

H. Lu et al. (Eds.): ICIG 2023, LNCS 14356, pp. 149–161, 2023.
https://doi.org/10.1007/978-3-031-46308-2_13

ing the broad application of hyperspectral images possible. Compared with RGB images, hyperspectral images contain more spectrum, which helps distinguish objects with similar colors and cope with complex scenes. Therefore, hyperspectral semantic segmentation has received increasing attention, especially using deep learning methods.

Although the high dimensionality of hyperspectral images provides abundant information, it also poses a challenge to model training [16]. In order to enhance the generalization ability of the hyperspectral model, more training samples are required. Otherwise, performance will be compromised due to the data-hungry problem [18]. Furthermore, hyperspectral imaging entails high storage costs and computational burdens, which restricts the availability of publicly accessible hyperspectral datasets. The absence of large-scale datasets like ImageNet or COCO for RGB images in hyperspectral tasks hinders the feasibility of hyperspectral deep models to leverage general pre-training in the hyperspectral modality.

Considering that RGB-based semantic segmentation is a mature task, and there are many accessible pre-trained models with prior knowledge, we propose a dual fusion network for hyperspectral semantic segmentation. It uses pseudo-color images to fit the pre-trained models and improve the generalization capabilities. The hyperspectral images are used as supplements to improve the segmentation accuracy further. Simultaneously processing the images, the dual encoder generates distinct features which are then merged through a spectral feature fusion module to obtain a more discriminative representation. The resulting representation is fed into a multi-scale decoder to predict the segmentation map. Our contributions can be summarized as follows:

1) We propose a dual fusion network for hyperspectral semantic segmentation, which can deal with the data-hungry problem of hyperspectral data by using the knowledge of pre-trained RGB models.
2) We design a spectral feature fusion module to fuse the pseudo-color and hyperspectral image features effectively.
3) The proposed hyperDF network achieves state-of-the-art performance on the Hyperspectral City V2.0.

2   Related Work

2.1   Segmentation Task

Semantic segmentation is a visual task that predicts semantic categories for each pixel of an input image. With the rise of deep learning methods, researchers have focused on designing various neural network structures for segmentation. Encoder-decoder networks have been proven effective, as the encoder can generate feature maps at different scales, fully capturing high-level semantics, and the decoder gradually restores the resolution to obtain per-pixel classification results at the original resolution. FCN [17] is a milestone work in the encoder-decoder form. Subsequent works such as UNet [20], SegNet [2], PSPNet [30], Deep-Labv3

[5], HRNet [22], etc. have made significant progress. Afterward, attention mechanisms became a focus of research, with researchers incorporating non-local and self-attention modules into semantic segmentation networks, for example, DANet [8]. Recently, transformer-based structures have led to a new wave of research, producing works such as SegFormer [26] in semantic segmentation.

2.2 HSI Data Augmentation

The scarcity of hyperspectral data has become a common problem in the field. Li et al. [14] summarized the problem of sample limitation in remote sensing. Liu et al. [16] discovered the impact of the data-hunger problem on hyperspectral object tracking tasks. These findings demonstrate the importance of research in addressing data scarcity.

Data augmentation is the most intuitive solution to address the aforementioned problems. The data augmentation methods for hyperspectral images can be mainly categorized into handcrafted methods and deep generative models. Data augmentation through transformations and random noise has been widely used in hyperspectral data augmentation. Sun et al. [21] proposed a permutation-based sample generation method. Zhu et al. [31] used GAN to generate pseudo-samples with class labels and used them to train the discriminative network to improve the generalization performance. Wang et al. [25] proposed a conditional variational autoencoder with an adversarial training process to generate training samples that satisfy spectral constraints, which improved the diversity and spectral realism of generated samples. Besides, there are many other similar approaches to generating synthetic samples. However, due to the spectral complexity of hyperspectral images, it is difficult to judge whether the generated spectral fingerprints are realistic. Therefore, the stability of these methods in more diverse scenarios still needs further verification.

2.3 Transfer Learning

Transfer learning is a method that can apply knowledge learned from source domain data to target data. Research on transfer learning in HSI focuses on cross-scene transfer learning.

Early studies on cross-scene transfer learning often used the approach of directly transferring network parameters. Yang et al. [28] directly copied the middle and low-level network trained on the source domain and trained the top layer on the target domain data. Kemker and Kanan [13] proposed to extract features from a large number of unlabeled samples using unsupervised methods and then apply them to the source domain. However, these methods can only be applied to data collected by the same sensor, as only then can the same spectral setting be shared. Subsequent research focused on learning domain adaptation from both source and target data. Wang et al. [24] designed a dual-stream network with a cross-domain attention module to learn the transfer process end-to-end. Zhang et al. [30] proposed a cross-domain learning framework based on graph information aggregation, which aligns cross-domain graphs at the feature and distribution levels to mitigate the impact of domain shift. Overall, these studies make full use of existing remote sensing datasets and effectively alleviate the performance degradation problem of networks under small samples. However, their performance in autonomous driving scenarios still needs further research.

3   Proposed Method

Overview: We propose a dual fusion network for processing hyperspectral and pseudo-color images, as shown in Fig. 1. The network consists of three main parts: 1. dual encoders for hyperspectral and pseudo-RGB features; 2. spectral feature fusion module(SFF); 3. multi-scale decoders with low-level feature injection. The network first learns features for hyperspectral and pseudo-color inputs separately and then obtains modality-fused features through the spectral feature fusion module. Finally, the multi-scale decoder with low-level feature injection is used to obtain accurate semantic segmentation results.

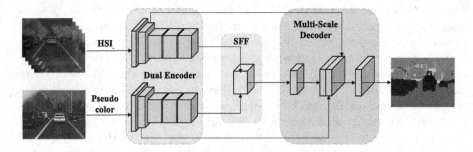

Fig. 1. The flowchart of the proposed dual fusion network.

3.1   Dual Encoder

Firstly, we use HSI to generate pseudo-color images to simulate RGB signals. For real-time applications, we simplify the color space conversion and do not consider the influence of the spectral response curves of different sensors. Based on the spectral resolution of hyperspectral images, we select three channel responses in the RGB bands and then perform channel normalization to synthesize the pseudo-color image. These pseudo-color images are distributed similarly to RGB images, so using common backbone structures as encoders is very effective. It is also easy to train and converge after initializing with pre-trained parameters.

Then, we use a backbone initially designed for RGB as the HSI encoder, using a deep stem module consisting of multiple convolution blocks to adjust different input channels. We initialize the model with the pre-trained parameters of RGB images. Similar research has already existed in related fields [15,16,19].

Intuitively, there may be a gap between HSI data and RGB-based pre-training. However, many studies have shown that pre-trained models may be beneficial for training cross-modal data tasks, even if the target modality has never been used during pre-training, such as 2D-3D [27], RGB-infrared [29].

As mentioned above, we propose a dual-feature encoder that takes the hyperspectral image and the generated pseudo-color image as inputs and learns separate backbones to extract features for each modality. By independently training each encoder branch and then jointly training the two encoders for subsequent network learning, we ensure that the features learned for each modality have distinct characteristics and can complement each other by filling in the missing information.

3.2 Spectral Feature Fusion Module

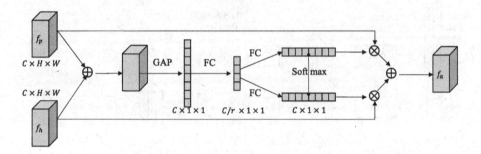

Fig. 2. The spectral feature fusion module.

To handle the hyperspectral features f_h and pseudo-color features f_p obtained by the encoder, our method uses a spectral feature fusion module to obtain the fused feature f_a for information complementation, as shown in Fig. 2. Considering that the main difference between the two modalities lies in the spectral dimension information, we borrow the SE block design from SENet [10] to create the channel attention fusion module. First, the global channel feature f_c with coarse fusion is predicted as follows:

$$f_c = \mathrm{GAP}(f_h + f_p) \tag{1}$$

where GAP stands for global average pooling.

The squeeze and excitation operations are performed by three fully connected layers. First, the f_c feature is compressed to a dimension of C/r. Then, two C-dimensional attention vectors for the two modalities are expanded, which can be represented as:

$$a_h = \mathrm{FC}_h(\mathrm{FC}_g(f_c)) \tag{2}$$

$$a_p = \mathrm{FC}_p(\mathrm{FC}_g(f_c)) \tag{3}$$

The attention weights w_h and w_p can be obtained by applying softmax between the corresponding positions of the two attention vectors. The final calculation for attention-weighted feature fusion is as follows:

$$f_a = w_h * f_h + w_p * f_p \tag{4}$$

With the proposed spectral feature fusion module, we obtain a comprehensive feature in the spectral dimension, compensating for the spectral information lost during the excessive dimension reduction process and enhancing the discriminative power of the RGB modality representation.

3.3   Multi-Scale Decoder with Low-Level Feature Injection

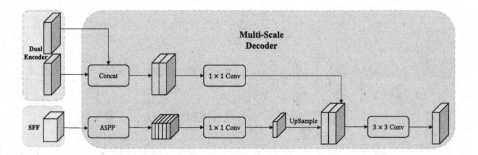

Fig. 3. The multi-scale decoder with low-level feature injection.

Referring to the work of Deeplabv3+ [6], we construct a multi-scale decoder that fuses low-level features, as shown in Fig. 3. The previously fused feature f_a is input into an Atrous Spatial Pyramid Pooling (ASPP) module [5], which obtains contextual information at different scales through dilated convolutions and image pooling with different dilation rates, and then aggregates multi-scale semantic features through 1×1 convolution along the channel dimension. We use low-level features encoded from the HSI and pseudo-color images to inject details into semantic feature resolution. Specifically, we connect the outputs of the first layer of the dual encoder, which are aggregated through 1×1 convolution, to the high-dimensional semantic features used for upsampling, and jointly predict the semantic segmentation results.

3.4   Training and Loss

We adopt a multi-stage training strategy to ensure that the features learned by the hyperspectral and pseudo-color branches do not interfere with each other and meet the need for complementary missing information. Specifically, we first separately train the segmentation network of each encoder and then fix the learned encoders before training the SFF module and multi-scale decoder. It is worth noting that the pseudo-color image comes from the hyperspectral image, so no additional RGB image assistance is required during training or testing.

During the multi-stage training process, we use the same form of loss function. The loss function for the segmentation network is defined as follows:

$$L = \lambda_1 L_{ce} + \lambda_2 L_{lovasz} \tag{5}$$

where L_{ce} and L_{lovasz} are the cross-entropy loss and the Lovasz-softmax [3] loss, respectively. The Lovasz-softmax loss is a network loss that optimizes the mean intersection over union (IoU) and is based on the convex Lovasz extension of submodular losses. The combination of pixel-level cross-entropy loss and region-based Lovasz-softmax loss improves prediction accuracy, stabilizes the training process, and speeds up convergence.

4   Experiment

4.1   Implementation Details

The proposed method is implemented in the experiment using the Pytorch framework on a server with 2 NVIDIA TITAN RTX GPUs and 64GB RAM. SGD is used to optimize the entire model. The batch size is set to 8 during the training of the pseudo-color branch and 4 at other times due to memory limitations. In the step-by-step training process, the initial learning rate for training the independent encoder is set to 0.01 for 30 epochs, and the learning rate for training SFF and multi-scale decoders is set to 0.001 for 20 epochs. We use a polygon learning rate policy, where the initial learning rate is multiplied by $(1 - \frac{epoch}{total\_epoch})^{0.9}$ after each epoch. The momentum and weight decay coefficients are set to 0.9 and 0.0005, respectively. After experimental validation, we finally set the loss function coefficients to $\lambda_1 = 0.5$ and $\lambda_2 = 1.0$. The widely used ResNet50 [9] is used as the backbone. We initialize the backbone with pre-trained weights on ImageNet during the encoder training phase. Only the trained encoder is loaded in the training of SFF and multi-scale decoders, and the decoder is retrained. During training and testing, we use the $[63, 19, 1]$ channels of hyperspectral images to synthesize three-channel images for input to the pseudo-color branch. Due to the relationship between spectral signals and physical reflection properties, we do not use data augmentation during training.

4.2   Dataset and Evaluation

Hyperspectral City V2 is a hyperspectral image dataset of urban scenes used in the 2021 ICCV Hyperspectral City Challenge [1]. The dataset includes hyperspectral and RGB images, but our method only uses the HSI. The LightGene HS video camera provides 128 spectral channels from 450 to 950nm with 4nm spectral resolution. The RGB and HSI images were cropped to a resolution of

1889×1422 to align perfectly. The dataset contains diverse urban scenes, including crowded city areas, CBDs, highways, suburban roads, university campuses, overpasses, and technology parks, and was collected in various lighting conditions, including day, night, sunset, front lighting, backlighting, and complicated light conditions in the city with many tall buildings.

The dataset is divided into a train set with 1054 images and a test set with 276 images, labeled into 19 classes following the Cityscapes [7] setting by professional labelers. Like many driving datasets, it suffers from severe sample imbalance problems, with the proportion of labeled pixels in different classes presenting a long-tailed distribution.

Intersection-over-union (IoU) and pixel-wise accuracy (Acc) are used to evaluate the performance of different semantic segmentation networks. The mean IoU and Acc of all classes will be used as the comprehensive evaluation metrics of the network on the entire test set.

4.3   Comparisons with State-of-the-Art Methods

We compare our proposed method with several widely used semantic segmentation models in the Hyperspectral City benchmark [12], including FCN [17], CCNet [11], PSPNet [30], HRNet [22], Deeplabv3 [6], and SegFormer [26]. Since we could not obtain the method that won the challenge, we could only list the scores posted on the website [1]. These models initially designed for RGB input are modified by changing the input channel of the first layer to 128 to adapt to the HSI input while keeping other layers unchanged. Due to the high memory consumption of HSIs, we downsample the dataset by 0.5x and set the batch size to 4. In addition, we also compare the performance of these methods on the RGB data provided in the dataset, where the results without using pre-trained parameters are denoted as RGB_non. The experimental results are shown in Table 1, where the best results are highlighted in bold black font.

As shown in Table 1, our experimental result outperforms the simple modifications based on RGB methods in all category evaluation metrics when only using HSI as input. It is 0.28% better than the current known best result in mIoU.

It can be observed that pre-training parameters have a significant impact on the model results under the RGB modality and can improve the mIoU of HRNet by up to 8.55%, bringing it to the best result. Compared with the RGB training results without pre-training parameters, the performance of using an existing network to learn from HSI directly is still inferior. This is because the hyperspectral dataset has high-dimensional features and a lack of sufficient samples, leading to severe problems of the curse of dimensionality and data-hungry. Our method generates pseudo-color images from HSI to simulate RGB signals, which can borrow RGB prior knowledge to achieve better results than the RGB modality without additional input signals.

Upon comparing the segmentation outcomes across various categories, it becomes apparent that the network's learning performance is impressive for most categories. However, the performance could be better for categories with scarce data and small targets. This can be attributed to small targets having limited

Table 1. Comparison of the performance on segmentation models w.r.t mIoU, mAcc and mIoU of each class.

	FCN50	FCN101	CCNet	PSPNet	HRNet	DeepLabv3	SegFormer	hyperDF	champion's
road	89.79	90.44	89.25	89.1	90.41	85.67	44.21	**94.01**	–
sidewalk	27.69	24.53	24.81	25.69	20.69	21.94	12.22	**34.68**	–
building	64.4	65.47	64.34	60.9	61.5	59.86	37.4	**73.2**	–
wall	28.36	31.69	42.59	45.43	43.59	38.84	33.73	**56.99**	–
fence	8.87	14.06	13.04	6.43	8.62	8.32	3.43	**17.53**	–
pole	20.85	20.09	20.23	18.09	18.45	15.89	9.13	**39.59**	–
traffic light	40.79	41.42	41.69	39.96	35.65	39.61	13.46	**66.82**	–
traffic sign	52.91	54.67	55.27	51.52	45.34	45.94	23.08	**65.14**	–
vegetation	77.25	77.63	77.92	76.09	76.68	76.15	39.96	**82.68**	–
terrain	0.81	0.55	0.07	1.01	2.47	1.76	0.14	**2.74**	–
sky	80.71	80.4	80.67	80.29	80.8	81.6	42.08	**88.66**	–
person	19.54	20.8	18.37	15.67	11.89	10.93	8.28	**33.98**	–
rider	30.17	29.55	25.66	29.35	23.4	21.98	11.54	**43.48**	–
car	83.65	85.62	83.54	83.01	82.06	78.05	44.22	**89.86**	–
truck	47.1	48.78	47	40.3	42.01	40.91	19.7	**74.43**	–
bus	65.38	68.22	60.2	70.88	63.81	52.62	43.08	**84.03**	–
train	0	0	0	0	0	0	0	0	–
motorcycle	0	0	0	0	0	0	0	0	–
bicycle	26.21	27.55	5.24	31.46	14.96	26.98	19.54	**34.16**	–
mAcc	53.84	52.19	51.19	53.01	49.42	49.92	28.58	**61.39**	–
mIoU	40.24	41.13	39.47	40.27	40.13	37.21	21.33	**51.68**	51.4
mIoU(RGB)	50.55	51.02	50.78	51.26	**51.76**	50.95	44.34	–	–
mIoU(RGB_non)	47.88	**49.72**	48.72	49.35	43.21	46.84	40.87	–	–

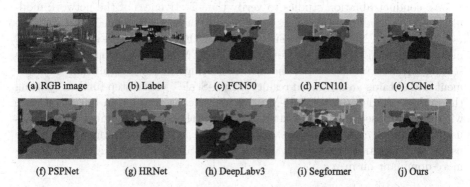

(a) RGB image   (b) Label   (c) FCN50   (d) FCN101   (e) CCNet

(f) PSPNet   (g) HRNet   (h) DeepLabv3   (i) Segformer   (j) Ours

Fig. 4. Semantic segmentation results on Hyperspectral City testing set.

distinguishable features and challenging to differentiate from neighboring categories like fences. Furthermore, as stated earlier, the dataset suffers from a long-tail distribution problem, which leads to a scarcity of training and testing samples for categories such as terrain, train, and motorcycle. These concerns require further investigation in the future.

Fig. 4 displays the semantic segmentation results of models using hyperspectral images as input. It can be observed that most models lose many details.

While the transformer-based SegFormer can identify differences in details, it fails to preserve the spatial shape of the objects. In contrast, our proposed method successfully captures finer details and better maintains the overall shape of the objects. These results demonstrate that the network that incorporates prior knowledge from the RGB modality can effectively capture the targets' spatial and spectral characteristics.

4.4 Ablation Study

Table 2. Ablation study to verify the effectiveness of the module

Method	Modality	mAcc	mIoU
Baseline	hsi	53.84	40.24
FCN	pseudo-color	59.5	50.21
FCN	hsi	60	49.83
Multi-Scale	pseudo-color	61.34	51.52
Multi-Scale	hsi	61.6	51.21
Dual + Multi-Scale	fusion	61.39	51.68

We conduct ablation studies to verify the effectiveness of the network modules, and the experimental results are shown in Table 2. "Baseline" represents the results of the FCN50 model trained directly with hyperspectral images. "FCN" means to train the branch network with the FCN head under our initialization setting and loss function. Our modification brings about a significant improvement and obtains an advanced result. "Multi-Scale" goes a step further by using the multi-scale decoder. "Dual+Multi-Scale" means training in full accordance with our proposed framework. It can be seen that as the number of modules used increases, the mIoU results gradually increase. The learning results of the pseudo-color branch are slightly better than HSI results on mIoU, but HSI is more dominant on mAcc.

5 Conclusion

In this paper, we propose a dual fusion network for hyperspectral semantic segmentation. To solve the training difficulties caused by the hyperspectral image's high dimensionality and data-hungry, it generates pseudo-color images to simulate RGB modality information and fully uses the RGB pre-training knowledge. The dual encoder extracts features from the pseudo-color and hyperspectral images and fuses them through a spectral fusion module. The multi-scale decoder can inject low-level features and capture multi-scale content of fused features to improve segmentation accuracy. Experiments on the Hyperspectral

City V2.0 dataset demonstrate the effectiveness of the proposed method, and our method achieves state-of-the-art results. In the future, we will continue to improve the task of hyperspectral semantic segmentation in urban scenes in the following aspects, including: 1) dimension reduction and efficient feature extraction of hyperspectral data; 2) generation of realistic hyperspectral data; 3) neural network structures that are suitable for hyperspectral characteristics.

Acknowledgment. This work was supported in part by the National Natural Science Foundation of China under Grant 62106106.

References

1. Hyperspectral city challenge (2021). https://pbdl-ws.github.io/pbdl2021/challenge/index.html
2. Badrinarayanan, V., Kendall, A., Cipolla, R.: Segnet: a deep convolutional encoder-decoder architecture for image segmentation. IEEE Trans. Pattern Anal. Mach. Intell. **39**(12), 2481–2495 (2017)
3. Berman, M., Triki, A.R., Blaschko, M.B.: The lovász-softmax loss: a tractable surrogate for the optimization of the intersection-over-union measure in neural networks. In: Proceedings of the IEEE Conference on Computer Vision and Pattern Recognition, pp. 4413–4421 (2018)
4. Cao, X., Tong, X., Dai, Q., Lin, S.: High resolution multispectral video capture with a hybrid camera system. In: CVPR 2011, pp. 297–304. IEEE (2011)
5. Chen, L.C., Papandreou, G., Schroff, F., Adam, H.: Rethinking atrous convolution for semantic image segmentation. arXiv preprint arXiv:1706.05587 (2017)
6. Chen, L.-C., Zhu, Y., Papandreou, G., Schroff, F., Adam, H.: Encoder-decoder with atrous separable convolution for semantic image segmentation. In: Ferrari, V., Hebert, M., Sminchisescu, C., Weiss, Y. (eds.) ECCV 2018. LNCS, vol. 11211, pp. 833–851. Springer, Cham (2018). https://doi.org/10.1007/978-3-030-01234-2_49
7. Cordts, M., et al.: The cityscapes dataset for semantic urban scene understanding. In: Proceedings of the IEEE Conference on Computer Vision and Pattern Recognition, pp. 3213–3223 (2016)
8. Fu, J., et al.: Dual attention network for scene segmentation. In: Proceedings of the IEEE/CVF Conference on Computer Vision and Pattern Recognition, pp. 3146–3154 (2019)
9. He, K., Zhang, X., Ren, S., Sun, J.: Deep residual learning for image recognition. In: Proceedings of the IEEE Conference on Computer Vision and Pattern Recognition (CVPR) (2016)
10. Hu, J., Shen, L., Sun, G.: Squeeze-and-excitation networks. In: Proceedings of the IEEE Conference on Computer Vision and Pattern Recognition, pp. 7132–7141 (2018)
11. Huang, Z., Wang, X., Huang, L., Huang, C., Wei, Y., Liu, W.: CCNet: criss-cross attention for semantic segmentation. In: Proceedings of the IEEE/CVF International Conference on Computer Vision, pp. 603–612 (2019)

12. iori2333: Hyperspectral city v2 benchmark. https://github.com/iori2333/HSICity V2-Benchmark

13. Kemker, R., Kanan, C.: Self-taught feature learning for hyperspectral image classification. IEEE Trans. Geosci. Remote Sens. **55**(5), 2693–2705 (2017)

14. Li, S., Song, W., Fang, L., Chen, Y., Ghamisi, P., Benediktsson, J.A.: Deep learning for hyperspectral image classification: an overview. IEEE Trans. Geosci. Remote Sens. **57**(9), 6690–6709 (2019)

15. Li, Z., Xiong, F., Zhou, J., Wang, J., Lu, J., Qian, Y.: Bae-net: a band attention aware ensemble network for hyperspectral object tracking. In: 2020 IEEE International Conference on Image Processing (ICIP), pp. 2106–2110. IEEE (2020)

16. Liu, Z., Wang, X., Zhong, Y., Shu, M., Sun, C.: Siamhyper: learning a hyperspectral object tracker from an RGB-based tracker. IEEE Trans. Image Process. **31**, 7116–7129 (2022)

17. Long, J., Shelhamer, E., Darrell, T.: Fully convolutional networks for semantic segmentation. In: Proceedings of the IEEE Conference on Computer Vision and Pattern Recognition, pp. 3431–3440 (2015)

18. Lu, J., Gong, P., Ye, J., Zhang, C.: Learning from very few samples: a survey. arXiv preprint arXiv:2009.02653 (2020)

19. Pan, B., Shi, Z., Xu, X., Shi, T., Zhang, N., Zhu, X.: CoinNet: copy initialization network for multispectral imagery semantic segmentation. IEEE Geosci. Remote Sens. Lett. **16**(5), 816–820 (2018)

20. Ronneberger, O., Fischer, P., Brox, T.: U-net: convolutional networks for biomedical image segmentation. In: Navab, N., Hornegger, J., Wells, W.M., Frangi, A.F. (eds.) MICCAI 2015. LNCS, vol. 9351, pp. 234–241. Springer, Cham (2015). https://doi.org/10.1007/978-3-319-24574-4_28

21. Sun, H., Zheng, X., Lu, X.: A supervised segmentation network for hyperspectral image classification. IEEE Trans. Image Process. **30**, 2810–2825 (2021)

22. Sun, K., et al.: High-resolution representations for labeling pixels and regions. arXiv preprint arXiv:1904.04514 (2019)

23. Vunckx, K., Charle, W.: Accurate video-rate multi-spectral imaging using imec snapshot sensors. In: 2021 11th Workshop on Hyperspectral Imaging and Signal Processing: Evolution in Remote Sensing (WHISPERS), pp. 1–7. IEEE (2021)

24. Wang, C., Ye, M., Lei, L., Xiong, F., Qian, Y.: Cross-domain attention network for hyperspectral image classification. In: IGARSS 2022–2022 IEEE International Geoscience and Remote Sensing Symposium, pp. 1564–1567. IEEE (2022)

25. Wang, X., Tan, K., Du, Q., Chen, Y., Du, P.: Cva 2 e: a conditional variational autoencoder with an adversarial training process for hyperspectral imagery classification. IEEE Trans. Geosci. Remote Sens. **58**(8), 5676–5692 (2020)

26. Xie, E., Wang, W., Yu, Z., Anandkumar, A., Alvarez, J.M., Luo, P.: Segformer: simple and efficient design for semantic segmentation with transformers. Adv. Neural. Inf. Process. Syst. **34**, 12077–12090 (2021)

27. Xu, C., et al.: Image2point: 3D point-cloud understanding with 2d image pretrained models. In: ECCV 2022, Part XXXVII. LNCS, vol. 13697, pp. 638–656. Springer, Cham (2022). https://doi.org/10.1007/978-3-031-19836-6_36

28. Yang, J., Zhao, Y.Q., Chan, J.C.W.: Learning and transferring deep joint spectral-spatial features for hyperspectral classification. IEEE Trans. Geosci. Remote Sens. **55**(8), 4729–4742 (2017)

29. Zhang, P., Zhao, J., Wang, D., Lu, H., Ruan, X.: Visible-thermal UAV tracking: a large-scale benchmark and new baseline. In: Proceedings of the IEEE/CVF Conference on Computer Vision and Pattern Recognition, pp. 8886–8895 (2022)

30. Zhao, H., Shi, J., Qi, X., Wang, X., Jia, J.: Pyramid scene parsing network. In: Proceedings of the IEEE Conference on Computer Vision and Pattern Recognition, pp. 2881–2890 (2017)
31. Zhu, L., Chen, Y., Ghamisi, P., Benediktsson, J.A.: Generative adversarial networks for hyperspectral image classification. IEEE Trans. Geosci. Remote Sens. **56**(9), 5046–5063 (2018)

Strip-FFT Transformer for Single Image Deblurring

Lei Liu[1], Yulong Zhu[2], Haoyu Zhang[2], Weifeng Zhang[2], and Hong Peng[3(✉)]

[1] Medical College, Shantou University, Shantou 515041, China
[2] College of Engineering, Shantou University, Shantou 515063, China
[3] College of Computer and Information Engineering, Hanshan Normal University, Chaozhou 521041, China
stp_ph@126.com

Abstract. The purpose of image deblurring is to restore the origin image from the blurred image. With the development of deep learning, better performance for image deblurring can be obtained through the deblurring methods based on CNNs, while limited ability to model the global relationship, therefore its treatment of the correlation between the original resolution pixels is relatively weak. The hot Transformer approaches have a better ability to model the global context in the early stage, howerver, the disadvantage is that it is computational complexity. In addition, using only spatial features for image deblurring may lead to poor recovery of frequency domain information from the deblurred images, and frequency domain information is also key features for image deblurring. Therefore, we propose the SFT (Strip-FFT Transformer) method, which uses a hybrid architecture of CNNs and transformers to reduce the computational complexity, and a strip-fft Attention Block that integrates attention and Res-FFT mechanism to simultaneously process spatial and frequency domain information. After experiments, it is proved that SFT can obtain state-of-the-art effect in dynamic scene deblurring with relatively low memory consumption and computational complexity.

Keywords: image deblurring · transformer · FFT

1 Introduction

Blurring is a common phenomenon that occurs during digital signal transmission. It usually caused by camera shakes and moving of the subject during shooting process, and this phenomenon is unwanted for most people. Dynamic scene image deblurring is a more difficult and meaningful way of deblurring scenes, including global and local non-uniform blurring that is closer to real scene blurring.

Traditional blind deblurring methods are usually limited by the requirement of estimating blur kernel [14,20]. Since image deblurring is a highly ill-posed problem and real scenes may contain both global and local nonuniform blurs, the estimated blur kernel approach may not suitable for complex real scene deblurring. To solve the dynamic deblurring problem of real scenes, some approaches

H. Lu et al. (Eds.): ICIG 2023, LNCS 14356, pp. 162–174, 2023.
https://doi.org/10.1007/978-3-031-46308-2_14

try to use convolution neural networks (CNNs) [11,13,15] to improve performance of image deblurring. Comparing with the traditional methods, CNN-based methods has advantages of increasing deblurring performance, suitable for more complex blur scene and saving time of manual adjustment to parameters and complex iterating inference.

In order to make the best use of the powerful non-linear capabilities of CNNs to solve the problem of image deblurring. Recent methods mainly using architecture like single-scale (SS) [17] and recurrent architectures like multi-scale (MS) [2,3,10,11,15], multi-patch (MP) [23,24]. Recently, the self attention mechanism based transformers achieve great success in natural language processing (NLP) domain. Using transformer based architectures in deblurring task is relatively novel, and some major architectures and modules are not satisfactory. Flattening the images or feature maps as input of transformer model will greatly increase the complexity and cost of computation and memory. Therefore, it requires some methods to reduce complexity when using transformer in image debulrring area. Wang et al. [19] proposed Uformer similar to the idea of ViT (Vision Transformer) [6] using a fixed slicing window approach. Zamir et al. [22] propose Restormer, which explicitly generates the global contextual attention graph by computing cross-covariance across channels. hybrid architecture [16], specifically based on the U-shaped network architecture, where the front layer uses stacked CNNs to embedding input features and reduce the spatial dimension of features.

Inspired by the strip attention (SA) [16] which is more comply with characteristic of blur and the idea of using frequency domain information [1,10]. We applied a new network SFT (Strip-FFT Transformer) and a new attention module in the deblurring task. Our proposed SFA (Strip-FFT-Attention Block) is capable of simultaneously taking both spatial directionality and frequency domain information into consideration in blurred information, and better modeling long-range dependence. Specifically, our method can greatly reduce computation complexity compared with Transformer architecture, and it can more efficiently exploit embedded features of images by using the Res Block [11] of CNNs with localization and other inductive bias modules in the front layer. Secondly, for the bottom layer, we will use the interleaved overlapping intra and inter- SFA similar with [16] to model blur features in multiple dimensions to promote model convergence. Since our proposed SFA (Strip-FFT-Attention Block) module has a Res-FFT branch, it enables the attention module with global modeling capability to control the features in the frequency domain at the same time. For downstream tasks such as image deblurring, the information in the frequency domain is also crucial, especially for solving the cases where the blur is more severe due to faster object motion, and some boundaries, etc. The information in the frequency domain can be used to supplement the information in cases where information is lost.

SFT adopts the SFA (Strip-FFT-Attention Block). It is a attention mechanism based module that is more suitable to blur characteristic, easier to form the corresponding inductive bias, can better fuse the information in the space and frequency domains. In addition, SFT requires much less memory and computational complexity than a normal transformer. According to the experiments, SFT achieves state-of-the-art (SOTA) results in terms of image recovery quality and computational speed compared to other deblurring methods.

2   Related Works

CNN-Based Deblurring Method. CNN-based method is good at capturing local and high frequency features, and it has local connectivity and translation equivariance, which makes CNN-based method achieves considerable performance with less parameters comparing with Transformer-based method. The CNN-based methods mainly includes network architectures like MS (multi-scale), MP (multi-patch) and SS (single-scale). Nah *et al.* [11] proposed a muti-scale network architecture that process image from coarse one to explicit one, and the stacked Res Block is adopted to singly remove the blurs at corresponding scale and its output will be up sampled then combining with next layer to supplement deblurring information at bottom scale. Zhu *et al.* [26] applied the deformable convolution in multi-scale network. Cho *et al.* [3] proposed a Encoder-Decoder structure which is the combination of three layers of Encoder-Decoder branch, and added a Asymmetric feature fusion (AFF) module between largest and secondly largest scale to fuse information at different scales. This method can substantially reduce parameters of network and improve information transmission in network. Zhang *et al.* [24] proposed multi-patch architecture (MP), which alters down-sampling methods that change different feature scales to method that splits blocks at spatial dimension. Zamir *et al.* [23] proposed a cross-stage feature fusion (CSFF) module based on multi-patch architecture, which connects scales of two adjacent Encoder-Decoder layers. [17] proposed a deblurring method based on single-scale architecture (SS), which adopts multi-kernel strip pooling (MKSP) to capture blurs within rectangular range. And it also uses parallel dilated convolution (PDC) to expand range of receptive field.

Transformer-Based Deblurring Method. Due to the demand of large numbers of data in pre-training stage, Transformer-based deblurring method has considerable potentiality although it has shorter development time. Wang *et al.* [19] suggested to substitute global attention mechanism with locally-enhanced window (LeWin) Transformer block which has non-overlapping widow. Thus, making the Transformer model can be applied in image deblurring. Zamir *et al.* [22] proposed a transformer-based deblurring method called Restormer. They also designed a Multi-Dconv Head Transposed Attention (MDTA) module that is capable of saving large computation cost by calculating cross-covariance of channel dimension. Tsai *et al.* Stripformer suggested to reduce model complexity through hybrid CNNs and Tansformer architectures. Their network can exploit original feature by stacking Res Block [11]. And using U-shaped network to generating multi-scale features. Finally, the Inductively biased parameters that corresponding with blurring direction and amplitude can be learned by the bottom strip transformer.

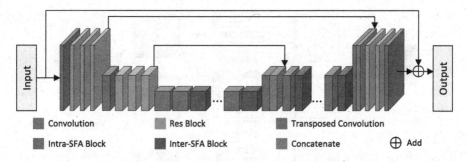

Fig. 1. Architecture of SFT (Strip-FFT Transformer). Convolution layer and Res Blocks [11] are used to embed the features of front layer and back layer. The bottom layer adopts Intra-SFA Block and Inter-SFA.

Fast Fourier Transform Applications. FFT method has been applied in downstream vision task such as image deblurring for a long time. Due to its success in traditional methods [5,12,18], more and more researchers started to use frequency domain information in deep learning based methods [10,21,25,27]. Yang *et al.* [21] proposed the FDA which is able to exploit frequency domain information then apply in semantic segmentation tasks. Zhao *et al.* [25] proposed a module to exploit frequency domain information to help with image classification. For image deblurring tasks, [27] adopted wavelet transform to help deblurring of image. Mao *et al.* [10] recommended to apply FFT residual branch in Res Block, and designed a Res FFT-Conv Block to exploit information from frequency domain to help deblurring of image.

3   Methods

3.1   Overview

The overview of our proposed Strip-FFT-Trans architecture is depicted in Fig. 1. The multi-scale U-shaped Transformer is adopted as our basic structure, which is capable of processing the features at different scales including full, half and quarter of the original resolution through layer 1, 2 and 3 respectively. The Encoder-Decoder structure has used to encode the different feature scales through down sampling which is able to keep the spatial consistency between deblurring images and blurring images and also convenient for the network to exploit features.

3.2   Basic Flow

Firstly, the blurring image B will be passed to a single convolution layer to do embedding encode to produce embedding features before transmit it to the whole Transformer. As shown in Fig. 3, the embedding features that has same resolution to original image B will be processed by three layer of Res-Conv Block [11],

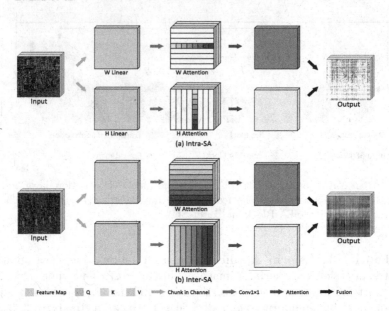

Fig. 2. Illustration of (a) Intra-Strip Attention (Intra-SA) Block and (b) Inter-Strip Attention (inter-SA) Block [16].

which can ensure desirable balance between network performance and complexity. Subsequently, after process of learnable down sampling implemented by 3×3 convolution, the resolution of output features will be half to the original image. Then, the features will be transmitted to another 3 layer Res-Conv Block and 3×3 convolution, the output feature resolution will be quarter to the original image. At the bottom of network, we will stack Strip-FFT-Transformer to process the features with smallest resolution. For Strip-FFT-Transformer, the design of Intra-FFT-SA and Inter-FFT-SA is inspired by [16]. As shown in Fig. 3, the interactively multi-dimension and multi-direction features are generated by attention between intra- and inter- that is vertical, and the FFT branch can exploit frequency domain features then further blend with spatial feature. Through this step interaction between long and short distance can be better controlled. After crossed process of Intra-FFT-SA and Inter-FFT-SA, the transposed convolution will be used as learnable up sampling. Next, according to the U-shaped network structure, the corresponding half scale features exploited by Encoder will combine with features processed by up sampling up at the channel dimension then this output will be transmitted to second layer as input features. For the consideration of keeping details of corresponding scale, the stacked Transformer is still used in the second layer of Decoder instead of using stacked Res-Conv Block. Besides, in order to ensure network has better performance and shorter training time, the first layer of Decoder will use the similar up sampling and fusion mechanism. And after stacking Res-Conv Block layers, we can get decoding features with same resolution to original image. Finally, the deblurring image obtained by residual connection of input blurring image and the decoding features.

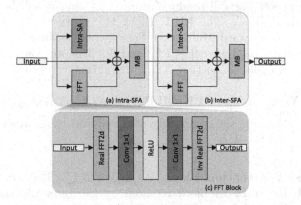

Fig. 3. The process of (a) Intra-SFA (Intra-Strip-FFT Attention), (b) Inter-SFA (Inter-Strip-FFT Attention) and (c) Res-FFT brach.

3.3   Strip-FFT Attention Block

Similar to [16], the underlying processing of the SFT is alternated between the Intra-SFA block and the Inter-SFA block. Its detailed implementation will be described as follow.

Intra-Strip-FFT Attention Block. As shown in Fig. 3(a), an Intra-SFA (Intra-Strip-FFT Attetion Block) is constituted by parallel Intra-SFA-H (horizontal intra-strip attention) and Intra-SFA-V (vertical intra-strip attention), which is corresponding to horizontal and vertical direction respectively. The process of Intra-SA [16] is shown in Fig. 2(a). The process of Res-FFT brach is shown in Fig. 3(c). The blur has characteristic of motion direction. So, using strip attentions that corresponding to horizontal and vertical direction is able to make the transformer module more conform to inductive bias of blur. In addition, for the purpose of better capturing frequency domain information that useful to low-level image tasks. We add the Res-FFT branch to extract frequency domain information that generated by fast fourier transform of images, and residual connection is also used between Res-FFT branch and two parallel strip attentions. The formula is shown below.

$$
\begin{aligned}
\left(X^h, X^v\right) &= \mathbf{Conv}(\mathbf{Norm}(X)), \\
A^h, A^v &= \mathbf{Intra} - \mathbf{SA}\left(X^h, X^v\right), \\
X_{out} &= \mathbf{Conv}\left(\mathbf{Concate}\left(A^h, A^v\right)\right) + \mathbf{FFT_{Res}}\left(X\right) + X.
\end{aligned}
\tag{1}
$$

Norm represents LayerNorm layer, **Conv** stands for 1×1 convolution layer, **Intra** − **SA** indicate horizontal and vertical Intra-strip attention mechanism. **FFT**$_{Res}$ indicates fast fourier processing branch.

The above processing will produce result X_{out}, and it will be further processed by a **MLP** Block. The **MLP** Block is constructed by a single layer of LayerNorm, feed-forward MultiLayer Perceptron, residual connection, Conditional Positional Encodings [4] (CPE) and 3×3 depth convolution, and all connections are residual connection. The formula is shown below.

$$X_{Intra-SFA} = \mathbf{CPE}\left(\mathbf{MLP}\left(\mathbf{Norm}\left(X_{out}\right)\right) + X_{out}\right) \tag{2}$$

By using strip attention, the complexity of the overall transformer module corresponds to $\mathcal{O}\left(HW^2 + WH^2\right)$.

Inter-Strip-FFT Attention Block. As shown in Fig. 3(b), similar to Intra-SFA, but with the Intra-SA block replaced by the Inter-SA block [16]. The process of Intra-SA is shown in Fig. 2(b). In contrast to the Intra-SA block, the Inter-SA block merges the channel direction with the other two directions (H or W) separately for the calculation of the Self-Attention mechanism. This method has advantage of learning more direction information and disadvantage of difficult to convergence in the training. Thus, we use the similar Intra-FFT-SA and Inter-FFT-SA that has interactively stacked structure to facilitate convergence of our model. Its total mathematical expression is shown below.

$$\begin{aligned}
\left(X^h, X^v\right) &= \mathbf{Conv}(\mathbf{Norm}(X)), \\
A^h, A^v &= \mathbf{Inter} - \mathbf{SA}\left(X^h, X^v\right), \\
O_{attn} &= \mathbf{Conv}\left(\mathbf{Concate}\left(A^h, A^v\right)\right) + \mathbf{FFT}_{branch}\left(X\right) + X, \\
O_{Inter-SFA} &= \mathbf{CPE}\left(\mathbf{MLP}\left(\mathbf{Norm}\left(O_{attn}\right)\right) + O_{attn}\right).
\end{aligned} \tag{3}$$

where **Inter** − **SA** denotes Inter-SA block calculation

3.4   Loss Function

In order to ensure improvement of network performance and prove that the our proposed FFT branch is capable of increasing performance. We decided to use the same loss function with [16]. The formula is shown below.

$$L = L_{char} + \lambda_1 L_{edge} + \lambda_2 L_{con} \tag{4}$$

where L_{char} and L_{edge} are the Charbonnier loss and the edge loss from MPRNet [23], and L_{con} is the contrastive loss from [16]. We set $\lambda_1 = 0.05$ and $\lambda_2 = 0.0005$.

4   Experiments

4.1   Dataset and Implementation Details

The baseline GoPro [11] datasets will be used to train our model. All blur images in this datasets are obtained by average result of a series of photo from a fast camera, which can more similar with blurs from real scene. Training set includes 2,013 blurred and sharp pairs, and the test set includes 1,111 pairs. All image size are 1280×720. In addition, the Lai's dataset will be used to test our model quanlitative analysis comparison.

(a) Blur   (b) MPRNet   (c) Stripformer   (d) SFT (ours)   (e) sharp

Fig. 4. Image deblurring comparisons. Left is (a) original blur image from GoPro test dataset. From left to right are (b) MPRNet [23], (c) Stripformer [16], (d) SFT (ours), (e) sharp image.

We adopts Adam [7] optimizer with learning rate of 10^{-4}, and the learning rate will fade to 10^{-7} by csoine annealing strategy. The random flipping and rotation will be applied in data augmentation. We will test our well-trained SFT model on GoPro testing set [11] and Lai's dataset [9]. As for the training process, we will use randomly cropped images with size of 256×256 at pretraining stage; Then, we will train our model with randomly cropped images with size of 512×512. The epoch is 3000 and 1000 respectively, the batch size will be 4 and 1. Experimental device: an NVIDIA 4090 GPU.

4.2   Experimental Results

Quantitative Analysis. We compared our model with current CNN-based [3,8,11,15,23,24] and Transformer-based [16,19,22] SOTA deblurring methods on GoPro testing set. And the comparison results are shown in Table 1. Our proposed strip-FFT-Attention module can better learn inductive bias parameters that related to deblurring and it is also capable of exploit the combined information of spatial domain and frequency domain. Thus, compared with other methods, our SFT method achieves SOTA scores on both PSNR and SSIM evaluation standard. [16] said the deblurring tasks need modules similar with strip attention to learn inductive bias parameters to reduce influences from less data

Table 1. Performance comparasion on GoPro test dataset [11]. The best score in each column is highlighted, and second best is underlined.

Model	PSNR	SSIM	Params
CNN-based models			
DeepDeblur [11] (2017, cvpr)	29.23	0.916	<u>12</u>
DeblurGAN-v2 [8] (2019, cvpr)	29.55	0.934	68
SRN [15] (2018, cvpr)	30.26	0.934	**7**
DMPHN [24] (2019, cvpr)	31.20	0.945	22
MIMO-UNet [3] (2021, cvpr)	32.45	0.957	16
MPRNet [23] (2021, cvpr)	32.66	0.959	20
Transformer-based models			
Uformer [19] (2022, cvpr)	32.97	0.967	–
Restormer [22] (2022, cvpr)	32.92	0.961	–
Stripformer [16] (2022, eccv)	<u>33.08</u>	<u>0.962</u>	20
SFT (ours)	**33.15**	**0.963**	31

numbers at pre-training stage. Experiment results on Lai's dataset [9] are shown in Fig. 5. All model are only trained on GoPro training set.

Quanlitative Analysis. Qualitative comparisons of SFT and other methods on GoPro testing dataset and Lai's dataset [9] are shown in Fig. 4 and Fig. 5. And the Fig. 4 shows the deblurring results of GoPro test set, we can notice that our method has better deblurring performance compared with other methods. Our method has more details and texture especially for numbers and characters. SFT use the extra frequency domain information. Thus, we can obtain exquisite results for severe blurs. Figure 5 shows the restoration effects for people and scenery respectively on Lai's datasets. We can see that SFT is capable of achieving considerable deblurring performance for images like People and natural scenery. Therefore, our method is more suitable for image deblurring on real scene.

4.3   Ablation Study

We conducted a ablation study to demonstrate the effectiveness of our proposed modules especially for the Transformer-based hybrid architecture. The comparison results of using FFT branch and not using FFT branch is shown in Table 2. For the purpose of ensuring validity, our architecture and modules are similar to Stripformer [16]. Therefore, the experimental results of without FFT-Res branch is used to compare with Stripformer. Additionally, the 512×512 image size

(a) Blurry	(b) MPRNet [23]	(c) SFT (ours)

Fig. 5. Image deblurring comparisons. Left is (a) original blur image form Lai's test dataset. From left to right are (b) MPRNet [23], (c) SFT (ours).

and merge method as [10,27] is adopted for testing. Our proposed Strip-FFT-Attention has larger number of parameters and FLOPs compared with other methods when tested on GoPro data set, but PSNR, SSIM and other indexes can achieve better scores.

Table 2. Ablation study performance on GoPro test dataset [11]. * means using the slicing crop method [10,27], illustrate as Sect. 4.3.

Model	PSNR	Params(M)	FLOPs(G)
Stripformer* [16]	33.07	**20**	**118.9**
SFT (ours)	**33.15**	31	154.4

4.4   Conclusion

We proposed a novel Transformer-based method SFT (Strip-FFT-Transformer) for single image deblurring. SFT adopts a new Strip-FFT Attention Block which combines strip attention and FFT branch to better capture global contextual information and fuse with features from frequency domain. And it is a hybrid architecture based on Transformer and CNN. The CNN will be applied in front layer to exploit embedded features. The down sampling also included in CNN. For the bottom layer, the Strip-FFT Attention module will be used to finish the cross processing between intra- and inter-band. Thus, we can reduce computational complexity of Transformer and obtain better performance. Thanks to the Intra-SA Block and Inter-SA Block propose by [16], which proved that Transformer could be used in relatively small image deblurring baseline datasets such as GoPro. Our experiments shows that SFT can achieve SOTA performance on GoPro datasets and it is more suitable with circumstances like severely blurring image and images with boundary problems. Compared with previous SOTA methods, Stripformer [16] can achieve desirable performance on the basis of less parameters and computation cost. We hope that our proposed SFT could enlighten more people to design better Transformer-based deblurring methods in the future.

Acknowledgments. This study was supported by Guangdong Provincial Department of Education Characteristic Innovation Project and HanShan Normal university Doctoral Initiation Program.

References

1. Brigham, E.O.: The Fast Fourier Transform and its Applications. Prentice-Hall, Inc., Hoboken (1988)
2. Chen, L., Lu, X., Zhang, J., Chu, X., Chen, C.: HINet: half instance normalization network for image restoration. In: Proceedings of the IEEE/CVF Conference on Computer Vision and Pattern Recognition, pp. 182–192 (2021)
3. Cho, S.J., Ji, S.W., Hong, J.P., Jung, S.W., Ko, S.J.: Rethinking coarse-to-fine approach in single image deblurring. In: Proceedings of the IEEE/CVF International Conference on Computer Vision, pp. 4641–4650 (2021)

4. Chu, X., Tian, Z., Zhang, B., Wang, X., Wei, X., Xia, H., Shen, C.: Conditional positional encodings for vision transformers. arXiv preprint arXiv:2102.10882 (2021)
5. Donatelli, M., Huckle, T., Mazza, M., Sesana, D.: Image deblurring by sparsity constraint on the fourier coefficients. Numer. Algorithms **72**, 341–361 (2016)
6. Dosovitskiy, A., et al.: An image is worth 16×16 words: transformers for image recognition at scale. arXiv preprint arXiv:2010.11929 (2020)
7. Kingma, D.P., Ba, J.: Adam: a method for stochastic optimization. arXiv preprint arXiv:1412.6980 (2014)
8. Kupyn, O., Martyniuk, T., Wu, J., Wang, Z.: Deblurgan-v2: deblurring (orders-of-magnitude) faster and better. In: Proceedings of the IEEE/CVF International Conference on Computer Vision, pp. 8878–8887 (2019)
9. Lai, W.S., Huang, J.B., Hu, Z., Ahuja, N., Yang, M.H.: A comparative study for single image blind deblurring. In: Proceedings of the IEEE Conference on Computer Vision and Pattern Recognition, pp. 1701–1709 (2016)
10. Mao, X., Liu, Y., Shen, W., Li, Q., Wang, Y.: Deep residual fourier transformation for single image deblurring. arXiv preprint arXiv:2111.11745 (2021)
11. Nah, S., Hyun Kim, T., Mu Lee, K.: Deep multi-scale convolutional neural network for dynamic scene deblurring. In: Proceedings of the IEEE Conference on Computer Vision and Pattern Recognition, pp. 3883–3891 (2017)
12. O'Connor, D., Vandenberghe, L.: Total variation image deblurring with space-varying kernel. Comput. Optim. Appl. **67**, 521–541 (2017)
13. Schuler, C.J., Hirsch, M., Harmeling, S., Schölkopf, B.: Learning to deblur. IEEE Trans. Pattern Anal. Mach. Intell. **38**(7), 1439–1451 (2015)
14. Shan, Q., Jia, J., Agarwala, A.: High-quality motion deblurring from a single image. ACM Trans. Graph. (tog) **27**(3), 1–10 (2008)
15. Tao, X., Gao, H., Shen, X., Wang, J., Jia, J.: Scale-recurrent network for deep image deblurring. In: Proceedings of the IEEE Conference on Computer Vision and Pattern Recognition, pp. 8174–8182 (2018)
16. Tsai, FJ., Peng, YT., Lin, YY., Tsai, CC., Lin, CW.: Stripformer: strip transformer for fast image Deblurring. In: Avidan, S., Brostow, G., Cissé, M., Farinella, G.M., Hassner, T. (eds.) Computer Vision - ECCV 2022. ECCV 2022. LNCS, vol. 13679, pp. 146–162. Springer, Cham (2022). https://doi.org/10.1007/978-3-031-19800-7_9
17. Tsai, F.J., Peng, Y.T., Tsai, C.C., Lin, Y.Y., Lin, C.W.: Banet: a blur-aware attention network for dynamic scene deblurring. IEEE Trans. Image Process. **31**, 6789–6799 (2022)
18. Wang, R., Tao, D.: Recent progress in image deblurring. arXiv preprint arXiv:1409.6838 (2014)
19. Wang, Z., Cun, X., Bao, J., Zhou, W., Liu, J., Li, H.: Uformer: a general u-shaped transformer for image restoration. In: Proceedings of the IEEE/CVF Conference on Computer Vision and Pattern Recognition, pp. 17683–17693 (2022)
20. Xu, L., Jia, J.: Two-phase kernel estimation for robust motion deblurring. In: Daniilidis, K., Maragos, P., Paragios, N. (eds.) ECCV 2010. LNCS, vol. 6311, pp. 157–170. Springer, Heidelberg (2010). https://doi.org/10.1007/978-3-642-15549-9_12
21. Yang, Y., Soatto, S.: FDA: fourier domain adaptation for semantic segmentation. in: Proceedings of the IEEE/CVF Conference on Computer Vision and Pattern Recognition, pp. 4085–4095 (2020)

22. Zamir, S.W., Arora, A., Khan, S., Hayat, M., Khan, F.S., Yang, M.H.: Restormer: efficient transformer for high-resolution image restoration. In: Proceedings of the IEEE/CVF Conference on Computer Vision and Pattern Recognition, pp. 5728–5739 (2022)

23. Zamir, S.W., Arora, A., Khan, S., Hayat, M., Khan, F.S., Yang, M.H., Shao, L.: Multi-stage progressive image restoration. In: Proceedings of the IEEE/CVF Conference on Computer Vision and Pattern Recognition, pp. 14821–14831 (2021)

24. Zhang, H., Dai, Y., Li, H., Koniusz, P.: Deep stacked hierarchical multi-patch network for image deblurring. In: Proceedings of the IEEE/CVF Conference on Computer Vision and Pattern Recognition, pp. 5978–5986 (2019)

25. Zhao, X., et al.: Fractional fourier image transformer for multimodal remote sensing data classification. IEEE Trans. Neural Netw. Learn. Syst. (2022)

26. Zhu, K., Sang, N.: Multi-scale deformable deblurring kernel prediction for dynamic scene deblurring. In: Peng, Y., Hu, S.-M., Gabbouj, M., Zhou, K., Elad, M., Xu, K. (eds.) ICIG 2021. LNCS, vol. 12890, pp. 253–264. Springer, Cham (2021). https://doi.org/10.1007/978-3-030-87361-5_21

27. Zou, W., Jiang, M., Zhang, Y., Chen, L., Lu, Z., Wu, Y.: SdwNet: a straight dilated network with wavelet transformation for image deblurring. In: Proceedings of the IEEE/CVF International Conference on Computer Vision, pp. 1895–1904 (2021)

Vision-Language Adaptive Mutual Decoder for OOV-STR

Jinshui Hu[1,2], Chenyu Liu[1,2], Qiandong Yan[2], Xuyang Zhu[2], Jiajia Wu[2], Jun Du[1], and Lirong Dai[1(✉)]

[1] University of Science and Technology of China, Hefei, China
{jshu,cyliu7}@mail.ustc.edu.cn, {jundu,lrdai}@ustc.edu.cn
[2] IFLYTEK Research, Hefei, China
{qdyan,xyzhu8,jjwu}@iflytek.com

Abstract. Recent works have shown huge success of deep learning models for common in vocabulary (IV) scene text recognition. However, in real-world scenarios, out-of-vocabulary (OOV) words are of great importance and SOTA recognition models usually perform poorly on OOV settings. Inspired by the intuition that the learned language prior have limited OOV preformence, we design a framework named Vision Language Adaptive Mutual Decoder (VLAMD) to tackle OOV problems partly. VLAMD consists of three main conponents. Firstly, we build an attention based LSTM decoder with two adaptively merged visual-only modules, yields a vision-language balanced main branch. Secondly, we add an auxiliary query based autoregressive transformer decoding head for common visual and language prior representation learning. Finally, we couple these two designs with bidirectional training for more diverse language modeling, and do mutual sequential decoding to get robuster results. Our approach achieved 70.31% and 59.61% word accuracy on IV+OOV and OOV settings respectively on Cropped Word Recognition Task of OOV-ST Challenge at ECCV 2022 TiE Workshop, where we got 1st place on both settings.

Keywords: Out-of-vocabulary · Scene text recognition

1 Introduction

Scene text recognition (STR) plays an important part on general visual understanding. Despite of the fast developing in computer vision [5,9,10,23] and text recognition [2,6,16,24,25], there are still some problems unsolved in real world scenarios, e.g., the OOV problem. [29] reveals that SOTA methdos perform well on images with words within vocabulary but generalize poorly to images with words outside vocabulary. However, in real-world scenarios OOV words are common and of great importance, for example, toponyms, business names, URLs, random strings, etc. Hence, addapting current systems to recognize OOV instances is a crucial next step forward in terms of both research and application.

H. Lu et al. (Eds.): ICIG 2023, LNCS 14356, pp. 175–186, 2023.
https://doi.org/10.1007/978-3-031-46308-2_15

To help explore this problem, [7] firstly propose a new benchmark that can specifically measure performance over OOV instances. Besides, a challenge named ECCV 2022 Challenge on Out of Vocabulary Scene Text Understanding (OOV-ST) is simultaneously come up, which is held at ECCV 2022 Workshop on Text in Everything (TiE). This benchmark combines common scene-text datasets as training set, i.e. Syn90k [11], ICDAR 2015 [12], TextOCR [26], MLT-19 [22], HierText [20], OpenTextImages [13]. As for the final testset, images with text instances will never occur in the above-mentioned training datasets. This benchmark will serve as the footstone of OOV research and OCR community, we also build our work on it.

In this paper, we aim to build up an adaptive and unified recognition framwork for both IV and OOV instances. Our motivation is, the recognizer shall be able to make decision on how much visual and lingustic info is used, when handling different inputs and decode steps. Our contributions can be summarized as follows:

- We put forward VLAD module, which can adaptively fuse visual or linguistic features at every decode step, leading to a great improvement on OOV instances.
- Besides, we propose a mutual decoding method together with a TransD head and a bidirectional modeling mechanism, which prevent recognizer from overfitting a undirectional language prior and get robuster co-decoding results both in OOV and IV settings.
- We carefully evaluate our proposed VLAMD on official OOV-ST Challenge, which achieves 1st places on both OOV and IV+OOV metric, with a word accuracy of 59.61% and 70.31% respectively. Experimental results have proved the effectiveness of our method.

2   Related Works

With the development of computer vision and deep learnring, performance of STR has been improved significantly. In this section we'll give a brief review of related works for STR and OOV Recogintion.

2.1   Scene Text Recognition

In the past ten years, STR methods evolved from HMM based [2], CTC based [24], to Attention based [4,6,15,16,25,31]. Limited by conditional independence assumption, both HMM and CTC based methods perform a language-free fragmented prediction, and usually need an external language model (LM) [19]. On the other hand, attention based approaches adopt an autoregressive framework, bringing an implicit LM and a more flexible spatial recognition ability. Moreover, ASTER [25] combines a rectification module with an attention decoder to tackle irregular STR, SAR [16] illustrates that a decoder with 2D attention is a strong baseline that achieves SOTA performance on irregular STR, while SATRN [15] extends Transformer [28] to SAR and outperforms most STR methods. Recently, query based parallel decoders are shown comparable preformance on STR, with a dynamic position enhancement branch [31] or an iterative language modeling [6]. Thanks to the development and application of these methods, machines are now able to recognize text in common scenes with a level of accuracy that rivals that of humans, marking a significant breakthrough in the field of text recognition.

2.2 Out-of-vocabulary Text Recognition

Despite the considerable development in STR, its application in scenarios with a high number of OOV words still may fail, e.g. ~20% absolute performance drop from IV to OOV setting [7,29]. However, there are few works aim to tackle OOV problems in text recognition. [29] firstly points a quantitative analysis of OOV text recognition out, reveals the week OOV performance of attention based methods, and proposes a joint learning baseline of attentioned based and segmentation based methods. Inspired by the STR framework of non-autoregressive recognition + LM refinement, RobustScanner [31] designs a decoupled position queried module and dynamicly fuses the positional and language hybrid features, yielding a considerable improvements. These two works have relieved OOV troubles from different views of feature enhancing. On the other direction, [18] proposes context decoupling modules to solve open-set recognition, while [1,21,30] attempt to study self supervised learning in STR, we point out here that these directions will also benifit OOV researches further.

3 Approach

3.1 Overview

The overall training framework can be seen in Fig. 1a. Given an image $\mathbf{I} \in \mathbb{R}^{3 \times H \times W}$, the backbone will firstly encode it to a downsampled visual contextual feature $\mathbf{F} \in \mathbb{R}^{C \times \frac{H}{4} \times \frac{W}{4}}$. Then, both the VLAD module and the TransD module will decode out two results respectively, i.e., the left to right (L2R) and the right to left (R2L) target strings. These different decode modules together with the backbone are jointly trained, where the loss contains four cross entropy loss guided by the GT target and four mutual KL loss between L2R and R2L sequences, see Eq. (12).

3.2 Backbone

For simplicity, a small CNN Plain-ViT backbone is adopted: 1) we use two Conv blocks with each stride 2 to fast downsample, getting a feature map of size $512 \times \frac{H}{4} \times \frac{W}{4}$; 2) we flatten the feature map to $512 \times \frac{HW}{16}$, and send it to a standard transformer encoder used in [28]; 3) Finally, the feature map is reshaped to $512 \times \frac{H}{4} \times \frac{W}{4}$ for decoding.

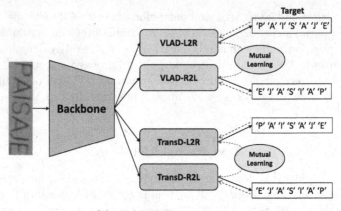

(a) VLAMD Training Framework.

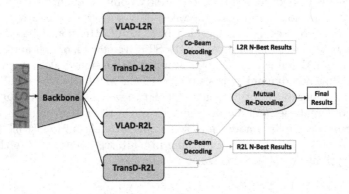

(b) VLAMD Testing Framework.

Fig. 1. Overall framwork of our proposed VLAMD. VLAMD have three key components: VLAD module, TransD module and the Mutual Decoding strategy. VLAD is designed for dynamicly using visual-lingustic infos, TransD is a common query based transformer decoder, and Mutual Decoding is aiming to get robuster resuls and is used both in training and testing. (a) While training, each of VLAD and TransD will take a bidirectional training head, named L2R and R2L. In addition to commom CE loss, VLAD applies a mutual learning manner through cross KL Divergence to distill extra knowledge. Red dashed lines denote the gradient flows back from losses. (b) During testing, different modules with same decoding direction are combined to form a co-beam decoding, then L2R and R2L N-Best results will do a cross teacher forcing re-decoding, named Mutual Re-Decoding. (Color figure online)

3.3   VLAMD

As mentioned before, our vision-language adaptive mutual decoders for text recognition are made up of three building blocks. One is the key Vision Language Adaptive Decoder (VLAD), one is a query based transformer decoder (TransD), and another is the bidirectional training and the mutual decoding strategy.

VLAD. The main decoding branch is based on LAS [4] architecture and coverage attention mechanism [27]. Our key insight for vision-language balanced recognition is that, the adaptive choice ability from vision or language shall be a basic component of our system. To achieve this, we additionally design a position query branch named Positional Aware Attention (PAA) module, together with the reusing of the Visual Aware Attention (VAA), to extract visual-only context. Besides, an Adaptive Gated Fusion module is proposed to adaptively fuse the linguistic enhanced feature and the visual-only features. Figure 2 illustrates VLAD in a detailed manner.

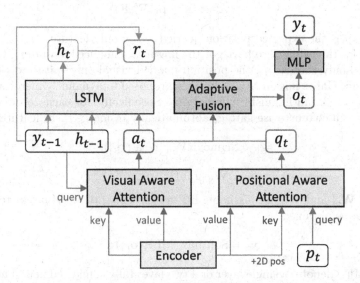

Fig. 2. Detailed structure of VLAD. In addition to the main LSTM decoder, VLAD consists of three sub-modules: a) VAA module in light blue, output a visual-only feature a_t; b) PAA module in light orange red, output a positional aware visual-only feature q_t; c) Adaptive Fusion module in green, form a key dynamic visual-lingustic fusion strategy.

Mathematically, during one decoding step t, a visual-only context is firstly computed using last step's result $\mathbf{y}_{t-1}$, hidden state $\mathbf{h}_{t-1}$, image feature $\mathbf{F}$:

$$\mathbf{a}_t = \text{Attention}([\mathbf{y}_{t-1}; \mathbf{h}_{t-1}], \mathbf{F}, \mathbf{F}), \tag{1}$$

where Attention(*query, *key, *value) denotes a basic attention layer, $\mathbf{a}_t$ is the obtained visual-only feature. For simplicity, we omit coverage attention here, please refer to [27] for detail.

Then, the hidden state $\mathbf{h}_t$ for LSTM cell and the linguistic enhanced feature $\mathbf{r}_t$ are updated by

$$\mathbf{h}_t = \text{LSTM}([\mathbf{y}_{t-1}; \mathbf{a}_{t-1}], \mathbf{h}_{t-1}), \tag{2}$$

$$\mathbf{r}_t = \text{Concat}(\mathbf{h}_t, \mathbf{y}_{t-1}). \tag{3}$$

For position aware attention module, firstly a position embedding layer $\mathbf{P} = [\mathbf{p}_1, \mathbf{p}_2, \cdots, \mathbf{p}_{t'}]$ is learnt for querying, where the index t' denotes the decoding token id. Following [31], a postion enhanced feature $\mathbf{F}'$ is used as the key, and the oringnal $\mathbf{F}$ is used as the value:

$$\mathbf{q}_t = \text{Attention}(\mathbf{p}_t, \mathbf{F}', \mathbf{F}), \tag{4}$$

in which $\mathbf{q}_t$ is the expected position queried visual-only feature.

Now, for time step t, we have got the linguistic enhanced feature $\mathbf{r}_t$, the original visual-only context $\mathbf{a}_t$, the position queried visual-only feature $\mathbf{q}_t$. Finally, an Adaptive Gated Fusion (AGF) block is proposed to dynamicly merge and balance the visual and linguistic infomations. Specifically, for each decoding step, AGF learns a channel-wise gate $\mathbf{g}_t$ aotumatically to merge these features:

$$\mathbf{g}_t = \text{Sigmoid}(\mathbf{W}_m[\mathbf{r}_t; \mathbf{a}_t; \mathbf{q}_t]), \tag{5}$$

$$\mathbf{o}_t = \mathbf{W}_o[\mathbf{g}_t \odot [\mathbf{r}_t; \mathbf{a}_t; \mathbf{q}_t]], \tag{6}$$

in which $\mathbf{W}_m$ and $\mathbf{W}_o$ are learnable FC layers. Then, the final ouput token for step t can be obtained by

$$\mathbf{y}_t = \text{Softmax}(\text{MLP}(\mathbf{o}_t)), \tag{7}$$

Here MLP($\cdot$) denotes a single layer or a two layer fully connected neural network.

TransD. The second branch in our framework is formed by a naive transformer decoder [28]. Given the encoded map $\mathbf{F}$, and a learned position enbedding $\mathbf{Q}'$ similar to Eq. (4), the finaly features $\mathbf{O}' = [\mathbf{o}'_1, \cdots, \mathbf{o}'_t]$ and the ouputs $\mathbf{Y}' = [\mathbf{y}'_1, \cdots, \mathbf{y}'_t]$ can be formulated as:

$$\mathbf{O}' = \text{TransD}(\mathbf{Q}', \mathbf{F}), \tag{8}$$

$$\mathbf{Y}' = \text{Softmax}(\text{MLP}(\mathbf{O}')), \tag{9}$$

where TransD($\cdot$) represents a stack of tranformer decoder layers, with self attention and cross attention in it.

Mutual Decoding. As mentioned before, for each branch, we copy it and construst two decoding targets during training and testing. Specifically, for one target string sequence $\mathbf{S}_{\text{L2R}} = [s_1, s_2, \cdots, s_L]$, we reverse it to $\mathbf{S}_{\text{R2L}} = [s_L, \cdots, s_2, s_1]$ which will be used as the other target. As shown in Fig. 1a, both

VLAD and TransD will be added twice and supervised by $\mathbf{S}_{L2R}$ and $\mathbf{S}_{R2L}$, respectively. We define VLAD's output distribution as $\mathbf{Y}_{L2R}$ and $\mathbf{Y}_{R2L}$, TransD's output distribution as $\mathbf{Y}'_{L2R}$ and $\mathbf{Y}'_{R2L}$, our main loss is:

$$
\begin{aligned}
\mathcal{L}_{main} =\, & \text{CE}(\mathbf{S}_{L2R}, \mathbf{Y}_{L2R}) + \text{CE}(\mathbf{S}_{R2L}, \mathbf{Y}_{R2L}) \\
& + \text{CE}(\mathbf{S}_{L2R}, \mathbf{Y}'_{L2R}) + \text{CE}(\mathbf{S}_{R2L}, \mathbf{Y}'_{R2L}),
\end{aligned} \tag{10}
$$

where $\text{CE}(*gt, *pred)$ is a standard cross entropy loss.

In order to prevent our model from overfiting an unidirectional single language prior, we propose to apply a bidirectional mutual learning strategy: for the same branch, we make them distill from each other using the L2R and R2L head on the every same token. Hence, two cross Kullback-Leibler Divergence (KLD) loss with stop gradient is used:

$$
\begin{aligned}
\mathcal{L}_{mut}(\mathbf{Y}_{L2R}, \mathbf{Y}_{R2L}) =\, & \text{KL}(\mathbf{Y}_{L2R} \,\|\, \text{RS}(\mathbf{Y}_{R2L})) \\
& + \text{KL}(\mathbf{Y}_{R2L} \,\|\, \text{RS}(\mathbf{Y}_{L2R})),
\end{aligned} \tag{11}
$$

where $\text{KL}(p\|q) = \sum_{i=1}^{N} p(x) \log \frac{p(x)}{q(x)}$ denotes a KLD function, $\text{RS}(\cdot)$ denotes a sequence reverse operation followed by a stop gradient layer. The overall loss of our system is:

$$
\begin{aligned}
\mathcal{L}_{total} =\, & \mathcal{L}_{main} + \lambda \cdot \mathcal{L}_{mut}(\mathbf{Y}_{L2R}, \mathbf{Y}_{R2L}) \\
& + \lambda \cdot \mathcal{L}_{mut}(\mathbf{Y}'_{L2R}, \mathbf{Y}'_{R2L}),
\end{aligned} \tag{12}
$$

and λ is a hyper parameter.

VLAMD's inference process is shown clearly in Fig. 1b. Firstly, the two branch VLAD and TransD will do joint co-beam search process twice, yield a left to right N-Best list and a right to left N-Best list. Then, using a cross teacher forcing scheme, our system applys a mutual decoding method:

$$
\mathbb{P}(\mathbf{y}_{pred}|\mathbf{F}) = \mathbf{Y}_{L2R}(\mathbf{y}_{pred}) + \mathbf{Y}_{R2L}(\text{Reverse}(\mathbf{y}_{pred})). \tag{13}
$$

According to Eq. (13), for a decoding path $\mathbf{y}_{pred} = [y_{pred}^1, y_{pred}^2, \cdots, y_{pred}^T]$ from L2R joint co-beam search result, we will send it to R2L joint co-beam search module and vice versa. We found it efficient to acquire robuster results not only in OOV sets but also in IV+OOV settings.

4   Experiments

4.1   Datasets

We evaluate our method on OOV-ST Challenge [7] mentioned in Sect. 1, which contains fine-grained validation and test sets with OOV or IV tags. For training, OOV-ST contains a total of 4.29M real cropped line images collected from several public datasets [12,13,20,22,26], and a corpus of 90K common words [11] for

Table 1. OOV-ST Challenge Results [7] on test set. All results are from the official [7], and we list top 5 methods here accroding to the official OOV CRW metric. Submits from the same affiliation are filted out. Our VLAMD obtains best performance on both OOV and IV+OOV metrics.

Rank	Method	CRW (%)	
		OOV	IV+OOV
1	**VLAMD**	**59.61**	**70.31**
2	SCATTER	59.45	69.58
3	dat	59.03	69.90
4	MaskOCR	58.65	69.63
5	Summer	58.06	68.77

Table 2. Comparison with SOTA STR methods on OOV-ST testset. Our method outperforms others by a large margin. (Note that the SCATTER method here is different with Eq. Table 1 SCATTER, SCATTER in Eq. Table 1 is just a team name.)

Method	CRW (%)	
	OOV	IV+OOV
ABINet [6]	48.55	59.84
UnifiedSTR [3]	53.96	64.97
SCATTER [17]	55.38	66.68
Ours	**59.61**	**70.31**

synthetising new data. Besides, there are 113K cropped lines for validation and 313K cropped lines for testing, respectively (Table 2).

In our experiments, we do not synthesise any data ourselves. Only a subset of Synth90K [11] and SynthText [8] are used for a short pretaining [15], where both are public synthetic datasets using the 90K words. Moreover, we filter out training samples that contain out of dictionary characters, remaining 3.98M real cropped lines for training.

4.2   Training Details

For simplicity, all images are resized to 32×100 for both training and testing, and we do not use any data augmentation tricks. We firstly pretrain the backbone using a simple decoder on synthetic data for 4 epochs, and finetune it on 3.98M real image lines using the proposed VLADM for 10 epochs. An ADAM optimizer with multistep lr decay is adopted, and the base learning rate is set to 1e-4, weight decay is set to 1e-5, batch size is set to 128. λ in Eq. (12) is set to 0.4 after applying a grid search method.

Table 3. Abalation study on OOV-ST validation set. Both OOV and OOV+IV metric used in the challenge are evaluated here. BS means our baseline, and VLAD, TD, MT denotes our proposed VLAD, TransD, bidirectional and mutual decoding strategy respectively. ES denotes our 4-ensemble final model submitted to OOV-ST, in which different seeds and heads are used.

BS	VLAD	TD	MT	S	CRW (%)	
					OOV	IV+OOV
RobustScanner [31]					60.36	71.85
✓					60.42	72.04
✓	✓				60.82	72.35
✓	✓	✓			61.84	73.42
✓	✓	✓	✓		**62.61**	**73.92**
✓	✓	✓	✓	✓	**64.85**	**75.83**

4.3 Comparison with State-of-the-Art Methods

We evaluate VLAMD's performance against state-of-the-art methods using the Correcly Recognized Words (CRW) rate, which is a commonly used metric in speech-to-text recognition (STR) tasks. In Table 1, we compare VLAMD's results with those of other participants on the OOV-ST dataset. It is worth noting that most existing methods struggle to balance performance between in-vocabulary (IV) and out-of-vocabulary (OOV) words, while VLAMD achieves the highest CRW rate in both settings, demonstrating its superior performance.

To further illustrate VLAMD's competitiveness, we compare it with other public state-of-the-art STR methods, including ABINet [6], UnifiedSTR [3], and SCATTER [17], on the OOV-ST dataset [7]. These methods are reimplemented using their source code and evaluated their performance using the CRW rate. As shown in Tab. 2, VLAMD outperforms these methods in both the IV and OOV settings, achieving a CRW rate of 59.61% and 70.31%, respectively, outperform the second-best method SCATTER's 55.38% and 66.78% by a large margin. These results indicate that VLAMD has achieved state-of-the-art performance in STR tasks, especially in handling and balancing both IV and OOV words.

In addition to quantitative evaluations, we also conducted a visual comparison of the outputs generated by different methods. As depicted in Eq. Fig. 3, our analysis indicates that prior techniques suffer from recognition instability and errors when confronted with challenging OOV scenarios, while our proposed VLAMD model exhibits superior and consistent recognition performance. Our conclusion is further bolstered by the compelling evidence presented in the visual comparison, which underscores the effectiveness of our approach.

4.4 Ablation Study

We show the effectiveness of each module in VLAMD on validatioin set, see Tab. 3. Firstly we' reproduce RobustScanner [31] as a strong baseline for

SAR [15]:	tickets.wonsetticktickels	http://www.ameibo.com/bund_...
RobustScanner [25]:	tickets.wonsetticktickels	http://www.ameiba.com/bund_...
SATRN [16]:	bickets.www.sunsettickets	http://www.amelbo.com/bundl.._
Ours:	tickets:www.sunsettickets	http://www.ameibo.com/bundl...

SAR [15]:	heatthCity	BURDICAL_	4580
RobustScanner [25]:	heatthCity	BURDICAL	4580
SATRN [16]:	HealthCriting	BURDICALLY	+580
Ours:	HealthCity	BURDIGALA	￥580

Fig. 3. Visualization of recognition results across different methods. The images samples are from OOV-ST OOV validation set [7]. For the sake of fairness, all models are trained using the same training data and hyperparameters. Wrong charaters are shown in red color.

comparison, using the public code in [14]. And VLAMD's baseline in Table 3 is a simple decoder based on Eq. (3), using [4, 27]. Then, each module designed in Sect. 3 is added to our baseline cumulatively for ablation study. As shown, even our baseline can achieve comparable performance with SOTA OOV method, the proposed VLAD, TransD, Mutual Decoding modules are all effective. Finally, our submitted VLAMD in Table 1 is formed by 4-ensemble models, shown in the last line of Table 3.

5   Conclusion

In this paper, we present VLAMD, an adaptive and unified recognition framework for scene text recognition that addresses the OOV problem and balances both IV and OOV scenarios. Our VLAMD dynamically fuses visual and linguistic information and enables bidirectional mutual learning and decoding, resulting in a significant improvement in both OOV and IV STR. Experimental results show the effectiveness of our proposed method, which outperforms SOTA STR methods by a large margin and won the 2022 ECCV OOV-ST Challenge. We hope this work will inspire further research on this important topic.

References

1. Aberdam, A., et al.: Sequence-to-sequence contrastive learning for text recognition. In: Proceedings of the IEEE/CVF Conference on Computer Vision and Pattern Recognition, pp. 15302–15312 (2021)
2. Alsharif, O., Pineau, J.: End-to-end text recognition with hybrid hmm maxout models. arXiv preprint arXiv:1310.1811 (2013)
3. Baek, J., et al.: What is wrong with scene text recognition model comparisons? dataset and model analysis. In: Proceedings of the IEEE/CVF International Conference on Computer Vision, pp. 4715–4723 (2019)

4. Chan, W., Jaitly, N., Le, Q., Vinyals, O.: Listen, attend and spell: a neural network for large vocabulary conversational speech recognition. In: 2016 IEEE International Conference on Acoustics, Speech and Signal Processing (ICASSP), pp. 4960–4964. IEEE (2016)

5. Dosovitskiy, A., et al.: An image is worth 16×16 words: transformers for image recognition at scale. arXiv preprint arXiv:2010.11929 (2020)

6. Fang, S., Xie, H., Wang, Y., Mao, Z., Zhang, Y.: Read like humans: autonomous, bidirectional and iterative language modeling for scene text recognition. In: Proceedings of the IEEE/CVF Conference on Computer Vision and Pattern Recognition, pp. 7098–7107 (2021)

7. Garcia-Bordils, S. et al.: Out-of-vocabulary challenge report. In: Karlinsky, L., Michaeli, T., Nishino, K. (eds.) Computer Vision - ECCV 2022 Workshops. ECCV 2022, Part IV, LNCS, vol. 13804, pp 359–375. Springer, Cham (2023). https://doi.org/10.1007/978-3-031-25069-9_24

8. Gupta, A., Vedaldi, A., Zisserman, A.: Synthetic data for text localisation in natural images. In: Proceedings of the IEEE Conference on Computer Vision and Pattern Recognition, pp. 2315–2324 (2016)

9. He, K., Gkioxari, G., Dollár, P., Girshick, R.: Mask r-cnn. In: Proceedings of the IEEE International Conference on Computer vision, pp. 2961–2969 (2017)

10. He, K., Zhang, X., Ren, S., Sun, J.: Deep residual learning for image recognition. In: Proceedings of the IEEE Conference on Computer Vision and Pattern Recognition, pp. 770–778 (2016)

11. Jaderberg, M., Simonyan, K., Vedaldi, A., Zisserman, A.: Synthetic data and artificial neural networks for natural scene text recognition. arXiv preprint arXiv:1406.2227 (2014)

12. Karatzas, D., et al.: Icdar 2015 competition on robust reading. In: 2015 13th international conference on document analysis and recognition (ICDAR), pp. 1156–1160. IEEE (2015)

13. Krylov, I., Nosov, S., Sovrasov, V.: Open images v5 text annotation and yet another mask text spotter. In: Asian Conference on Machine Learning, pp. 379–389. PMLR (2021)

14. Kuang, Z., et al.: Mmocr: a comprehensive toolbox for text detection, recognition and understanding. arXiv preprint arXiv:2108.06543 (2021)

15. Lee, J., et al.: On recognizing texts of arbitrary shapes with 2d self-attention. In: Proceedings of the IEEE/CVF Conference on Computer Vision and Pattern Recognition Workshops, pp. 546–547 (2020)

16. Li, H., Wang, P., Shen, C., Zhang, G.: Show, attend and read: a simple and strong baseline for irregular text recognition. In: Proceedings of the AAAI Conference on Artificial Intelligence, vol. 33, pp. 8610–8617 (2019)

17. Litman, R., Anschel, O., Tsiper, S., Litman, R., Mazor, S., Manmatha, R.: Scatter: selective context attentional scene text recognizer. In: Proceedings of the IEEE/CVF Conference on Computer Vision and Pattern Recognition, pp. 11962–11972 (2020)

18. Liu, C., Yang, C., Yin, X.C.: Open-set text recognition via character-context decoupling. In: Proceedings of the IEEE/CVF Conference on Computer Vision and Pattern Recognition, pp. 4523–4532 (2022)

19. Liu, Q., Wang, L., Huo, Q.: A study on effects of implicit and explicit language model information for DBLSTM-CTC based handwriting recognition. In: 2015 13th International Conference on Document Analysis and Recognition (ICDAR), pp. 461–465. IEEE (2015)

20. Long, S., Qin, S., Panteleev, D., Bissacco, A., Fujii, Y., Raptis, M.: Towards end-to-end unified scene text detection and layout analysis. In: Proceedings of the IEEE/CVF Conference on Computer Vision and Pattern Recognition, pp. 1049–1059 (2022)

21. Luo, C., Jin, L., Chen, J.: Siman: exploring self-supervised representation learning of scene text via similarity-aware normalization. In: Proceedings of the IEEE/CVF Conference on Computer Vision and Pattern Recognition, pp. 1039–1048 (2022)

22. Nayef, N., et al.: ICDAR 2019 robust reading challenge on multi-lingual scene text detection and recognition-RRC-MlT-2019. In: 2019 International Conference on Document Analysis and Recognition (ICDAR), pp. 1582–1587. IEEE (2019)

23. Ren, S., He, K., Girshick, R., Sun, J.: Faster r-cnn: Towards real-time object detection with region proposal networks. In: Advances in Neural Information Processing Systems, vol. 28 (2015)

24. Shi, B., Bai, X., Yao, C.: An end-to-end trainable neural network for image-based sequence recognition and its application to scene text recognition. IEEE Trans. Pattern Anal. Mach. Intell. **39**(11), 2298–2304 (2016)

25. Shi, B., Yang, M., Wang, X., Lyu, P., Yao, C., Bai, X.: Aster: an attentional scene text recognizer with flexible rectification. IEEE Trans. Pattern Anal. Mach. Intell. **41**(9), 2035–2048 (2018)

26. Singh, A., Pang, G., Toh, M., Huang, J., Galuba, W., Hassner, T.: TextOcr: towards large-scale end-to-end reasoning for arbitrary-shaped scene text. In: Proceedings of the IEEE/CVF Conference on Computer Vision and Pattern Recognition, pp. 8802–8812 (2021)

27. Tu, Z., Lu, Z., Liu, Y., Liu, X., Li, H.: Modeling coverage for neural machine translation. arXiv preprint arXiv:1601.04811 (2016)

28. Vaswani, A., et al.: Attention is all you need. In: Advances in Neural Information Processing Systems, vol. 30 (2017)

29. Wan, Z., Zhang, J., Zhang, L., Luo, J., Yao, C.: On vocabulary reliance in scene text recognition. In: Proceedings of the IEEE/CVF Conference on Computer Vision and Pattern Recognition, pp. 11425–11434 (2020)

30. Yang, M., et al.: Reading and writing: discriminative and generative modeling for self-supervised text recognition. arXiv preprint arXiv:2207.00193 (2022)

31. Yue, X., Kuang, Z., Lin, C., Sun, H., Zhang, W.: RobustScanner: dynamically enhancing positional clues for robust text recognition. In: Vedaldi, A., Bischof, H., Brox, T., Frahm, J.-M. (eds.) ECCV 2020. LNCS, vol. 12364, pp. 135–151. Springer, Cham (2020). https://doi.org/10.1007/978-3-030-58529-7_9

DensityLayout: Density-Conditioned Layout GAN for Visual-Textual Presentation Designs

HsiaoYuan Hsu[1,2], Xiangteng He[1,2], and Yuxin Peng[1,2(✉)]

[1] Wangxuan Institute of Computer Technology, Peking University, Beijing, China
kslh99@stu.pku.edu.cn, {hexiangteng,pengyuxin}@pku.edu.cn
[2] National Key Laboratory for Multimedia Information Processing, Peking University, Beijing, China

Abstract. Generating layouts for visual-textual presentation designs aims at arranging elements such as logo, text, and underlay on the given images, which is the key to automating poster designs. It is challenging since *the compositions of images, the spatial patterns of layout elements,* and *their cross-relationships* need to be simultaneously considered. Existing works focus on the cross-relationships and either (1) suffer from the instability of adopting off-the-shelf saliency maps as prior knowledge or (2) require the semantic content of each element. To this end, this paper presents an efficient density paradigm that requires *neither* off-the-shelf models *nor* additional training data other than image-layout pairs. Under this paradigm, a three-stage approach using GAN is proposed, entitled **DensityLayout**. First, a density mapping network weakly supervised by the custom *consistency loss* will translate given images to spatial distributions of elements. Second, a *multi-scale strategy* is proposed to enhance understanding of the maps, and a generator conditioned on these visual features will generate preliminary layouts. Finally, a *directed graph representation* illustrating the inclusion relationships between elements is presented, and a graph convolution network will fine-tune the layouts. The effectiveness of the proposed approach is validated on CGL-Dataset, showing it achieves the best performance by generating visually appealing layouts for visual-textual presentation designs of diverse images.

1 Introduction

Visual-textual presentation [22] is known as overlaying informative and decorative elements on images, such as posters and magazine covers. Its effectiveness and visual appeal are strongly influenced by the layout, i.e., spatial arrangements of elements. Generally, to simplify and speed up the design process, pre-defined template layouts are used at the expense of *flexibility* and *visual attraction*. In such circumstances, generating layouts adaptive to given images becomes the key to automating high-quality visual-textual representation designs, as shown in Fig. 1. While research has demonstrated the potential of artificial intelligence in presentation layout generation [5,14,18], previous works that assume no images as input fail to adapt to the target task for two reasons. First, it requires considering the compositions of given images, the spatial patterns of layout elements, and their cross-relationships simultaneously. Second, design styles are very subjective and diverse for different presentation purposes. These issues make the target task challenging.

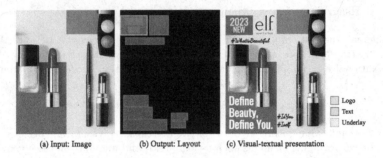

(a) Input: Image   (b) Output: Layout   (c) Visual-textual presentation

Fig. 1. Layout generation for visual-textual presentation designs.

With the advance in big data and crowdsourcing platforms, a data-driven approach becomes a feasible solution and enables implicit learning of aesthetic rules from collected designs. However, some related works [8,23,25] require additional data as supervision besides image and layout. As for those which do not [2,26], they instead rely on off-the-shelf salient object detection (SOD) models. Specifically, these approaches take saliency maps as prior knowledge when processing cross-relationships between images and layouts, explicitly introducing the association between non-salient and layout-overlaid regions. It is straightforward; however, the inconsistency between regions occurs frequently and can harm the robustness of models, especially if there is a discrepancy in training data, e.g., DUTS [20] for SOD models but CGL-Dataset [26] for layout GAN. Therefore, saliency-independent approaches that only demand paired image-layout data are studied in this paper. Modeling the density of the spatial distribution of layout elements on the images is the first idea that comes to mind to perceive cross-relationships. We find conditioning layout generation with density maps not only alleviates the inconsistency or discrepancy mentioned above, but also transfers the subtle design styles implied in collected designs. To this end, a density-conditioned layout GAN, DensityLayout, is presented. It consists of three stages: (1) dedicated density mapping, (2) density-conditioned layout generation, and (3) graph-based pattern fine-tuning.

To evaluate generated layouts, we adopt graphic metrics and composition-aware metrics. The former is commonly used in ordinary layout generation tasks and only considers the spatial relationship between elements, including overlap and alignment. The latter is specific to this task and considers cross-relationships between images and layouts, including readability and occlusion. Even though design styles are subjective, the density maps surely capture those in collected designs in the spatial domain. Therefore, the consistency between the map and the layout will also be used as a quantitative indicator. We conduct experiments on CGL-dataset and compare the proposed approach with the state-of-the-art one. Both quantitative and visualized results show that DensityLayout achieves the best performance by generating suitable layouts for visual-textual presentation designs of diverse images.

The main contribution of this paper can be summarized as follows:

- An **efficient density paradigm** for layout generation for visual-textual presentation designs. It requires *only* paired image-layout data while improves the robustness of generative models in the pipeline.
- A **density-conditioned layout GAN** implemented using LSTM, whose generator and discriminator networks *share a multi-scale network* that extracts visual features of density maps as their initial hidden states. It considers all key aspects of the target task, which are the compositions of images, the spatial patterns of layout elements, and their cross-relationships.
- A **graph representation of layouts** using *directed* edges to indicate spatial relationships between elements. It enables graph convolution networks to model patterns of layouts and fine-tune them to be more plausible.

2 Related Work

Most previous works for layout generation focus on only the intra-relationship between layout elements. For enhancing relationship modeling, they introduce attention mechanisms [1,13], graph representation (GCN) [11], latent-space optimization [10], element dropout [14], and hierarchical decoding [9]. Although these works show strong abilities to improve graphic metrics in layout generation, they cannot cope directly with visual-textual presentation designs since they do not consider cross-relationships between images and layouts. Some recent works notice the shortages; however, they often require extra data as supervision. LayoutNet [25] additionally utilizes the presentation topics and contents of texts to get multimodal features that condition the layout GANs. Similarly, [8,23] demand textual features of elements and fuse them with visual ones to get cross-modal features. In the former, features guide region proposal, and in the latter, they condition Transformer-based generative models. There are still very few works that require only paired image-layout data, which adopt off-the-shelf saliency maps as prior knowledge. CGL-GAN [26] simply utilizes self-attention and cross-attention layers in the standard Transformer decoder in GANs to model simultaneously spatial patterns of layout elements and their cross-relationships with compositions of images. ICVT [2] further introduces custom geometry terms in cross-attention to facilitate aligning geometric parameters, i.e., bounding boxes, with visual features. Most recently, DS-GAN [7] involves human design experience as a helpful heuristic and achieves remarkable results on the newly proposed benchmark, PKU PosterLayout. These one-stage works associate non-salient and layout-overlaid regions in a very intuitive way, as emphasized in Sect. 1. However, inconsistency between the two regions harms the robustness of models, and an imbalanced focus on cross-relationships is still witnessed to some extent. These drawbacks encourage us to research and propose a density paradigm that demands only paired image-layout data and fully considers all three key aspects of the task to generate the most proper layout for visual-textual presentation designs of the given image.

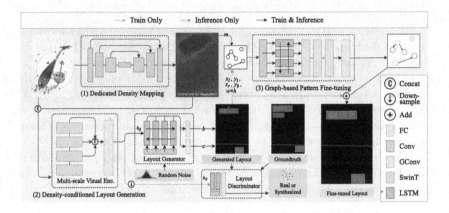

Fig. 2. An overview of the proposed approach, DensityLayout.

3   Density-Conditioned Layout GAN for Visual-Textual Presentation Designs

After analyzing the weaknesses of previous works, we propose DensityLayout. As shown in Fig. 2, it is composed of three stages: (1) dedicated density mapping, (2) density-conditioned layout generation, and (3) graph-based pattern fine-tuning. This section elaborates on details of each stage.

3.1   Dedicated Density Mapping

Predicting density maps that indicate the number and spatial distribution of objects of interest in an image is widely used in object counting. However, unlike general ones for crowds [4], layout elements are not present in images during inference. Instead of capturing features of objects, the target mapping network should perceive common attributes of regions where layout elements are usually present and identify their location and density. Precisely, it is what the cross-relationships focus on and distinguishes layout generation for visual-textual presentation designs from ordinary layout generation. The mapping is formulated as a pixel-to-pixel regression problem. That is, $\mathcal{M}(I) = M$, saying that the given image $I \in \mathbb{R}^{3 \times H \times W}$ is translated to its density map $M \in \mathbb{R}^{H \times W}$ through network $\mathcal{M}$. Based on the previous analysis, a preprocessing scheme is designed to take geometric parameters of layouts, i.e., bounding boxes, to render n binary bitmap images $B \in \{0,1\}^{H \times W}$, where n is the number of elements in the layout. Then, these bitmap images are aggregated as ground truth density maps of their corresponding source RGB images to supervise the model.

Since the final goal of obtaining density maps in this work is to identify accurate *regions* suitable for placing layout elements, the continuity of density in the spatial domain needs to be concerned. Considering the stiff shape of objects of interest, a dedicated continuity loss function is designed referring to the maximum area of a rectangle inscribed in a circle, as

$$\mathcal{L}_{con}(M', M) = (\frac{2}{\pi} - \frac{\Sigma M + \epsilon}{\Sigma M' + \epsilon})^2, \tag{1}$$

where M' is the predicted density map, and ϵ is a small number to avoid division by zero. It encourages the availability of density maps by filling vacancies between adjacent elements and smoothing the outline of the region of interest. Finally, network $\mathcal{M}$ is implemented using a feature pyramid network [16] trained with continuity loss $\mathcal{L}_{con}$ and mean squared error loss $\mathcal{L}_{mse}$.

3.2 Density-Conditioned Layout Generation

After obtaining a density map of an image, traditional density paradigms [8,12,24] for layout generation directly resort to handcrafted algorithms and formulate a constrained optimization problem to find a *single* anchor box. All layout elements are then assigned in the anchor box one below another, making presentation designs inflexible and rigid. To this end, a density-conditioned layout GAN is proposed in this paper to generate visually appealing layouts. The problem is formulated as a sequence-to-sequence problem. That is, $\}(N, I, M) = \{e_i \mid i \in [0, n)\}$, saying that a set of random noise N is translated to a set of layout elements $\{e\}$ through the generator $\}$, conditioning on the given image I and the corresponding density map obtained in the previous stage. More precisely, each element e_i is composed of a one-hot vector c_i indicating its class label and a 4-dimensional vector indicating center position coordinates and size of its bounding box b_i.

In order for GAN to be fully aware of density maps and compositions of the images before generating layouts, it is crucial to use an effective visual feature encoder $\mathcal{V}$. Therefore, Swin Transformer [17] architecture accompanying a new multi-scale strategy is utilized. It takes the concatenation along the channel axis of M and I as input, and consequently, the input channel is set to four. Excluding the classifier head, there are four basic blocks following the patch partition, denoted as stages in the original paper. The multi-scale strategy is introduced into blocks 2, 3, and 4 to combine high-level and low-level features and output fused features F, as

$$A_2' = \mathbf{AvgPool}_d(\mathbf{Conv}_{11}(A_2)),$$
$$A_3' = \mathbf{AvgPool}_d(A_3),$$
$$A_4' = \mathbf{AvgPool}_d(\mathbf{LayerNorm}(A_4)),$$
$$F = \mathbf{Concat}(A_2', A_3', A_4'),$$

(2)

where A_i represents activations of i-th basic block, operator $\mathbf{AvgPool}_d$ represents an average pooling of output size d, and operators $\mathbf{Conv}_{11}$ represents a convolution of kernel size 1. As a rule of thumb, since the consistency of conditions is helpful to stabilize the minimax game in GANs, the generator and discriminator share one visual encoder, and only the former is responsible for updating its weights.

Next to consider is the main component of GAN, i.e., sequence-to-sequence models, which needs to understand both visual features of images and patterns of layout elements. Among numerous network architectures, bidirectional LSTM architecture is chosen regarding its ability to remember the attributes of generated elements. Intuitively, this trait is expected to be very helpful for avoiding overlay in layout generation. Even more advisable, since recurrent models are triggered by initial hidden states h_0, an elegant way of introducing visual features in the process is to take the fused feature F after linear projection as h_0. Last but not least, 1D CNNs are attached to extract patterns of layout elements before they are passed into LSTM, known as CNN-LSTM architecture. Both the generator and discriminator are built in this manner but with different ending blocks according to their goal. The former takes the output sequence of LSTM and projects them with two fully connected layers, one for class labels and another for bounding boxes. The latter takes the output of the last cell only and projects it as a probability of the input layout being real or synthesized. During training, besides commonly-used adversarial loss $\mathcal{L}_{adv}$ [15] and reconstruction loss $\mathcal{L}_{rec}$ [3], alignment loss $\mathcal{L}_{ali}$ [10] are also applied.

3.3 Graph-Based Pattern Fine-Tuning

All key aspects of the task, namely the compositions of images, the spatial patterns of layout elements, and their cross-relationships, have been considered in previous stages. Moreover, to take a step further in making generated layouts more plausible, a fine-tuning procedure is designed. The plausibility of layouts is highly relevant to the category of elements; for example, when two elements almost or completely overlap, one of them, more likely the larger one, must be an underlay element. Therefore, it is formulated as a classification problem. That is, $\mathbf{C}(M, \{e\}) = \{c'\}$, where c' is the re-predicted logit values. Since handcrafting the principles is impractical and hurts the generality of the procedure, a graph convolution network (GCN) [21] that automatically models them is presented. Correspondingly, a graph representation that embeds layouts as directed graphs is proposed. Each node in graphs is naturally an element, and its feature f is a 6-dimensional vector. The first four values are the top-left and bottom-right coordinates of the corresponding bounding box b_i, and the fifth is the amount of its area. The last one indicates whether b_i shows out in a high-density region by checking the maximum value it corresponds to on the density map M. Denoting w and h as the width and height of the bounding box, th as the threshold, and $M[:]$ as the operator obtaining pixel-level values in the slicing area on the density map, a node feature f constructed from an element is as

$$m = \begin{cases} 1, & \text{if } \max(M[x_l : x_r, y_t : y_b]) > th, \\ 0, & \text{otherwise}, \end{cases} \tag{3}$$

$$f = [x_l, y_t, x_r, y_b, w \times h, m].$$

All nodes that illustrate valid elements are then connected, and the connectivity implies the plausibility of layouts in terms of availability. That is, nodes that have insufficient amounts of areas will be isolated. Remember that the constructed graph is directed, and the edge weights ε can explicitly indicate the inclusion relationship between nodes, as

$$\varepsilon_{i \to j} = \begin{cases} 1, & \text{if } e_j \subseteq e_i, \\ 0, & \text{otherwise}. \end{cases} \tag{4}$$

Now, with directed weighted graphs and ground-truth class labels of nodes, a GCN is trained with cross-entropy loss L_{ce}. During inference, the final class label c^* of a node is determined by the weighted sum of logits c and logits c', as

$$c^* = \arg\max(\omega \times c + (1 - \omega) \times c'), \tag{5}$$

where ω is a hyperparameter. Finally, the layout is obtained with c^* and the corresponding b^* that discards nodes predicted to be isolated.

Table 1. Comparison of quantitative results on CGL-Dataset.

	$Val \uparrow$	$Con \uparrow$	$Rea \downarrow$	$Uti \uparrow$	$Occ \downarrow$	$Ove \downarrow$	$Ali \downarrow$	$Pla_l \uparrow$	$Pla_s \uparrow$
CGL-GAN [26]	0.7461	0.3383	0.2885	0.1566	0.4707	0.0665	0.0017	**0.8891**	0.3573
DensityLayout (Ours)	**0.9675**	**0.3714**	**0.2769**	**0.2012**	**0.4283**	**0.0358**	**0.0001**	0.8812	**0.5407**

4 Experiment

4.1 Datasets

To validate the effectiveness of the proposed DensityLayout, experiments are conducted on CGL-Dataset [26]. It represents layouts as a set of bounding boxes, each with class labels, either text, logo, underlay, or embellishment. Considering the actual amount of elements in each category, embellishment elements are omitted without loss of generality. Totally, it contains 60,546 eligible image-layout pairs for training and 1,000 images for testing.

4.2   Evaluation Metrics

Eight composition-aware and graphic metrics are adopted to evaluate generated layouts, but first of all, an element-level validity is considered, denoted as $Val \uparrow$. An up arrow behind indicates a higher value is preferred, and vice versa. It represents the proportion of elements that occupy more than 0.1% of the image area. The following metrics will only consider valid elements to keep the results meaningful. For better observation, all metrics are normalized to 0–1 range.

- **Composition-aware metrics.** (1) $Con \uparrow$ indicates the consistency between density maps and layouts, defined as the average value that layouts correspond to on the maps. A higher consistency demonstrates more accurate style transfer from collected designs to generated layouts. (2) $Rea \downarrow$ indicates the *hard* readability of information on the presentation rendered according to the layout, implemented following [26]. (3) $Uti \uparrow$ and (4) $Occ \downarrow$ demonstrate relationships between layouts and salient objects on images by regarding the off-the-shelf saliency maps [12,19]. The former indicates the utilization rate of non-salient areas, and the latter indicates occlusion between layouts and those objects, calculated in the same way as for $Con \uparrow$.
- **Graphic metrics.** (5) $Ove \downarrow$ indicates the overlay ratio between informative elements. (6) $Ali \downarrow$ indicates the extent of spatial *non*-alignment between elements, implemented following [14]. (7) $Pla_l \uparrow$ and (8) $Pla_s \uparrow$ demonstrate the plausibility of layouts concerning the loose or strict inclusion relationship between informative elements e_I and decorative elements e_D, as

$$Pla_l = \frac{1}{|e_D|} \Sigma_i^{|e_D|} \{ \max_j \{ \frac{e_{D_i} \cap e_{I_j}}{e_{I_i}} \}\},$$

$$Pla_s = \frac{|\{e_{D_i} \mid \exists e_{I_j} \subseteq e_{D_i}\}|}{|e_D|}. \tag{6}$$

4.3   Implementation Details

The proposed DensityLayout has five components in three stages, namely the density mapping network $\mathcal{M}$, the multi-scale network $\mathcal{V}$, generator $\mathcal{G}$, discriminator $\mathcal{D}$ of layout GAN, and the fine-tuning network $\mathcal{C}$. The backbone of $\mathcal{M}$ is ResNet-50 [6], and that of $\mathcal{V}$ is Swin-Tiny [17]. Considering the complexity of the respective tasks, $\mathcal{G}$ and $\mathcal{D}$ are implemented using 4- and 2-layer stacked LSTM models, respectively. $\mathcal{C}$ is composed of a 4-layer stacked CNN-LSTM model, a 3-layer GCN, and a fully connected layer. These components are trained using Adam optimizers with initial learning rates of 10^{-6}, 10^{-4}, 10^{-5}, 10^{-3}, and 10^{-3}. Moreover, the feature dimension d in Eq. 2 is 256, the threshold th in 3 is 128, and the weight ω in Eq. 5 is determined by a grid search. All experiments are carried out under the Pytorch framework using four NVIDIA A100-SXM4-80GB GPUs.

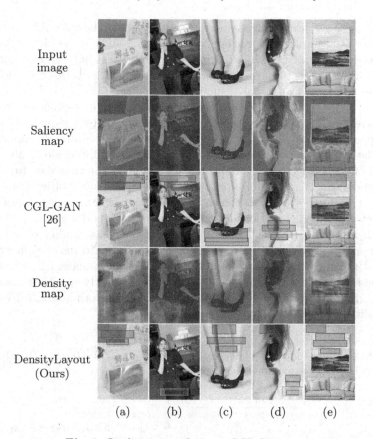

Input
image

Saliency
map

CGL-GAN
[26]

Density
map

DensityLayout
(Ours)

(a)   (b)   (c)   (d)   (e)

Fig. 3. Qualitative analysis on CGL-Dataset.

4.4   Comparisons with State-of-the-art Method

CGL-GAN [26] is a saliency paradigm-based approach known as the current
state-of-the-art method dedicated to layout generation for visual-textual presentation designs requiring only paired image-layout data. Table 1 shows the comparison of quantitative results on CGL-Dataset. Comprehensively, it is observed
that our approach outperforms the SOTA method in most metrics. First, notice
that most elements in the layouts it generates are valid, and then let the content-
aware metrics in the second column block tell us more. As expected, Density-
Layout brings a better $Con \uparrow$ since the density maps are visible to it during
training. On the other hand, although saliency maps are visible to CGL-GAN,
it still cannot beat DensityLayout in either $Uti \uparrow$ or $Occ \downarrow$. This finding proves
the effectiveness of the new paradigm presented in this paper. Even without off-
the-shelf saliency maps, it can still improve the utilization of non-salient areas
while avoiding occluding salient objects. Further effects of density maps will be
depicted in the ablation study. Now, turning to the third column block, a more
significant advantage of DensityLayout is observed in graphic metrics. As men-

tioned in Sect. 3.2, leveraging memory gate structures in layout GAN is expected helpful to avoid unpleasant overlay $Ove \uparrow$ between informative elements, which is indeed demonstrated by the experimental results. Last but not least, although DensityLayout seems to be slightly behind in $Pla_l \uparrow$, it is aware of a much more accurate pattern of layouts, as demonstrated in $Pla_s \uparrow$.

Figure 3 shows several layouts generated by different approaches, together with corresponding saliency maps [19] and density maps for qualitative analysis. Apparently, our density paradigm models more accurate and informative cross-relationships between images and layouts. It carefully considers all objects, including those neglected by the saliency paradigm, as shown in case (a). On the other hand, it can find an appropriate region overlaying salient objects and brings a better visual experience, as shown in cases (b) and (c). It also shows higher consistency between conditioned maps and layout-overlaid regions, as shown in cases (d) and (e). Moreover, visualized results verify the ability of our multi-stage approach to dominate in recognizing the spatial patterns of elements, e.g., $Ove \downarrow$, $Ali \downarrow$, and $Pla \uparrow$. In a comprehensive view, the proposed DensityLayout based on the new density paradigm generates more visually appealing layouts for visual-textual presentation designs of different images. Both quantitative results and qualitative results have validated this conclusion.

Table 2. Ablation study on (A) density maps, (B) multi-scale strategy, (C) alignment loss, and (D) graph-based fine-tuning.

A	B	C	D	$Con \uparrow$	$Rea \downarrow$	$Uti \uparrow$	$Occ \downarrow$	$Ove \downarrow$	$Ali \downarrow$	$Pla_l \uparrow$	$Pla_s \uparrow$
✓				0.3699	0.3003	0.1666	0.4791	0.1443	0.0024	-	-
	✓			0.3081	0.2940	0.1593	0.5171	0.0384	0.0025	0.8777	0.4146
✓	✓			**0.3833**	0.2884	0.1612	0.4695	0.0378	0.0039	**0.8863**	0.4987
✓	✓	✓		<u>0.3748</u>	**0.2767**	<u>0.1892</u>	<u>0.4396</u>	0.0358	**0.0001**	0.8747	<u>0.5363</u>
✓	✓	✓	✓	0.3714	<u>0.2769</u>	**0.2012**	0.4283	0.0358	**0.0001**	<u>0.8812</u>	**0.5407**

4.5 Ablation Study

To gain insight into the effects of components in DensityLayout, an ablation study is carried out. Although key aspects of the target task are considered throughout all stages of the proposed approach, each aspect can still correspond to a component that is the most relevant. Specifically, the density maps conditioning layout GAN is for cross-relationships between images and layouts, the multi-scale strategy introduced to the visual encoder is for compositions of images, and the graph-based fine-tuning network is for spatial patterns of layout elements. Moreover, the impact of introducing alignment loss into the training phase of layout GAN is also interesting since it normally degrades network stability for its contradiction to reconstruction loss. According to the order in which they appear in the pipeline, each of (A) density maps, (B) multi-scale strategy,

(C) alignment loss, and (D) graph-based fine-tuning will be attached to a vanilla image-conditioned layout GAN based on LSTM architecture in an accumulating manner. Experimental results are shown in Table 2.

Through rows 2 and 3, the effect of conditioning layout generation with (A) density maps is observed to bring a significant improvement, especially in $Con \uparrow$, $Occ \downarrow$, and $Pla_s \uparrow$. Since these three metrics are highly specific to the target task, the overall improvement strongly demonstrates the effectiveness and necessity of the density paradigm presented in this paper. Through rows 1 and 3, the advantage of introducing the (B) multi-scale strategy is observed, especially in $Rea \downarrow$, $Ove \downarrow$, and both $Pla \uparrow$, which is very reasonable. Specifically, whether placing informative elements along with a decorative element, e.g., underlay, is determined by both local information, i.e., region complexity, and global information, i.e., overall compositions. Due to the lack of perceiving multi-level features, the one in row 2 does not arrange any decorative elements. Through rows 3 and 4, a slight drop in $Val \uparrow$, $Con \uparrow$, and Pld_l is indeed observed after introducing (C) alignment loss. It is analyzed that as the loss makes the geometric parameters in the layout more regular, those bounding boxes on the boundary of the insufficient area directly collapse to zero sizes. On the other hand, it is found helpful in improving $Rea \downarrow$, $Uti \uparrow$, and $Occ \downarrow$ for its caution in expanding bounding boxes. Finally, after the (D) fine-tuning procedure, the generated layouts have the best quality comprehensively. The collapsed bounding boxes are isolated, and the inclusion relationships between informative and decorative elements are refined, bringing further improvement in $Val \uparrow$, $Ocl \downarrow$, and $Pla_s \uparrow$. In this way, the ablation study verifies the indispensability of each component in DensityLayout.

5   Conclusion

In this paper, we study a new paradigm for layout generation for visual-textual presentation designs, and propose a density-conditioned layout GAN, DensityLayout. It consists of three stages to fully consider the compositions of images, the spatial patterns of layout elements, and their cross-relationships. Specifically, among its five components, a density mapping network and an LSTM-based layout generator and discriminator focus on the cross-relationships; a multi-scale visual encoder and a graph-based fine-tuning procedure focus on enhancing the process of images and layouts, respectively. Several experiments conducted on CGL-dataset verify the effectiveness of the proposed paradigm and approach.

In future work, we suggest exploring (1) a single-stage approach under the density paradigm that achieves competitive performance compared to multi-stage ones and (2) a denoising diffusion probabilistic model-based approach.

Acknowledgements. This work was supported by grants from Beijing Natural Science Foundation (4232005), National Natural Science Foundation of China (61925201, 62132001, 62272013) and Meituan.

References

1. Arroyo, D.M., Postels, J., Tombari, F.: Variational transformer networks for layout generation. In: Proceedings of the IEEE/CVF Conference on Computer Vision and Pattern Recognition, pp. 13642–13652 (2021)
2. Cao, Y., et al.: Geometry aligned variational transformer for image-conditioned layout generation. In: Proceedings of the ACM International Conference on Multimedia, pp. 1561–1571 (2022)
3. Carion, N., Massa, F., Synnaeve, G., Usunier, N., Kirillov, A., Zagoruyko, S.: End-to-end object detection with transformers. In: Proceedings of the European Conference on Computer Vision, pp. 213–229 (2020)
4. Gao, G., Gao, J., Liu, Q., Wang, Q., Wang, Y.: Cnn-based density estimation and crowd counting: a survey. arXiv preprint arXiv:2003.12783 (2020)
5. Guo, S., Jin, Z., Sun, F., Li, J., Li, Z., Shi, Y., Cao, N.: Vinci: an intelligent graphic design system for generating advertising posters. In: Proceedings of the CHI Conference on Human Factors in Computing Systems, pp. 1–17 (2021)
6. He, K., Zhang, X., Ren, S., Sun, J.: Deep residual learning for image recognition. In: Proceedings of the IEEE Conference on Computer Vision and Pattern Recognition, pp. 770–778 (2016)
7. Hsu, H.Y., He, X., Peng, Y., Kong, H., Zhang, Q.: PosterLayout: a new benchmark and approach for content-aware visual-textual presentation. In: Proceedings of the IEEE/CVF Conference on Computer Vision and Pattern Recognition. pp. 6018–6026 (2023)
8. Huang, D., Li, J., Liu, C., Liu, J.: AUPOD: end-to-end automatic poster design by self-supervision. IEEE Access **10**, 47348–47360 (2022)
9. Jiang, Z., Sun, S., Zhu, J., Lou, J.G., Zhang, D.: Coarse-to-fine generative modeling for graphic layouts. In: Proceedings of the AAAI Conference on Artificial Intelligence, vol. 36, pp. 1096–1103 (2022)
10. Kikuchi, K., Simo-Serra, E., Otani, M., Yamaguchi, K.: Constrained graphic layout generation via latent optimization. In: Proceedings of the ACM International Conference on Multimedia, pp. 88–96 (2021)
11. Lee, H.Y., et al.: Neural design network: Graphic layout generation with constraints. In: Proceedings of the European Conference on Computer Vision, pp. 491–506 (2020)
12. Li, C., Zhang, P., Wang, C.: Harmonious textual layout generation over natural images via deep aesthetics learning. IEEE Trans. Multimedia **24**, 3416–3428 (2021)
13. Li, J., Yang, J., Hertzmann, A., Zhang, J., Xu, T.: LayoutGAN: synthesizing graphic layouts with vector-wireframe adversarial networks. IEEE Trans. Pattern Anal. Mach. Intell. **43**(7), 2388–2399 (2020)
14. Li, J., Yang, J., Zhang, J., Liu, C., Wang, C., Xu, T.: Attribute-conditioned layout GAN for automatic graphic design. IEEE Trans. Visual Comput. Graphics **27**(10), 4039–4048 (2020)
15. Lim, J.H., Ye, J.C.: Geometric GAN. arXiv preprint arXiv:1705.02894 (2017)
16. Lin, T.Y., Dollár, P., Girshick, R., He, K., Hariharan, B., Belongie, S.: Feature pyramid networks for object detection. In: Proceedings of the IEEE Conference on Computer Vision and Pattern Recognition, pp. 2117–2125 (2017)
17. Liu, Z., et al.: Swin transformer: Hierarchical vision transformer using shifted windows. In: Proceedings of the IEEE/CVF International Conference on Computer Vision, pp. 10012–10022 (2021)

18. Patil, A.G., Ben-Eliezer, O., Perel, O., Averbuch-Elor, H.: READ: recursive autoencoders for document layout generation. In: Proceedings of the IEEE/CVF Conference on Computer Vision and Pattern Recognition Workshops, pp. 544–545 (2020)
19. Wang, B., Chen, Q., Zhou, M., Zhang, Z., Jin, X., Gai, K.: Progressive feature polishing network for salient object detection. In: Proceedings of the AAAI Conference on Artificial Intelligence, pp. 12128–12135 (2020)
20. Wang, L., et al.: Learning to detect salient objects with image-level supervision. In: Proceedings of the IEEE Conference on Computer Vision and Pattern Recognition, pp. 136–145 (2017)
21. Welling, M., Kipf, T.N.: Semi-supervised classification with graph convolutional networks. In: Proceedings of the International Conference on Learning Representations (2016)
22. Yang, X., Mei, T., Xu, Y.Q., Rui, Y., Li, S.: Automatic generation of visual-textual presentation layout. ACM Trans. Multimed. Comput. Commun. Appl. 12(2), 1–22 (2016)
23. Yu, N., et al.: LayoutDETR: detection transformer is a good multimodal layout designer. arXiv preprint arXiv:2212.09877 (2022)
24. Zhang, P., Li, C., Wang, C.: SmartText: learning to generate harmonious textual layout over natural image. In: Proceedings of the IEEE International Conference on Multimedia and Expo, pp. 1–6 (2020)
25. Zheng, X., Qiao, X., Cao, Y., Lau, R.W.: Content-aware generative modeling of graphic design layouts. ACM Trans. Graph. 38(4), 1–15 (2019)
26. Zhou, M., Xu, C., Ma, Y., Ge, T., Jiang, Y., Xu, W.: Composition-aware graphic layout GAN for visual-textual presentation designs. In: Proceedings of the International Joint Conference on Artificial Intelligence, pp. 4995–5001 (2022)

GLTCM: Global-Local Temporal and Cross-Modal Network for Audio-Visual Event Localization

Xiaoyu Wu[1](✉), Jucheng Qiu[2], and Qiurui Yue[2]

[1] Communication University of China, Beijing, China
wuxiaoyu@cuc.edu.cn
[2] State Key Laboratory of Media Convergence and Communication, Communication University of China, Beijing, China
925825044@qq.com, 790314825@qq.com

Abstract. With the explosive growth of network video, how to better solve the problem of video understanding has become a hot topic, and the task of Audio-Visual Event Localization will help us solve more higher-semantic and challenging video understanding problems in the future. The existing methods in AVE lack utilizing local temporal information fully and ignore constructing cross-modal fusion relationships well with different scales. In this paper, we propose a Global-Local Temporal and Cross-Modal Network(GLTCM) for supervised/weakly-supervised audio-visual event localization task, which is composed of a feature extraction module, global-local temporal module, cross-modality module, and localization module. The global-local temporal module is exploited to model the temporal relationship between the entire and surrounding segments, the cross-modality module is utilized to model the cross-modal information of multi-modal features, and the localization module is based on multi-task learning. Our proposed method is verified for two tasks of supervised and weakly-supervised audio-visual event localization. The experimental results demonstrated that our method is competitive on the public AVE dataset.

Keywords: GLTCM · Audio-Visual Event Localization · Cross-Modal Fusion

1 Introduction

The video understanding problem has been applied in our daily life. With the rapid development of the online video industry, the video understanding problem will have more application scenarios. As illustrated in Fig. 1, an Audio-Visual Event(AVE) is defined as an event that is both audible and visible (i.e., hearing a sound from an object and seeing that object at the same time). The goal of the Audio-visual Event Localization(AVEL) task is to predict the start and end time and audio-visual event categories in a video. The audio-visual event localization task will help us solve more difficult, higher-level, and higher-semantic video understanding problems in the future, such as video subtitles [1], video question answering [2], and other issues that have been widely used in video understanding, but there is a lack of effective modeling. The AVEL task studied in this paper helps to model visual and auditory coherence. In general, visual and auditory events often occur simultaneously, but not always: the scene is turned away during a speech, the train has left the frame but the train horn can still be heard. Audio-visual event localization research contributes to video understanding related research and provides better auxiliary information for multiple application fields.

AVEL [3] used an audio-guided visual attention model to generate a context vector, then employed LSTM to model the temporal dependencies of visual and audio features, and finally applied a bimodal residual structure to fuse the two modal features. Similar.

to AVEL [3], AVSDN [4] used LSTM to construct temporal information and a bimodal residual structure to fuse the features of the two modalities to obtain the global representation. The attention methods including self-attention or co-attention are utilized to model temporal information of visual and audio features respectively [5, 6]. MPN [7] can compute global semantic information and local information in parallel, and it is composed of a classification self-network for classifying event categories and a location sub-network for locating event occurrence boundaries. The above methods exploited dual-modality features and adapted global-local cues for locating audio-visual events. However, how to capture audio-visual complementarity effectively and fusion them with global-local different scales, and suppress the interference between different modal information is vital for audio-visual location tasks.

To solve the above problems, this paper proposed Global-Local Temporal and Cross-Modal Network (GLTCM) for supervised and weakly-supervised tasks of audio-visual event localization. Firstly, we extract visual and audio features through the existing deep neural network. Then, the features are sent to the global-local temporal module to model the global and local temporal relations fully. Then, the two-stage cross-modal module is presented to fully model the cross-modal information of the two modes, which is very important for the multi-modal information. Finally, the multi-task is constructed by determining whether the event occurs and the event category to realize audio-visual event localization and classification. Global-Local Temporal and Cross-Modal Network (GLTCM) for supervised and weakly-supervised tasks have achieved competitive results in audio-visual event localization tasks. It is hoped that the framework can provide new ideas for cross-modal related tasks.

2   Related Work

The task of audio-visual event location was proposed by Tian et al. [3] in AVEL, which requires locating the start and end time of the audio-visual events in the video and identifying the event category. AVEL used an audio guide for the visual attention model to generate a context vector, and then LSTM was used to simulate the visual and audio temporal dependencies respectively, finally using the double modal residual structure fusion of two modal features. AVSDN [4] constructed an end-to-end audio-visual event location task network based on an encoder and decoder, which adopted the LSTM module to simulate the temporal dependence of audio-visual features, and a dual-mode residual structure was designed to obtain the global representation of the features. But it concatenated multi-modal features without the LSTM module as local features, and finally fed global feature expression and local feature expression into the decoder. The cross-modal information was exploited through cross-checking mechanism and modeled high-level semantic event information in the works of literature [8–10]. CMRA [11] network proposed two relation-aware modules that capture both intra-modality relations and inter-modality relations for accurate event localization. Zhou et al. [12] presented positive sample propagation (PSP) module to only aggregate the features from the pairs with high similarity scores and reduce the interference caused by irrelevant audio-visual segment pairs. Afterwards, they proposed CPSP [13], which includes not only PSP, but also segment-level and video-level positive sample activation, these modules activate more positive samples from the segment and video levels through contrastive strategies. Lin et al. [14] proposed a Latent Audio-Visual Hybrid (LAV$_{IS}$H) adapter that adapts pre-trained Vision Transformers (ViTs) to audio-visual tasks by injecting a small number of trainable parameters into each layer of a frozen ViT, achieving competitive or even better performance without relying on costly audio pre-training or external audio encoders. However, the above methods focus on the global temporal information at the video level and ignore the local temporal information at the segment level.

Fig. 1. An illustrative example of an audio-visual event location task, the train horn is heard and the train is seen in the first three segments, it's considered an audio-visual event. In the last two segments, only the sound is heard without any visual event, so it's considered background.

The following work like the MPN [7] and the M2N [15] leverage local-to-global interactions and learned the information correlation between segments of two modes and between multi-scale event locations. But they only adapt simple fusion methods or fusion between modalities and didn't consider mutual guidance for sufficient intra-modal and inter-modal fusion. In this paper, the GLTCM (Global-Local Temporal and Cross-Modal) Network is proposed for supervised and weakly-supervised audio-visual event localization tasks, in which we present the global-local temporal module to model its temporal information and the two-stage cross-modal module to interact with two modal information to achieve the purpose of fusion.

3   Methods for Global-Local Temporal and Cross-Modal (GLTCM)

To solve the audio-visual event localization task, we divide the video S into T non-overlapping video segments, namely $S = \{S_t = (V_t, A_t)\}_t^T$, where V_t and A_t denote the visual content of segment t and the corresponding audio content. Here, we divide the 10-s video into 10 segments, and each is 1 s long. For a given video sequence S, the audio-visual event localization task needs to predict whether each segment S_t has audio-visual events and event category labels (including background) based on the visual

V_t and audio A_t of each segment S_t. As illustrated in Fig. 2, an audio-visual event is defined as an event that is both audible and visible (i.e., hearing a sound from an object and seeing that object at the same time).

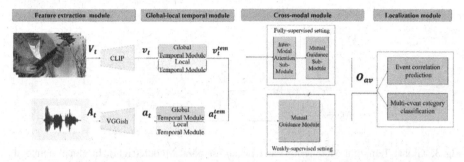

Fig. 2. The framework of GLTCM for audio-visual event localization. The GLTCM for audio-visual event localization is mainly composed of four parts: the feature extraction module, the global-local temporal module, the cross-modal module, and the localization module.

The GLTCM for supervised audio-visual event location is mainly composed of four parts in Fig. 2: the feature extraction module, the global-local temporal module, the cross-modal interaction module, and the localization module. Firstly, we use the CLIP [16] network to extract visual features v_t and VGGish [17] network to extract audio features a_t. Then, we send the visual features and audio features into the global-local temporal module, respectively, modeling the global and surrounding segments' temporal relations of visual features and audio features, and obtain v_t^{tem} and a_t^{tem}. The visual features and audio features with temporal dependence are fed into the two-stage cross-modal module to model the cross-modal relationship between the two modalities, and then the two modal features are fused by concatenation. Finally, the fusion feature O_{av} is sent to the localization module. The localization module is mainly composed of two parts: the event-relevant and the event classification modules.

3.1 Feature Extraction Module

It has been suggested that models learned from large-scale datasets (e.g. WebText, AudioSet) are highly general and consequential. So, we make use of the CLIP [16] models pre-trained on WebText and the VGGish [17] models pre-trained on AudioSet to extract visual features v_t and audio features a_t for video segments.

3.2 Global-Local Temporal Module

Temporal information is unique for video data and we think that local temporal information and global temporal information are equally crucial for the audio-visual event localization task. When modeling temporal information, we consider the information of the surrounding segments of the current video segment to help reduce the noisy information caused by too far segments. Therefore, inspired by the encoder for Temporal Action

Proposal Refinement [18], we present the global-local temporal module to model the intra-level local and global temporal relationships of audio features and visual features respectively.

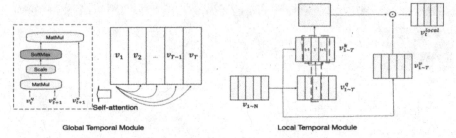

Global Temporal Module   Local Temporal Module

Fig. 3. Global Temporal Module(left) and Local Temporal Module(right). In global temporal module, we use self-attention operation for all visual features, outputting visual global temporal feature v_t^{global}. The local temporal module is operated for all visual features, outputting v_t^{local}.

As illustrated in Fig. 3, the global-local temporal module is divided into two sub-modules: the global temporal sub-module and the local temporal sub-module. We exploit the global temporal sub-module to model the temporal relationship of the entire video sequence and use the local temporal sub-module to model the temporal relationship of the surrounding segments and realize the efficient modeling method of global temporal modeling and local temporal modeling simultaneously through channel grouping. The global temporal sub-module interacts with all segments in the temporal dimension to simulate long-term dependence. We use the global-local temporal module in the visual path and the audio path in the existing network. The local temporal sub-module also uses the principle of the self-attention mechanism to model the temporal relationship, but the local temporal sub-module only considers the influence of the surrounding segments in the temporal dimension. For this short video with a length of 10 s, we only need to consider the surrounding two segments, and the farther segments will bring the noise. Finally, we concatenate v_t^{global} and v_t^{local} to get v_t^{tem} visual global-local temporal feature, and a_t^{global} and a_t^{local} to get a_t^{tem} audio global-local temporal feature.

$$v_t^{global} = Softmax\left(\frac{v_t^q\left(v_1^{k^T}, ..., v_T^{k^T}\right)}{\sqrt{d}}, \left(v_1^v, ..., v_T^v\right)\right) \tag{1}$$

$$v_t^{local} = Softmax\left(\frac{v_t^q\left(v_{t+1}^k, v_{t-1}^k\right)^T}{\sqrt{d}}, \left(v_{t+1}^v, v_{t-1}^v\right)\right) \tag{2}$$

In Fig. 3 and formulas (1) and (2), only the global-local temporal module of the visual path is listed. In the actual network, a_t^{global} and a_t^{local} are obtained by using the same just-shot in the audio path, respectively. Where v_t^q, v_t^k, v_t^v represent the visual query feature, visual key feature, and visual value feature, and d is the dimension of the input feature, $(.)^T$ is the transpose of the matrix.

3.3 Cross-Modal Interaction Module

A Two-Stage Cross-Modal Interaction Module is Used for Supervised AVEL. For multi-modal tasks, effectively fusing the two modal features is very important. In this paper, the two-stage cross-modal module is used to achieve the purpose of feature fusion. Finally, the interactive features are directly concatenated to obtain the final feature. The two-stage cross-modal module includes the inter-modal attention sub-module and the mutual guidance sub-module. As illustrated in Fig. 4, the inter-modal attention sub-module models the mutual importance of visual and audio features, and the mutual guidance sub-module adjusts the weights of the modes through the mutual guidance mechanism.

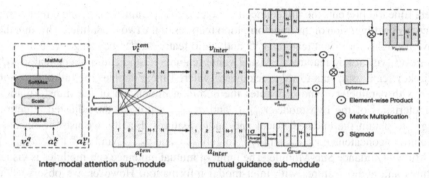

Fig. 4. Two-Stage Cross-Modal Module. The two-stage cross-modal module includes the inter-modal attention sub-module and the mutual guidance sub-module.

Inter-Modal Attention Sub-Module: The inter-modal attention sub-module can identify the cross-mode relationship between visual features and audio features, and capture the importance of each pair of visual features and audio features. In the network, visual features and audio features calculate the cross-modal weight of each other. Taking the attention of audio features to visual features as an example, the visual features of the first segment and the corresponding audio features all segment features calculate the attention weight. Specifically, we use different linear layers to transform visual features v_t^{tem} and audio features a_t^{tem} into the corresponding query features $v_t^q a_t^q$, key feature $v_t^k a_t^k$ and value feature $v_t^v a_t^v$. By calculating the inner product $v_t^q a_t^{k^T}$ between each pair of the visual query feature v_t^q and the audio key feature a_t^k, the original attention weight from the aggregation information of the audio feature to each visual feature is obtained, and vice versa, as shown in Fig. 4 the inter-modal attention sub-module. The original weights are normalized by the square root of the dimension and the Softmax nonlinear function. Two attention matrices $softmax(v_t^q a_t^{k^T}/\sqrt{d}) \in R^{10 \times \dim}$ are obtained for weighting the information flow from audio to visual, and $softmax(a_t^q v_t^{k^T}/\sqrt{d}) \in R^{10 \times \dim}$ for weighting the information flow from visual to audio. These two bidirectional Inter matrices capture the importance between each visual segment and each audio segment. Taking $softmax(v_t^q a_t^{k^T}/\sqrt{d})$ as an example, each row represents the attention weight between a visual fragment and all audio fragment features. Information from all audio features to this visual segment feature can be aggregated into a weighted summation of audio features. We represent the information flow of the Inter module to update the visual and audio fragment features as $v_{update} \in R^{10 \times dim}$ and $a_{update} \in R^{10 \times dim}$:

$$v_t^q = Linear\left(v_t^{tem^T}, \theta_{vq}\right), a_t^q = Linear\left(a_t^{tem^T}, \theta_{aq}\right) \tag{3}$$

$$v_{update} = softmax\left(\frac{v_t^q a_t^{k^T}}{\sqrt{d}}\right) \times a_t^v, a_{update} = softmax\left(\frac{a_t^q v_t^{k^T}}{\sqrt{d}}\right) \times v_t^v \tag{4}$$

$$v_{inter} = Linear\left(\left[v_t^{tem}, v_{update}\right]^T; \theta_{vt}\right), a_{inter} = Linear\left(\left[a_t^{tem}, a_{update}\right]^T; \theta_{at}\right) \tag{5}$$

where Linear represents the full connection layer whose parameter is θ, and d represents the common dimension of the transformation features of the two modalities. Through the above formulas for visual features v_t^{tem} and audio features a_t^{tem}, we can get visual query features v_t^q, visual key features v_t^k, visual value features v_t^v and audio query features a_t^q, audio key features a_t^k, audio value features a_t^v. where Linear denotes the full connection layer with parameter θ and d denotes the common dimension of the transformation characteristics of the two modes. v_{update} and a_{update} represent the adjusted attention weight to obtain the updated visual and audio features. Finally, we use the residual structure to concatenate v_{update} and v_t^{tem} to get v_{inter}, and a_{update} and a_t^{tem} to get a_{inter}.

Mutual Guidance Sub-Module: The input of mutual guidance sub-modules is visual features and audio features with inter-modal information. However, we observe that the relationships within each modality in the audio-visual event localization task are complementary. Some basic intra-modal attention module only takes advantage of intra-modal information to estimate the importance of visual-to-visual and audio-to-audio. However, some relationships are essential for multi-modal tasks, but they can only be identified based on information from other modes. We can generate visual-based audio attention flow and audio-based visual attention flow by visual and audio mutual guidance, and adjust the importance weight in the mode. Specifically, we averaged visual and audio features in the temporal dimension to summarize all information from other modes. The Sigmoid nonlinear function is used to process the average features and expand them to generate the channel adjustment gates $G_{v \leftarrow a}$, $G_{a \leftarrow v}$ that can multiply the query features and key features by elements.

$$G_{v \leftarrow a} = \sigma\left(Linear\left(Avg_{pool(a_{inter})}; \theta_{ap}\right)\right), G_{a \leftarrow v} = \sigma\left(Linear\left(Avg_{pool(v_{inter})}; \theta_{vp}\right)\right). \tag{6}$$

$$\hat{v}_q = (1 + G_{v \leftarrow a}) \odot v_{inter}^q, \hat{v}_k = (1 + G_{v \leftarrow a}) \odot v_{inter}^k \tag{7}$$

We can get $G_{v \leftarrow a}$ and $G_{a \leftarrow v}$ by formulas (6) and obtain the visual features of $\hat{v}_q$ and $\hat{v}_k$ by formula (7). Similar formulas are utilized to get $\hat{a}_q$ and $\hat{a}_k$ in the audio path. Where $\odot$ represents the multiplication of the corresponding elements of the matrix, $\sigma(\cdot)$ is the hyperbolic tangent function.

The channels of query and key features will be activated or disabled by channel gates based on other modes. The channel-based gated vector is generated based on cross-modal information. Then, the mutual guided intra-modal attention flow matrices

$DyIntra_{v \leftarrow v} \in R^{10 \times \dim}$ and $DyIntra_{a \leftarrow a} \in R^{10 \times \dim}$ are obtained by gated query features and key features to weight different intra-modal relationships. Visual features are updated through residual structure:

$$DyIntra_{v \leftarrow v} = softmax\left(\frac{\hat{v}_q \hat{v}_k^{\mathrm{T}}}{\sqrt{d}}\right), v_{update} = DyIntra_{v \leftarrow v} \times v_{inter}^v \qquad (8)$$

$$F_v = Linear\left(F_v + v_{update}\right) \qquad (9)$$

Similar formulas are utilized to get $DyIntra_{a \leftarrow a}$, a_{update} and a feature in the audio path. Finally, we concatenate the visual features F_v and audio features F_a output by the two-stage cross-modal module to generate the final fusion features O_{av}.

A Mutual Guidance Sub-module is Used for Weakly-Supervised AVEL. Unlike supervised audio-visual event localization tasks, the weakly-supervised audio-visual event localization task is only sent to coarse-grained labels such as video-level in the training phase. But we still need to predict segment-level labels during testing. Since the fine-grained clip-level label is unavailable for the weakly-supervised task, as is shown in Fig. 2, GLTCM for weakly-supervised audio-visual event localization makes corresponding adjustments to the two-stage cross-modal module. This paper only uses the mutual guidance sub-module in the weakly-supervised audio-visual event localization task.

The reason for abandoning the inter-modal attention sub-module is that this sub-module is to compute fine-grained attention between cross-modal segments to segments, namely, the fine-grained calculation at the segment level. In the current weakly-supervised audio-visual event localization task, the coarse video-level label available conflicts with the segment-level fine-grained calculation of the inter-modal attention sub-module and is not conducive to network training. Therefore, visual features v_t^{tem} and audio features a_t^{tem} from global-local temporal module ignore the inter-modal attention sub-module and are directly input into the mutual guidance sub-module to obtain the final fusion features O_{av}. The role of the mutual guidance sub-module is the same as one of the supervised tasks and is to generate a global expression of the video level for the features of one mode to adjust the characteristics of another mode.

3.4 Localization Module

The audio-visual event localization is decomposed into two scores in the supervised audio-visual event localization prediction. The first score predicted an event-relevant score ($\hat{s}_t$), predicted whether there was an event in the t video segment, and the second predicted event category score ($\hat{s}_c \in \mathbb{R}^C$), C represented the number of foreground categories. The final fusion feature can be obtained from the previous network module O_{av}. Send O_{av} to the classifier to get event-relevant scores $\hat{s}_t$. When $\hat{s}_t \geq 0.5$, it is considered that there is an event in the tth video segment. When $\hat{s}_t < 0.5$, it is considered that there is no event in the tth video segment, which is the background. Then we maximized O_{av} in the temporal dimension, and O_{av} is generated and sent to the event category classifier to obtain the event category score $\widehat{s_c}$. The specific calculation is as follows:

$$\widehat{s_t} = \sigma(\boldsymbol{O_{av}}W_s), \widehat{s_c} = Softmax(\boldsymbol{O_{av}}W_c)\#(10) \tag{10}$$

W_s and W_c denote learning parameters. We send the segment-level labels in the training phase, including event-relevant labels and event category labels. The object function is composed of the common-used cross-entropy function for multiply category classification and binary cross-entropy for discriminating relevant/irrelevant audio-visual events.

4 Experimental and Results

4.1 Dataset

AVEL Dataset: AVEL proposed the Audio-Visual Event (AVE) dataset, including 4,143 videos and 28 event categories. The AVE dataset extracts 4143 10-s videos and labels them with audio-visual event boundaries. The AVE dataset covers a wide range of audio-visual events (e.g., male speech, female speech, bark, playing guitar, frying (food), etc.). Each event category contains at least 60 videos and up to 188 videos in the AVE dataset. Each video contains at least one audio-visual event of 2 s, of which 66.4% contain audio-visual events spanning 10 s.

4.2 Implementation Details

In Global-Local Temporal and Cross-Modal Network (GLTCM) for supervised audio-visual event localization, we cut a 10-s video in the AVE dataset into 10 segments. Each segment is 1 s long. The pre-trained CLIP model is used to extract 2 frame image features per segment, and the visual features with a dimension of 20×512 are output. Then we use global average pooling to get segment-level features with a dimension of 10×512. The VGGish model pre-trained is used to obtain the segment-level audio feature with dimension 128, and the audio feature with dimension 10×128. For the global-local temporal module, we set the number of parallel headers to 8. The number of channel groups N is 8, A is 4, and the window size of the local temporal sub-module is 3. For the two-stage cross-modal module, we set the number of parallel heads to 8, and stack two groups of two-stage cross-modal modules. The number of training batches in the network is 32, and Adam is adopted as the optimizer. The initial learning rate is set to 5 $\times 10^{-4}$, and it is gradually reduced by 0.5 multiplying every 10, 20, and 30 rounds. We use the overall accuracy as the evaluation index.

In Global-Local Temporal and Cross-Modal Network (GLTCM) for weakly-supervised audio-visual event localization, the initial learning rate is set to 5×10^{-4} and is gradually reduced by 0.5 multiplied every 5, 20, and 40 rounds. The overall accuracy is applied as the evaluation index.

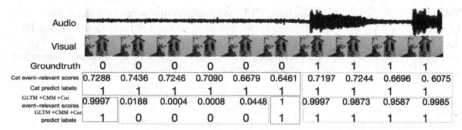

Audio									
Visual									
Groundtruth	0	0	0	0	0	0	1	1	1	1
Cat event–relevant scores	0.7288	0.7436	0.7246	0.7090	0.6679	0.6461	0.7197	0.7244	0.6696	0.6075
Cat predict labels	1	1	1	1	1	1	1	1	1	1
GLTM +CMM +Cat event–relevant scores	0.9997	0.0188	0.0004	0.0008	0.0448	1	0.9997	0.9873	0.9587	0.9985
GLTM +CMM +Cat predict labels	1	0	0	0	0	1	1	1	1	1

Fig. 5. Visualization of GLTCM for supervised Audio-Visual Event Localization on AVE dataset. "1" means an audio-visual event occurred, and "0" means no audio-visual event occurred.

4.3 Ablation Experimental Result of GLTCM for Audio-Visual Event Localization

GLTCM for Supervised Audio-Visual Event Localization: We perform ablation experiments to show the relative importance of each component. The results of the ablations are shown in Table 1. From the ablation experiment, it can be seen that the modeling of temporal relationships brings certain improvements to the audio-visual event localization task. Specifically, modeling global temporal relationships and local temporal relationships is crucial, and the simultaneous application of the global temporal module and local temporal module through channel grouping can bring greater benefits. We exploit the two-stage cross-modal module to model the cross-modal relationship between visual features and audio features so that the two modal information complement each other and achieve a certain fusion effect. After we put visual and audio features into the two-stage cross-modal module, we use a simple concatenation method to fuse features and then send them into the localization module. The accuracy of GLTCM for supervised audio-visual event localization is 81.49%, which improves 4.59% compared to the method with simple feature concatenation in the second row of Table 1.

4.4 Comparisons with the Previous Methods for Audio-Visual Event Localization

Table 2 presents a comparison between GLTCM's research results for audio-visual event localization tasks and those of other recent networks. This paper presents the GLTCM model for audio-visual event localization, which extracts multi-modal features using an appropriate method, fully models the temporal relationship of surrounding segments and the entire video with a global-local temporal module, uses two two-stage cross-modality modules to model two modal features, and finally concatenates the two features. The GLTCM model achieves 81.49% accuracy in the supervised audio-visual event localization task and 77.5% accuracy in the weakly-supervised audio-visual event localization task. These results demonstrate the advanced performance of the GLTCM model for audio-visual event localization. We compared the parameters of AVEL and CMRA based on the published code and found tha our proposed GLTCM achieved better audio-visual event localization accuracy without significantly increasing the number of parameters. Moreover, our method has a computational cost of only 6.18 M, and during testing, it takes only 6.5 ms to infer a 10-s video.

Table 1. Ablation study on AVE dataset in GLTCM for audio-visual event localization. Cat, GTM, LTM, GLTM, IMA, MG, and CMM denote concatenation, Global Temporal Module, Local Temporal Module, Global-Local Temporal Module, Inter-Modal Attention Sub-Module, Mutual Guidance Sub-Module, Two-stage Cross-Modal Module, respectively. Sup, W-Sup denote supervised and weakly- supervised audio-visual event localization.

Methods	Sup. Acc.	W-Sup. Acc.
Cat with clip features	76.91	76.19
GTM + Cat	79.72	76.24
LTM + Cat	79.13	76.20
GLTM + Cat	79.95	76.81
IMA + Cat	78.51	74.05
MG + Cat	78.81	76.51
CMM + Cat	79.55	75.50
GLTCM (ours)	**81.49**	**77.51**

As illustrated in the visualized result in Fig. 5, only simple concatenation of features is performed, and the first to sixth segments are predicted incorrectly; after the multi-modal feature passes GLTM and CMM, the predicted labels of the second to fifth segments can be corrected to improve the accuracy of audio-visual event localization. The first and sixth segments are still mispredicted because the first segment has no previous information, which makes it difficult to predict; the seventh segment has an event that occurred, which causes the sixth segment to be affected.

Table 2. Experimental comparison with existing methods on the AVE dataset in the supervised audio-visual event localization task. "Parms" denotes the number of parameters(M) of the model.

Networks	Sup. Acc.	Sup. Params.	W-Sup. Acc.	W-Sup Params.
AVEL [3]	72.7	2.32	66.7	1.34
AVSDN [4]	72.6	–	68.4	–
DAM [8]	74.5	–	–	–
AVIN [9]	75.2	–	69.4	–
JOA [6]	76.2	–	–	–
AV-transformer [10]	76.8	–	68.9	–
MPN [7]	77.6	–	72.0	–
CMRA [11]	77.4	15.86	72.9	15.86
PSP [12]	77.8	–	73.5	–
CPSP [13]	78.6	–	74.2	–
M2N [15]	79.5	–	–	–
LAV$_{IS}$H [14]	81.1	10.1	–	–
GLTCM (ours)	**81.49**	4.02	**77.5**	3.37

5 Conclusions

This paper proposed Global-Local Temporal and Cross-Modal Network (GLTCM) for supervised/weakly-supervised audio-visual event localization. Experimental results demonstrate that our proposed GLTCM method achieves excellent results on supervised and weakly-supervised audio-visual event localization tasks in the AVE dataset.

References

1. Xu, J., Mei, T., Yao, T., Rui, Y.: MSR-VTT: a large video description dataset for bridging video and language. In: CVPR 2016, pp. 5288–5296 (2016)
2. Tapaswi, M., Zhu, Y., Stiefelhagen, R., Torralba, A., Urtasun, R., Fidler, S.: MovieQA: understanding stories in movies through question-answering. In: CVPR 2016, pp. 4631–4640 (2016)
3. Tian, Y., Shi, J., Li, B., Duan, Z., Xu, C.: Audio-Visual Event Localization in Unconstrained Videos. In: ECCV, vol. 2, pp. 252–268 (2018)
4. Lin, Y.B., Li, Y.J., Wang, Y.C.F. Dual-modality Seq2Seq network for audio-visual event localization. In: ICASSP 2019, pp. 2002–2006 (2019)
5. Xuan, H., Zhang, Z., Chen, S., Yang, J., Yan, Y.: Cross-modal attention network for temporal inconsistent audio-visual event localization. In: AAAI 2020, pp. 279–286 (2020)
6. Duan, B., Tang, H., Wang, W., Zong, Z., Yang, G., Yan, Y.: Audio-visual event localization via recursive fusion by joint co-attention. In: WACV 2021, pp. 4012–4021 (2021)
7. Yu, J., Cheng, Y., Feng, R.: MPN: multimodal parallel network for audio-visual event localization. In: ICME 2021, pp. 1–6 (2021)
8. Wu, Y., Zhu, L., Yan, Y., Yang, Y.: Dual attention matching for audio-visual event localization. In: ICCV 2019, pp. 6291–6299 (2019)
9. Ramaswamy, J.: What makes the sound?: A dual-modality interacting network for audio-visual event localization. In: ICASSP 2020, pp. 4372–4376 (2020)
10. Lin, Y.B., Wang, Y.C.F.: Audiovisual transformer with instance attention for audio-visual event localization. In: ACCV, vol. 6, pp. 274–290 (2020)
11. Xu, H., Zeng, R., Wu, Q., Tan, M., Gan, C.: Cross-modal relation-aware networks for audio-visual event localization. In: ACM Multimedia 2020, pp. 3893–3901 (2020)
12. Zhou, J., Zheng, L., Zhong, Y., Hao, S., Wang, M.: Positive sample propagation along the audio-visual event line. In: CVPR 2021, pp. 8436–8444 (2021)
13. Zhou, J., Guo, D., Wang, M.: Contrastive positive sample propagation along the audio-visual event line. IEEE Trans. Pattern Anal. Mach. Intell. (2022)
14. Lin, Y.B., Sung, Y.L., Lei, J., et al. Vision transformers are parameter-efficient audio-visual learners. arXiv preprint arXiv:2212.07983 (2022)
15. Wang, H., Zha, Z.J., Li, L., et al.: Multi-modulation network for audio-visual event localization. arXiv preprint arXiv:2108.11773 (2021)
16. Radford, A., et al.: Learning transferable visual models from natural language supervision. In: ICML 2021, pp. 8748–8763 (2017)
17. Hershey, S., et al.: CNN architectures for large-scale audio classification. ICASSP 2017, pp. 131–135 (2017)
18. Qing, Z., et al.: Temporal context aggregation network for temporal action proposal refinement. In: CVPR 2021, pp. 485–494 (2021)

Recent Advances in Class-Incremental Learning

Dejie Yang, Minghang Zheng, Weishuai Wang, Sizhe Li, and Yang Liu[✉]

Wangxuan Institute of Computer Technology, Peking University, Beijing, China
ydj@stu.pku.edu.cn, {minghang,wangweishuai,lisizhe,yangliu}@pku.edu.cn

Abstract. A large number of deep learning models have been applied in a wide range of fields nowadays. However, most existing models can only generalize to the categories in the training set and are unable to learn new categories incrementally. In practical applications, new categories or tasks will constantly emerge, which requires models to continuously learn new category knowledge like humans while maintaining existing category knowledge. Such the learning process, i.e., *class-incremental learning* (CIL), abstracts more attention from the research community. CIL faces several challenges, such as imbalanced data distribution, limited model memory capacity, and the catastrophic forgetting of category representation. Therefore, we provide an up-to-date and detailed overview of CIL methods in this survey, including data-based, model-based, and representation-based approaches. We also discuss the impact of pre-trained models on CIL and compare the latest methods on widely-used benchmarks. Finally, we summarize the challenges and future directions of CIL.

Keywords: Class-Incremental Learning · Continual Learning · Lifelong Learning

1 Introduction

Both humans and animals possess the remarkable ability to learn a wide variety of new tasks while retaining previously acquired knowledge. In practical applications, this ability to learn continuously is essential, as new data become available and older data may become obsolete due to storage constraints [15], privacy concerns [5], or other factors. Therefore, developing learning algorithms that can learn incrementally and adapt to changing environments is crucial for many real-world applications. Unfortunately, existing AI systems, particularly those based on deep learning techniques, often significantly decline performance on previously learned tasks when trained on new data, aka. *catastrophic forgetting* [40]. *Incremental learning* (IL) is a promising approach to addressing this challenge. And IL has been successfully applied to solve a wide range of real-world problems, including medical diagnosis [52], autonomous driving [53], human-machine interaction [42], etc.

H. Lu et al. (Eds.): ICIG 2023, LNCS 14356, pp. 212–224, 2023.
https://doi.org/10.1007/978-3-031-46308-2_18

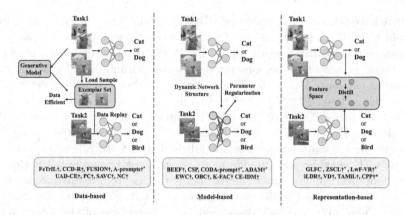

Fig. 1. We have divided the latest class-incremental learning methods into three major categories, with each major class method more precisely divided into two specific methods. The methods correspond to the colors of the works below. * represents the method utilizing pre-trained model and † shows the work is proposed in 2023. (Color figure online)

Incremental learning, also known as *continual* or *lifelong* learning, aims to continuously learn new knowledge while retaining most of the previously learned knowledge [38]. At the stage for a particular 'new' task, the model is trained with only the data from this current task. The trained model is then required to complete all previous tasks. For example, in animal image classification as shown in Fig. 1, at the first stage, a model learns 'cat' and 'dog' with the data of the first task. In the second stage, the model learns 'bird' with the data of the second task. Then it is required to recognize images of all seen classes ('cat', 'dog', and 'bird'). Incremental learning can be divided into three types based on the nature of the tasks and categories that the model needs to learn: Task-Incremental Learning (TIL), Domain-Incremental Learning (DIL), and Class-Incremental Learning (CIL). In TIL, the task is known and the data category for a given task is determined. In DIL, the tasks are unknown during testing, but the category space remains the same under different tasks. In CIL, both the tasks and the categories are unknown and constantly changing. This survey focuses on **Class-Incremental Learning** for its more stringent settings.

There are three challenges in CIL according to the levels of machine learning. Firstly, for aforementioned *catastrophic forgetting*, it is important to handle the imbalanced and distribution-unstable data of different tasks or utilize additional data to improve CIL. Secondly, due to the limitation of computational cost and memory of the model, it is also a challenge to adjust the architecture and parameters of the model to fit new data without forgetting old data. Thirdly, it is critical for CIL how to optimize the representation of different categories to learn new knowledge from new data while preserving old knowledge. Our survey focuses on the three challenges and provides a comprehensive overview of CIL.

There have been several surveys on CIL [19,22,56,63]. Our survey differs from theirs in the following aspects: (1) Different from these surveys, we pay more attention to **pre-trained models** (PTMs). With the rapid development of pre-trained models, they have demonstrated strong performance and generalization capabilities on many tasks [16,46], and may have a significant impact on CIL by providing a knowledge foundation. In this survey, we investigate the recent CIL methods using PTMs and analyze the impact of the strong transfer ability of PTMs on CIL. (2) Unlike [19,22] that focus on some sub-domains of CIL, such as predictive maintenance [19] and label-efficient CIL [22], we focus on the **general CIL setting** and provide more comprehensive methods towards the above challenges. (3) We adopt the taxonomy of CIL from [63] while pay more attention to the **latest (2023) developments** in CIL. [56,63] only include CIL methods up to 2022 and lack discussion and comparison of the latest SOTA methods.

The contributions of our survey can be summarized as follows: (1) We present an up-to-date and comprehensive review of CIL with the latest methods and analyze the works related to PTMs. (2) We offer a holistic overview of the latest CIL methods with elaborated taxonomy of application scenarios. And we also provide detailed problem definitions, comparisons on different datasets, and analysis of the results. (3) To inspire future research, we provide an in-depth analysis of current challenges and outline potential future directions for research and applications in class-incremental learning.

2   Taxonomy and Approaches

2.1   Problem Definition

Class-incremental learning aims to sequentially learn a series of tasks containing different sets of categories. Formally, let there be a sequence of T training tasks $\{\mathcal{D}^1, \mathcal{D}^2, ..., \mathcal{D}^T\}$, where $\mathcal{D}^t = \{(\boldsymbol{x}_i^t, y_i^t)\}_{i=1}^{n_t}$ is the t-th task with n_t training instances. $\boldsymbol{x}_i^t$ is the i-th instance in input space $\mathcal{X}$, and $y_i^t \in \mathcal{Y}_t$ is its corresponding label, where $\mathcal{Y}_t$ is the category set of t-th task. The sets of categories for different tasks are not intersected, i.e. if $i \neq j$, $\mathcal{Y}_i \cap \mathcal{Y}_j = \emptyset$. When training the t-th task, we can only access the data in $\mathcal{D}^t$. The ultimate goal of CIL is to continuously establish classification models for all classes. When the training process of the t-th task is finished, we get a model $f(x) : \mathcal{X} \sim \mathbf{Y}_t$ which can minimize the predefined loss functions on $\mathcal{D}^t$ as well as maintain the ability to distinguish between previously learned categories $\{\mathcal{Y}^i\}_{i=0}^{t-1}$.

2.2   Data-Based Class-Incremental Learning

Due to the limited data availability, in each new task, CIL models are trained with the data of current task $\mathcal{D}^t$ and can not get access to the whole data of previous tasks $\{\mathcal{D}^i\}_{i=0}^{t-1}$. So we need the data-based method to get a high-quality subset of the base class or reduce deviation from the base set.

Data Replay-Based Methods. To avoid the *catastrophic forgetting* (Sect. 1), most data-based CIL methods store a few training samples or extra data for seen categories as the *exemplar set*: $\mathcal{E} = \{(\boldsymbol{x}_j, y_j)\}_{j=1}^{M}, y_j \in \mathbf{Y}_{t-1}$, where M is the number of samples or data of previous dataset. With the joint optimization of the exemplar set and current task data $\mathcal{E} \cup \mathcal{D}^t$, i.e., data replay, the CIL models can relive the catastrophic forgetting effectively. To our knowledge, [61] is the first study to apply data replay in CIL, which involved storing a subset of the training data from previous tasks and replaying it during training a new task to prevent catastrophic forgetting. [44] propose a combination of a pseudo-sample generator based on the centroid representations of past-task datasets and a fixed feature extractor of the current task. Similarly, to tackle the continual domain drift problem, CCD-R [33] samples data points for exemplar set based on constructed centroids to reduce the sample bias in data replay. To better utilize the knowledge extracted from former tasks, FUSION [2] proposes a learning strategy based on the construction of meta-examples and exploits the update through meta-examples to improve supervised and unsupervised CIL. In order to better guarantee the separation between old and new classes, ISM [45] proposes an incremental semantics mining approach to reduce the confusion between old and new classes by excluding the semantics of old classes from the representation of new classes. To save space for storing exemplar set, [35] compress exemplars by generating 0-1 masks on pixel level from class activation maps.

Inspired by the pre-trained model's outstanding performance, A-prompts [37] introduce a prompt-generating mechanism on top of the pre-trained vision transformer (ViT). Samples of the particular current task can be remapped to the features of any previous task with the help of the learned prompts. Besides, [28] quantitatively shows the substantial benefits of pre-trained models over from-scratch trained models and finds that pre-trained models are particularly gainful for existing data-replay methods.

Data Efficient-Based Methods. To avoid model overfitting without catas-trophically forgetting all seen classes, some data efficient-based methods have attracted increasing attention, which incrementally and data-efficiently learn novel classes from limited labeled samples,i.e., few-shot CIL. UAD-CE [8] employs a class-balanced self-training to avoid the gradual dominance of easy-to-classified classes on pseudo-label generation for unlabeled data and combines uncertainty-guided knowledge refinement with adaptive distillation to distill reli-able knowledge from the reference model. PC [57] proposes a prototype con-tainer to store each class prototype to retain old knowledge and update the container with new classes to enhance the representation of extracted features and supplement few-shot scenes. SAVC [49] finds that the cross-entropy loss suffers poor class separation in terms of representations and limits to the novel classes generalization and introduces semantic-aware virtual contrastive learn-ing by introducing virtual classes via pre-defined transformations. In order to update a learnable classifier as a geometric structure, NC [59] proposes a neural collapse framework by pre-assigning an optimal feature-classifier alignment as a fixed target throughout incremental training.

Discussions. Data-based methods explore many ways to reduce catastrophic forgetting, including building an exemplar set to replay, prototype learning with unlabeled data, or contrastive learning. And these methods obtain a certain performance improvement for CIL on the data level. However, few methods consider the data-imbalance problem of different classes, especially the emerging new data, and tasks in real-world applications, which hurts the performance of CIL [31]. On the other hand, for some privacy protection scenarios, the methods also need to avoid exposing user data, like introducing Federated Learning [13].

2.3   Model-Based Class-Incremental Learning

Model-based class-incremental learning forces the model itself to evolve during the training process. There are two main categories, dynamic network structure, and parameter regularization. When introduced to a new task, the former expands the network to enhance its representation capacity, while the latter tries to regularize important parameters to relieve catastrophic forgetting.

Dynamic Network Structure-Based Methods. The premise of dynamic network structure methods is to assume that the network's ability of representation is finite and is positively correlated with model size. As a result, when the model is expanded, it represents features which contain richer information. Dynamic network structure methods design the network structure to dynamically match the representation capacity required by a specific task. DEN [60] first enhances the representation ability by adding neurons. It expands new neurons top-down, then removes useless ones using group-sparsity regularization. Some methods use reinforcement learning to search for appropriate neural structures for each specific task. For example, CSP [14] builds a subspace of policies to train the agent on the task sequence, which grows adaptively according to the task sequence. In addition to learning new neurons, some methods also duplicate the backbone networks, train them on new tasks and fit them with former tasks. Expert Gate [1] learns a mapping gate to distinguish the task class of each instance and choose a suitable pathway for each instance during inference. However, the above methods train different models in a coupled manner, which leads to the spoilage of eventual predictions. BEEF [55] considers the bi-directional capacity among modules and aggregates those modules into a unifying classifier by proposing an energy-based method. It conducts an energy function to measure the uncertainty of predicting the label of the input x as y. Generally, methods of learning new backbones require extra memory, and some methods try to optimize the expansion cost. For example, MEMO [64] finds when changing tasks, deeper layers of different models always differ more than the shallow layers. So models for different tasks can share generalizable shallow layers, and each model has its specialized task-specific deeper layers, and the loss function as:

$$\mathcal{L} = \sum_{k=1}^{|y_b|} -\mathbb{I}(y = k) \log S_k(W_{new}^{T}[\phi_{s_{old}}(\phi_g(\mathbf{x})), \phi_{s_{new}}(\phi_g(\mathbf{x}))]), \qquad (1)$$

where ϕ_s and ϕ_g represent the deep and shallow layers separately. S_k represents the softmax function, and W_{new} is a mapping matrix.

Recently, with the prevalence of Vision Transformer (ViT), some methods borrow from its idea, using prompt expansion to adjust to new tasks and reduce memory requirements. Also, large-scale pre-train models contain more task-agnostic knowledge, which benefits the training process. For example, CODA-Prompt [48] adopts the attention-based end-to-end key-query scheme to extend the prompt search. ADAM [65] introduces the model adapt and model merge method which aggregates the advantages of the pre-trained model's generalizability and the adapted model's flexibility.

Parameter Regularization-Based Methods. Some methods propose that the importance of model parameters is not equivalent, so if keeping the important ones static, the model can maintain the former knowledge to avoid catastrophic forgetting. As a result, these methods focus on evaluating the importance of each parameter. EWC [24] first conducts an importance matrix that introduces a regularization loss to remember old tasks, as shown in.

$$\mathcal{L} = \ell(f(\mathbf{x}), y) + \frac{1}{2}\lambda \sum_k \Omega_k (\theta_k^{b-1} - \theta_k)^2. \tag{2}$$

where θ_k represents the parameter of the k-th model and θ_k^{b-1} the parameter after learning the $(b-1)$-th task. Ω is the importance matrix. In other words, θ_k with more importance has a larger Ω_k. OBC [7] only modifies the parameters of the final layer to mitigate the prediction bias. In order to learn new class in the incremental sessions, WaRP [23] transforms the original parameter space into a new space and try to select the important parameters while freezing the useless ones properly. In order to dynamically optimize the parameters during training instead of conducting optimization at the end of each task, some existing methods propose to estimate the importance matrix online. Based on this idea, K-FAC [27] mixes the Gaussian posteriors and uses the estimated Fisher information matrix to find a maximum, and CE-IDM [58] analyzes the capacity difference of parameters in different layers to learn layer-wise importance matrix.

Discussions. Model-based methods achieve good performance on CIL tasks. However, they need to design specific modules for new tasks where task-specific prior knowledge is required. In detail, dynamic network structure methods always need a pre-train model and extra budgets when expanding the model, so they are unsuitable for unexpandable client devices. Besides, the guidance from the importance matrix in parameter regularization methods may conflict at different training stages, leading to the difficulty of model optimization.

2.4   Representation-Based Class-Incremental Learning

Representation-based CIL focuses to learn the representation, which preserves a model's knowledge from previous tasks. A common idea is to use knowledge distillation (KD) [17] to require the new model to retain the characteristics of the old model. Some methods also aim to optimize the feature space, ensuring that adding new classes affects the old class feature space as little as possible.

Knowledge Distillation-Based Methods. Knowledge distillation (KD) can transfer the prior knowledge in the old model to new model and prevent catastrophic forgetting. In general, knowledge distillation-based approaches learn new categories through classification loss (e.g. cross entropy) and prevent old categories from being forgotten through knowledge distillation loss (e.g. KL divergence):

$$\mathcal{L} = \mathcal{L}_{CLS}(f^t(x), y) + \mathcal{L}_{KD}(\phi^t(x), \phi^{t-1}(x)) \tag{3}$$

where f^t is the new model which outputs the logits of the input sample, ϕ^t and ϕ^{t-1} can be either the feature extractor of the new and old model which outputs the representations or the full model, which outputs the logits. Chen et al. [6] combine the uncertainty in model predictions with knowledge distillation by minimizing the uncertainty of old class predictions to help the new model keep old knowledge. Some methods also consider the knowledge from the relationship between samples. For example, GLFC [13] uses a class-semantic relation distillation loss to address the issue of forgetting old classes. This loss helps maintain consistent inter-class semantic similarity relations between old and new models.

Largely pre-trained vision-language models have recently achieved remarkable performance on various downstream tasks. LwF-VR [12] fine-tunes the pre-trained CLIP model [46] for CIL while preventing forgetting by generating random sentences for distillation. ZSCL [62] introduces a reference dataset to distill both visual and language knowledge from old models.

Feature Space-Based Methods. Some methods achieve incremental learning from the perspective of feature space. For example, iLDR [51] utilizes a closed-loop data transcription system [9] to learn a linear discriminative representation (LDR). The LDR of each class is positioned in a low-dimensional linear subspace, which is highly incoherent for each class. When learning new classes, to retain the memory of an old class, iLDR simply needs to preserve the subspace. IVoro [36] is the first to utilize prototypical networks for CIL, which involves constructing a Voronoi Diagram (VD) in a fixed feature space. VD can be incrementally constructed, with newly added classes only affecting proximate classes and making non-contiguous classes difficult to forget. TAMiL [3] creates a communication bottleneck to reduce the interference between different tasks by allowing only task-relevant information to reach the global workspace. LwP [20] proposes that forgetting can be positive if it removes biases or spurious correlations in the training data. LwP encourages benign forgetting through label-free contrastive learning, which helps the model learn unbiased representations by avoiding false correlations between features and labels. CPP [32] takes advantage of ViT and explicitly aligns the embedding functions generating prototypes, which reduces prototype interference in the embedding space.

Discussions. Representation-based methods achieve class-incremental learning by distilling knowledge from the old model or directly learning highly incoherent feature spaces for each class. They have advantages in model size and computational complexity because they do not require a large expansion of model parameters when facing new classes compared to dynamic networks. However, as the number of new classes increases, approaching or even surpassing the base classes, constrained by the limited model capacity, the representation-based approach is more likely to suffer from catastrophic forgetting.

3   Evaluation

CIL methods are used in many tasks, like VQA [29], object detection [43], semantic segmentation [4,41], language modeling [34,39,50] and robotics [21,30]. Most CIL methods are designed to deal with image classification. In this section, we focus on CIL in the image classification task.

3.1   Datasets and Metrics

Commonly-used datasets for image classification in early are MNIST [11] and CIFAR-10 [25]. These two datasets have low resolutions (20×20 and 32×32) and contain 10 categories. With the development of CIL, datasets with a larger number of categories and higher resolution are used to validate the performance of approaches. The datasets used in recent class-incremental learning work include CIFAR-100 [25], CUB-200 [54], Tiny-ImageNet [26], ImageNet-100 [10,47], ImageNet-Full [10], etc.

We use the metric 'average accuracy' to evaluate the performance of different methods. We denote the accuracy of the i-th task as a_i, and the 'average accuracy' can be calculated as $\frac{1}{T} \sum_{i=1}^{T} a_i$, where T is the total number of tasks.

3.2   Performance Comparisons

The performance comparison is shown in Table 1. On small-scale datasets (CIFAR-100 and CIFAR-10), the model-based method CODA-Prompt [48] utilizes the large-scale pre-trained models and achieves the best performance under the 'B0Inc10' setting. For the methods without pretraining, the representation-based iVoro [36] achieves the best performance, demonstrating the effectiveness of introducing the Voronoi diagram. The data-based approach shows strengths on the large-scale dataset (ImageNet-100), and ISM achieves the best performance under the 'B0Inc10' setting. We also found that the number of base classes has a certain impact on model performance. For example, the model-based BEEF [55] performs best under the 'B50Inc10' setting, while its performance is generally average under other settings.

The methods above take different models as backbones and have different model sizes. A-prompts [37] shows the best performance on B0Inc10, yet it uses the backbone ViT/B-16, which has the highest parameter count. Similarly, CPP [32] also performs best on B0Inc5 while employing the ViT/B-16 backbone. Nonetheless, some methods can achieve solid performance with a significantly smaller number of parameters. Among all the model-based methods, ADAM [65] exceeds the performance of other model-based methods, even though its model parameter count is far lower (only 0.15M). CIL methods should have strong classification performance while considering the model's parameter size and operational efficiency to save inference costs and apply to more low-resource scenarios.

Table 1. Average accuracy and resources consumption comparison of different methods. 'BxIncy' indicates different settings, where x is the number of base classes, y the number of new classes in each task.* represents the method utilizing the pre-trained model. ˣ represents this work is published in 2022, otherwise in 2023.

Taxonomy	Method	#Params	CIFAR-100				ImageNet-100		CIFAR-10	
			B0Inc5	B60Inc5	B0Inc10	B50Inc10	B0Inc10	B50Inc10	B0Inc1	B0Inc2
Data-based	FeTrIL [44]	11.4M	61.5	–	65.2	–	71.20	–	–	–
	FUSIONˣ [2]	–	–	–	–	–	–	–	–	83.95
	CCD-R [33]	–	70.69	–	–	–	–	–	–	–
	ISM [45]	22.7M	74.96	–	–	–	92.67	–	–	–
	UAD-CE [8]	–	–	63.93	–	–	–	–	–	–
	PC [57]	11.4M	–	61.71	–	–	–	–	–	–
	NC [59]	12.4M	–	67.50	–	–	–	–	–	–
	A-prompts* [37]	86M	–	–	87.87	–	–	–	–	–
Model-based	BEEF [55]	0.43M	73.05	–	72.93	71.71	79.34	80.52	–	–
	MEMOˣ [64]	2.1M	73.57	–	72.37	69.39	72.55	–	–	–
	DNE [18]	–	–	74.86	–	–	78.56	–	–	–
	CODA-Prompt* [48]	86M	–	86.25	–	–	–	–	–	–
	CIM-CIL [35]	11.4M	–	–	–	69.53	–	–	–	–
	WaRP [23]	0.27M	65.83	–	–	–	–	–	–	–
	ADAM* [65]	0.15M	90.65	–	–	–	–	–	–	–
Rep-based	GLFCˣ [13]	–	–	66.9	–	57.0	–	–	–	–
	Chen et al. [6]	11.4M	71.70	–	72.51	68.61	81.21	80.69	–	–
	ZSCL* [62]	86M	80.39	–	82.15	–	–	–	–	–
	iLDR [51]	4.5M	–	–	–	–	–	–	72.7	72.3
	TAMiL [3]	3.3M	–	50.11	–	–	–	74.45	–	–
	iVoro [36]	–	81.24	–	83.52	–	90.04	–	–	–
	CPP* [32]	86M	93.49	–	–	–	–	–	–	–

4   Discussion and Challenges

In this section, we discuss the current challenges and possible future directions of class-incremental learning.

CIL with PTMs. A potential research direction is exploring how to better transfer the ability to new classes while retaining the generalization of PTMs. Although some methods [12,62] have made preliminary attempts, they still face catastrophic forgetting, as the data for knowledge distillation struggles to cover the data used for pre-training.

CIL with Multi-modal. The data in real-world applications is usually multi-modalities, including images, videos, texts, audio, 3D, etc. CIL models need to adapt to more modal scenarios [21,39]. And how to utilize the complementary of multi-modality to enhance CIL is also a worthwhile research problem.

CIL with Edge Devices. Models deployed on edge devices will pose new challenges, such as limited storage and computing resource and real-time high-performance requirements [44]. Hence, CIL models on edge should take more metrics into account, like memory cost and inference efficiency.

5   Conclusion

In practical applications, class-incremental learning (CIL) methods can incrementally learn knowledge from data of new categories without catastrophic forgetting of previous categories. This survey focuses on the mainstream methods of CIL, including data, model, and representation, and provides an overview and analysis of the latest methods in these three aspects. To identify critical factors for improving CIL, we compare these methods to widely-used benchmarks. We also discuss current challenges and future research directions of CIL to facilitate subsequent works in this field and beyond.

References

1. Aljundi, R., Chakravarty, P., Tuytelaars, T.: Expert gate: lifelong learning with a network of experts. In: CVPR (2017)
2. Bertugli, A., Vincenzi, S., Calderara, S., Passerini, A.: Generalising via meta-examples for continual learning in the wild. In: Machine Learning, Optimization, and Data Science: 8th International Workshop, LOD (2022)
3. Bhat, P., Zonooz, B., Arani, E.: Task-aware information routing from common representation space in lifelong learning. arXiv (2023)
4. Cermelli, F., Mancini, M., Bulò, S.R., Ricci, E., Caputo, B.: Modeling the background for incremental learning in semantic segmentation. In: CVPR (2020)
5. Chamikara, M.A.P., Bertók, P., Liu, D., Camtepe, S., Khalil, I.: Efficient data perturbation for privacy preserving and accurate data stream mining. Pervasive Mob. Comput. (2018)
6. Chen, K., Liu, S., Wang, R., Zheng, W.S.: Adaptively integrated knowledge distillation and prediction uncertainty for continual learning. arXiv (2023)
7. Chrysakis, A., Moens, M.F.: Online bias correction for task-free continual learning. In: ICLR (2022)
8. Cui, Y., Deng, W., Chen, H., Liu, L.: Uncertainty-aware distillation for semi-supervised few-shot class-incremental learning. arXiv (2023)
9. Dai, X., et al.: Closed-loop data transcription to an LDR via minimaxing rate reduction. arXiv (2021)
10. Deng, J., Dong, W., Socher, R., Li, L.J., Li, K., Fei-Fei, L.: Imagenet: a large-scale hierarchical image database. In: CVPR (2009)
11. Deng, L.: The mNIST database of handwritten digit images for machine learning research. IEEE Sig. Process. Mag. (2012)
12. Ding, Y., Liu, L., Tian, C., Yang, J., Ding, H.: Don't stop learning: towards continual learning for the clip model. arXiv (2022)

13. Dong, J., et al.: Federated class-incremental learning. In: CVPR (2022)
14. Gaya, J.B., Doan, T.V., Caccia, L., Soulier, L., Denoyer, L., Raileanu, R.: Building a subspace of policies for scalable continual learning. arXiv (2022)
15. Golab, L., Özsu, M.T.: Issues in data stream management. ACM SIGMOD Rec. (2003)
16. Han, K., et al.: A survey on vision transformer. IEEE TPAMI (2022)
17. Hinton, G., Vinyals, O., Dean, J.: Distilling the knowledge in a neural network. arXiv (2015)
18. Hu, Z., Li, Y., Lyu, J., Gao, D., Vasconcelos, N.: Dense network expansion for class incremental learning. In: CVPR (2023)
19. Hurtado, J., Salvati, D., Semola, R., Bosio, M., Lomonaco, V.: Continual learning for predictive maintenance: overview and challenges. arXiv (2023)
20. Jeon, M., Lee, H., Seong, Y., Kang, M.: Learning without prejudices: continual unbiased learning via benign and malignant forgetting. In: ICLR (2022)
21. Julian, R.C., Swanson, B., Sukhatme, G.S., Levine, S., Finn, C., Hausman, K.: Efficient adaptation for end-to-end vision-based robotic manipulation. arXiv (2020)
22. Kilickaya, M., van de Weijer, J., Asano, Y.M.: Towards label-efficient incremental learning: a survey. arXiv (2023)
23. Kim, D.Y., Han, D.J., Seo, J., Moon, J.: Warping the space: weight space rotation for class-incremental few-shot learning. In: ICLR (2022)
24. Kirkpatrick, J., et al.: Overcoming catastrophic forgetting in neural networks. Proc. Natl. Acad. Sci. (2016)
25. Krizhevsky, A., Hinton, G., et al.: Learning multiple layers of features from tiny images (2009)
26. Le, Y., Yang, X.: Tiny imagenet visual recognition challenge. CS 231N (2015)
27. Lee, J., Hong, H.G., Joo, D., Kim, J.: Continual learning with extended Kronecker-factored approximate curvature. In: CVPR (2020)
28. Lee, K.Y., Zhong, Y., Wang, Y.X.: Do pre-trained models benefit equally in continual learning? In: WACV (2023)
29. Lei, S.W., et al.: Symbolic replay: scene graph as prompt for continual learning on VQA task. arXiv (2022)
30. Lesort, T., Lomonaco, V., Stoian, A., Maltoni, D., Filliat, D., Rodríguez, N.D.: Continual learning for robotics: definition, framework, learning strategies, opportunities and challenges. Inf. Fusion (2020)
31. Li, Y., Bai, L., Liang, Z., Du, H.: Incremental label propagation for data sets with imbalanced labels. Neurocomputing (2023)
32. Li, Z., et al.: Steering prototype with prompt-tuning for rehearsal-free continual learning. arXiv (2023)
33. Liu, D., Lyu, F., Li, L., Xia, Z., Hu, F.: Centroid distance distillation for effective rehearsal in continual learning. arXiv (2023)
34. Liu, T., Ungar, L., Sedoc, J.: Continual learning for sentence representations using conceptors. arXiv (2019)
35. Luo, Z., Liu, Y., Schiele, B., Sun, Q.: Class-incremental exemplar compression for class-incremental learning. arXiv (2023)
36. Ma, C., Ji, Z., Huang, Z., Shen, Y., Gao, M., Xu, J.: Progressive Voronoi diagram subdivision enables accurate data-free class-incremental learning. In: ICLR (2022)
37. Ma, Z., Hong, X., Liu, B., Wang, Y., Guo, P., Li, H.: Remind of the past: incremental learning with analogical prompts. arXiv (2023)
38. Masana, M., Liu, X., Twardowski, B., Menta, M., Bagdanov, A.D., van de Weijer, J.: Class-incremental learning: survey and performance evaluation on image classification. IEEE TPAMI (2022)

39. de Masson d'Autume, C., Ruder, S., Kong, L., Yogatama, D.: Episodic memory in lifelong language learning. arXiv (2019)
40. McCloskey, M., Cohen, N.J.: Catastrophic interference in connectionist networks: the sequential learning problem. In: Psychology of Learning and Motivation (1989)
41. Michieli, U., Zanuttigh, P.: Incremental learning techniques for semantic segmentation. In: ICCV Workshop (2019)
42. OpenAI: Gpt-4 technical report (2023)
43. Pérez-Rúa, J.M., Zhu, X., Hospedales, T.M., Xiang, T.: Incremental few-shot object detection. In: CVPR (2020)
44. Petit, G., Popescu, A., Schindler, H., Picard, D., Delezoide, B.: Fetril: feature translation for exemplar-free class-incremental learning. In: WACV (2023)
45. Qiu, Z., Xu, L., Wang, Z., Wu, Q., Meng, F., Li, H.: ISM-net: mining incremental semantics for class incremental learning. Neurocomputing (2023)
46. Radford, A., et al.: Learning transferable visual models from natural language supervision. In: ICML (2021)
47. Rebuffi, S.A., Kolesnikov, A., Sperl, G., Lampert, C.H.: ICARL: incremental classifier and representation learning. In: ICCV (2017)
48. Smith, J., et al.: Coda-prompt: continual decomposed attention-based prompting for rehearsal-free continual learning. In: CVPR (2023)
49. Song, Z., Zhao, Y., Shi, Y., Peng, P., Yuan, L., Tian, Y.: Learning with fantasy: semantic-aware virtual contrastive constraint for few-shot class-incremental learning. arXiv (2023)
50. Sun, F.K., Ho, C.H., Yi Lee, H.: Lamol: language modeling for lifelong language learning. In: ICLR (2019)
51. Tong, S., Dai, X., Wu, Z., Li, M., Yi, B., Ma, Y.: Incremental learning of structured memory via closed-loop transcription. arXiv (2022)
52. van de Ven, G.M., Tuytelaars, T., Tolias, A.S.: Three types of incremental learning. Nat. Mach. Intell. (2022)
53. Verwimp, E., et al.: Clad: a realistic continual learning benchmark for autonomous driving. Neural Netw. (2023)
54. Wah, C., Branson, S., Welinder, P., Perona, P., Belongie, S.: The caltech-ucsd birds-200-2011 dataset (2011)
55. Wang, F.Y., Zhou, D.W., Liu, L., Ye, H.J., Bian, Y., Zhan, D.C., Zhao, P.: Beef: bi-compatible classincremental learning via energy-based expansion and fusion (2023)
56. Wang, L., Zhang, X., Su, H., Zhu, J.: A comprehensive survey of continual learning: theory, method and application. arXiv (2023)
57. Xu, X., Wang, Z., Fu, Z., Guo, W., Chi, Z., Li, D.: Flexible few-shot class-incremental learning with prototype container. Neural Comput. Appl. (2023)
58. Yang, Y., Zhou, D., Zhan, D., Xiong, H., Jiang, Y., Yang, J.: Cost-effective incremental deep model: matching model capacity with the least sampling. IEEE TKDE (2023)
59. Yang, Y., Yuan, H., Li, X., Lin, Z., Torr, P., Tao, D.: Neural collapse inspired feature-classifier alignment for few-shot class incremental learning. arXiv (2023)
60. Yoon, J., Yang, E., Lee, J., Hwang, S.J.: Lifelong learning with dynamically expandable networks. arXiv (2017)
61. Zenke, F., Poole, B., Ganguli, S.: Continual learning through synaptic intelligence. In: ICML (2017)
62. Zheng, Z., Ma, M., Wang, K., Qin, Z., Yue, X., You, Y.: Preventing zero-shot transfer degradation in continual learning of vision-language models. arXiv (2023)
63. Zhou, D.W., Wang, Q.W., Qi, Z.H., Ye, H.J., Zhan, D.C., Liu, Z.: Deep class-incremental learning: a survey. arXiv (2023)

64. Zhou, D.W., Wang, Q., Ye, H.J., Chuan Zhan, D.: A model or 603 exemplars: towards memory-efficient class-incremental learning. arXiv (2022)
65. Zhou, D.W., Ye, H.J., Zhan, D.C., Liu, Z.: Revisiting class-incremental learning with pre-trained models: generalizability and adaptivity are all you need. arXiv (2023)

TTA-GCN: Temporal Topology Aggregation for Skeleton-Based Action Recognition

Haoming Meng[1], Yangfei Zhao[2], Yijing Guo[2], and Pei Lv[2,3,4(✉)]

[1] Henan Institute of Advanced Technology, Zhengzhou University, Zhengzhou, China
[2] School of Computer and Artificial Intelligence, Zhengzhou University, Zhengzhou, China
ielvpei@zzu.edu.cn
[3] Engineering Research Center of Intelligent Swarm Systems, Ministry of Education, Zhengzhou, China
[4] National Supercomputing Center in Zhengzhou, Zhengzhou, China

Abstract. Graph Convolutional Networks (GCNs) have been widely used in skeleton-based action recognition. In GCN-based approaches, graph topology dominates feature aggregation, and therefore extraction of the complex relationships between joints is the key to generate spatial-temporal skeletal graph topology structure. We note that current methods are more inclined to construct the topology matrix from the spatial dimension and rarely combine the features from the temporal dimension. This paper proposes a Temporal Topology Aggregation Graph Convolutional Network (TTA-GCN) to learn temporal topology dynamically and efficiently aggregating topology structure in channel dimensions for skeleton-based action recognition. In addition, the multi-stream ensemble framework has a significant effect on improving action recognition accuracy, and more than single natural skeleton modality are required to fuse multi-streams. Therefore, we present a multi-modal representation according to the semantics of human skeleton to capture relationships between non-naturally connected joints. Extensive experiments show that our model results achieved state-of-the-arts performance on three large accepted datasets: NTU-RGB+D 60, NTU-RGB+D 120, and Northwestern-UCLA. Finally, we evaluated the effectiveness of our model through various comparison experiments.

Keywords: Skeleton · Action Recognition · Temporal Attention · GCN

1 Introduction

Human Action Recognition (HAR) is a task of classifying action and has a wide range of applications in video surveillance, human-computer interaction, and virtual reality. Current HAR methods can be categorized into RGB-based [18]

H. Lu et al. (Eds.): ICIG 2023, LNCS 14356, pp. 225–237, 2023.
https://doi.org/10.1007/978-3-031-46308-2_19

and skeleton-based [15, 22], which use the video and skeleton sequences as inputs. Skeleton data is a 3D coordinates sequences of skeleton joints, which can be quickly obtained from static images by human pose estimation technology [5] or directly collected by 3D depth cameras. The RGB-based methods are vulnerable to the strong impact of environmental noise, such as variations of illuminations, weather conditions, and background changes. Compared to RGB-based methods, skeleton-based methods have attracted extensive attention due to their highly compact input and robustness against these noises.

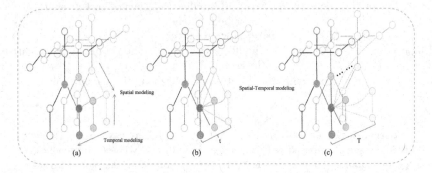

Fig. 1. (a) ST-GCN modeling. Without the direct information stream across space and time. (b) MS-G3D modeling. t is a manually fixed sliding temporal window. (c) TTA modeling. T is a global temporal window. The method can aggregate weights on the global time dimension.

The early HAR algorithm based on deep learning [12] did not consider the inherent spatial correlations between body joints, only regarded the node features as a time series and input RNNs or CNNs to predict the action label. Subsequently, [20] first manually modeled the physical connection between human skeleton joints as a topology and used graph convolution networks (GCNs) and temporal convolution networks (TCNs) to extract the motion features. After that, the research based on GCNs has gradually increased, and most existing algorithms continue to use the handcrafted human skeleton topology proposed by [20]. However, both the connections between adjacent joints and relationship between distant joints are significant and crucial for HAR. The handcrafted topology cannot recognize the relationship between disconnected joint nodes but can only aggregate features according to the physical connection in the human skeleton. Although some methods [13, 15] have considered this deficiency, their networks still have yet to eliminate this effect, as they continue to use physically connected topology. Based on this, we propose a semantic connection skeleton topology which is different from a physical connection skeleton topology, to infer the potential relationships between nonadjacent joints.

In terms of extracting spatial-temporal information in networks, [20] adopted the decomposition modeling method. As shown in Fig. 1(a), first extract the spatial node features of the current frame by GCNs, then extract the temporal information between frames by TCNs. It seems that both spacial information and temporal information have been fused, but the cross spatial-temporal combined relation is not fully considered. For example, human motion can usually be seen as the simultaneous motion of each joint in space and time, but there is a priority problem under subdivision. That is, the motion of the upper body in the previous frame (leaning forward) will drive the future motion of the lower body in the next frame (standing up), which prevents the direct information stream across space and time for capturing complex regional spatial-temporal joint dependencies because decomposition modeling unable to aggregate the information of the next frame in a previous frame. To some extent, it weakens the representation ability of GCNs. Therefore, an ideal HAR algorithm should simultaneously aggregate spatial-temporal features effectively. To address this issue, [13] proposed a multi-scale aggregation scheme with graph convolution to aggregate spatial features across time and space. However, due to the limitation of the size of sliding temporal window, the number of frames that can be seen between nodes in the topology matrix is limited when modeling topology across time and space (in Fig. 1(b)). In this work, we address the limitation of fixed sliding temporal window size in above-mentioned method. We propose a temporal topology aggregation graph convolution network (TTA-GCN) to model spatial-temporal topology: The topology of each feature channel can be aggregated to select from the global temporal topology, which is generated purely based on input data. There is no limit on the size of the sliding window when modeling the topology matrix across space and time (in Fig. 1(c)).

In addition, most recent state-of-the-arts networks [1,16] adopt multi-stream fusion frameworks. Such as [1] employ four-stream data, with one topology of the skeleton, composed of the joint, bone edge, joint motion, and bone motion flow, which are the original human joints coordinates, the differential space value between adjacent joint coordinates, the temporal differential of joints, and the temporal differential of bones. We note that the accuracy of the motion stream data is significantly lower than the spatial stream data, which reduces the lower accuracy limit after fusion. To address this problem, we discard the motion data and only adopt spatial data. To achieve the same scale of multi-stream fusion, we present a semantic topology method, which is multi-modal representation of the skeleton.

Our main contributions are summarized as follows. We propose a semantic-based method to divide the human skeleton into several subgraphs, add the multi-modal topology of the skeleton, and promote the multi-stream performance. We proposed TTA-GCN to model topological matrix across spatial-temporal dynamically. The proposed model is evaluated and achieves state-of-the-arts performance on three large datasets: NTU-RGB+D 60, NTU-RGB+D 120, and Northwestern-UCLA, among which in the NTU-RGB+D 120 datasets outperform the most advanced method.

2   Related Work

2.1   Skeleton-Based Human Action Recognition

Previous approaches [4,8,12] for skeleton-based HAR focus on designing hand-crafted features and parts relationships to simulate human motion patterns for downstream classifiers. These approaches mainly processed the data with translation between joints and 3D rotation, ignoring the essential physical connectivity of human body. Recently, the development of deep learning has led to the application of various neural network architectures in skeleton-based HAR. Among these, recurrent neural networks (RNNs), convolutional neural networks (CNNs), and graph convolutional networks (GCNs) have become more widely adopted. RNN-based [10] and CNN-based [6,7] approaches do not explicitly model the joint relationship. It is difficult to fully use the natural topology of human body, leading to poor recognition performance. To improve this, [20] firstly introduced GCN-based methods and proposed ST-GCN to construct spatial-temporal graphs, which are separate spatial modeling and temporal modeling.

2.2   GCN-Based Spatial Modeling

The ST-GCN employs three segmentation strategies to manually define static topology, while it is challenging to model the spatial relationship between unnaturally connected joints. Based on this work, many approaches have been proposed. Multi-scale GCNs [9,13] are proposed to capture the dependencies of multi-level neighbors among joints, which effectively improves spatial-temporal topological modeling. 2S-AGCN [15] creates an adaptive adjacency matrix using random trainable parameters. It can make spatial modeling more flexible but lacks the accuracy of modeling function dependence due to its random value. Dynamic-GCN [21] introduces the contextual features of all joints to learn skeleton topology automatically, then CTR-GCN [1] proposes a non-shared dynamic graph convolution with a channel topology refinement method, which can spatially implement dynamic topology modeling. Although these methods achieve considerable performance, a common deficiency of these works is ignoring the balance of spatial and temporal dimensions. They mostly favor using spatial information for modeling, such as [1] performing an average pooling operation on the temporal sequence before the spatial modeling. Therefore, we have made some explorations in spatial modeling by temporal information.

3   Method

In this section, we introduce the proposed skeleton-based HAR method. We define the relevant symbols representation for the preliminaries work in Sect. 3.1. Then, we introduce the method of constructing semantic topology and the multi-stream fusion method in Sect. 3.2. Afterward, we elaborate on the specific architecture of our TTA-GC module in Sect. 3.3. Finally, we illustrate the structure of our TTA-GCN in Sect. 3.4.

3.1   Preliminaries

In skeleton-based HAR, a human skeleton is represented by a graph denoted as $G = (V, E, X)$, where set V represents all the human joints. The set of edges E is formulated as an adjacency matrix $A \in R^{V \times V}$, which defines connectivity among joints. The temporal sequence skeleton data is denoted as $X \in R^{T \times V \times C}$, where T represents the sequence size, and C represents the feature dimension of each joint. We adopt a spatial partition method based on [20], and the operation of GCN with input X mapping is as follows:

$$F_{out} = \sum_{s \in S} A_s X W_s \qquad (1)$$

where $S = \{s_{id}, s_{cf}, s_{cp}\}$ denotes graph subsets of spatial partition, the s_{id}, s_{cf}, and s_{cp} indicate identity, centrifugal, and centripetal connections according to different partition method [20]. W_s is a trainable parameter of convolution operation for each subset.

3.2   Construction of Semantic Topology

Recent methods have used the handcrafted graph proposed by [20], but it is challenging to model the relationships between non-naturally connected joints. We propose a new representation method for multi-modal skeleton graphs that fully exploits the potential information between non-connected joints. We divide the representation of the skeleton graph into two categories: natural topology and semantic topology, as shown in Fig. 2.

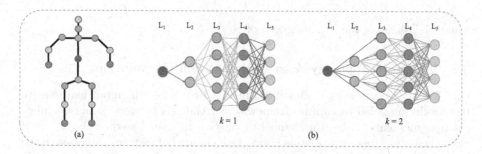

Fig. 2. (a) Structure of nature skeletal. The red node is the center point, and the nodes with the same distance from the center point have the same color. (b) Structure of Semantic skeletal. Nodes of the same color are on the same layer and connected with the k value. (Color figure online)

Semantic Topology. The natural topology refers to the physical connections of the human body, and its structure is represented as $A \in R^{3 \times V \times V}$. We take the midpoint of the body as the center point and decompose the natural skeletal according to the distance from the center point (e.g., if the hands and feet are at the same distance from the central point, they are grouped together and belong to the same semantic space). After decomposition, the joints in the same semantic space are grouped into a set (layer), as shown in Fig. 2(b). The construction of semantic topology is formally defined as:

$$A_{s_{cf}} = [(\ \underset{i=1}{\overset{N_L-k}{\|}}\ f(L_i \rightarrow L_{i+k}))\ \|\ (\ \underset{i=N_L-k+1}{\overset{N_L-1}{\|}}\ f(L_i \rightarrow L_{i+1}))] \tag{2}$$

Where i represents the layer number of the semantic sets, L_i represents the joints set within the i-th layer, and $f(L_i \rightarrow L_{i+k})$ represents a set of fully connected edges from layer i to $i + k$. N_L is the number of layers, and k represents the distance between two layers. To be consistent with partition method [20], we use $\leftarrow$ and $+$ to replace $\rightarrow$ to obtain $A_{s_{cp}}$ and $A_{s_{id}}$, where $\leftarrow$ denote centripetal edge, $\rightarrow$ denote centrifugal edge and $+$ denote identity edge. $\|$ is a concatenation operation. Therefore, we get the semantic adjacency matrix $A_k \in R^{(N_L-1) \times 3 \times V \times V}$.

Compared to natural topology, semantic topology A_k has a different number of edge sets and multiple subgraphs. The joints in the two semantic spaces are fully connected through the step size k, and the connectivity of the graph is denser than before. Due to the addition of subgraphs, the graph convolution formula (1) needs to be adjusted when calculating semantic topology:

$$F_{out}^{(i)} = \underset{s \in S}{\|}\ A_{ks}^{(i)} X W_s^{(i)} \tag{3}$$

where $A_{ks}^{(i)}$ denotes the i-th subgraph of A_{ks}.

3.3 Temporal Topology Aggregation Graph Convolution

Our TTA-GC framework is illustrated in Fig. 3(c). First, the input features are temporally modeled to capture framewise correlations between joints at different time moments. Then, the channel topology is inferred based on the obtained global temporal topology. At this point, each channel of features can observe the joint connectivity from the global topology and generate an adapted dynamic non-shared topology matrix. Finally, the features in each channel are aggregated with the corresponding topology to achieve cross spatial-temporal graph convolution and obtain the final output. Specifically, our TTA-GC consists of four parts.

Temporal Topology Modeling. The purpose of this part is to capture the framewise correlation between joints of input features at different time steps, with input $X \in R^{T \times V \times C}$ and output $A_{tmp} \in R^{T \times V \times V}$. The correlation modeling

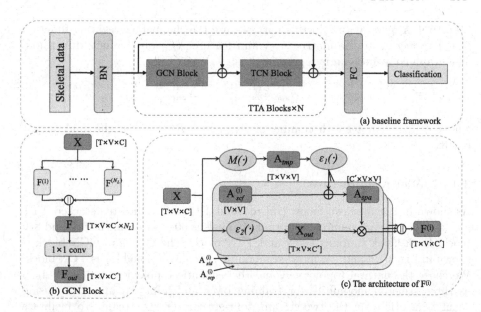

Fig. 3. The illustration of the proposed network. (a) The architecture of TTA-GCN, it receives skeleton sequence as input and obtains an action label. (b) Each GCN block contains N_L subgraphs, and using 1×1 conv to match the output channel. (c) TTA-GC block with correlation function.

function $M(\cdot)$ employs the ConvLSTM network [17], with setting the cell size of the last hidden layer to V so that each node can predict the long-term correlation with the other nodes through forget gates and other mechanisms. We obtain a temporal matrix A_{tmp}, which can be expressed as:

$$A_{tmp} = M(X) = \sigma(ConvLSTM(X)) \tag{4}$$

Spatial Topology Modeling. This part aims to further refine the temporal topology matrix into a channel-wise matrix using the linear transformation function $\varepsilon(\cdot)$. We use the channel-wise topology [1] method to obtain a matrix $A_{spa} \in R^{C' \times V \times V}$ of space dynamically. Since the topology of each channel feature is derived from the temporal topology transformation, it can achieve the effect of modeling across time and space. The formula is represented as:

$$A_{spa} = \alpha\varepsilon(A_{tmp}) + A = \alpha A_{tmp}W + A \tag{5}$$

where α is a trainable scalar using a broadcast way, and A is a handcraft topology matrix.

Input Feature Transformation. The input features X are converted into high level feature representations through $\varepsilon(X)$ to fit the output channel, and get the transformed feature $X_{out} \in R^{T \times V \times C'}$.

Channel Aggregation. In this part, we use the channel aggregating function $CA(\cdot)$ to aggregate the matrix A_{spa} and feature X_{out} on channels dimension. The graph convolutional is represented as:

$$F = CA(X_{out}, A_{spa}) = (A_{spa}^{(1)} X_{out}^{(1)}) \big|\big| (A_{spa}^{(2)} X_{out}^{(2)}) \big|\big| \cdots \big|\big| (A_{spa}^{(C')} X_{out}^{(C')}) \quad (6)$$

where $A_{spa}^{(c)}$ is denotes c-th channel of A_{spa}. $F \in R^{T \times V \times C'}$ is the final output result.

3.4   Model Architecture

As shown in Fig. 3(a), we follow [15] to build TTA-GCN with ten stacked TTA blocks. The primary number of output channels is 60, double on the 5th and 8th block. Each block contains GCN and TCN block. The details of GCN block is shown in Fig. 3(b), and use multi-scale temporal convolutional [1] as TCN block. We chose the natural topology A and the semantic topologies $A_{k=1}$ and $A_{k=2}$ as three skeleton modalities for training bone and joint streams, then fusing them sequentially in the two-stream, four-stream, or six-stream. To facilitate the construction of the model structure, we conduct dimension expansion on the natural topology $A \in R^{1 \times 3 \times V \times V}$.

4   Experiments

4.1   Datasets

NTU-RGB+D 60&120. NTU-RGB+D 60 [14] is a large-scale HAR dataset with 60 action classes performed by 40 volunteers. The dataset has 56,880 skeleton action sequences, and each sample contains 25 human skeleton joints. The authors recommend two benchmarks: (1) Xsub: training data comes from 20 subjects, and testing data comes from the other 20 subjects. (2) Xview: training data comes from camera views 2 and 3, and testing data comes from camera view 1. The NTU-RGB+D 120 [11] is an extended version of the NTU-RGB+D 60 with an additional 57,367 skeleton sequences over 60 extra action classes. The actions are performed by 106 volunteers with three camera views and contain 32 setups. Similarly, two benchmarks are suggested: (1) Xsub: training data comes from 53 subjects, and testing data comes from the other 53 subjects. (2) Xset: training data comes from samples with even setup IDs, and testing data comes from samples with odd setup IDs.

Northwestern-UCLA. [19] contains 1494 video clips over ten classes. Each action is performed by 10 different subjects. The benchmarks are suggested: Two camera views for training and another for validation.

4.2 Implementation Details

All the experiments are implemented on a single Tesla V100 GPU with the PyTorch framework. We use the SGD optimizer in models with a Nesterov momentum of 0.9 and a weight decay of 0.0004. The number of epochs is set to 90, and the warm-up strategy is adopted to the first five epochs to obtain more stable learning. We set the decay strategy of the learning rate to cosine annealing, with a maximum learning rate of 0.1 and the minimum learning rate of 0.0001. For NTU RGB+D datasets, we set the batch size to 32 and used the pre-processing data method from [22]. For the NorthwesternUCLA dataset, we set the batch size to 16 and used the pre-processing data method from [2].

4.3 Comparison with the State-of-the-Arts

We compared our models with the state-of-the-arts methods on three datasets. The comparison of each dataset is shown in Table 1. For NTU-RGB+D 60 and Northwestern-UCLA, our model has reached the advanced result of the current methods; For NTU-RGB+D 120, our accuracy is 0.1% higher than InfoGCN [3] on both benchmarks.

Table 1. Comparison of the top-1 accuracy (%) on the NTU-60 & 120 and Northwestern-UCLA. 4s means four-stream fusion.

Methods	NTU-60		NTU-120		N-UCAL
	Xsub	Xview	Xsub	Xset	
ST-GCN(2018) [20]	81.5	88.3	70.7	73.2	–
2S-AGCN(2019) [15]	88.5	95.1	82.9	84.9	–
SGN(2020) [22]	89.0	94.5	79.2	81.5	92.5
4s Shift-GCN(2020) [2]	90.7	96.5	85.9	87.6	96.5
MS-G3D(2020) [13]	91.5	96.2	86.9	88.4	–
4s CTR-GCN(2021) [1]	92.4	96.8	88.9	90.6	96.5
6s InfoGCN(2022) [3]	**93.0**	**97.1**	89.8	91.2	**97.0**
2s TTA-GCN(Ours)	92.1	96.6	88.8	90.1	96.3
4s TTA-GCN(Ours)	92.8	96.8	89.7	91.0	96.8
6s TTA-GCN(Ours)	92.9	97.0	**89.9**	**91.3**	**97.0**

For multi-stream fusion, we list the results of stream fusion at different scales in Table 1. Among them, the two-stream fusion uses joint and bone stream data with natural topology skeleton modality like previous networks to ensure fair comparison. We abandoned the motion stream data for the four-stream and six-stream fusion but added skeleton representation modality, only using their joint and bone stream data. It can be seen that the result fused with motion stream data [1] is lower than the spatial data of other skeleton modalities at the same scale. Overall, the multi-scale fusion results of our model on NTU-RGB+D 120 dataset outperform existing methods.

4.4   Ablation Study

In this section, we compare our TTA-GC block with the cross spatial-temporal modeling G3D block proposed by MS-G3D [13] to verify the effectiveness of our method. Concretely, we employ 2S-AGCN [15] as the backbone, adopt the same natural connection skeleton modality as the topology structure, then replace the spatial convolution block with the G3D block as a baseline for fair comparison. We take Xsub of NTU-RGB+D 120 dataset as the benchmark to explore the performance of various modules on the bone stream and further explore the configuration of the model.

Table 2. Comparison of accuracies when replaced TTA-GC block.

Methods	Params	Acc (%)
MS-G3D(code)	3.20M	84.9
Baseline	5.93M	85.0
2 TTA-GC	3.56M	84.8
5 TTA-GC	3.65M	85.0
TTA-GC w/o $\varepsilon(\cdot)$	1.46M	85.8
TTA-GCN	1.64M	**86.2**

Table 3. Configuration exploration with TTA-GC block.

Methods	$M(\cdot)$	$\sigma(\cdot)$	Layers	Units	Acc (%)
A	M_2	$Tanh$	–	–	85.4
B	M_1	$Tanh$	2	$[32, V]$	**86.2**
C	M_1	$Tanh$	1	$[V]$	86.0
D	M_1	$Tanh$	3	$[64,32,V]$	85.8
E	M_1	Sig	2	$[32, V]$	85.3
F	M_1	$ReLU$	2	$[32, V]$	85.4

Effectiveness of TTA-GC. The experimental results are shown in Table 2. We gradually replaced the G3D block in the baseline with TTA-GC (as shown in Fig. 3(c)). We observed that the accuracy slightly decreased at first when two blocks were replaced, then the accuracy remained the same as the baseline when half of the blocks were replaced. When TTA-GC replaced all the G3D modules, the number of trainable parameters significantly decreased, and the accuracy reached the highest, with a 1.2% improvement compared to the baseline.

In addition, we also explored the impact of the temporal topological channel transformation operation in Sect. 3.3 on the model. We removed the channel transformation formula $\varepsilon(\cdot)$ from TTA-GC and directly used the temporal topology matrix generated by $M(\cdot)$ as the shared matrix. The result shows an improvement of 0.8% compared to the baseline but decrease of 0.4% compared to the non-shared topology method in TTA-GC. The results indicate that: Inferring the topology matrix based on temporal sequences information is more effective than adaptive topology or modeling topology based on spatial information; Adding the non-shared method can further improve the accuracy.

Configuration Exploration. We further explored the configuration of the TTA-GC block, including the selection of the related modeling function $M(\cdot)$, activation function $\sigma(\cdot)$, the number of hidden layers and the hidden unit size of ConvLSTM in the modeling function $M_1(\cdot)$. $M_2(\cdot)$ is another modeling function that only randomly initializes the weight matrix to compare with the temporal modeling function $M_1(\cdot)$. As shown in Table 3, comparing models A and B, using ConvLSTM to establish temporal topology can significantly improve accuracy. Comparing B, C, and D, the performance is better with two hidden layers in ConvLSTM, and more hidden layers impair the accuracy and increase training time. Comparing B, E, and F, the $Tanh(\cdot)$ activation function performs the best, possibly because $Tanh(\cdot)$ has negative values, which can get a broader and more flexible range of parameter selection. Overall, we choose model B as our final model and observe that all models under different configurations outperformed the baseline, demonstrating the robustness of TTA-GC.

5   Conclusion

In this paper, we propose a temporal topology aggregation graph convolution network for skeleton-based action recognition that can infer spatial topology with temporal sequence information. We also propose a multi-modal representation method for skeletons to use multi-stream fusion. Extensive experiments have shown that our method has improvements on the baseline model.

Acknowledgements. Thanks for the suggestions of all the anonymous reviewers. This work was supported in part by National Key R&D Program Project under Grant 2022YFC3803203 and Joint Fund of the Ministry of Education for Equipment Pre Research with Grant 8091B032257.

References

1. Chen, Y., Zhang, Z., Yuan, C., Li, B., Deng, Y., Hu, W.: Channel-wise topology refinement graph convolution for skeleton-based action recognition. In: Proceedings of the IEEE/CVF International Conference on Computer Vision, pp. 13359–13368 (2021)
2. Cheng, K., Zhang, Y., He, X., Chen, W., Cheng, J., Lu, H.: Skeleton-based action recognition with shift graph convolutional network. In: Proceedings of the IEEE/CVF Conference on Computer Vision and Pattern Recognition, pp. 183–192 (2020)
3. Chi, H.g., Ha, M.H., Chi, S., Lee, S.W., Huang, Q., Ramani, K.: InfoGCN: representation learning for human skeleton-based action recognition. In: Proceedings of the IEEE/CVF Conference on Computer Vision and Pattern Recognition, pp. 20186–20196 (2022)
4. Du, Y., Wang, W., Wang, L.: Hierarchical recurrent neural network for skeleton based action recognition. In: Proceedings of the IEEE Conference on Computer Vision and Pattern Recognition, pp. 1110–1118 (2015)
5. Fang, H.S., Xie, S., Tai, Y.W., Lu, C.: RMPE: regional multi-person pose estimation. In: Proceedings of the IEEE International Conference on Computer Vision, pp. 2334–2343 (2017)
6. Kim, T.S., Reiter, A.: Interpretable 3d human action analysis with temporal convolutional networks. In: 2017 IEEE Conference on Computer Vision and Pattern Recognition Workshops (CVPRW), pp. 1623–1631. IEEE (2017)
7. Li, B., Dai, Y., Cheng, X., Chen, H., Lin, Y., He, M.: Skeleton based action recognition using translation-scale invariant image mapping and multi-scale deep CNN. In: 2017 IEEE International Conference on Multimedia & Expo Workshops (ICMEW), pp. 601–604. IEEE (2017)
8. Li, C., Xie, C., Zhang, B., Han, J., Zhen, X., Chen, J.: Memory attention networks for skeleton-based action recognition. IEEE Trans. Neural Netw. Learn. Syst. **33**(9), 4800–4814 (2021)
9. Li, M., Chen, S., Chen, X., Zhang, Y., Wang, Y., Tian, Q.: Actional-structural graph convolutional networks for skeleton-based action recognition. In: Proceedings of the IEEE/CVF Conference on Computer Vision and Pattern Recognition, pp. 3595–3603 (2019)
10. Li, W., Wen, L., Chang, M.C., Nam Lim, S., Lyu, S.: Adaptive RNN tree for large-scale human action recognition. In: Proceedings of the IEEE International Conference on Computer Vision, pp. 1444–1452 (2017)
11. Liu, J., Shahroudy, A., Perez, M., Wang, G., Duan, L.Y., Kot, A.C.: NTU RGB+ D 120: a large-scale benchmark for 3d human activity understanding. IEEE Trans. Pattern Anal. Mach. Intell. **42**(10), 2684–2701 (2019)
12. Liu, M., Liu, H., Chen, C.: Enhanced skeleton visualization for view invariant human action recognition. Pattern Recogn. **68**, 346–362 (2017)
13. Liu, Z., Zhang, H., Chen, Z., Wang, Z., Ouyang, W.: Disentangling and unifying graph convolutions for skeleton-based action recognition. In: Proceedings of the IEEE/CVF Conference on Computer Vision and Pattern Recognition, pp. 143–152 (2020)
14. Shahroudy, A., Liu, J., Ng, T.T., Wang, G.: NTU RGB+ D: a large scale dataset for 3d human activity analysis. In: Proceedings of the IEEE Conference on Computer Vision and Pattern Recognition, pp. 1010–1019 (2016)

15. Shi, L., Zhang, Y., Cheng, J., Lu, H.: Two-stream adaptive graph convolutional networks for skeleton-based action recognition. In: Proceedings of the IEEE/CVF Conference on Computer Vision and Pattern Recognition, pp. 12026–12035 (2019)

16. Shi, L., Zhang, Y., Cheng, J., Lu, H.: Skeleton-based action recognition with multi-stream adaptive graph convolutional networks. IEEE Trans. Image Process. **29**, 9532–9545 (2020)

17. Shi, X., Chen, Z., Wang, H., Yeung, D.Y., Wong, W.K., Woo, W.c.: Convolutional LSTM network: a machine learning approach for precipitation nowcasting. In: Advances in Neural Information Processing Systems, vol. 28 (2015)

18. Simonyan, K., Zisserman, A.: Two-stream convolutional networks for action recognition in videos. In: Advances in Neural Information Processing Systems, vol. 27 (2014)

19. Wang, J., Nie, X., Xia, Y., Wu, Y., Zhu, S.C.: Cross-view action modeling, learning and recognition. In: Proceedings of the IEEE Conference on Computer Vision and Pattern Recognition, pp. 2649–2656 (2014)

20. Yan, S., Xiong, Y., Lin, D.: Spatial temporal graph convolutional networks for skeleton-based action recognition. In: Proceedings of the AAAI Conference on Artificial Intelligence, vol. 32 (2018)

21. Ye, F., Pu, S., Zhong, Q., Li, C., Xie, D., Tang, H.: Dynamic GCN: context-enriched topology learning for skeleton-based action recognition. In: Proceedings of the 28th ACM International Conference on Multimedia, pp. 55–63 (2020)

22. Zhang, P., Lan, C., Zeng, W., Xing, J., Xue, J., Zheng, N.: Semantics-guided neural networks for efficient skeleton-based human action recognition. In: Proceedings of the IEEE/CVF Conference on Computer Vision And Pattern Recognition, pp. 1112–1121 (2020)

A Stable Long-Term Tracking Method for Group-Housed Pigs

Shibo Gao[1,2], Jinmeng Gong[4], Peipei Yang[2,3]([✉]), Chao Liang[4,5], and Linlin Huang[1]

[1] Beijing Jiaotong University, Beijing, China
[2] State Key Laboratory of Multimodal Artificial Intelligence Systems, Institute of Automation, Chinese Academy of Sciences, Beijing, China
ppyang@nlpr.ia.ac.cn
[3] School of Artificial Intelligence, University of Chinese Academy of Sciences, Beijing, China
[4] College of Water Resources and Civil Engineering, China Agricultural University, Beijing, China
[5] Key Laboratory of Agricultural Engineering in Structure and Environment, Ministry of Agriculture and Rural Affairs, Beijing, China

Abstract. In recent years, computer vision technologies have been increasingly applied to livestock farming for improving efficiency and reducing the labor force in surveillance. Tracking of group-housed pigs is an important task for monitoring the daily behaviors of pigs, which can be used to preliminarily evaluate the health status of pigs. Most researchers directly apply existing multi-object tracking algorithms to this task, but often suffer from tracking failures due to false detection, stacking, occlusion, video jamming, etc. It usually produces a lot of incorrect ID switches that are disastrous for follow-up tasks. In this paper, we propose a group-housed pigs tracking method that can achieve stable long-term tracking. As the identity and number of monitored pigs remain unchanged during a feeding period, we introduce a new object matching mechanism with a classifier, which avoids most incorrect ID switches and effectively improves the matching accuracy. Thus, our tracking method is more robust to complex posture variations of the pig and achieves stable long-term tracking. The experimental results on real videos captured in a pigs farm prove the effectiveness of our method.

Keywords: multi-object tracking · pigs tracking · long-term tracking

1 Introduction

According to the US Department of Agriculture, the global pork production has grown to 114.1 million tons and the number of group-housed pigs has exceeded

Supported by "Scientific and Technological Innovation 2030" Program of China Ministry of Science and Technology (2021ZD0113803).

1.29 billion in 2023 [19]. As the increasing production scale of group-housed pigs, the demand for intelligent and automatic breeding is raised for both improving efficiency and reducing the labor force of human being [13].

Monitoring the daily behaviors of group-housed pigs is an important task in pig production. By analyzing the behavior of each pig, we can obtain its exercise amount, feeding frequency/duration, drinking frequency/duration, sleep quality, social level, stress sate, etc. They can be used for preliminarily evaluating the health status of pigs and early warning of diseases such as PRRS or mycoplasma pneumonia [5]. The sub-healthy or sick individuals can thus be identified and get more attentions. In spite of its importance, this task is difficult to be accomplished in a modern large-scale breeding mode [6].

First, since there are quite a large number of pigs in modern pig farms, it's impossible for farmers to focus on so many individual pigs. Second, for accurately evaluating the health status of all pigs, long-term monitoring of their behaviors is needed, which is a rather burdensome work for human being [13,14]. Considering that surveillance cameras have been widely deployed in piggeries, it's an attractive idea to automatically analyze the behaviors of pigs from videos by exploiting the technologies of computer vision.

To achieve this aim, a series of methods have been proposed and applied in practice to replace manual monitoring. The basic idea is to fist track each group-housed pigs to obtain its trajectory, and then analyze its behavior based on the trajectory [15]. Most of these methods directly exploit existing multi-object tracking (MOT) methods to track the pigs [17,18]. However, there are obvious differences between the group-housed pigs tracking and the ordinary multi-object tracking. (a) The number of individuals that need to be tracked is known before starting the tracking process; (b) The appearance of different individuals are similar; (c) There are obviously more irregular movements of individuals in the scene of group-housed pigs tracking; (d) The scene of group-housed pigs tracking is more complex due to the dark environment and the frequent mutual shielding/stacking of individual pigs.

Although some approaches have been proposed to solve these problems [4, 10,17,20], they are not well solved yet. First, existing methods cannot utilize the prior knowledge of known number of individuals to be tracked, and thus false detection and mutual stacking of individuals often cause much incorrect ID switches. Second, the mainstream feature extraction network may cause false Reid due to the similar appearances of different individuals. Third, the frequent irregular movements make ordinary trajectory prediction fail.

In this paper, we propose a tracking method for group-housed pigs, which fully utilizes the prior knowledge about the number of pigs to be tracked by introducing a classification network, and can effectively improve the accuracy and stability of long-term tracking. Different from most existing tracking approaches, objects matching between adjacent frames in our method depends on the change in number of detected objects. According to the case of number change, the corresponding object matching strategy is adopted, which can well cope with false detection, missed detection, stacking, and occlusion.

Besides, different from the scenes of ordinary MOT, each individual pig in our problem appears as various postures during the tracking processing, which deteriorates the performances of traditional Re-ID methods. Thus, we introduce a classifier for objects matching so that it can well adapt to posture variations. Experimental results show that our method can track the pigs stably and accurately without incorrect ID switches even in long-term tracking, which reflects the effectiveness of our method.

The contributions of this paper are summarized as follows:

- We propose a tracking method for group-housed pigs, where objects of adjacent frames are matched by different strategies according to the number change of objects. It is able to keep a stable and accurate performance even in long-term tracking.
- We introduce a classifier to replace the traditional Re-ID mechanism in order to adapt to posture variations.

2   Related Work

In the early stages of research, scholars usually directly use general multi-objective tracking methods such as Deep-sort [21] or Bytetrack [22] to solve pigs tracking. However, as we mentioned earlier, these methods do not effectively track group-housed pigs. With the further development of multi-object tracking, MOT based on joint detection and tracking [23,24] and MOT based on attention mechanism [12,16] have also been applied to this problem. Although these new methods improved tracking performance to some extent, the fundamental problem are not solved.

In recent years, scholars have conducted a lot of research on this specific application scenarios. Kashiha et al. [10] first used ellipses to identify individuals by writing or marking patterns on the back of pigs, and attempted to track them based on 15600 individuals. Cowton et al. [4] use Fast R-CNN to detect live pig individuals, and then use Kalman filtering and Hungarian methods to correlate individuals in different frames. They achieved good results within 7 min and resolved sudden movements of piglets. Most previous studies have achieved high accuracy in short-term tracking, but their performances on long-term tracking are unsatisfactory, making it difficult to put into actual production. Psota et al. [17] attempt to solve the problem of long-term tracking with key point detection and ear tags, but this invasive behavior can lead to animal injury and frequent loss of markers. Wang et al. [20] attempt to accurately track individuals through Kalman filtering and partially limiting the number of IDs. All these methods suffer from frequent incorrect ID switches and cannot obtain satisfactory performances.

3   Method

3.1   Overview

Our proposed method follows the classic two stage tracking approach, which first detects the objects of individuals within each video frame and then matches the objects of adjacent frames. In this paper, we exploit YOLO-V5 [8] for detecting the objects.

For accommodating to the scene of group-housed pigs, the key ideas of our method include a novel multi-strategy object matching mechanism, and a classifier-based Re-ID mechanism. The strategy for object matching is selected according to the change in number of objects, while the classifier-based Re-ID makes our method robust to posture variations. In this section, we will analyze the differences of scenes between traditional MOT and group-housed pigs tracking, and then introduce the details of our method.

3.2   Motivation

In an ordinary scene, multi-object tracking detects multiple objects such as pedestrians, cars, and animals in the video without knowing the number of objects in advance, and assigns IDs to track them [9]. Each object is assigned with a unique ID in order to accomplish subsequent trajectory prediction, accurate search, and other work. Any individual usually appears in a video for only a short time and the movement trends are relatively regular. Existing MOT methods usually resort to tricks such as Kalman filtering and Re-ID networks to deal with the short-term occlusion problems. However, these methods cannot handle long tracking processes or object occlusion situations well, resulting in the serious problem of frequent incorrect ID switches [11].

In addition, an important characteristic of group-housed pigs tracking is that the number and approximate appearances of the individuals to be tracked can be known in advance, and they will not change for a considerable period. This provides us additional information for tracking and identifying individuals. In our method, based on the number of individuals to be tracked, we can use a classifier to accurately initialize the IDs of individuals within the first frame. In the entire tracking process, we divide all possible cases of the number change of objects into three categories:

– **All objects matched**: normal situation.
– **New object entry**: false detection.
– **Object lost**: individual occlusion or missed detection.

We only match according to IOU when the number of objects is unchanged. When there are objects lost, we match the existing objects with the ones in last frame and maintain the lost objects until they are matched again. When multiple new objects appear or a new object appear close to existing objects, we will use the classifier to accurately identify individuals for complete the matching.

3.3   Tracking with Multi-strategy Object Matching

In real pigsties, the movements of individual pigs are constrained in a enclosed area, and thus the total number of individuals to be tracked is known in advance. Based on this important information, we adopt different matching strategies according to the number change of objects. In this scene, Kalman filtering is no longer accurate due to the irregular movement of individuals. Instead, we summarize the scenarios of long-term group-housed pigs tracking into different situations and propose a new tracking method using the previously known knowledge. The flow chart of our method is shown in Fig. 1.

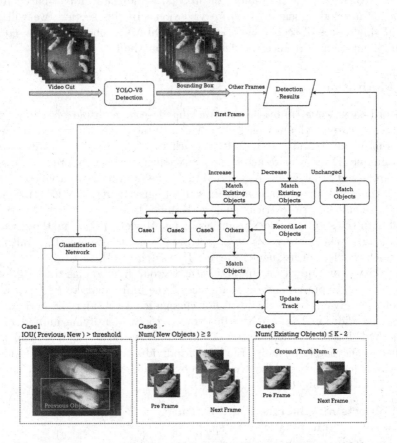

Fig. 1. The figure lists three situations where classifier need to be enabled, except for initialization. The network which has been trained on a certain amount of data can handle situations that can easily cause an ID switch. For other situations, we only match them through methods.

We also showed the pseudo code of our method in Algorithm 1 to show the details more clearly.

For the initialization of the first frame, the classifier detects objects within the image and assigns each object with an accurate ID. After that, we will maintain a dynamic dictionary for recording the position of each ID at each frame.

In the best case where all objects are still being tracked at next frame, each individual will be matched according to IOU and the extra objects will be

---

Algorithm 1: Algorithm Processing

---

input : Frame I, Detection(I), Target Num, Iou Threshold, Cls, M_{wait}
output: Frame I, ID, Bbox

1 **if** $I = 1$ **then**
2 | ID = ID.init(Detection(I))

3 **else**
4 | **if** *len(New bbox) = len(Pre bbox)* **then**
5 | | Match ID with IOU
6 | **if** *len(New bbox) < len(Pre bbox)* **then**
7 | | Match existing ID with IOU
8 | | M_{wait}.append(Loss ID)
9 | **else**
10 | | Match existing ID with IOU
11 | | **if** *Target num = len(Pre bbox)* **then**
12 | | | Delete new object
13 | | **if** *Target num - 1 = len(Pre bbox)* **then**
14 | | | **if** *IOU(New Object, Existing Object) < Iou Threshold* **then**
15 | | | | Match(M_{wait})
16 | | | **else**
17 | | | | ID = Cls(New Object, Existing Object)
18 | | **else**
19 | | | ID = Cls(New Multi-objects)
20 | ID.update

---

deleted. If some objects disappear, the existing objects are matched according to IOU and then the IDs of the unmatched objects will be recorded. Unlike other tracking methods, if an object is missed, its ID will be kept until being matched again. For one isolated object entry, if there is only one ID in the unmatched queue, it will be assigned to the new object. In the above cases, we can match the objects without classifier. Under the following scenarios, we should resort to the classifier for reassign the IDs for some objects: (1) Confused objects entry; (2) Multiple objects entry; (3) Insufficient objects entry.

This method avoids the incorrect ID switch caused by long-time occlusion or false detection. Our method can also well handle the stacking, blocking, and even slight video jams between individuals using the classifier.

3.4   Classifier-Based Re-ID

Mainstream tracking methods typically reassigns IDs based on distance metric of the features. When an object is lost, the current Re-ID network records the crop of the object in the previous frame and then extracts its feature representation. By calculating the cosine distances of the feature representations between the newly detected objects and missing objects, the lost IDs can be correctly reassigned to the corresponding objects.

However, this approach is based on the assumption that there is no obvious change in the objects' appearance or posture. For example, people's clothing and walking posture do not change much before and after the occlusion. For an individual pig, changes in body orientation and posture can cause the variation of its feature, which makes it difficult to match. Thus, exploiting the specialty of the enclosed environment, we use a ResNet-101 classifier to classify objects in an frame for matching objects. The classifier is trained using object crops under various situations rather than just on frame, and thus more robust to body orientation and posture variations.

We crop the group-housed pigs in the videos under the same monitor and resize them to 224×224 as the input. Then the classifier generates a normalized category probability of each pig for matching. In our work, the multi-category cross entropy is used for training the classifier:

$$L = \frac{1}{N} \sum_i L_i = -\frac{1}{N} \sum_i \sum_{c=1}^{M} y_{ic} \log(p_{ic}),$$

where M and p_{ic} represent the number of categories and the prediction probability of observation sample i belonging to category c, respectively. The y_{ic} takes 1 if the category of i is equal to c, otherwise take 0.

4   Experiments

4.1   Data

We used a wide-angle camera installed in the center of the ceiling of the enclosed pigsty for video recording (1920×1080, 29 fps). The camera covers the entire pigsty and some aisles. Due to the viewing angle, there may be some blocking situations in the corners. We conduct a continuous recording of the pigsty for 14×24 h, and utilize the collected data to evaluate our method with three experiments.

- First, we label two video segments containing 570 and 420 consecutive frames respectively for multi-object tracking evaluation.
- Second, we capture a video of 20 min to evaluate the effectiveness of the method in long-term tracking.
- Last, we randomly cut 30 shot videos of 30 s from all the videos for evaluating the ability of tracking without ID switches.

4.2   Performances on MOT

Following the common practice in multi-object tracking (MOT), Multiple Object Tracking Accuracy (MOTA) [1] is adopted to evaluate the overall performance of model. The MOTA is defined as

$$MOTA = 1 - \frac{\sum_i (FN_i + FP_i + ID_{switch})}{\sum_i gt},$$

where i represents the index of frames. FN_i, FP_i, ID_{switch} and gt represent the false negatives, false positives, ID switch and ground truth number of objects.

In addition, to better measure the tracking quality, $IDF1$, ratio of mostly tracked (MT), and ratio of mostly lost (ML) are generally used. The definition of $IDF1$ is defined based on ID precision (IDP) and ID recall (IDR):

$$IDF1 = \frac{2}{\frac{1}{IDP} + \frac{1}{IDR}} = \frac{2IDTP}{2IDTP + IDFP + IDFN},$$

where $IDTP$ represents the number of correctly detected objects and $IDFN$ means the number of missed objects. $IDFP$ represents the number of false detection. Besides, MT is defined as the number of tracks where at least 80% of its life span is successfully tracked. Similarly, ML is defined as the number of tracks where at most 20% of its total length is successfully tracked. Table 1 shows the evaluation results of our method, Deep-sort and Byte-track on general MOT indicators.

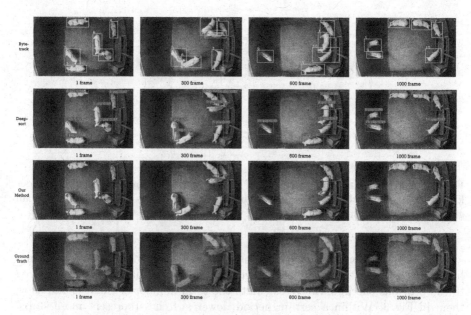

Fig. 2. A test video containing long-term occlusion (1000 frame). Deep-sort and Byte-track are prone to lead to ID switches when encountering occlusion, while our method is very stable.

Figure 2 presents specific visualization results to more intuitively describe the advantages of our method.

From the results, it can be seen that our method greatly improves the tracking accuracy, and has a surprising effect on avoiding incorrect ID switches. The tracks without errors ensure the reliability of tracking information, which makes a great benefit to group-housed pigs farming.

Table 1. Comparison of our method with Deep-sort and Byte-track

	MOTA	IDF1	MT	ML
Deep-sort [21]	90.6%	84.6%	66.7%	33.3%
Byte-track [22]	94.7%	91.2%	83.3%	8.3%
Our Method	99.5%	95.3%	100%	0.00

4.3 Performances on Long-Term Tracking

The stability under long-term condition is an important evaluation index for group-housed pigs tracking methods in enclosed environments. Previous works [4, 15, 20] evaluate the stability of the method by calculating the average number of ID switches over a long period of time.

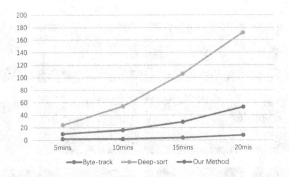

Fig. 3. This figure shows the numbers of ID switches given by three methods under long-term tracking, where the method giving fewer ID switches is more stable and can give more reliable results.

In this paper, we test our method on a video of about 20 min. We perform a frame extraction every 5 s and check whether the object has changed compared to the previous checkpoint. We calculate the total number of changes and show them in Fig. 3. Within a certain period, fewer switches represent more stable tracking. It is obvious that our method is still stable in long-term tracking. In fact, several ID switches are due to the group-housed pigs' flash move caused by the video jamming.

4.4 Ability of Tracking Without ID Switches

In practical applications, tracking is to obtain the feeding/drinking time and exercise amount of pigs. Thus, just one ID switch may invalidate previously obtained information, leading to catastrophic consequences [3]. We randomly sample thirty videos for evaluating the ability of our method to track without any incorrect ID switches, and each video segment will be sampled every five seconds (145 fps). We check whether the IDs are correct in each sampling frame, and only videos that completely match correctly are considered to be correctly tracked. We compared our method with Deep-sort, and the results are shown in Fig. 4.

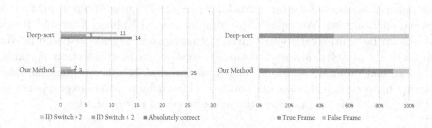

Fig. 4. In addition to the number of ID switches, we also compare the accuracies of correctly predicted frames, which is calculate every five frames.

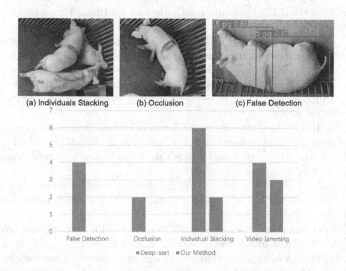

Fig. 5. Compared to Deep-sort, our method significantly reduces ID switches caused by false detection and occlusion, which are the most important factors to make difficulties to long-term group-housed pigs tracking in an enclosed environment.

In addition, we observe that ID switches are mainly caused by false detection, occlusion, individual stacking, and video jamming. Some examples and specific statistics are shown in Fig. 5. It is worth noting that there may be more than one situations that cause false tracking, which are classified as the category of the most important of failure.

These results show that our method can effectively deal with false detection and occlusion while improving the tracking accuracy. It can handle the cases of pigs stacking and video jamming.

5   Conclusion

This paper proposes a long-term tracking method for group-housed pigs in an enclosed environment. We replace the commonly used Kalman filter and Re-ID network with a multi-strategy matching mechanism and a classifier-based Re-ID. This method can well deal with tracking false caused by false detection, stacking, occlusion, and maintain stable in long-term tracking. It can even handle video jamming in some extent. Our method is evaluated by multiple experiments on real videos, and the results prove the effectiveness of our method.

References

1. Bernardin, K., Stiefelhagen, R.: Evaluating multiple object tracking performance: the clear mot metrics. EURASIP J. Image Video Process. **2008**, 1–10 (2008)
2. Bewley, A., Ge, Z., Ott, L., Ramos, F., Upcroft, B.: Simple online and realtime tracking. In: 2016 IEEE International Conference on Image Processing (ICIP), pp. 3464–3468. IEEE (2016)
3. Chen, C., Zhu, W., Norton, T.: Behaviour recognition of pigs and cattle: journey from computer vision to deep learning. Comput. Electron. Agric. **187**, 106255 (2021)
4. Cowton, J., Kyriazakis, I., Bacardit, J.: Automated individual pig localisation, tracking and behaviour metric extraction using deep learning. IEEE Access **7**, 108049–108060 (2019)
5. Cronin, G., Rault, J., Glatz, P., et al.: Lessons learned from past experience with intensive livestock management systems. Rev. Sci. Tech. **33**(1), 139–51 (2014)
6. Gan, H., et al.: Automated piglet tracking using a single convolutional neural network. Biosys. Eng. **205**, 48–63 (2021)
7. He, K., Zhang, X., Ren, S., Sun, J.: Deep residual learning for image recognition. In: Proceedings of the IEEE Conference on Computer Vision and Pattern Recognition, pp. 770–778 (2016)
8. Jocher, G., et al.: ultralytics/yolov5: v5. 0-YOLOv5-P6 1280 models AWS super-vise. ly and YouTube integrations. Zenodo 11 (2021)
9. Kalake, L., Wan, W., Hou, L.: Analysis based on recent deep learning approaches applied in real-time multi-object tracking: a review. IEEE Access **9**, 32650–32671 (2021)
10. Kashiha, M., et al.: Automatic identification of marked pigs in a pen using image pattern recognition. Comput. Electron. Agric. **93**, 111–120 (2013)
11. Luo, W., Xing, J., Milan, A., Zhang, X., Liu, W., Kim, T.K.: Multiple object tracking: a literature review. Artif. Intell. **293**, 103448 (2021)
12. Meinhardt, T., Kirillov, A., Leal-Taixe, L., Feichtenhofer, C.: Trackformer: multi-object tracking with transformers. In: Proceedings of the IEEE/CVF Conference on Computer Vision and Pattern Recognition, pp. 8844–8854 (2022)
13. Pedersen, L.J.: Overview of commercial pig production systems and their main welfare challenges. In: Advances in Pig Welfare, pp. 3–25. Elsevier (2018)

14. Sherwin, C., et al.: Ethical treatment of animals in applied animal behavior research. Int. Soc. Appl. Ethol. (2017)
15. Sun, L., et al.: Multi target pigs tracking loss correction algorithm based on faster R-CNN. Int. J. Agric. Biol. Eng. **11**(5), 192–197 (2018)
16. Sun, P., et al.: TransTrack: multiple object tracking with transformer. arXiv preprint arXiv:2012.15460 (2020)
17. T. Psota, E., Schmidt, T., Mote, B., C. Pérez, L.: Long-term tracking of group-housed livestock using keypoint detection and map estimation for individual animal identification. Sensors **20**(13), 3670 (2020)
18. USDA, F., et al.: Livestock and poultry: world markets and trade. United States Department of Agriculture, Foreign Agricultural Service (2006)
19. USDA, F., et al.: Livestock and poultry, world markets and trade. US Department of Agriculture Foreign Agricultural Service, Washington, DC, pp. 08–09 (2023)
20. Wang, M., Larsen, M.L., Liu, D., Winters, J.F., Rault, J.L., Norton, T.: Towards re-identification for long-term tracking of group housed pigs. Biosys. Eng. **222**, 71–81 (2022)
21. Wojke, N., Bewley, A., Paulus, D.: Simple online and realtime tracking with a deep association metric. In: 2017 IEEE International Conference on Image Processing (ICIP), pp. 3645–3649. IEEE (2017)
22. Zhang, Y., et al.: ByteTrack: multi-object tracking by associating every detection box. In: Avidan, S., Brostow, G., Cissé, M., Farinella, G.M., Hassner, T. (eds.) ECCV 2022, Part XXII. LNCS, vol. 13682, pp. 1–21. Springer, Cham (2022)
23. Zhang, Y., Wang, C., Wang, X., Zeng, W., Liu, W.: A simple baseline for multi-object tracking. arXiv preprint arXiv:2004.01888 7(8) (2020)
24. Zhou, X., Koltun, V., Krähenbühl, P.: Tracking objects as points. In: Vedaldi, A., Bischof, H., Brox, T., Frahm, J.-M. (eds.) ECCV 2020, Part IV. LNCS, vol. 12349, pp. 474–490. Springer, Cham (2020). https://doi.org/10.1007/978-3-030-58548-8_28

Dynamic Attention for Isolated Sign Language Recognition with Reinforcement Learning

Shiquan Lin, Yuchun Fang$^{(\boxtimes)}$, and Liangjun Wang

School of Computer Engineering and Science, Shanghai University, Shanghai, China
{funterlin,ycfang}@shu.edu.cn

Abstract. With computer vision developing rapidly, sign language recognition (SLR) can be realized to bridge the communication gap for deaf people. In this paper, we propose a novel deep reinforcement learning model imitating the dynamic attention of humans for isolated SLR that selectively pays attention to keyframes of video and exclude noise from the redundant frames. We construct a Partially Observable Markov Decision Process (POMDP) to learn dynamic attention for SLR from the non-differentiable sequence of interactions. The proposed model adopts Inflated 3D ConvNets as the feature learner. Following the policy learned by the deep reinforcement learning method, the proposed model "observes" a clip from the video to infer the position of keyframes and move the focus for the following observation. As a result, dynamic attention excludes interference from redundant frames and improves performance. We validate the effectiveness of the proposed method and compare it with benchmark methods on the Chinese Sign Language dataset.

Keywords: reinforcement learning · sign language · attention

1 Introduction

Sign language is a significant bridge for communication among deaf people and between deaf people and ordinary people, which eases deaf people's lives and bridges the obstacle hindering exchanging ideas. However, communication between deaf and ordinary people is still hard to achieve without understanding sign language. Therefore sign language recognition (SLR) systems have been widely studied and developed for facilitating communication during the past few decades. The sign language recognition task consists of isolated SLR and continuous SLR. The isolated SLR is a word-level system that requires recognizing sign language word by word. The continuous SLR is sentence-level or text-level, which requires the system to recognize and translate sign language into text in the context. Since the isolated SLR system maps actions to words, it is a fundamental task in SLR. This paper focuses on isolated SLR with recent advanced techniques in pattern recognition and computer vision.

© The Author(s), under exclusive license to Springer Nature Switzerland AG 2023
H. Lu et al. (Eds.): ICIG 2023, LNCS 14356, pp. 250–262, 2023.
https://doi.org/10.1007/978-3-031-46308-2_21

Conventional methods for SLR recognition are mainly statistical learning based on data acquired in a costly way. For example, collecting with datagloves worn by signers is time-consuming and restricted by tough conditions. Chen et al. [1] leveraged Hidden Markov Models like Starner et al. [2] and Vogler et al. [3] to build a sign language dialog system. Based on the manifold analysis, Fang et al. [4] adopted a hierarchical decision model with a fuzzy decision tree as the final classifier to recognize a large vocabulary of 5,113 signs. Sun et al. [5] proposed a discriminative exemplar coding approach to build a set of exemplar-based classifiers for SLR. They show the competitive performance of SLR and facilitate the study in this field.

With the significant progress in computer vision, recognizing actions from videos is promising for practical applications. As a result, SLR from videos can be more acceptable and flexible in practice. Laptev et al. [6] detected events by maximizing a normalized Spatio-temporal Laplacian operator over spatial and temporal scales from videos, built on the idea of the Harris and Förstner interest point operators. Wang et al. [7] adopted improved dense trajectories as video representation for action recognition. Tang et al. [8] proposed a two-stage hand posture recognition system for Sign Language Recognition that first detects and tracks the hands and then automatically learn feature from hand posture images with deep neural networks. Pigou et al. [9] proposed an end-to-end deep neural networks model incorporating temporal convolutions and bidirectional recurrence to improve gesture recognition performance significantly. Hu et al. proposed a Global-Local Enhancement Network with two mutually promoted streams toward different crucial aspects of SLR to combat the ambiguity of the non-manual feature [10].

Attention has become an effective mechanism in deep learning methods in recent years. Mnih et al. [11] constructed a recurrent neural network with spatial attention for image recognition that learns only from the significant regions rather than globally, directly reducing the computation. Bahdanau et al. [12] introduced soft attention into the model for natural language processing in which each sequence element is weighted. Luong et al. [13] proposed two kinds of novel attention mechanisms: global attention and local attention. Global attention is similar to soft attention, and local attention is calculated to construct a window at a point in the sequence. The model only takes the information in that window into consideration. Huang et al. [14] proposed an attention-based 3D–Convolutional Neutral Networks (CNNs) learn Spatio-temporal feature from raw video without prior knowledge, and the attention mechanism helps select the clue for SLR.

Since understanding sign language is a process of visual observation, imitating the human attention mechanism can selectively process the frames of the videos for SLR tasks. Hence, we propose to learn dynamic attention to selectively observe frames for isolated SLR. However, the discrete annotation of sequence states makes the interaction sequence non-differentiable in training. Hence, a new learning scheme beyond general backpropagation is necessary to make the training feasible.

We propose a dynamic attention deep reinforcement learning model for isolated SLR from videos as illustrated in Fig. 1. The proposed model recognizes sign language words from videos by repeatedly observing the clips in the video and looking for the keyframes. As humans do, the agent infers the next position of keyframes according to what it has observed and then moves there for more information. After a sequence of observations, the model predicts the word. To tackle the non-differentiable problem in the interaction sequence, we propose to learn the policy by reinforcement learning methods with policy gradient and construct a Partially Observable Markov Decision Process (POMDP) [15] to learn the dynamic attention for SLR. The learned humanlike dynamic attention can enhance the ability of recognition and improve accuracy. We also adapt the proposed framework for a multimodal isolated SLR.

The major contributions of our work are listed below.

– We propose a novel dynamic attention mechanism for isolated SLR from videos. The dynamic attention mechanism mimics the action of humans in watching video sequences. The mechanism can enhance the ability of recognition and improve accuracy by excluding noise and redundancy.
– For learning the dynamic attention for SLR, we construct a Partially Observable Markov Decision Process (POMDP), which makes learning from the non-differentiable sequence of interactions possible for a deep reinforcement learning model.

The remainder of this paper is organized as follows. The details of the proposed model is introduced in Sect. 2. The experimental analysis is summarized in Sect. 3. Finally We draw conclusions in Sect. 4.

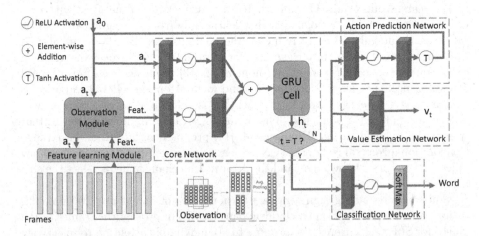

Fig. 1. The framework of the proposed dynamic attention deep reinforcement learning model. The blocks in the orange box illustrate the observation module of the model. a_t is the action predicted by the action prediction network except the initial a_0. h_t is the hidden state of GRU. v_t is the state value. 'Feat.' denotes the feature of the clip. (Color figure online)

2 Methodology

2.1 Framework of the Proposed Model

The proposed dynamic attention deep reinforcement learning model comprises three modules, as illustrated in Fig. 1. The first is for feature learning module. The second module is the observation module for selecting critical information. The third module is the deep reinforcement structure, which comprises a core network, a value estimation network, an action prediction network, and a classification network.

For recognition from video, the proposed model selectively focuses on the keyframes found through a sequence observation of clips to mimic human actions in searching events from videos. First, the information from each observation is combined to build up the representation of the whole video. Then classification is made by the information gained from selective observation. We construct a Markov Decision Process (MDP) and apply the reinforcement learning method to learn an optimal policy.

2.2 Feature Learning Module

Learning the relatedness of all frames along the time dimension requires the model to combine frames in temporal succession. 3D CNN is a competent candidate for this task, so we adopt it as the feature learner for videos. In addition to the convolutional operation on two spatial dimensions, 3D CNN also does along the time dimension to capture the relatedness. We adopt Inflated 3D ConvNets (I3D) [16] as backbone, extending from 2D CNN Inception-V1 [17].

2.3 Observation Module with Dynamic Attention

The observation module selects the clip for the deep reinforcement learning module as the sensation from the environment. Meanwhile, the deep reinforcement learning module determines the clipping frames, which allows the model to focus on the region of interest through a sequence of observations. As shown in the orange box in Fig. 1, each observation module chooses some continuous frames and a more extended clip at the same position. Their feature is extracted with the representation learning module. The extended clip is reshaped to the same length as the short by average pooling. Hence, the model can focus on the region of interest with a blurred view. Denote the video sequence as V, the action as a_t, the feature learning module is defined in Equation (1).

$$x_t^{clipped} = f_r(V, a_{t-1}) . \tag{1}$$

2.4 Deep Reinforcement Module

The MDP to solve the video recognition problem contains a set of states, actions, and rewards.

- **States.** Denote the step state at the time t as s_t, which contains the information gained from all the historical observations. The representation of the states is learned by the core network that encodes the sequence of states.
- **Rewards.** The target is to maximize the cumulative reward $R = \sum_{t=1}^{T} r_t$, in which T is the number of observations the model would make. For the model to learn beneficial policies in action recognition, the agent is rewarded $r_T = 1$ only if a correct classification is achieved at the final step T, and $r_t = 0$ at all the other steps.
- **Action.** The action determines where to observe the sequence. The action a outputted by the action prediction network is a scalar between -1 and 1, indicating a normalized position in the video.

Learning the parameters θ of the model is learning the policy π because θ determines the model behavior. The policy π generates a distribution of the interaction sequence, in which the expected cumulative reward is denoted as in Equation (2).

$$J(\theta) = \mathbb{E}_{p(s_{(1:T)};\theta)} \left[\sum_{t=1}^{T} r_t \right] = \mathbb{E}_{p(s_{(1:T)};\theta)} [R] . \tag{2}$$

In Equation (2), The sequence of states is denoted as $s_{(1:T)}$, and $p(s_{(1:T)}; \theta)$ is determined by policy π. It is impractical to solve the maximization of J accurately, since it involves the sequence of high-dimension interactions generated from an unknown dynamic environment. But if it is regarded as a POMDP, it can be solved by reinforcement learning methods. In the reinforcement learning method, the gradient of J is calculated as an approximation in Equation (3) . In the Equation (3), s^i $(i = 1 \dots M)$ denotes the sequence of interaction.

$$\nabla_\theta J = \sum_{t=1}^{T} \mathbb{E}_{p(s_{(1:T)};\theta)} \left[\nabla_\theta log(\pi(a_t|s_{(1:t)}; \theta))R \right]$$
$$\approx \frac{1}{M} \sum_{i=1}^{M} \sum_{t=1}^{T} \nabla_\theta log(\pi(a_t^i|s_{(1:t)}^i; \theta))R^i . \tag{3}$$

As an agent interacts with the environment in training, the current model generates a sequence $s = s_1 s_2 \dots s_T$, updates the parameters θ to increase the probability of choosing the action with a high expected cumulative reward. In practice, it is with relatively high variance at the beginning of training, resulting from arbitrary initialization. Hence, Equation (4) takes the place of Equation (3).

$$\frac{1}{M} \sum_{i=1}^{M} \sum_{t=1}^{T} \nabla_\theta log(\pi(a_t^i|s_{(1:t)}^i; \theta))(R_t^i - v_t) . \tag{4}$$

In Equation (4), $R_t^i = \sum_{j=t}^{T} r_j^i$ is the cumulative reward and v_t is the baseline of value estimate relies on $s_{(1:t)}$ but not on action a_t^i and t directly. Equation (4) is equivalent to Equation (3) but with lower variance, which brings more stable training. $v_t = \mathbb{E}_\pi [R_t]$ is learned by the aforementioned value estimation network to estimate the cumulative reward from the current state.

The proposed MDP to solve deep reinforcement learning can guide the model to learn video keyframes based on only the reward signal from the final classification.

2.5   Dynamic Attention Learning

The deep reinforcement learning module receives the feature of a clip $x_t^{clipped}$ as the sensation from the environment and then combines it with the action a_t to comprehend the clip. Meanwhile, it decides where to observe in the next step. Finally, the classification is made after T times of observations based on the information observed. The deep reinforcement learning module comprises four networks: the core network, value estimation network, action prediction network, and classification networks, which cooperate to achieve the above behaviors.

The core network comprises four fully-connected layers and a Gate Recurrent Unit-Cell(GRU-Cell) as shown in Fig. 1. The feature of the observation module and its action are passed through two fully-connected layers with a ReLU activation. Then they are fused before sending into the GRU-Cell. At the very beginning, the position of the clip is arbitrary. Denote the parameters of the branch receiving the feature and the action signal respectively as θ_c^{feat} and θ_c^a, and denote the GRU-Cell as θ_c^g, the core network can be denoted as in Equation (5) and Equation (6).

$$g_t = f_c^{feat}(x_t^{clipped}; \theta_c^{feat}) + f_c^a(a_{t-1}; \theta_c^a) . \tag{5}$$

$$h_t = f_c^g(g_t, h_{t-1}; \theta_c^g) . \tag{6}$$

where h_{t-1} is the hidden state of GRU-Cell calculated by f_c^g at the last time step, and h_0 is initially filled with zeros.

The action prediction network comprises two fully-connected layers with a ReLU activation and a *tanh* activation, taking the output of the core network as input. The *tanh* activation guarantees that the output is between -1 and 1. The action a_t is sampled from a Gaussian Distribution whose mean μ is the output of *tanh* activation. The variance σ is a hyperparameter. Denote its parameters as θ_a, the action prediction network can be denoted as in Equation (7) and Equation (8).

$$\mu = Tanh(f_a(h_t; \theta_a)) . \tag{7}$$

$$a_t \sim Normal(\mu, \sigma^2) . \tag{8}$$

The value estimation network and the classification network have the structure of fully-connected layers, taking the output of the core network. The classification network works only at the last observation. Denote its parameters as θ_{cls}, the classification network can be denoted as in Equation (9). And denote its parameters as θ_v, the value estimation network is defined in Equation (10).

$$o = Softmax(f_{cls}(h_T; \theta_{cls})) \, . \tag{9}$$

$$v_t = f_v(h_t; \theta_v) \, . \tag{10}$$

Denote the parameters of the proposed model as θ, the interaction at time step t can be denoted as in Equation (11).

$$a_t, v_t, h_t = f_\theta(V, a_{t-1}, h_{t-1}; \theta) \, . \tag{11}$$

2.6   Loss Function

The deep reinforcement learning model is trained based on the policy gradient method with a loss with three components.

Loss for Classification. After the last observation step, the action classification determines the output of the essential task. So we adopt the Cross-Entropy Loss for classification denoted as in Equation (12).

$$L_{cls} = -\log(\frac{\exp(o_y)}{\Sigma_i \exp(o_i)}) = -\hat{y} + \log(\Sigma_i \exp(o_i)) \, . \tag{12}$$

where o is the output of the classification network and y is the class label.

Loss for Value Estimation. The supervision for the value estimation network also comes from the final classification. Denote the classification output as R, and the loss for value estimation can be denoted as in Equation (13). If the prediction is correct, $R = 1$, otherwise $R = 0$.

$$L_v = \frac{\Sigma_t^N \|R - v_t\|_2^2}{N} \, . \tag{13}$$

Loss for Action Prediction. The deep reinforcement learning model is trained based on policy gradient. Denoting $p(a_t)$ as the probability of a_t in Equation (8). The loss for action prediction can be denoted as in Equation (14).

$$L_a = -\frac{\Sigma_t^N \log p(a_t) \times (R - v_t)}{N} \, . \tag{14}$$

The total loss of the proposed model is the sum of the above three components as in Equation (15), in which λ is the weight of the loss for action prediction. The final classification supervises the training of the model.

$$L = L_{cls} + L_v + \lambda L_a \, . \tag{15}$$

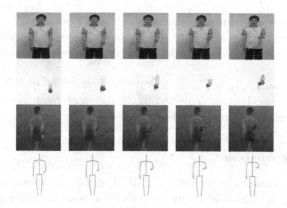

Fig. 2. The examples of four modalities from top to bottom are RGB, optical flow, depth, and skeleton joints.

3   Experiments

3.1   Dataset

We construct experiments on the SLR500 dataset [18] to estimate model performance. SLR500 dataset consists of three modalities, i.e., RGB, depth, and skeleton joints, as shown in Fig. 2.

The RGB videos are in a resolution of 1280px × 720px and a frame rate of 30 FPS. The depth videos are in a resolution of 512px × 424px and also a frame rate of 30 FPS. The skeleton joints videos contain 25 joints of the human body. All videos of action last from 2 to 4 s. In addition, we extract the optical flow videos from RGB videos with the TV1 [19] algorithm to enrich the motion representation.

There are 500 words in SLR500 dataset in which the action of each word is performed by 50 different signers and repeated 5 times per signer. We adopt all full videos in the experiments.

3.2   Experimental Setting

According to the CSL protocol, the data of the first 36 signers is used as the training set, and the rest is the test set. All videos are adjusted to 224px × 224px.

We pretrain the I3D as the feature learner first. Then, we clip the videos with the sliding-window method of 75% overlapping and 16 frames per window. When training the I3D, we tag each clip from the same video with the same label. The output of the last pooling layer is the clip feature, a vector of 1024 dimensions. Besides, all other fully-connected layers and GRU-Cell in the proposed model are 1024 units. Adam optimizer is adopted in all experiments with a learning rate of 10^{-4}.

For the deep reinforcement learning module, we set that $T = 7$, meaning that each prediction is made after seven observations. For each module, the prediction is made based on observing a clip of 6 windows with a broader glance of 12 windows.

For multimodal SLR, we build independent modules except classification network for each modalities. The feature of different modalities are fused by concatenation before fed into classification network.

3.3   Modality Analysis

We perform experiments to compare the RGB, depth, skeleton joints, and optical flow modalities and their different combinations with optimized settings of hyperparameters. The results of single and multiple modalities are summarized in Table 1.

Table 1. Results for modality comparison analysis.

	Modalities				Accuracy
	RGB	Depth	Joints	Flow	
Single Modality	✓				0.900
		✓			0.963
			✓		0.796
				✓	0.828
Double Modalities	✓	✓			**0.974**
	✓			✓	0.870
	✓		✓		0.896
		✓		✓	0.936
	✓	✓			0.965
			✓	✓	0.872
Triple Modalities	✓	✓	✓		0.971
	✓		✓	✓	0.906
		✓	✓	✓	0.967
	✓	✓		✓	0.970
All Modalities	✓	✓	✓	✓	0.971

For single modality, the results in Table 1 indicate that depth and optical flow are more competitive than others. Even though RGB provides details of hands, resulting from massive redundancy, such as clothes, gender, and characteristics irrelevant to action, it is less superior but close to them. Skeleton joints exclude most of the redundancy. Nevertheless, the lack of details about hands makes the actions less discriminative as it provides only three joints in each hand.

For multiple modality combinations, Table 1 shows that accuracy increases with the combination of modalities. The increase indicates that the accuracy benefits from the compensation information among multiple modalities. For example, joining the RGB and depth modalities achieves the best performance of 97.4% in double-modality combinations. For triple-modality combinations, joining the RGB, depth, and skeleton joints modalities achieves the best performance of 97.1%. Hence, the compensation effect is the greatest between the RGB and depth modality among all combinations.

The accuracy decreases when using modalities which are incompatibility, indicating that feature-level combination is not a proper solution in heterogenous modality combination.

3.4   Ablative Studies

To validate the effectiveness we construct a basic model without dynamic attention and compare the performance on four single-modality tasks. Specifically, the basic model takes the feature of full video as input and then passes it through the GRU-Cell and classification network. Results in Table 2 demonstrate that the performance on each modality decreases without dynamic attention. Moreover, performance deteriorates dramatically on skeleton joints and optical flow as there are information is sparse in these two modalities. These results demonstrate the effectiveness and necessity of the proposed dynamic attention.

Table 2. Comparison of the accuracy of the basic model without dynamic attention and proposed model with dynamic attention on four modalities.

Modality	No Attention	Dynamic Attention
RGB	0.838	0.900
Depth	0.937	0.963
Skeleton Joints	0.548	0.796
Optical Flow	0.472	0.828

3.5   Comparison Analysis

We also compare the proposed model with the benchmark methods on SLR500 dataset, such as detecting spatio-temporal interest points (STIP) [6], improved Dense Trajectories (iDT) [7], Hidden Markov Model with Gaussian Mixture Model (GMM-HMM) [8], Visual Geometry Group Networks (VGG) [20], 3D convolution networks(C3D) [21], attention-based 3d-CNNs (attn-3DCNN) [14] and Global-Local Enhancement Network (GLE-Net) [10]. For STIP [6] and iDT [7], the extracted features are encode with the fisher vector [22]. The details of the compared benchmark methods can be found in [10], which reaches the peak of research on isolated SLR in recent years. Our work makes an effort to boost the topic to fill in the gap of recent years.

The comparison results are summarized in Table 3. Though the research on isolated SLR has been a less attractive topic in recent years, our research indicates that the newly developed machine learning techniques are promising in boosting the topic further.

Table 3. Comparison with benchmark methods.

Method	Modalities				Accuracy
	RGB	Depth	Joints	Flow	
STIP [6]-FV-SVM	✓				0.618
iDT [7]-FV-SVM	✓			✓	0.685
GMM-HMM [8]	✓	✓	✓		0.563
VGG [20]	✓				0.607
C3D [21]	✓	✓			0.747
attn-3DCNN [14]	✓	✓	✓		0.887
GLE-Net [10]	✓				0.968
ours	✓	✓			**0.974**

4   Conclusions

This paper presents a deep reinforcement learning model to realize dynamic attention in video watching for isolated SLR. The model interacts with data following the learned policy gradient method. The policy gradient method allows the deep reinforcement module to learn non-differentiable interactions in the sequences. The model observes and comprehends a video clip and generates the inner state in each iteration. Based on the inner state, the learned policy guides the model to search the keyframes of the video. Repeating the interaction, the model can focus on the keyframes of the videos and exclude the interference from redundant frames. All modules in the proposed model can be trained in an end-to-end supervised manner with only the video labels. Moreover, the fusion of multimodal data enhances the result by compatible advantages. The results on SLR500 dataset show the superiority of the proposed method over other compared methods.

References

1. Chena, Y., Gao, W., Fang, G., Yang, C., Wang, Z.: CSLDS: Chinese sign language dialog system. In: IEEE International SOI Conference. Proceedings (Cat. No. 03CH37443). IEEE, vol. 2003, pp. 236–237 (2003)

2. Starner, T., Weaver, J., Pentland, A.: Real-time American sign language recognition using desk and wearable computer based video. IEEE Trans. Pattern Anal. Mach. Intell. **20**(12), 1371–1375 (1998)

3. Vogler, C., Metaxas, D.: ASL recognition based on a coupling between HMMs and 3D motion analysis. In: Sixth International Conference on Computer Vision (IEEE Cat. No. 98CH36271), pp. 363–369. IEEE (1998)

4. Fang, G., Gao, W., Zhao, D.: Large vocabulary sign language recognition based on fuzzy decision trees. IEEE Trans. Syst. Man Cybern. Part A Syst. Hum. **34**(3), 305–314 (2004)

5. Sun, C., Zhang, T., Bao, B.-K., Xu, C., Mei, T.: Discriminative exemplar coding for sign language recognition with kinect. IEEE Trans. Cybern. **43**(5), 1418–1428 (2013)

6. Laptev, I.: On space-time interest points. Int. J. Comput. Vision **64**(2), 107–123 (2005)

7. Wang, H., Schmid, C.: Action recognition with improved trajectories. In: Proceedings of the IEEE International Conference on Computer Vision, pp. 3551–3558 (2013)

8. Tang, A., Lu, K., Wang, Y., Huang, J., Li, H.: A real-time hand posture recognition system using deep neural networks. ACM Trans. Intell. Syst. Technol. (TIST) **6**(2), 1–23 (2015)

9. Pigou, L., Van Den Oord, A., Dieleman, S., Van Herreweghe, M., Dambre, J.: Beyond temporal pooling: recurrence and temporal convolutions for gesture recognition in video. Int. J. Comput. Vision **126**(2), 430–439 (2018)

10. Hu, H., Zhou, W., Pu, J., Li, H.: Global-local enhancement network for NMF-aware sign language recognition. ACM Trans. Multimedia Comput. Commun. Appl. (TOMM) **17**(3), 1–19 (2021)

11. Yosinski, J., et al.: Advances in neural information processing systems. vol. 27 (2014)

12. Bahdanau, D., Cho, K.H., Bengio, Y.: Neural machine translation by jointly learning to align and translate. In: 3rd International Conference on Learning Representations, ICLR 2015 (2015)

13. Luong, M.-T., Pham, H., Manning, C.D.: Effective approaches to attention-based neural machine translation. arXiv e-prints, pp. arXiv-1508 (2015)

14. Huang, J., Zhou, W., Li, H., Li, W.: Attention-based 3D-CNNs for large-vocabulary sign language recognition. IEEE Trans. Circuits Syst. Video Technol. **29**(9), 2822–2832 (2018)

15. Monahan, G.E.: State of the art-a survey of partially observable markov decision processes: theory, models, and algorithms. Manage. Sci. **28**(1), 1–16 (1982)

16. Carreira, J., Zisserman, A.: Quo vadis, action recognition? A new model and the kinetics dataset. In: Proceedings of the IEEE Conference on Computer Vision and Pattern Recognition, pp. 6299–6308 (2017)

17. Szegedy, C., et al.: Going deeper with convolutions. In: Proceedings of the IEEE Conference on Computer Vision and Pattern Recognition, pp. 1–9 (2015)

18. Zhang, J., Zhou, W., Xie, C., Pu, J., Li, H.: Chinese sign language recognition with adaptive HMM. In: IEEE International Conference on Multimedia and Expo (ICME). vol. 2016, pp. 1–6. IEEE (2016)

19. Zach, C., Pock, T., Bischof, H.: A duality based approach for realtime TV-L^1 optical flow. In: Hamprecht, F.A., Schnörr, C., Jähne, B. (eds.) DAGM 2007. LNCS, vol. 4713, pp. 214–223. Springer, Heidelberg (2007). https://doi.org/10.1007/978-3-540-74936-3_22

20. Simonyan, K., Zisserman, A.: Very deep convolutional networks for large-scale image recognition. arXiv preprint arXiv:1409.1556 (2014)
21. Tran, D., Bourdev, L., Fergus, R., Torresani, L., Paluri, M.: Learning spatiotemporal features with 3D convolutional networks. In: Proceedings of the IEEE International Conference on Computer Vision, pp. 4489–4497 (2015) .
22. Oneata, D., Verbeek, J., Schmid, C.: Action and event recognition with fisher vectors on a compact feature set. In: Proceedings of the IEEE International Conference on Computer Vision, pp. 1817–1824 (2013)

A Segmentation Method Based on SE Attention and U-Net for Apple Image

Liang Gao, Jinrong He$^{(\boxtimes)}$, Longlong Zhai, and Yiting He

College of Mathematics and Computer Science, Yan'an University, Yan'an 716000, China
hejinrong@yau.edu.cn

Abstract. Apple image segmentation is the basis for apple target recognition and positioning in apple intelligent picking. Traditional apple image segmentation methods have problems such as low accuracy and poor recall rate. Based on the U-Net model, a SE attention mechanism fusion improved U-Net apple image segmentation method is proposed to utilize contextual information of features. First, 344 apple images were collected in the orchard and manually labeled using LabelMe software. The samples were expanded to 1700 using data augmentation. Then the U-type network structure is used to connect the feature maps of the low-level network and the high-level network. The skip connection is used to reduce the network complexity, and the number of feature map channels is superimposed. The SE attention mechanism is added to the decoder part to enhance the channel features of the effective feature maps for apple image segmentation tasks and suppress unimportant channel features to obtain rich contextual information for more refined feature maps. Finally, apple target segmentation is predicted based on the obtained feature maps. The results show that the U-Net model with SE attention fusion can accurately segment the apple region, especially for small-scale apples, and can further optimize the segmentation effect of the edge. The segmentation precision of the model can reach 98.86%, and F1 score is 98.96%, verifying that the proposed model can accurately segment apple targets of different scales in complex environments.

Keywords: apple picking · image segmentation · U-Net · feature maps · SE attention mechanism

1 Introduction

Yan'an is one of the important production bases for apple export in China. Yan'an apples have a wide variety and excellent quality, which are renowned both domestically and abroad. However, until now, apple picking still heavily relies on human labor due to low efficiency and high labor intensity. Moreover, the apple picking season is concentrated, making it necessary to develop intelligent apple picking robots. Image segmentation is the first step of object recognition. When an intelligent apple picking robot is in operation, it needs to accurately recognize and locate the apple first before it can perform picking. Therefore, accurate segmentation of the apple is necessary [1].

© The Author(s), under exclusive license to Springer Nature Switzerland AG 2023
H. Lu et al. (Eds.): ICIG 2023, LNCS 14356, pp. 263–276, 2023.
https://doi.org/10.1007/978-3-031-46308-2_22

Image segmentation has been studied for decades, but a universal segmentation method applicable to all types of images is yet to be found. Many scholars and experts have proposed and researched several methods for the segmentation of targeted objects. Liu et al. [2] proposed an apple-picking robot fruit segmentation method based on superpixel features, which extracted the texture features of superpixels and achieved segmentation of apple with uneven color distribution, with a segmentation accuracy of 92.14%. Liu et al. [3] proposed a Lingwu long jujube image segmentation method based on the watershed algorithm. They optimized the threshold value using a genetic algorithm and used methods like maximum between-class variance to process images for segmentation with an accuracy of 89.99%. Zhao et al. [4] established a geometric model of Lingwu long jujube and used its geometric curves to fit the segmentation line of the target object in the jujube image. Their method could also solve the issue of object adhesion with an accuracy of 92.31%. Zhang et al. [5] proposed an apple image segmentation method based on color-texture fusion features and machine learning, which selected three color features to segment apple pixels from background pixels, and used GLCM to extract texture features. The method achieved an accuracy of 94%. Fan et al. [6] proposed an apple segmentation method based on gray-RGB color space, which could accurately segment apple pixels from other pixels. They also proposed a feature segmentation algorithm based on patches with higher accuracy. Peng et al. [7] proposed a segmentation method based on disparity images, which improved the segmentation performance of overlapping fruits, with a final edge detection error of only 5.74%. Although these methods could segment large-scale objects well, they fail to meet the accuracy and stability requirements for target object segmentation under complex backgrounds.

In recent years, deep learning has been commonly applied in agricultural image detection and segmentation. Minaee et al. [8] provided a comprehensive summary of image segmentation methods, analyzed the similarities of various image segmentation models, and their advantages and disadvantages. Liu et al. [9] proposed an improved DeepLab V3 + segmentation model, which made three improvements on the basis of the original network. The improved model achieved better segmentation performance and increased speed. The segmentation accuracy of trees reached 95.61%. Chen et al. [10] established a grain image segmentation model of harvested rice based on the improved U-Net network, which was able to effectively segment grains, stems and stalks in rice grain images. The segmentation accuracy of rice grain was 99.42%, of stem 88.56%, and of stalk 86.84%. Zhang et al. [11] proposed a cucumber leaf disease segmentation method based on a multi-scale fusion convolutional neural network. The average segmentation accuracy of crop disease leaf images under complex backgrounds reached 93.12%. Zhang et al. [12] proposed a research on tree image segmentation based on the U-Net network, which can automatically locate the tree area, divide the tree area, and achieve end-to-end image segmentation. Duan et al. [13] proposed deep fully convolutional neural network-based segmentation of rice panicles in farmland. This method is based on an improved SegNet network. The principle is to first divide and crop the original image into several sub-images, segment these sub-images with PanicleNet, and then combine them to obtain the segmentation results. It is also suitable for irregular rice panicle edges, different varieties, and complex environments such as external lighting, significantly improving the accuracy and efficiency of rice panicle segmentation, but the best segmentation accuracy is only 86%. Liu et al. [14] proposed a cotton field canopy image segmentation method based on the improved fully convolutional neural network model, which was 16.22 percentage points higher in segmentation performance compared to traditional fully convolutional neural network models. Xiong et al. [15] proposed a litchi flower and leaf segmentation method based on a deep semantic segmentation network, which improved the DeepLab V3 network with an accuracy of 87%.

At present, more and more scholars have proposed methods to identify and segment fruits. Jia et al. [16] proposed a network framework specifically for fruit network segmentation. This framework is based on the improved Mask R-CNN model and introduces Gaussian attention module, which has good segmentation performance for overlapping target objects, but is time-consuming. Xue et al. [17] proposed an image segmentation method of Lingwu long jujube based on improved FCN-8s, which mainly targets the segmentation problem of long jujubes with different maturity levels and achieves a segmentation accuracy of 98.44%. Ni et al. [18] proposed a research method for testing the maturity and fruit quantity of blueberries as well as evaluating the compactness of four cultivated varieties. The network model used is Mask R-CNN, which finally has a good effect on the segmentation of blueberry fruits and the evaluation of the compactness of different blueberry varieties. Wang et al. [19] proposed an apple image segmentation algorithm based on BP neural network, which can effectively segment apples and backgrounds. Through subsequent erosion and dilation algorithm processing, good results were obtained. Jia et al. [20] proposed a harvesting robot visual detector model based on Mask R-CNN, which can better identify overlapping apples, and the accuracy is 97.31%, and the recognition speed is relatively fast, but the problem of sample shortage has not been solved. Li et al. [21] proposed a small-scale U-Net segmentation algorithm suitable for recognizing green apples in a complex orchard environment, which can accurately identify green apples under conditions such as occlusion and overlap, and has high accuracy in the segmentation of the edge of green apples. The model also has high generalization ability. Nicolai et al. [22] introduced a new dataset for detecting and segmenting apples in orchards, which contains a number of object instances and apple varieties and is also suitable for small object detection. The segmentation performance of four models was compared, and the experimental results showed that the U-Net with pre-training weights performed better than other methods. They also mentioned methods for solving yield estimation problems. Currently, image segmentation algorithms based on deep learning have some shortcomings to varying degrees, such as low segmentation accuracy and weak generalization ability.

In order to meet the requirements of the intelligent picking robot in complex environment for the precision of apple target segmentation and the algorithm robustness, this paper presents an apple image segmentation method of integrating the SE attention mechanism and U-Net. By changing the backbone network and the upsampling method in the decoder part, the feature map with the same size as the original image is obtained, and the SE attention mechanism is integrated into the decoder part to obtain a more detailed feature map. The main contributions of this paper are as follows:

(1) The Apple image object segmentation dataset is established. The dataset includes 1700 training images, 40 test images and the improved U-Net network structure code, which has been shared on github: https://github.com/Planet82/SE-UNet.

(2) By integrating the SE attention mechanism into the U-Net model (denoted as SE-U-Net), which adaptively assigns channel weights to the feature layers that are effective for the current task, and adding the SE module does not change the size of the feature layers. The precision and robustness of apple segmentation in orchard are improved.

(3) Design experiments are conducted to compare and analyze the target segmentation methods such as U-Net, PsPNet and DeepLab V3 +. It is verified that the improved U-Net model with SE attention in apple image segmentation task is effective, and the segmentation accuracy of SE-U-Net reaches 98.86%.

2   Material

2.1   Image Acquisition and Dataset Construction

The image collection site was located in Zhuangtou Village and surrounding villages in Yanshuiguan Town, and apple orchard images were collected in different environments in the morning, noon, and evening using a Huawei Honor 20s phone. A total of 344 images were collected, including apples in different environments. Among them, the initial training set has 304 images, and the test set has 40 images, all stored in PNG format.

The collected apple images were manually labeled with LabelMe, and the contour edges of Yan'an apples were marked by hand. As shown in Fig. 1, the generated json file of the labeled image was converted into PNG format, and the labeled image was binarized and saved in the corresponding file path.

(a) Labeled images

(b) Ground truth

Fig. 1. Labeled Yan 'an apple images and Ground truth

2.2 Data Augmentation

To improve the generalization ability of the neural network model, the original images and ground truth of each apple are subjected to rotation, flipping, and random scaling operations with different probabilities. This is done to augment the dataset and expand the training set to 1700 images. Some samples of the augmented data for a particular apple image in the dataset are shown in Fig. 2.

Fig. 2. Part of the images after data augmentation (a) Original image; (b) Rotate left; (c) Rotate left and zoom in; (d) Flip; (e) Flip and zoom in; (f) Flip, rotate right and zoom in; (g) Flip, rotate left and zoom in; (h) Flip and rotate right

3   Methods

3.1   U-Net Network

U-Net, proposed by Ronneberger et al. [23], is a symmetrical network structure. It is named U-Net because of its U-shaped network structure, as shown in Fig. 3. Similar to FCN, U-Net consists of an encoder-decoder structure. The left of the network is the encoder module, which extracts the main features of the image using convolutions and max pooling. The convolutional structure used uniform 3×3 kernel. VGG16 is used as the backbone network, which produces five initial effective feature layers with shapes of $512 \times 512 \times 64$, $256 \times 256 \times 128$, $128 \times 128 \times 256$, $64 \times 64 \times 512$, and $32 \times 32 \times 512$. The right of the network is the decoder module, which upsamples the initial effective feature layers obtained from the encoder module and performs skip connections. Upsampling is used to restore dimensions, and skip connections fuse the feature maps obtained from downsampling by stacking them according to the number of channels. The upsampling is two times that of the original paper's decoder module for ease of feature fusion. After the first upsampling and skip connection, a $64 \times 64 \times 1024$ feature map is obtained, following two convolutions to reduce the number of channels to 512. Three more upsamplings are performed, followed by two final convolutions to obtain a $512 \times 512 \times 64$ feature map.

To facilitate network construction and generalization, when upsampling the feature maps, two times the upsampling is performed. This step is to facilitate feature fusion. The final map uses 1×1 convolution to adjust the channel number to 2 for pixel-wise classification of the image. Finally, the size of the output is resized to match the size of the input image, and segmentation is performed based on the obtained feature map.

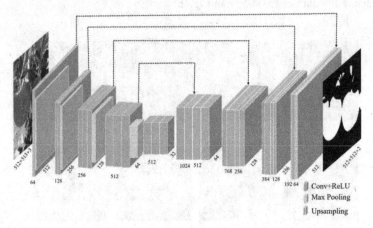

Fig. 3. U-Net Network structure

3.2   SE-U-Net Network

3.2.1   SE attention Mechanism

The SE (Squeeze and Excitation) attention module was proposed in SENet, which achieved the first place in ImageNet 2017 and achieved good results in the 2017 ILSVRC classification. The SE module can effectively improve performance and can be easily integrated into other network structures, achieving plug and play [24]. Moreover, it is lightweight in computation, which will not make the computation become overly complex and makes it cost-effective.

Conventional convolution operations convolve over each channel and sum the results to fuse channel and spatial features together. The importance of each channel is assumed to be equal. In contrast, the SE module allows the model to directly learn channel features. By explicitly modeling the interdependence between channel features, the SE module can re-adjust channel characteristics [25]. It learns the importance of each channel and assigns weight values to each feature according to its importance, emphasizing important features and allowing the neural network to focus on channels with high weight values. The SE module structure is shown in Fig. 4.

The SE attention mechanism consists of three stages: squeeze, excitation, and reweight. In the squeeze stage, as shown in Fig. 4, since the previous convolution was only operated in local space, it is difficult to get enough information to obtain the importance of each channel. To obtain the importance of each channel, global average pooling is used to compress the spatial features of each channel into a global feature, resulting in a $1 \times 1 \times C$ dimensional feature map. After obtaining the global feature, it enters the excitation stage and two FC fully connected layers are added to learn channel features, obtaining an attention feature map with dimensions of $1 \times 1 \times C$. The first fully connected layer compresses the C channels into C/R channels to reduce the number of channels and computation costs, whereas the second fully connected layer restores the C channels to increase dimensionality. Using two fully connected layers has the advantage of having more non-linearity, which can fit complex relationships between channels. Next, the Sigmoid activation function is used for normalization and to normalize the channel weights to [0,1]. Finally, it enters the reweight stage, where the obtained weight feature map of $1 \times 1 \times C$ and the original feature map of $H \times W \times C$ are multiplied channel-wise by the weight coefficients, allowing for the acquirement of feature maps where channel importance varies. The final output is a feature map with channel attention.

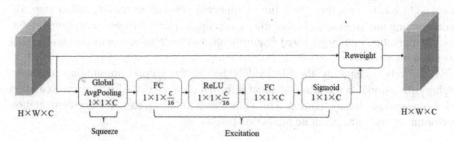

Fig. 4. SE module

3.2.2 Network Structure

SE-U-Net network mainly adds SE attention mechanism to the decoder part. SE-U-Net algorithm is still based on the Encoder-Decoder structure, and uses the most classic VGG16 network structure in the VGGNet model series as the backbone feature extraction network. The improved U-Net network performs 3×3 convolution operations twenty-two times, 2×2 max pooling operations four times, upsamplings four times, and skip connections four times. The specific implementation process is as follows. In the left part, which is the encoder module, the input image is subjected to convolution and max pooling operations in the VGG16 structure for feature extraction, obtaining five preliminary effective feature maps. In the right part, which is the decoder module, the preliminary effective feature maps are upsampled and skip-connected. Before the second upsampling, the SE attention mechanism module is added for processing, in order to enhance the channel features of the feature map, and adaptively give channel weights to enhance the channels of effective feature maps that are effective for the current task, obtaining a more fine-grained feature map. Adding the SE module does not change the size of the feature map, and the feature map after the second upsampling is still $128 \times 128 \times 768$. Then continue to perform two times upsamplings to obtain a final effective feature map that fuses all features. Finally, a 1×1 convolution is used for predicting segmentation image. The simplified image of SE-U-Net network structure is shown in Fig. 5.

In the SE-U-Net algorithm, the decision to incorporate the SE module before the second upsampling is based on the following considerations. Firstly, during the feature fusion stage, the decoder module upsamples the low-resolution feature maps and merges them with the corresponding encoder module's feature maps. As the dimension of the feature maps gradually increases, integrating the SE module before the upsampling operation can better handle high-dimensional features. Secondly, regarding channel-wise adjustment, the SE module adjusts the importance of each channel in the feature map by learning weight coefficients. In the decoder module, the number of channels in the feature maps decreases gradually. Therefore, introducing the SE module before the second upsampling can better adjust the channel information, highlight important features. Lastly, the consideration of attention mechanism scope is crucial. The SE module utilizes global average pooling to capture global feature information and learns the weight coefficients through a fully connected network in the excitation step. By incorporating the SE module before the second upsampling, we ensure applying global pooling operations on larger-sized feature maps to obtain more comprehensive global attention information.

Ultimately, integrating the SE module before the second upsampling leverages higher-dimensional features and channel information to enhance feature representation while preserving global attention. This contributes to improved semantic segmentation performance and more accurate prediction results.

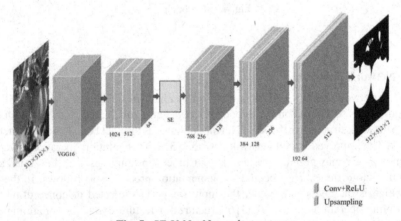

Fig. 5. SE-U-Net Network structure

3.2.3 Loss Function

The loss function of SE-U-Net consists of two parts, the Cross Entropy loss that measures pixel classification and the Dice loss that measures region correlation. Cross Entropy loss function is commonly used in neural networks to estimate the similarity of model's prediction and true value. It is a non-negative real-valued function and the smaller the loss, the better the training effect and robustness [26]. The loss function can make the training effect approximate to the true value. The expression of cross-entropy loss function used in U-Net model is shown above:

$$Loss = -\sum_{i=1}^{N} y_i log \hat{y}_i \tag{1}$$

where N represents the number of classes, y_i denotes the label value of apple pixel i and $\hat{y}_i$ denotes the predicted value of apple pixel i.

Dice loss can solve the problem of unbalanced positive and negative samples well. It is famous for the Dice coefficient, which is a measure function used to evaluate the similarity of two samples. The larger the Dice value, the more similar the two samples, and vice versa. Therefore, the Dice coefficient is better when it is larger. Dice loss is often used in image segmentation, where X represents the pixel class of the true label image and Y represents the pixel class of the predicted segmentation image. It can be regarded as the dot product between the pixels of the true label image and the predicted segmentation image, and then the dot product result is added. |X| and |Y| can be regarded as the sum of the respective pixels in the two types of images. The expression of Dice loss is shown above:

$$Dice\ Loss = 1 - \frac{2|X \cap Y|}{|X| + |Y|} = 1 - \frac{2\sum_{i=1}^{N} y_i \hat{y}_i}{\sum_{i=1}^{N} y_i \sum_{i=1}^{N} \hat{y}_i} \tag{2}$$

where N represents the total number of pixels, y_i denotes the label value of pixel i and $\hat{y}_i$ denotes the predicted value of pixel i.

4 Experiment and Result Analysis

4.1 Experimental Environment

The experimental environment is a personal computer with the Windows 10 operating system, Intel(R) Core(TM) i5-8250U CPU @ 1.60GHz, 8.00GB of memory, the graphics card is NVIDIA GeForce RTX 3060, and the PyTorch deep learning programming framework.

4.2 Evaluation Indicator

In this experiment, we selected Intersection over Union (IoU), Pixel Accuracy (PA), Precision (CPA), Recall, and F1 score as evaluation indicator for model performance. *IoU* is the ratio of the intersection to the union of the model's predicted results and the true values for apples. PA is the proportion of correctly predicted apple class pixels to total pixels. CPA corresponds to Precision, which is the probability of correctly predicting apple class in the prediction results. Recall is the proportion of pixels correctly identified as apple class to all pixels actually classified as apple class. The F1 score indicator simultaneously considers Precision and Recall and ranges from 0 to 1. The formulas for calculating each evaluation indicator are shown below:

$$IoU = \frac{TP}{FP + TP + FN} \tag{3}$$

$$PA = \frac{TP + TN}{TP + TN + FP + FN} \tag{4}$$

$$CPA = \frac{TP}{TP + FP} \tag{5}$$

$$Recall = \frac{TP}{TP + FN} \tag{6}$$

$$F1 = \frac{2 \times CPA \times Recall}{CPA + Recall} \tag{7}$$

where TP represents the number of correctly segmented pixels, TN represents the number of correctly segmented background pixels, FP represents the number of incorrectly segmented pixels, and FN represents the number of missed segmented pixels.

4.3 Result Analysis

From Fig. 6, it can be seen that SE-U-Net and other network models have completed the segmentation task of Yan'an apples under different environments, including the red and green parts of Yan'an apples and Yan'an apples in different environments in the morning, noon, and evening, all achieving relatively good segmentation results. The segmentation results of U-Net, PsPNet, DeepLab V3 +, and SE-U-Net models on the Yan'an apple dataset are shown in Fig. 6, and the evaluation indicator results based on U-Net, PsPNet, DeepLab V3 +, and SE-U-Net are shown in Table 1.

From Table 1, we can compare and analyze the pros and cons of U-Net, PsPNet, DeepLab V3 +, and SE-U-Net semantic segmentation models. The results in Table 1 show that the segmentation effect of the SE-U-Net model is better than that of the U-Net model, the segmentation effect of the U-Net model is better than that of the DeepLab V3 + model, and the segmentation effect of the DeepLab V3 + model is better than that of the PsPNet model.

The segmentation precision of the U-Net model reached 98.68%, and the F1 score reached 98.79%. The segmentation performance of this model is relatively high and can accurately segment most apples in the image, but the segmentation effect of some apple boundaries is still not clear enough, and the boundaries are not refined enough. For example, the fifth image in Fig. 6c. The segmentation precision of the PsPNet model reached 96.24%, and the F1 score reached 96.14%. Although the segmentation precision and F1 score were both above 96%, the segmentation effect for sticky, occluded, and small-scale apples was poor, as shown in the red rectangle in Fig. 6d. PsPNet failed to segment the smaller-scale apples in the second, third, and fourth images of Fig. 6d, and the edge segmentation effect of the sticky apple in the first image of Fig. 6d was also rough. The segmentation precision of the DeepLab V3 + model reached 98.01%, and

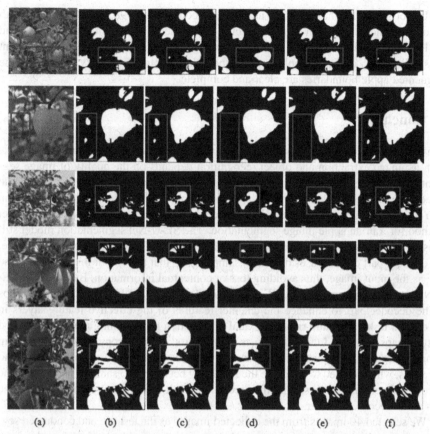

Fig. 6. Segmentation results of several models (a) Original images; (b) Ground truth; (c) U-Net segmentation results; (d) PsPNet segmentation results; (e) DeepLab V3 + segmentation results; (f) SE-U-Net segmentation results

Table 1. Comparison of segmentation results from different semantic segmentation models

Segmentation model	IoU/%	PA/%	Precision rate/%	Recall rate/%	F1 score/%
U-Net	97.63	99.13	98.68	98.91	98.79
PsPNet	92.65	97.42	96.24	96.05	96.14
DeepLab V3 +	95.85	98.54	98.01	97.75	97.88
SE-U-Net	**97.96**	**99.26**	**98.86**	**99.07**	**98.96**

the F1 score reached 97.88%. From the segmentation results, this model is better than PsPNet but still cannot segment small targets and occluded apples. For example, the first and second images in Fig. 6e. However, the boundary contour segmentation effect for sticky apples is clearer than that of the PsPNet model. The segmentation precision of the

SE-U-Net model reached 98.86%, and the F1 score reached 98.96%. Compared with the original model, the segmentation precision increased by 0.18 percentage points, and the F1 score increased by 0.17 percentage points. The segmentation effect is excellent for small targets, occluded apples, and the boundary contours of sticky apples, and the segmented apple boundaries are clear and complete.

5 Conclusion

Image segmentation is the first step in image analysis, and the quality of subsequent tasks such as image extraction and object recognition depends on the quality of image segmentation. The segmentation result directly affects the accuracy and precision of apple detection and recognition. In response to the problem of low segmentation precision of Yan'an apple images using traditional methods, this paper proposes the SE-U-Net method for Yan'an apple image segmentation. The SE-U-Net segmentation model still consists of the encoder and decoder parts. Based on the SE-U-Net network structure, the decoder part directly uses double upsampling, so that the output image is the same size as the input image, thus avoiding loss of contextual information. Based on the SE-U-Net segmentation model, the SE attention mechanism is added to the feature maps in the decoder part to enhance the channel features of the effective feature layers in the current task and obtain rich contextual information for obtaining more fine-grained feature maps. The loss function consists of two parts: cross-entropy, commonly used in semantic segmentation models, which is used when using softmax to classify pixels, and Dice loss, which is used to calculate the similarity between two samples. The larger the Dice coefficient, the more similar the prediction result is to the true label image, so the loss value becomes smaller.

We selected 40 images from the collected images as the test set, and conducted segmentation predictions on the test set, and compared them with classical deep learning models such as PsPNet, DeepLab V3 +, and U-Net. The experimental results show that the SE-U-Net model can meet the needs of apple segmentation in complex environments, with a IoU of 97.96%, a pixel accuracy of 99.26%, a precision of 98.86%, a recall of 99.07%, and a F1 score of 98.96%. Among them, the precision is 0.18 percentage points higher than U-Net, 2.72 percentage points higher than PsPNet, and 0.87 percentage points higher than DeepLab V3 +. The F1 score is 0.17 percentage points higher than U-Net, 2.93 percentage points higher than PsPNet, and 1.10 percentage points higher than DeepLab V3 +. The proposed method can accurately segment apples in complex environments and smaller scales, further improving the accuracy and robustness of Yan'an apple image segmentation and laying a foundation for further realization of intelligent apple picking.

Acknowledgement. This work is supported in part by National Natural Science Foundation of China under grant No. 61902339, by the Natural Science Basic Research Plan in Shaanxi Province of China under grants No. 2021JM-418, by the Epidemic Emergency Research Projects of Yan'an University under grant No. YDFK073, by Doctoral Starting up Foundation of Yan'an University under grant No. YDBK2019–06, by Yan'an Special Foundation for Science and Technology (2019–01, 2019–13).

References

1. Zhang, Y.J., Li, M.Z., Qiao, J., Liu, G.: Segmentation algorithm for apple recognition using image features and artificial neural network. Acta Optica Sinica **28**(11), 2104–2108 (2008)
2. Liu, X.Y., Zhao, D.A., Jia, W.K., Ruan, C.Z., Ji, W.: Fruits segmentation method based on superpixel features for apple harvesting robot. Trans. Chin. Soc. Agric. Mach. **50**(11), 15–23 (2019)
3. Liu, X.N., Wang, Y.T., Zhao, C., Zhu, C.W., Li, L.K.: Research on image segmentation method of Lingwu Long Jujubes based on watershed. Comput. Eng. Appl. **54**(15), 169–175+184 (2018)
4. Zhao, C., Wang, Y.T., Zhu, C.W.: Lingwu long jujubes image segmentation algorithm based on geometric features. Comput. Eng. Appl. **55**(15), 204–212 (2019)
5. Zhang, C.L., Zou, K.L., Pan, Y.: A method of apple image segmentation based on color-texture fusion feature and machine learning. Agronomy **10**(7) (2020)
6. Fan, P., et al.: A method of segmenting apples based on gray-centered RGB color space. Remote Sens. **13**(6), 1211 (2021)
7. Peng, H., Wu, P.F., Zhai, R.F., Liu, S.M., Wu, L.L., Jing, X.: Image segmentation algorithm for overlapping fruits based on disparity map. Trans. Chin. Soc. Agric. Mach. **43**(06), 167–173 (2012)
8. Minaee, S., Boykov, Y.Y., Porikli, F., et al.: Image segmentation using deep learning: a survey. IEEE Trans. Pattern Anal. Mach. Intell. **44**(7), 3523–3542 (2022)
9. Liu, H., Jiang, J.B., S.Y., Jia, W.D., Zeng, X., Zhuang, Z.Z.: Multi-category segmentation of orchard scene based on improved DeepLab V3+. Trans. Chin. Soc. Agric. Mach. **53**(11), 255–261 (2022)
10. Chen, J., Han, M.N., Lian, Y., Zhang, S.: Segmentation of impurity rice grain images based on U-Net model. Trans. Chin. Soc. Agric. Eng. **36**(10), 174–180 (2020)
11. Zhang, S.W., Wang, Z., Wang, Z.L.: Method for image segmentation of cucumber disease leaves based on multi-scale fusion convolutional neural networks. Trans. Chin. Soc. Agric. Eng. **36**(16), 149–157 (2020)
12. Zhang, B.Y., Ni, H.M., Hu, X.Y., Qi, D.W.: Research on tree image segmentation based on U-net network. For. Eng. **37**(02), 67–73 (2021)
13. Duan, L.F., Xiong, X., Liu, Q., Yang, W.N., Huang, C.L.: Field rice panicles segmentation based on deep full convolutional neural network. Trans. Chin. Soc. Agric. Eng. (Transactions of the CSAE) **34**(12), 202–209 (2018)
14. Liu, L.B., Cheng, X.L., Lai, J.C.: Segmentation method for cotton canopy image based on improved fully convolutional network model. Trans. Chin. Soc. Agric. Eng. (Transactions of the CSAE) **34**(12), 193–201 (2018)
15. Xiong, J.T., Liu, B.L., Zhong, Z., Chen, S.M., Zheng, Z.H.: Litchi flower and leaf segmentation and recognition based on deep semantic segmentation. Trans. Chin. Soc. Agric. Mach. **52**(06), 252–258 (2021)
16. Jia, W.K., Zhang, Z.H., Shao, W.J., Ji, Z., Hou, S.J.: RS-Net: robust segmentation of green overlapped apples. Precis. Agric. **23**(2), 492–513 (2022)
17. Xue, J.R., et al.: Image Segmentation method for Lingwu long jujubes based on improved FCN-8s. Trans. Chin. Soc. Agric. Eng. (Transactions of the CSAE) **37**(05), 191–197 (2021)
18. Ni, X., Li, C., Jiang, H., Takeda, F.: Deep learning image segmentation and extraction of blueberry fruit traits associated with harvestability and yield. Horticult. Res. (1) (2020)
19. Wang, J.J., Zhao, D.A., Ji, W., Cai, J.H., Li, F.Z.: Segmentation of apple image by BP neural network using in apple harvesting robot. J. Agric. Mech. Res. (11), 19–21 (2008)
20. Wjpd, A., Yt, A., Rong, L.B., et al.: Detection and segmentation of overlapped fruits based on optimized mask R-CNN application in apple harvesting robot. Comput. Electron. Agric. **172** (2020)

21. Li, Q.W., Jia, W.K., Sun, M.L., Hou, S.J., Zheng, Y.J.: A novel green apple segmentation algorithm based on ensemble U-Net under complex orchard environment. Comput. Electron. Agric. **180**, 105900 (2021)
22. Nicolai, H., Pravakar, R., Volkan. I., MinneApple: a benchmark dataset for apple detection and segmentation. IEEE Robot. Autom. Lett. **5**(2) (2020)
23. Ronneberger, O., Philipp, F., Brox, T.: U-Net: convolutional networks for biomedical image segmentation. CoRR, abs/1505.04597 (2015)
24. Jie, H., Li, S., Albanie, S., Gang, S., Wu, E.H.: Squeeze-and-excitation networks. IEEE Trans. Patt. Anal. Mach. Intell. **PP**(99) (2017)
25. Zhong, Z., Lin, Z.Q., Bidart, R., et al.: Squeeze-and-attention networks for semantic segmentation. CoRR, abs/1909.03402 (2019)
26. Qiu, Y.F., Wen, J.Y.: Image semantic segmentation based on combination of DeepLabV3+ and attention mechanism. Laser Optoelec. Prog. **59**(04), 130–139 (2022)

Human Action Recognition Method Based on Spatio-temporal Relationship

Haigang Yu[1], Ning He[2(✉)], Shengjie Liu[1], and Wenjing Han[2]

[1] Laboratory of Information Service Engineering, Beijing Union University, Beijing 100101, China

[2] Smart City College, Beijing Union University, Beijing 100101, China
xxthening@buu.edu.cn

Abstract. Traditional human motion recognition algorithms cannot fully utilize the spatio-temporal information in the video. In this paper, we propose a human motion recognition method with spatio-temporal modeling from local to global perspective. For local spatio-temporal information, the motion feature extraction module and the multi-scale spatio-temporal feature extraction module are designed. The local motion features are extracted by establishing cross-frame level correspondence within the network and combined into spatial features to obtain local spatio-temporal information. For global spatio-temporal information, the segmented network fusion module is designed. The representative recognition results are filtered from the video segments, and the fused filtered recognition results predict the final classification results. The results show that the model can effectively obtain the spatio-temporal dynamic information in the video for action recognition, achieve high recognition accuracy, and greatly reduce the model's complexity.

Keywords: Motion Recognition · Motion Features · Attention Mechanism

1 Introduction

Human action recognition is one of the important research directions in the field of computer vision, and the main task is to recognize the actions of people in videos. However, the inherent complexity and variability of videos make it difficult for traditional image recognition algorithms to effectively handle the dynamic information in videos. Therefore, modeling for spatio-temporal information to obtain dynamic information in videos for recognition is a challenging problem for the current human action recognition task.

To better learn the spatio-temporal information in videos. Many approaches use 3D convolutional network models to learn spatio-temporal features by spatio-temporal convolution across multiple frames. For example, Tran et al. [1] proposed the C3D network, which effectively demonstrated the spatio-temporal modeling capability of 3D convolutional networks. However, related studies [2] showed that 3D convolution actually does not learn the change of information on the temporal sequence well but more on the aggregation of temporal information, and adding a dimension brings higher computational cost. To reduce the computational cost, the work of Tran et al. [3], Xie et al. [4], and Li et al. [5] decomposes the 3D convolution into a combination of 2D convolution and 1D convolution. These methods reduce the computational cost to some extent but lead to a degradation of the model's performance. There are also methods that effectively improve the accuracy of action recognition by using optical flow to characterize motion information in the video. However, extracting optical flow requires a large amount of computation and requires a separate network in the model to learn spatio-temporal features, leading to a doubling of the number of parameters and their computational cost. Zhao et al. [6] used RGB temporal difference maps to simulate motion features instead of optical flow for action recognition, but in their work only the temporal difference maps were used as another output, again requiring a separate network to be trained and fused with the spatial network. Jiang et al. [7] extracted motion features by spatial shifting and subtraction operations between spatial features. This method is computationally efficient but does not achieve the classification accuracy of the dual-stream network. In summary, in order to improve the spatio-temporal modeling capability of 2D networks while maintaining the advantage of computational complexity, This paper focuses on the following research:

1. A network framework is designed for spatio-temporal information fusion from local to global, which can capture both short-term and long-term spatio-temporal information and improve the accuracy of action recognition.
2. A motion feature extraction module and a multi-scale spatio-temporal feature extraction module are designed to be embedded in the 2D network to improve the spatio-temporal feature extraction capability of the 2D network.
3. A segmented network fusion module is designed to be able to detect video clips and eliminate video clips with interference to improve the classification accuracy.

2 Related work

2.1 Action Recognition Method Based on Temporal Modeling

Temporal modeling is crucial to obtaining dynamic information in video for motion recognition. In 2014, Simonyan et al. [8] proposed a dual-stream convolutional network to extract optical streams to input separate temporal networks to capture motion information. In 2016, Wang et al. [9] proposed a TSN (Temporal Segment Networks) network structure that combines sparse sampling strategy to segment the video and effectively solves the temporal modeling problem of long-range video. In 2018, Zhou et al. [10] proposed the Temporal Relation Network (TRN) to learn and reason about the temporal correlation between video frames at multiple time scales. In 2019, Lin et al. [11] proposed the TSM (Temporal Shift Module) network to design a temporal shift module for the temporal modeling problem, i.e., information exchange between adjacent frames by shifting part of the channel information between adjacent frames. 2020: Kwon et al. [12] proposed an end-to-end trainable module that can efficiently extract motion features. In 2021, Liu et al. [2] proposed a temporal adaptive module that generates specific convolution kernels to capture temporal information at different scales according to the corresponding feature maps.

2.2 Attentional Mechanisms

Attention models are also widely used in action recognition tasks. In 2015, Xu et al. [13] first applied attention mechanisms to the image domain and used visualization techniques to visually represent the role of attention mechanisms. In 2018,Roy et al. [14] proposed the SENet attention model to focus on the relationship between channels and automatically learn the importance of different channel features. In 2019, Woo et al. [15] proposed a CBAM attention model combining temporal attention mechanisms and spatial attention mechanisms to filter important information. In 2019, Gao et al. [16] proposed the GSoP-Net structure to capture long-range statistical information by modeling the relevance of overall image information, making full use of the contextual information of the image. In 2020, Liu et al. [17] proposed a new self-calibrating convolution that explicitly extends the field of view of each convolutional layer through internal communication, thus enriching the output characteristics. In 2021, Wang et al. [18] proposed the ACTION-NET network, combining spatio-temporal attention, channel attention, and motion attention to significantly improve feature extraction in each dimension.

3 The Proposed Approach

3.1 Spatio-Temporal Information Fusion Network

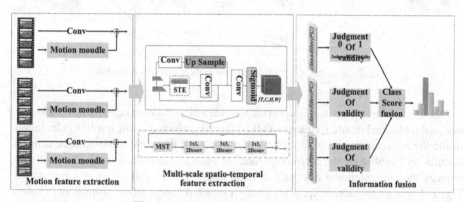

Fig. 1. Overall network structure diagram

Both short-term temporal information and long-term temporal information are crucial in action recognition tasks. In this paper, we design a human motion recognition model with spatio-temporal modeling from local to global. The overall structure of the model is divided into three parts, as shown in Fig. 1. The first part is a motion feature extraction module, which calculates the correspondence between video frames and transforms them into motion features, adds motion features to spatial features, and sends them to the next layer of the network. The second part designs the spatio-temporal attention mechanism and multi-scale learning structure to construct the multi-scale spatio-temporal feature extraction module, through which the spatio-temporal features in the video are further extracted. The third part is the information fusion module, which detects video clips, eliminates misleading or unrepresentative video clips, fuses the remaining video clip information, and predicts the final classification result.The overall modeling approach is shown in Eqs. (1) and (2):

$$G = g(F(K_1; W), F(K_2; W), \ldots, F(K_n; W)) \tag{1}$$

$$L(y, G) = -\sum_{i=1}^{c} y_i(G_i - \log \sum_{j=1}^{c} \exp^{G_j}) \tag{2}$$

where K represents video clips, randomly sampled from the video; F represents training for each video clip individually with parameter W; finally, the score of each clip is returned; the consensus result of the category hypothesis is deduced by combining the scores of multiple clips through the segment consensus function G, L represents the loss function, C is the total number of categories, and i represents the true value of the ith category.

3.2 Motion Feature Extraction Module

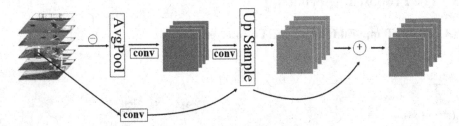

Fig. 2. Structure diagram of motion feature extraction module

Motion information is very important for video classification tasks.In this paper, we design the Motion Feature Extraction (MFE) module, which uses the implicit calculation inside the network instead of the calculation of optical flow, and represents the motion features by establishing the correspondence between adjacent frames, which effectively reduces the computational cost and storage space. The overall structure is shown in Fig. 2. For a given video clip, a randomly extracted image frame from it is denoted as $T = [T_1, T_2, \ldots, T_k]$, and T_i denotes an extracted image frame with dimension $[T, C, H, W]$. Firstly, the appearance features are extracted by convolving the central frame, then the difference between the central frame and the preceding and following video frames is calculated, and the motion features are established by the time difference between frames. Finally, the motion features are added to the appearance features and sent to the next layer of the network. The calculation process is shown in Eq. (3):

$$F_{i'} = F_i + M(T_i) \tag{3}$$

where F_i denotes the features obtained by convolution of the central frame, $F_{i'}$ denotes the final output features, and $M(T_i)$ is expressed in Eq. (4) as:

$$M(T_i) = Upsample(CNN(Downsample(S_i))) \tag{4}$$

where $S(T_i) = [S_{-2}, S_{-1}, S_1, S_2]$ denotes the result of local frame difference, the result of frame difference is downsampled and input to the convolutional layer to extract high level features, and finally its shape is recovered by upsampling and fused with the central frame features.

3.3 Multi-scale Spatio-temporal Feature Extraction Module

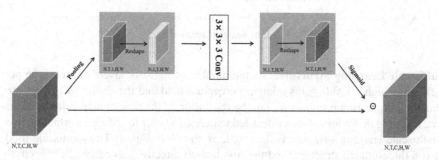

Fig. 3. Spatio-temporal attention mechanism structure diagram

Temporal Attention Mechanism. The use of attention mechanisms can efficiently help models focus on important regions in an image. Traditional spatial attention mechanisms cannot meet the needs of video tasks. Because of video frames, it is necessary to analyze the temporal information between video frames in addition to focusing on the spatial features of the images. Therefore, this paper designs a Spatio-temporal Attention (STA) mechanism, which introduces a three-dimensional convolutional layer to enhance the model's temporal information extraction capability by operating on multiple video frames simultaneously. The overall structure is shown in Fig. 3. Firstly, the global pooling operation of the feature map in the channel dimension is performed to obtain the feature F, and then its dimension is changed and sent to the 3D convolutional layer to extract spatio-temporal features, as shown in Eq. (5):

$$F^* = A * F \tag{5}$$

where F^* is the feature vector of F after 3D convolution extraction. The feature vector L is obtained using the sigmoid activation function for F^*. As shown in Eq. (6):

$$L = \delta(F^*) \tag{6}$$

Finally, L is multiplied pointwise with the original feature X, as shown in Eq. (7):

$$Y = X + X * L \tag{7}$$

Each round of original features is vector-aware of the importance of spatio-temporal information, and the spatio-temporal features in the video are effectively extracted.

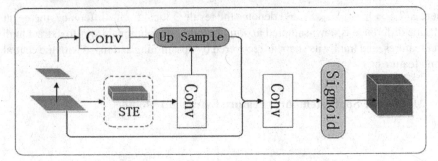

Fig. 4. Multi-scale structure diagram

Multi-scale Learning Structure. As the number of network layers deepens, the network at the higher levels gains a larger perceptual field and the ability to characterize semantic information is enhanced, but the resolution of the feature map is lower at this time, resulting in the loss of many detailed features. In order to reduce information loss, a multiscale learning structure is designed, as shown in Fig. 4. The multiscale module is a three-branch structure, and the first branch directly does residual connectivity for feature enhancement. The second branch does feature information extraction on the existing feature map. The third branch first downsamples the feature map to get a smaller image before extracting features. In this way, each branch gets the semantic information of different resolutions, and finally the feature information of the three branches is fused to solve the problem of feature information loss. The calculation process is shown in Eq. (8):

$$X(F_i) = Sigmoid(Conv(\sum_{j=1}^{N} CNN_j(F_i))) \tag{8}$$

where $N = 3$ denotes the three branches, F_i denotes the input feature vector, and X denotes the final output feature vector.

3.4 Information Fusion Module

In the original TSN method, the prediction results of each video clip are fed directly into the final fusion function for weighted fusion to calculate the final classification results. In practical action recognition applications, the original video sequences usually contain many irrelevant and misleading clips that affect the classification results. In order to eliminate those unrepresentative video clips, a judgment of validity (JOV) mechanism is introduced in this paper to identify and determine each video clip, and only those video clip results that are judged to be reliable can be used in the final information fusion.

Specifically, if the video clips are valid, the distribution of category scores is usually relatively sparse, i.e., only individual categories will have high scores, and the total scores will be low. Conversely, if the video clips are not discriminative, their category results are relatively evenly distributed, and the total score is high. Therefore, a binary weight is assigned to each video clip, and the value of representative clips is set to 1, while the clips with discriminative properties are set to 0. During the training process, only representative video clips are used to update the parameters of the network. Finally, only the prediction results of the video clips with an assigned value of 1 are selected and fused to derive the final category score, which is calculated as shown in Eq. (9):

$$H(K_i) = -\sum_{i=1}^{c} P_i(K_i) \log_{P_i} K_i \qquad (9)$$

where $H(K_i)$ denotes the video clip reliability result, $P(K_i)$ denotes the category score, and C is the number of categories for the action, denoting c-dimensional vector.the final fusion follows the fusion method in the TSN model. The predicted results of the video clips judged to be reliable are fed into the aggregation function G for fusion, which can be expressed as:

$$G_i = g(F_i(T_1), ..., F_i(T_K)) \qquad (10)$$

For different forms of aggregation functions, we evaluated them experimentally by using the uniform average, maximum value, and weighted average methods, respectively. Among them, the mean average method achieved the best identification results.

4   Experimental Results and Analysis

4.1   Dataset

The UCF101 action recognition dataset contains a total of 101 categories of actions and a total of 13320 videos at a resolution of 320 * 224, for a total of 6.5 GB. The 101 categories of actions can be divided into 5 major categories: human-object interaction, human action, human-human interaction, musical instrument playing, and sports. Some of the action schematics are shown in Fig. 5.

The Something-SomethingV2 [19] dataset is a large dataset of video clips with annotations that records the basic actions between humans and some objects in daily life. Some of the actions are shown schematically in Fig. 6. The dataset contains a total of 220,847 videos, of which 168,913 are in the training set, 24,777 are in the validation set, and 27,157 are in the test set. There are 174 action categories listed.

Fig. 5. Example of UCF101 dataset   **Fig. 6.** Example of somethingV2 dataset

4.2   Experimental Details and Evaluation Indexes

In the experiments, RexNet [20] is used as the backbone network in this paper. First, the video is segmented, and 8 or 16 frames of images are extracted from each subsequence as the input data. Position dithering, horizontal flipping, corner cutting, and scale dithering are used for data processing, and the maximum crop size of the video is set to 224 * 224 and pre-trained on the ImageNet [21] dataset. The model training batch size was 64, with an initial learning rate of 0.01 and a decay rate of 0.1, for a total of 100 training rounds using a stochastic gradient descent (SGD) optimizer. For the UCF dataset, the official evaluation scheme is followed, using three divisions of cross-validation, first calculating the accuracy of each category, and finally taking the average of all categories as the final accuracy. For the something-somethingV2 dataset, the evaluation metric is top-1 accuracy.

4.3   Experimental Results

The algorithm of this paper is compared with other advanced action recognition algorithms in recent years, and Table 1 shows the experimental results obtained by the algorithm of this paper on the UCF101 dataset. The recognition accuracy of 95.7% was achieved by this algorithm on this dataset, which is comparable to the current optimal recognition results and significantly better than the recognition results of the traditional two-stream network model.

Table 1. Comparison of the recognition rate of existing methods with the method in this paper on the UCF101 dataset.

Method	backbone	Acc
Two stream	VGG	93.5
TSN	BNInception	94.2
AttentionClusters [22]	ResNet50	94.6
Interpretable ST-attention [23]	ResNet50	87.1
TS-VIB-LSTM [24]	LSTM	93.2
Ours	ResNet50	95.7

Table 2 shows the experimental results of the algorithm in this paper and the current mainstream algorithm on the something-somethingV2 dataset. In comparison, the algorithm in this paper achieves 65.7% recognition accuracy, which is significantly better than the accuracy of the literature [9–11, 25–27]. The experimental results show that the model in this paper can effectively fuse the dynamic information of the video and improve the recognition accuracy without introducing optical flow information.

Figure 7 shows the visual heat map of the regions of interest to the model, where the first row is the original image, the second row is the result identified by the ResNet network, and the third row is the result identified by the method in this paper. The area

Table 2. Comparison of the recognition rate of existing methods with this paper on the something-somethingV2 dataset.

Method	backbone	frames	Gflops	Top1	Top-5
TSN	ResNet50	8	33	27.8	57.6
		16	65	30	60.5
TSM [11]	ResNet50	8	33	59.1	85.6
		16	65	63.4	88.5
TRN-Multiscale [10]	BNInception	8	33	48.8	77.6
TAM [25]	blResNet50	16x2	47.7	61.7	88.1
GST [26]	ResNet50	16	59	62.6	87.9
SmallBigNet [27]	ResNet50	8 + 16	157	63.3	88.8
Ours	ResNet50	8	37	64.5	88.4
		16	74	65.7	89.5

inside the aperture indicates the part that the model pays more attention to, i.e., the more representative part, and the area outside the aperture represents the background part in the video. By observing the visual heat map, we can find that the method in this paper enables the model to focus on the part of the video where people and objects interact, so as to extract the key information and improve the recognition accuracy.

Fig. 7. Visualized Heat Map

4.4 Ablation Experiments

Table 3 shows the results of the ablation experiments on the UCF101 dataset with the addition of MFE, STA, and JOV, respectively. It can be seen that the model recognition accuracy is improved after the model is added to the MFE, STA, and JOV modules alone. The improvement effect is more significant after adding MFE, which indicates that this method can effectively obtain motion information and improve the accuracy of action recognition. Secondly, the addition of the STA method also achieves better results, which further confirms the effectiveness of the spatio-temporal attention mechanism designed in this paper, which can effectively filter background information. In contrast, the effect of adding the JOV module alone is not outstanding, but further combination of the modules shows that the combination of STA and JOV modules achieves excellent results, which are analyzed in this paper because the STA method can help the network focus on the main areas of the video, eliminate redundant information, and achieve clearer classification results for most of the video clips, followed by the JOV method to further refine the classification results. Then, the JOV method can efficiently eliminate the remaining misleading video clips and finally fuse the scores of the filtered video clips to improve the classification accuracy.

Table 3. Ablation experiments on UCF101

Backbone	MFE	STA	JOV	UCF101
ResNet-50				92.5
ResNet-50	✓			94.1
ResNet-50		✓		93.7
ResNet-50			✓	92.9
ResNet-50	✓	✓		95.3
ResNet-50	✓		✓	94.1
ResNet-50		✓	✓	94.6
ResNet-50	✓	✓	✓	95.7

5   Conclusion

In order to solve the problem of difficult spatio-temporal modeling and complex computation of the human action recognition network, this paper proposes an action recognition network with spatio-temporal modeling from local to global. First, the motion information is characterized by establishing the correspondence between video frames; then, the motion information is added to the spatial features to further extract local spatio-temporal features; and finally, the representative video clips are selected using a video clip filtering strategy to calculate the category scores. The model in this paper can achieve end-to-end training and can effectively capture video-based dynamic information. Experiments are conducted on the UCF101 and something-somethingV2 datasets, and the results show that this model can significantly improve action recognition accuracy and reduce computational cost. In the future, the scenarios of human action recognition will become more diversified, and we will continue to study human action recognition methods in order to achieve higher action recognition accuracy with a smaller number of parameters.

Acknowledgements. This work is supported by the National Natural Science Foundation of China (62272049, 62236006, 61972375, 62172045), the Key Project of Beijing Municipal Commission of Education (KZ201911417048), the Major Project of Technological Innovation 2030 – "New Generation Artificial Intelligence" (2018AAA0100800), Premium Funding Project for Academic Human Resources Development in Beijing Union University (BPHR2020AZ01, BPH2020EZ01), the Science and Technology Project of Beijing Municipal Commission of Education (KM202111417009, KM201811417005).

References

1. Tran, D., Bourdev, L., Fergus, R., et al.: Learning spatiotemporal features with 3D convolutional networks. In: Proceedings of the IEEE International Conference on Computer Vision, pp. 4489–4497 (2015)
2. Liu, Z., Wang, L., Wu, W., et al.: Tam: temporal adaptive module for video recognition. In: Proceedings of the IEEE/CVF International Conference on Computer Vision, pp. 13708–13718 (2021)
3. Tran, D., Wang, H., Torresani, L., et al.: A closer look at spatiotemporal convolutions for action recognition. In: Proceedings of the IEEE Conference on Computer Vision and Pattern Recognition, pp. 6450–6459 (2018)
4. Xie, S., Sun, C., Huang, J., Tu, Z., Murphy, K.: Rethinking spatiotemporal feature learning: speed-accuracy trade-offs in video classification. In: Ferrari, V., Hebert, M., Sminchisescu, C., Weiss, Y. (eds.) ECCV 2018. LNCS, vol. 11219, pp. 318–335. Springer, Cham (2018). https://doi.org/10.1007/978-3-030-01267-0_19
5. Li, K., Li, X., Wang, Y., et al.: CT-net: channel tensorization network for video classification. arXiv preprint arXiv:2106.01603 (2021)
6. Zhao, Y., Xiong, Y., Lin, D.: Recognize actions by disentangling components of dynamics. In: Proceedings of the IEEE Conference on Computer Vision and Pattern Recognition (2018)
7. Jiang, B., Wang, M.M., Gan, W., et al.: STM: spatiotemporal and motion encoding for action recognition. In: Proceedings of the IEEE/CVF International Conference on Computer Vision, pp. 2000–2009 (2019)
8. Simonyan, K., Zisserman, A.: Two-stream convolutional networks for action recognition in videos. arXiv preprint arXiv:1406.2199 (2014)
9. Wang, L., Xiong, Y., Wang, Z., et al.: Temporal segment networks: Towards good practices for deep action recognition. In: Leibe, B., Matas, J., Sebe, N., Welling, M. (eds.) ECCV 2016. LNCS, vol. 9912, pp. 20–36. Springer, Cham (2016). https://doi.org/10.1007/978-3-319-46484-8_2
10. Zhou, B., Andonian, A., Oliva, A., Torralba, A.: Temporal relational reasoning in videos. In: Ferrari, V., Hebert, M., Sminchisescu, C., Weiss, Y. (eds.) ECCV 2018. LNCS, vol. 11205, pp. 831–846. Springer, Cham (2018). https://doi.org/10.1007/978-3-030-01246-5_49
11. Lin, J., Gan, C., Han, S.: TSM: temporal shift module for efficient video understanding. In: Proceedings of the IEEE/CVF International Conference on Computer Vision, pp. 7083–7093 (2019)
12. Kwon, H., Kim, M., Kwak, S., Cho, M.: Motionsqueeze: neural motion feature learning for video understanding. In: Vedaldi, A., Bischof, H., Brox, T., Frahm, J.-M. (eds.) ECCV 2020. LNCS, vol. 12361, pp. 345–362. Springer, Cham (2020). https://doi.org/10.1007/978-3-030-58517-4_21
13. Xu, K., Ba, J., Kiros, R., et al.: Show, attend and tell: neural image caption generation with visual attention. In: International Conference on Machine Learning, pp. 2048–2057. PMLR (2015)

14. Roy, A.G., Navab, N., Wachinger, C.: Concurrent spatial and channel 'squeeze & excitation' in fully convolutional networks. In: Frangi, A.F., Schnabel, J.A., Davatzikos, C., Alberola-López, C., Fichtinger, G. (eds.) MICCAI 2018. LNCS, vol. 11070, pp. 421–429. Springer, Cham (2018). https://doi.org/10.1007/978-3-030-00928-1_48

15. Woo, S., Park, J., Lee, J.-Y., Kweon, I.S.: Cbam: convolutional block attention module. In: Ferrari, V., Hebert, M., Sminchisescu, C., Weiss, Y. (eds.) ECCV 2018. LNCS, vol. 11211, pp. 3–19. Springer, Cham (2018). https://doi.org/10.1007/978-3-030-01234-2_1

16. Gao, Z., Xie, J., Wang, Q., et al.: Global second-order pooling convolutional networks. In: Proceedings of the IEEE/CVF Conference on Computer Vision and Pattern Recognition, pp. 3024–3033 (2019)

17. Liu. J.J., Hou, Q., Cheng, M.M., et al.: Improving convolutional networks with self-calibrated convolutions. In: Proceedings of the IEEE/CVF Conference on Computer Vision and Pattern Recognition, pp. 10096–10105 (2020)

18. Wang, Z., She, Q., Smolic, A.: Action-net: multipath excitation for action recognition. arXiv preprint arXiv:2103.07372 (2021)

19. Materzynska, J., Xiao, T., Herzig, R., et al.: Something-else: compositional action recognition with spatial-temporal interaction networks. In: Proceedings of the IEEE/CVF Conference on Computer Vision and Pattern Recognition, pp. 1049–1059 (2020)

20. He, K., Zhang, X., Ren, S., et al.: Deep residual learning for image recognition. In: Proceedings of the IEEE Conference on Computer Vision and Pattern Recognition, pp. 770–778 (2016)

21. Deng, J., Dong, W., Socher, R., et al.: Imagenet: a large-scale hierarchical image database. In: 2009 IEEE Conference on Computer Vision and Pattern Recognition, pp. 248–255. IEEE (2009)

22. Long, X., Gan, C., De Melo, G., et al.: Attention clusters: purely attention based local feature integration for video classification. In: Proceedings of the IEEE Conference on Computer Vision and Pattern Recognition, pp. 7834–7843 (2018)

23. Meng, L., Zhao, B., Chang, B., et al.: Interpretable spatio-temporal attention for video action recognition. In: Proceedings of the IEEE/CVF International Conference on Computer Vision Workshops (2019)

24. Srivastava, A., Dutta, O., Gupta, J., et al.: A variational information bottleneck based method to compress sequential networks for human action recognition. In: Proceedings of the IEEE/CVF Winter Conference on Applications of Computer Vision, pp. 2745–2754 (2021)

25. Fan, Q., Chen, C.F.R., Kuehne, H., et al.: More is less: learning efficient video representations by big-little network and depthwise temporal aggregation. In: Advances in Neural Information Processing Systems, vol. 32 (2019)

26. Luo, C., Yuille, A.L.: Grouped spatial-temporal aggregation for efficient action recognition. In: Proceedings of the IEEE/CVF International Conference on Computer Vision, pp. 5512–5521 (2019)

27. Li, X., Wang, Y., Zhou, Z., et al.: Smallbignet: integrating core and contextual views for video classification. In: Proceedings of the IEEE/CVF Conference on Computer Vision and Pattern Recognition, pp. 1092–1101 (2020)

Facial Expression Recognition from Occluded Images Using Deep Convolution Neural Network with Vision Transformer

Mingxiu Li[1], Shanshan Tu[1(✉)], and Sadaqat ur Rehman[2]

[1] Beijing University of Technology, Beijing 100124, China
sstu@bjut.edu.cn
[2] University of Salford, Manchester, UK

Abstract. Facial expression recognition (FER) is a challenging task due to various unrestricted conditions. Normal facial expression algorithms work well on frontal faces. However, detection expression from the occluded faces is still a challenging task. In this paper, we propose a novel deep convolution neural network with self-attention mechanism in order to detect the occlusion regions in the face for efficient recognition of facial expression. Firstly, we use a backbone CNN to extract feature maps of the facial images. Then the global self-attention with relative position encodings is utilized to process and aggregate the information contained in the feature maps. The global self-attention can learn the relationships between the single feature and entire facial information. In order to pay attention to the highly relative region and ignore the information-deficient regions. To evaluate the efficiency of the proposed model, we use two wild benchmark datasets RAF and AffectNet for FER. The results show that proposed model is effective to recognize the facial expression from the occluded images.

Keywords: Facial expression recognition · Deep convolution neural network · Transformer · Computer vision

1 Introduction

Facial expression recognition (FER) plays an important role in the application of computer vision, such as human-computer interaction, medical treatment, behaviour analysis. Most of the researches have paid attention to the development of FER algorithm. However, it is still a challenging task to recognize the facial expression because of the variations including head pose, illumination and occlusion. Majority of the FER systems perform well on the lab-collected datasets such as CK+ [1], MMI [2], Oulu-CASIA [3], however, the performance degraded in the recognition of facial expression in the wild.

Due to the uncertainties of facial expression and insufficient high-quality data, the experiments on datasets from the real world are difficult to achieve a high accuracy. Especially for the occlusion problem, which may lead the recognition accuracy to decrease. It is challenging to address the occlusion issue because there are different occlusions and positions on face expression. The convolutional neural networks (CNNs) for the FER

© The Author(s), under exclusive license to Springer Nature Switzerland AG 2023
H. Lu et al. (Eds.): ICIG 2023, LNCS 14356, pp. 289–299, 2023.
https://doi.org/10.1007/978-3-031-46308-2_24

usually require big data to implement [4]. While deep convolution operation can capture local feature in facial image, it may lead to the over-fitting problem.

Numerous efforts have since continued to solve the problem of occluded facial expression. Previous methods are mainly based facial part feature or global face. We argue that extracting feature directly from face with deep neural network ignores the occluded information. Otherwise, part-based methods utilize the patches and landmarks to detect the occluded parts [5, 6]. Then they compensate or discard the miss part, or re-weight the occluded and non-occluded patches [7]. Very recently, Zhang et al. [8] adopted the deep regression networks coupled with de-corrupt autoencoders to explicitly handle partial occlusion problem which recover the genuine appearance for the occluded parts. In addition, Juefei-Xu et al. [9] proposed a progressive convolutional neural network training paradigm to enforce the attention shift during the learning process. Besides, attention mechanism have been applied in FER. Minaee et al. [10] designed an end-to-end deep learning models using attentional convolutional network that achieves significant improvement. Generative adversarial networks (GAN) has also been utilized in model architecture for FER [11, 12].

Although the convolution operation can effectively capture the local information and have great performance in vision tasks, it is more powerful to aggregate the global dependencies. Nowadays transformer [13] has a dominant position in natural language processing (NLP). It also has been applied in some vision tasks. Self-attention was firstly introduced in vision task for capturing long-range dependencies [14]. A simple approach to using self-attention in vision is to replace spatial convolutional layers with the multi-head self-attention (MHSA) layer proposed in the Transformer [15].

It has been investigated that human could effectively utilized the local regions of face to aware the global face information. According to this, we can recognize the facial expression easily. Inspired by this and the global vision of Transformer, We proposed a deep convolution neural network with self-attention mechanism model. Firstly, we use a backbone CNN to efficiently learn abstract feature maps from facial images. Secondly, the global self-attention is utilized to process and aggregate the information contained in the feature maps captured by the convolutional layers. Thirdly, two fully connected layers realize the facial expression classification.

The main contribution of our work can be summarized as follows:

1. We propose a deep convolution neural network with self-attention mechanism model for FER from occluded images, which integrates local CNN features and global self-attention for improving expression recognition accuracy.
2. We applied self-attention with relative position encodings in the FER. The global self-attention can learn the relationships between the single feature and entire facial information. Therefore, we can pay attention to the highly relative region and ignore the information-deficient regions.
3. Experiments conducted on RAF-DB and AffectNet datasets demonstrate that our CNNT model is effective to recognize the occluded facial images (Fig. 1).

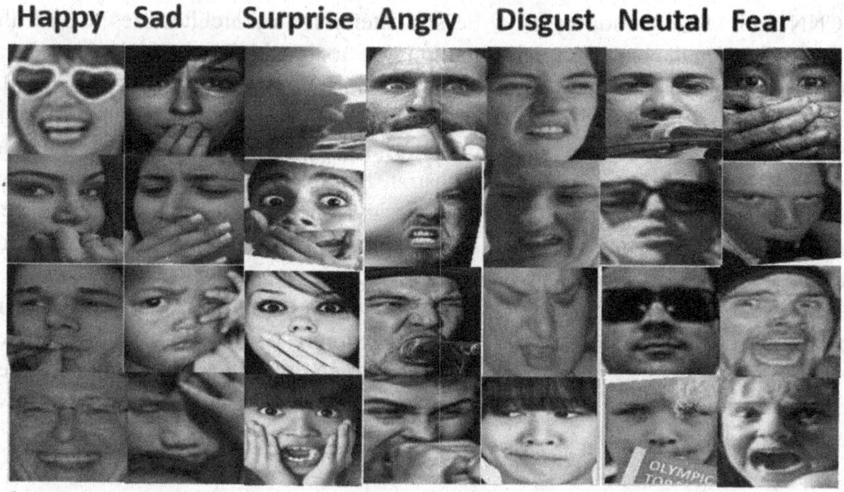

Happy   Sad   Surprise Angry   Disgust Neutal   Fear

Fig. 1. Example of images picked from RAF-DB datasets. The occludes are various in occlusion types, positions, ratio etc.

2 Related Work

2.1 Facial Expression Recognition in the Wild

Great attention has been paid to the FER in the wild. Li et al. [16] proposed a deep locality-preserving CNN (DLP-CNN) method to enhance the discriminative power of deep features by preserving the locality closeness while maximizing the inter-class scatters. Some works focus on combining the CNN and attention mechanism to improve the performance. A convolution neutral network (CNN) with attention mechanism (ACNN) was introduced to improve the performance, which combined patch-based ACNN (pACNN) with global-local-based ACNN (gACNN) [17]. More recently, to address the real-world pose and occlusion robust FER problem, Wang et al. [18] proposed a Region Attention Network (RAN) to adaptively capture the importance of facial regions. Importantly, Self-Cure Network (SCN) model achieved a new state-of-the-art. It suppresses the uncertainties efficiently and prevents deep networks from over-fitting uncertain images [19].These methods all used CNN to extract abstract feature from facial images.

It is worth mentioned that Visual Transformers with Feature Fusion (VTFF) firstly apply Transformers for FER to learn the relationships between elements of visual feature sequences [20].

2.2 Transformers in Computer Vision

In the recent year, attention mechanism has widely been used in Natural Language Processing (NLP). The improvement in various tasks is largely attributed to the Transformer [13]. Moreover, the pre-trained model-based transformer can obtain better result in the experiment [21]. Inspired by its capacity to learn global information, some studies have considered utilizing self-attention in computer vision tasks. They either combined the CNN with self-attention or used the self-attention-only architectures to lead the improvements. On the one hand, self-attention was firstly added into CNN by non-local operations to capture long-range dependencies [14]. Bello et al. [22] firstly introduced a two-dimensional relative self-attention mechanism that proves competitive in replacing convolutions as a stand-alone computational primitive for image classification. On the other hand, Ramachandran et al. [23] demonstrate that self-attention can be a stand-alone layer. Moreover, Cordonnier et al. [24] provides evidence that attention layers can perform convolution and a multi-head self-attention layer with sufficient number of heads is at least as expressive as any convolutional layer.

More recently, Vision Transformer (ViT) was utilized to train on a large dataset and then fine-tuned for downstream tasks [25]. Interestingly, Srinivas et al. [15] designed a Bottleneck Transformer and replaced the final three bottleneck blocks of a ResNet. These Transformer methods designed for vision tasks has provide us a new perspective to resolve the problem of FER.

3   Method

3.1   Framework Overview

We propose a deep convolutional neural network with Transformer mechanism (CNNT) to recognize the facial expression wih occlusion. As can be seen in the Fig. 2, the model contains mainly three components.1) CNN Backbone, 2) Bottleneck Transformer, 3) Classification module.

At the beginning, the input images are resized as $224 \times 224 \times 3$ tensors. And then they are fed into the CNN backbone to extract abstract feature. We mainly use VGG16 [26] and ResNet-18[27] for the backbone CNN. In order to compare with other state-of-the-art methods, we conduct the experiment on both VGG16 and ResNet-18. Inspired from the architecture [15], we adopt the Bottleneck Transformer architecture based on Multi-head Self-Attention (MHSA) to obtain the relationship between the occluded regions and entire global face. It also applies the residual function to optimize the model. Finally, two fully connected layers adjust the weights of these features and realize the facial expression classification.

3.2   CNN Backbone

We adopted the VGG16 or ResNet-18 as the backbone network because their simple structure and great performance in image classification. The CNN backbone can learn the abstract feature maps of form the occluded images, which can be utilized by the next self-attention module. If we use the VGG16, the first nine convolution layers are chosen as the feature maps extractor. Otherwise, we employ the first five stages of ResNet18 to extract feature maps. The pre-trained VGG16 based on ImageNet dataset is downloaded directly and the ResNet-18 is pre-trained on MS-Celeb-1M face recognition dataset. In detail, we adopt the first nine layers of VGG16, which can be seen as Table 1.

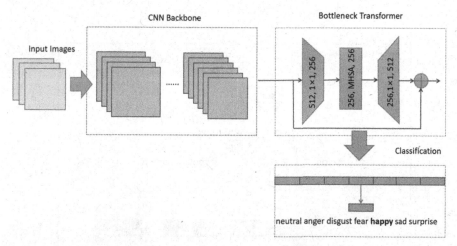

Fig. 2. An overview of our proposed CNNT. It can be divided into three parts, CNN backbone, bottleneck Transformer and classification. The pre-trained VGG16 or ResNet-18 is used as the backbone to extract feature maps. And then all the extract features are fed into the bottleneck Transformer to further process the information and model the relationships between the single feature and entire facial features. The network finally realizes the facial expression classification by two fully connected layers and a softmax function.

3.3 Bottleneck Transformer

The vision transformer used in the proposed work consists of blocks with self-attention [20]. The spatial (3 × 3) convolutional layer are replaced by the Multi-head Self-Attention(MHSA) layer (Fig. 3).

Self-Attention Over Images. After the CNN backbone, we obtained the feature maps which represent the face global features. Suppose the shape of tensor is (H, W, F_{in}), we flatten it into a matrix $X \in R^{HW \times F_{in}}$ and feed it into the multi-head attention. The output of the self-attention mechanism for a single head h can be computed as:

$$O_h = Soft\max\left(\frac{(XW_q)(XW_k)^T}{\sqrt{d_k^h}}\right)(XW_v) \tag{1}$$

where $W_q, W_k \in R^{F_{in} \times d_k^h}$ and $W_v \in R^{F_{in} \times d_v^h}$ that satisfied queries $Q = XW_q$, key $K = XW_k$ and values $V = XW_v$. The outputs of all heads are then concatenated and projected again as follows:

$$MHA(X) = Concat[O_1, \ldots, O_{Nh}]W^o$$

where $W^o \in R^{d_v \times d_v}$ is a learned linear weight. $MHA(X)$ is then reshaped into a tensor of shape (H, W, d_v) to match the original spatial dimensions.

Relative Position Encodings. It has been investigated that relative position encodings is better suit for vision tasks [16, 17].The attention can not only capture the content

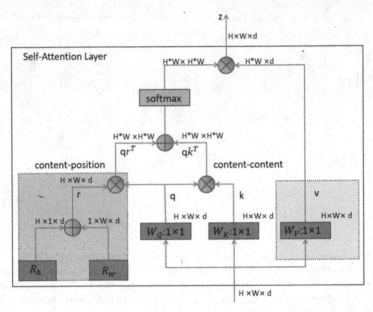

Fig. 3. Multi-Head Self-Attention (MHSA) layer used in the BoT block. Here we use 4 heads and relative distance encodings. The attention logits are $qk^T + qr^T$ where q, k, r represent query, key and position encodings respectively. $\oplus$ and $\otimes$ represent element wise sum and matrix multiplication respectively. 1×1 represents a pointwise convolution.

information, but also relative distances between features at different locations. Therefore, we implement the two-dimensional relative position encodings in self-attention by independently adding relative height information and relative width information. The attention logit for how much pixel $i = (i_x, i_y)$ attends to pixel $j = (j_x, j_y)$ is computed as:

$$l_{i,j} = \frac{q_i^T}{\sqrt{d_k^h}} \left(k_j + r_{j_x-i_x}^W + r_{j_y-i_y}^H \right) \tag{2}$$

where q_i is the query vector for pixel i (the i-th row of Q),

k_j is the key vector for pixel j(the j-th row of K). The $r_{j_x-i_x}^W$ and $r_{j_y-i_y}^H$ are learned embeddings for relative width $j_x - i_x$ and relative height $j_y - i_y$, respectively. The output of head h now becomes:

$$O_h = Soft \max \left(\frac{QK^T + S_H^{rel} + S_W^{rel}}{d_k^h} \right) V \tag{3}$$

where $S_H^{rel}[i,j] = q_i^T r_{j_x-i_x}^W$ and $S_H^{rel}[i,j] = q_i^T r_{j_y-i_y}^H$. As we consider relative height and width information separately, S_H^{rel} and S_W^{rel} also satisfy the properties $S_W^{rel}[i,j] = S_W^{rel}[i,j+W]$ and $S_H^{rel}[i,j] = S_H^{rel}[i+H,j]$, which prevents from having to compute the logits for all (i,j) pairs.

Table 1. The network configuration of the first nine layers of VGG16.

Name	Input	Operation	Kernel	Output
Conv_11	$224 \times 224 \times 3$	Convolution	3×3, ReLU	$224 \times 224 \times 64$
Conv_12	$224 \times 224 \times 64$	Convolution	3×3, ReLU	$224 \times 224 \times 64$
Max_pool	$224 \times 224 \times 64$	Pooling	2×2	$112 \times 112 \times 64$
Conv_21	$112 \times 112 \times 64$	Convolution	3×3, ReLU	$112 \times 112 \times 128$
Conv_22	$112 \times 112 \times 128$	Convolution	3×3, ReLU	$112 \times 112 \times 128$
Max_pool	$112 \times 112 \times 128$	Pooling	2×2	$56 \times 56 \times 128$
Conv_31	$56 \times 56 \times 128$	Convolution	3×3, ReLU	$56 \times 56 \times 256$
Conv_32	$56 \times 56 \times 256$	Convolution	3×3, ReLU	$56 \times 56 \times 256$
Conv_33	$56 \times 56 \times 256$	Convolution	3×3, ReLU	$56 \times 56 \times 256$
Max_pool	$56 \times 56 \times 256$	Pooling	2×2	$28 \times 28 \times 256$
Conv_41	$28 \times 28 \times 256$	Convolution	3×3, ReLU	$28 \times 28 \times 512$
Conv_42	$28 \times 28 \times 512$	Convolution	3×3	$28 \times 28 \times 512$

4 Experiments

This section describes the implementation details of the experiments conducted. Before diving in to the results, it is important to describe the datasets in detail. Next, the experimental conditions are demonstrated in order to confirm the efficacy of the proposed model. Finally, we assess the proposed CNNT model against the benchmark models on the same datasets.

4.1 Datasets

RAF-DB [16] contains 30,000 facial images annotated with basic or compound expressions by 40 trained human coders. We only used basic emotions images which include 12271 images as training data and 3068 images as test data. The basic emotions images have seven basics expressions: Happy, Sad, Fear, Surprise, Disgust, Anger, Neutral. The details are shown in Table 2.

AffectNet [28] is the largest dataset with annotated facial emotions which contains about 400,000 images manually annotated for the presence of seven discrete facial expressions and the intensity of valence and arousal. In our experiment, we only used the images with seven basic emotions including 280,000 training samples and 3,500 test samples.

4.2 Implementation Details

In our experiments, we firstly detect and align the facial images using MTCNN [29], and then resize them to the size of 224×224. We implement the model with Pytorch toolbox and conduct the experiments on a single NVIDIA RTX 3090Ti GPU card. For

Table 2. The statistics of RAF-DB.

Emotion	Happy	Sad	Fear	Surprise	Disgust	Anger	Neutral	Total
Train_datasets	4772	1982	281	1290	717	705	2524	12271
Test_datasets	1185	478	74	729	160	162	180	3068

the backbone CNN, we mainly use the VGG16 [26] and ResNet-18[27]. The pre-trained VGG16 based on ImageNet dataset is downloaded directly and the ResNet-18 is pre-trained on MS-Celeb-1M face recognition dataset. The learning rate of the model is initialized as 0.0001 and is reduced by polynomial policy with gamma of 0.1. We use the Adam optimizer [30] to optimize the whole network with a batch size of 32 and 100 epoch. The standard cross-entropy loss is applied to supervise the model to generalize well for expression recognition.

4.3   Exploring CNNT on FER Datasets for Pretraining

To further explore the potential of CNNT, we use the Web Emotion dataset [19] to pretrain our model and boost the performance. With pretraining, we obtain obvious improvements on RAF-DB and AffectNet. The detail of results is showed on Table 3. As can be seen, the experiments which adopt CNNT (VGG16) based on RAF-DB and AffectNet both increase by 13.86%, 2.89% respectively. The CNNT based ResNet-18 also obtains an increase of 9.89% and 13.55%. It can be demonstrated that the importance of pretraining with big dataset and our model has talent on learn deep features in occluded images.

Table 3. CNNT on real-world FER datasets.

Pretrain	CNNT	RAF-DB	AffectNet
×	×	72.00%	45.58%
×	CNNT(VGG16)	74.39%	47.69%
×	CNNT(ResNet-18)	78.45%	48.35%
√	CNNT(VGG16)	88.25%	60.58%
√	CNNT(ResNet-18)	88.34%	61.90%

4.4   Comparison with State-of-the-Art Methods

In this section, we compare the CNNT model with several state-of-the-art methods on RAF-DB and AffectNet. Generally, our model performance better than other methods on the same dataset and baseline. The detail of the results are explicitly shown in Table 4.

Results on RAF-DB: As can be seen in the Table 4, we compare our model with other different methods conducted on RAF-DB. We use the VGG16 and ResNet-18 as the baseline for the model. They outperforms these recent state-of-the-art methods with 88.25%, 88.35% on RAF-DB. In detail, our method on RAF-DB has obtained gains of 7.38% and 0.20% over Gacnn [17] and SCN [19], which are the baseline method and the previous state-of-the-art method, respectively. The better performance demonstrates the superiority of our proposed methods.

Results on AffectNet: Table 4 presents the comparison of methods based on Affect-Net. We obtain 61.90% accuracy with oversampling. As is mentioned above, AffectNet has imbalanced distribution. To solve the imbalance problem, we adopt the oversampling methods in our experiments as RAN [18] and SCN [19]. Our CNNT based ResNet-18 achieves 61.90% accuracy on AffectNet, which is the best performance. The results compared with other methods suggests that the CNNT has better generalization ability on large-scale expression recognition datasets like AffectNet and can effectively handle the occluded facial images.

Table 4. Comparison with state-of-the-art methods on RAF-DB and AffectNet.

Methods	Network	RAF-DB	AffectNet
VGG16 [26]	VGG16	80.96%	51.11%
gACNN [17]	VGG16	85.07%	58.78%
RAN [18]	ResNet-18	86.90%	59.50%
SCN [19]	ResNet-18	88.14%	60.23%
VTFF [20]	ResNet-18	88.14%	61.85%
CNNT (VGG16)	VGG16	88.25%	60.58%
CNNT (ResNet-18)	ResNet-18	88.34%	61.90%

5 Conclusion

In this paper, we propose a deep convolution neural network with self-attention (CNNT) model for Facial expression recognition from occluded images. The CNNT consists of three modules including CNN backbone, Bottleneck Transformer and Classification. The CNN backbone learns abstract feature maps from occluded facial images. After-ward, we apply self-attention with relative position encodings to obtain the weights based facial importance for classification. The global self-attention can learn the rela-tionships between the single feature and entire facial information. Therefore, we can pay attention to the highly relative region and ignore the information-deficient regions. Finally, two fully connected layers and a SoftMax layer were utilized to complement the classification. Experiments conducted on the RAF-DB and AffectNet demonstrate that our CNNT can effectively recognize the occluded facial images. We hope that our research based on self-attention mechanism could provide a new perspective of FER in the future.

Acknowledgements. This work is supported in part by the Beijing Natural Science Foundation (No. 4212015), China Ministry of Education-China Mobile Scientific Research Foundation (No. MCM20200102).

References

1. Lucey, P., Cohn, J.F., Kanade, T.: The Extended Cohn-Kanade Dataset (CK+): a complete dataset for action unit and emotion-specified expression. In: Computer Society Conference on Computer Vision and Pattern Recognition - Workshops, pp. 94–101. IEEE, San Francisco (2010)
2. Pantic, M., Valstar, M., Rademaker, R.: Web-based database for facial expression analysis. In: IEEE International Conference on Multimedia & Expo, pp. 5. IEEE, Amsterdam (2005)
3. Zhao, G., Huang, X., Taini, M.: Facial expression recognition from near-infrared videos. Image Vis. Comput. **29**(9), 607–619 (2011)
4. LeCun, Y., Boser, B., Denker, J.S.: Backpropagation applied to handwritten zip code recognition. Neural Comput. **1**(4), 541–551 (1989)
5. Zhong, L., Liu, Q., Yang, P.: Learning active facial patches for expression analysis. In: Conference on Computer Vision and Pattern Recognition, pp. 2562–2569 IEEE, RI (2012)
6. Dapogny, A., Bailly, K., Dubuisson, S.: Confidence-weighted local expression predictions for occlusion handling in expression recognition and action unit detection. Int. J. Comput. Vision **126**(2), 255–271 (2017)
7. Li, W., Abtahi, F., Zhu, Z.: Action unit detection with region adaptation, multi-labeling learning and optimal temporal fusing. In: Conference on Computer Vision and Pattern Recognition, pp. 6766–6775. IEEE, Honolulu (2017)
8. Jie, Z., Kan, M., Shan, S.: Occlusion-free face alignment: deep regression networks coupled with de-corrupt AutoEncoders. In: Conference on Computer Vision and Pattern Recognition, pp. 3428–3437. IEEE, Las Vegas (2016)
9. Juefei-Xu, F., Verma, E., Goel, P.: DeepGender: occlusion and low resolution robust facial gender classification via progressively trained convolutional neural networks with attention. In: Conference on Computer Vision and Pattern Recognition Workshops, pp. 136–145 IEEE, Las Vegas (2016)
10. Minaee1, S., Abdolrashidi2, A.: Deep-emotion: facial expression recognition using attentional convolutional network (2019)
11. Zhang, F., Zhang, T., Mao, Q.: Joint pose and expression modeling for facial expression recognition. In: Proceedings of the IEEE Conference on Computer Vision and Pattern Recognition, pp. 3359–3368. IEEE, Salt Lake City 2018)
12. Lai, Y.-H., Lai, S.-H. : Emotion-preserving representation learning via generative adversarial network for multi-view facial expression recognition. In: 13th IEEE International Conference on Automatic Face & Gesture Recognition, pp. 263–270. IEEE, Xi'an (2018)
13. Vaswani, A., Shazeer, N., Parmar, N.: Attention is all you need. In: Advances in Neural Information Processing Systems, 5998–6008 (2017)
14. Wang, X., Girshick, R., Gupta, A.: Non-local neural networks. In Proceedings of the IEEE Conference on Computer Vision and Pattern Recognition, pp. 7794–7803. IEEE (2016)
15. Srinivas, A., Lin, T.-Y., Parmar, N.: Bottleneck transformers for visual recognition. In: 2021 IEEE/CVF Conference on Computer Vision and Pattern Recognition, pp. 16514–16524. IEEE, Nashville 2021)
16. Li, S., Deng, W., Du, J.P.: Reliable crowd sourcing and deep locality-preserving learning for expression recognition in the wild. In: 2017 IEEE Conference on Computer Vision and Pattern Recognition, pp. 2584–2593. IEEE, Honolulu (2017)

17. Li, Y., Zeng, J., Shan, S.: Occlusion aware facial expression recognition using CNN With attention mechanism. IEEE Trans. Image Process. **28**(5), 2439–2450 (2019)
18. Wang, K., Peng, X., Yang, J.: Region attention networks for pose and occlusion robust facial expression recognition. IEEE Trans. Image Process. **29**, 4057–4069 (2020)
19. Wang, K., Peng, X., Yang, J.: Suppressing uncertainties for large-scale facial expression recognition. In: 2020 IEEE/CVF Conference on Computer Vision and Pattern Recognition, pp. 6896–6905. IEEE, Seattle (2020)
20. Ma, F., Sun, B., Li, S.: Facial expression recognition with visual transformers and attentional selective fusion. IEEE Trans. Affect. Comput. (2021)
21. Devlin, J., Chang, M.W., Lee, K.: BERT: pre-training of deep bidirectional transformers for language understanding (2018)
22. Bello, I., Zoph, B., Le, Q.: Attention augmented convolutional networks. In: IEEE/CVF International Conference on Computer Vision, pp. 3285–3294. IEEE, Seoul (2019)
23. Ramachandran, P., Parmar, N., Vaswani, A.: Stand-alone self-attention in vision models. In: Proceedings of the 33rd International Conference on Neural Information Processing Systems, pp. 68–80 (2019)
24. Cordonnier, J.B., Loukas, A., Jaggi, M..: On the relationship between self-attention and convolutional layers. In: International Conference on Learning Representations (2019)
25. Dosovitskiy, A., Beyer, L., Kolesnikov, A., Weissenborn, D.: An image is worth 16×16 words: transformers for image recognition at scale. In: International Conference on Learning Representations (2020)
26. Simonyan, K., Zisserman, A.: Very deep convolutional networks for large-scale image recognition. In: Computer Vision and Pattern Recognition (2014)
27. He, K., Zhang, X., Ren, S.: Deep residual learning for image recognition. In: 2016 IEEE Conference on Computer Vision and Pattern Recognition (CVPR), pp. 770–778. IEEE, Las Vegas (2016)
28. Mollahosseini, A., Hasani, B., Mahoor, M.H.: Affectnet: a database for facial expression, valence, and arousal computing in the wild. IEEE Trans. Affect. Comput. **10**, 18–31 (2019)
29. Zhang, K., Zhang, Z., Li, Z.: Joint face detection and alignment using multitask cascaded convolutional networks. IEEE Signal Process. Lett. **23**(10), 1499–1503 (2016)
30. Kingma, D.P., Ba, J.: Adam: a method for stochastic optimization. In: Computer Science (2014)

Learning Discriminative Proposal Representation for Multi-object Tracking

Yejia Huang[1], Xianqin Liu[2], Yijun Zhang[2], and Jian-Fang Hu[1(✉)]

[1] Sun Yat-sen University, GuangZhou, China
huangyj275@mail2.sysu.edu.cn , hujf5@mail.sysu.edu.cn
[2] National Information Center of GACC (Guangdong), GuangZhou, China
zhangyijun@customs.gov.cn

Abstract. Multiple object tracking (MOT) by tracklets rather than discrete detections has received more attention in recent years. Following the tracking-by-detection paradigm, many approaches treat tracklets as individual units in data association, aiming at exploiting local or global relationships among them. However, the problem of fragmentations still remains. When severe occlusions occur, adjacent trajectories will collapse into many ambiguous tracklets, which renders tracklet representations to be unreliable. To address this, we treat potential tracklets to be linked as a proposal and propose a trainable tracklet-to-proposal embedding framework based on graph attention network (GAT). Guided by tracklet-wise information, our framework mainly designs two tracklet-embedding modules to extract intra- and inter-tracklet features to generate discriminative representations of tracklet-based proposals, enhancing the accuracy of proposal classification. We experimentally demonstrate that the proposed method significantly outperforms previous state-of-the-art techniques on MOT17 public benchmarks.

Keywords: Multi-object Tracking · Tracklet · Proposal-Based Framework · GAT

1 Introduction

Multiple object tracking (MOT) is a fundamental task in computer vision that aims to track multiple objects over time in a video sequence. The goal of MOT is to maintain the identities of objects across frames while dealing with various challenges such as occlusion, motion blur, and illumination changes. It is critical for the task of MOT to relate with many real-world applications such as video surveillance, autonomous driving, robotics, and human-computer interaction.

In recent years, most MOT algorithms have adopted the tracking-by-detection (TBD) paradigm [1–4,12]: firstly, detecting targets in each frame; secondly, linking the frame-wise detections and form trajectories. However, due to the happening of more challenging scenes with serious occlusion, TBD-based trackers become sensitive to error detector responses and individual missing

H. Lu et al. (Eds.): ICIG 2023, LNCS 14356, pp. 300–310, 2023.
https://doi.org/10.1007/978-3-031-46308-2_25

detections. Consequently, the use of tracklets (short trajectories) in trackers has been proposed to generate more complete and reliable trajectories. In this way, the size of hypothesis space decreases dramatically from detection-level to tracklet-level.

Various tracklet-based methods leverage tracklets as a building block for robust tracking, combined with MHT [16,18,24], network flow [17,20–22], motion model [6,23], graph neural network [8,26] and etc. Most of them only focus on global or adjacent relationships among tracklets, struggling to alleviate the fragmentation issue but less considering to model tracklet association in a feasible search space. Recent work [11] proposes a novel proposal-based learnable framework, which effectively simplify the problem of tracklet association by clustering potential tracklets to be linked within a proposal, and serves MOT as a proposal classification task to be solved. However, it still faces some limitations related to generating reliable representations of proposals.

In this work, we build our pipeline by developing the key strategy of proposal-based methods, and try to mitigate the problem by learning discriminative representations for tracklet-based proposals. Therefore, we design a tracklet-to-proposal embedding framework to distinguish positive and negative proposals. The framework consists of two tracklet-related module of intra and inter-embedding designed with multi-head graph attentions [26], which focus on different aspects of tracklets; besides, temporal embedding module is employed to extract proposal's discriminative features guided with tracklet's spatio-temporal information.

The main contribution of the paper is in two folds: 1) We propose a tracklet-to-proposal embedding framework to learn discriminative representations for tracklet-based proposals; 2) We demonstrate that our method achieves state-of-the-art results of our method on MOTChallenge public benchmarks MOT17 [28].

2   Related Work

Graph-Based Methods in MOT. Multi-object tracking can fundamentally be viewed as a graph optimization problem. A graph is an effective way to represent relational information, and Graph Neural Network (GNN) can learn higher-order relational information through a message passing process that propagates and aggregates neighboring features. Early work by [5] integrated CNN and LSTM to simultaneously learn appearance and motion features, with a subsequent application of GCN [7] for feature refinement. Xu et al. [40] proposes an online MOT method with a spatio-temporal relation network that consists of a spatial relation module and a temporal relation module. The features from these two modules are fused to predict the affinity score for association. Brasó et al. [8] adopts a message passing network [10] with time-aware node update module that aggregates past and future features separately and solves MOT problem as edge classification. Dai et al. [11] clusters and ranks tracklets through a graph convolution network and shows promising results. However, these trackers do not fully capitalize on the potential of tracklets to effectively reduce identity switches and generate more extended and continuous trajectories.

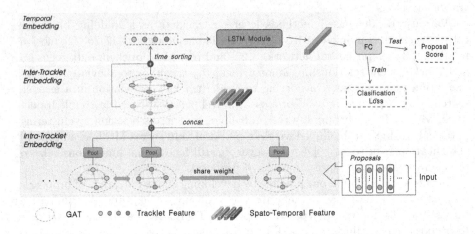

Fig. 1. Overview of our pipeline. Our work comprises 4 steps: (1) Given a set of proposals containing several tracklets as input. (2) Intra- and Inter-tracklet embedding modules based on multi-head GAT generates tracklet-level embeddings. (3) Temporal embedding module concatenates spatio-temporal features with tracklet embeddings and produces representative proposal-level embeddings. (4) Two fully connected layers convert proposal embeddings into proposal scores.

Tracklet Embedding in MOT. In line with the tracking-by-detection paradigm, many approaches [6,7,13–15] treat tracklets as separate entities instead of individual detections, aiming to exploit both local and global temporal information within the embedding. Wang et al. [13] utilized epipolar geometry to generate tracklets and constructed a multi-scale TrackletNet to group tracklets based on appearance and temporal features. Zhang et al. [14] measures the input tracklets whether they belong to the same track using CNN and LSTM to model appearance and motion in two respectively designed networks. Wang et al. [6] proposes a reconstruct-to-embed strategy to embed the tracklet based on motion features, and GCN [7] is adopted to learn the interaction among tracklets. Chu et al. [15] uses a spatial-temporal graph Transformer encoder to encode tracklets and uses spatial graph decoder to estimate the association between tracklets and detections. However, these methods still fall short in producing discriminative representation for tracklets in crowded scenes.

3   Method

Given a batch of video frames and corresponding detections $D = \{d_1, ..., d_k\}$, where k is the total number of detections for all frames. Each detection d_i contains its 2D image coordinates and its timestamp. A set of time-ordered detections forms a trajectory $\mathcal{T}_i = \{d_{i_1}, \cdots, d_{i_{n_i}}\}$, where n_i is the number of detections that belong to trajectory i. The goal of MOT is to assign a unique track ID to each detection and generate a set of m trajectories $\mathcal{T}_* = \{\mathcal{T}_1, \cdots, \mathcal{T}_m\}$ that accurately preserves the identities of the objects.

3.1   Intra-Tracklet Embedding

As shown in Fig. 1, our work takes tracklet-based proposals $\mathcal{P} = \{\mathcal{P}_i\}$ as input. To obtain tracklets, we firstly preprocess each detection with a pretrained ReID model [29] to extract its appearance feature, and then apply Hungarian algorithm [30] to generate low-level tracklets by linking detections based on three affinities of their appearance, position and timestamps. Subsequently, cluster tracklets possibly to be linked as a proposal $\mathcal{P}_i = \{\mathcal{T}_{i_1}, \cdots, \mathcal{T}_{i_{m_i}}\}$, where m_i is the number of tracklets in proposal i, which can be selected randomly in training and generated iteratively in inference similar to [11].

Each tracklet is represented by a 2048-dimensional vector average pooled by all its box ReID features. To capture a more representative feature of a tracklet, we averagely divide each tracklet input feature into N_b parts at the channel dimension, and take their part features as nodes, utilizing a Graph Attention Network (GAT) [26] to learn the representative information of the tracklet, with its independent multi-head attention mechanism. Finally, the node part features are aggregated by using max pooling to generate intra-tracklet embeddings $F_s = \{f_{s_i}\}$ within a proposal.

3.2   Inter-Tracklet Embedding

We consistently employ a GAT-based network to learn inter-tracklet information, making it well-suited for inductive tasks that involve discerning patterns of positive or negative proposals based on diverse relationships among tracklets.

Considering the tracklet-level embedding lacks explicit spatial and temporal information, which are important cues for MOT task, we follow [11] to encode the information of relative positions, sizes, and temporal distances among nodes as spatio-temporal features. Given a proposal $\mathcal{P} = \{v_i\}_{i=1}^{m_i}$ with m_i vertices, sorted in the ascending time-order, the bounding box at the ending timestamp $(t_{e_i}, x_i, y_i, w_i, h_i)$ and the bounding box at the starting timestamp $(t_{s_{i+1}}, x_{i+1}, y_{i+1}, w_{i+1}, h_{i+1})$ between two temporal adjacent vertices are used to calculate the spatio-temporal feature for each vertex v_i, which is defined as:

$$f_{st_i} = (t_{s_{i+1}-t_{e_i}}, \frac{2(x_{i+1} - x_i)}{(x_{i+1} + x_i)}, \frac{2(y_{i+1} - y_i)}{(y_{i+1} + y_i)}, \log\frac{w_{i+1}}{w_i}, \log\frac{h_{i+1}}{h_i}) \qquad (1)$$

and later concatenated with intra-tracklet embeddings to form spatio-temporal encoding features $f_{c_i} = concat(f_{s_i}, f_{st_i})$. Then, the GAT takes spatio-temporal encoding features $F_c = \{f_{c_i}\}_{i \in m_i}$ as nodes, and stacks L layers with residual connections to output inter-trackelet embeddings $F'_c = \{f'_i\}_{i \in m_i}$.

$$\mathbf{a}_{i,j}^{(l)} = softmax_j(LeakyReLU(\mathbf{a}^T[W^{(l)}\mathbf{f}_{c_i}^{(l)}||W^{(l)}\mathbf{f}_{c_j}^{(l)}])) \tag{2}$$

$$\mathbf{f}_{c_i}'^{(l)} = \overset{K}{\underset{k=1}{||}} \sigma(\sum_{j\in\mathcal{N}_i} \mathbf{a}_{i,j}^{(l)}W^{(l)}\mathbf{f}_{c_j}^{(l)}) + \mathbf{f}_{c_i}'^{(l-1)} \tag{3}$$

where $f_{c_i}^{(l)}$ is the feature vector of node i in the l-th layer, and W is a learnable weight matrix. $a_{i,j}^{(l)}$ is the normalized attention coefficient between nodes i and j. $||$ denotes concatenation, and K indicates the number of attention heads. σ is a non-linear activation function (ELU in our implementation).

3.3 Temporal Embedding

In temporal embedding, we simply implement a LSTM module to aggregate tracklet-level embeddings $F_c' = \{f_i'\}_{i\in m_i}$ in time-ascending order into proposal-level embeddings. The ablation study shows its significant improvements on ID switches. The proposal embedding is finally represented by the output sequence in the last step of LSTM , and later fed into two fully connected layers to estimate the scores of the given proposals.

3.4 Training and Inference

Training Loss. In the training procedure, we randomly collect tracklets with the same object ID or different object ID to generate negative or positive proposals as training data, assigned to a classification label with a value of 0 or 1, respectively. Besides, we make sure the same numbers of two kinds of proposals for label balance. According to the above, the score confidence of proposal can be learned with the classification loss L_{cls} based on binary cross-entropy loss.

Inference. In the inference, we follow the iterative clustering strategy from [11], which builds an affinity graph for tracklets as nodes and cluster them iteratively by using their connected component. In the original proposal generation, the clustering constraints are too strict that only produces proposals without long-term possibility, so we loose the constraints for more potential proposals.

After calculating the scores for all proposals, we arrange them in descending order and select those with the highest rankings. Each tracklets within the same proposal is assigned with the same object ID. To avoid duplicate assignment of object IDs, we ensure that tracklets within different proposals do not overlap. Then, linear interpolation of bounding boxes is employed to post-process tracklets sharing the same ID, merging them into a longer trajectory.

4 Experiments

4.1 Experiments Settings

Datasets and Metrics. We conduct experiments on MOT17 [28] dataset, which comprises multiple challenging pedestrian tracking sequences characterized by frequent occlusions and crowded scenes. The dataset consists of 7 videos for train and 7 videos for test. Each video sequence is provided with 3 sets of detections, i.e. DPM [9], Faster-RCNN [33] and SDP [19]. To ensure a fair comparison with other approaches, we utilize the public detections supplied by MOTChallenge and preprocess them by using the tracking results from [3]. This strategy is commonly employed in published methods [8,31].

Following standard protocols, we utilize CLEAR MOT Metrics [32] and HOTA [35] for evaluation. The Multiple Object Tracking Accuracy (MOTA) [32] and ID F1 Score (IDF1) [34] are deemed the most critical metrics, as they accurately measure object coverage and identity preservation, respectively. Compared with them, HOTA offers a comprehensive balance between detection, association, and localization performance.

Implementation Details. In intra-tracklet embedding, the module is built by 1 GAT layer with 8 attention heads, and the divided number of each tracklet feature N_b is set to 8. In inter-tracklet embedding module, the number of GAT layers L is set to 2, with 4 attention heads per layer. In temporal embedding module, 2 hidden layers of LSTM and 2 FC layers are used. During training, the batch size is set to 128, and the model parameters are updated using the Adam optimizer with weight decay of 1×10^{-4}. To prevent network training from overfitting, we train for 600 iterations in total with a learning rate of 5×10^{-4}.

4.2 Comparison with the State-of-the-Art Methods

We present the quantitative results of our method on MOT17 in Table 1, respectively, and compare them with officially published methods on the MOTChallenge public benchmark. As illustrated in Table 1, our approach achieves state-of-the-art results. For fair comparison, we compare with those MOT methods using Tracktor [3] to refine the public detection. In MOT17 public benchmark, our method achieves the best tracking accuracy (i.e. 67.5% IDF1, 51.9% HOTA and 59.5% MOTA, etc.). This demonstrates that our proposed tracklet-to-proposal embedding network delivers robust performance in object coverage and identity preservation, with significant improvement in ID switches metric.

4.3 Ablation Study

In this subsection, we aim to evaluate the performance of each module in our framework. We conduct all of our experiments on the whole MOT17 [28] train set. Besides, we visualize tracking results of robust trajectories on MOT17 test set shown in Fig. 2.

Table 1. Performance comparison with start-of-the art on MOT17 test set. For fair comparison, only MOT methods using [3] to refine the public detection are listed.

Method	IDF1 ↑	MOTA ↑	HOTA ↑	FP ↓	FN ↓	ID Sw. ↓
Tracktor [3]	55.1	56.3	44.8	**8866**	235449	1987
LPT [17]	57.7	57.3	-	15187	224560	1424
MPNTrack [8]	61.7	58.8	49.0	17413	213594	1185
Lif_T [36]	65.6	60.5	51.3	14966	206619	1189
ApLift [27]	65.6	60.5	51.1	30,609	**190,670**	1709
GMT [41]	65.9	60.2	51.2	13142	209812	1675
LPC_MOT [11]	66.8	59.0	51.5	23102	206948	1122
Ours	**67.5**	**59.5**	**51.9**	21390	205922	**924**

Fig. 2. Samples results from the results on MOT17 [28]. Each bounding box's color represents the target identity, and the dotted line below every bounding box signifies the latest tracklet for each target. The proposed tracker predicts trajectories over a large interval with substantially robust and temporally coherence.

Table 2. Ablation study of different network layers for tracklet-related embedding modules

Alg	IDF1 ↑	MOTA ↑	FP ↓	FN ↓	ID Sw. ↓
GCN [7]	74.4	65.1	5277	111820	533
GAT [26]	**74.7**	**65.2**	5161	**111512**	**477**
GATv2 [37]	74.5	65.1	5203	111801	492
Self-Attn [39]	74.1	64.9	**3896**	113904	535

Effects of Different Network Layers for Tracklet-Related Embedding Modules. It is worth mentioning that our framework is flexible to allow different deep neural network layers to be plugged into our two tracklet-related embedding modules, including GCN [7], GAT [26], GATv2 [37] and Self-Attention [39]. To evaluate the embedding abilities of these network layers, we extend the training iterations to 1200 and choose the best iteration of these models before overfitting. Table 2 presents the results by evaluating these neural network layers. By comparing GAT with other neural network layers, it is clear that GAT achieves better performance on all metrics listed, attributed to its capability of capturing more discriminative information to measure the score of each proposals. For the GATv2 and Self-attention network layers, we believe that the limited size of our dataset could be the reason of their poor performance.

Table 3. Ablation study of the aggregation methods for proposal embedding.

Agg	IDF1 ↑	MOTA ↑	FP ↓	FN ↓	ID Sw. ↓
Sum	73.8	64.9	3771	113910	735
Avg-pool	74.1	65.0	4119	113153	671
Max-pool	74.6	**65.2**	5260	111581	523
Temporal-embed	**74.7**	**65.2**	**5161**	**111512**	**477**

Effects of the Aggregation Methods for Proposal Embeddings. We test different aggregation methods to generate the final proposal embeddings, compared with our temporal embedding module. As shown in Table 3, using temporal module can achieve improvement when aggregating the tracklet-level embeddings into the proposal-level embeddings, especially with significant decreases on FP, FN and ID switches metrics.

5   Conclusions

In this paper, we introduce three learnable embedding modules designed to enhance the proposal-based MOT framework. Our experimental results demonstrate that our method effectively distinguishes positive proposals from negative ones. We employ a GAT-based network for intra- and inter-tracklet embeddings, combined with explicit spatio-temporal cues, to capture higher-order information from tracklets to proposals. Additionally, we integrate a temporal embedding module to extract temporal features and enhance proposal representation in crowded scenes with severe occlusions. Our approach achieves a significant performance improvement compared to the previous state-of-the-arts. We discovered that our work is primarily limited by low-quality detections. In the future, we aim to conduct more experiments on MOT private benchmarks and generalize our framework to other challenging tracking datasets.

Acknowledgements. This work was supported partially by the NSFC (U19114 01, U1811461, 62076260, 61772570), Guangdong Natural Science Funds Project (2020B1515120085), Guangdong NSF for Distinguished Young Scholar (2022B151 5020009), and the Key-Area Research and Development Program of Guangzhou (202007030004).

References

1. Schulter, S., Vernaza, P., Choi, W., Chandraker, M.: Deep network flow for multi-object tracking. In: Proceedings of the IEEE Conference on Computer Vision and Pattern Recognition, pp. 6951–6960 (2017)
2. Wojke, N., Bewley, A., Paulus, D.: Simple online and realtime tracking with a deep association metric. In: ICIP, pp. 3645–3649 (2017)
3. Bergmann, P., Meinhardt, T., Leal-Taixe, L.: Tracking without bells and whistles. In: Proceedings of the IEEE/CVF International Conference on Computer Vision, pp. 941–951 (2019)
4. Zhang, Y., Wang, C., Wang, X., Zeng, W., Liu, W.: FairMOT: on the fairness of detection and re-identification in multiple object tracking. Int. J. Comput. Vis. **129**, 3069–3087 (2021)
5. Jiang, X., Li, P., Li, Y., Zhen, X.: Graph neural based end-to-end data association framework for online multiple-object tracking. arXiv preprint arXiv:1907.05315 (2019)
6. Wang, G., Gu, R., Liu, Z., Hu, W., Song, M., Hwang, J.N.: Track without appearance: learn box and tracklet embedding with local and global motion patterns for vehicle tracking. In: Proceedings of the IEEE/CVF International Conference on Computer Vision, pp. 9876–9886 (2021)
7. Kipf, T. N., Welling, M.: Semi-supervised classification with graph convolutional networks. arXiv preprint arXiv:1609.02907 (2016)
8. Brasó, G., Leal-Taixé, L.: Learning a neural solver for multiple object tracking. In: Proceedings of the IEEE/CVF Conference on Computer Vision and Pattern Recognition, pp. 6247–6257 (2020)
9. Felzenszwalb, P.F., Girshick, R.B., McAllester, D., Ramanan, D.: Object detection with discriminatively trained part-based models. IEEE Trans. Pattern Anal. Mach. Intell. **32**(9), 1627–1645 (2010)
10. Gilmer, J., Schoenholz, S.S., Riley, P.F., Vinyals, O., Dahl, G.E: Neural message passing for quantum chemistry. In: International Conference on Machine Learning, pp. 1263–1272. PMLR (2017)
11. Dai, P., Weng, R., Choi, W., Zhang, C., He, Z., Ding, W.: Learning a proposal classifier for multiple object tracking. In: Proceedings of the IEEE/CVF Conference on Computer Vision and Pattern Recognition, pp. 2443–2452 (2021)
12. Bewley, A., Ge, Z., Ott, L., Ramos, F., Upcroft, B.: Simple online and realtime tracking. In: ICIP, pp. 3464–3468 (2016)
13. Wang, G., Wang, Y., Zhang, H., Gu, R., Hwang, J.N.: Exploit the connectivity: multi-object tracking with trackletnet. In: Proceedings of the 27th ACM International Conference on Multimedia, pp. 482–490 (2019)
14. Zhang, Y., et al.: Long-term tracking with deep tracklet association. IEEE Trans. Image Process. **29**, 6694–6706 (2020)
15. Chu, P., Wang, J., You, Q., Ling, H., Liu, Z.: TransMOT: spatial-temporal graph transformer for multiple object tracking. In: Proceedings of the IEEE/CVF Winter Conference on Applications of Computer Vision, pp. 4870–4880 (2023)

16. Chen, J., Sheng, H., Zhang, Y., Xiong, Z.: Enhancing detection model for multiple hypothesis tracking. In: Proceedings of the IEEE Conference on Computer Vision and Pattern Recognition Workshops, pp. 18–27 (2017)
17. Li, S., Kong, Y., Rezatofighi, H.: Learning of global objective for network flow in multi-object tracking. In: Proceedings of the IEEE/CVF Conference on Computer Vision and Pattern Recognition, pp. 8855–8865 (2022)
18. Sheng, H., Chen, J., Zhang, Y., Ke, W., Xiong, Z., Yu, J.: Iterative multiple hypothesis tracking with tracklet-level association. IEEE Trans. Circuits Syst. Video Technol. **29**(12), 3660–3672 (2018)
19. Yang, F., Choi, W., Lin, Y.: Exploit all the layers: fast and accurate CNN object detector with scale dependent pooling and cascaded rejection classifiers. In: CVPR (2016)
20. Shitrit, H.B., Berclaz, J., Fleuret, F., Fua, P.: Multi-commodity network flow for tracking multiple people. IEEE Trans. Pattern Anal. Mach. Intell. **36**(8), 1614–1627 (2013)
21. Wang, B., Wang, G., Luk Chan, K., Wang, L.: Tracklet association with online target-specific metric learning. In: Proceedings of the IEEE Conference on Computer Vision and Pattern Recognition, pp. 1234–1241 (2014)
22. Wang, B., Wang, G., Chan, K.L., Wang, L.: Tracklet association by online target-specific metric learning and coherent dynamics estimation. IEEE Trans. Pattern Anal. Mach. Intell. **39**(3), 589–602 (2016)
23. Yang, B., Nevatia, R.: Multi-target tracking by online learning of non-linear motion patterns and robust appearance models. In: 2012 IEEE Conference on Computer Vision and Pattern Recognition, pp. 1918–1925 (2012)
24. Kim, C., Li, F., Ciptadi, A., Rehg, J. M.: Multiple hypothesis tracking revisited. In: Proceedings of the IEEE International Conference on Computer Vision, pp. 4696–4704 (2015)
25. Wang, Y., Kitani, K., Weng, X.: Joint object detection and multi-object tracking with graph neural networks. In: 2021 IEEE International Conference on Robotics and Automation (ICRA), pp. 13708–13715 (2021)
26. Veličković, P., Cucurull, G., Casanova, A., Romero, A., Lio, P., Bengio, Y.: Graph attention networks. arXiv preprint arXiv:1710.10903 (2017)
27. Hornakova, A., Kaiser, T., Swoboda, P., Rolinek, M., Rosenhahn, B., Henschel, R.: Making higher order mot scalable: an efficient approximate solver for lifted disjoint paths. In: Proceedings of the IEEE/CVF International Conference on Computer Vision, pp. 6330–6340 (2021)
28. Milan, A., Leal-Taixé, L., Reid, I., Roth, S., Schindler, K.: MOT16: a benchmark for multi-object tracking. arXiv preprint arXiv:1603.00831 (2016)
29. He, L., Liao, X., Liu, W., Liu, X., Cheng, P., Mei, T.: FastReID: a pytorch toolbox for general instance re-identification. arXiv preprint arXiv:2006.02631 (2020)
30. Munkres, J.: Algorithms for the assignment and transportation problems. J. Soc. Industr. Appl. Math. **5**(1), 32–38 (1957)
31. Liu, Q., Chu, Q., Liu, B., Yu, N.: GSM: graph similarity model for multi-object tracking. In: IJCAI, pp. 530–536 (2020)
32. Bernardin, K., Stiefelhagen, R.: Evaluating multiple object tracking performance: the clear MOT metrics. EURASIP J. Image Video Process. **2008**, 246309 (2008). https://doi.org/10.1155/2008/246309
33. Ren, S., He, K., Girshick, R., Sun, J.: Faster R-CNN: towards real-time object detection with region proposal networks. In: NIPS (2015)

34. Ristani, E., Solera, F., Zou, R., Cucchiara, R., Tomasi, C.: Performance measures and a data set for multi-target, multi-camera tracking. In: Hua, G., Jégou, H. (eds.) ECCV 2016. LNCS, vol. 9914, pp. 17–35. Springer, Cham (2016). https://doi.org/10.1007/978-3-319-48881-3_2

35. Luiten, J., et al.: HOTA: a higher order metric for evaluating multi-object tracking. Int. J. Comput. Vis. **129**, 548–578 (2021)

36. Hornakova, A., Henschel, R., Rosenhahn, B., Swoboda, P.: Lifted disjoint paths with application in multiple object tracking. In: International Conference on Machine Learning, pp. 4364–4375. PMLR (2020)

37. Brody, S., Alon, U., Yahav, E.: How attentive are graph attention networks? arXiv preprint arXiv:2105.14491 (2021)

38. Lin, T. Y., Goyal, P., Girshick, R., He, K., Dollár, P.: Focal loss for dense object detection. In: Proceedings of the IEEE International Conference on Computer Vision, pp. 2980–2988 (2017)

39. Vaswani, A., et al.: Attention is all you need. In: Advances in Neural Information Processing Systems 30 (2017)

40. Xu, J., Cao, Y., Zhang, Z., Hu, H.: Spatial-temporal relation networks for multi-object tracking. In: Proceedings of the IEEE/CVF International Conference on Computer Vision, pp. 3988–3998 (2019)

41. He, J., Huang, Z., Wang, N., Zhang, Z.: Learnable graph matching: incorporating graph partitioning with deep feature learning for multiple object tracking. In: Proceedings of the IEEE/CVF Conference on Computer Vision and Pattern Recognition, pp. 5299–5309 (2021)

Virtual-Violence: A Brand-New Dataset for Video Violence Recognition

Pengpeng Ou[(✉)], Xiaoyu Wu, and Yimeng Shang

Communication University of China, Beijing, China
1261015866@qq.com, {wuxiaoyu,ym_s}@cuc.edu.cn

Abstract. As the development of intelligent terminals, a large number of online videos are uploaded to the video platforms. Thus, violence detection has been a significant part of online video content review. Suitable datasets are an important prerequisite for deep learning network training. However, considering the particularity of violence actions, it is both time and labor consuming to collect sufficient and various data. To address the problem, we generate the Virtual-Violence, a brand-new dataset containing 809 videos in total. Besides, we propose a violence detection model based on global-local visual and audio contrastive learning, which demonstrates the Virtual-Violence can improve the performance on the current datasets. Experimental results prove Virtual-Violence performs well on violence recognition task.

Keywords: Violence Recognition · Multimodality · Virtual Dataset

1 Introduction

With the increasing interest in video violence recognition and advancing in related algorithms (e.g., TSM [12], TSN [26], C3D [24]), there are large numbers of datasets for violence recognition [1,3,5–7,10,14,16,17,22,27]. Most of existing datasets are collected from real-world, which have some limitations of small-scale, unitary category and low resolution of the videos. On the one hand, it is difficult to collect sufficient data of various abnormal actions as excessively violent videos are not allowed to be distributed. On the other hand, some datasets originate from surveillance camera videos. Limited by the recording device, the videos are not high resolution generally. In addition, there are some datasets collected from films and television dramas or virtual scenes, which contains abundant types of violence actions. However, the violent elements in movies are usually artistically embellished and exaggerated, and therefore differ from real-world violence actions.

To address the above issues, we propose the Virtual-Violence as showed in Fig. 1, a new video dataset consisting of multiple virtual scenes and characters for violence recognition. In order to make our dataset more realistic, we set weather and light in addition to human actions that are close to real-world. For the purpose of validating the performance of Virtual-Violence and its effect for

H. Lu et al. (Eds.): ICIG 2023, LNCS 14356, pp. 311–322, 2023.
https://doi.org/10.1007/978-3-031-46308-2_26

Fig. 1. Example video frames in the Virtual-Violence including both non-violence type and violence type.

the current datasets, we propose a violence recognition model based on global-local visual and audio contrastive learning, which can make full use of the audio and visual information.

To summarize our work, contributions of the paper are threefold:

- We introduce the Virtual-Violence, a new virtual dataset consisting of 809 videos in total used for video violence recognition.
- We propose a violence recognition model, which better copes with the limitations of the current datasets and makes full use of the audio and visual information.
- We conduct the experiments to show that the Virtual-Violence dataset can enhance the performance of violence recognition model on both real-world and virtual datasets.

2   Related Work

2.1   Violence Recognition Datasets

At present, most of violence recognition datasets originate from real world. According to the acquisition source of videos, there are mainly two kinds of datasets: online videos and surveillance camera.

Hassner et al. [10] propose the ViF (Violent-Flows) dataset focusing on violence in crowded scenes. The dataset contains 246 videos downloaded from YouTube, including a wide variety of recording conditions. It therefore causes the problem that some videos are low resolution and too crowed to recognize violence actions. The length of each video lasts from 1.04 seconds to 6.52 seconds. The videos are stored as AVI files with 320×240 frame size and annotated at video-level labels.

Perez et al. [16] collected $1,000$ videos comprised of various fighting elements from YouTube, named the CCTV-Fights dataset. There are 280 videos from CCTV lasting from 5 s to 12 min, and rest 720 videos are recorded by mobile cameras, car cameras and drones or helicopters lasting from 3 s to 7 min.

Each video is annotated at frame-level labels. However, limited by the recording device, there is no background sounds of all the videos in the CCTV-Fights dataset.

Cheng et al. [6] present the RWF-2000 (Real-World Fighting) dataset consisting of 2000 clips without audio information captured all by surveillance cameras in the real world. The RWF-2000 dataset involves various violence activities such as fighting, robbing, shooting and etc. All of the videos are edited into clips with the length of 5 s at 30 FPS, and annotated at video-level labels.

Sultani et al. [22] establish the UCF-Crime dataset of 1900 clips collected from YouTube and LiveLeak. There are 13 types of violence actions in UCF-Crime including abuse, arrest, arson and etc. All clips are long unedited surveillance videos with a duration of 1 to 10 min. However, only videos in testing set are annotated at both video-level and frame-level labels, while videos in training set are annotated at video-level labels. It is a tough task to recognize the violence elements from long videos.

In spite of the works mentioned above, there are also some videos datasets generated from films and television dramas or the virtual world.

Nievas et al. [3] propose the Movies Fight, a dataset of 200 videos captured from the hockey games, which contains the events of clash between the athletes and the sound at the moment. The Movies Fight are annotated at video-level labels. However, the Movies Fight dataset is small-scale and unitary variety of scene and violence action.

Demarty et al. [7] present the VSD dataset comprising 1, 317 audio videos collected from 18 Hollywood movies. The elements about bleeding, fighting, fire, guns and etc. are defined as violence. Under the above criteria, each video is annotated at frame-level label as violence or non-violence.

Acsintoae et al. [1] generated the UBnormal dataset in the Cinema4D consisting of 543 videos. Differ from all the datasets mentioned above, the UBnormal dataset is comprising of various virtual scenes and characters. All videos are generated at 30 FPS and set 720 pixels as the minimum height of frame size. Each video in UBnormal is annotated at pixel-level label. There is the segmentation and the object label for both normal and abnormal synthetic object. However, the videos in UBnormal dataset are lack of audio information.

Summarizing these datasets proposed for violence recognition task, each of them has one or more of the following limits:

- Small-scale
- Low resolution of videosinformation in the videos.
- Low resolution of videos
- Unitary variety of violence actions, some of which are not close enough to real-world life

To cope with the issues, we generated a new virtual dataset in Unity consisting of 809 video clips with audio information. The detailed description and generation methods of the dataset we present will be introduced in Sect. 3 (Table 1).

Table 1. Comparisons between our dataset Virtual-Violence and the previous video dataset for violence recognition.

Dataset	Scale	Annotation	Resource	Audio
ViF [10]	246 videos	Video-Level	Real-World	✓
CCTV-Fights [16]	1,000 videos	Frame-Level	Real-World	✗
RWF-2000 [6]	2,000 videos	Video-Level	Real-World	✗
UCF-Crime [22]	1,900 videos	Frame-Level and Video-Level	Real-World	✗
Movie Fights [3]	200 videos	Video-Level	Real-World	✓
VSD [7]	1,317 videos	Video-Level	Real-World	✓
UBnormal [1]	543 videos	Pixel-Level and Video-Level	Virtual	✗
Virtual-Violence (ours)	809 videos	Video-Level	Virtual	✓

2.2 Violence Recognition Methods

Existing algorithms mainly extract spatial and temporal features through CNN (Convolutional Neural Network) to distinguish violent behaviors. Some early studies extract the spatial features based on 2D-CNN and the temporal features based on LSTM (Long Short-Term Memory) [19].

Dong et al. [8] adopt apparent flows, optical flows and acceleration flows as three input branches for 2D-CNN. Then utilize the LSTM to processing the temporal information and obtain the results of violence recognition by feature fusion.

Sudhakaran et al. [21] improve the ConvLSTM with the difference of adjacent frames instead of a sequence of raw frames as input. At the same time, the frame differences suppress background information, therefore reducing the computational resource.

However, the separate extraction of spatial and temporal features ignores their intrinsic connection, reducing the representational ability. Therefore, some studies introduce 3D-CNN, which enables more complete extraction of spatial and temporal features than the 2D-CNN and RNN structure.

Perez et al. [16] introduce the CCTV-Fights dataset and develop a pipeline consisting of Two-Stream CNN [20], 3D-CNN and a local interest point descriptor, in addition to variety of classifiers. Extensive experiments prove that the method achieves good results in recognizing the violence actions.

Cheng et al. [6] present the Flow Gated Network that utilizes both the merits of 3D-CNN and optical flow. The Flow Gated Network model adopt RGB images and optical flows as input to process the spatial and temporal information.

3D-CNN performs well in extracting the spatial and temporal features from videos with high computing cost. Thus, there is also a lot of work devoted to improving 3D-CNN by reducing the number of parameters in order to save computing resources.

Tran et al. [25] propose the R(2+1)D structure, which factorizes the 3D convolutional filters into separate spatial and temporal components yields. Shang et al. [18] introduce the MD-VR model on the basis of the R(2+1)D structure to recognize violence more efficiently.

Acsintoae et al. [1] introduces some new methods. They first develop a pre-trained detector to capture objects in the videos, and then train a 3D-CNN to generate distinguishable violence information by four jointly learning multiple proxy tasks.

In addition, considering that parts of the violence data contain audio information in addition to visual information, some scholars utilize multi-stream networks to extract features from different modalities, and complete the task of violence recognition by means of feature fusion. To our knowledge, there are several works [2,9,11,13,15,27] extracting the audio information for violence recognition.

In summary, the approaches of violence recognition mainly utilize CNN to extract the desired features. To make full use of the multimodal information in the videos, in this paper we adopt both visual and audio features as the input. More details of the violence recognition model we use will be introduced in Sect. 4.

3   Generation of Virtual-Violence

Figure 2 shows the whole process of dataset construction. We first set up the scenes. Then we expand the dataset in terms of characters, weather and light to ensure the diversity and realism of our dataset. Finally, the video is created in batches by adjusting the pose and position of the camera. The details are as follows and Fig. 3 shows the virtual models and effects used.

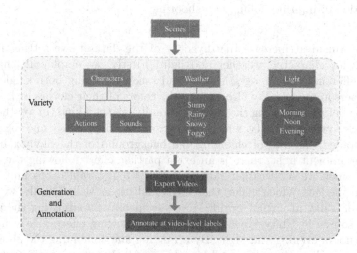

Fig. 2. The process of establishing the Virtual-Violence.

Scenes. The Virtual-Violence dataset is created with the game engine Unity, in which we can generate, import and place various 3D models freely. We totally choose 9 scenes collected from Unity Store and other online shopping platforms. The scenes we select include both outdoor ones: factory, street, building site, old port, countryside, city and town, and indoor ones: hospital and office building. For all the scenes selected, we remove excess lights, light baking and LOD, delete excess resources, and ensure occlusion culling to optimize each map and save the memory. All scenes mentioned above are large enough, so we can record large number of different videos by adjusting the position and pose of the camera in each scene.

Actions and Sounds. We get the action data from an open-source website. Then we set the start-and-end time and the cycle of the actions based on the animation machine in Unity. For all videos in Virtual-Violence, the following 7 actions are considered normal: walking, talking, running, standing, sitting, dancing and rocking while listening. While the following 12 actions are considered abnormal: falling, fighting, crawling, convulsion, having a seizure, having a stomachache, walking drunk, groan while laying down, kicked by others, shooting, fire and smoke. In our dataset, normal videos contain only normal actions, which include one or more types. As for the abnormal videos, all of them contain at least one type abnormal action, and some of them include one or more types normal actions also. Furthermore, in order to make the videos more realistic and meet the need of multimodality, we binding appropriate sound effects for each set of actions. For example, we add the sound of moans, crashes and booming in the action of injuring, falling and shooting.

Variety. Aimed at increase the diversity of the dataset, we setting multiple categories for character, weather and light. Firstly, we employ 12 characters covered different genders, ages, shapes and races, including both single-person and two-person models. We also change the colors of their clothes or hair using photoshop before animating the videos. Secondly, we set 4 kinds of weather using the particle system in Unity, which involve sunny, rainy, snowy and foggy days. To be detailed, in spite of changing the background of the Skybox in Unity to set the ambient light, there is an extra particle effect following the lens. In addition, when we set weather rainy, snowy or foggy, rain drops and fog will appear on the lens, which makes the videos realistic as well. Thirdly, we control the time of a day in virtual world. More specifically, by adjusting the angle of the light source in Unity, we can achieve the following effects: early morning, morning, noon, evening and night. By arranging and combining the above three variables, as well as the scenes and camara, we fill the gap of single content and low resolution on the current real-world datasets.

Generation and Annotation. By adjusting the position and pose of the main camera in Unity, we can easily record videos from various angles, some of which

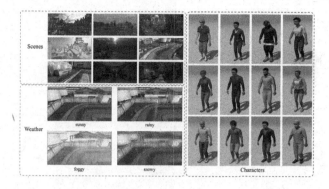

Fig. 3. Various scenes, characters and weather we used to generate the Virtual-Violence dataset.

may be difficult to achieve in the real world. Then, we utilize the video recording function built in Unity to generate all videos at 30 FPS. Each of the videos in Virtual-Violence lasts from 2 s to 15 s. It takes us about a month and a half to simulate the events and create all of the videos. We number all the videos, while checking each video for gravity issues of the characters, incorrect occlusions and other exceptional cases. And we annotate the dataset at video-level label, which indicates whether the video includes violence elements.

4 Methods

Considering that the violence elements are reflected on the audio information in addition to visual information, we propose a Violence Recognition Model Based on Global-Local Visual and Audio Contrastive Learning (GLVAC) as our baseline. The GLVAC model consists of following two parts as showed in Fig. 4: visual and audio feature contrastive learning module and feature fusion module. The former module includes global and local apparent feature extraction and audio feature positive sample selection.

Visual and Audio Feature Extraction. Both global and local apparent feature extractions require preprocessing. For global features, we frame the input sequences with a low sampling rate to capture coarse-grained timing information. While for local features, a high sampling rate is used to capture fine-grained information. Then based on the R(2+1)D structure with different parameters, we extract the global apparent feature v_g, $v_g \in \mathbf{R}^{512 \times 1}$ and local apparent feature v_l, $v_l \in \mathbf{R}^{512 \times 1}$.

We used the LibROSA to process the raw audio waveform to obtain a matrix of 80 frequency bands. Then based on the audio feature extractor we obtain the audio feature f_a, $f_a \in \mathbf{R}^{512 \times T}$, T is proportional to the length of the input audio.

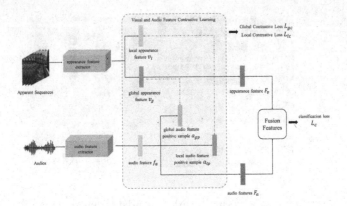

Fig. 4. The pipeline of the GLVAC model

Visual and Audio Feature Contrastive Learning. We obtain the global audio feature positive sample a_{gp} according to v_g and local audio feature positive sample a_{lp} according to v_l. We calculate the similarity between the apparent features and the audio features. The distance between the apparent features and the audio positive samples is reduced, while the distance to the audio negative samples is increased. Based on audio features f_a and the global apparent feature v_g, we obtain audio features F_a and the apparent feature F_v respectively.

Loss Function. According to the contrastive learning module, we obtain the global contrastive loss L_{gc} from the Eq. 1.

$$L_{gc} = -\log\left(\frac{\exp\left(v_g^T \cdot a_{gp}/\tau\right)}{\exp\left(v_g^T \cdot a_{gp}/\tau\right) + \sum_B \exp\left(v_g^T \cdot a_{gn}/\tau\right)}\right) \tag{1}$$

where the superscript T denotes the transpose matrix, τ is the temperature coefficient hyperparameter set to 5, a_{gn} indicates global audio feature negative sample and B denotes the batch size. Similarly, we obtain the local contrastive loss L_{lc}.

We input the fusing result of the audio features F_a and the apparent feature F_v into the fully connected layer with softmax function to formulate the non-violent prediction score q_0 and violent prediction score q_1. We regard the classification loss L_c corresponding to the violence recognition task as the main loss, and we adopt the cross-entropy loss as the classification loss. The classification loss is formulated as follows:

$$L_c = -c\log\left(q_1\right) + (1-c)\log\left(q_0\right) \tag{2}$$

where $c \in \{0, 1\}$ is the true label of the current input video, $c = 0$ denotes a non-violent video while $c = 1$ denotes violent.

The total loss function L is calculated as shown in Eq. 3, which consists of global contrastive loss L_{gc}, local contrastive loss L_{lc} and classification loss L_c.

$$L = \lambda(L_{gc} + L_{lc}) + L_c \tag{3}$$

where λ is the scale hyperparameter set to 0.5.

5 Experiments

5.1 Implementation Details

Datasets. Apart from our dataset Virtual-Violence, we also consider the VCD and GTAV dataset generated by our laboratory. The VCD dataset consists of 7,396 audio videos collected from movies, and the GTAV dataset consists of 1,000 audio videos collected from the virtual game GTA. Both two datasets are annotated at video-level labels. In addition, of all the datasets presented in Sect. 2.1, only the ViF, Movie Fights and VSD datasets contain audio information. Considering the dataset scale, we finally choose the ViF dataset.

Evaluation Metrics. The number of normal and abnormal videos is evenly distributed in the VCD, GTAV and ViF dataset. Thus, we consider the accuracy score (ACC) as the measure of our experiment.

Parameter Settings. The experiments we implement is based on PyTorch. The network is trained for 150 epochs and the batch size is 64. The learning rate varies from 10^{-4} to 8×10^{-4} according to the parameter fine-tuning result.

5.2 Ablation Experiments

We split the VCD, GTAV and ViF dataset into training and test sets with a proportion of 4 : 1. Besides, aiming to validate the performance improvement of the Virtual-Violence for the above two datasets, we add the Virtual-Violence to the training set of all three datasets while the two test sets are unchanged.

In Table 2, we show the experiment results we obtain on the GLVAC model. The first column represents whether the Virtual-Violence added, and the last three columns represent the ACC score gained on the VCD, GTAV and ViF dataset each.

We can see that the GLVAC model attains an ACC score of 92.29% on VCD, 96.75% on GTAV and 91.45% on ViF. Besides with the addition of the Virtual-Violence dataset, the GLVAC model scores 99.47% on VCD, 99.94% on GTAV and 94.95% on ViF, which improves by 5.80% on VCD, 3.19% on GTAV and 3.50% on ViF respectively.

The data demonstrates that the Virtual-Violence dataset can improve the performance of the violence detection model to a certain extent on both real-world and virtual datasets. Furthermore, the results show that our dataset can be applied to multimodality tasks and has a better improvement for violence detection.

Table 2. ACC scores of the GLVAC models on the VCD, GTAV and ViF datasets with the addition of the Virtual-Violence. Best results are highlighted in bold.

Methods		VCD ACC (%)	GTAV ACC (%)	ViF ACC (%)
GLVAC	Virtual-Violence Added			
✓		92.3	96.8	91.5
✓	✓	**98.1**	**99.9**	**95.0**

In Table 3, we show comparisons between our method and other state-of-the-art methods on the VCD, GTAV and ViF dataset. Due to the lack of existing experiments, we implement and train the fifth method on the VCD and GTAV dataset by ourselves. Our method surpasses the other state-of-the-art methods by at least 0.5% on the VCD dataset, while 2.0% on the GTAV dataset. As for the ViF dataset, our method obtains a competitive ACC score among the state-of-the-art methods.

Table 3. Comparisons between our method and others on the VCD and ViF dataset. Best results are highlighted in bold.

Methods	VCD ACC (%)	GTAV ACC (%)	ViF ACC (%)
DMRN [23]	95.5	–	–
3DCNN [14]	–	–	94.3
MA-Net [18]	96.2	-	-
Keyframes [4]	–	–	95.0
Mutual Distillation [18]	97.3	97.9	–
Semantic Correspondence [9]	97.6	–	**97.7**
GLVAC + Virtual-Violence (ours)	**98.1**	**99.9**	95.0

6   Conclusion

In this paper, we introduce a novel dataset named Virtual-Violence. We then propose the GLVAC model for verifying whether the inclusion of Virtual-Violence improves the performance on the violence recognition task. The experiment results show that the Virtual-Violence can enhance the accuracy scores on both real-world and virtual datasets for violence recognition and our dataset performs well in multimodality tasks.

In future work, we aim to expand the scale of Virtual-Violence, and develop an application for batch production of virtual videos efficiently. Besides, we plan to test and improve the performance over other state-of-the-art violence recognition models on Virtual-Violence.

References

1. Acsintoae, A., et al.: UBnormal: new benchmark for supervised open-set video anomaly detection. In: Proceedings of the IEEE/CVF Conference on Computer Vision and Pattern Recognition, pp. 20143–20153 (2022)
2. Adão Teixeira, M.V., Avila, S.: What should we pay attention to when classifying violent videos? In: Proceedings of the 16th International Conference on Availability, Reliability and Security, pp. 1–10 (2021)
3. Bermejo Nievas, E., Deniz Suarez, O., Bueno García, G., Sukthankar, R.: Violence detection in video using computer vision techniques. In: Real, P., Diaz-Pernil, D., Molina-Abril, H., Berciano, A., Kropatsch, W. (eds.) CAIP 2011, Part II. LNCS, vol. 6855, pp. 332–339. Springer, Heidelberg (2011). https://doi.org/10.1007/978-3-642-23678-5_39
4. Bi, Y., Li, D., Luo, Y.: Combining keyframes and image classification for violent behavior recognition. Appl. Sci. **12**(16), 8014 (2022)
5. Blunsden, S., Fisher, R.: The behave video dataset: ground truthed video for multi-person behavior classification. Ann. BMVA **4**(1–12), 4 (2010)
6. Cheng, M., Cai, K., Li, M.: RWF-2000: an open large scale video database for violence detection. In: 2020 25th International Conference on Pattern Recognition (ICPR), pp. 4183–4190. IEEE (2021)
7. Demarty, C.H., Penet, C., Soleymani, M., Gravier, G.: VSD, a public dataset for the detection of violent scenes in movies: design, annotation, analysis and evaluation. Multimed. Tools Appl. **74**, 7379–7404 (2015)
8. Dong, Z., Qin, J., Wang, Y.: Multi-stream deep networks for person to person violence detection in videos. In: Tan, T., Li, X., Chen, X., Zhou, J., Yang, J., Cheng, H. (eds.) CCPR 2016, Part I. CCIS, vol. 662, pp. 517–531. Springer, Singapore (2016). https://doi.org/10.1007/978-981-10-3002-4_43
9. Gu, C., Wu, X., Wang, S.: Violent video detection based on semantic correspondence. IEEE Access **8**, 85958–85967 (2020)
10. Hassner, T., Itcher, Y., Kliper-Gross, O.: Violent flows: real-time detection of violent crowd behavior. In: 2012 IEEE Computer Society Conference on Computer Vision and Pattern Recognition Workshops, pp. 1–6. IEEE (2012)
11. Korbar, B., Tran, D., Torresani, L.: Cooperative learning of audio and video models from self-supervised synchronization. In: Advances in Neural Information Processing Systems, vol. 31 (2018)
12. Lin, J., Gan, C., Han, S.: TSM: temporal shift module for efficient video understanding. In: Proceedings of the IEEE/CVF International Conference on Computer Vision, pp. 7083–7093 (2019)
13. Lou, J., Zuo, D., Zhang, Z., Liu, H.: Violence recognition based on auditory-visual fusion of autoencoder mapping. Electronics **10**(21), 2654 (2021)
14. Nievas, E.B., Suarez, O.D., Garcia, G.B., Sukthankar, R.: Hockey fight detection dataset. In: Computer Analysis of Images and Patterns, pp. 332–339. Springer, Heidelberg (2011)
15. Peixoto, B., Lavi, B., Bestagini, P., Dias, Z., Rocha, A.: Multimodal violence detection in videos. In: ICASSP 2020-2020 IEEE International Conference on Acoustics, Speech and Signal Processing (ICASSP), pp. 2957–2961. IEEE (2020)
16. Perez, M., Kot, A.C., Rocha, A.: Detection of real-world fights in surveillance videos. In: ICASSP 2019-2019 IEEE International Conference on Acoustics, Speech and Signal Processing (ICASSP), pp. 2662–2666. IEEE (2019)

17. Rota, P., Conci, N., Sebe, N., Rehg, J.M.: Real-life violent social interaction detection. In: 2015 IEEE International Conference on Image Processing (ICIP), pp. 3456–3460. IEEE (2015)

18. Shang, Y., Wu, X., Liu, R.: Multimodal violent video recognition based on mutual distillation. In: Yu, S., et al. (eds.) PRCV 2022, Part III. LNCS, vol. 13536, pp. 623–637. Springer, Cham (2022). https://doi.org/10.1007/978-3-031-18913-5_48

19. Shi, X., Chen, Z., Wang, H., Yeung, D.Y., Wong, W.K., Woo, W.C.: Convolutional LSTM network: A machine learning approach for precipitation nowcasting. In: Advances in Neural Information Processing Systems, vol. 28 (2015)

20. Simonyan, K., Zisserman, A.: Two-stream convolutional networks for action recognition in videos. In: Advances in Neural Information Processing Systems, vol. 27 (2014)

21. Sudhakaran, S., Lanz, O.: Learning to detect violent videos using convolutional long short-term memory. In: 2017 14th IEEE International Conference on Advanced Video and Signal Based Surveillance (AVSS), pp. 1–6. IEEE (2017)

22. Sultani, W., Chen, C., Shah, M.: Real-world anomaly detection in surveillance videos. In: Proceedings of the IEEE Conference on Computer Vision and Pattern Recognition, pp. 6479–6488 (2018)

23. Tian, Y., Shi, J., Li, B., Duan, Z., Xu, C.: Audio-visual event localization in unconstrained videos. In: Proceedings of the European Conference on Computer Vision (ECCV), pp. 247–263 (2018)

24. Tran, D., Bourdev, L., Fergus, R., Torresani, L., Paluri, M.: Learning spatiotemporal features with 3D convolutional networks. In: Proceedings of the IEEE International Conference on Computer Vision, pp. 4489–4497 (2015)

25. Tran, D., Wang, H., Torresani, L., Ray, J., LeCun, Y., Paluri, M.: A closer look at spatiotemporal convolutions for action recognition. In: Proceedings of the IEEE Conference on Computer Vision and Pattern Recognition, pp. 6450–6459 (2018)

26. Wang, L., et al.: Temporal segment networks: towards good practices for deep action recognition. In: Leibe, B., Matas, J., Sebe, N., Welling, M. (eds.) ECCV 2016. LNCS, vol. 9912, pp. 20–36. Springer, Cham (2016). https://doi.org/10.1007/978-3-319-46484-8_2

27. Wu, P., et al.: Not only look, but also listen: learning multimodal violence detection under weak supervision. In: Vedaldi, A., Bischof, H., Brox, T., Frahm, J.-M. (eds.) ECCV 2020, Part XXX. LNCS, vol. 12375, pp. 322–339. Springer, Cham (2020). https://doi.org/10.1007/978-3-030-58577-8_20

A Novel Attention-DeblurGAN-Based Defogging Algorithm

Xintao Hu[1], Xiaogang Cheng[1(✉)], Zhaobin Wang[2], Jie Ni[2], Bo Zhang[2], Bo Gao[2], Yan Zhang[2], Xin Geng[1], and Limin Song[1]

[1] School of Communications and Information Engineering, Nanjing University of Posts and Telecommunication, Nanjing, China
chengxg@njupt.edu.cn
[2] Nanjing Public Security Bureau Science and Technology Information Department, Nanjing, China

Abstract. With the rapid development of machine learning, deep learning-based image defogging algorithms are receiving more and more attention from scholars compared to traditional image defogging method. A novel method for synthesizing high-quality haze images in fixed surveillance scenes is proposed, based on a dark channel-based approach for image fusion. The method also contributes a synthetic haze image dataset, which accurately corresponds to real-world scenarios, for use in deep learning network training and evaluation of defogging effects. To address the issue of chromatic aberration in the sky and local areas when using a deblurring network for defogging, the SKNet module in the Attention mechanism is integrated into DeblurGAN. The defogging network is trained using the synthetic haze image dataset, and is tested on various sets of synthetic and actual haze images, yielding improved results in metrics such as SSIM, PSNR, and MSE.

Keywords: Image defogging · Generative adversarial networks · Attention mechanism · Computer vision

1 Introduction

As computer vision technology advances, deep learning techniques have become increasingly prevalent in various outdoor scenarios, such as intelligent traffic [1–3] and autonomous driving [4–6]. Nonetheless, the majority of computer vision systems necessitate clear images as input. Unfortunately, the rapid industrialization of recent years has resulted in a high occurrence of foggy weather conditions, severely impacting aerospace [7, 8], automatic driving of vehicles [9], traffic monitoring [10, 11], and especially high-speed road monitoring [12]. Thus, research on image defogging methods holds significant practical importance.

In recent times, image defogging has garnered significant attention, with various single-image defogging methods being developed based on the atmospheric scattering model [13]. These methods mainly rely on different image priors, such as the dark channel priors [14] and color attenuation priors [15]. Mat Nor et al. used a per-pixel

H. Lu et al. (Eds.): ICIG 2023, LNCS 14356, pp. 323–334, 2023.
https://doi.org/10.1007/978-3-031-46308-2_27

alpha mixing method to estimate the transmission image by distinguishing between the light source and non-light source regions [16]. Liu et al. estimated the local aerial components of the image and then utilized a multiscale fusion approach to restore the fog-free image [17]. However, these methods may not be ideal when dealing with foggy images under complex imaging conditions.

Deep learning-based defogging methods have gained popularity as the leading approach to address the limitations of conventional algorithms. GAN(Generative Adversarial Network) is an unsupervised method that can be trained without supervised labeling, avoiding the expensive cost of labeling data and has received a lot of attention in image defogging methods [18–21], and these methods have achieved good defogging results. Kupyn et al. proposed DeblurGAN-v2 [22], a single image motion deblurring end-to-end GAN based on a relativistic conditional GAN with a double-scale discriminator. In terms of deblurring quality and efficiency, DeblurGAN-V2 performs competitively on several well used benchmarks. However, DeblurGAN-v2 has a relatively weak ability to capture features of local areas and sky, DeblurGAN-v2's defogging method still needs to be improved in terms of detailed texture, sky area chromatic aberration, and local artifact restoration.

To solve the above problems, this paper proposes an image defogging algorithm named Attention-DeblurGAN. (1) The FPN architecture of DeblurGAN-v2 is enhanced with the SKNet [23] module, which enables the network to selectively choose the appropriate convolutional kernel size. (2) Attention [24] mechanism is introduced to empower the network to automatically select the essential features for fusion mechanism. (3) A dataset with true values corresponding to haze images is established using a dark channel-based haze image fusion method, which can be utilized for image defogging.

The paper is structured as follows: Sect. 2 presents a defogging algorithm that employs Attention-DeblurGAN with an embedded SKNet module to address challenges such as poor defogging effects and chromatic aberration. Section 3 details the establishment of the dataset, training process and comparison of results. Finally, Sect. 4 summarizes the paper.

2 Methods

This study presents a novel image defogging algorithm named Attention-DeblurGAN, which addresses the challenges related to poor defogging effects and chromatic aberration. The proposed method incorporates the SKNet module into the FPN architecture of DeblurGAN-v2 to enhance the feature extraction process. Additionally, the Attention mechanism is utilized to enable the network to selectively choose the optimal convolutional kernel size and automatically select crucial features for fusion. The overall structure of our proposed algorithm is illustrated in Fig. 1. Overall workflow of the proposed Attention-DeblurGAN-Based Defogging Algorithm.

2.1 Attention Mechanism

Attention mechanisms have proven to be effective in various fields such as natural language processing (NLP) and computer vision (CV) since their introduction in 2015.

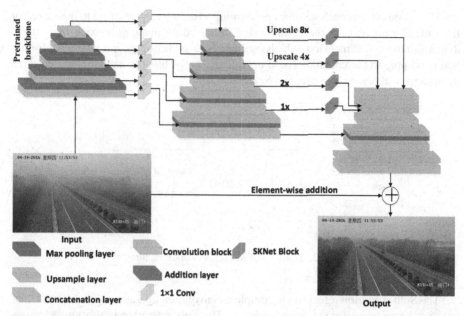

Fig. 1. Overall workflow of the proposed Attention-DeblurGAN-Based Defogging Algorithm

Typically, attention mechanisms can be classified into two types, namely, Spatial Attention [25] and Temporal Attention [26]. Spatial Attention is used to focus on the overall contour or a particular texture of an object, where the focus of attention varies depending on the application. On the other hand, Temporal Attention is employed to highlight the relevance of contextual information.

In the Encoder-Decoder model, the attention mechanism assigns weights to the output of the Encoder to determine the importance of each feature. These weights are then multiplied with the output of the Encoder to form the input of the Decoder. This allows the model to effectively extract key information from complex data, leading to improved performance with a minimal increase in parameters.

2.2 SKNet Module

The core idea of SKNet is to intelligently select channels for multi-scale feature information and guide which convolution kernel information to focus on for feature fusion. The input original feature map is convolved with several convolution kernels of different sizes (3×3, 5×5...) to obtain different feature maps U1, U2..., and then the information in these perceptual fields is fused to obtain a feature map U with the shape [C, H, W], (where C represents the channel, H represents the height, and W represents the width). Averaged along the dimensions H and W, respectively, a vector of dimension C $\times 1 \times 1$ was finally output to characterize the importance of each channel information in turn. The overall network structure is shown in Fig. 2. Diagram of SKNet network structure.

The proposed approach involves performing a linear transformation to map a vector from the C dimension to the Z dimension, followed by mapping it back from the Z dimension to the C dimension, which facilitates the extraction of dimensional information pertaining to the channel. These operations can be broadly categorized into three main steps, namely, Split, Fuse, and Select.

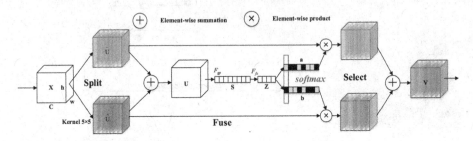

Fig. 2. Diagram of SKNet network structure

The Split operation refers to the complete convolution operation with different convolution kernel sizes for the input vector X. The Fuse operation is to sum the results $(\widetilde{U}_c, \widehat{U}_c)$ of the convolution of different convolution kernels ($3 \times 3, 5 \times 5$) to obtain (U) and then downscale and then upscale the operation, F_{gp} is the global average pooling operation, and F_{fc} is the fully connected layer of downscaling and then upscaling; the Select operation is to use several weight matrices a, b with weight sum 1 to b for different convolution kernels to obtain the final output vector V.

$$V_c = a_c \cdot \widetilde{U}_c + b_c \cdot \widehat{U}_c, a_c + b_c = 1 \tag{1}$$

DeblurGAN-v2 can be viewed as an Encoder-Decoder architecture that utilizes the FPN architecture. Specifically, the bottom-up extraction of features at different scales in DeblurGAN-v2 is equivalent to the encoding operation of the Encoder, while the top-down feature reconstruction is equivalent to the decoding operation of the Decoder. The integration of SKNet in the Decoder can potentially enhance the selection of features and filter out unnecessary perceptual fields, thereby facilitating the recovery of detailed textures. In contrast, the use of different channel selection attention in DeblurGAN-v2 is effective in limiting the chromatic aberration effect that is inherent in generative adversarial networks. This attention mechanism is particularly helpful for color recovery of the sky region and the elimination of artifacts.

The proposed method involves integrating the SKNet module into the FPN architecture of DeblurGAN-v2, which enables the intelligent selection of appropriate feature maps for each of the four branches. This is done after the top-down path and before feature fusion, ensuring the effectiveness of the fused features. The SKNet module defaults to two sizes of convolutional kernels (i.e., $3 \times 3, 5 \times 5$).

3 Experiments

3.1 Establishment of Haze Image Dataset

Since the traditional method of binocular vision estimation requires the binocular camera to capture image data and the participation of camera internal parameters and external camera parameters in the calculation process of depth map estimation, this paper uses a haze image fusion method based on a dark channel from the relatively fixed scene monitoring camera. This method only requires the same camera to have fog and fog-free image data at different times. The main steps are shown in Fig. 3. Flowchart of the dark channel-based haze image fusion method.

Based on the surveillance video frame of Jiangsu Tongqi Expressway, we took 10 different degrees of haze images as templates for each scene in 6 scenes, and then randomly selected a total of 285 clear images from 6 scenes. The template method, and then set the corrected extinction coefficient alpha to 0.2,0.3,0.4, respectively, to synthesize a haze image data set with 855 clear images and haze images.

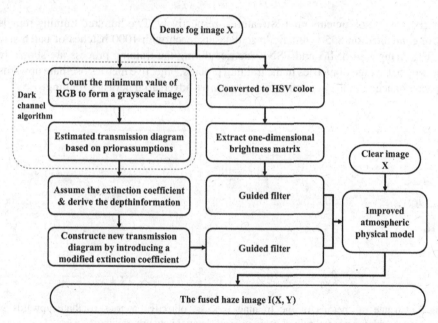

Fig. 3. Flowchart of the dark channel-based haze image fusion method

The effect of some synthetic haze images is shown in the Fig. 4. Examples of original images and fogged images in the data set.

3.2 Training Process

In this paper, SKNet is embedded in the PFN architecture of DeblurGAN-v2, and Split operations are performed with 3×3 and 5×5 convolutional kernels to train attention

Fig. 4. Examples of original images and fogged images in the data set

matrix weight coefficients on 128 features, respectively. Two hundred training rounds were conducted on 855 synthetic haze datasets, each with 1000 batches of batch size 8. The changes in SSIM and PSNR metrics during the training process are shown in the Fig. 5. Change of metrics in the training process, objective metrics oscillate upwards in accordance with the general rule of generative adversarial network training.

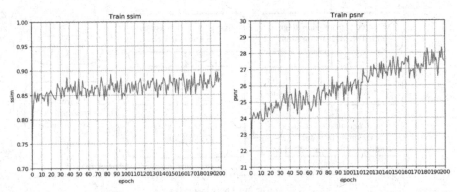

Fig. 5. Change of metrics in the training process, objective metrics oscillate upwards in accordance with the general rule of generative adversarial network training

As can be seen from Fig. 6 below, verification is carried out once every 100 batches of training, and SSIM and PSNR indexes are gradually improved during the verification process.

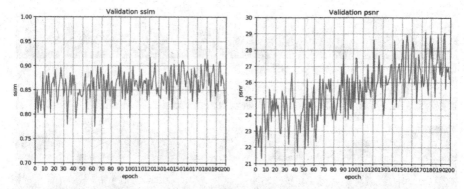

Fig. 6. Variation of validation metrics, objective metrics oscillate upwards in accordance with the general rule of generative adversarial network training

3.3 Comparison of Results

Firstly, we compared four different defogging methods on a test set consisting of 171 synthetic haze images: the classical dark channel priori defogging method (DCP), Deblur-Gan-v1, Deblur-Gan-v2, and Attention-Deblur-Gan-v2. To evaluate their effectiveness, we measured their average Structural Similarity (SSIM, reflects the similarity between the two images, the value range is [0, 1], the higher the value means the higher the similarity), Peak Signal to Noise Ratio (PSNR, measures image distortion and noise levels as a whole, with higher values of PSNR indicating less distortion), and Mean Square Error (MSE, commonly used in pixel-level image quality assessment) scores. Additionally, we invited 32 observers to evaluate the defogging results subjectively, scoring them on a scale from 1–5 (poor defogging, fair defogging, good defogging) and obtaining a subjective Mean Opinion Score (MOS) through data analysis.

Table 1. Comparison table of defogging quality assessment

Defogging method	DCP	Deblur-Gan-v1	Deblur-Gan-v2	Attention-Deblur-Gan-v2
SSIM	0.482	0.735	0.777	0.804
MSE	1523.608	269.984	182.513	162.238
PSNR	16.508	24.181	25.896	26.061
MOS	1.524	2.499	4.419	4.444

As can be seen from Table 1, both subjective and objective indexes of the DeblurGAN-v2 method were improved after the improvement. The effect plots of the three defogging methods are summarized to yield Fig. 7, where from left to right are clear image (ground truth), image to be defogged (fused haze image), Deblur-GAN-v2-based defogging effect, DeblurGAN-based defogging effect, and Attention-DeblurGAN-based defogging effect.

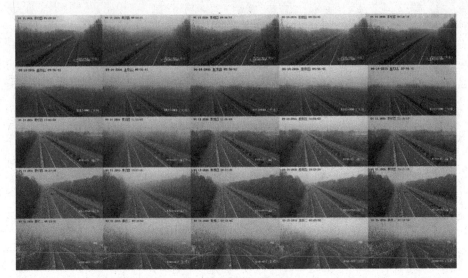

Fig. 7. Comparison graph of the defogging effect, from making to the right are: clear image (ground truth), synthetic haze image, DeblurGAN-v2 defogging method, DeblurGAN-v1 defogging method, Attention-DeblurGAN defogging method

From Fig. 7 above, it can be found that the DeblurGAN-v2-based defogging method after the introduction of the SKNet module does not over-correct the chromatic aberrations in the sky region and the local tree colors, and is closer to Ground Truth in terms of color, thus its test average structural similarity SSIM has been slightly improved.

Combined with Table 1 and Fig. 7, the test set data show that with the introduction of SKNet based on DeblurGAN-v2, both the objective evaluation metrics and subjective evaluation scores improved compared to the DeblurGAN-v2 defogging method, with the average SSIM improving by 3.47%, MSE decreasing by 11.1%, average PSNR improving by 0.165 dB, and subjective evaluation score slightly improved from 4.419 to 4.444.This shows that introducing SKNet on top of DeblurGAN-v2 can better limit the local color reproduction, making this part neither as insensitive to defogging as the DeblurGAN-v1 defogging method nor as overcorrection as the DeblurGAN-v2 defogging method.

To verify the defogging performance of the trained model on real haze data, we tested the Attention-DeblurGAN-Based defogging method on real haze images of the Tongqi Expressway, and the test results are shown in the Fig. 8.

Compared with the test results of the DeblurGAN-v2 method for haze removal, the average SSIM of the Attention-DeblurGAN-Based defogging method improved from 0.792 to 0.816, the average PSNR decreased slightly from 26.289 to 26.195, and the MSE decreased slightly from 163.570 to 157.706. The trend of each index is consistent with our performance on the synthetic haze dataset of Tongqi Expressway, and the haze removal effect does not appear to be good on the synthetic dataset but poor on the real haze image data, which verifies the authenticity and validity of the haze data synthesized by our dark channel-based haze image fusion method from another aspect.

Fig. 8. Improved Attention-DeblurGAN real haze image defogging effect, from left to right: clear image approximate true value, real haze image & Attention-DeblurGAN defogging effect.

In addition, we did tests using the Attention-DeblurGAN method on some images of the haze image dataset synthesized from Cityscape data[27], and the defogging effect is shown in the Fig. 9.

Compared with the previous DeblurGAN-v2 defogging method, it can be found that after the introduction of the Attention mechanism, the color aberration phenomenon is significantly suppressed, and the "green variation" of the road surface is improved, the average SSIM is improved from 0.722 to 0.743, the average PSNR is improved from 27.524 to 27.560, and the MSE is reduced from 27.524 to 127.208. The objective indexes were all improved and combined with our previous evaluation of the haze removal effect in synthetic and real haze images, and we again verified the conclusion that the introduction of the Attention mechanism could improve the haze removal effect by effectively suppressing the chromatic aberration variation.

Fig. 9. Defogging effect of Attention-DeblurGAN on Cityscape haze data

4 Conclusion

To further improve the detail restoration of image defogging and to solve the problems of color difference in the sky and "excessive vividness" in local area restoration, this chapter introduces the SKNet module in the Attention mechanism based on the DeblurGAN-v2 defogging method to intelligently guide the FPN architecture to choose the appropriate convolutional kernel size for convolutional operations. The unified test results of the three methods on the synthetic haze image test set show that the DeblurGAN-v2-based defogging method with the introduction of the SKNet module is better in the subjective and objective evaluation indexes such as SSIM, PSNR, MSE, MOS, etc., and better balances the color difference after local defogging reduction, making the sky part and local area more similar to the real scene after defogging. The method proposed can be used to improve the quality of images affected by fog, and has potential applications in various domains such as surveillance, autonomous driving, and aerial photography.

References

1. Liu, S., Huang, S., Xu, X., Lloret, J., Muhammad, K.: Efficient visual tracking based on fuzzy inference for intelligent transportation systems. IEEE Trans. Intell. Trans. Syst. (2023)
2. Mangla, C., Rani, S., Herencsar, N.: A misbehavior detection framework for cooperative intelligent transport systems. ISA Trans. **132**, 52–60 (2023)

3. Hijji, M., et al.: 6G connected vehicle framework to support intelligent road maintenance using deep learning data fusion. IEEE Trans. Intell. Trans. Syst/ (2023)

4. Wang, L., et al.: SAT-GCN: Self-attention graph convolutional network-based 3D object detection for autonomous driving. Knowl.-Based Syst..-Based Syst. **259**, 110080 (2023)

5. Zhao, C., Song, A., Zhu, Y., Jiang, S., Liao, F., Du, Y.: Data-driven indoor positioning correction for infrastructure-enabled autonomous driving systems: A lifelong framework. IEEE Trans. Intell. Trans. Syst. (2023)

6. Alaba, S.Y., Ball, J.E.: Deep learning-based Image 3D object detection for autonomous driving. IEEE Sensors J. (2023)

7. Kulkarni, R., Jenamani, R.K., Pithani, P., Konwar, M., Nigam, N., Ghude, S.D.: Loss to aviation economy due to winter fog in New Delhi during the winter of 2011–2016. Atmosphere **10**, 198 (2019)

8. Huang, H., Chen, C.: Climatological aspects of dense fog at Urumqi Diwopu International Airport and its impacts on flight on-time performance. Nat. Hazards **81**, 1091–1106 (2016)

9. Saffarian, M., Happee, R., de Winter, J.: Why do drivers maintain short headways in fog? A driving-simulator study evaluating feeling of risk and lateral control during automated and manual car following. Ergonomics **55**, 971–985 (2012)

10. Liang, C.-W., Chang, C.-C., Liang, J.-J.: The impacts of air quality and secondary organic aerosols formation on traffic accidents in heavy fog–haze weather, Heliyon (2023)

11. Peng, Y., Abdel-Aty, M., Lee, J., Zou, Y.: Analysis of the impact of fog-related reduced visibility on traffic parameters. J. Trans. Eng. Part A: Syst. **144**, 04017077 (2018)

12. Sitao, H., Xuemei, W., Chuchu, D., Jing, Z.: Influence mechanism of mass fog on highway traffic safety. In: Proceedings 2011 International Conference on Transportation, Mechanical, and Electrical Engineering (TMEE), pp. 791–794. IEEE (2011)

13. He, S., Chen, Z., Wang, F., Wang, M.: Integrated image defogging network based on improved atmospheric scattering model and attention feature fusion. Earth Sci Inform. **14**, 2037–2048 (2021)

14. Dong, T., Zhao, G., Wu, J., Ye, Y., Shen, Y.: Efficient traffic video dehazing using adaptive dark channel prior and spatial-temporal correlations. Sensors. **19**, 1593 (2019)

15. Kuanar, S., Mahapatra, D., Bilas, M., Rao, K.R.: Multi-path dilated convolution network for haze and glow removal in nighttime images. Vis. Comput.Comput. **38**, 1121–1134 (2022)

16. Mat Nor, M.N., Rupenthal, I.D., Green, C.R., Acosta, M.L.: Differential action of connexin hemichannel and pannexin channel therapeutics for potential treatment of retinal diseases. Int. J. Mol. Sci. **22**, 1755 (2021)

17. Liu, X., Liu, C., Lan, H., Xie, L.: Dehaze enhancement algorithm based on retinex theory for aerial images combined with dark channel. Open Access Library J. **7** (2020)

18. Wu, M., Li, B.: Single image dehazing based on generative adversarial networks. In: Intelligent Computing Theories and Application: 18th International Conference, ICIC 2022, Xi'an, China, 7–11 August 2022, Proceedings, Part II, pp. 460–469. Springer (2022). https://doi.org/10.1007/978-3-031-13829-4_40

19. Ma, D., Fang, H., Wang, N., Zheng, H., Dong, J., Hu, H.: Automatic defogging, deblurring, and real-time segmentation system for sewer pipeline defects. Autom. Constr. **144**, 104595 (2022)

20. Li, Y., Cheng, J., Li, Z., Pan, Q., Zeng, R., Tian, T.: Single image defogging method based on improved generative adversarial network. In: 2022 IEEE Asia-Pacific Conference on Image Processing, Electronics and Computers (IPEC), pp. 781–787. IEEE (2022)

21. Deqiang, C., Yangyang, Y., Qiqi, K., Jinyang, X.: A generative adversarial network incorporating dark channel prior loss used for single image defogging. Opto-Elect. Eng. **49**, 210448–210451 (2022)

22. Kupyn, O., Martyniuk, T., Wu, J., Wang, Z.: Deblurgan-v2: Deblurring (orders-of-magnitude) faster and better. In: Proceedings of the IEEE/CVF International Conference on Computer Vision, pp. 8878–8887 (2019)

23. Li, X., Wang, W., Hu, X., Yang, J.: Selective kernel networks. In: Proceedings of the IEEE/CVF Conference on Computer Vision and Pattern Recognition, pp. 510–519 (2019)

24. Vaswani, A., et al.: Attention is all you need. In: Advances in Neural Information Processing Systems 30 (2017)

25. Laskar, Z., Kannala, J.: Context aware query image representation for particular object retrieval. In: Sharma, P., Bianchi, F.M. (eds.) SCIA 2017. LNCS, vol. 10270, pp. 88–99. Springer, Cham (2017). https://doi.org/10.1007/978-3-319-59129-2_8

26. Pei, W., Baltrusaitis, T., Tax, D.M., Morency, L.-P.: Temporal attention-gated model for robust sequence classification. In: Proceedings of the IEEE Conference on Computer Vision and Pattern Recognition, pp. 6730–6739 (2017)

27. Cordts, M., et al.: The cityscapes dataset. In: CVPR Workshop on the Future of Datasets in Vision. sn (2015)

Multi-modal Context-Aware Network for Scene Graph Generation

Junjie Ye, Bing-Kun Bao, and Zhiyi Tan[✉]

School of Telecommunications and Information Engineering, Nanjing University of
Posts and Telecommunications, Nanjing, China
tzy@njupt.edu.cn

Abstract. Scene graphs are structured represetations of the visual scene,
composed of relationship triplets, i.e., <subject, predicate, object>.
Recently, existing studies tend to promote the performance of scene graph
generation (SGG) models with the help of knowledge graphs and graph
neural networks (GNNs). However, they neither comprehensively consider
the correlations between predicates in the knowledge graph, nor explore
an efficient message-passing mechanism to sufficiently propagate different
modal messages. Therefore, they can hardly detect informative predicates.
In this work, we propose a novel **Multi-Modal Context-Aware Network**
(**MMCA-Net**) for SGG, which alleviates the above problems from two
aspects: (1) We construct multi-hop connections in the knowledge graph
through Graph Transformer Layers, aiming to comprehensively consider
the high-order graph-structured correlations between predicate classes. (2)
We devise a cross-modal graph attention mechanism to uncover the cross-
modal context between the scene and knowledge graph. By aggregating
the collected cross-modal context, the representations of nodes can be discriminatory enough to differentiate relationships. Extensive experiments
on the Visual Genome dataset demonstrate that the proposed MMCA-Net
is of superior promotion compared with previous methods.

Keywords: Scene Graph Generation · Knowledge Graph · Graph
Neural Networks

1 Introduction

Scene graph generation, which aims to generate a structured description for an
input image, is proposed to achieve a comprehensive understanding of visual
semantics. The structured scene usually consists of nodes that represent the objects
in the image and edges that represent the relationships between objects.

Recently, numerous methods [1,2,7,16,17] concentrate on promoting the SGG
models' performance by incorporating adequate prior knowledge. However, there
are two main limitations causing the performance drop of their approaches. Firstly,
a series of works [2,7] introduce the language prior (e.g., word embeddings) and statistical regularity [1,17] into the SGG task, without carefully considering the correlations between language entities. So, there appears the work [16] which combines

H. Lu et al. (Eds.): ICIG 2023, LNCS 14356, pp. 335–347, 2023.
https://doi.org/10.1007/978-3-031-46308-2_28

the language entities and the correlations between them as knowledge graph. However, it ignores the high-order structured information in the knowledge graph. The traditional one-hop connected structure of the graph restricts nodes only to aggregate messages from the first-hop neighbors, which results in the SGG model insufficiently considering the high-order correlations between nodes in the knowledge graph. As shown in Fig. 1(a), the trivial predicate "on" cannot directly aggregate the message of the informative predicate "standing on" in the knowledge graph, which leads to the model underestimating the correlation between them and hardly generalizing from "on" to "standing on". Secondly, the language prior based works [2,7,16] fail to comprehensively consider the modality propagation and fusion process in the SGG model. Typically, most of them just concatenate the vision and the language representations. To propagate cross-modal node messages, [16] designs a bridging mechanism that bridges an entity in the scene graph to the most relevant one in the knowledge graph. This mechanism still fails to sufficiently discover the cross-modal messages between the scene and knowledge graph. As shown in Fig. 1(a), since the relationship <car on road> may occur 1000 times more than <car parked on road>, the bridging mechanism could be highly biased towards the trivial predicate "on" in the knowledge graph. When propagating messages, the mechanism enables the predicate node <car1, street> in the scene graph to aggregate the message of "on" in the knowledge graph, but is incapable of exploring the textual context of predicates which benefits the prediction of informative predicates (e.g., "parked on").

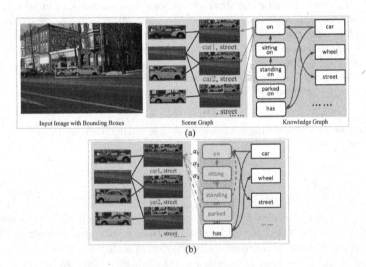

Fig. 1. (a) Illustration of the method in [16]. (b) Illustration of our ideas. (Color figure online)

Inspired by the above observations, we take action from two aspects to alleviate the above limitations. On the one hand, we adopt a multi-hop connections constructor, Graph Transformer Layers (GTran) [15], to model the high-order multi-hop connections between predicate nodes in the knowledge graph. As shown in Fig. 1(b), with the built 2-hop connections (red arrow), our model can comprehensively capture the correlations between predicate classes and preserve high-order graph-structured information. On the other hand, we design a Cross-modal Graph Attention module (CGA) to discover the cross-modal context of different modal graphs. With a visual node in the scene graph as a query, CGA first finds the potentially relevant textual nodes in the knowledge graph and then fuses these textual messages as the cross-modal context of the query node. As depicted in Fig. 1(b), the textual context (green region) of the visual predicate node <car1, street> is constructed via the attention coefficients generated by a cross-modal attention mechanism. Analogously, per node in the knowledge graph can gain access to relevant visual-modal context, ensuring sufficient cross-modality fusion. By aggregating the collected cross-modal context, the representations of predicate nodes can be discriminatory enough, which benefits predicting informative relationships.

To this end, we propose a novel scene graph generation model, **Multi-Modal Context-Aware Network (MMCA-Net)**, which generates scene graphs through three stages: (1) graph initializing, (2) message passing, (3) message aggregating. In the first stage, our model builds on Faster-RCNN [8] to initialize the scene graph. Meanwhile, GTran is adopted to model the multi-hop connections for the knowledge graph. In the second stage, the proposed CGAs extract the cross-modal context between nodes of different modalities. At the same time, the node messages flow along the initialized edges in the scene graph and knowledge graph to form the self-modal context of graph nodes. In the last stage, we adopt Gated Recurrent Units (GRU) to aggregate the collected cross- and self-modal context and enhance the node representations. The whole framework is optimized end-to-end.

Our contributions can be summarized as follows:

(1) We propose a new scene graph generation model, MMCA-Net, which achieves superior performance in detecting informative relationships that possess more semantics by sufficiently exploring the structure of the knowledge graph and the cross-modal context of different modalities.
(2) We adopt Graph Transformer Layers (GTran) to model the multi-hop connections in the knowledge graph, which can catch the high-order graph-structured information by exploiting the multi-hop connections between nodes in the knowledge graph.
(3) We design a Cross-modal Graph Attention module (CGA), which can extract the cross-modal context of each node. Consequently, by fusing the collected cross-modal context, the representations of nodes can be discriminatory enough to promote the prediction of relationships.

2   Related Work

Scene Graph Generation. Over the past few years, numerous researchers attempt to advance the Scene graph generation task by adopting different ways to encode the contextual information, ranging from early recurrent neural networks [12,17] to novel graph neural networks [7,9,16].

The RNN-based models are able to extract the visual context around objects and infer the interactions between them. Xu *et al.* [12] utilize a node GRU and edge GRU to aggregate the local and global visual context and iteratively update the node and edge representations in the scene graph. Zellers *et al.* [17] adopt two independent bi-LSTMs to respectively encode the object context and edge context and then use them to inform the local predictors.

With the development of GNNs, a lot of approaches utilize GNNs to propagate visual messages distilled from the image. To incorporate the language prior and global context, Qi *et al.* [7] introduce a semantic transformation module to capture the semantic embedded feature and a graph self-attention module to embed a joint graph representation. Sharifzadeh *et al.* [9] take the language prior as inductive bias by injecting them into visual features and adopt a transformer-based graph neural network to extract global context. Recently, Zareian *et al.* [16] introduce the knowledge graph into SGG task and design a bridging mechanism to propagate messages between scene graph and knowledge graph.

Prior Knowledge. Prior knowledge serves a crucial role in generating a more accurate scene graph. There are several types of prior knowledge adopted by previous works, such as language prior [2], statistical prior [1,17] from the dataset, and knowledge graph [16] from the external knowledge base [5,10]. Cui *et al.* [2] build a semantic graph through language priors to model the semantic correlations across objects and use a diffusion network to aggregate contextual information. Meanwhile, Zellers *et al.* [17] introduces a strong frequency-based model FREQ that demonstrates the importance of statistical co-occurrences. Chen *et al.* [1] explicitly incorporates statistical correlations into scene graphs to regularize the visual features. The knowledge graph-based work [16] is the most representative of previous work because the knowledge graph can not only describe the prior knowledge structurally but also possess greater interpretability.

Summary. Unlike the previous methods, we comprehensively consider the structural information of the knowledge graph by exploring hierarchical node connections (multi-hop connection) and design a cross-modal attention mechanism to extract the context between different modalities, thereby capturing the messages of informative predicates.

3 Proposed Method

In this section, we will present the proposed MMCA-Net, as depicted in Fig. 2.

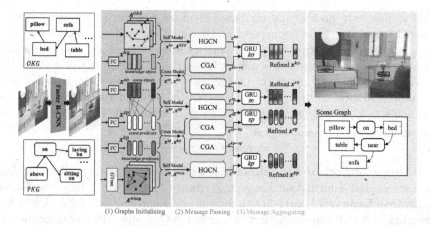

(1) Graphs Initializing   (2) Message Passing   (3) Message Aggregating

Fig. 2. The framework of MMCA-Net. The whole model takes the raw image, predicate knowledge graph (PKG), and object knowledge graph (OKG) as inputs. It contains three stages: graphs initialization, message passing, and message aggregating.

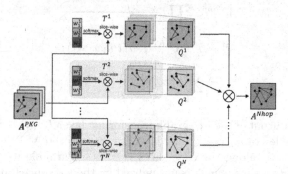

Fig. 3. Illustration of the stacked graph transformer layers used to generate the $Nhop$ connected PKG (A^{Nhop}). This figure only shows the case where the number of heads is 1.

3.1 Graphs Initializing

Scene Graph: Given an image I, the scene graph is initialized by the widely used Faster R-CNN detector [8]. The detector outputs the bounding box of the i-th object and the ROI feature of the object can be denoted as $\mathbf{x}_i^{so}$ (so is short for scene object). Besides, the feature of the k-th predicate node $v_k^p \in \mathcal{V}^p$ is the ROI feature of the union box of the i-th and j-th object (sp is short for scene predicate). Then, two linear layers are used to map features to $\mathbb{R}^{1 \times d}$. Similar to previous works [9,16,17], we set the edges between nodes in the scene graph as (subject $v_i^o \rightarrow$ predicate $v_k^p \rightarrow$ object v_j^o).

Knowledge Graph: There are two heterogeneous knowledge graphs in our model, respectively object knowledge graph $OKG(\mathcal{V}^o, \mathcal{E}, \mathcal{T}^{e,o})$ composed of object nodes from object label set $\mathbb{C}^o$ and predicate knowledge graph $PKG(\mathcal{V}^p, \mathcal{E}, \mathcal{T}^{e,p})$ composed of predicate nodes from predicate label set $\mathbb{C}^p$. Each node feature $\mathbf{x}_i^*$ is achieved by mapping the corresponding GloVe [6] embeddings of class labels to $\mathbb{R}^{1 \times d}$, where $* \in \{ko, kp\}$ (ko, kp is short for knowledge object and predicate). The structure of OKG and PKG mainly follow [16] (collect from ConceptNet [10] and WordNet [5]). Additionally, we calculate the semantic similarity between node embeddings to measure the relevance between the i-th and j-th entity, which can be denoted as $s_{ij}^* = \mathbf{x}_i^* \cdot (\mathbf{x}_j^*)^\mathsf{T} / (\|\mathbf{x}_i^*\|_2 \times \|\mathbf{x}_j^*\|_2)$. At last, the heterogeneous adjacency matrices can be denoted as $\mathbf{A}^{OKG} \in \mathbb{R}^{|\mathbb{C}^o| \times |\mathbb{C}^o| \times q}$ and $\mathbf{A}^{PKG} \in \mathbb{R}^{|\mathbb{C}^p| \times |\mathbb{C}^p| \times l}$, where $q = |\mathcal{T}^{e,o}|$ and $l = |\mathcal{T}^{e,b}|$ represent the number of edge types.

Multi-hop Connection Modeling: In order to comprehensively utilize the high-order structured information between predicate classes, we deploy the Graph Transformer Layers (GTran) [15] to build the multi-hop connected PKG, which is shown in Fig. 3. With the adjacency matrix of PKG as input, the $Nhop$ connected adjacency matrix $A^{Nhop} \in \mathbb{R}^{|\mathbb{C}^p| \times |\mathbb{C}^p|}$ can be obtained by matrix multiplication of the outputs of N graph transformer layers:

$$A^{Nhop} = \prod_{i=1}^{N} Q^i$$

$$Q^i = T^i(\mathbf{A}^{PKG}; softmax(\mathbf{w}^i)) \tag{1}$$

$$= \sum_{t=1}^{l} w_t^i \times A_t^{PKG}$$

where Q^i is the output of the i-th graph transformer layer T^i, $\mathbf{w}^i \in \mathbb{R}^{1 \times l}$ is a learnable vector. Single graph transformer layer compresses the $\mathbf{A}^{PKG} \in \mathbb{R}^{|\mathbb{C}^p| \times |\mathbb{C}^p| \times l}$ to $Q^i \in \mathbb{R}^{|\mathbb{C}^p| \times |\mathbb{C}^p|}$ along the edge slices l. w_t^i is a learnable weight parameter assigned to the t-th slice, which is normalized by the $softmax$ function and represents the importance of the t-th edge type. Then, we adopt the multi-head mechanism to learn different graph structures, i.e., $\mathbf{A}^{Nhop} = stack(A_1^{Nhop}, \ldots, A_L^{Nhop})$. $\mathbf{A}^{Nhop} \in \mathbb{R}^{|\mathbb{C}^p| \times |\mathbb{C}^p| \times L}$ represents the multi-hop adjacency matrix of PKG and L means the number of heads.

3.2 Message Passing

In this section, we will describe the message passing stage in Fig. 2.

Cross-modal Context Extraction: The Cross-modal Graph Attention module (CGA) is designed to propagate cross-modal information between different modal graphs. Given graphs of two different modalities, we mark one as the source modality and the other as the target modality. Then, with the node features of different modalities as inputs of the CGA, the cross-modal context $\mathbf{c}_i^{src \leftarrow tgt} \in \mathbb{R}^{1 \times d}$ of the i-th source modality node can be simplified to:

$$\mathbf{c}_i^{src \leftarrow tgt} = CGA(\mathbf{x}_i^{src}, \mathbf{X}^{tgt}) \tag{2}$$

where $\mathbf{x}_i^{src} \in \mathbb{R}^{1 \times d}$ is the i-th node feature of the source modality; $\mathbf{X}^{tgt} \in \mathbb{R}^{N \times d}$ is · the feature matrix of the target modality and N is the number of nodes in target modality graph.

Concretely, with the i-th source modality node as a query, CGA adaptively attends to the target modality nodes and gets the attention vector:

$$
\begin{cases}
\boldsymbol{\alpha}_i^{src \leftarrow tgt} = [\alpha_{i1}^{src \leftarrow tgt}, \alpha_{i2}^{src \leftarrow tgt}, ..., \alpha_{iN}^{src \leftarrow tgt}] \\
\alpha_{ij}^{src \leftarrow tgt} = \dfrac{exp(\sigma(\mathbf{q} \cdot (\mathbf{x}_i^{src} || \mathbf{x}_j^{tgt})^\mathsf{T}))}{\sum_{k=1}^{N} exp(\sigma(\mathbf{q} \cdot (\mathbf{x}_i^{src} || \mathbf{x}_k^{tgt})^\mathsf{T}))}
\end{cases}
\tag{3}
$$

where σ is the LeakyRelu activation function; $\mathbf{q} \in \mathbb{R}^{1 \times 2d}$ is a learnable vector. The superscript $src \leftarrow tgt$ denotes that the source modality node queries the target modality to get the attentive vector $\boldsymbol{\alpha}_i^{src \leftarrow tgt} \in \mathbb{R}^{1 \times N}$. Then, the output of CGA is the cross-modal context of the i-th source node and can be formulated by the weighted sum of the target node features:

$$
\mathbf{c}_i^{src \leftarrow tgt} = \sum_{j=1}^{N} \alpha_{ij}^{src \leftarrow tgt} \times \mathbf{x}_j^{tgt} = \boldsymbol{\alpha}_i^{src \leftarrow tgt} \cdot \mathbf{X}^{tgt}
\tag{4}
$$

We utilize four CGA modules to sufficiently extract the cross-modal context of each node type in the OKG, PKG, and scene graph. The cross-modal context corresponding to the knowledge object can be expressed as $\mathbf{c}^{ko \leftarrow so} = CGA(\mathbf{x}^{ko}, \mathbf{X}^{so})$ and the cross-modal context of the knowledge predicate $\mathbf{c}^{kp \leftarrow sp}$, the scene object $\mathbf{c}^{so \leftarrow ko}$, the scene predicate $\mathbf{c}^{so \leftarrow ko}$ are obtained in the same way.

Self-modal Context Extraction: Besides the cross-modal message extraction, we utilize the traditional heterogeneous graph convolution network to extract the self-modal context of a node in the graph. A heterogeneous graph can be defined as $\mathcal{G}(\mathcal{V}, \mathcal{E}, \mathcal{T}^e)$, where $\mathcal{V}$ and $\mathcal{E}$ respectively represent the node and edge set of the graph, $\mathcal{T}^e$ represent the set of edge types. Then, by collecting messages from the neighborhood, the self-modal context $\mathbf{c}_i \in \mathcal{R}^{1 \times d}$ of the i-th node in the graph can be formulated as:

$$
\begin{aligned}
\mathbf{c}_i &= HGCN(\mathcal{V}, \mathcal{N}_i; \mathbf{W}) \\
&= \Phi(\,||_{k \in \mathcal{T}^e} (\sum_{j \in \mathcal{N}_i} e_{ij}^k \times \phi(\mathbf{x}_j)))
\end{aligned}
\tag{5}
$$

where $\mathcal{N}_i$ is the neighborhood of the i-th node, $\mathbf{W}$ is the learnable weight matrix. $\mathbf{x}_j \in \mathcal{R}^{1 \times d}$ is the feature of node $j \in \mathcal{V}$. $e_{ij}^k \in \mathcal{E}$ is the weight of the k-th type edge from the j-th to i-th node. $\phi(\cdot)$ and $\Phi(\cdot)$ are multi-layer perceptrons composed of two linear layers and a ReLU activation function.

With HGCNs, the self-modal context of each node type in the OKG, PKG, and scene graph can be denoted as $\mathbf{c}^{ko}$, $\mathbf{c}^{kp}$ and $\mathbf{c}^{so}$, $\mathbf{c}^{sp}$. It is worth noting that with the multi-hop structure (adjacency matrix is $\mathbf{A}^{Nhop}$ at the end of Sect. 3.1), predicate nodes in the PKG can possess a wider neighborhood from 1-hop to N-hop, which enables the model to more comprehensively consider the correlations between predicates.

3.3   Message Aggregating and Training

After the message passing stage, we get the (cross-modal, self-modal) context pair with respect to each node type, i.e., $sp : (c^{sp\leftarrow kp}, c^{sp})$, $so : (c^{so\leftarrow ko}, c^{so})$, $kp : (c^{kp\leftarrow sp}, c^{kp})$, $ko : (c^{ko\leftarrow so}, c^{ko})$. In the aggregating stage, four independent Gated Recurrent Units (GRUs) are used to update the node representations by aggregating the related context pairs, which are defined as:

$$\begin{cases} z^{\triangle} = \sigma(W_z^{\triangle} c^{\triangle\leftarrow} + U_z^{\triangle} c^{\triangle}) \\ r^{\triangle} = \sigma(W_r^{\triangle} c^{\triangle\leftarrow} + U_r^{\triangle} c^{\triangle}) \\ h^{\triangle} = tanh[W_h^{\triangle}(c^{\triangle\leftarrow} + c^{\triangle}) + U_h^{\triangle}(r^{\triangle} \odot x^{\triangle})] \\ x^{\triangle} \Leftarrow (1 - z^{\triangle}) \odot x^{\triangle} + z^{\triangle} \odot h^{\triangle} \end{cases} \tag{6}$$

where $\triangle \in \{sp, so, kp, ko\}$; $c^{\triangle\leftarrow}$ and $c^{\triangle}$ respectively represents the cross-modal context and self-modal context of node type $\triangle$; $W^{\triangle}$ and $U^{\triangle}$ are trainable matrices shared across the same node type; $\odot$ means Hadamard Product and $\Leftarrow$ stands for updating node representations.

After iteratively updating node representations for T times, the classification scores of objects and predicates can be defined as:

$$y_{ij}^{so} = \frac{exp[(\psi^{so}(x_i^{so})^{\top} \psi^{ko}(x_j^{ko})]}{\sum_k exp[(\psi^{so}(x_i^{so})^{\top} \psi^{kp}(x_k^{ko})]} \tag{7}$$

$$y_{ij}^{sp} = \frac{exp[(\psi^{sp}(x_i^{sp})^{\top} \psi^{kp}(x_j^{kp})]}{\sum_k exp[(\psi^{sp}(x_i^{sp})^{\top} \psi^{kp}(x_k^{kp})]} \tag{8}$$

where $\psi^{\triangle}$ are MLPs for different node types; y_{ij}^{so} denotes the probability that the i-th scene object is predicted to be the j-th class and y_{ij}^{sp} has the same meaning for the scene predicate.

We follow the training stage mentioned in [16] which utilizes the cross-entropy loss for object classification and a cross-entropy loss controlled by predicate frequency for predicate classification, which can be defined as:

$$L_i^{obj} = -log(y_{ij}^{so}) \tag{9}$$

$$L_i^{pred} = -\frac{1 - \beta}{1 - \beta^{n_k}} log(y_{ik}^{sp}) \tag{10}$$

where n_k is the number of training samples of the k-th predicate class. β is a hyper-parameter. The total loss L^{total} can be formulated as $L^{total} = L^{obj} + L^{pred}$.

4   Experiments

We conduct extensive experiments on the Visual Genome [3] benchmark to evaluate our method.

4.1 Dataset and Knowledge Graph

Visual Genome [3] consists of 108,077 images with average annotations of 38 objects and 22 relationships per image. Following previous works [1,9,16,17], we utilize a cleaned version [12] of VG, known as VG150. In order to avoid noisy labels, Xu *et al.* [12] manually filter the VG dataset and reserve the most frequent 150 object classes and 50 predicate classes.

Predicate and Object Knowledge Graph respectively contain 50 predicate nodes and 150 object nodes according to VG150. The structure of the knowledge graph is constructed from two aspects: (1) edges between classes extracted from the dataset [3] and knowledge base [5,10] (refer to [16] for details), (2) semantic correlations between classes computed by word embeddings. Finally, the number of edge types in the predicate knowledge graph is equal to 3, i.e., $l = 3$ for l in $A^{PKG} \in \mathbb{R}^{|\mathbb{C}^p| \times |\mathbb{C}^p| \times l}$. The number of edge types in the object knowledge graph is equal to 5, i.e., $q = 5$ for q in $A^{OKG} \in \mathbb{R}^{|\mathbb{C}^o| \times |\mathbb{C}^o| \times q}$.

4.2 Implementation Details

We set the dimension of node representations to 1024 (i.e., $d = 1024$), and the iteration step T to 3. The number of heads L and hops N in $A^{Nhop} \in \mathbb{R}^{|\mathbb{C}^p| \times |\mathbb{C}^p| \times L}$ is set to 3 and 2 (the best we have found experimentally). Following [16], β in Eqn. (15) is set to 0.999. The Faster R-CNN that we employ is based on the VGG-16 backbone and pre-trained by [17]. We employ Adam optimizer to optimize MMCA-Net with a batch size of 4. The learning rate is initialized as 0.0001 and is divided by 10 after training for 5 epochs. All experiments are terminated after 15 epochs. We implement the MMCA-Net on Pytorch. Experiments are conducted on an NVIDIA Tesla V100 GPU.

We evaluate the proposed model with three subtasks, respectively: Predicate Classification (PredCls), Scene Graph Classification (SGCls), and Scene Graph Generation (SGGen). The three tasks are of increasing difficulty. We employ the widely used mean Recall@K (abbreviated to mR@K) [1] to evaluate the MMCA-Net. Results are reported under the setting: **with** and **without Constraint**. The latter setting allows an object pair to have multiple reasonable predicates in the model output, thus resulting in a more comprehensive evaluation.

4.3 Experiment Results

Quantitative Analysis: We compare the proposed MMCA-Net with several outstanding models, including IMP [12], FREQ [17], SMN [17], KERN [1], GB-Net [16], Schemata [9], GPS-Net [4], CapSGG [18] and some model-agnostic methods PCPL [13], PUM [14], and EBM [11]. Results are shown in Table 1.

Compared with Previous SGG Models: Our MMCA-Net achieves competitive performance on mR metric. The highest average mR is **16.3%** and **33.1%** under the setting with and without constraint, with an improvement of **1.7%** and **1.6%** compared with the **GB-Net** (the best SGG model among previous works). Besides,

Table 1. Comparison of the mR@50 and mR@100 in % with and without constraint. †
means the model is re-implemented by [17] and "–" denotes unknown results. ‡ means
the SGG model is equipped with a model-agnostic learning strategy or post-processing
method.

	methods		PredCls		SGCls		SGGen		Mean
			mR@50	mR@100	mR@50	mR@100	mR@50	mR@100	
Constraint	IMP†	baseline [12]	9.8	10.5	5.8	6.0	3.8	4.8	6.8
		PUM ‡ [14]	11.3	12.3	6.4	6.8	4.5	5.5	7.8
		EBM ‡ [11]	11.8	12.8	6.8	7.2	4.2	5.4	8.0
	SMN	baseline [17]	13.3	14.4	7.1	7.6	5.3	6.1	9.0
		PUM ‡ [14]	16.4	18.1	9.4	10.1	7.5	8.6	11.7
		EBM ‡ [11]	18.0	19.5	10.2	11.0	7.7	9.3	12.6
	KERN	baseline [1]	17.7	19.2	9.4	10.0	6.4	7.3	11.7
		PUM ‡ [14]	18.7	20.4	9.9	10.6	6.5	7.4	12.3
	GE	baseline [13]	17.3	18.7	9.3	9.8	5.5	6.5	11.2
		PCPL ‡ [13]	**35.2**	**37.8**	**18.6**	**19.6**	**9.5**	**11.7**	**22.1**
	FREQ [17]		13.3	15.8	6.8	7.8	4.3	5.6	8.9
	GB-Net [16]		22.1	24.0	12.7	13.4	7.1	8.5	14.6
	GPS-Net [4]		21.3	22.8	11.8	12.6	8.7	9.8	14.5
	Schemata [9]		19.1	20.7	10.1	10.9	–	–	–
	CapSGG-fully [18]		17.7	19.5	10.4	11.1	7.3	8.7	12.5
	MMCA-Net (ours)		27.0	29.0	11.6	12.4	8.0	9.6	16.3
Without Constraint	IMP† [12]		20.3	28.9	12.1	16.9	5.4	8.0	15.3
	SMN [17]		27.5	37.9	15.4	20.6	9.3	12.9	20.6
	KERN [1]		36.3	49.0	19.8	26.2	11.7	16.0	26.5
	FREQ [17]		24.8	37.3	13.5	19.6	5.9	8.9	18.3
	GB-Net [16]		44.5	58.7	25.6	32.1	11.7	16.6	31.5
	Schemata [9]		40.1	54.9	21.4	28.8	–	–	–
	GE	baseline [13]	32.7	44.0	18.3	23.8	8.3	11.6	23.1
		PCPL ‡ [13]	**50.6**	62.6	**26.8**	**32.8**	10.4	14.4	32.9
	MMCA-Net (ours)		48.9	**63.6**	24.0	31.7	**12.5**	**17.6**	**33.1**

our MMCA-Net outperforms the **GPS-Net** by **1.8**% from 14.5% to 16.3% and
the **CapSGG-fully** by **3.8**% from 12.5% to 16.3% with constraint. **Compared
with model-agnostic methods**: Under the constraint setting, our model outperforms most model-agnostic methods (e.g., **SMN+EBM**, an increment of **3.7**%)
except the **GE+PCPL** [13] (Note that MMCA-Net is better than [13]'s baseline
model **GE**). However, under the without constraint setting, our MMCA-Net can
still achieve comparable performance compared with **GE+PCPL**, an increment
of **0.2**%.

Qualitative Analysis: (1) In Fig. 4, we visualize several scene graph examples. Compared with GB-Net which prefers trivial predicate classes such as "on",
scene graphs generated by MMCA-Net are more informative. For instance, in
Fig. 4(a), <man sitting on bench> is predicted correctly by MMCA-Net, while
GB-Net prefers predicting the simple predicate "on". Additionally, in scenes like
Fig. 4(b, c) where there are many people walking, MMCA-Net is inclined to predict <people walking on sidewalk> which is more appropriate than the triplet
<people on sidewalk>. In Fig. 4(d), our MMCA-Net precisely predicts the triplet
<motorcycle parked on street>, while GB-Net only gives the "on" broadly. (2)

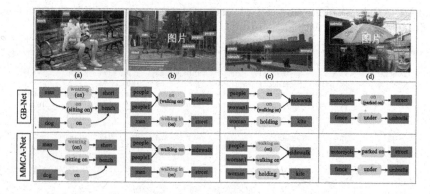

Fig. 4. Examples of scene graph generated by GB-Net and MMCA-Net under the setting of PredCls task. The scarlet predicates are the wrong prediction results.

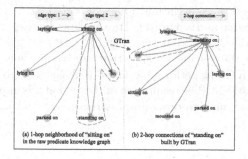

Fig. 5. Visualization of PKG and the 2-hop connected PKG.

In Fig. 5, we visualize the raw predicate knowledge graph and the 2-hop predicate knowledge graph generated by GTran. Figure 5(a) exhibits the 1-hop neighborhood of "sitting on". After routing twice, "standing on" can reach "on" via the path in the dashed box. After building 2-hop connections in Fig. 5(b), "standing on" and "on" can directly interact with each other by routing once, which demonstrates that utilizing the high-order structured information of the predicate knowledge graph is essential.

4.4   Ablation Study

In this subsection, we will test the effectiveness of the Cross-modal Graph Attention (**CGA**) module and the multi-hop (**mhop**) connected predicate knowledge graph. The ablative results are present in Table 2.

(1) To verify the necessity of sufficient modality propagation and fusion in the SGG task, we compare the **CGA** module with the **bridging** mechanism proposed in GB-Net [16]. Comparing **exp1** with **exp3** in Table 2, we find that: when utilizing the CGA module to fully exploit the cross-modal node context, our work performs better than the model equipped with the bridging mechanism, both with

Table 2. Ablation studies of our work under the evaluation metrics of mR@50 and mR@100 in % with and without constraint.

	exp	methods	PredCls		SGCls		SGGen		mean
			mR@50	mR@100	mR@50	mR@100	mR@50	mR@100	
Constraint	1	MMCA-Net+bridging	25.4	27.1	11.3	12.0	7.6	9.0	15.4
	2	MMCA-Net+bridging+mhop	24.7	26.4	11.0	11.9	7.8	9.2	15.2
	3	MMCA-Net+CGA	25.5	27.6	**11.7**	**12.5**	7.6	8.9	15.6
	4	MMCA-Net+CGA+mhop	**27.0**	**29.0**	11.6	12.4	**8.0**	**9.6**	**16.3**
Without Constraint	1	MMCA-Net+bridging	47.1	61.9	23.4	30.3	12.0	17.1	32.0
	2	MMCA-Net+bridging+mhop	47.6	62.1	23.5	30.5	12.2	17.5	32.3
	3	MMCA-Net+CGA	48.5	63.3	23.4	30.3	12.5	**18.0**	32.7
	4	MMCA-Net+CGA+mhop	**48.9**	**63.6**	**24.0**	**31.7**	12.5	17.6	**33.1**

and without constraint. The same conclusion can be received from the experiment setting **exp2** and **exp4**. These results demonstrate that our CGA module is more effective in passing and aggregating cross-modal messages.

(2) To verify the effectiveness of the multi-hop connected PKG, we simply carry out ablative studies **with** and **without** GTran module. The experiment with **mhop** means utilizing the GTran to construct multi-hop connected PKG. Comparing **exp3** with **exp4**, the conclusion comes that: when deploying the GTran to build the multi-hop PKG, the performance of MMCA-Net gets promotion both with and without constraint. The results demonstrate that it is important to comprehensively consider the high-order graph-structured correlations between predicate classes.

5   Conclusion

In this paper, we propose a new scene graph generation model, Multi-Modal Context-Aware Network (MMCA-Net), which can alleviate the problems of insufficient predicate correlations consideration and insufficient cross-modality propagation in previous works, thereby achieving outstanding performance in detecting informative relationships. Both quantitative and qualitative results demonstrate that our model is capable of detecting informative relationships compared with several strong baselines. In the future, we will continue to explore ways to generate informative scene graphs.

Acknowledgement. This work was supported by National Key Research and Development Project (No. 2020AAA0106200), the National Nature Science Foundation of China under Grants (No. 61936005, 61872424), and the Natural Science Foundation of Jiangsu Province (Grants No. BK20200037 and BK20210595).

References

1. Chen, T., et al.: Knowledge-embedded routing network for scene graph generation. In: Proceedings of the IEEE Conference on Computer Vision and Pattern Recognition, pp. 6163–6171 (2019)

2. Cui, Z., et al.: Context-dependent diffusion network for visual relationship detection. In: Proceedings of the ACM International Conference on Multimedia, pp. 1475–1482 (2018)

3. Krishna, R., et al.: Visual genome: connecting language and vision using crowd-sourced dense image annotations. Int. J. Comput. Vis. **123**(1), 32–73 (2017)

4. Lin, X., et al.: GPS-net: graph property sensing network for scene graph generation. In: Proceedings of the IEEE Conference on Computer Vision and Pattern Recognition, pp. 3746–3753 (2020)

5. Miller, G.A.: WordNet: a lexical database for English. Commun. ACM **38**(11), 39–41 (1995)

6. Pennington, J., et al.: GloVe: global vectors for word representation. In: Proceedings of the conference on Empirical Methods in Natural Language Processing, pp. 1532–1543 (2014)

7. Qi, M., et al.: Attentive relational networks for mapping images to scene graphs. In: Proceedings of the IEEE Conference on Computer Vision and Pattern Recognition, pp. 3957–3966 (2019)

8. Ren, S., et al.: Faster R-CNN: towards real-time object detection with region proposal networks. Proceedings of the Advances in Neural Information Processing Systems, vol. 28, pp. 91–99 (2015)

9. Sharifzadeh, S., et al.: Classification by attention: scene graph classification with prior knowledge. In: Proceedings of the AAAI Conference on Artificial Intelligence, vol. 35, pp. 5025–5033 (2021)

10. Speer, R., Havasi, C.: ConceptNet 5: a large semantic network for relational knowledge. In: Gurevych, I., Kim, J. (eds.) The People's Web Meets NLP. TANLP, pp. 161–176. Springer, Heidelberg (2013). https://doi.org/10.1007/978-3-642-35085-6_6

11. Suhail, M., et al.: Energy-based learning for scene graph generation. In: Proceedings of the IEEE Conference on Computer Vision and Pattern Recognition, pp. 13936–13945 (2021)

12. Xu, D., et al.: Scene graph generation by iterative message passing. In: Proceedings of the IEEE Conference on Computer Vision and Pattern Recognition, pp. 5410–5419 (2017)

13. Yan, S., et al.: PCPL: predicate-correlation perception learning for unbiased scene graph generation. In: Proceedings of the ACM International Conference on Multimedia, pp. 265–273 (2020)

14. Yang, G., et al.: Probabilistic modeling of semantic ambiguity for scene graph generation. In: Proceedings of the IEEE Conference on Computer Vision and Pattern Recognition, pp. 12527–12536 (2021)

15. Yun, S., et al.: Graph transformer networks. In: Proceedings of the Advances in Neural Information Processing Systems, vol. 32, pp. 11983–11993 (2019)

16. Zareian, A., Karaman, S., Chang, S.-F.: Bridging knowledge graphs to generate scene graphs. In: Vedaldi, A., Bischof, H., Brox, T., Frahm, J.-M. (eds.) ECCV 2020. LNCS, vol. 12368, pp. 606–623. Springer, Cham (2020). https://doi.org/10.1007/978-3-030-58592-1_36

17. Zellers, R., et al.: Neural motifs: scene graph parsing with global context. In: Proceedings of the IEEE Conference on Computer Vision and Pattern Recognition, pp. 5831–5840 (2018)

18. Zhong, Y., et al.: Learning to generate scene graph from natural language supervision. In: Proceedings of the IEEE International Conference on Computer Vision, pp. 1823–1834 (2021)

VQA-CLPR: Turning a Visual Question Answering Model into a Chinese License Plate Recognizer

Gang Lv[1,2], Xuhao Jiang[3], Yining Sun[1,2(✉)], Weiya Ni[3], and Fudong Nian[3,4]

[1] University of Science and Technology of China, Hefei, China
[2] Hefei Institutes of Physical Science, Chinese Academy of Sciences, Hefei, China
ynsun@iim.ac.cn
[3] School of Advanced Manufacturing Engineering, Hefei University, Hefei, China

[4] Anhui Provincial Engineering Technology Research Center of Intelligent Vehicle
Control and Integrated Design Technology, Hefei, China

Abstract. This paper proposes a new method, VQA-CLPR, to transfer multimodal pretrained Visual Question Answering (VQA) model to Chinese License Plate Recognition (CLPR). Specifically, we recast CLPR as VQA and directly transfer a vision-language pretrained model to the end task. The length of the license plate characters is the answer to the question "How many characters in the image?" and the character at position i is the answer to the question "What is the $i-th$ character in the image?". All the answers combine to form the final result of Chinese license plate recognition. With pre-training on large-scale annotated general Chinese VQA data, the extensive experimental results on four large-scale synthetic and real Chinese license plate recognition datasets indicate that our VQA-CLPR achieves competitive results while possessing the best generalization performance compared to existing state-of-the-art methods.

Keywords: License plate recognition · VQA · Transfer learning

1 Introduction

Chinese License Plate Recognition (CLPR) is a long-standing research topic aiming to develop computer vision algorithms and systems that can accurately and efficiently recognize Chinese license plates from images or videos, which has a wide range of applications, including traffic control, toll collection, parking management, law enforcement, and security surveillance.

Before the era of deep learning, Chinese license plate recognition algorithms were based on traditional computer vision techniques, such as edge detection, feature extraction, and pattern recognition. These algorithms usually consisted of several steps, including image preprocessing, character segmentation, and character recognition. However, these methods were limited by their reliance on

H. Lu et al. (Eds.): ICIG 2023, LNCS 14356, pp. 348–359, 2023.
https://doi.org/10.1007/978-3-031-46308-2_29

handcrafted features and the performance was often affected by the quality of the input images, lighting conditions, and variations in license plate designs.

In the deep learning era, the development of deep learning has revolutionized license plate character recognition technology due to their ability to learn discriminative features directly from raw image data [10,17], leading to significant improvements in accuracy and robustness [25]. As shown in Fig. 1(a), these models typically employ a combination of convolutional layers to extract spatial features and recurrent layers to model temporal dependencies in the sequence of characters [6,15,19,22]. In recent years, inspired by the application of Transformers in natural language processing, some researchers have proposed Transformer-based OCR (optical character recognition) algorithms [5] and applied them to the field of Chinese license plate recognition [14].

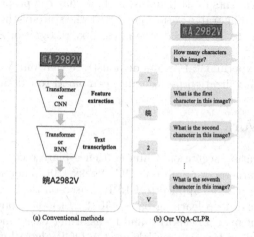

Fig. 1. Comparison of different paradigms for Chinese license plate recognition.

Although the aforementioned methods have made significant progress in the field of Chinese license plate recognition, their generalization performance (such as zero-shot recognition) is still unsatisfactory. The recent large-scale Vision-Language Models (VLM) has shown great potential in various downstream vision tasks [24], e.g., image classification [26], object detection [23], and semantic segmentation [13]. Lin et al.. [16] deemed the OCR as image captioning task, and transferred the unified multi-modal pretrained model (OFA) [21] to text recognition.

Unlike all existing CLPR algorithms, this paper proposes a novel CLPR framework. Since Chinese license plate image presents with both visual and rich character information, which has a natural connection with the visual question answering (VQA) model, as shown in Fig. 1(b), this paper proposes a new method, VQA-CLPR, to transfer multimodal pretrained Visual Question Answering model to Chinese License Plate Recognition. Specifically, We design a visual question answering model based on Transformer and an encoder-decoder framework, which is pre-trained on a large-scale open-source Chinese visual question answering dataset. Then, we fine-tune the model on the Chinese license plate recognition dataset. The length of the license plate characters is the answer to the question "How many characters in the image?" and the character at position i is the answer to the question "What is the $i-th$ character in the image?". All the answers combine to form the final result of Chinese license plate recognition. Extensive experimental results on four synthetic and real benchmark datasets validate the effectiveness and superiority of our proposed method.

The main contributions of this work are three-fold:

- To the best of our knowledge, our proposed VQA-CLPR model is the first work to introduce a visual question answering multimodal machine learning framework for Chinese license plate recognition tasks.
- Extensive experiments on four datasets show that the proposed VQA-CLPR model achieves comparable performance with the state-of-the-art visual-based OCR algorithm (SVTR [5], $i.e.$, the latest text recognition algorithm in PP-OCRv3[1]).
- Cross-dataset experimental results demonstrate that our VQA-CLPR model has superior generalization performance compared to existing algorithms.

2   Related Work

In terms of application scenarios, Chinese license plate recognition is a special type of optical character recognition (OCR) task [20]. Therefore, in principle, all OCR algorithms can be applied to CLPR. Based on this, this section mainly reviews some typical deep learning-based OCR methods. Convolutional neural networks, recurrent neural networks, and transformer-based models are some of the most popular deep learning models used in OCR algorithms.

The architecture of CNN-based OCR algorithms [7,25] typically consists of a convolutional layer, a pooling layer, and a fully connected layer. The convolutional layer applies a set of filters to the input image, generating a set of feature maps. The pooling layer reduces the size of the feature maps while preserving the important features. The fully connected layer takes the flattened feature maps as input and produces the final classification output.

Recurrent Neural Networks (RNNs) have also been widely used in OCR algorithms [15,19], particularly for recognizing text in images with variable length. The main advantage of RNNs is their ability to capture sequential information from the input data. One popular type of RNN for OCR is the Long Short-Term Memory (LSTM) network, which can handle the vanishing gradient problem and effectively model long-term dependencies. Another type is the Gated Recurrent Unit (GRU), which has a simpler structure than LSTM but can still effectively capture long-term dependencies. In RNN-based OCR algorithms, the input image is typically preprocessed and converted into a sequence of feature

---

[1] https://github.com/PaddlePaddle/PaddleOCR.

vectors, which are then fed into the RNN. The RNN outputs a sequence of predictions, which are often post-processed to obtain the final recognized text. The
most famous RNN-based OCR algorithm is CRNN (Convolutional Recurrent
Neural Network) [19], which combines a CNN with an LSTM network, and uses
an attention-based mechanism to selectively attend to different parts of the input
image during recognition.

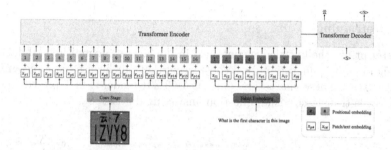

Fig. 2. The overall framework of our approach.

The transformer architecture, initially proposed for natural language processing tasks, has been adapted for OCR tasks by several researchers [1,5,18].
One of the advantages of transformer-based OCR algorithms is that they can
learn global dependencies between characters in a sequence, which is important
for accurately recognizing characters in license plates. The transformer model
is trained on large amounts of labeled data to learn the relationships between
the characters in different positions in the sequence. This model then uses this
learned knowledge to predict the characters in a new, unseen image of a license
plate. Several studies have shown that transformer-based OCR algorithms outperform previous state-of-the-art models in terms of accuracy and robustness [2].

Despite significant advances in CLPR with the aforementioned methods, their
ability to generalize, such as in zero-shot recognition, remains inadequate. Our
approach is distinct from all existing CLPR algorithms, as we transform the
single visual modality semantic recognition task of CLPR into a multimodal
VQA task.

3   Method

3.1   Framework

To turn the visual question answering model into the Chinese license plate recognizer, we propose VQA-CLPR, a VQA framework shown in Fig. 2 and Fig. 3.
Due to the outstanding performance of OFA's multi-modal architecture on various multi-modal tasks including visual question answering [21], we directly adopt
its visual question answering sub-module as the framework for our VQA-CLPR

model. Specifically, VQA-CLPR is a Transformer encoder-decoder framework, which utilizes visual backbones such as ResNet [9] and ViT [4] as adaptors for Chinese license plate images, and word embeddings as adaptors for texts, making information from different modalities adaptable to the Transformer. Information from modalities is encoded as discrete tokens, which enables the decoder to perform generation. For more details on the model structure, refer to the original OFA paper.

3.2 Pretraining

To better utilize the knowledge contained in the large-scale multimodal datasets with high-quality annotations and considering that our license plate recognition task involves Chinese characters, our VQA-CLPR model is first pre-trained on a large-scale translated visual question answering dataset [8].

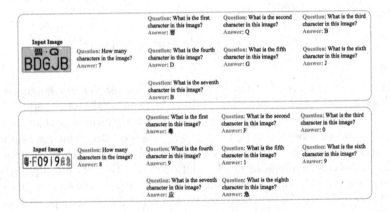

Fig. 3. Selected examples to illustrate the questions design in our VQA-CLPR.

3.3 Finetuning on CLPR Dataset

It is natural to recast Chinese license plate recognition as visual questioning answering, as Chinese license plate recognition also requires the model to answer the total number of characters on the license plate and what each character is. Therefore, CLPR is equivalent to finetuning VQA model on different visual question answering dataset. Our specific approach is as follows: as shown in Fig. 3, we first define two questions applicable to Chinese license plate recognition, namely "How many characters in the image?" and "What is the $i - th$ character in the image?". For each image in the Chinese license plate recognition dataset, we create question-answer pairs based on its license plate annotation and all the defined questions. Then, we fine-tune the VQA-CLPR model pretrained on the large-scale Chinese visual question answering dataset on the Chinese license plate dataset, where each training sample consists of a triplet of a Chinese license plate image, a question, and an answer. Finally, We finetune our VQA-CLPR model with maximum likelihood estimation for optimization.

3.4 Inference

As illustrated in Fig. 3, After training our VQA-CLPR model, the steps to use it to recognize a Chinese license plate character are as follows: first, ask the model "How many characters in the image?" and determine the index of the maximum character position based on the answer. Then different character positions can be calculated in parallel using the question "What is the $i - th$ character in the image?" All of the answers from the different positions are merged to form the complete string corresponding to the input Chinese license plate image.

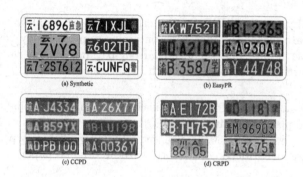

Fig. 4. Example images in the Synthetic, EasyPR, CCPD and CRPD datasets.

4 Experiments

We perform experiments on four CLPR datasets, the Synthetic dataset, the EasyPR dataset[2], the CCPD dataset [22] and the CRPD dataset [6]. Data samples from the four datasets are shown in Fig 4. In this section, we first introduce these datasets, evaluation metric and our implementation details, and then compare the performance of VQA-CLPR with other state-of-the-art approaches. Finally, we investigate the impact of different components via a set of ablation studies.

It is worth noting that the experiments in this paper were conducted to demonstrate the effectiveness of the newly proposed visual question answering-based Chinese license plate recognition framework VQA-CLPR, rather than to exhaust all possible methods to achieve the best performance.

---

[2] https://github.com/liuruoze/EasyPR.

4.1   Dataset

The Synthetic Dataset. We synthesized 50,000 license plate images, including various types such as blue, white, yellow, and double-layer plates, using open-source Chinese license plate generation code[3]. Among them, 40,000 license plates were used as the training set, 2,000 as the validation set, and the remaining 8,000 as the test set.

The EasyPR Dataset. The EasyPR dataset was a popular open-source Chinese license plate recognition dataset during the traditional machine learning era. It was mainly used to train SVM models, and contained 1,400 license plates in the training set and 517 license plates in the testing set. The license plates in the dataset were of two types: blue plates and yellow plates, but all were single-layered.

The CCPD Dataset. CCPD is currently the largest publicly available Chinese license plate recognition dataset, containing approximately 250,000 single-layered Chinese license plates collected from parking lots in Hefei City. The dataset was partitioned consistently with the original paper.

The CRPD Dataset. CRPD dataset is the latest publicly available large-scale Chinese license plate recognition dataset that covers the widest range of license plate types. It contains over 30,000 license plates from different types and scenes. The dataset was partitioned consistently with its original paper.

4.2   Evaluation Metric

Due to extreme class label imbalance in some datasets (such as CCPD dataset where the majority of license plates start with the same Chinese character, and the proportion of special license plates is very small in all datasets except for the synthesized dataset), we use F-measure as the evaluation metric.

F-measure is a commonly used performance evaluation metric in OCR (Optical Character Recognition) tasks, which is a combination of precision and recall. Precision measures the accuracy of the OCR system in identifying correct characters in the recognized text, while recall measures the OCR system's ability to identify all relevant characters. F-measure is the harmonic mean of precision and recall, where the maximum value of F-measure is 1, indicating perfect precision and recall. F-measure is calculated using the following formula:

$$F - measure = 2 * (precision * recall)/(precision + recall). \qquad (1)$$

OCR systems aim to achieve high F-measure scores, indicating a high level of accuracy in character recognition. Since Chinese license plate recognition is a special type of OCR task, using F-measure as the evaluation metric is also appropriate.

---

[3] https://github.com/Pengfei8324/chinese_license_plate_generator.

4.3   Implementation Details

All experiments are conducted on 2 NVIDIA 3090 GPUs using PyTorch library. Our algorithms are trained with Adaptive Moment Estimation (Adaw) [11] optimizer and the mini-batch size is set to 16. For input embeddings of Transformer Encoder and Transformer Decoder, consistent with the data processing in the original OFA [21], we use the pre-trained CoAtNet [3] to extract visual features and the pre-trained SentencePiece [12] to extract textual features. When the training loss value does not decrease for 10 consecutive epochs, we consider the model has converged.

Table 1. Results on four CLPR benchmarks tested against existing methods. Syn indicates the Synthetic dataset. "First, ..., Seventh" represent the position of each character in the license plate, and "Full Plate" indicates the situation where all characters of the license plate are recognized correctly. F-measure (%) is used to evaluate performance of all methods.

Dataset	Methods	First	Second	Third	Fourth	Fifth	Sixth	Seventh	Full Plate
CRPD	CRNN	95.7	99.4	98.3	98.3	98.6	98.2	97.9	91.1
	SVTR	96.2	99.4	98.8	98.4	98.7	98.4	98.1	92.3
	VQA-CLPR	96.3	99.5	99.1	98.3	98.4	98.1	98.3	91.5
CCPD	CRNN	96.7	99.3	98.8	98.4	98.7	98.1	98.7	91.7
	SVTR	97.9	99.3	99.1	99.2	98.8	98.7	98.0	93.4
	VQA-CLPR	96.9	99.4	98.4	99.1	98.5	98.7	99.4	92.8
EasyPR	CRNN	95.8	98.7	97.6	98.1	97.5	98.1	98.1	90.7
	SVTR	96.9	99.1	97.9	98.8	98.8	98.1	98.9	92.1
	VQA-CLPR	95.9	98.9	97.5	98.3	97.9	98.3	98.3	91.0
Syn	CRNN	99.7	99.3	99.6	99.4	99.5	99.1	98.7	95.7
	SVTR	99.9	99.9	99.9	99.9	99.8	99.7	98.7	99.7
	VQA-CLPR	100	100	100	100	100	100	100	100

4.4   Comparison to State-of-the-Art Methods

We evaluate the proposed VQA-CLPR on four benchmark datasets, and compare it with two state-of-the-art methods, i.e., CRNN [19] and SVTR [5]. The results are summarized in Table 1. The results show that our proposed VQA-CLPR model achieved competitive results in both individual character recognition accuracy and complete license plate string recognition accuracy. This demonstrates (1) the feasibility of using a visual question answering framework for Chinese license plate recognition; (2) our method can accurately predict the number of characters in the license plate and identify characters at different index positions. In addition, we can also see that the accuracy of recognizing the entire license plate string is significantly lower than that of recognizing individual characters. This indicates that there is still significant room for improvement in the framework proposed in this paper for predicting the length of the string.

4.5 Ablation Study

To better understand VQA-CLPR, we conducted two groups of ablation experiments, which are described in detail as follows.

The Advantage of VQA Model. The main difference of the Chinese license plate recognition framework proposed in this paper compared to existing algorithms is the use of the visual question answering (VQA) multimodal framework. To evaluate the advantages of VQA over traditional visual classification methods, we replaced our framework with a ResNet-50 based multi-class convolutional neural network framework for the task of predicting the number of characters in a license plate. The experimental results are shown in Table 2, which clearly indicates that traditional CNN classification algorithms are not suitable for character counting tasks, while our VQA-CLPR model achieved excellent performance on three real-world datasets.

Table 2. Comparison of license plate character count prediction performance using different methods on three public datasets. F-measure (%) is used to evaluate performance of all methods.

Method	CRPD	CCPD	EasyPR
ResNet-50	70.8	72.5	68.2
VQA-CLPR	95.2	96.8	94.1

Pre-trained VQA Backbone. During the training phase of our VQA-CLPR model, we first trained it on a general Chinese visual question answering dataset and then transferred the parameters to the Chinese license plate dataset for further fine-tuning. To verify the necessity of this strategy, we compared the performance of the VQA-CLPR model with and without pre-training on character recognition. The experimental results are shown in Fig. 5, and it can be seen that the character recognition accuracy is significantly improved after adopting the pre-training strategy. This means that our VQA-CLPR model can learn transferable knowledge through pre-training on a large-scale general Chinese visual question answering dataset.

4.6 Generalization Ability

The existing Chinese license plate recognition algorithms are basically trained and tested on the same dataset, because the data distribution varies greatly across different datasets. In addition, for the field of Chinese license plate recognition, it is extremely important to collect a large amount of real-world license plate data and annotate it for model training, but collecting and annotating real-world data is very resource-intensive. A natural idea is to synthesize a batch of

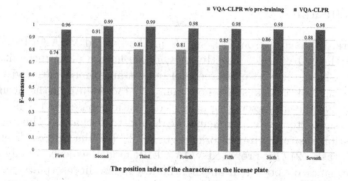

Fig. 5. A comparison between the performance with or without general VQA pretraining on CRPD dataset.

license plate data, pre-train on the synthesized license plates, and then fine-tune on a small amount of real data. This approach requires the model to have strong generalization ability. To evaluate the generalization ability of our VQA-CLPR model and existing models, we conducted zero-shot Chinese license plate experiments across datasets, that is, training on one dataset and directly testing on another dataset. Specifically, we conducted the following four experiments:

- Syn → CRPD: Train on synthetic dataset, test on CRPD dataset.
- CRPD → Syn: Train on CRPD dataset, test on synthetic dataset.
- CCPD→Syn: Train on CCPD dataset, test on synthetic dataset.
- Syn → CCPD: Train on synthetic dataset, test on CCPD dataset.

The experimental results are shown in Table 3. From the results, we can see that due to the huge visual differences between synthesized license plate data and real license plate data (as shown in Fig. 4), commonly used pure visual recognition methods do not have cross-dataset generalization ability, while our VQA-CLPR model demonstrates good generalization ability, which has a broader application prospect.

Table 3. Cross-dataset zero-shot license plate recognition results. F-measure (%) is used to evaluate performance of all methods.

Method	Syn → CRPD	CRPD → Syn	CCPD→Syn	Syn → CCPD
CRNN	0	0	0	0
SVTR	0	0	0	0
VQA-CLPR	29	43	32	57

5   Conclusion

In this work, we have presented a simple method called VQA-CLPR, focusing on turning the VQA model directly for Chinese license plate recognition. The problem of Chinese license plate recognition is transformed into a visual question answering task that answers how many characters are in the license plate image and what the character is for a series of positions based on the license plate image. Through extensive experiments, we demonstrate that (1) The multimodal visual question answering framework can be applied to the Chinese license plate recognition task. (2) Our proposed VQA-CLPR model achieved highly competitive performance on both real and synthetic Chinese license plate recognition datasets. (3) Compared to pure visual recognition methods, our model has significantly improved cross-dataset generalization ability. We hope that VQA-CLPR will foster further research in general text recognition. In the future, we will explore integrating our proposed VQA-CLPR model with existing license plate detection algorithms to form a complete high-precision Chinese license plate recognition system.

Acknowledgments. This work was supported in part by the University Synergy Innovation Program of Anhui Province (No. GXXT-2022-043), and Anhui Provincial Key Research and Development Program (No. 2022a05020042). Weiya Ni is a student of Haikou Middle School, Hainan Province, this work is done during internship at Hefei University, thanks for her contribution to server management and maintenance.

References

1. Atienza, R.: Vision transformer for fast and efficient scene text recognition. In: Lladós, J., Lopresti, D., Uchida, S. (eds.) ICDAR 2021. LNCS, vol. 12821, pp. 319–334. Springer, Cham (2021). https://doi.org/10.1007/978-3-030-86549-8_21
2. Azadbakht, A., Kheradpisheh, S.R., Farahani, H.: Multipath vit ocr: A lightweight visual transformer-based license plate optical character recognition. In: 2022 12th International Conference on Computer and Knowledge Engineering (ICCKE), pp. 092–095. IEEE (2022)
3. Dai, Z., Liu, H., Le, Q.V., Tan, M.: Coatnet: Marrying convolution and attention for all data sizes. Adv. Neural. Inf. Process. Syst. **34**, 3965–3977 (2021)
4. Dosovitskiy, A., et al.: An image is worth 16x16 words: Transformers for image recognition at scale. arXiv preprint arXiv:2010.11929 (2020)
5. Du, Y., et al.: Svtr: Scene text recognition with a single visual model. arXiv preprint arXiv:2205.00159 (2022)
6. Gong, Y., et al.: Unified Chinese license plate detection and recognition with high efficiency. J. Vis. Commun. Image Represent. **86**, 103541 (2022)
7. Goodfellow, I.J., Bulatov, Y., Ibarz, J., Arnoud, S., Shet, V.: Multi-digit number recognition from street view imagery using deep convolutional neural networks. arXiv preprint arXiv:1312.6082 (2013)
8. Goyal, Y., Khot, T., Summers-Stay, D., Batra, D., Parikh, D.: Making the V in VQA matter: Elevating the role of image understanding in visual question answering. In: Proceedings of the IEEE Conference on Computer Vision and Pattern Recognition, pp. 6904–6913 (2017)

9. He, K., Zhang, X., Ren, S., Sun, J.: Deep residual learning for image recognition. In: Proceedings of the IEEE Conference on Computer Vision and Pattern Recognition, pp. 770–778 (2016)

10. Jiang, Y., et al.: An efficient and unified recognition method for multiple license plates in unconstrained scenarios. IEEE Trans. Intell. Transport. Syst. (2023)

11. Kingma, D.P., Ba, J.: Adam: A method for stochastic optimization. arXiv preprint arXiv:1412.6980 (2014)

12. Kudo, T., Richardson, J.: Sentencepiece: A simple and language independent subword tokenizer and detokenizer for neural text processing. arXiv preprint arXiv:1808.06226 (2018)

13. Li, B., Weinberger, K.Q., Belongie, S., Koltun, V., Ranftl, R.: Language-driven semantic segmentation. arXiv preprint arXiv:2201.03546 (2022)

14. Li, C., et al.: Pp-ocrv3: More attempts for the improvement of ultra lightweight OCR system. arXiv preprint arXiv:2206.03001 (2022)

15. Li, H., Wang, P., Shen, C., Zhang, G.: Show, attend and read: A simple and strong baseline for irregular text recognition. In: Proceedings of the AAAI Conference on Artificial Intelligence, vol. 33, pp. 8610–8617 (2019)

16. Lin, J., et al.: Transferring general multimodal pretrained models to text recognition. arXiv preprint arXiv:2212.09297 (2022)

17. Shashirangana, J., Padmasiri, H., Meedeniya, D., Perera, C.: Automated license plate recognition: a survey on methods and techniques. IEEE Access 9, 11203–11225 (2020)

18. Sheng, F., Chen, Z., Xu, B.: NRTR: A no-recurrence sequence-to-sequence model for scene text recognition. In: 2019 International Conference on Document Analysis and Recognition (ICDAR), pp. 781–786. IEEE (2019)

19. Shi, B., Bai, X., Yao, C.: An end-to-end trainable neural network for image-based sequence recognition and its application to scene text recognition. IEEE Trans. Pattern Anal. Mach. Intell. 39(11), 2298–2304 (2016)

20. Subramani, N., Matton, A., Greaves, M., Lam, A.: A survey of deep learning approaches for ocr and document understanding. arXiv preprint arXiv:2011.13534 (2020)

21. Wang, P., et al.: OFA: Unifying architectures, tasks, and modalities through a simple sequence-to-sequence learning framework. In: International Conference on Machine Learning, pp. 23318–23340. PMLR (2022)

22. Xu, Z., et al.: Towards end-to-end license plate detection and recognition: A large dataset and baseline. In: Proceedings of the European Conference on Computer Vision (ECCV), pp. 255–271 (2018)

23. Yu, W., Liu, Y., Hua, W., Jiang, D., Ren, B., Bai, X.: Turning a clip model into a scene text detector. arXiv preprint arXiv:2302.14338 (2023)

24. Zhang, J., Huang, J., Jin, S., Lu, S.: Vision-language models for vision tasks: A survey. arXiv preprint arXiv:2304.00685 (2023)

25. Zherzdev, S., Gruzdev, A.: Lprnet: License plate recognition via deep neural networks. arXiv preprint arXiv:1806.10447 (2018)

26. Zhou, K., Yang, J., Loy, C.C., Liu, Z.: Conditional prompt learning for vision-language models. In: Proceedings of the IEEE/CVF Conference on Computer Vision and Pattern Recognition, pp. 16816–16825 (2022)

Unsupervised Vehicle Re-Identification via Raw UAV Videos

Shangzhi Teng[1]([envelope]) [iD] and Tingting Dong[2]

[1] Beijing Information Science and Technology University, Beijing, China
tengshangzhi@bistu.edu.cn
[2] Beijing Special Engineering Design and Research Institute, Beijing, China

Abstract. For matching vehicles across different camera views, vehicle Re-Identification has made great progress in supervised learning. However, supervised approach would require extensive manual labeling which is costly and unfeasible for large-scale vehicle Re-ID dataset. Therefore, we propose an unsupervised method to overcome the difficulty of vehicle ID labeling. Inspired by self-supervised methods in object tracking, we utilize self-supervised tracker to associate vehicle images in each unlabeled raw videos. We also utilize object sequence clustering method to associate vehicles from different videos and ensure the quality of the predicted pseudo labels. Based on these vehicle images and predicted labels discriminative vehicle features can be learned. In this paper, we construct a large-scale Unmanned Aerial Vehicle (UAV) vehicle video dataset to facilitate the study of video-based unsupervised vehicle Re-ID. Extensive experiments show that our method is effective and achieves competitive performance compared with recent unsupervised works. In addition, using the data obtained by the proposed method as the pre-training data can further improve the performance of the fully-supervised methods.

Keywords: UAV videos · Vehicle Re-Identification · Unsupervised tracking · Feature clustering

1 Introduction

Vehicle Re-Identification (Re-ID) targets to match and identify query vehicles against a large vehicle image gallery set. It is an important technique to achieve efficient traffic control and smart city surveillance. For the convenience of data collection, existing vehicle Re-ID systems [14,22] are mainly conducted with videos taken by fixed traffic surveillance cameras. Although their number is already large in many cities, traffic surveillance cameras exhibit limited coverage due to their fixed locations and viewpoints.

In recent years, the UAV technology has been substantially improved in terms of flight time, automatic control algorithm, and wireless image transmission, *etc.*

Therefore, UAV-based vision applications have been drawing increasing attention from both industry and academia [30, 35, 36]. Existing UAV-related research and datasets mainly focus on the tasks of object detection [35], single, multiple object tracking [15, 36], and human trajectory analysis [23]. UAVs exhibit good mobility and flexibility. Compared with fixed traffic surveillance cameras, mobile cameras on UAVs present better mobility and more flexible viewing scope, making it possible to achieve more efficient and active vehicle Re-ID based on UAV videos. Currently, there is a limited number of works focus on the UAV-based vehicle Re-ID. The main reason is that manual annotation of vehicle ID from UAV videos is expensive. Therefore, it is difficult to collect and release large scale UAV vehicle Re-ID datasets. For instance, Wang *et al.* [30] constructed a large-scale vehicle Re-ID dataset VRAI. The annotation of VRAI costs more than 3,500 man-hours.

Recent Re-ID research efforts to focus on unsupervised methods. Compared with supervised learning, unsupervised learning relieves the requirement of expensive data annotation, hence shows better potential to push Re-ID towards real scenarios. Recent unsupervised Re-ID methods are mainly proposed for person Re-ID [2, 3, 39]. Those works have achieved significant success. Most of them define unsupervised Re-ID as a transfer learning task, which leverages labeled data on other domains for model initialization or label transfer. However, existing vehicle Re-ID datasets are collected by surveillance cameras, which differs with UAV-mounted cameras in the viewpoints and image qualities. There is a considerable gap between traditional vehicle Re-ID datasets and UAV-based vehicle Re-ID dataset. As discussed in many works [32, 34], large domain gap degrades the performance of feature representation. It is inappropriate to use the traditional vehicle Re-ID data set for transfer learning of UAV vehicle Re-ID.

This work aims to study a more efficient unsupervised training algorithm for UAV vehicle Re-ID. Instead of relying on costly ID annotations, we propose to automatically detect and annotation vehicles from raw video frames. After associating vehicles from different video frames, we finally obtain the training data with pseudo-labels and learn discriminative features with these data.

This work also constructs a large-scale dataset for unsupervised UAV vehicle Re-ID. This dataset contains 76,000 video frames for unsupervised training. Extensive experimental results indicate that our method is effective and achieves promising performance combined with supervised vehicle Re-ID methods. We also compare with several unsupervised Re-ID models, which also shows the superiority of our method.

2   Related Work

2.1   Vehicle Re-Identification

Most studies of vehicle Re-ID are based on supervised learning, which can be categorized into three groups including global feature optimization by distance metric learning [14, 17, 22], local feature learning [10, 19, 26] and viewpoint robust feature learning [4, 20, 27]. However, supervised learning require expensive data annotation, which is time-consuming and may not be reliable. Compared with supervised learning, unsupervised learning shows better potential to push vehicle Re-ID towards real applications.

2.2   Unsupervised Re-Identification

Recently, more and more people pay attention to unsupervised Re-ID methods [2, 3, 25, 39]. [5, 32] aim to translate images from the source domain to the target domain by GAN. [21] develops a camera-aware domain adaptation method to reduce the discrepancy not only between source and target domains but also across camera-level sub-domains. [33] proposes a camera-aware similarity consistency loss to learn consistent pairwise similarity distributions for intra-camera matching and cross-camera matching. These methods utilize transfer learning to deal with the discrepancy between different datasets or different cameras. [7, 16, 25] use source data for pre-training and estimate pseudo labels from unlabelled target data by clustering and fine-tuning. [7] proposes a self-similarity grouping approach that exploits the potential similarity of unlabeled samples to build multiple clusters from different views automatically. These methods explore unlabeled data progressively by alternately assigning pseudo-labels to unlabeled data and updating the model according to these pseudo-labeled data.

Most of the unsupervised Re-ID methods leverage other labeled source datasets to improve the performance of target dataset. It is inappropriate to use transfer learning methods and clustering methods for unsupervised vehicle Re-ID, because the gaps between aerial vehicle images and traditional vehicle images are significant. In contrast, we focus on boosting unsupervised vehicle Re-ID from raw videos with no prior knowledge of relevant source domains.

2.3   Self-supervised Learning

One of the key elements of our proposed method is the self-supervised learning. It has been applied successfully in a variety of applications, including 3D shape matching [12, 41], structure from motion [38], image or video alignment [6, 41], image-to-image translation [1, 42], visual correspondence learning [31], video segmentation [13] and visual object tracking [29]. For example, [31] uses cycle consistency in time as free supervisory signal for learning visual representations from scratch. [29] proposes an unsupervised tracking method based on the Siamese correlation filter network, which is learned via forward and backward tracking. These two methods aim to learn a generic feature representation, while not being strictly required to track a complete object. They all use the randomly cropped bounding boxes as tracking initialization which could result in ambiguity, *e.g.*, tracking a patch that only contain the background or contain multiple objects does not make sense. In this paper, we initialize the tracking target from the vehicle locations which are obtained by vehicle detection model. Therefore our model is more efficient. Furthermore there are many vehicles around the target vehicle. So we introduce self-supervised triplet loss to ensure the effectiveness and efficiency of self-supervised tracking module.

3 Unsupervised Vehicle Re-ID Framework

3.1 Formulation

Given the consecutive vehicle video frames $\mathcal{I} = \{I_1, I_2, \cdots, I_n\}$ and the bounding boxes (location parameters) of all vehicles $\Theta = \{\theta_1, \theta_2, \cdots, \theta_m\}$, we can obtain vehicle images $\mathcal{X} = \{x_1, x_2, \cdots, x_m\}$. Our goal is to train a vehicle Re-ID model on $\mathcal{X}$ and obtain the feature embedding model ϕ. For any query vehicle image q, the vehicle Re-ID model ϕ is expected to produce a feature vector f to retrieve image g containing the same vehicle ID from a gallery set G.

To make the training without ID label possible, we propose a novel framework of utilizing the a Self-supervised Tracking Module (STM) to learn a generic vehicle feature representation and a localization model with unlabeled data. As shown in Fig. 1, STM takes a target vehicle T_t and search patch P_t and P_{t+1} as input and outputs the embedding model φ, i.e.,

$$\varphi = \text{STM}(T_t, P_{t+1}, P_t). \tag{1}$$

According to φ and Sequence Labelling and Learning Module (SLLM), we annotate vehicle images $\mathcal{X}$ with IDs $\bar{y}_i$ automatically, i.e.,

$$\bar{y}_i = \text{SLLM}(x_i, \varphi). \tag{2}$$

After remove outlier images in vehicle sequence, we enhance the accuracy of the predicted labels $\bar{y}_i$. We training embedding model ϕ by taken vehicle image x_i and label $\bar{y}_i$ as inputs.

$$\phi = \mathcal{L}_{id}(x_i, \bar{y}_i), \tag{3}$$

where $\mathcal{L}_{id}$ is softmax loss. In the inference stage, we extract vehicle features through ϕ and retrieve the query vehicle image from gallery set.

3.2 Self-supervised Tracking Module

An overview of the self-supervised tracking procedure is presented in Fig. 1. The goal of self-supervised learning is to learn a feature space φ and a localization model LM by tracking a initial target T_t from image I_t forwards and then backwards in the subsequent frames, while minimizing the cycle consistency loss l_θ (yellow arrow in Fig. 1).

Cycle Consistency Loss. Given two consecutive frames I_t and I_{t+1}, we crop the initial target T_t and search patch P_t from I_t based on the location parameter θ_{T_t}. The search patch P_t is centered around the initial vehicle target

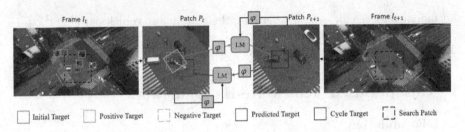

Fig. 1. Overview of self-supervised tracking module (STM) for vehicle Re-ID between two consecutive frames. The initial target (blue box) is simply the beginning of the cycle. The predicted target (purple box) is the location that obtained by localization model (LM). The cycle target (red box) is the end of the cycle that obtained by tracking backward. The yellow arrow between the start and end represents the cycle consistency learning signal. To ensure the efficiency of our localization model, we attempt to exploit triplet samples online in each cycle during training. Better viewed in color. (Color figure online)

T_t with four times region size. We crop the search patch P_{t+1} from I_{t+1} also based on the location parameter θ_{T_t}. *i.e.*,

$$T_t = \mathrm{C}(I_t, \theta_{T_t}), P_t = \mathrm{C}(I_t, \theta_{T_t}), P_{t+1} = \mathrm{C}(I_{t+1}, \theta_{T_t}), \qquad (4)$$

where $\mathrm{C}(\cdot)$ is the crop operation. These pixel inputs are mapped to a feature space by an encoder φ, such that:

$$F_t^T = \varphi(T_t), F_t^P = \varphi(P_t), F_{t+1}^P = \varphi(P_{t+1}). \qquad (5)$$

The role of localization model LM is to locate a target features F_{t+1}^T in patch features F_{t+1}^P that are most similar to F_t^T:

$$(F_{t+1}^T, \theta_{T_{t+1}}) = \mathrm{LM}(F_t^T, F_{t+1}^P). \qquad (6)$$

where θ is the learned location parameter. By convention, the localization model LM can be applied backwards from time $t + 1$ to t:

$$(\hat{F}_t^T, \hat{\theta}_{T_t}) = \mathrm{LM}(F_{t+1}^T, F_t^P). \qquad (7)$$

where $\hat{\theta}_{T_t}$ and $\hat{F}_t^T$ are the location parameter and corresponding features of the cycle target as depicted in Fig. 1.

The cycle consistency loss $\mathcal{L}_\theta$ is defined as

$$\mathcal{L}_\theta = l_\theta(F_t^T, \hat{F}_t^T) = \frac{1}{n} \sum_i^n \|\mathcal{T}(\theta_{T_t})_i - \mathcal{T}(\hat{\theta}_{T_t})_i\|_2^2. \qquad (8)$$

where $\mathcal{T}(\cdot)$ corresponds to the transform operation. We follow the formulation introduced by [24]. They construct a grid of points in image A, transform it using the ground truth and neural network estimated transformations $\mathcal{T}(\theta_{T_t})$ and

$\mathcal{T}(\hat{\theta}_{T_t})$ with parameters θ_{T_t} and $\hat{\theta}_{T_t}$, respectively, and measure the discrepancy between the two transformed grids by summing the squared distances between the corresponding grid points. Assuming $\mathcal{T}(\theta)$ contains n sampling coordinates. It measures the error in alignment between the initial target and cycle target.

Self-supervised Triplet Loss. To ensure the efficiency of our localization model and obtain a robust representation that is able to model wide range of appearance changes, we attempt to exploit triplet samples in each frame during training. It is clear in Fig. 1 that we define the initial target as anchor sample S_a (the blue box in frame I_t), the other vehicle targets as negative sample S_n (the orange dashed box in frame I_t). We conduct random image transformation on S_a and generate a positive sample S_p (the green box in patch P_t). The triplet loss can be defined as:

$$\mathcal{L}_{triplet}(f_a, f_p, f_n) = \max(0, \mathrm{d}(f_a, f_p) - \mathrm{d}(f_a, f_n) + m), \qquad (9)$$

$$(f_a, f_p, f_n) = \mathrm{GAP}(\varphi(S_a), \varphi(S_p), \varphi(S_n)), \qquad (10)$$

where $\mathrm{d}(\cdot)$ represents the L_2 distance, $\varphi(\cdot)$ denote the encoder network, $\mathrm{GAP}(\cdot)$ denote Global Average Pooling operation and m is a constant threshold value. Note that the triplet loss is carried out in a self-supervised manner and only needed in training process.

The overall learning objective could be represented as:

$$\mathcal{L} = \mathcal{L}_\theta + \lambda\mathcal{L}_{triplet}. \qquad (11)$$

where λ control the contribution of $\mathcal{L}_\theta$ and $\mathcal{L}_{triplet}$.

3.3   Sequence Labelling and Learning Module

Sequence Labelling. Since STM can locate the initial target position of the current frame in the next frame, we could use STM many times to obtain a vehicle sequence for each initial vehicle target. For the first frame of each video, we choose all the detected vehicle instances as the initial tracking target and assign them with different identities. Then predict their location in the second frame with STM. For the second frame, we examine all the detected vehicle instances. Find the vehicle instances that have different locations from the vehicle targets that predicted from the first frame and then label them with new identities. Then we set the predicted vehicle locations and the new detected vehicle locations in the second frame as the initial tracking target and predict their location in the third frame. By that analogy, we can apply STM iteratively in a forward manner from the first frame to the end of the video frame. By doing this, we can obtain a set of vehicle sequences with different identities:

$$\{S_1, S_2, \cdots, S_C\}, S_j = \{x_{i,j}\}_{i=1}^{l_j}, j = \{1, \cdots, C\} \qquad (12)$$

where C is the number of vehicle identities and each sequence contains l_j vehicle images. With these labeled vehicle images, we can optimise a vehicle Re-ID model.

Sequence Clustering with KNN: Because the same vehicle may appear in different videos, we need to associate the same vehicle images from different videos. Inspired by k-reciprocal nearest neighbor [40], we assume that, if two vehicle sequences belong to the same class, their neighbor image sequences should also be similar. In other words, two sequences should be mutual neighbor for each other if they can be assigned with similar labels. We first calculate the center feature f_j of each sequence. Then we compute the sequence distance based on these center features. When two vehicle sequences (selected from two different videos) are both k-reciprocal nearest neighbors, we regard the two vehicle sequences as true matches.

Sequence Discrimination Learning. We choose ResNet50 [11] as the supervised learning backbone. Then we use softmax loss to train the automatically annotated data. We compute the softmax loss as:

$$\mathcal{L}_{id}(f_i) = \sum_{j=1}^{C} -y_i(j) \cdot \log(\frac{\exp(\omega_j^\mathsf{T} f_i)}{\sum_{k=1}^{C} \exp(\omega_k^\mathsf{T} f_i)}), \tag{13}$$

where f_i and y_i refer to the extracted feature vector and the assigned vehicle ID for the i-th training image. C denotes the number of vehicle categories in the training set, and ω_k denotes the classifier parameters of the k-th category. Finally, we obtain the network parameters ϕ and use it to extract image features f at the inference stage.

4   Experiments

4.1   Datasets and Settings

We use two UAVs to simultaneously shoot videos at two adjacent locations or at the same location with different viewpoints (in total we select 16 locations), in order to capture vehicle instances with a diverse set of view-angles. With more than 60 man-hours of UAV flying and video shooting, we finally collect 40 of videos, with approximately 500 min.

Unsupervised Training Data Construct. We select 30 of videos from the collected UAV-based videos, with a total length of 320 min. In each video, we sample frames at every 0.25 s and obtain approximately 76,000 image frames in total. The bounding boxes we used were automatically generated by the object detection model in advance for all the training data.

Detection Module. There are many off the shelf object localization algorithms. In this paper we use SSD [18] to detect the vehicle bounding boxes from training frames. We select 300 frames from our UAV-based vehicle video dataset. For these selected frames, four corners of all visible vehicles are manually marked and stored. The SSD model is trained with these annotated bounding box labels, which is hence used to generate the location labels on all of the UAV-based vehicle video frames. In the inference stage of detection, each bounding box is assigned a confidence score that indicates the possibility of that bounding box belonging to vehicle class. We set a threshold $\delta = 0.3$ for excluding the samples with confidence scores below the threshold. All input images for SSD model are resized to 512×512. Compared to a large number of vehicle IDs labeling, bounding box annotation on 300 image frames is relatively easier to carry out.

Testing Data. We use UAV-VeID [28] dataset to verify the performance of proposed methods. The training set contains 18,709 bounding boxes of 1797 identities, the validation set contains 4150 bounding boxes of 596 identities and the test set contains 19,058 bounding boxes of 2208 identities, respectively. During testing, we follow [28] to split the query and gallery set. One image is randomly selected from each vehicle to generate a gallery set with 1,386 images. The remaining 14,080 images are used as query images.

4.2 Experimental Details

All the experiments are executed on a computer with 4.00GHz Intel Core i7 and one NVIDIA GTX 1080Ti GPU. During self-supervised tracking training, we use the Adam with weight decay 0.0003 to optimize the parameters for 100 epochs. The batch size is set to 8. The initial learning rate is set to 3×10^4 and decays to 3×10^5 after 50 epochs. We empirically set $m = 0.3$ for Eq. 9, $\lambda = 0.1$ for Eq. 11. We resize the original frame size to 1280×2428. The size of the vehicle box and search patch are set as 128×128 and 512×512. We learn the feature encoder φ with ResNet50 [11] architecture without res5 for larger spatial outputs. The size of the spatial features of the vehicle target and search patch are $8 \times 8 \times c$ and $32 \times 32 \times c$ (c is the channel num of the last feature map of res4). For sequence discrimination learning model ϕ we resize vehicle images to 224×224. The initial learning rate is set to 1×10^3 and decays to 1×10^4 after 20 epochs. The maximal training epoch was set to 40.

At the Re-ID inference stage, given a test probe vehicle image and a set of gallery vehicle images, we first compute feature vector f by forward-feeding each image to the trained network ϕ. Then, we compute the distance between query and each gallery image with the L_2 distance, and rank all gallery images according to their distance to the probe image. The top-ranked images are supposed as the true positives of the Re-ID result. The widely used cumulative matching characteristics (CMC) curve and mean average precision (mAP) are used for quantitative measurement.

4.3 Ablation Study and Parameter Analysis

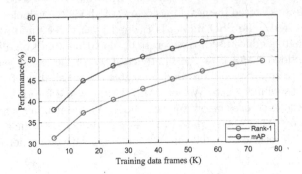

Fig. 2. Evaluating the unlabeled training frame size.

Different Size of Unlabeled Training Frame. We utilize different size of training frame for training our proposed model. Different proportions of video frames are used to train our framework. Figure 2 shows that gradually increase the amount of video frames can advance the performance on UAV-VeID dataset. Utilizing STM and SLLM on approximately 76,000 frames of unsupervised video frames can yield 49.1% in rank-1 accuracy.

Table 1. Effectiveness of KNN for sequence clustering.

Methods	Rank-1	Rank-5	Rank-10	mAP
SLLM-w/o-KNN	49.1	62.66	68.95	55.57
SLLM-w/-KNN	**52.39**	**68.86**	**75.78**	**59.26**

Effectiveness of KNN. If the value of k is too small, the clustering effect between vehicle sequences will be very weak. If the value of k is too large, there will be more false matches included in the k-reciprocal set, resulting in a decline in performance. We set k to 5 according to the characteristics of the data set. Experiment results are shown in Table 1. It can be seen that, SLLM-w/-KNN consistently improves the rank-1 accuracy and mAP, which demonstrate that the KNN operation is effective.

4.4 Comparison with the State of the Art

One of the most popular solutions for unsupervised Re-ID issue is transfer learning. It leverages labeled data on other domains for model initialization

Table 2. Comparison with the state of the art on UAV-VeID dataset.

Methods	Supervised	Source-Data	Rank-1	Rank-5	Rank-10
Direct Transfer	-	✓	16.96	27.34	33.22
RevGrad [8]	-	✓	20.30	34.81	42.67
UDAR [25]	-	✓	23.14	40.92	49.93
MMT [9]	-	✓	31.26	49.63	56.31
CMSN [37]	-	✓	41.22	53.63	60.61
PPLR [3]	-	✓	47.78	62.16	71.89
Ours	-	-	**52.39**	**68.86**	**75.78**
Baseline	✓	-	61.70	80.36	88.53
MVAN [27]	✓	-	65.33	83.02	91.78
VSCR [28]	✓	-	70.59	88.33	92.51
S + U	✓	-	63.52	79.58	86.91
U → S (Ours)	✓	-	**72.25**	**89.93**	**95.36**

or label transfer. We use VehicleID [17] as the source data and UAV-VeID as target data for vehicle Re-ID experiments. The training set of VehicleID have 100,182 images and 13,164 identities. In Table 2, Direct Transfer denotes that directly using the initial source-trained encoder network on the target data. RevGrad [8] proposes a gradient reversal layer (GRL) and integrate it into a standard deep neural network for minimizing the classification loss in source data while minimizing the distribution discrepancy between different datasets. UDAR [25] iteratively performs clustering on unlabeled target data and then fine tuning the network on selected samples with pseudo labels. MMT [9] proposes an unsupervised Mutual Mean-Teaching (MMT) framework to tackle the problem of noisy pseudo labels in clustering-based unsupervised domain adaptation methods. CMSN [37] is a multiple object tracking (MOT) method. We use this MOT method to replace our self-supervised tracking method to associate vehicle images. PPLR [3] is a part-based pseudo label refinement method. As shown in Table 2, our unsupervised method significantly outperforms the traditional unsupervised Re-ID methods. There is a significant domain gap between UAV-VeID and the traditional vehicle Re-ID datasets VehicleID [17]. Cross-domain transfer methods are limited on the significant gaps of images between different datasets. Thus they still yield weak performances. Compared with CMSN [37] and PPLR [3] we also have better results. Because the pretrain data in [37] and PPLR [3] is different from our dataset in viewpoints and scales.

We report results of fully-supervised methods on UAV-VeID dataset. We integrate the training samples obtained by our method and the supervised dataset together to further improve the performance on UAV-VeID dataset. MVAN [27] proposes a multi-view spatial attention network to alleviate negative effects of vehicle viewpoint variance. VSCR [28] proposes a viewpoint adversarial training strategy to alleviate the negative effects of viewpoint variance. Table 2 sum-

marizes the results of different data training strategies. Our method already
achieves fairly strong performance 72.25% in Rank-1 accuracy on UAV-VeID
dataset. In Table 2, S + U shows the performance that incorporating the training samples obtained by our framework and the UAV-VeID training sets. U → S
shows the performance of pre training with our proposed pseudo label datasets
and then fine-tuning with UAV-VeID training sets. U → S method outperforms
other supervised methods by a large margin. This indicates that our method not
only has good generalization ability, but also can help supervised data to further
improve the performance.

5   Conclusion

In this paper, we propose a method of implementing unsupervised UAV vehicle
Re-ID using self supervised tracking. This design reduces the cost of manual
annotation for vehicle identities and achieves scalable vehicle Re-ID in practical applications. We construct a large-scale video dataset for unsupervised UAV
vehicle Re-ID. Extensive experiments demonstrate the effectiveness of the proposed method in unsupervised vehicle Re-ID.

Acknowledgements. This work is supported in part by The National Natural Science
Foundation of China (62202061); Beijing Natural Science Foundation (4232025); R&D
Program of Beijing Municipal Education Commission (KM202311232002).

References

1. Bansal, A., Ma, S., Ramanan, D., Sheikh, Y.: Recycle-gan: Unsupervised video
   retargeting. In: ECCV (2018)
2. Chen, H., Wang, Y., Lagadec, B., Dantcheva, A., Bremond, F.: Learning invariance
   from generated variance for unsupervised person re-identification. IEEE Trans.
   Pattern Analysis Mach. Intell. (2022)
3. Cho, Y., Kim, W.J., Hong, S., Yoon, S.E.: Part-based pseudo label refinement for
   unsupervised person re-identification. In: CVPR, pp. 7298–7308 (2022)
4. Chu, R., Sun, Y., Li, Y., Liu, Z., Zhang, C., Wei, Y.: Vehicle re-identification with
   viewpoint-aware metric learning. In: ICCV (2019)
5. Deng, W., Zheng, L., Ye, Q., Kang, G., Yang, Y., Jiao, J.: Image-image domain
   adaptation with preserved self-similarity and domain-dissimilarity for person rei-
   dentification. In: CVPR (2018)
6. Dwibedi, D., Aytar, Y., Tompson, J., Sermanet, P., Zisserman, A.: Temporal cycle-
   consistency learning. In: CVPR (2019)
7. Fu, Y., Wei, Y., Wang, G., Zhou, Y., Shi, H., Huang, T.S.: Self-similarity grouping: A simple unsupervised cross domain adaptation approach for person re-
   identification. In: ICCV (2019)
8. Ganin, Y., Lempitsky, V.: Unsupervised domain adaptation by backpropagation.
   In: ICML (2015)
9. Ge, Y., Chen, D., Li, H.: Mutual mean teaching pseudo label refinery for unsupervised domain adaption on person reid. In: ICLR (2020)

10. He, B., Li, J., Zhao, Y., Tian, Y.: Part-regularized near-duplicate vehicle re-identification. In: CVPR (2019)
11. He, K., Zhang, X., Ren, S., Sun, J.: Deep residual learning for image recognition. In: CVPR (2016)
12. Kulkarni, N., Gupta, A., Tulsiani, S.: Canonical surface mapping via geometric cycle consistency. In: ICCV (2019)
13. Lai, Z., Lu, E., Xie, W.: Mast: A memory-augmented self-supervised tracker. In: CVPR (2020)
14. Li, M., Liu, J., Zheng, C., Huang, X., Zhang, Z.: Exploiting multi-view part-wise correlation via an efficient transformer for vehicle re-identification. IEEE Trans. Multimedia **25**, 919–929 (2023)
15. Li, Y., Fu, C., Ding, F., Huang, Z., Lu, G.: Autotrack: Towards high-performance visual tracking for UAV with automatic spatio-temporal regularization. In: CVPR (2020)
16. Lin, Y., Dong, X., Zheng, L., Yan, Y., Yang, Y.: A bottom-up clustering approach to unsupervised person re-identification. In: AAAI (2019)
17. Liu, H., Tian, Y., Yang, Y., Pang, L., Huang, T.: Deep relative distance learning: Tell the difference between similar vehicles. In: CVPR (2016)
18. Liu, W.: SSD: Single shot multibox detector. In: ECCV (2016)
19. Lou, Y., Bai, Y., Liu, J., Wang, S., Duan, L.: Veri-wild: A large dataset and a new method for vehicle re-identification in the wild. In: CVPR (2019)
20. Meng, D., et al.: Parsing-based view-aware embedding network for vehicle re-identification. In: CVPR (2020)
21. Qi, L., Wang, L., Huo, J., Zhou, L., Shi, Y., Gao, Y.: A novel unsupervised camera-aware domain adaptation framework for person re-identification. In: ICCV (2019)
22. Qian, W., Luo, H., Peng, S., Wang, F., Chen, C., Li, H.: Unstructured feature decoupling for vehicle re-identification. In: ECCV (2022). https://doi.org/10.1007/978-3-031-19781-9_20
23. Robicquet, A., Sadeghian, A., Alahi, A., Savarese, S.: Learning social etiquette: human trajectory understanding in crowded scenes. In: Leibe, B., Matas, J., Sebe, N., Welling, M. (eds.) ECCV 2016. LNCS, vol. 9912, pp. 549–565. Springer, Cham (2016). https://doi.org/10.1007/978-3-319-46484-8_33
24. Rocco, I., Arandjelovic, R., Sivic, J.: Convolutional neural network architecture for geometric matching. In: CVPR (2017)
25. Song, L., et al.: Unsupervised domain adaptive re-identification: Theory and practice. In: PR (2020)
26. Teng, S., Liu, X., Zhang, S., Huang, Q.: SCAN: spatial and channel attention network for vehicle re-identification. In: Hong, R., Cheng, W.-H., Yamasaki, T., Wang, M., Ngo, C.-W. (eds.) PCM 2018. LNCS, vol. 11166, pp. 350–361. Springer, Cham (2018). https://doi.org/10.1007/978-3-030-00764-5_32
27. Teng, S., Zhang, S., Huang, Q., Sebe, N.: Multi-view spatial attention embedding for vehicle re-identification. In: TCSVT (2020)
28. Teng, S., Zhang, S., Huang, Q., Sebe, N.: Viewpoint and scale consistency reinforcement for UAV vehicle re-identification. Int. J. Comput. Vision **129**, 719–735 (2021)
29. Wang, N., Song, Y., Ma, C., Zhou, W., Liu, W., Li, H.: Unsupervised deep tracking. In: CVPR (2019)
30. Wang, P., et al.: Vehicle re-identification in aerial imagery: Dataset and approach. In: ICCV (2019)
31. Wang, X., Jabri, A., Efros, A.A.: Efros. Learning correspondence from the cycle-consistency of time. In: CVPR (2019)

32. Wei, L., Zhang, S., Gao, W., Tian, Q.: Person transfer GAN to bridge domain gap for person re-identification. In: CVPR (2018)

33. Wu, A., Zheng, W.S., Lai, J.H.: Unsupervised person re-identification by camera-aware similarity consistency learning. In: ICCV (2019)

34. Yan, H., Ding, Y., Li, P., Wang, Q., Xu, Y., Zuo, W.: Mind the class weight bias: Weighted maximum mean discrepancy for unsupervised domain adaptation. In: CVPR (2017)

35. Yang, F., Fan, H., Chu, P., Blasch, E., Ling, H.: Clustered object detection in aerial images. In: ICCV (2019)

36. Yu, H., et al.: The unmanned aerial vehicle benchmark: object detection, tracking and baseline. Int. J. Comput. Vision **128**(5), 1141–1159 (2019). https://doi.org/10.1007/s11263-019-01266-1

37. Yu, H., et al.: The unmanned aerial vehicle benchmark: Object detection, tracking and baseline. IJCV **128**(5), 1141–1159 (2020)

38. Zach, C., Klopschitz, M., Pollefeys, M.: Disambiguating visual relations using loop constraints. In: CVPR (2010)

39. Zhang, X., et al.: Implicit sample extension for unsupervised person re-identification. In: CVPR, pp. 7359–7368 (2022)

40. Zhong, Z., Zheng, L., Cao, D., Li, S.: Reranking person re-identification with k-reciprocal encoding. In: CVPR (2017)

41. Zhou, T., Krahenbuhl, P., Aubry, M., Huang, Q., Efros, A.A.: Learning dense correspondence via 3D-guided cycle consistency. In: CVPR (2016)

42. Zhu, J.Y., Park, T., Isola, P., Efros, A.A.: Unpaired image-to-image translation using cycle-consistent adversarial networks. In: ICCV (2017)

Distance-Aware Vector-Field and Vector Screening Strategy for 6D Object Pose Estimation

Lichun Wang[1,2]($\boxtimes$) , Chao Yang[1,2] , Jianjia Xin[1,2], and Baocai Yin[1,2]

[1] Faculty of Information Technology, Beijing University of Technology, Beijing 100124, China
wanglc@bjut.edu.cn, {yangchaoyc,xinjianjia}@emails.bjut.edu.cn
[2] Beijing Key Laboratory of Multimedia and Intelligent Software Technology, Beijing University of Technology, Beijing 100124, China

Abstract. 6D object pose estimation calculates the rotation and translation matrices from the object coordinate system to the camera coordinate system and plays an important role in tasks such as robotic grasping. The voting-based 6D pose estimation method PVNet votes on a set of hypotheses to determine one as the estimation for real keypoint, and uses Perspective-n-Point (PnP) algorithm to calculate 6D pose based on the estimated keypoints. For improving the accuracy of estimated keypoints, the accuracy of hypotheses should be improved firstly. Since each hypothesis is an intersection computed with extended lines of two predicted unit vectors, three factors should be considered for improving its accuracy. The deviation of angle between predicted vector and real vector should be as small as possible. The angular deviation for predicted vectors of pixels farther away from keypoints should be smaller than that of those nearer. Any two approximately parallel or coincident predicted vectors should be prohibited to compute intersection. In light of the three points, this paper predicts vector-field instead of unit vector-field to take into account the distance from pixel to real keypoint, and proposes a distance-aware vector-field prediction loss which requires that the farther pixels from keypoints, the smaller the angular deviation for predicted vectors, and suggests a strategy for preventing approximately parallel or coincident predicted vectors from computing hypothesis. Experiments on LINEMOD and OCC-LINEMOD datasets show that our method achieves 5.9% and 8.4% improvement for the average accuracy of pose estimation in terms of ADD(-S) respectively compared with PVNet.

Keywords: 6D Pose estimation · Distance-aware vector-field · Vector screen · Deep learning

This research was supported by The National Key R & D Program of China (No.2021ZD0111902), NSFC(U21B2038, 61876012), Foundation for China university Industry-university Research Innovation (No.2021JQR023).

H. Lu et al. (Eds.): ICIG 2023, LNCS 14356, pp. 373–388, 2023.
https://doi.org/10.1007/978-3-031-46308-2_31

1   Introduction

Estimating the 6D pose of object with RGB image has a wide range of applications in autonomous driving, industrial robot, and augmented reality. However, in the real world, affected by illumination changes, object occlusion, insufficient texture information, and cluttered scenes, accurately estimating the 6D object pose becomes a challenging problem. Traditional methods [1–4] usually extract manually defined features from image, then establish the corresponding relationship between object 2D image and 3D model, finally solve 6D pose parameters through geometric methods. However, the manually defined features are not robust to complex scenes. With the rise of deep learning, many deep learning-based 6D pose estimation algorithms [5–25] extract features with CNN automatically and achieve better performance than traditional methods.

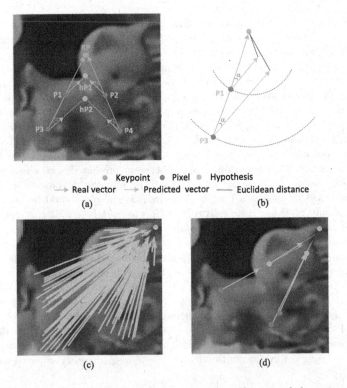

Fig. 1. Influence of predicted vectors on computing hypotheses and the necessity of vector screening. (a) When the angle deviation is same, the distance from pixel to keypoint has greater impact on the accuracy of the computed hypothesis. (b) Euclidean distance between the predicted vector and the real vector reflects two points, the modulus length of the predicted vector whose ground-truth is the distance from pixel to keypoint, the angle deviation between the predicted vector and the real vector. (c) Vector-field. (d) Parallel or nearly parallel vectors, filtered out before calculating hypotheses.

However, using network to extract object features is still not ideal, when there is occlusion or truncation in the image. Recently, some works make efforts to deal with occlusion [5–9], among which PVNet [5] suggests pixel-wise estimation to deal with occlusion or truncation. Instead of directly predicting the position of each keypoint, PVNet creates a unit vector-field representation for each 2D keypoint, by voting on the unit vector-field, which can accurately locate keypoints from the visible part even if the object is occluded or outside of the image. PVNet constrains the angular deviation of each predicted unit vector as small as possible to gain hypotheses with high accuracy, but it is not always effective due to the influence of the distance from pixel to keypoint. In Fig. 1(a), p_1 and p_2 are two pixels having same distance from the keypoint KP, p_3 and p_4 are another two pixels having the same distance from KP. p_3 and p_4 locate more farther from KP than p_1 and p_2. The predicted vectors for all the four pixels have small enough angular deviation α. The hypothesis $hp2$ computed with p_3 and p_4 has worse accuracy than the hypothesis $hp1$ computed with p_1 and p_2, which means that both the angular deviation of predicted vector and the distance from pixel to keypoint affect the accuracy of the hypothesis. As shown in Fig. 1(b), this paper predicts vector-field and uses Euclidean distance between predicted vector and real vector as loss, which gives a larger penalty to the predicted vector having larger difference to the real vector, thereby constraining the angular deviation of the predicted vectors of pixels far from the keypoint to be smaller. Figure 1(c) shows the vector-field predicted in this paper. Figure 1(d) shows that when calculating hypotheses, if the predicted vectors used to calculate the intersection are approximately parallel, the error of the calculated hypothesis is large, so it is necessary to perform vector screening before calculating hypotheses.

For improving the accuracy of voting-based 6D object pose estimation, the main contributions of our work are as follows:

• Learn distance-aware vector-field instead of unit vector-field and suggest distance-aware vector-field prediction loss, by which the predicted vectors of pixels far from keypoints are constrained to smaller angular deviations.

• Propose screening strategy for preventing two approximately parallel or coincident predicted vectors from computing hypotheses.

• Compared with PVNet, our method has significant performance improvement on two popular datasets(LINEMOD and OCC-LINEMOD). The accuracy of ADD(-S) is improved by 5.9% and 8.4% respectively, the accuracy of 5 cm 5° is improved by 1.7% and 4.66% respectively, the accuracy of 2 cm 2° is improved by 13.6% and 3.23% respectively.

2   Related Work

Existing RGB-based 6D pose estimation methods first construct correspondence between 2D keypoints in image and 3D points which locate on 3D object model or vertex of 3D bounding box for object model, then use PnP algorithm [26] to calculate 6D pose based on the constructed 2D-3D correspondence. The correspondence between 2D keypoints and 3D keypoints is intermediate representation for the 6D pose. According to the intensity of intermediate representation, RGB-based 6D pose estimation methods can be divided into two kinds, sparse correspondence-based method and dense correspondence-based method. The dense correspondence-based method is more time consuming because of needing more object model information for predicting dense correspondence.

Traditional sparse correspondence-based methods [1–3] directly located 2D keypoints based on feature detection and establish 2D-3D correspondence through feature matching. However, these methods can only work well on objects with rich textures. To address this problem, some deep learning-based works [10–14] firstly defined 3D model keypoints and predicted their projections on the image, the projections are regarded as 2D keypoints. Bb8 [10] and Yolo-6D [11] defined the eight vertices of object model's 3D bounding box as 3D model keypoints. Bb8 [10] segmented object from image and regressed coordinates of the 3D model keypoints from the segmented object using CNN. For promoting computation speed, Yolo-6D [11] regressed coordinates of the 3D model keypoints using the lightweight network YOLO9000 [22]. The traditional methods considered general cases, so the locating accuracy was seriously affected while dealing with occlusion scenes, resulting in significant decrease for the accuracy of pose estimation.

Some recent deep learning-based methods [5–9] define the 3D model keypoints on the surface of 3D object model to avoid locating 2D keypoints outside of the object piexs in the image. There would be bigger error for the locating of 2D keypoints while the projections are located outside of the object region. PVNet [5] defined the keypoints on the model surface and proposed voting-based method, which first predicted a unit vector-field for each 2D keypoint and then voted to estimate a spatial probability distribution for the 2D keypoint, which ensures the 2D keypoint at the occluded position can be robustly estimated by the visible part of object. Based on PVNet, DPVR [6] added a differentiable proxy voting loss item to make the network to predict unit vectors having smaller angular deviation for pixels farther away from the keypoints. Because the proxy voting loss item computes the length of vertical segment from real keypoint to the extended line of predicted unit vector, so two unit vectors having reverse directions receive same loss, which is ambiguous for constraining the network. HybridPose [7] utilized multiple intermediate representations to represent different geometric information in images, including keypoints, edge vectors, and symmetric correspondences, which greatly improved the accuracy of estimating 6D pose compared to using one intermediate representation. KDFNet [8] used a neural network to regress the keypoint distance field(KDF) for each keypoint, and proposed a distance-based voting scheme to localize hypotheses by calculating the intersection of circles, which implicitly using all directions from the pixel to the keypoint, rather than a specific direction. So, KDFNet prompts that predicting correct direction is important for locating keypoints.

The dense correspondence-based method predicted 3D coordinates for each object pixel, thereby constructed pixel-level correspondences. Traditional methods [27–29] predicted 3D coordinates for all pixels using random forest. Recently, some works [16–21] used CNN to predict dense 3D coordinates to build 2D-3D correspondence. SO-Pose [16] established a two-layer intermediate representation to utilize self-occlusion information. EPOS [17] divided the 3D model into a certain number of patches, then predicted multiple possible corresponding 3D points for each pixel, meaning that EPOS constructed many-to-many 2D-3D correspondences. Considering the translation is more affected by size and position of object, the rotation is more affected by appearance of object, CDPN [18] decoupled rotation and translation and computed separately. The translation was regressed through the network directly, the rotation was calculated through RANSAC-PnP algorithm based on the dense correspondence between object image and 3D model.

3   Methodology

For improving accuracy of hypotheses, this paper predicts distance-aware vector-field instead of unit vector-field, defines distance-aware vector-field prediction loss and suggests a strategy for excluding inappropriate predicted vectors from computing hypotheses. Figure 2 is an overview of the proposed method, this paper uses the same network architecture as PVNet, takes H × W × 3 images as input, and output the H × W × (2 × I) tensor representing vector-field (I represents the number of keypoints on the object), then appropriate vectors are selected to calculate the intersection as a hypotheses, next, the 2D keypoints are located by voting on the hypotheses, finally the 6D pose parameters of the object are calculated through PnP algorithm.

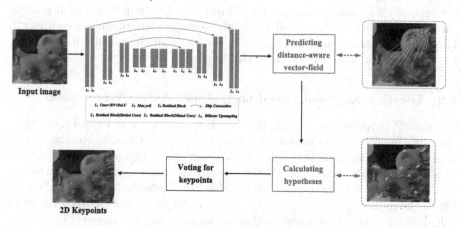

Fig. 2. Vector-field based pose prediction network which backbone and network flow are same with PVNet. The blue rectangles are implemented with new proposals of this paper. (Color figure online)

3.1   Distance-Aware Vector-Field Prediction

Existing voting-based method predicts pixel-level unit vector-field, which makes the network pay more attention to the local area of image to handle the occluded object. As shown in Fig. 1(a), predicting vector with smaller angular deviation for the pixel farther away from the real keypoint is benefit for improving the accuracy of hypothesis, so considering the distance from pixel to real keypoint is necessary. Instead of predicting unit vector, for the ith real keypoint of the object O, this paper predicts a vector $v^i(p)$ for each pixel p. As shown in Eq. 1, $v^i(p)$ is the vector pointing from the pixel p to the keypoint kp_i of the object O.

$$v^i(p) = kp_i - p \tag{1}$$

The modulus length of $v^i(p)$ is an estimation of the distance from pixel p to keypoint kp_i. Then, the predicted vector-field for the keypoint kp_i of object O is gotten. The vector-field is noted as $V(kp_i) \in R^{H \times W \times 2}$, where $V(kp_i)[h, w, :] = v^i(p)$.

In order to simultaneously consider the deviation angle of the prediction vector and the distance from pixel to keypoint, this paper suggests distance-aware vector-field prediction loss to minimize Euclidean distance between pixel's predicted vector and its real vector, as shown in Eq. 2.

$$L_{vf} = \sum_i \sum_{p \in O} smooth\ell_1 \left(\left\| v^i(p) - g^i(p) \right\|_2 \right) \tag{2}$$

where $g^i(p)$ is the real vector pointing from the pixel p to the keypoint kp_i. The loss L_{vf} not only constrains the direction of predicted vector more closer to the corresponding ground-truth, but also is sensitive to the position of pixel. For the pixel farther away from real keypoint, corresponding predicted vectors will be punished more even if its angular deviation is small, which stimulates the hypotheses to be more closer to the real keypoint.

3.2   Locating Keypoint Based on Distance-Aware Vector-Field

For the ith keypoint of the object O, using the vector-field $V(kp_i)$, the corresponding hypotheses are generated according to **Algorithm** 1. For the vector-field $V(kp_i)$, we calculate the angle between each pair of vectors in the vector-field to obtain the angle matrix A and then calculate the indicator matrix A' which is used for filtering the vector pairs not suitable for calculating hypotheses. According to the indicator matrix, N vector pairs are selected from the vector-field to calculate the lines where these vectors are located, and the intersection of each pair of lines is taken as a hypothesis. After generating the hypotheses, the distributions of the hypotheses corresponding to each real keypoint is calculated, then the object's pose is computed based on the distributions using the same operation with PVNet.

Algorithm 1 Calculating hypotheses with qualified vectors.

Input: $V(kp_i) \in R^{H \times W \times 2}$, predicted vector-field for the keypoint kp_i of object O;
    threshold of angular deviation $\gamma = \pi/60$; number of hypotheses N.

Output: $K_h^i = \{hk_n^i \mid n = 0, 1, \ldots, N - 1\}$, set of hypotheses for the keypoint kp_i.

 1: Compute the angle between each pair of vectors in $V(kp_i)$ and save the results in
    angle matrix $A \in R^{t \times t}$;

 2: **for** $i = 0$; $i \leq t - 1$; $i + +$; **do**

 3:    **for** $j = 0$; $j \leq t - 1$; $j + +$; **do**

 4:      **if** $A[i][j] > \gamma$ **then**

 5:        $A'[i][j] = 1$;

 6:      **else**

 7:        $A'[i][j] = 0$;

 8:      **end if**

 9:    **end for**

10: **end for**   // Compute indicator matrix $A' \in R^{t \times t}$ according to the angle matrix A,
    the vectors have too smaller included angle are excluded from computing hypothesis
    by setting the corresponding indicator as 0.

11: Initialize: $n \leftarrow 0$;

12: **while** $(n < N)$ **do**

13:    randomly select $A'[x][y]$ from A';

14:    **if** $A'[x][y] == 1$ **then**

15:      calculate intersection hk_n^i using the $v^i(x)$, $v^i(y) \in V(kp_i)$;

16:      $A'[x][y] == 0$;

17:      $n = n + 1$;

18:    **end if**

19: **end while**   // Compute hypotheses.

3.3   Overall Objective

The overall objective function consists of semantic segmentation term and
distance-aware vector-field prediction term.

$$L = L_{se.g.} + L_{vf} \tag{3}$$

where the semantic segmentation loss L_{seg} adopts cross-entropy loss.

$$L_{seg} = -a_p \log a'_p - (1 - a_p) \log \left(1 - a'_p\right) \tag{4}$$

where a'_p is the probability that pixel p is predicted as the target object pixel,
and a_p is the semantic ground-truth.

4   Experiments

In order to prove the effectiveness and superiority of the proposed method,
we conduct experiments on two widely used 6D pose estimation datasets:
LINEMOD and OCC-LINEMOD, and compare the experiment results with popular sparse correspondence-based methods.

4.1   Datasets

(1) LINEMOD [30] is a standard 6D pose estimation dataset. The dataset contains 13 weakly textured objects and each of them has different semantic labels. The dataset has a total of 15783 images, and each object is corresponded with about 1200 images. LINEMOD dataset is challenging because of the lighting conditions, occlusion, and cluttered scenes. Usual splitting for training and testing data is adopted, 15% for training and 85% for testing. For each object, about 180 images are used for training and more than 1000 images for testing.

(2) OCC-LINEMOD [27] dataset is a subset of the LINEMOD dataset and mainly focuses on occluded objects. Each image in this dataset contains multiple annotated objects, and the objects are heavily occluded, making the 6D pose estimation more challenging.

4.2   Training Strategy

In order to avoid overfitting, synthetic data generation and data enhancement scheme are used by 6D pose estimation methods [5–9]. In our experiments, we follow the usual synthetic data generation and data enhancement scheme proposed in [5]. For LINEMOD dataset, 10000 images are rendered from different viewpoints. In addition, 10000 images are synthesized by pasting the cut object to the SUN397 dataset images. For improving the robustness of the learned model, data enhancement is imposed on the training data including random rotation, random cropping, adding noise, and color jittering.

4.3   Evalutation Metrics

(1) ADD/ADD-S [30]. ADD refers to the average distance between two-point sets, one set is generated by transforming the 3D object model with the estimated pose $(\tilde{R}, \tilde{T})$ and the other is generated by transforming the 3D object model with ground-truth pose (R, T).

$$\text{ADD} = \frac{1}{m} \sum_{x \in M} \|(Rx + T) - (\tilde{R}x + \tilde{T})\|_2 \tag{5}$$

where M is the set of 3D model points, m is the number of model points.

For symmetric objects, due to the pose ambiguity, ADD-S [23] metric is defined, where the average distance is calculated with the point pairs which are the closest.

$$\text{ADD-S} = \frac{1}{m} \sum_{\substack{x_1 \in M \\ x_2 \in M}} \|(Rx_1 + T) - (\tilde{R}x_2 + \tilde{T})\|_2 \tag{6}$$

$$\text{st. } x_2 = \arg \min_{x_i \in M} \|x_1 - x_i\|_2$$

According to [30], the estimated pose is considered correct while the average distance is less than 10% of the largest distance of all point pairs(the largest distance between all point pairs is the model diameter).

(2) Kcm K° [24]: The estimated pose is considered correct if the error of translation is lower than Kcm and the error of rotation error is lower than K°. In this paper, K is set as 5 and 2 to calculate the accuracy of estimated poses. 2cm 2° is more strict than 5cm 5°, and can better reflect the applicability of estimated pose for augmented reality tasks or fine operation of robots.

4.4   Experiments on LINEMOD and OCC-LINEMOD Datasets

Performance on LINEMOD Dataset. Table 1 shows accuracy of pose estimation according to ADD(-S) on LINEMOD dataset. Compared with other methods in this paper, by estimating more accurate hypothesis, our method achieves the highest average accuracy and improves 5.9% compared with PVNet.

Table 1. Accuracy comparison in terms of ADD(-S) on the LINEMOD dataset. The objects signed with "*" are symmetric and evaluated with ADD-S, the other objects are evaluated with ADD.

Method	Yolo-6D [11]	Bb8 [10]	PVNet [5]	HybridPose [7]	DPVR [6]	Ours
Ape	21.6	40.0	43.6	63.1	69.1	**70.4**
Benchvise	81.8	91.8	99.9	99.9	**100.0**	100.0
Cam	36.6	55.7	86.9	90.4	**94.1**	94.0
Can	68.8	64.1	95.5	98.5	**98.5**	96.1
Cat	41.8	62.6	79.3	**89.4**	83.1	88.5
Driller	63.5	74.4	96.4	98.5	**99.0**	98.3
Duck	27.2	44.3	52.6	65.0	63.5	**69.2**
Eggbox*	69.6	57.8	99.2	**100.0**	100.0	99.9
Glue*	80.0	41.2	95.7	**98.8**	98.0	98.2
Holepuncher	42.6	67.2	81.9	**89.7**	88.2	87.9
Iron	74.9	84.7	98.9	**100.0**	99.9	99.5
Lamp	71.1	76.5	99.3	99.5	**99.8**	**99.8**
Phone	47.7	54.0	92.4	94.9	96.4	**96.5**
Average	55.9	62.7	86.3	91.3	91.5	**92.2**

Table 2 shows accuracy of pose estimation of all objects according to Kcm K°. Our method outperforms PVNet for almost all categories, and the average accuracy is improved by 1.7% and 13.6%, respectively. In particular, our method improved the accuracy in terms of 2cm 2° significantly, which is very favorable for supporting fine operations, such as robotic grasping small objects.

Performance on OCC-LINEMOD dataset. Table 3 shows accuracy of pose estimation according to ADD(-S) on OCC-LINEMOD dataset. Our method achieves significant improvements, with an average accuracy increase of 8.4% compared to PVNet. Compared with KDFNet, our method achieves competitive accuracy and outperforms it on some objects. Accuracy of pose estimation

Table 2. Accuracy comparison of all objects in terms of Kcm K° with PVNet on the LINEMOD dataset.

Method	PVNet [5]		Ours	
Threshold	5cm 5°	2cm 2°	5cm 5°	2cm 2°
Ape	91.90	27.05	**96.57**	**63.05**
Benchvise	99.52	79.46	**100.0**	**86.82**
Cam	99.02	64.22	**99.22**	**79.61**
Can	**99.31**	78.05	99.21	**89.17**
Cat	98.50	58.28	**99.20**	**73.95**
Driller	97.72	73.84	**99.70**	**80.18**
Duck	91.27	32.86	**94.46**	**49.39**
Eggbox*	97.84	55.40	**99.34**	**65.16**
Glue*	90.15	37.74	**95.75**	**60.91**
Holepuncher	97.43	53.95	**98.19**	**65.84**
Iron	97.65	60.67	**99.69**	**74.46**
Lamp	**99.42**	**78.98**	99.33	74.95
Phone	98.17	61.96	**99.33**	**75.70**
Average	96.76	58.65	**98.46**	**72.25**

of all objects according to Kcm K° is shown in Table 4. Our method outperforms PVNet for almost all categories, and the average accuracy is improved by 4.66% and 3.23%, respectively. Because the OCC-LINEMOD dataset includes seriously occluded cases, the accuracy of pose estimation on OCC-LINEMOD dataset is lower than that of the LINEMOD dataset, and improving the accuracy is more difficult.

Table 3. Accuracy comparison in terms of ADD(-S) on the OCC-LINEMOD dataset. The objects signed with "*" are symmetric and evaluated with ADD-S, the other objects are evaluated with ADD.

Method	Yolo-6D [11]	Oberweger [15]	PVNet [5]	DPVR [6]	RPVNet [9]	HybridPose [7]	KDFNet [8]	Ours
Ape	2.5	17.6	15.8	19.2	17.9	20.9	19.5	**23.3**
Can	17.5	53.9	63.3	69.8	69.5	75.3	**78.4**	75.4
Cat	0.7	3.3	16.7	21.1	19.0	24.9	**28.2**	23.8
Driller	1.1	19.2	65.7	71.6	63.7	70.2	**75.1**	72.3
Duck	7.7	62.4	25.2	34.3	31.1	27.9	**38.6**	36.2
Eggbox*	-	25.9	50.2	47.3	**59.2**	52.4	51.2	53.6
Glue*	10.1	39.6	49.6	39.7	46.6	53.8	52.1	**58.0**
Holepuncher	5.5	21.3	39.7	45.3	42.8	54.2	**59.0**	50.7
Average	6.4	30.4	40.8	43.5	43.7	47.5	**50.3**	49.2

Table 4. Accuracy comparison of all objects in terms of Kcm K° with PVNet on the OCC-LINEMOD dataset.

Method	PVNet [5]		Ours	
Threshold	5cm 5°	2cm 2°	5cm 5°	2cm 2°
Ape	39.15	4.27	**39.32**	**4.79**
Can	69.51	24.19	**77.56**	**34.55**
Cat	18.70	1.68	**23.93**	**3.88**
Driller	66.80	23.23	**71.42**	**30.07**
Duck	16.48	2.01	**17.44**	**2.80**
Eggbox*	**1.28**	0	0.77	0
Glue*	22.70	1.0	**28.24**	**1.44**
Holepuncher	46.95	8.12	**60.17**	**12.80**
Average	35.20	8.06	**39.86**	**11.29**

4.5 Ablation Study

In this section, we explore the ablation between the distance-aware vector-field and the vector screening strategy. Table 5 and Table 6 show the ablation results on LINEMOD dataset and OCC-LINEMOD dataset respectively. Comparing the first and the third column in Table 5 or 6, it can be seen that the accuracy of pose estimation is significantly improved by predicting distance-aware vector-field. Gain of 3.62% and 5.93% are achieved on LINEMOD and OCC-LINEMOD respectively, which is due to considering the distance from the pixel to the keypoint and the angle deviation between the prediction vector and the real vector. Comparing the first and the second column in Table 5 or 6, it can be seen that the accuracy of pose estimation is improved by adding vector screening strategy. Gain of 0.28% and 0.52% are achieved on LINEMOD and OCC-LINEMOD respectively, which indicates that there has unreasonable intersection when calculating hypotheses directly. Comparing the first column with the fourth column in Table 5 or 6, it can be seen that the accuracy of pose estimation is further improved by combining distance-aware vector-field and vector screening strategy. Gain of 3.89% and 6.23% are achieved on LINEMOD and OCC-LINEMOD respectively.

4.6 Visualization

For further demonstrating the effect of our method, Fig. 3 visualizes hypotheses and real keypoints for the model "Ape" and "Cat" in LINEMOD. The hypotheses in images are respectively computed with PVNet and our method without using the vector screening strategy. The Distributions of the hypotheses in images on the right column are more concentrated than that in images on the left, which shows that the hypotheses computed with our method have higher accuracy than those computed with PVNet. The more concentrated hypotheses benefit from

Table 5. Ablation study in terms of ADD(-S) on the LINEMOD dataset. The objects signed with "*" are symmetric and evaluated with ADD-S, the other objects are evaluated with ADD.

Distance-aware vector-field	×	×	✓	✓
Screening strategy	×	✓	×	✓
Ape	60.52	61.18	68.48	**70.38**
Benchvise	**100.0**	99.81	**100.0**	**100.0**
Cam	82.76	83.04	93.63	**94.02**
Can	97.70	**98.62**	95.67	96.06
Cat	80.22	80.44	**88.52**	**88.52**
Driller	96.74	97.12	**98.41**	98.32
Duck	58.40	58.12	68.64	**69.20**
Eggbox*	99.33	99.72	99.34	**99.91**
Glue*	96.86	97.20	**98.45**	98.17
Holepuncher	85.69	85.63	87.82	**87.91**
Iron	99.70	**99.80**	99.49	99.49
Lamp	99.61	99.72	99.71	**99.81**
Phone	90.24	90.97	**96.64**	96.54
Average	88.29	88.57	91.91	**92.18**

Table 6. Ablation study in terms of ADD(-S) on the OCC-LINEMOD dataset. The objects signed with "*" are symmetric and evaluated with ADD-S, and the other objects are evaluated with ADD.

Distance-aware vector-field	×	×	✓	✓
Screening strategy	×	✓	×	✓
Ape	18.12	18.37	**23.33**	**23.33**
Can	69.01	70.67	74.82	**75.39**
Cat	19.55	19.46	23.51	**23.76**
Driller	70.68	71.58	**72.41**	72.32
Duck	26.10	26.28	35.32	**36.20**
Eggbox*	41.49	41.62	**53.70**	53.62
Glue*	51.60	52.24	57.48	**58.03**
Holepuncher	46.95	47.43	50.38	**50.71**
Average	42.94	43.46	48.87	**49.17**

the predicted vector-field having higher accuracy, which is computed using the distance-aware vector-field prediction loss.

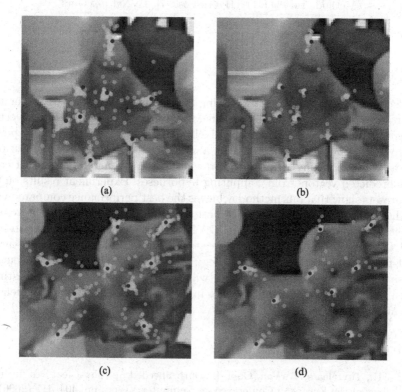

(a)   (b)

(c)   (d)

Fig. 3. Visualization of hypotheses and real keypoints for the model "Ape" (a), (b) and "Cat" (c), (d). The blue points are real keypoints and the yellow points are hypotheses. Hypotheses in images (a) and (c) are computed with PVNet, and hypotheses in images (b) and (d) are computed with our method without using the vector screening strategy. (Color figure online)

4.7   Efficiency of Prediction

Table 7 lists the FPS of several methods which are tested on a computer with Intel i9-10900X 3.7GHz CPU and GTX 3090 GPU. The experiment results show that our method achieves similar inference speed to the comparative methods. Combing the experiments listed in Table 1 and Table 3, our method achieves higher comprehensive performance for pose estimation, which is beneficial to real-time pose estimation.

Table 7. Efficiency in terms of FPS(frame/sec), tested on a computer with GPU (GTX 3090).

Method	Yolo-6D [11]	HybridPose [7]	PVNet [5]	Ours
FPS	41	40	35	34

5   Conclusion

In order to improve the accuracy of voting-based pose estimation, this paper suggests to predict distance-aware vector-field and defines a distance-aware vector-field prediction loss, which makes the pixels farther away from the real keypoints acquire predict vectors having smaller angular deviations, this paper also proposes a vector screening strategy for preventing approximately parallel or coincident predicted vectors from computing hypotheses. Experiment results on the two datasets show that our method achieves the best performance compared with the other sparse representation-based pose estimation methods, and achieves significant improvement compared with PVNet. The ablation experiment results on LINEMOD and OCC-LINEMOD datasets show that both distance-aware vector-field and vector screening strategy can effectively improve the accuracy of pose estimation. In future work, we will focus on how to apply pose estimation to practical robot grasping tasks, in order to have an impact on related applications in the real world.

References

1. Bay, H., Tuytelaars, T., Van, Gool. L.: Surf: Speeded up robust features. In: Proceedings of the European Conference on Computer Vision, pp. 404–417 (2006)
2. Lowe, D. G.: Object recognition from local scale-invariant features. In: Proceedings of the IEEE International Conference on Computer Vision, pp. 1150–1157 (1999)
3. Rublee, E., Rabaud, V., Konolige, K., Bradski, G.: ORB: an efficient alternative to SIFT or SURF. In: Proceedings of the IEEE International Conference on Computer Vision, pp. 2564–2571 (2011)
4. Rosten, E., Drummond, T.: Fusing points and lines for high performance tracking. In: Proceedings of the IEEE International Conference on Computer Vision, pp. 1508–1515 (2005)
5. Peng, S., Liu, Y., Huang, Q., Zhou, X., Bao, H.: Pvnet: pixel-wise voting network for 6dof pose estimation. In: Proceedings of the IEEE Conference on Computer Vision and Pattern Recognition, pp. 4561–4570 (2019)
6. Yu, X., Zhuang, Z., Koniusz, P., Li, H.: 6dof object pose estimation via differentiable proxy voting regularizer. In: British Machine Vision Conference, pp. 1–12 (2020)
7. Song, C., Song, J., Huang, Q.: HybridPose: 6d object pose estimation under hybrid representations. In: Proceedings of the IEEE Conference on Computer Vision and Pattern Recognition, pp. 431–440 (2020)
8. Liu, X., Iwase, S., Kitani, K. M.: KdfNet: Learning keypoint distance field for 6d object pose estimation. In: 2021 IEEE/RSJ International Conference on Intelligent Robots and Systems, pp. 4631–4638 (2021)

9. Xiong, F., Liu, C., Chen, Q.: Region pixel voting network (RPVNet) for 6d pose estimation from monocular image. Appl. Sci. **11**(2), 743–757 (2021)

10. Rad, M., Lepetit, V.: Bb8: a scalable, accurate, robust to partial occlusion method for predicting the 3d poses of challenging objects without using depth. In: Proceedings of the IEEE International Conference on Computer Vision, pp. 3828–3836 (2017)

11. Tekin, B., Sinha, S. N., Fua, P.: Real-time seamless single shot 6d object pose prediction. In: Proceedings of the IEEE Conference on Computer Vision and Pattern Recognition, pp. 292–301 (2018)

12. Zhao, W., Zhang, S., Guan, Z., Zhao, W., Peng, J., Fan, J.: Learning deep network for detecting 3d object keypoints and 6d poses. In: Proceedings of the IEEE Conference on Computer Vision and Pattern Recognition, pp. 14134–14142 (2020)

13. Pavlakos, G., Zhou, X., Chan, A., Derpanis, K. G., Daniilidis, K.: 6-dof object pose from semantic keypoints. In: 2017 IEEE International Conference on Robotics and Automation, pp. 2011–2018 (2017)

14. Hu, Y., Hugonot, J., Fua, P., Salzmann, M.: Segmentation-driven 6d object pose estimation. In: Proceedings of the IEEE Conference on Computer Vision and Pattern Recognition, pp. 3385–3394 (2019)

15. Oberweger, M., Rad, M., Lepetit, V.: Making deep heatmaps robust to partial occlusions for 3d object pose estimation. In: Proceedings of the European Conference on Computer Vision, pp. 119–134 (2018)

16. Di, Y., Manhardt, F., Wang, G., Ji, X., Navab, N., Tombari, F.: So-pose: exploiting self-occlusion for direct 6d pose estimation. In: Proceedings of the IEEE International Conference on Computer Vision, pp. 12396–12405 (2021)

17. Hodan, T., Barath, D., Matas, J.: Epos: Estimating 6d pose of objects with symmetries. In: Proceedings of the IEEE Conference on Computer Vision and Pattern Recognition, pp. 11703–11712 (2020)

18. Li, Z., Wang, G., Ji, X.: Cdpn: Coordinates-based disentangled pose network for real-time RGB-based 6-DOF object pose estimation. In: Proceedings of the IEEE International Conference on Computer Vision, pp. 7678–7687 (2019)

19. Wang, G., Manhardt, F., Tombari, F., Ji, X.: GDR-net: geometry-guided direct regression network for monocular 6d object pose estimation. In: Proceedings of the IEEE Conference on Computer Vision and Pattern Recognition, pp. 16611–16621 (2021)

20. Zakharov, S., Shugurov, I., Ilic, S.: Dpod: 6d pose object detector and refiner. In: Proceedings of the IEEE International Conference on Computer Vision, pp. 1941–1950 (2019)

21. Chen, B., Parra, A., Cao, J., Li, N., Chin, T. J.: End-to-end learnable geometric vision by backpropagating pnp optimization. In: Proceedings of the IEEE Conference on Computer Vision and Pattern Recognition, pp. 8100–8109 (2020)

22. Redmon, J., Farhadi, A.: YOLO9000: better, faster, stronger. In: Proceedings of the IEEE Conference on Computer Vision and Pattern Recognition, pp. 7263–7271 (2017)

23. Xiang, Y., Schmidt, T., Narayanan, V., Fox, D.: PoseCNN: a convolutional neural network for 6d object pose estimation in cluttered scenes. In: Robotics: Science and Systems Conference, pp. 19–32 (2018)

24. Shotton, J., Glocker, B., Zach, C., Izadi, S., Criminisi, A., Fitzgibbon, A.: Scene coordinate regression forests for camera relocalization in RGB-D images. In: Proceedings of the IEEE Conference on Computer Vision and Pattern Recognition, pp. 2930–2937 (2013)

25. Nigam, A., Penate-Sanchez, A., Agapito, L.: Detect globally, label locally: Learning accurate 6-DOF object pose estimation by joint segmentation and coordinate regression. IEEE Robot. Autom. Lett. **3**(4), 3960–3967 (2018)
26. Lepetit, V., Moreno-Noguer, F., Fua, P.: EPnP: an accurate O(n) solution to the PnP problem. Int. J. Comput. Vision **81**(2), 155–166 (2009)
27. Brachmann, E., Krull, A., Michel, F., Gumhold, S., Shotton, J., Rother, C.: Learning 6d object pose estimation using 3d object coordinates. In: Proceedings of the European Conference on Computer Vision, pp. 536–551 (2014)
28. Michel, F., et al.: Global hypothesis generation for 6D object pose estimation. In: Proceedings of the IEEE Conference on Computer Vision and Pattern Recognition, pp. 462–471 (2017)
29. Brachmann, E., Michel, F., Krull, A., Yang, M. Y., Gumhold, S.: Uncertainty-driven 6d pose estimation of objects and scenes from a single RGB image. In: Proceedings of the IEEE Conference on Computer Vision and Pattern Recognition, pp. 3364–3372 (2016)
30. Hinterstoisser, S., et al.: Model based training, detection and pose estimation of texture-less 3d objects in heavily cluttered scenes. In: Asian Conference on Computer Vision, pp. 548–562 (2012)

SSTA-Net: Self-supervised Spatio-Temporal Attention Network for Action Recognition

Yihan Li, Wenwen Zhang, and Zhao Pei[✉]

School of Computer Science, Shaanxi Normal University, Xi'an 710119, China
zpei@snnu.edu

Abstract. Action recognition aims to identify the action categories and features in the video by analyzing the actions and behavior patterns that are significant to the development of intelligent security, automatic driving, smart home, and other fields. However, current methods fail to adequately model the spatio-temporal relationships of actions in videos, and video annotation is a time-consuming and expensive process. This paper proposes a Self-Supervised Spatio-Temporal Attention Network (SSTA-Net) for action recognition to solve the above problems. Firstly, we use a self-supervised method for training, which does not require a large amount of labeled data and can explore unknown or hidden information in the data. Secondly, in the feature extraction part, Multi-Scale Convolution Attention Module (MC-AM) is proposed. By performing convolution operations on the input image at different scales, the details and edge information in the image are enhanced, and the image quality of the original sampling frame is improved. Finally, a Spatio-Temporal Attention Module (ST-A) is proposed. The module is used to capture the spatio-temporal signal sensitivity in the video, which effectively improves the accuracy of action recognition.

Keywords: Action recognition · Self-supervised · Transformer · Multi-Scale · Spatio-Temporal Attention

1 Introduction

Action recognition has rapidly become a research hotspot in computer vision because of its wide application in video surveillance [1], human-computer intelligent interaction [2], and other fields. With the introduction of deep learning networks [3], a series of significant progress are made in the field of action recognition. However, the current action recognition technology still fails to adequately meet the actual needs.

Firstly, many action recognition methods are based on supervised training methods. They train by minimizing the error between the predicted value and the ground truth. However, such methods require expensive annotation of action recognition datasets. Secondly, the feature extraction part of the current methods fails to distinguish key information and important action regions effectively. Some regions may have interference factors such as background and noise. To improve the accuracy of action recognition, researchers propose feature extraction methods, such as [4,5], etc. However, many methods incorporate multiple features, increasing computational complexity, which adds a certain degree of difficulty for model training. Finally, unlike images, features of actions are distribut along the temporal dimension. Before action recognition, we need to sample the video. If the sampling rate is too low, the features of changes between actions are not obvious enough (weak discriminative). If the sampling rate is too high, the actions are too obvious (discriminative). Both may lose key actions and ignore sensitive spatio-temporal signals, which brings difficulties to the spatio-temporal modeling of action recognition.

To mitigate these problems, we propose a novel Self-supervised Spatio-Temporal Attention Network (SSTA-Net) to capture long-range relations along the spatial and temporal dimensions for action recognition in video. Afterward, we propose a Multi-Scale Convolution Attention Module (MC-AM). This module integrates different features of the image to solve the problem of not effectively distinguishing critical information and essential action areas when extracting action recognition features. At last, the transformer-based method [6] can better capture the dependencies between different positions in the sequence. Therefore, we propose a Spatio-Temporal Attention Module (ST-A) based on the transformer, focusing on the spatio-temporal modeling of video data, capturing sensitive spatio-temporal action signals, and improving the accuracy of action recognition.

We consider using a self-supervised approach for training, which does not require labels and extracts useful features from massive data. During training, we use the self-distillation method to learn self-supervised features from unlabeled videos [7,8], both the teacher and the student network process different spatio-temporal views of the same video. The parameters of the teacher network are updated as the exponential moving average of the learner network, which enables SSTA-Net to learn robust features that are invariant to the spatio-temporal of actions in the videos.

Our main contributions are summarized as follows:

- A novel Spatio-Temporal Attention Network trained by Self-supervised (SSTA-Net) is proposed for action recognition to learn self-supervised features from unlabeled videos.
- As for feature extraction, we propose a Multi-Scale Convolution Attention Module (MC-AM) to enhance the details and edge information in the image and improve the image quality of the original sampled frame.
- We propose a Spatio-Temporal Attention Module (ST-A), focusing on combining spatio-temporal information and capturing sensitive spatio-temporal action signals.
- The experimental results accomplish new accuracy of 94.9% using Kinetics-400, and 91.2% accuracy using UCF101.

2   Related Work

2.1   Self-supervised Learning

In recent years, self-supervised learning has been widely used in the field of image and video [8]. Initially, self-supervised learning does not consider the temporal factor, and the image-based self-supervised method is directly extended to each frame in the video [9]. This method ignores the characteristics of temporal series information and dynamic changes in the video. Many self-supervised research methods use videos' unique temporal information to solve the factors, such as CoCLR [10] and CVRL [11]. These methods use the feature similarity between frames of different perspectives or different time points in the video as a self-supervised signal, and the trained model can distinguish between positive and negative sample pairs. Methods Pace [12] use the temporal relationship between frames in the video as a self-supervised signal, and the training model can verify whether the frame sequence is correct, predict future frames, estimate motion speed, etc. Nevertheless, these methods may be affected by the quality and stability of video data and does not consider the ambiguity and diversity present in videos, such as orientations, objects, etc.

To better utilize spatio-temporal information, [13] proposes to extract temporal labels as well as spatial labels as supervisory signals. However, the above method only considers the supervisory signal of the information in the videos and fails to adequately use the object category information in the videos. In this paper, through the self-supervised method based on self-distillation, the different views are used to expand the corresponding relationship between views and narrow the gap between the feature representations of different spatio-temporal views from the same video. A shared network method is used instead of large-scale network training to avoid the resulting bias caused by massive calculations.

2.2   Transformer in Video Action Recognition

The transformer model is a sequence modeling method based on a self-attention mechanism, which has achieved great success in natural language processing. Meanwhile, it also explores the field of computer vision [11,14]. The Transformer model can effectively capture spatio-temporal features and long-term dependencies, which is suitable for processing video data. Currently, some Transformer-based action recognition models have been proposed. ViTAA [15] proposes a novel Spatio-Temporal Attention Module, which can consider the information of the current frame and future frames at the same time. It uses a separable Spatio-Temporal Attention module. However, this mechanism may have the problem of missing or duplicating information when processing long sequence data. ViViT [14] extracts spatio-temporal markers from input videos, proposing several efficient model variants, which have higher computational efficiency and parameter efficiency. Nevertheless, ViViT requires a large amount of data and computing resources to train, relies on pre-trained models for transfer learning, and fails to adequately exploit the multi-scale and structural information present in video data.

TimeSformer [6] uses two different attention mechanisms to model spatio-temporal information in videos separately to improve the performance of video understanding. However, it requires attention mechanisms and full connectivity layer calculations on three dimensions and difficulty in processing multi-resolution data, which will limit its application in some application scenarios. MViT [16] is a multi-scale visual Transformer, which uses the Transformer model for feature extraction and fusion, but it ignores the principle of translation invariance, resulting in changes in absolute position encoding. In addition, its computational load is still large. These works show the potential and advantages of Transformer in action recognition, but there are also some challenges and limitations, such as how to deal with large-scale video data, how to improve spatio-temporal modeling capabilities, etc.

3   Method

In this section, we present our Self-supervised Spatio-Temporal Attention Network (SSTA-Net) for action recognition. Our goal is to capture spatio-temporal relations by a Self-supervised Spatio-Temporal Attention Network to obtain a more effective action representation. In what follows, we begin with an overview of our framework and then describe each essential building block of our network in detail.

3.1   The Whole Framework

As shown in Fig. 1, we use the self-distillation method [8,17]. During the training process, both the teacher and student networks process different spatio-temporal views of the same video. We represent input video as $V = \{v_t\}_{t=1}^{N}$, where N represents the number of frames, then we sample the same video at different frame rates. Our sampling methodology generates two types of clips (also termed view interchangeably). Evenly sample 90% (A) and 40% (B) of the extracted frames from the video timeline. Send A to the teacher SSTA-Net, and send A and B to the student SSTA-Net at the same time.

The teacher network and student network are SSTA-Net with different parameters. During each training step, we update the weights of the student model by backpropagation, while the weights of the teachers are updated with the exponential moving average (EMA) of the student weights. This method integrates rich spatio-temporal backgrounds into feature representation while maintaining differences between features. SSTA-Net is mainly divided into two modules, the Multi-Scale Convolution Attention Module (MC-AM) and the Spatio-Temporal Attention Module (ST-A). In the network, the information first passes through MC-AM, then extracts the required tokens and inputs the information into ST-A, which consists of L components. Tokens represent the common features of SSTA-Net learning along a video spatial dimension. Finally, we use a multi-layer perceptron (MLP) as a projection head over the classification token from the final encoder block [18].

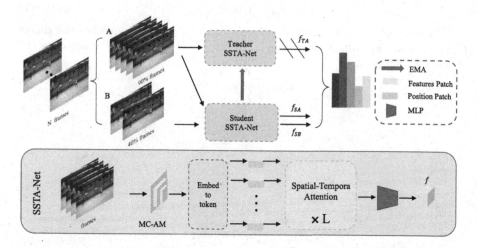

Fig. 1. The Self-supervised Spatio-Temporal Attention Network (SSTA-Net) structure.

3.2   Multi-scale Convolution Attention Module

We propose a Multi-Scale Convolution Attention Module (MC-AM), which uses convolution kernels of different sizes to perform convolution operations on the feature map. MC-AM does not change the size of the original feature map.

The structure of MC-AM is shown in Fig. 2. Assume that we extract a sequence of features in a video as $X = \{x_1, x_2, ..., x_T\}$ where T denotes the number of frames in the sequence. $x_i \in R^{C \times H \times W}$ represents a frame feature map. C is the number of feature channels, and H, W represent the feature height and width, respectively.

Given the above defined operations, we define three branched modules which takes in an input tensor and outputs a refined tensor of the same shape. The three branches have pooling layers, and the next two branches have convolutions of different scales.

The pooling layer is responsible for combining the average merge feature and the maximum merge feature on this dimension, which enables the layer to retain the rich representation of the actual tensor while reducing its depth. We used max pooling and average pooling. x_i is the tensor of the input model. It can be represented by the following equation:

$$MixedPool(x_i) = MaxPool(x_i) + AvgPool(x_i) \qquad (1)$$

Convolution is an enhancement of the extracted features. a is the order of branches, and b is the number of convolutions of branches. It can be represented by the following equation:

$$x_{ab} = Conv(x_i) \tag{2}$$

The convolution operation of different convolution cores enriches the image features, and the output is through the $sigmoid(\sigma)$ layer. x_j represents the output of each branch.

$$X_{out} = \frac{1}{\sum_{j=1}^{3} \sigma(x_j)} \tag{3}$$

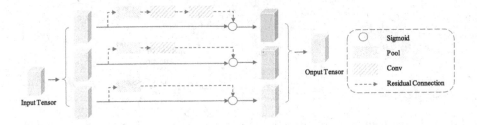

Fig. 2. Multi-Scale Convolution Attention Module (MC-AM).

3.3   Spatio-Temporal Attention Module

Unlike traditional image recognition, people focus on certain spatial and temporal regions when discriminating an action in a video sequence. Therefore, a Spatio-Temporal Attention Module (ST-A) based on the transformer is proposed, which can fully extract the spatial and temporal features of video data. As shown in Fig. 3, ST-A has two parts: Temporal Attention Module (TA) and Spatial Attention Module (SA).

TA can be seen as a dynamic temporal selection mechanism, which to learn the contribution of each sampled frame to an action and obtain their importance scores. Concretely, we compute attention weights for each token separately over the temporal dimensions using different heads. The embeddings compute into three latent subspaces, including queries Q, keys K, and values V. We note that the attention operation for each head is defined as:

$$Attention(Q^t, K^t, V^t) = softmax(\frac{Q^t(K^t)^T}{\sqrt{d_k}}V^t) \tag{4}$$

$$head_t = Attention(Q^t, K^t, V^t) \tag{5}$$

$$MultiHead(Q^t, K^t, V^t) = add(head_1, ..., head_k) \tag{6}$$

where $add(*)$ denotes the add layer to merge k heads of different self-attention. $Attention_t$ represents the self-attention of the $t - th$ head modules.

Then we utilize the final fully connected layer to produce outputs containing temporal dependencies. In our model, long-term temporal dependencies are efficiently captured in each layer of the transformer, as the TA focuses on the attributes of the action at each frame.

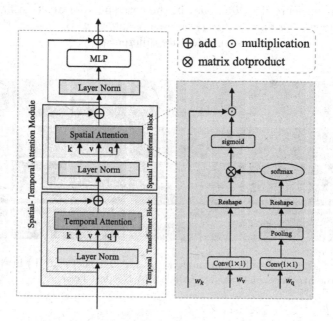

Fig. 3. Spatio-Temporal Attention Module (ST-A).

The SA as shown in Fig. 3, we extract all tokens from the same spatial index, after that, each token performs different operations.

$$O_{sp} = W_k \odot \sigma[softmax(F_R(F_P(W_q))) \otimes F_R(W_v)] \qquad (7)$$

Where W_q and W_v are 1×1 convolution layers respectively, F_R are two tensors reshape operators, $\otimes$ is the matrix dot product operation, and F_P is a pooling operator. $\odot$ is a spatial-wise multiplication operator.

Our spatial attention not only keeps the full $[W, H]$ spatial resolution but also internally keeps learnable parameters in W_q and W_v for the nonlinear Softmax reweighting. Our experiments demonstrate that ST-A is an efficient module for temporal dependencies modeling.

3.4 Loss

We match the correspondence between two different views in the feature space. Compare the target characteristics of the teacher network in view A with the target features of the student network to obtain the loss item. The loss function consists of two parts:

$$L = -f_{TA} \cdot \log(f_{SA}) - f_{TA} \cdot \log(f_{SB}) \qquad (8)$$

This loss measures the difference in the corresponding relationship between the two networks in view A (f_{TA}). Views A and view B through the student network (f_{SA} and f_{SB}) to reduce feature differences.

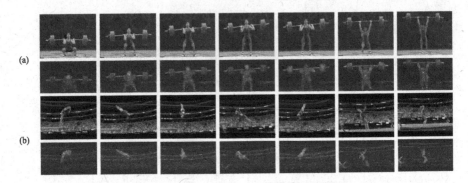

Fig. 4. The feature maps of CleanAndJerk (a) and BalanceBeam (b) in the UCF101 dataset on the attention mechanism of the SSTA Net last layer.

4   Experiments

4.1   Experimental Setup

We use the Kinetics-400 [19] dataset and the UCF101 [20] dataset.

Kinetics-400: The dataset contains 400 human action classes, and each action has at least 400 video clips. Each clip lasts about 10 s. These actions are human-centered and cover a wide range of categories, including the interaction between people who play musical instruments and objects and the interaction between people who shake hands.

UCF101: There are 13320 clips in total, with a total video duration of 27 h and 101 actions in total. UCF101 has the broadest flexibility in motion, including camera motion, object appearance and posture, object size, angle of view, and chaotic scenes. UCF101 is the most challenging data set for human action recognition due to the great changes in the lighting environment.

We train our models for 20 epochs on the train set of the Kinetics-400 dataset without any labels using a batch size of 16 across 2 NVIDIA GPUs. We randomly initialize weights.

4.2   Results

We compare SSTA-Net with other approaches for action recognition. Figure 4 clearly shows the feature maps of BalanceBeam and CleanAndJerk in the UCF101 dataset generated by the attention mechanism of the last layer in SSTA-Net. Our network can focus on action and related objects while ignore the background. In the second group of pictures, the background is noisy but the network can still capture the movements of the gymnasts.

Accuracy (*Acc*) is used as the evaluation standard to evaluate the model. We present our results Kinetics-400 in Table 1 on and UCF101 in Table 2. The strong performance of this dataset shows the advantages of our proposed method.

Table 1. Comparison on Kinetics-400

Method	Backbone	Top-1	Top-5
R(2+1)D [21]	ResNet-18	72.0	90.0
SlowFast-R50 [22]	ResNet-50	75.6	92.1
SMNet [23]	ResNet-50	76.8	93.3
X3D-XL [24]	SlowFast-R50	79.1	93.9
MViT-S [16]	ViT-S	76.0	92.1
MViT-B [16]	ViT-B	80.2	94.4
X-ViT-B [25]	ViT-B	80.2	94.7
ViViT-L [14]	ViT-L	81.3	94.7
OURS	ViT-T	**81.5**	**94.9**

Table 2. Comparison on UCF101

Method	Backbone	Top-1	Top-5
IICv2 [26]	R3D	55.1	72.1
TCLR [27]	R3D	56.2	72.2
SLIC [28]	R3D	81.0	84.9
ViViT-L [14]	ViT-L	64.4	89.8
MViT-B [16]	ViT-B	67.1	90.8
SVT [29]	ViT-T	75.3	90.3
OURS	ViT-T	**77.4**	**91.2**

4.3   Ablation Studies

We perform ablation studies on MC-AM and ST-A using the UCF101 dataset. Specifically, we systematically dissect the contribution of each component of our method. We study the effect of two elements: a) Single-Scale and Multi-Scale; b) TA and SA Modules. Evaluate using the same setup as described in Sect. 4.

Single-Scale vs. Multi-Scale: Because scaling or cropping can destroy image information, single-scale models may not perform well when processing images. While capturing different spatio-temporal relationship information on multiple scales and obtaining more comprehensive action representation, MC-AM achieved a significant performance improvement in top-1 accuracy (Table 3).

TA and SA Modules: We investigate the effect of TA and SA modules. We compared the experimental results of the TA module and SA module. To increase the richness of the ablation experiment, we also exchanged the order of TA and SA. As shown in Table 4, adding ST-A can effectively improve the performance of our model.

Table 3. Ablation study on the effect of Single-Scale and Multi-Scale

Model	Scales	Top-1	Top-5
	None	76.1	90.4
SSTA-Net	Single	75.7	89.8
	Multi	**77.4**	**91.2**

Table 4. Ablation study on the effect of TA and SA modules

Model	Modules	Top-1	Top-5
	None	70.1	82.3
	TA	76.4	90.1
SSTA-Net	SA	75.1	88.2
	TS-A	77.1	90.6
	ST-A	**77.4**	**91.2**

5   Conclusion and Future Work

Overall, this paper proposes a method of Self-supervised Spatio-Temporal Attention Network (SSTA-Net) for action recognition. This network is to learn the characteristics of different views through the network of students and teachers. Additionally, SSTA-Net allows modeling spatio-temporal and clearly explains how the Multi-Scale Convolution Attention Module (MC-AM) and Spatio-Temporal Attention Module (ST-A) improve the accuracy of action recognition models. The results indicate that the SSTA-Net achieved results. In the future, we will expand our work and apply it to practical scenarios to solve problems such as anomaly detection, and road traffic pedestrian behavior.

Acknowledgement. This work was supported in part by the National Natural Science Foundation of China under Grant 61971273 and in part by the Fund Program for the Scientific Activities of Selected Returned Overseas Professionals in Shaanxi Province of China under Grant 2021-012.

References

1. Beye, F., Shinohara, Y., Itsumi, H., Nihei, K.: Recognition-aware bitrate allocation for ai-enabled remote video surveillance. In: Proceedings of the IEEE 20th Consumer Communications & Networking Conference, pp. 158–163 (2023)
2. Gupta, S., Maple, C., Crispo, B., Raja, K., Yautsiukhin, A., Martinelli, F.: A survey of human-computer interaction (hci) & natural habits-based behavioural biometric modalities for user recognition schemes. Pattern Recogn. **139**, 109453 (2023)
3. Herath, S., Harandi, M., Porikli, F.: Going deeper into action recognition: a survey. Image Vis. Comput. **60**, 4–21 (2017)
4. Suh, S., Rey, V.F., Lukowicz, P.: Adversarial deep feature extraction network for user independent human activity recognition. In: Proceedings of the IEEE International Conference on Pervasive Computing and Communications, pp. 217–226 (2022)
5. Hwang, Y.M., Park, S., Lee, H.O., Ko, S.K., Lee, B.T.: Deep learning for human activity recognition based on causality feature extraction. IEEE Access **9**, 112257–112275 (2021)
6. Bertasius, G., Wang, H., Torresani, L.: Is space-time attention all you need for video understanding? In: Proceedings of the 38th International Conference on Machine Learning, pp. 813–824 (2021)
7. Hou, Y., Ma, Z., Liu, C., Loy, C.C.: Learning lightweight lane detection cnns by self attention distillation. In: Proceedings of the IEEE/CVF International Conference on Computer Vision, pp. 1013–1021 (2019)
8. Caron, M., Touvron, H., Misra, I., Jégou, H., Mairal, J., Bojanowski, P., Joulin, A.: Emerging properties in self-supervised vision transformers. In: Proceedings of the IEEE/CVF International Conference on Computer Vision, pp. 9650–9660 (2021)
9. He, K., Fan, H., Wu, Y., Xie, S., Girshick, R.: Momentum contrast for unsupervised visual representation learning. In: Proceedings of the IEEE/CVF Conference on Computer Vision and Pattern Recognition, pp. 9729–9738 (2020)
10. Han, T., Xie, W., Zisserman, A.: Self-supervised co-training for video representation learning. Adv. Neural. Inf. Process. Syst. **33**, 5679–5690 (2020)
11. Qian, R., Meng, T., Gong, B., Yang, M.H., Wang, H., Belongie, S., Cui, Y.: Spatiotemporal contrastive video representation learning. In: Proceedings of the IEEE/CVF Conference on Computer Vision and Pattern Recognition, pp. 6964–6974 (2021)
12. Wang, J., Jiao, J., Liu, Y.H.: Self-supervised video representation learning by pace prediction. In: Proceedings of the European Conference on Computer Vision, pp. 504–521 (2020)

13. Luo, D., Liu, C., Zhou, Y., Yang, D., Ma, C., Ye, Q., Wang, W.: Video cloze procedure for self-supervised spatio-temporal learning. In: Proceedings of the AAAI Conference on Artificial Intelligence, pp. 11701–11708 (2020)

14. Arnab, A., Dehghani, M., Heigold, G., Sun, C., Lučić, M., Schmid, C.: Vivit: a video vision transformer. In: Proceedings of the IEEE/CVF International Conference on Computer Vision, pp. 6836–6846 (2021)

15. Wang, Z., Fang, Z., Wang, J., Yang, Y.: Vitaa: visual-textual attributes alignment in person search by natural language. In: Proceedings of the European Conference on Computer Vision, pp. 402–420 (2020)

16. Fan, H., Xiong, B., Mangalam, K., Li, Y., Yan, Z., Malik, J., Feichtenhofer, C.: Multiscale vision transformers. In: Proceedings of the IEEE/CVF International Conference on Computer Vision, pp. 6824–6835 (2021)

17. Hinton, G., Vinyals, O., Dean, J.: Distilling the knowledge in a neural network. arXiv preprint arXiv:1503.02531 (2015)

18. Grill, J.B., et al.: Bootstrap your own latent-a new approach to self-supervised learning. Adv. Neural. Inf. Process. Syst. **33**, 21271–21284 (2020)

19. Carreira, J., Zisserman, A.: Quo vadis, action recognition? a new model and the kinetics dataset. In: Proceedings of the IEEE Conference on Computer Vision and Pattern Recognition, pp. 6299–6308 (2017)

20. Soomro, K., Zamir, A.R., Shah, M.: Ucf101: A dataset of 101 human actions classes from videos in the wild. arXiv preprint arXiv:1212.0402 (2012)

21. Tran, D., Wang, H., Torresani, L., Ray, J., LeCun, Y., Paluri, M.: A closer look at spatiotemporal convolutions for action recognition. In: Proceedings of the IEEE Conference on Computer Vision and Pattern Recognition, pp. 6450–6459 (2018)

22. Feichtenhofer, C., Fan, H., Malik, J., He, K.: Slowfast networks for video recognition. In: Proceedings of the IEEE/CVF International Conference on Computer Vision, pp. 6202–6211 (2019)

23. Yang, Q., Lu, T., Zhou, H.: A spatio-temporal motion network for action recognition based on spatial attention. Entropy **24**, 368 (2022)

24. Feichtenhofer, C.: X3d: Expanding architectures for efficient video recognition. In: Proceedings of the IEEE/CVF Conference on Computer Vision and Pattern Recognition, pp. 203–213 (2020)

25. Dosovitskiy, A., et al.: An image is worth 16×16 words: transformers for image recognition at scale. In: Proceedings of the 9th International Conference on Learning Representations, pp. 132–141 (2021)

26. Tao, L., Wang, X., Yamasaki, T.: An improved inter-intra contrastive learning framework on self-supervised video representation. IEEE Trans. Circuits Syst. Video Technol. **32**, 5266–5280 (2022)

27. Dave, I., Gupta, R., Rizve, M.N., Shah, M.: Tclr: temporal contrastive learning for video representation. Comput. Vis. Image Underst. **219**, 103406 (2022)

28. Khorasgani, S.H., Chen, Y., Shkurti, F.: Slic: Self-supervised learning with iterative clustering for human action videos. In: Proceedings of the IEEE/CVF Conference on Computer Vision and Pattern Recognition,. pp. 16091–16101 (2022)

29. Ranasinghe, K., Naseer, M., Khan, S., Khan, F.S., Ryoo, M.S.: Self-supervised video transformer. In: Proceedings of the IEEE/CVF Conference on Computer Vision and Pattern Recognition, pp. 2874–2884 (2022)

Gesture Recognition Method Based on Sim-ConvNeXt Model

Yupeng Huo, Jie Shen$^{(\boxtimes)}$, Li Wang, and Yuxuan Wu

College of Electrical Engineering and Control Science, Nanjing Tech University,
Nanjing 211816, China
shenjienj@163.com

Abstract. Gesture recognition has become an important subject for researchers dealing with the problem of human-computer interaction, with computer vision enabling significant advancements in this field. Existing gesture recognition methods based on vision typically rely on traditional pure convolutional neural networks. However, these models face challenges in terms of low feature extraction efficiency and poor representation ability when encountering complex backgrounds, leading to complex parameter optimization. To address this issue, we propose an improved ConvNeXt algorithm, which is called as Sim-ConvNeXt network. SimAM (A Simple, Parameter-Free Attention Module for Convolutional Neural Networks) was introduced to address the issue of complex gesture recognition environments and unbalanced feature coupling between gestures. Additionally, the optimal fusion mode of SimAM was analyzed to resolve the problem of feature information loss between channels after the Depthwise Convolution module in the ConvNeXt model. Finally, the experiment on the HaGRID dataset showed that our model improved the identification accuracy effectively with a very small increase in the number of parameters, and achieved better performance compared with other models.

Keywords: Gesture Recognition · Feature Extraction · Sim · Convolutional · Neural Network

1 Introduction

Gesture recognition is the process of extracting human gestures, recognizing their features, and assigning them correct labels, which can be utilized to control devices and interact with digital interfaces. Gesture recognition is a rapidly evolving field that has seen significant advancements in recent years, thanks to the increasing utilization of sensors and machine learning algorithms in computer vision and other downstream applications [1].

Gesture recognition technology is utilized in a wide range of fields, including computer vision, entertainment, healthcare image processing, and industrial automation. In computer vision, gesture recognition can be utilized to control characters and objects in virtual environments, providing a more immersive and interactive experience for users

© The Author(s), under exclusive license to Springer Nature Switzerland AG 2023
H. Lu et al. (Eds.): ICIG 2023, LNCS 14356, pp. 401–412, 2023.
https://doi.org/10.1007/978-3-031-46308-2_33

[2]. In the healthcare field, gesture recognition can be utilized to assist patients with disabilities or injuries to communicate and interact with others.

The continuous development of gesture recognition technology has made it possible by exploring advances in computer vision, machine learning, and sensor technology. These technologies allow systems to recognize and analyze patterns in human movement, enabling them to accurately identify and interpret gestures in real-time [3]. Currently, there are several primary existing methods for gesture recognition, including rule-based systems, which rely on a set of pre-defined models to recognize specific gestures [4]. Specifically, a system might be programmed to recognize a specific hand gesture as a sign. Template matching is another method that involves comparing an input gesture to a pre-defined set of templates to identify the most similar match. The matching method performs accurately on simple gestures [5], but can be less precise for more complex gestures with noise. Neural networks are novel machine learning algorithms that can be trained to recognize patterns in gesture data. They are particularly effective for complex gestures that involve multiple movements and variations [6].

Convolutional neural network is a type of deep learning algorithm that is particularly effective for analyzing visual data such as images and videos. The architecture of a convolutional neural network is devised to mimic the organization of the human visual cortex, which allows it to recognize and classify complex patterns in visual data. Indeed, convolutional neural networks have been utilized in a wide range of applications, from image and video classification to object detection and facial recognition [7]. Convolutional neural networks are particularly useful in downstream tasks that involve large amounts of visual data, as they are able to learn and extract features from this data in a way that is both accurate and efficient [8].

One of a most essential advantages of convolutional neural network is the ability to automatically learn and extract features from images without the need for manual feature engineering. The characteristic ensures the model is a powerful tool for tasks including image classification, where the goal is to identify the presence of specific objects or features within an image [9]. However, in 2021, researchers [10] at Microsoft Research proposed a layered vision Swin Transformer that shifted computing across windows, which could be used as a universal backbone network for computer vision. And it has achieved excellent performance in each data set. However, it cannot replace convolutional neural networks in image processing. At the same time, Transformer's excellent performance is probably due to its built-in structure. Based on this assumption, Facebook AI Research (FAIR) [11] proposed a new CNN architecture influenced by Swin et al., named ConvNeXt. The model is not self-attention-based, and they perform better than other methods on different visual tasks. Since then, ConvNeXt has become one of the best performing convolutional neural networks in existence.

Therefore, we propose a deep convolutional neural network called Sim-ConvNeXt that incorporates attention mechanisms to process extracted gesture features and recognize gestures. We first selected the public gesture recognition dataset HaGRID and preprocessed the data. Subsequently, Sim-ConvNeXt is utilized to calculate the extracted features, and a neural network is trained using the training sets. The rest of this paper is organized as follows: related work is introduced in Sect. 2, the method framework and principles are illustrated in Sect. 3, experimental results and analysis are presented in Sect. 4, and finally, we conclude the paper in Sect. 5.

2 Related Work

ConvNeXt mainly draws inspiration from the design principles of Swin Transformer in terms of Macro Design, Micro Design, Depthwise Convolution, and applies them to ResNet. Its overall structure is shown in Fig. 1.

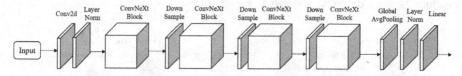

Fig. 1. ConvNeXt Network structure.

2.1 Macro Design

At the macro level, ConvNeXt has a total of four stages, with a block stacking ratio of 3:3:9:3 for each stage. At the same time, ConvNeXt sets the initial layer to a convolution operation with a kernel size of 4 and a stride of 4, which plays a role in partitioning the image data into local regions.

2.2 Micro Design

At the micro level, ConvNeXt differs from traditional convolutional neural networks such as ResNet. ConvNeXt replaces ReLU with GELU and reduces the number of activation functions. It also uses fewer normalization layers and replaces Batch Norm with Layer Norm, as shown in Fig. 2. Additionally, ConvNeXt uses 2×2 convolution with a stride of 2 for spatial downsampling.

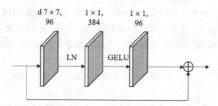

Fig. 2. LN and GELU in the ConvNeXt Block.

2.3 Depthwise Convolution

This part adopts the idea from ResNeXt [12] and uses Depthwise Convolution. It can reduce the number of parameters while allowing features to interact spatially only within each channel.

ResNet uses the Bottleneck structure to reduce computation, while previous models like MobileNetV2 [13] use the Inverted Bottleneck structure to reduce information loss. FAIR researchers believe that the Inverted Bottleneck is very similar to a multi-layer perceptron and can allow information exchange between different dimensions of the feature vector. Therefore, ConvNeXt also adopts this design. The Inverted Bottleneck structure used in ConvNeXt is shown in Fig. 3.

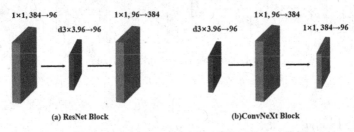

(a) ResNet Block   (b)ConvNeXt Block

Fig. 3. Inverted Bottleneck on ResNeXt and ConvNeXt.

3 Sim-ConvNeXt Model

In this section, we present Sim-ConvNeXt model and explain the execution procedures and function of each steps. The general framework is demonstrating in following subsection.

3.1 Model Framework

The framework of the Sim-ConvNeXt model is shown in Fig. 4. The A-stage mainly implements data preprocessing and partitioning, and the output of this part is represented as $F_{A\text{-out}}$. The B-stage mainly demonstrates the design methods at the micro-scale of the image and the integration of the SimAM module, and the output of this part is represented as $F_{B\text{-out}}$. The C-stage mainly shows the 2×2 convolution downsampling module of Sim-ConvNeXt, the stacked Sim-ConvNeXt feature extraction network, and the classification head of the network, and the output of this part is the final recognition result.

Indeed, following items describe the detail execution of proposed model.

- Data preprocessing involves cleaning and preparing the raw gesture Data for use in the model. This may include the tasks such as segmenting the data into individual gestures, rotate crop and variability and converting the data into a suitable format. The processed data is then convolved with LayerNorm (LN) by 4×4 to obtain $F_{A\text{-out}}$.

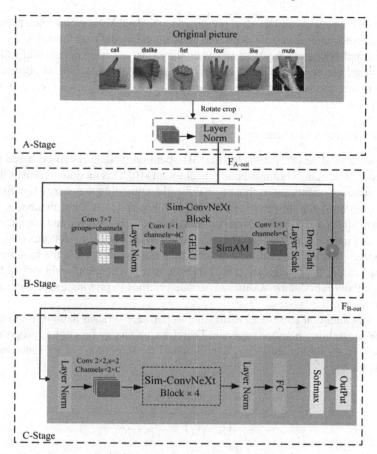

Fig. 4. Architecture of Sim-ConvNeXt.

- ConvNeXt including the certain number and type of layers, the size of the input and output layers and the type of activation functions utilization. In our proposed In the gesture recognition model, the feature graph is first followed by depth-separable convolution (DW), and the LayerNorm (LN) Normalization is used instead of the Batch Normalization (BN). After that, the channel size is increased by 1×1 convolution and GELU activation function is used to enter the Sim attention mechanism. The final feature diagram is restored to the input channel size by 1×1 convolution, and $F_{B\text{-out}}$ is obtained by fusing the output of LayerScale layer [14], DropPath layer [15] and $F_{A\text{-out}}$.

- $F_{B\text{-out}}$ is normalized by LayerNorm (LN), and the size of feature graph is reduced and the size of channel is increased by 2×2 convolution. After extracting feature information through 4 blocks, the output F is finally obtained. F is normalized by LN and transmitted to the full connection layer. Finally, the recognition result is obtained by Softmax classification.

- To train Sim-ConvNeXt, we use a labeled gesture dataset for both training and validation. During training, the model learns to recognize and classify different gestures based on the patterns and features presented in the data. Validation is then performed on a separate labeled gesture dataset to evaluate the model's performance.

- Testing and evaluation are executed when the model has been trained and validated. The model can then be used to classify unseen gesture data, and its accuracy and performance can be evaluated using metrics such as classification precision and F1 score.

3.2 Sim Attention Mechanism

Sim attention module is a parameter-free 3D attention module proposed based on the characteristics of human brain attention mechanism [16].This module improves the calculation speed of attention weights by analytically computing the energy function, and has the advantages of lightweight and flexibility compared to existing channel or spatial attention modules.To reduce interference from hair, other body parts, and complex backgrounds and enhance the anti-interference ability of the model in gesture recognition, we propose to add the SimAM module after the Depthwise Convolution module in the ConvNeXt model. This enables a more comprehensive and efficient evaluation of feature weights without introducing additional parameters, thus improving the performance of the basic model.

The Sim attention module evaluates the importance of each neuron by measuring the linear separability between neurons. Therefore, an energy function is proposed and after a series of simplifications, the expression of the minimum energy function $e_t{}^*$ is shown as Eq. (1).

$$e_t{}^* = \frac{4\left(\hat{\sigma}^2 + \lambda\right)}{\left(t - \hat{\mu}^2\right) + 2\hat{\sigma}^2 + 2\lambda} \tag{1}$$

Here, t represents the neuron, $\hat{\mu}$ represents the mean of all neurons on a single channel, $\hat{\sigma}^2$ represents the variance of all neurons on a single channel., λ is a hyperparameter, and the expressions for $\hat{\mu}$ and $\hat{\sigma}^2$ are shown in Eqs. (2) and (3).

$$\hat{\mu} = \frac{1}{M} \sum_{i=1}^{M} x_i \tag{2}$$

$$\hat{\sigma}^2 = \frac{1}{M} \sum_{i=1}^{M} (x_i - \hat{\mu})^2 \tag{3}$$

In Eq. (2), i represents the index of a neuron, M represents the number of neurons per channel, x_i represents the adjacent neuron of neuron t. According to Eq. (1), the smaller value of $e_t{}^*$, the target neuron of the current feature map is more separate from other neurons, which means the neuron is more important. As a result, the importance of the neuron can be obtained by the value of $1/e_t{}^*$. Finally, the feature is enhanced through the method shown in Eq. (4).

$$\tilde{X} = sigmoid\left(\frac{1}{E}\right) \odot X \tag{4}$$

The output result $\tilde{X}$ is the enhanced feature, where X is the input feature, $\odot$ represents dot product operation, E is the energy function on each channel, and the sigmoid function is used to limit the possible occurrence of excessively large values in E. This method differs from the serial combination of SE [17] channel attention and CBAM [18] spatial attention and channel attention. SimAM directly evaluates the importance of independent neurons, and can assign higher weights to important neurons without increasing the number of parameters of the model.

Figure 5 illustrates a SimAM module, which can be viewed as a computational unit that takes any intermediate feature tensor of a neural network as input and transforms it into an output feature tensor with the same size and enhanced representation. In Fig. 5, X represents the input feature tensor, and C, H, W represent the number of channels, height, and width of the feature map.

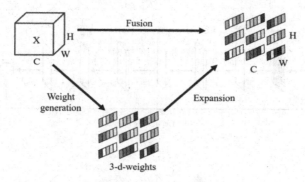

Fig. 5. SimAM module.

4 Experimental Results Evaluation and Analysis

4.1 Data-Set Description

The HaGRID [19] dataset contains 18 common general gestures such as one, two, ok, etc., marked with gesture boxes and gesture category labels, which can be used for tasks such as image classification or image detection. The HaGRID dataset contains 552,992 FullHD (1920 × 1080) RGB images. The data is divided into 92% of the training set and 8% of the test set, of which 509,323 images are used for training and 43,669 images are used for testing. Due to the HaGRID dataset is extremely large, we utilize 40% as training set and 8% as the testing set.

4.2 Design Experiments for SimAM

The original ConvNeXt block structure is shown in Fig. 6. To analyze the efficient fusion method of the SimAM module, this experiment added attention modules to different layers of ConvNeXt.

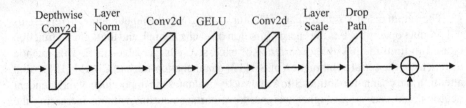

Fig. 6. ConvNeXt Block.

We conducted experiments by integrating the SimAM module into three different positions as shown in Fig. 7. One was integrated after the Depthwise Convolution, as shown in (a); another was integrated after the first 1x1 Convolution, as shown in (b); and the last one was integrated after the second 1x1 Convolution, as shown in (c).

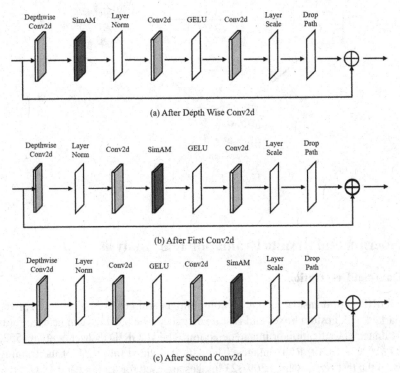

(a) After Depth Wise Conv2d

(b) After First Conv2d

(c) After Second Conv2d

Fig. 7. SimAM fusion location.

Table 1 shows the performance of the ConvNext model with the SimAM module added at different positions.

According to Table 1, adding the SimAM module after the Depthwise Convolution layer results in higher precision. The reason for this can be attributed to the network structure of ConvNeXt, which incorporates the design philosophy of Swin Transformer

Table 1. ConvNeXt model with SimAM added at different positions.

SimAM Insertion Position	HaGRID dataset		
	Precision	Recall	F1-score
After Depth Wise Conv2d	96.83%	95.74%	96.28
After First Conv2d	96.21%	95.69%	95.95
After Second Conv2d	96.35%	95.80%	96.07

and utilizes Depthwise Convolution. However, in Depthwise Convolution, each convolution kernel only operates on a single channel, and the information between different channels is not communicated, resulting in the loss of information between channels in the subsequent information flow and ultimately leading to a decrease in network performance. By adding the SimAM module in the experiment, important neurons can be better explored, thereby improving the performance of Depthwise Convolution.

4.3 Experimental Results and Analysis

In this section, we compared our proposed model with conventional convolutional neural networks including ResNet, ResNeXt, and MobileNet, as well as the current state-of-the-art Swin Transformer. The comparison results are shown in Fig. 8 below.

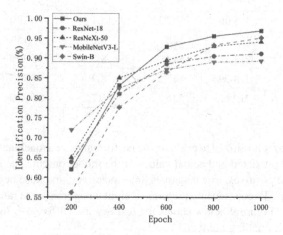

Fig. 8. Comparison results on accuracy.

Indeed, another essential evaluation indicator is F1-score, which is a commonly used metric for evaluating the performance of a machine learning model. It is a measure of a model accuracy and taking into account both precision and recall. F1-score is particularly useful in cases where the distribution of classes is imbalanced as it provides a more accurate representation of a model performance than other metrics such as accuracy. Table 2 demonstrates the different methods results.

In order to verify the impact of Sim attention mechanism proposed in this paper on model performance, we also conducted ablation experiments using other attention modules such as SE and CBAM. As shown in the last four rows of Table 2, when Sim attention mechanism was not used, the ConvNeXt model achieved an precision of 95.18% on the HaGRID dataset. Compared with the original convnext model, the precision of the model was improved by 1.68% after using the Sim module, with only an additional 0.37M parameters. This demonstrates the effectiveness of Sim attention mechanism in improving the recognition precision of the ConvNeXt model.

Table 2. Comparison results on Precision and F1-score.

Models	Model size (MB)	Parameters (M)	FLOPs(G)	Precision	F1-score
Resnet-18	44.8	11.19	1.8	93.08%	92.90%
Resnet-152	233.7	58.19	11.2	94.45%	94.27%
Resnext-50	92.5	23.02	3.4	95.04%	94.42%
Resnext-101	348.2	86.79	12.0	96.11%	95.31%
MobileNetV3-small	8.7	2.13	0.4	87.20%	86.15%
SMobileNetV3-large	22.0	5.46	2.1	89.39%	89.27%
ViT-B/32pretrained	353.1	88.24	7.4	94.42%	93.95%
Swin-S	199.65	50.09	8.7	94.93%	94.27%
Swin-B	355.06	88.72	15.4	96.29%	95.81%
ConvNeXt-S	209.16	52.5	8.7	95.15%	94.97%
SE-ConvNeXt	218.81	54.69	8.7	96.39%	96.02%
CBAM-ConvNeXt	218.99	54.72	8.9	95.97%	95.83%
Sim-ConvNeXt	219.62	52.87	8.7	96.83%	96.28%

Confusion matrix is utilized to evaluate the performance of a machine learning model by comparing the predicted and actual values of the model output. The matrix displays the number of true positives, true negatives, false positives, and false negatives for each class in the dataset. Twenty gesture pictures in eight categories were randomly selected in the experiment. Figure 9 below shows the test results. Different colors in the figure represent the corresponding number.

The experimental results presented above demonstrate the effectiveness of the Sim-ConvNeXt-based model in accurately identifying and classifying different gestures with high accuracy on the test dataset. The F1 score, which provides a balanced evaluation of the model's performance in both positive and negative aspects, is also reported. As shown in Table 2, the presented model achieves high F1 scores, which indicates more accurate classifying ability performance.

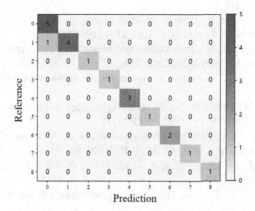

Fig. 9. Confusion matrix.

5   Conclusion

In this paper, we propose a gesture recognition method based on Sim-ConvNeXt model, which preserves the ConvNeXt model's main structure and adds SimAM attention module to the model. After analyzing its function position, we solve the problem of loss of feature information after Depthwise Convolution in ConvNeXt, and effectively improve the network's performance. Furthermore, experiments on the HaGRID dataset showed that the model improved the precision by 1.68% while adding only a few parameters. It has significant reference value for the existing problems in gesture recognition research and can solve the issues of low gesture recognition rate and poor generalization ability in practical applications to a certain extent.

References

1. Patel, S., Deepa, R.: Hand gesture recognition used for functioning system using OpenCV. Adv. Sci. Technol. **124**, 3–10 (2023)
2. Ullah, F., et al.: Fusion-based body-worn IoT sensor platform for gesture recognition of autism spectrum disorder children. Sensors **23**(3), 1672 (2023)
3. Wu, S., Liu, Q., et al.: Static gesture recognition algorithm based on improved YOLOv5s. Electronics **12**(3), 596 (2023)
4. Rawat, P., Kane, L., et al.: A review on vision-based hand gesture recognition targeting RGB-Depth sensors. Int. J. Inf. Technol. Decis. Mak.Decis. Mak. **22**(01), 115–156 (2023)
5. Riedel, A., Brehm, N., et al.: Hand gesture recognition of methods-time measurement-1 motions in manual assembly tasks using graph convolutional networks. Appl. Artif. Intell.Artif. Intell. **36**(1), 2014191 (2022)
6. Yuanyuan, S.H.I., Yunan, L.I., et al.: Review of dynamic gesture recognition. Virtual Reality Intell. Hardware **3**(3), 183–206 (2021)
7. Manikpure, S. V., Bankar, R. T., et al.: A Review on Robo Chair Assistance Using Head Gesture Recognition. Int. J. Innov. Sci. Modern Eng. (IJISME) **3**(2) (2015)
8. Wang, S., Ren, P., Takyi-Aninakwa, P., et al.: A critical review of improved deep convolutional neural network for multi-timescale state prediction of lithium-ion batteries. Energies **15**(14), 5053 (2022)

9. Saida, S.J., Sahoo, S.P., et al.: Deep convolution neural network based semantic segmentation for ocean eddy detection. Expert Syst. Appl. **219**, 119646 (2023)

10. Liu, Z., Lin, Y., Cao, Y., et al.: Swin transformer: hierarchical vision transformer using shifted windows. In: ICCV, pp. 10012–10022 (2021)

11. Liu, Z., Mao, H., Wu, C. Y., et al.: A convnet for the 2020s. In: CVPR, pp. 11976–11986 (2022)

12. Xie, S., Girshick, R., Dollár, P., Tu, Z., et al.: Aggregated residual transformations for deep neural networks. In: CVPR, pp. 1492–1500(2017)

13. Sandler, M., Howard, A., Zhu, M., Zhmoginov, A., et al.: Mobilenetv2: Inverted residuals and linear bottlenecks. In: CVPR, pp. 4510–4520 (2018)

14. Touvron, H., Cord, M., Sablayrolles, A., et al.: Going deeper with image transformers. In: ICCV, pp. 32–42 (2021)

15. Huang, G., Sun, Y., Liu, Z., Sedra, D., et al.: Deep networks with stochastic depth. In: ECCV, pp. 646–661 (2016)

16. Yang, L., Zhang, R. Y., Li, L., et al.: Simam: a simple, parameter-free attention module for convolutional neural networks. In: PMLR, pp. 11863–11874 (2021)

17. Hu, J., Shen, L., et al.: Squeeze-and-excitation networks. In: CVPR, pp. 7132–7141 (2018)

18. Woo, S., Park, J., Lee, J. Y., et al.: Cbam: convolutional block attention module. In: ECCV, pp. 3–19 (2018)

19. Kapitanov, A., Makhlyarchuk, A., et al.: Hagrid-hand gesture recognition image dataset. arXiv preprint arXiv:2206.08219 (2022)

Research on Airborne Infrared Target Recognition Method Based on Target-Environment Coupling

Yan Ouyang[1]([✉]), Pei Qi Deng[2], and Yin Bo Shao[1]

[1] Air Force Early Warning Academy, Hubei, China
oyy_01@163.com
[2] Hubei Academy of Social Sciences, Hubei, China

Abstract. Airborne infrared targets are easily influenced by environmental factors, imaging angles, imaging distances, etc., resulting in decreased recognition accuracy. To address this issue, this paper proposes an airborne infrared target recognition method based on target-environment coupled multi-feature fusion. This method first extracts multiple features including gradient histograms and deep convolutions from the infrared images containing both the airborne target and the sky environment. Then, a recognition framework based on sparse representation theory is used to perform sparse coding on each set of features, and finally, fusion decisions are made based on sparsity measurements. Through experiments conducted on an infrared simulation image dataset, the proposed method achieves the best recognition accuracy in complex environments with long distances, multiple angles, and small training samples, compared to current state-of-the-art recognition methods.

Keywords: Infrared Image · Target-Environment Joint Feature Extraction · Long-Range Multi-angle Imaging

1 Introduction

Airborne infrared target recognition has been one of the research hotspots in the field of infrared image analysis and processing. Zhang et al. [1] use wavelet moment invariants to identify different aircraft types in infrared images; Zeng et al. [2] achieve aircraft identification by extracting skeleton moment features; Li et al. [3] use D-S theory and Markov chains to identify 7 types of aircraft targets under three different flight attitudes; Jin et al. [4] use HOG features of the maximum gradient direction in infrared grayscale images combined with the SRC method to distinguish 8 aircraft types and achieved good recognition performance with a small number of training samples; Zhang et al. [5] mix deep convolution features and gradient histogram features and combine them with SVM classification methods to achieve identification of three types of infrared image styles: aircraft, interference points, and their combination under multi-angle observation conditions.

© The Author(s), under exclusive license to Springer Nature Switzerland AG 2023
H. Lu et al. (Eds.): ICIG 2023, LNCS 14356, pp. 413–422, 2023.
https://doi.org/10.1007/978-3-031-46308-2_34

Most of the current infrared image-based flight target recognition methods require prior target detection. In feature extraction, the focus is mainly on the infrared radiation characteristics [4] or shape features [1] of the aircraft itself, while ignoring the significant influence of different weather conditions on the infrared radiation characteristics of airborne targets, especially the infrared radiation energy on the surface of the aircraft [6, 7]. Although Zhang et al. [5] focused on this particularity, they did not use it for identifying various aircrafts. Under long-distance and multi-angle imaging conditions of the infrared detector, in addition to the aircraft target, a large amount of sky background will also be included in the field of view. Considering the effects of different weather conditions such as cloudy, sunny, rainy, and foggy, the infrared radiation on the surface of the aircraft will also undergo corresponding changes. Therefore, a feature extraction approach based on target-environment coupling needs to be proposed to address the challenge of the variability of meteorological conditions on airborne infrared target recognition.

We adopt the feature extraction methods of Zhang et al. [5], extracting gradient histogram features and deep convolution features from infrared images respectively. These features are directly used as training sample dictionaries, and then a recognition method framework based on sparse representation theory is employed to match different category features. Finally, due to analyzing the sparsity of the sparse coding results, a fusion weighting method is used to give the final judgement (Fig. 1).

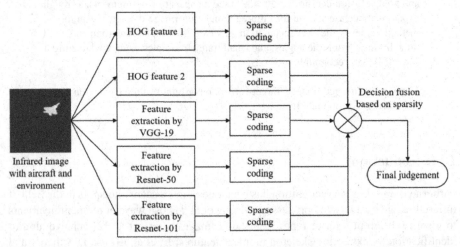

Fig. 1. Process of airborne infrared target recognition method based on target-environment coupled feature extraction

2 Infrared Image Feature Extraction Based on Target-Environment Coupling

2.1 Analysis of Far Distance Multi-view Infrared Target Radiative Characteristics

The infrared radiation characteristics of airborne targets, in addition to being affected by the environment, also change with different flight modes. For flying targets, the main sources of thermal radiation are exhaust gases ejected from the engine, engine heating components, exhaust valves, heat dissipation parts of the air conditioning system, aerodynamic thermal energy generated on the surface of the aircraft during flight, the cockpit top of the pilot, and reflection radiation generated by sunlight shining on the aircraft itself [8]. With changes in the observation angle, the main heating parts of the aircraft body will be obstructed during the target's motion, causing significant changes in the aircraft's infrared radiation characteristics relative to the background, as shown in Fig. 2.

As shown in Fig. 2(a), due to different viewing angles, the exhaust stream of the stealth fighter's tail nozzle will be obscured by the fuselage, and the airflow generated by the nozzle will also change, resulting in changes in radiance and length shape in the image. As shown in Fig. 2(b), for different viewing angles, the tail nozzle of the stealth bomber will also be obscured. As shown in Fig. 2(c), for different viewing angles, the four engines of the transport aircraft will be obscured by the fuselage, and the high heat generated by the engines will also exhibit different radiance in the infrared image. As shown in Fig. 2(d), the tail flow generated by the reconnaissance UAV's tail nozzle will also exhibit different length shapes and radiance in the infrared image under different viewing angles.

2.2 HOG Feature Extraction of Target-Environment Coupled Infrared Images

The main process of HOG feature extraction includes [9]: (1) normalization; (2) calculating the image gradient; (3) segmenting the image into several small regions (also known as "cells", with sizes that can be defined), selecting a suitable number of directions n, and accumulating the one-dimensional gradient histogram or edge direction of all pixels in the cell; (4) grouping 2×2 cells into a block called the HOG descriptor, normalizing the contrast between blocks, and overlapping cells between blocks by 50%; (5) gathering all HOG descriptors to construct the final HOG feature vector. In this paper, two scales of cells were selected for HOG feature extraction, with pixel sizes of 8×8 and 16×16, respectively. During the specific calculation process, adjacent cells overlap by 50%, as shown in Fig. 3. Six directions of 360°/n, where n = 2, 6, 8, 9, 12, 18, were selected for direction selection.

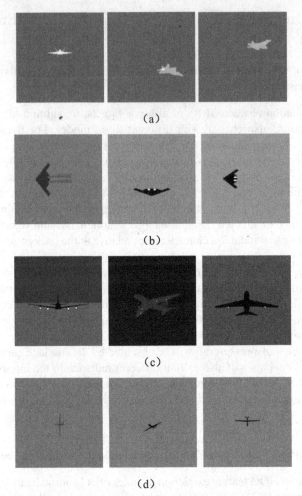

Fig. 2. Infrared simulation images of typical military airborne targets under ground-to-air obser-vation conditions at different viewing angles. Note: (a) Infrared simulation image of a stealth fighter under different viewing angles; (b) Infrared simulation image of a stealth bomber under different viewing angles; (c) Infrared simulation image of a transport aircraft under different viewing angles; (d) Infrared simulation image of a reconnaissance UAV under different viewing angles.

Therefore, two sets of HOG feature vectors were extracted for each image in this study, denoted as H_1 and H_2, respectively.

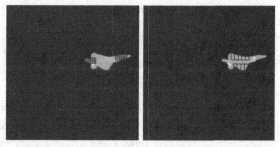

Fig. 3. Schematic diagram of different sizes of cell for HOG feature extraction. Note: (a) Cell size is 8 × 8 pixels; (b) Cell size is 16 × 16 pixels.

2.3 Deep Convolutional Feature Extraction for Infrared Image Based on Target-Environment Coupling

In this paper, pre-trained deep neural networks are used for feature extraction. Specifically, we employed three typical pre-trained deep neural network models, VGG-19, Resnet-50, and Resnet-101, as the network structures for feature extraction, with a convolutional kernel size of 3 × 3. For the VGG-19 network [10], we extracted the network layer output shown in Fig. 4. as feature V_1.

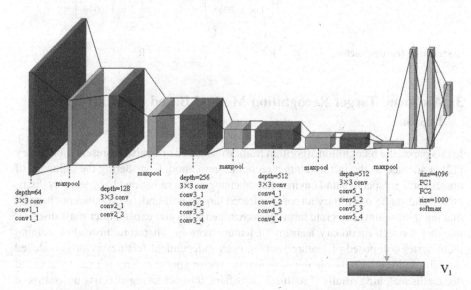

Fig. 4. Schematic diagram of feature extraction layer in VGG-19 network structure.

For Resnet-50 and Resnet-101 networks, we extract the output vector of the Average pool layer as the feature output of infrared simulation images, as shown in Table 1.

Table 1. ResNet Network

Layer Name	Output Size	50-layer	101-layer
conv1	112×112	7×7, 64, stride 2	
conv2_x	56×56	3×3 max pool, stride 2	
		$\begin{bmatrix} 1 \times 1 & 64 \\ 3 \times 3 & 64 \\ 1 \times 1 & 256 \end{bmatrix} \times 3$	$\begin{bmatrix} 1 \times 1 & 64 \\ 3 \times 3 & 64 \\ 1 \times 1 & 256 \end{bmatrix} \times 3$
Conv3_x	28×28	$\begin{bmatrix} 1 \times 1 & 128 \\ 3 \times 3 & 128 \\ 1 \times 1 & 512 \end{bmatrix} \times 4$	$\begin{bmatrix} 1 \times 1 & 128 \\ 3 \times 3 & 128 \\ 1 \times 1 & 128 \end{bmatrix} \times 4$
Conv4_x	14×14	$\begin{bmatrix} 1 \times 1 & 256 \\ 3 \times 3 & 256 \\ 1 \times 1 & 1024 \end{bmatrix} \times 6$	$\begin{bmatrix} 1 \times 1 & 256 \\ 2 \times 2 & 256 \\ 1 \times 1 & 1024 \end{bmatrix} \times 23$
Conv5_x	7×7	$\begin{bmatrix} 1 \times 1 & 512 \\ 3 \times 3 & 512 \\ 1 \times 1 & 2048 \end{bmatrix} \times 3$	$\begin{bmatrix} 1 \times 1 & 512 \\ 3 \times 3 & 512 \\ 1 \times 1 & 2048 \end{bmatrix} \times 3$
	1×1	Average pool	
Extracting feature vectors		R_1	R_2

3 Airborne Target Recognition Method Based on Multi-feature Fusion

In this paper, the recognition algorithm framework based on sparse representation theory [12] is adopted as the infrared target recognition method. Considering the influence of observation perspective and environmental changes, the radiation characteristics distribution and shape of military airborne infrared targets will undergo significant changes, making it difficult to integrate intra-class characteristics and expand inter-class discriminability through dictionary learning of feature vectors. Therefore, instead of training dictionaries composed of feature vectors, each independent feature vector is matched directly, and the sparsity obtained by feature vector sparse coding is used to fuse and decide the matching results of multiple classifiers, thus achieving effective utilization of different types of features. The specific steps are as follows:

Step 1: Input a set of 5 training samples labeled with i categories $\{H_1^i\}$, $\{H_2^i\}$, $\{V_1^i\}$, $\{R_1^i\}$, $\{R_2^i\}$, and a test sample y.

Step 2: Normalize all the feature vectors of the samples using l_2 norm.

Step 3: Extract 5 types of features H_1^y, H_2^y, V_1^y, R_1^y, R_2^y for the test sample y.

Step 4: Solve the $l_1 - minimization$ problem separately for the 5 groups of training samples consisting of different features:

$$\hat{x}_1 = argmin\|x_1\|_1 s.t. \left\|H_1^y - \left\{H_1^i\right\} \bullet x_1\right\|_2 \leq \varepsilon \tag{1}$$

$$\hat{x}_2 = argmin\|x_2\|_1 s.t. \left\|H_2^y - \left\{H_2^i\right\} \bullet x_2\right\|_2 \leq \varepsilon \tag{2}$$

$$\hat{x}_3 = argmin\|x_3\|_1 s.t. \left\|V_1^y - \left\{V_1^i\right\} \bullet x_3\right\|_2 \leq \varepsilon \tag{3}$$

$$\hat{x}_4 = argmin\|x_4\|_1 s.t. \left\|R_1^y - \left\{R_1^i\right\} \bullet x_4\right\|_2 \leq \varepsilon \tag{4}$$

$$\hat{x}_5 = argmin\|x_5\|_1 s.t. \left\|R_2^y - \left\{R_2^i\right\} \bullet x_5\right\|_2 \leq \varepsilon \tag{5}$$

Step 5: Multiply the 5 groups of sparse coding vectors by weight values w_j

$$p_i = \sum_{j=1}^{5} w_j \bullet \delta_i\left(\hat{x}_j\right) \tag{6}$$

Where, $w_j = \left(1/\|\hat{x}_j\|_1\right)^r$, $\|\hat{x}_j\|_1$ actually measures the sparsity, with smaller values indicating higher sparsity, and r represents the scale parameter. $\delta_i\left(\hat{x}\right) = [0, 0, 0, \ldots, \hat{x}_1^i, \hat{x}_2^i, \ldots, 0, 0, 0]$

Step 6: Determine which category the test sample y belongs to on the basis of the fused sparsity measure value.

$$identify(y) = argmax p_i \tag{7}$$

4 Experimental Analysis

4.1 Introduction to Experimental Environment

In order to verify that the method proposed in this paper can cope with the challenge of infrared image target recognition under different meteorological conditions (cloudy, sunny, rainy, and foggy), we simulated the infrared detection images of four types of aerial military targets (Stealth Fighter, Stealth Bomber, Transport Aircraft, Reconnaissance Drone) under different weather conditions (image size is 300 × 300 pixels). The observation elevation angle of the infrared image is 0–90°, and the observation azimuth angle is 0–360°. The observation distance is 35 km (Fig. 5).

The simulation experiment program was developed using Matlab2022b and the experimental computer had an Intel 8-core CPU and 32 GB of memory. To further verify the performance of the proposed method in this paper, a 5-fold cross-validation method was adopted for the experimental validation method. Specifically, the simulated data sample set was randomly divided into 5 folds for each category, with only one-fold of data used as training sample data and the remaining 4 folds of data used as test sample data. The average of the results obtained from 5 experiments was taken as the final result.

Fig. 5. Simulation images of infrared detection of reconnaissance drones under different meteorological conditions. Note: (a) Overcast environment; (b) Sunny environment; (c) Foggy environment; (d) Rainy environment.

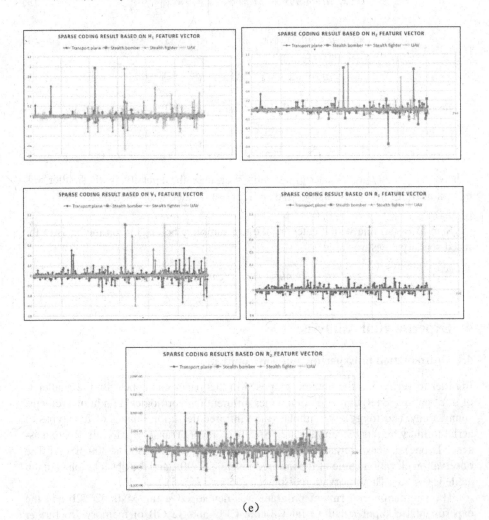

(e)

Fig. 6. Sparse coding results of different feature vectors. Note: (a) Sparse coding result based on H_1 feature vector; (b) Sparse coding result based on H_2 feature vector; (c) Sparse coding result based on V_1 feature vector; (d) Sparse coding result based on R_1 feature vector; (e) Sparse coding result based on R_2 feature vector.

4.2 Simulation Experiment Results Analysis

First, we present the results obtained from sparse coding of different feature vectors, as shown in Fig. 6.

According to the results shown in Fig. 6., there were variations in the sparse coding results obtained for identical target types using different feature vectors. For instance, H_1, H_2, and V_1 feature sets yielded better sparse coding results for the stealth bomber target type, whereas R_1 and V_1 feature sets yielded better results for the reconnaissance drone target type. Therefore, the ultimate objective of the proposed sparsity fusion decision-making approach is to fuse these results and determine the test sample category that best matches the training sample.

The identification results of the proposed method are presented in Table 2.

Table 2. Target recognition results based on small training samples

Method	Classification accuracy(%)
HOG+SRC[4]	59.1
Mixed features+SVM[5]	73.5
Skeleton Zernike moment+NN[2]	67.2
Proposed method	84.3

In Table 2, we have applied some existing infrared target recognition methods to the simulated dataset generated in this study. By comparing the identification results, our proposed method achieves the highest recognition accuracy when dealing with the problem of infrared target recognition under complex weather conditions.

To further validate the effectiveness of feature fusion, we attempted multiple decision strategies for feature fusion, and the results are shown in Table 3. Analysis shows that our proposed method based on six types of feature fusion decisions achieves the best recognition performance. This indicates that the gradient features of different categories of infrared images and the convolution features of different depths provide effective support for solving the problem of infrared aerial target recognition, especially when the gradient features and convolution features are fused for decision making, the accuracy of aerial infrared target recognition can be significantly improved.

Table 3. Decision fusion results based on different feature combinations

Feature combination	Fusion decision accuracy (%)
H_1	74.1
H_1+V_1	82.3
$H_1+V_1+R_1$	84.2

5 Summary

A target-environment coupled multi-feature fusion decision infrared air target recognition method is proposed for the problem of air infrared target identification under complex meteorological conditions. The method extracts gradient histogram and deep convolutional features from the infrared images respectively, utilizes the matching characteristics of the identification framework based on sparse representation theory, and fuses and decides on five features through sparse weighting. Through simulation experiments, it was found that this method can effectively deal with the difficulties of long-distance, multi-view, and small-sample air target recognition under complex environments. This summary is presented from the perspective of academic editing.

References

1. Zhang, F., Liu, S.Q., Wang, D.B., Guan, W.: Aircraft recognition in infrared image using wavelet moment invariants. Image Vis. Comput.Comput. **27**, 313–318 (2009)
2. Zeng, Y.L., et al.: Aircraft recognition based on improved iterative threshold selection and skeleton zernike moment. Optik **125**, 3733–3737 (2014)
3. Li, X., Pan, J., Dezert, J.: Automatic aircraft recognition using DSmT and HMM. In: 17th International Conference on Information Fusion (2014)
4. Jin, L., Li, F.M., Liu, S.J., Wang, X.: Rotation-invariant infrared aerial target identification based on SRC. J. Infrared Millim. Waves **38**(5), 578–586 (2019)
5. Zhang, K., Wei, J.Y., Wang, T.T., Li, S.Y., Yang, X.: Air target recognition algorithm based on mixed depth features in the interference environment. Optik **245**(167535), 1–19 (2021)
6. Huang, W., Ji, H.: Effect of environmental radiation on the long-wave infrared signature of cruise aircraft. Aerosp. Sci. Technol.. Sci. Technol. **56**, 125–134 (2016)
7. Pan, X., Wang, X., Wang, R., Wang, L.: Infrared radiation and stealth characteristics prediction for supersonic aircraft with uncertainty. Infrared Phys. Technol. **73**, 238–250 (2015)
8. Dragan, M.K., Peter, S.M., Zoran, M.N.: Modeling of aircraft infrared signature based on comparative tracking. Optik **225**, 165782 (2021)
9. Navneet, D., Bill, T.: Histograms of oriented gradients for human detection. In: International Conference on Computer Vision & Pattern Recognition, pp. 886–893 (2005)
10. Karen, S., Andrew, Z.: Very deep convolutional networks for large-scale image recognition. In: The 3rd International Conference on Learning Representations (2015)
11. He, K., Zhang, X., Ren, S., Sun, J.: Deep residual learning for image recognition. arXiv preprint arXiv:1512.03385 (2015)
12. Wright, J., Yang, A.Y., Ganesh, A., Sastry, S.S., Ma, Y.: Robust face recognition via sparse representation. IEEE Trans. Pattern Anal. Mach. Intell.Intell. **31**(2), 210–227 (2009)
13. Zhang, L., Yang, M., Feng, X.: Sparse representation or collaborative representation: Which helps face recognition? In: Proceedings of the International Conference on Computer Vision, pp. 471–478 (2011)

Semantic and Gradient Guided Scene Text Image Super-Resolution

Chengyue Shi, Wenbo Shi, Jintong Hu, and Wenming Yang$^{(\boxtimes)}$

Shenzhen International Graduate School, Tsinghua University, Beijing, China
yang.wenming@sz.tsinghua.edu.cn

Abstract. Scene text image super-resolution (STISR) aims to improve image quality and enhance downstream recognition tasks. Although recent works has made significant progress, there are still challenges to overcome. First, scene text images are subject to various forms of degradation, fonts, and deformations, previous methods are not robust enough. Second, the super-resolution results of character edges often appear distorted, broken, or stuck together, making the letters hard to recognize. To address these issues, we propose a semantic and gradient guided super-resolution network (SGGSR), which integrates two characteristics of text as guiding priors: semantics and gradient. Specifically, we present a semantic prior generator that is pre-trained with contrastive learning and a gradient direction loss. Experiments show that our SGGSR outperforms other methods in terms of image quality metrics such as PSNR and SSIM, as well as accuracy in downstream recognition tasks. The improvement in recognition performance is also observed for text instances from different datasets with varying degrees of degradation and deformation.

Keywords: Scene Text Images Super-Resolution · Contrastive learning · Gradient · Text Prior · Semantic Extraction

1 Introduction

Text images, being an ancient and vital information carrier, generally contain important information. But low resolution caused by motion blur or compression can impact the image quality as well as OCR performance. To address this issue, super-resolution techniques are utilized as a pre-processing step to enhance the resolution and clarity of low-resolution text images. It also enables downstream tasks, such as text recognition, to be performed more accurately.

Existing scene text image super-resolution (STISR) methods can be broadly categorized into two groups. The first group views text images as similar to natural images and employs general single image super-resolution (SISR) frameworks, but this often results in poor recognition performance due to the lack of consideration of text-specific features. In contrast, the second group aims to incorporate text-specific features into the STISR process, leading to improved recognition accuracy. For instance, Ma et al. [1] utilize recognition results as a

H. Lu et al. (Eds.): ICIG 2023, LNCS 14356, pp. 423–434, 2023.
https://doi.org/10.1007/978-3-031-46308-2_35

prior to iteratively perform super-resolution, and Chen et al. [2] employ stroke-level recognition information to generate more distinctive images.

Despite significant progress, several challenges still remain. 1) Lack of robustness across various fonts, deformations, and degradation methods in different text images. 2) The edges of characters often appear distorted, broken, or stuck together, which causes the letters to be difficult to identify.

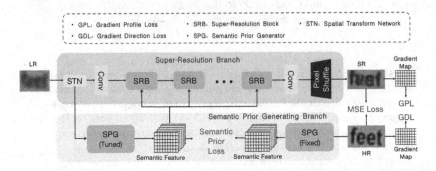

Fig. 1. The architecture of our method SGGSR.

In this paper, we present a semantic and gradient guided super-resolution network for text images, as illustrated in Fig. 1. The network consists of three parts, each with a specific purpose.

1) The first part is the super-resolution reconstruction branch, which uses the same architecture as TSRN [1] and includes an STN [13] alignment module and a series of sequential residual blocks.
2) The second part is the semantic prior fusion branch, where a semantic prior generator pre-trained through contrastive learning [14] is used to provide rich semantic guidance to the super-resolution reconstruction branch.
3) The Third part is a joint loss function, including the proposed gradient direction loss which aims to regularize the recovery of character edges.

Overall, the contributions of our work can be summarized as follows:

– In real-world scenarios, text images often experience various forms of degradation and deformation, and different fonts can also pose challenges for super-resolution. To address these issues, we utilize contrastive learning to generate robust semantic features to guide the recovery process.
– The reconstruction result of character edges often appear distorted, broken, or stuck together, which causes the letters to be difficult to identify. Given the fact that pixel gradient mainly appear at the edge of text, we design a gradient direction loss to regularize the recovery process.
– The results of the experiments show that SGGSR outperforms other methods in terms of both image quality metrics and recognition accuracy. The improvement in recognition performance is also observed for text instances

from different datasets with varying degradation and deformation, highlighting the generalizability of the proposed method.

2 Related Work

2.1 Single Image Super Resolution

Single Image Super-Resolution (SISR) is the task of recovering a high-resolution image from a low-resolution image. It is a challenging ill-posed problem, as the same low-resolution image can correspond to multiple high-resolution images due to different forms of degradation.

Traditionally, SISR methods have utilized hand-crafted priors to regularize the recovery process, such as self-similarity prior, sparsity prior, and statistical prior. However, recent advances in deep learning have led to the development of convolutional neural network (CNN) based methods for SISR. One of the earliest works, the Super-Resolution Convolutional Neural Network (SRCNN) [3], trains a three-layer CNN for SISR.

Subsequent works have proposed several improvements to optimize SISR performance. For instance, the use of residual blocks [4] and Laplacian pyramid structure [5] has been proposed to improve the accuracy of SISR. Additionally, densely connected networks [6] and attention mechanisms [7] have been used to further improve the results.

Recently, Generative Adversarial Networks (GANs) [8] have been employed to improve the perceptual quality of SISR results. These methods train a generator network to generate high-resolution images [29], while a discriminator network is used to distinguish the generated images from real high-resolution images. The generator and discriminator networks are trained together in an adversarial manner to produce high-quality super-resolution images.

2.2 Scene Text Image Super Resolution

Scene text Image Super Resolution (STISR) is a specialized form of single image super-resolution that focuses on text images captured from real scenes. The goal of STISR is not only to improve the statistical and perceptual quality of the image, but also to produce a semantically more reasonable image that is better suited for downstream recognition tasks.

Early STISR approaches used general SISR methods like Dong et al.'s extension of the SRCNN algorithm for text images [3], which achieved the best performance in the ICDAR 2015 competition.

More recent approaches focus on text-specific characteristics to improve quality. For example, Wang et al. introduced the TSRN [9] and gradient profile loss to capture sequential and text-specific information of text images . Ma et al. proposed the TPGSR method, which extracts predicted probability distributions or semantic features as clues to recover low-quality images [1]. Chen et al. proposed the TG method, which uses stroke-level clues to generate more distinguishable images [2].

While these approaches show potential for improving recognition accuracy, further research is needed to address challenges like robustness across different fonts, deformations, and degradation methods, and accounting for better reconstruction of character edges.

2.3 Scene Text Recognition

Scene text recognition techniques can be broadly divided into two categories: bottom-up approaches and top-down approaches. Bottom-up approaches recognize each character in the image first and then interpret the whole word, while top-down approaches view the image as a whole and perform word-level recognition.

One of the early works in this field is Convolutional Recurrent Neural Network (CRNN) [10]. CRNN employs a Convolutional Neural Network (CNN) to extract image features, and uses a Recurrent Neural Network (RNN) to model the semantic features from the image features. The Connectionist Temporal Classification (CTC) loss [15] is used to align the predicted sequence with the target sequence.

More recent work has focused on improving the performance of scene text recognition through contrastive learning. SeqCRL [11,28] is one such approach that promotes contrastive learning for visual sequence-to-sequence recognition. In this approach, each feature map is viewed as a sequence of individual instances, leading to contrastive learning at a sub-word level.

3 Method

3.1 Contrastive Learned Semantic Prior

Some recent works have focused on using the content of text images to guide super-resolution restoration. Textsr [16] uses a GAN with text-aware loss to create more realistic super-resolution images. TPGSR [1] incorporates character priors into the super-resolution process, while TATT [17] improves upon TPGSR by considering the influence of character priors on the corresponding spatial positions of text images, making it better suited for handling spatially deformed text images.

However, in real-world scenarios, text images often vary in terms of degradation, font, deformation, etc., leading to poor robustness of the aforementioned methods. To address this issue, we propose a contrastive Learned semantic prior generator(CLSP). As illustrated in Fig. 2, this method involves pretraining a semantic prior generator using the sequence-to-sequence contrastive learning presented in [11].

In general, we augment the input image to obtain two images for random data augmentation. To ensure that the augmentation does not negatively impact the task of text recognition, we avoid transformations such as flipping, aggressive rotations, and substantial horizontal translations, which can render the text in

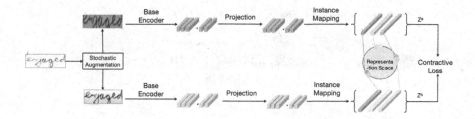

Fig. 2. Architecture of the contrastive learning process

the image unreadable. Instead, we consider augmentation types such as vertical cropping, blurring, adding random noise, and different perspective transformations.

After the input image passes through the backbone, we use a projection module to convert the overall features into a sequence of individual instances, leading to contrastive learning at a sub-word level. This approach is beneficial because words are composed of sequences of characters. The contrastive loss is calculated using the formulas presented below.

$$\mathcal{L}\left(\mathcal{Z}^a, \mathcal{Z}^b\right) = \sum_{r \in |\mathcal{Z}^a|} \ell_{\text{NCE}}\left(\mathbf{z}_r^a, \mathbf{z}_r^b; \mathcal{Z}^a \cup \mathcal{Z}^b\right)$$
$$+ \sum_{r \in |\mathcal{Z}^b|} \ell_{\text{NCE}}\left(\mathbf{z}_r^b, \mathbf{z}_r^a; \mathcal{Z}^a \cup \mathcal{Z}^b\right) \tag{1}$$

where $\ell_{\text{NCE}}(\cdot)$ is the noise contrastive estimation (NCE) loss function [12]

$$\ell_{\text{NCE}}\left(\mathbf{u}^a, \mathbf{u}^b; \mathcal{U}\right) = -\log \frac{\exp\left(\text{sim}\left(\mathbf{u}^a, \mathbf{u}^b\right)/\tau\right)}{\sum_{\mathbf{u} \in \mathcal{U} \setminus \mathbf{u}^a} \exp\left(\text{sim}\left(\mathbf{u}^a, \mathbf{u}\right)/\tau\right)} \tag{2}$$

We use the cosine distance as the similarity operator, that is, $\text{sim}(\mathbf{v}, \mathbf{u}) = \mathbf{v}^T \mathbf{u}/\|\mathbf{v}\|\|\mathbf{u}\|$.

To obtain a semantic feature generator robust to different font styles, degradation, and other factors, we pretrained it on publicly available datasets for both handwritten and scene text recognition. For handwritten text recognition, we use the IAM [18], CVL [19], and RIMES [20] datasets, which contain English and French text respectively. For scene text recognition, we train our model on the SyntText [21] synthetic dataset, and evaluate its performance on three real-world datasets: IIT5K [22], IC03 [23], and IC13 [24].

Finally, to enable the semantic generation module to balance both the good generalization brought by contrastive learning and the accuracy brought by supervised learning, we merge the features obtained from the semantic generator pre-trained by contrastive learning and a general OCR model, CRNN. This integration is shown in Fig. 3, and serves as the final output of the semantic prior branch.

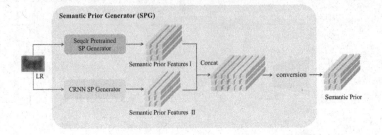

Fig. 3. Architecture of semantic prior generator.

3.2 Gradient Direction Loss

Mostly, the characters in text images have strong contrast with the backgrounds, since both internal and external regions of text are often flat, single-color areas. Therefore the gradient changes are mainly present along the edges of character.

The TSRN [9] method introduces the gradient profile loss, which is inspired by the gradient profile prior [25], to generate sharper edges.

However, this loss only takes into account the amplitude of the gradient and not its direction. For text edges, the gradient direction is perpendicular to the edge direction, so we designed a gradient direction loss to guide the edge direction of the text.

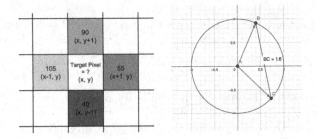

Fig. 4. Gradient Direction Loss

For a certain pixel, we can calculate the gradient as shown in Fig. 4. The vector $\overrightarrow{AB}$ and $\overrightarrow{AC}$ denotes the unit gradient in HR and SR. The direction loss is defined as the distance between the two unit gradient vectors:

$$\ell_{\mathrm{GD}(x,y)} = \left| \frac{\nabla I_{hr}(x,y)}{|\nabla I_{hr}(x,y))|} - \frac{\nabla I_{sr}(x,y)}{|\nabla I_{sr}(x,y))|} \right| \tag{3}$$

3.3   Overall Loss Function

The overall loss function is a joint loss function that includes MSE loss, semantic prior loss, gradient profile loss, and gradient direction loss, which can be expressed as follows:

$$L = L_{SR} + \alpha L_{SP} + \beta L_{GP} + \gamma L_{GD} \tag{4}$$

where the weighting factor are defined as $\alpha = 1e+2$, $\beta = 1e-4$, $\gamma = 1e-1$.

The semantic prior loss L_{SP} measures the difference between the semantic prior extracted from the LR image and the ground-truth using L1 norm and KL Divergence, as described in TPGSR [1].

4   Experiments

4.1   Implementation Details

To assess the similarity between the recovered image and the ground truth. We use two standard metrics for image super-resolution: Peak Signal-to-Noise Ratio (PSNR) and Structural Similarity Index Measure (SSIM). To further demonstrate the efficacy in downstream recognition applications, we test the recognition accuracy using the CRNN network with official PyTorch code.

The training was conducted using two NVIDIA RTX 2080Ti GPUs, with a batch size of 48 and a learning rate of 1e-4. The Adam optimizer, with a momentum term of 0.9, was used to update the model parameters.

4.2   Dataset

The proposed method is trained and evaluated using the TextZoom [9] dataset, which consists of 21,740 image pairs obtained by varying the camera's focal length in real-world scenarios. To further test the generalizability of our network, we conduct extra test on CUTE80 [26] and ICDAR2015 [27]. ICDAR2015 is a scene text recognition dataset includes 2,077 cropped images of street view photos. Meanwhile, CUTE80 includes 288 real-worldsamples, mostly having curved shapes.

4.3   Ablation Studies

In order to assess the effectiveness of our proposed components, we conduct experiments on the contrastive learned semantic prior (CLSP) generator, and the gradient direction loss (GDL).The results of these experiments will provide insights into how each component affects the quality of the super-resolution images.

Table 1. Ablation Study on Accuracy

Module		Accuracy(%)			
CLSP	GDL	easy	medium	hard	avg.
		61.00	49.90	36.70	49.80
✔		61.33	50.68	37.60	50.61
✔	✔	**62.26**	**51.89**	**37.61**	**51.34**

Table 2. Ablation Study on PSNR and SSIM

Module		PSNR				SSIM			
CLSP	GDL	easy	medium	hard	avg.	easy	medium	hard	avg.
		23.73	18.68	20.06	20.97	0.8805	0.6738	0.7440	0.7719
✔	-	24.36	**19.23**	20.02	**21.37**	0.8861	0.6746	0.7475	0.7749
✔	✔	**24.36**	19.17	**20.04**	21.36	**0.8936**	**0.6812**	**0.7627**	**0.7849**

Impact of the Contrastively Learned Semantic Prior. The results on the Textzoom dataset in terms of recognition accuracy are presented in Table 1 and Table 2. Our proposed method demonstrates superiority compared to the generator relying solely on CRNN as described in TPGSR [1]. This improvement is reflected in PSNR, SSIM and recognition accuracy.

Additionally, to assess the generalization performance to multiple degradation and deformantion of CLSP, we conducted recognition experiments on two extra datasets. As shown in Table 3, The results showed a marked improvement, with gains of 4.87% and 2.22% respectively on CUTE80 and ICDAR2015 compared to TPGSR.

Table 3. Generalization experiments

CLSP	ACC(%)	
	CUTE80	IC15
w/o	53.12	54.98
with	**57.99**	**57.20**

Impact of Gradient Direction Loss. To investigate the effect of GDL, we conducted an ablation study on TextZoom. The results, as shown in Table 1, demonstrate that the GDL can significantly improves recognition accuracy.

However, we observed a slight decrease in PSNR on some test sets in Table 2. This decrease is believed to be due to the incorporation of the GDL into the total loss function, which reduces the weight of the original MSE loss. As the calculation of PSNR is closely tied to the MSE value, the reduction in the weight of the MSE loss negatively impacts the PSNR metric.

4.4 Comparison with State-of-the-Arts

Our method was evaluated on the TextZoom dataset and compared to other super-resolution models using CRNN as the recognition model. The results, displayed in Table 4, highlight the significant improvement in recognition accuracy achieved by our method. The "-3" here means apply multi-stage training settings in [1]. In comparison to the state-of-the-art method TPGSR-3 , our method surpasses it, increasing recognition accuracy from 51.8% to 53.1% , PSNR from 21.18 to 21.86 and SSIM from 0.7774 to 0.7906. The proposed method demonstrates an advantage or equivalence with to the state-of-the-art, with a significant improvement compared to other methods.

Table 4. Performance comparison with major existing methods

Method	Accuracy(%)				PSNR Avg.	SSIM Avg.
	Easy	Medium	Hard	Avg.		
BICUBIC [17]	36.4	21.1	21.1	26.8	20.35	0.6961
SRCNN [17]	38.7	21.6	20.9	27.7	20.78	0.7227
SRResNet [17]	39.7	27.6	22.7	30.6	21.03	0.7403
TSRN [9]	52.5	38.2	31.4	41.4	21.42	0.7690
TBSRN [30]	59.6	47.1	35.3	48.1	20.91	0.7603
PCAN [31]	59.6	45.5	34.8	47.7	21.49	0.7752
TG [2]	61.2	47.6	35.5	48.9	21.40	0.7456
TATT [17]	62.6	53.4	39.8	52.6	21.52	**0.7930**
TPGSR(baseline) [1]	61.0	49.9	36.7	49.8	20.97	0.7719
TPGSR-3(baseline)	63.1	52.0	38.6	51.8	21.18	0.7774
SGGSR(ours)	62.3	51.9	37.6	51.3	21.36	0.7849
SGGSR-3(ours)	**64.0**	**54.2**	**38.9**	**53.1**	**21.86**	0.7906

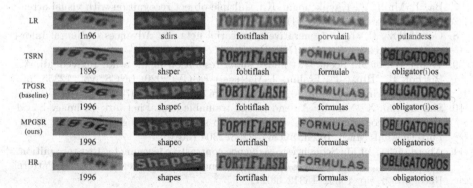

Fig. 5. Visual comparison with SOTA methods

In addition, we conduct a comparison of visual results, as shown in Fig. 5. It can be seen that our algorithm is able to create clearer and sharper edges, and the semantic recognition results are also more accurate.

5   Conclusion

In conclusion, the paper addresses the challenges in Scene Text Image Super-Resolution (STISR) by proposing a semantic and gradient guided super-resolution network (SGGSR) which integrates two key characteristics of text: semantics and gradient as guiding priors. The paper presents innovative approaches such as a pretrained semantic prior generator and a gradient direction loss. Extensive experiments demonstrate the effectiveness and superiority of the proposed method.

References

1. Ma, J., Guo, S., Zhang, L.: Text prior guided scene text image super-resolution. arXiv preprint arXiv:2106.15368 (2021)
2. Chen, J., Yu, H., Ma, J., et al.: Text gestalt: stroke-aware scene text image super-resolution. In: Proceedings of the AAAI Conference on Artificial Intelligence, vol. 36, no. 1, pp. 285–293 (2022)
3. Dong, C., Loy, C.C., He, K., Tang, X.: Image super-resolution using deep convolutional networks. In: Proceedings of the European Conference on Computer Vision (ECCV), pp. 184–199 (2014). https://doi.org/10.1007/978-3-319-10593-2_13
4. Kim, J., Kwon Lee, J., Mu Lee, K.: Accurate image super-resolution using very deep convolutional networks. In: Proceedings of the IEEE Conference on Computer Vision and Pattern Recognition (CVPR), pp. 1646–1654 (2016)
5. Lai, W.S., Huang, J.B., Ahuja, N., Yang, M.H.: Deep Laplacian pyramid networks for fast and accurate super-resolution. In: Proceedings of the IEEE Conference on Computer Vision and Pattern Recognition (CVPR), pp. 624–632 (2017)
6. Wang, X., Yu, Y., Dong, S., Qiao, Y.: Residual dense network for image super-resolution. In: Proceedings of the IEEE Conference on Computer Vision and Pattern Recognition (CVPR), pp. 2472–2481 (2018)
7. Ba, J., Mnih, V., Kavukcuoglu, K.: Multiple object recognition with visual attention. arXiv preprint arXiv:1412.7755 (2014)
8. Goodfellow, I., et al.: Generative adversarial nets. In: Advances in Neural Information Processing Systems (NIPS), pp. 2672–2680 (2014)
9. Wang, W., et al.: Scene text image super-resolution in the wild. In: Vedaldi, A., Bischof, H., Brox, T., Frahm, J.-M. (eds.) ECCV 2020. LNCS, vol. 12355, pp. 650–666. Springer, Cham (2020). https://doi.org/10.1007/978-3-030-58607-2_38
10. Shi, B., Bai, X., Yao, C.: An end-to-end trainable neural network for image-based sequence recognition and its application to scene text recognition. IEEE Trans. Pattern Anal. Mach. Intell. **39**(11), 2298–2304 (2016)
11. Aberdam, A., et al.: Sequence-to-sequence contrastive learning for text recognition. In: Proceedings of the IEEE/CVF Conference on Computer Vision and Pattern Recognition, pp. 15302–15312 (2021)
12. van den Oord, A., Li, Y., Vinyals, O.: Representation learning with contrastive predictive coding. arXiv preprint arXiv:1807.03748 (2018)

13. Jaderberg, M., et al.: Spatial transformer networks. In: Advances in Neural Information Processing Systems, pp. 2017–2025 (2015)
14. Chen, T., Kornblith, S., Norouzi, M., Hinton, G.: A simple framework for contrastive learning of visual representations. arXiv preprint arXiv:2002.05709 (2020)
15. Graves, A., Fern andez, S., Gomez, F., Schmidhuber, J. Connectionist temporal classification: labelling unsegmented sequence data with recurrent neural networks. In: Proceedings of the 23rd International Conference on Machine Learning (2006)
16. Wang, W., Xie, E., Sun, P., et al.: TextSR: content-aware text super-resolution guided by recognition. arXiv preprint arXiv:1909.07113 (2019)
17. Ma, J., Liang, Z., Zhang, L.: A text attention network for spatial deformation robust scene text image super-resolution. In: Proceedings of the IEEE/CVF Conference on Computer Vision and Pattern Recognition, pp. 5911–5920 (2022)
18. Marti, U.V., Bunke, H.: The IAM-database: an English sentence database for offline handwriting recognition. Int. J. Doc. Anal. Recogn. 5(1), 39–46 (2002). https://doi.org/10.1007/s100320200071
19. Kleber, F., Fiel, S., Diem, M., Sablatnig, R.: CVL-Database: an off-line database for writer retrieval, writer identification and word spotting. In: 2013 12th International Conference on Document Analysis and Recognition, pp. 560–564. IEEE (2013)
20. Grosicki, E., El Abed, H.: ICDAR 2009 handwriting recognition competition. In: 2009 10th International Conference on Document Analysis and Recognition, pp. 1398–1402. IEEE (2009)
21. Gupta, A., Vedaldi, A., Zisserman, A.: Synthetic data for text localisation in natural images. In: Proceedings of the IEEE Conference on Computer Vision and Pattern Recognition, pp. 2315–2324 (2016)
22. Mishra, A., Alahari, K., Jawahar, CV.: Scene text recognition using higher order language priors. In: BMVC-British Machine Vision Conference (2012)
23. Marti, U.-V., Bunke, H.: The IAM-database: an English sentence database for offline handwriting recognition. Int. J. Doc. Anal. Recogn. 5(1), 39–46 (2002). https://doi.org/10.1007/s100320200071
24. Karatzas, D., et al.: ICDAR 2013 robust reading competition. In: 2013 12th International Conference on Document Analysis and Recognition, pp. 1484–1493. IEEE (2013)
25. Sun, J., Sun, J., Xu, Z., Shum, H.: Gradient profile prior and its applications in image super-resolution and enhancement. Trans. Image Process. 20(6), 1529–1542 (2011)
26. Risnumawan, A., Shivakumara, P., Chan, C.S., Tan, C.L.: A robust arbitrary text detection system for natural scene images. Expert Syst. Appl. 41(18), 8027–8048 (2014)
27. Karatzas, D., et al.: ICDAR 2015 competition onrobust reading. In: 2015 13th International Conference on Document Analysis and Recognition (ICDAR), pp. 1156–1160. IEEE (2015)
28. Aberdam, A., Ganz, R., Mazor, S., et al.: Multimodal semi-supervised learning for text recognition. arXiv preprint arXiv:2205.03873 (2022)
29. Fang, C., Zhu, Y., Liao, L., et al.: TSRGAN: real-world text image super-resolution based on adversarial learning and triplet attention. Neurocomputing 455, 88–96 (2021)

30. Chen, J., Li, B., Xue, X.: Scene text telescope: text-focused scene image super-resolution. In: Proceedings of the IEEE/CVF Conference on Computer Vision and Pattern Recognition, pp. 12026–12035 (2021)
31. Zhao, C., Feng, S., Zhao, B.N., et al.: Scene text image super-resolution via parallelly contextual attention network. In: Proceedings of the 29th ACM International Conference on Multimedia, pp. 2908–2917 (2021)

Author Index

H. Lu et al. (Eds.): ICIG 2023, LNCS 14356, pp. 435–436, 2023.
https://doi.org/10.1007/978-3-031-46308-2

Printed in the United States
by Baker & Taylor Publisher Services